The
NEW WORLD
of WELFARE

REBECCA M. BLANK
RON HASKINS
Editors

BROOKINGS INSTITUTION PRESS
Washington, D.C.

Library of Congress Cataloging-in-Publication data

The new world of welfare / Rebecca M. Blank and Ron Haskins, editors.
    p.   cm.
Includes bibliographical references and index.
   ISBN 0-8157-1010-0 (alk. paper) — ISBN 0-8157-1011-9 (pbk. : alk.
paper)
    1. Public welfare—Government policy—United States. 2. United
States—Social policy. 3. United States—Economic policy. I. Blank,
Rebecca M. II. Haskins, Ron.
   HV95.N456   2001
   362.5'8'0973Cdc21   2001003367

9 8 7 6 5 4 3 2 1

Typeset in Adobe Garamond

Composition by Betsy Kulamer
Washington, D.C.

Printed by R. R. Donnelley and Sons
Harrisonburg, Virginia

Foreword

THE IDEA FOR THIS BOOK was born two years after the enactment of the sweeping 1996 welfare reform law, the Personal Responsibility and Work Opportunity Reconciliation Act (PRWORA) and its Temporary Assistance for Needy Families (TANF) block grant. In 1998 we realized that no one seemed to be thinking about the fact that the next round of the national debate regarding welfare, poverty, and other public policies affecting low-income families was about to begin. Funding for TANF will expire on October 1, 2002, and the 107th Congress and the Bush administration must decide by that date whether to continue TANF's block grant structure, whether to continue funding at the current level, and whether other structural or policy changes are needed.

The missions of both the Annie E. Casey Foundation and the Charles S. Mott Foundation emphasize the creation of an environment within which the nation's most at-risk children can grow up successfully. Key to this strategy is reducing the number of children growing up in poverty, especially in deep or persistent poverty. Since child well-being is inextricably linked to family well-being, the trustees of both foundations have a long-standing commitment to the promotion of public policies that promise to improve the economic and social circumstances of low-income families. Rethinking welfare and other support systems for low-income families is central to helping their children succeed. Sound, thoughtful, and creative approaches to the

welfare reform, work force development, and other economic security policies—in ways that better help the parents of dependent or poor families to
enter and remain in the workforce and that better enable them to raise their
families well—have been high priorities of the Casey Foundation and the
Mott Foundation for at least a decade.

Building upon a history of cross-foundation collaboration, we discussed
how the two organizations might work together to foster dialogue across ideological boundaries that would help delineate the most pressing or controversial issues for the 2002 reauthorization *before* the nation was in the thick of
the debates. Moreover, the Child Care and Development Fund and the Food
Stamp program are also scheduled for reauthorization in that year. Thus the
congressional review of TANF provides an exceptional opportunity and a
compelling hook for a far broader and more comprehensive discussion of
how America can further reduce family poverty, encourage intact and healthy
families, and improve the well-being of our children. In short, the discussions
are likely to involve wide-ranging and profound questions about the direction of federal and state social policies.

Regardless of which side of the aisle they were on in 1996, most observers
agree that passage of the 1996 welfare law marked an extraordinary turning
point in the nation's approach to poverty. Aided by vigorous economic
growth and related federal reforms, welfare rolls have plummeted and are
below half their 1994 peak; work and earnings of single mothers, especially
the poorest, have increased dramatically; child poverty has declined; and the
effects of parental work requirements on children appear either neutral or
slightly positive. But these impressive accomplishments notwithstanding,
most serious observers agree that the work of reforming welfare is not done.
Too many families have not fared well under the mandatory work regime;
some are clearly worse off. And even with the states' solid TANF achievements, the nation's income security agenda is far from completed. As Ron
Haskins—a prime architect of PRWORA—notes, "We shouldn't think welfare reform is a success because we've been able to move a mom with two kids
off welfare into a $12,000-a-year job. That may be great, but it's not enough."

Since Congress last considered these issues in 1995 and 1996, there have
been dramatic changes in the economy, labor force participation, welfare program participation, and the nature of state welfare and antipoverty efforts.
But one of the most remarkable changes has been a "detoxification" of the
debate about welfare, welfare reform, and poverty. Part of this change can be
attributed to the increased media coverage of life on welfare. These stories
have provided a more nuanced and multidimensional picture of families on
welfare, their problems, and their challenges. Another likely contributor is
the strong economy: people may be more charitable when they feel economi-

cally better off themselves. But the biggest factor is probably the collective belief that the new welfare system—and the people it serves—is much more closely aligned with basic American values and core beliefs about work, personal responsibility, equal opportunity, and support for families who "play by the rules." TANF has fundamentally realigned public perceptions by turning many of the dependent poor into the working poor. In this environment, there may also be more convergence around public policy responses and solutions to the continuing problems of welfare and poverty. If Americans feel we are solving the welfare problem, the nation may now be more ready to address the poverty problem.

Furthermore, there have developed new political opportunities to craft a more balanced set of policies to assist the working and dependent poor. The playing field—the realm of politically feasible debate—has narrowed considerably, making consensus more possible. Few liberals are pushing for restoration of the pre-1996 regime, and few conservatives are fighting hard for further cuts in the safety net or in support for the poor. Nevertheless, this toned-down rhetoric does not ensure that consensus will be easy to reach in the congressional debate on reauthorization. There will be no shortage of hot-button issues, such as attempts to curtail out-of-wedlock births, to reallocate resources to encouraging marriage, to slash federal spending, or to block grant additional federal programs.

Thus in 1998 we sought to contribute to a constructive debate and a positive outcome in 2002. In addition to initiating or seeking out and then funding a variety of projects that might inform and shape the public policy agenda in the welfare reform debate, we also wanted to be more directly engaged early on, to set the stage for the reauthorization deliberations and to inform other related policy decisions and discussions. We conceived of this policy-oriented effort as focused on translating research findings and analyses into policy recommendations. Moreover, given our optimism about the potential for some degree of political consensus, we wished very much to encourage a convergence of reasonable opinions from a wide range of perspectives and vantage points. We wanted to try to shape a bipartisan consensus out of the extensive research and analysis of the last decade, the detoxified environment surrounding welfare and poverty, the decline in caseloads, and the relatively healthy economy and fiscal circumstances the United States enjoys today.

Accordingly, we decided to sponsor a conference, the proceedings of which would be published as a book. To lead the project we chose two of the nation's most highly regarded policy researchers and advisers, one an influential liberal and the other a key conservative. Rebecca M. Blank is dean of the Gerald R. Ford School of Public Policy and professor of public policy and economics at the University of Michigan. She served as a member of the president's Council of Economic Advisers in 1997–99 and is the author of *It Takes A Nation: A New Agenda for Fighting Poverty* (Princeton University Press, 1997). Ron Haskins is both a senior fellow at the Brookings Institution, where he codirects the Welfare Reform and Beyond project, and a senior consultant to the Casey Foundation. Previously, he was staff director of the Subcommittee on Human Resources of the House Committee on Ways and Means, where he helped House Republicans write the 1996 welfare reform legislation.

The team then commissioned eighteen papers and comments on these pieces. In general, the political perspectives of the respondents differed from those of the paper's author. The Ford School of Public Policy was awarded funding to manage the project. The conference was held on February 1 and 2, 2001, only days after President Bush and the 107th Congress took office. Participants included some 900 policymakers at the federal and state levels, members of the media and other opinion leaders, policy analysts, grassroots organizers and advocates, and researchers and academics—representing the mix of players who determine national and state income security policy.

The papers presented at the conference and the commentators' responses constitute this book.

—What should be the purposes of TANF? Should states be required to focus more on marriage and other "family policy" issues? Or should TANF be revised as a program with the major goal of providing supports and assistance to the working poor?

—In light of caseload declines since 1994, should federal funding and state required spending levels be changed?

—Should federal time limits be modified? How should federal law address the families still receiving assistance? Is there need for discussion of the broader circumstances of these families, including issues relating to illness, disability, mental health, substance abuse, and domestic violence?

—What should be the key measures of state performance? And should there be more federal safeguards?

It seems likely that these will be among the questions raised in the discussions about reauthorization in 2002. It is our hope that this book will inform and guide the deliberations of Congress and the Bush administration on these and the many related issues.

We wish to acknowledge and thank the many individuals who have contributed to the conference and to this book. First, we wish to thank the trustees, the leadership, and our colleagues at the Annie E. Casey Foundation and the Charles S. Mott Foundation, without whose financial support, guidance, and encouragement this project would never have gotten off the ground. Benita Melton and Ami Nagle from the Mott Foundation were particularly helpful in maintaining support and continuity after Jennifer's transfer to the Joyce Foundation. In addition, we wish to acknowledge the special contributions of several colleagues, including the three dozen authors and respondents, as well as David Ellwood and Les Lenskowski, who served as raconteurs and general advisers on the draft papers.

We would also like to thank the staff of the Ford School of Public Policy who organized and implemented this project. Violet Elder, in particular, managed the conference and other public events with great skill. For their help in organizing the conference, we thank Diana Maly, Sonja Page, Jan Williams, and Andrea Balcena of the Ford School, and Nicole Gibby and Mike Dorer of the University of Michigan's Conference Management Services. Ed Hatcher, of Hatcher Communications, was invaluable in managing press and media relations for the conference. Martha Binderman at Finishing Touches and Jay Yurkshat at the Marriott also contributed greatly to the smooth operation of the conference, as did several graduate students at the Ford School.

At Brookings, we thank Robert Wooley for preparing the manuscript for publication and for coordinating our work with the Brookings Institution Press. We also thank the staff and directors of the Brookings Welfare Reform and Beyond initiative, as well as its funders, including the Annie E. Casey Foundation, Ford Foundation, Foundation for Child Development, Joyce Foundation, John D. and Catherine T. MacArthur Foundation, and David and Lucile Packard Foundation for their support of this volume. Vicky MacIntyre and Janet Mowery ably edited the manuscript, Carlotta Ribar proofread the pages, and Sherry Smith provided the index.

Finally, major endeavors like this one are never possible without the cooperation, patience, and support of one's spouse: our special thanks go to Hanns Kuttner, Eileen McGinnis, Ed Miller, and Susann Haskins.

The views expressed here are solely those of the authors and should not be attributed to any person or organization acknowledged above or to the trustees, officers, or other staff members of the Brookings Institution.

MICHAEL H. ARMACOST
President, Brookings Institution

MICHAEL C. LARACY
Senior associate, Annie E. Casey Foundation

JENNIFER PHILLIPS
Formerly program officer, Charles S. Mott Foundation

July 2001
Washington, D.C.

Contents

PART I

*Overview
and Policy
Recommendations*

1

RON HASKINS
REBECCA M. BLANK

Welfare Reform: An Agenda for Reauthorization

O N AUGUST 22, 1996, President Bill Clinton signed a revolutionary welfare reform bill crafted in Congress over the previous eighteen months,
the Personal Responsibility and Work Opportunity Reconciliation Act
(PRWORA). Everyone agreed that the law constituted a major break with
the past, although there was substantial disagreement about whether these
changes were for the better. The legislation passed Congress with a bigger
bipartisan majority—consisting of nearly all Republicans and about half the
Democrats in the House and Senate—than the bipartisan majority that
enacted Medicare in 1965. But there were those who bitterly criticized it.
Several administration officials, who urged the president to veto the bill,
resigned in protest when he approved it.

In passing this legislation, Congress placed a specific time limit on its
funding. Thus by October 1, 2002, Congress must enact new legislation in
order to continue federal funding for many of the provisions of the 1996 law.
Inevitably, as Congress considers whether and how much new spending to
authorize, most of the major provisions of the 1996 law will come under
scrutiny, including those that do not explicitly require reauthorization. In
this sense, all the provisions of the 1996 law are open to discussion and possible amendment during the reauthorization debate.

The Upcoming Reauthorization Debate

Given the importance of the 1996 reforms, Congress is likely to spend a great deal of time in 2001 and 2002 on the reauthorization debate. Extensive hearings in several House and Senate committees are likely; multiple bills by many members of the House and Senate, and in all probability a bill from the administration, can be expected; extensive and elaborate debates on the major provisions in subcommittees, full committees, and the floors of the House and Senate are a certainty. The best guess is that Congress will begin writing legislation in the late winter of 2002 and will enact final legislation in the fall of 2002.

During this process, many forces will influence congressional decision-making. These include the political philosophy of the Republican and Democratic parties, the particular alignment of power between the political parties in the House and Senate, the bitterness over the 2000 presidential election, the virtually even split of Republicans and Democrats in the House and Senate, the philosophy and goals of the leaders of the committees of jurisdiction, conservative interest groups that focus on limiting government power and spending while expanding personal responsibility in social programs, liberal interest groups hoping to ensure that the poor receive adequate public benefits and that some of the provisions of the 1996 legislation are modified, the states and their powerful lobbying groups working to ensure that states receive plenty of money and retain the vast flexibility they were given in the 1996 reforms, and a bewildering array of other individuals and groups lobbying on specific issues addressed by the 1996 reforms.

One other voice deserves a prominent place at the table during the lively debates that will accompany reauthorization. As the discussions in this volume show, the world of social science has produced a mountain of information about the provisions that were at the heart of the 1996 reforms, how the reforms have been implemented, and their effects on employment, income, poverty, family composition, and children's well-being. A major goal of social science is to inform policymakers about how policies have been carried out and the effects they have produced. The editors and authors of this volume, though equally divided between political conservatives and liberals, are advocates for the important role social science should play in the reauthorization debate. All of us have learned through experience, however, that there is no guarantee that social science will affect the debate or the decisions made by Congress and the president. Social scientists, like other actors who would influence Congress, must win a place at the table by delivering clear messages in prominent places.

Hence this volume. We certainly do not expect members of Congress to read a scholarly tome like this one. Nevertheless, we do expect congressional staff, social scientists, reporters, child advocates, and informed citizens to do so. In this way, we believe a consensus about the major findings will begin to grow, and this consensus will in turn influence media reports, congressional testimony, the analyses produced by congressional agencies such as the Congressional Research Service and the General Accounting Office, and the one-page summaries staff will give to members of Congress about specific reauthorization issues. It would be naive to think that social science will be the major force influencing Congress during reauthorization, but we have a lot to say about how the reforms have been working and believe that Congress—as well as those who would influence Congress—ignores this information at the peril of making poorer decisions.

An abundance of information is now available on the 1996 reforms from at least three sources. First, the 1996 law contained several provisions that required data collection, data reporting, and research or evaluation studies. Congress worked closely with the administration and the states to produce new administrative reporting requirements as part of the Temporary Assistance for Needy Families (TANF) block grant. In addition, the legislation required states to report, for the first time, fairly complete administrative data on child care subsidies. Although there have been problems with the state-reported child care data, other research has also focused on this topic, and information on child care utilization and funding has improved.

The 1996 law also provided the Department of Health and Human Services with about $15 million per year to fund research on a wide variety of issues relevant to the new legislation and to continue research, especially program evaluation studies of demonstration projects that had been authorized during the five or so years before the 1996 legislation. In addition, the law provided the Census Bureau with about $70 million in funding (which has since been increased by $6 million) to collect additional data on participants in two waves of the widely used and admired Survey of Income and Program Participation (SIPP). These funds allowed the Census Bureau to continue following the SIPP's representative sample of about 18,500 households and to expand their data on children's well-being. This important new study, called the Survey of Program Dynamics, was funded by Congress because it would permit comparisons of the condition of children and families before and after the 1996 reforms.

The second source of information about the effects of the 1996 reforms is research funded by foundations (see Research Forum on Children, Families, and the New Federalism, 2001). Although to our knowledge no one has yet produced an overview of all the welfare reform research funded by foundations since 1996, the Annie E. Casey Foundation, the Packard Foundation, the Foundation for Child Development, the Charles Stewart Mott Foundation, the Ford Foundation, the W. T. Grant Foundation, and the Rockefeller Foundation, among many others, have made extensive investments in studies on some aspect of welfare reform. Perhaps the most important among the foundation-funded projects is the Assessing the New Federalism project housed at the Urban Institute in Washington, D.C. The centerpiece of the New Federalism project is a large-scale national survey called the National Survey of America's Families. Other important research projects funded primarily by foundations are also being conducted by the Manpower Demonstration Research Corporation and by a consortium of scholars at Harvard University, Northwestern University, and Johns Hopkins University. Several of these studies have already produced important information and can be expected to provide additional information during the reauthorization debate.

Third, as the chapters in this volume amply testify, welfare reform has attracted the attention of many individual scholars, including some of the nation's most respected researchers. A growing number of scholarly studies either report new empirical data on some aspect of welfare reform or review the available evidence on specific issues.

In this volume, we bring many of these scholars together to examine the major issues that are bound to play a role in the reauthorization debate. Our goals are to describe changes in welfare programs that have taken place since the 1996 law was enacted, to assess the evidence on the effects of these changes, and to open debate on key issues that are likely to be important (and perhaps controversial) in the upcoming reauthorization debate. Many of these issues will be important well beyond reauthorization in 2002 and are relevant not only to federal decisionmaking, but also to ongoing efforts to design and implement effective welfare and work programs by states and localities. Before turning to a summary of the key parts of this volume, we outline the major provisions of the 1996 reforms.

Overview of the 1996 Welfare Reform Law

Since enactment of the sweeping welfare reforms in 1996, the attention of policymakers, researchers, and the media has focused on the state programs funded under the TANF block grant that replaced the Aid to Families with Dependent Children (AFDC) program. However, there were many other major and minor provisions in the legislation, any of which could come up during the reauthorization debate. Table 1-1 summarizes the major provisions of the 1996 law; it also indicates when the funding for each provision must be renewed and whether the funding for the renewed provision is assumed in the budget baseline. Many of the reforms enacted in 1996 became part of permanent federal law and do not need additional action to remain in effect after 2001 or 2002. Our guess is that this will not make much difference if members of Congress or powerful outside constituencies want the provision considered as part of the reauthorization debate.

For example, the restrictions on the access of legal immigrants to welfare were permanent and require no reauthorization. These provisions were among the most controversial during the original debate in 1995 and 1996 and were singled out by President Clinton when he signed the bill as an example of provisions he did not like and would try to change. In fact, in 1997 the president recommended and Congress accepted, and even expanded, legislation that reinstated some benefit eligibility to noncitizens, especially those who had been receiving benefits at the time of enactment. But many Democrats and advocacy groups believe these changes do not go far enough and remain strongly opposed to the general ban on welfare benefits for noncitizens who entered the country after August 22, 1996. These groups will make restoring benefit eligibility for noncitizens a major issue in the reauthorization debate.

As table 1-1 shows, the 1996 law covered eight major programs or policy domains: TANF, Supplemental Security Income (SSI) for children, child support enforcement, welfare for noncitizens, child protection, child care, child nutrition, and food stamps. In addition, the new law contained many provisions designed to reduce pregnancy outside marriage. This volume addresses most of these issues. Because we have elected to discuss what are in our opinion the most important issues for reauthorization, our review of the 1996 provisions is somewhat selective.

Temporary Assistance for Needy Families

Enactment of the TANF program was the most thorough and fundamental of the reforms because it replaced the AFDC program with a federal block grant. The most important elements of the TANF reforms can be captured in five provisions:

—States were given primary responsibility for designing their cash-assistance program and determining the rules under which families could receive assistance. The result is an increasingly diverse set of state programs since 1996.

—The entitlement to benefits provided under AFDC was abolished. In the past, destitute families with children who met joint federal-state income

Table 1-1. *Major Provisions in the 1996 Welfare Reform Law, Annual Funding, and Whether Funding Is Assumed in the Baseline*

Name	Description	Funding	Funding in baseline[a]
	Title I: Temporary Assistance for Needy Families		
Basic TANF grant	Block grant to states to help needy children, to reduce nonmarital births, and for other purposes	$16.5 billion annually, FY1996–2002	Yes
Illegitimacy bonus	Bonus grant to reward up to five states for greatest reduction in out-of-wedlock birth rates	$100 million annually, FY1999–2002	Yes
Performance bonus	Bonus grant to reward high performance by states for attaining goals of TANF	$1 billion for FY1999–2003; average annual bonus grants are $200 million	Yes
Population and poverty adjustor	Supplemental grant (of up to 2.5 percent of family assistance grant) for 17 qualifying states with above-average population growth and low (FY1994) federal welfare spending per poor person	Up to a total of $800 million for FY1998–2001	No
Contingency fund	Matching grants for needy states	Such sums as needed for FY1997–2001, up to a total of $2 billion; this original ceiling reduced by $40 million by P.L. 105-89	No
Indian tribes	Grants for Indian tribes and Alaskan native organizations that operated their own work programs before TANF	$7.6 million annually, FY1997–2002	Yes
Territories	Matching grants to Puerto Rico, Guam, the Virgin Islands, and American Samoa for TANF and foster care and adoption assistance programs	Such sums as needed annually for FY1997–2002 (about $116 million for TANF, Title IV-E, and aid to the aged, blind, and disabled in all the territories)	Yes

Loan fund	Interest-bearing loans for state welfare programs; total amount of loans made to a state during FY1997–2002 limited to 10 percent of the state's family assistance grant	Appropriates such sums as needed for the cost of the loans, with no specified years; limitation of 10 percent of state family assistance grant applies to FY1997–2002; total amount of loans outstanding may not exceed $1.7 billion	n.a.
Transitional increased federal matching for increased Medicaid administrative costs	Funds provided to states to compensate for increased costs of computing Medicaid eligibility for needy families	$500 million total without fiscal year limit	No
Research: Census Bureau	Census Bureau study to evaluate impact of TANF on random national sample of recipients and other low-income families	$10 million annually, FY1996–2002	No
Research by HHS on effects, costs, and benefits of state TANF programs	Funds for HHS to use to evaluate and conduct research on welfare reform	$15 million annually, FY1997–2002	No

Title II: Supplemental Security Income

SSI is a permanently authorized entitlement program. The amendments made in 1996 are permanent and do not require reauthorization. The most controversial amendments restricted benefits for children and are having an ongoing impact that reduces federal spending every year in relation to the spending that would have occurred without the 1996 reforms. Congress does not need to take any action during welfare reauthorization in order for the SSI program to continue operating as it does under current law.

continued on next page

Table 1-1. *Major Provisions in the 1996 Welfare Reform Law, Annual Funding, and Whether Funding Is Assumed in the Baseline* (continued)

Name	Description	Funding	Funding in baseline?[a]
	Title III: Child Support Enforcement		
	Child Support Enforcement is a permanently authorized entitlement program. All of the amendments made in 1996 are permanent. Congress does not need to take any action during welfare reauthorization in order for the Child Support Enforcement program to continue operating as it does under current law.		
	Title IV: Restricting Welfare and Public Benefits for Aliens		
	The amendments that restrict alien eligibility for welfare benefits are permanent, free-standing provisions of law. Congress does not need to take any action during welfare reauthorization in order for these provisions to continue operating as under current law.		
	Title V: Child Protection		
	This title made modest amendments in Title IV-B, Title IV-E, and section 1123 of the Social Security Act. These changes are permanent and require no reauthorizing action by Congress, although subpart 2 of Title IV-B must be reauthorized by the end of 2001. This title also authorized an important study of abused and neglected children as follows:		
National Random Sample Study of Child Welfare	Funds to conduct a longitudinal study of children with confirmed cases of abuse or neglect	$6 million per year, FY1996–2002	No
	Title VI: Child Care		
	The child care amendments in the 1996 welfare reform law were made to the Child Care and Development Block Grant (CCDBG) of 1990 and are a permanent part of the CCDBG. However, the CCDBG itself must be reauthorized in 2002.		
Child care: discretionary	The CCDBG contains both discretionary funds that require an annual appropriation and entitlement funds that require no annual appropriation	$1 billion authorized annually, FY1996–2002	n.a. (annual appropriation)

Child Care: Entitlement	The Child Care and Development Block Grant contains both discretionary funds that must be appropriated annually and entitlement funds that require no annual appropriation	Entitlement funding increases from $1.967 billion in 1997 to $2.717 billion in 2002; after 2002, the baseline amount is $2.717 billion annually	Yes

Title VII: Child Nutrition

The child nutrition program is authorized through 2003.

Title VIII: Food Stamps and Commodity Distribution

Food Stamp Employment and Training Program	Funds for states to operate training and employment programs for food stamp recipients	Reserves for allocation to state agencies specific amounts for FY1996–2002; about $220 million in grant funds plus additional funding at 50 percent federal contribution	Yes
Food Stamps	Provides coupons to purchase food to needy families	Authorizes general Food Stamp appropriations through FY2002 without specific dollar limits on appropriations or spending	Yes
Availability of commodities under the Food Stamp program	Funds for the federal government to purchase commodities for distribution to states	For FY1997–2002, mandates funding of $100 million annually for the Emergency Food Assistance Program	Yes

Title IX: Miscellaneous

This title contained twelve provisions. All except Abstinence Education were permanent provisions of law and do not need to be reauthorized by Congress. The particulars on reauthorization of the abstinence education provision follow:

Abstinence education grants	Grant funds distributed to states to conduct programs teaching abstinence to children	$50 million annually; FY1998–2002	No

n.a. Not applicable.

a. If funding is not assumed in the baseline, then Congress must find a revenue offset for the provision. If funding is assumed in the baseline, Congress can save money and use it for other purposes by not reauthorizing the provision or by reauthorizing it at a level below that assumed in the baseline.

eligibility rules had to be provided with cash benefits. Under TANF-funded programs, states have imposed a greater number of work and other behavioral requirements, along with income eligibility requirements, and states have authority to decide who receives benefits and under what circumstances. In most cases, cash benefits are now conditional on attempts to prepare for self-support.

—The AFDC funding mechanism of open-ended federal matching payments for state welfare expenditures was replaced by a block grant to each state. The block grant funding level for each state is fixed and is based on the level of federal expenditures in the mid-1990s under the old AFDC program. Because the block grant funding is fixed, if states can help families leave welfare, they retain the funds that used to pay their welfare benefit. This feature of the block grant was intended to provide states with a financial incentive to help families leave welfare, although some argue that it was intended to control federal spending. States must also maintain their own spending at a level equal to 75 or 80 percent of the amount they spent from state funds on the AFDC and Job Opportunities and Basic Skills Training programs in 1994.

—States are required to place an annually accelerating percentage of their caseload in work activities for a specific number of hours, although states can also meet this requirement by reducing their caseload below its 1995 level. By 2002, states must have 50 percent of their caseload involved in work for thirty hours a week; some or all of the 50 percent can be met by caseload reductions. States that fail to meet the work requirement have their block grant reduced. States in turn impose sanctions by reducing the cash benefits of individuals who fail to work. States with large caseload declines face less stringent work requirements.

—States are not allowed to use federal TANF dollars to pay the benefits of families who have been on welfare for more than five years. Twenty percent of the caseload may be exempted from this time limit.

Taken together, these five characteristics have made state-run TANF programs radically different from the AFDC program they replaced.

Supplemental Security Income for Children

The SSI provisions for children were intended to tighten the standards by which children qualified for cash SSI benefits and thereby reduce the number of children receiving SSI. The Individualized Functional Assessment test that a number of parties, including the U.S. General Accounting Office (GAO, 1995), thought too subjective in judging children to be disabled, was banned and the definition of childhood disability was made more specific and restrictive. These and similar measures were designed to ensure that only poor children with the most serious disabilities were admitted to the SSI program.

Child Support Enforcement

By sheer numbers alone, the child support enforcement amendments were the most extensive provisions in the 1996 legislation. They were exceptionally comprehensive and amended nearly every aspect of the child support enforcement program. The general thrust of the reforms was to increase the number of children with paternity established at birth, to provide access to new sources of employment and financial information for state programs, to reform state programs by automating information and case processing as much as possible, and to provide additional child support payments to mothers who left welfare. The major goal of these reforms was to improve the performance of the child support program so that more noncustodial parents would be located, more paternities established, more child support orders put in place, and more money collected to help single mothers leaving welfare and to reimburse the government for providing cash welfare payments for needy children.

Welfare for Noncitizens

Next to TANF, the most controversial provisions in the legislation were those that virtually ended welfare for noncitizens. When legislation on welfare for aliens was first enacted in the late 1880s, Congress made it clear that no alien should be admitted to the United States if immigration officials thought the alien could become a public charge (U.S. House of Representatives, 1998, appendix J). As welfare programs expanded in the 1960s and 1970s, however, noncitizens began to qualify for benefits, although illegal aliens never had access to public assistance. Even when Congress controlled alien access to welfare, as in the 1993 SSI provision that the elderly could not receive benefits until five years after entry, the underlying assumption was that noncitizens who were legally admitted to the United States did qualify for benefits. In 1996 Republicans wanted to reinstate the presumption that noncitizens should not receive welfare. Thus the 1996 legislation all but eliminated welfare for the first five years after aliens enter the country (except among refugees who continued to be eligible) and seriously restricted access even after the fifth year. More specifically, after five years the ban on SSI and Food Stamps continues, but states may, at their option, provide TANF benefits and Medicaid to legal aliens. Furthermore, as a condition of entry, aliens must sign an agreement stipulating that they understand they cannot receive welfare. Finally, the sponsorship agreements by which churches, relatives, and others agree to provide help to entering aliens if they fall on hard times were converted into legally binding obligations.

Child Care

The child care provisions in the 1996 welfare reform law were straightforward and in their final form and funding level, relatively noncontroversial. First, several programs that provided child care for low-income and welfare families were merged. This reform simplified state administration of federal child care subsidies by allowing states to run a single program, called the Child Care and Development Block Grant, that covered all poor and low-income families, including those leaving welfare. Second, the 1996 legislation increased total child care funding by about $4.5 billion over six years. States also were given even more flexibility in funding child care by provisions that allowed them to spend money directly from the TANF block grant on child care or to transfer funds from the TANF block grant into the Child Care and Development Block Grant to spend on child care. As it turned out, by 1999 states were using almost $3 billion in TANF funds to purchase child care. Finally, continuing a compromise between Republicans and Democrats first reached in the Family Support Act of 1988, regulation of child care quality was left to states and localities.

Food Stamps

The Food Stamp program provisions, considered to be the most extensive food stamp reforms since 1977, expanded state options and control of food stamps, especially with regard to sanctions for noncompliance with various state requirements. The 1996 reforms also limited eligibility for those 18 to 50 years old and without dependents, greatly restricted eligibility for aliens, reduced the basic food stamp benefit across the board by about 3 percent, increased penalties for fraud, and expanded the use of electronic cards to deliver food stamp benefits.

Reducing Illegitimacy

A host of provisions designed to reduce illegitimacy were scattered across several titles of the 1996 law. Conservatives inside and outside Congress argued that nonmarital births were the nation's major social problem and caused many of the nation's other social problems such as welfare use, delinquency and crime, poor school performance, and illegitimacy in subsequent generations. In fact, influential conservative activists such as William Bennett and Robert Rector, as well as conservative social scientists such as James Q. Wilson and Charles Murray, all but disparaged the emphasis on work requirements. They argued that unless something were done about illegitimacy, the emphasis on work, even if successful, would make little difference in the long run.

A problem with the legislative emphasis on nonmarital births was that evaluations of programs designed to reduce their frequency had consistently shown no impacts. Murray (1984) had suggested the remedy of completely ending welfare benefits for children born outside marriage, but, except in a highly modified version, complete termination of benefits was never seriously considered by Congress. Rather, Republicans decided to literally throw in a host of provisions that might have an impact on reducing nonmarital births. The most important measures are bonus money given to states that reduce their nonmarital birth rate and the number of abortions, an abstinence education grant program designed to teach children that abstinence is the standard for youth, and very strong and mandatory paternity establishment requirements.

Taken separately, any of these eight domains of reform would have been considered major legislation. Taken together, they constitute perhaps the most extensive and thorough reform of federal assistance policy since the creation of AFDC in 1935. The concept of entitlement to cash benefits for able-bodied parents and their children was ended, strong work requirements and time limits were established, the definition of children's disability was narrowed, child support was greatly strengthened, Food Stamp eligibility and benefits were significantly reduced, welfare for noncitizens was all but eliminated, child care subsidies were streamlined and federal spending was dramatically increased, and illegitimacy was brought to the top of the nation's social agenda and several new programs to fight it were put in place.

Organization of the Volume

The chapters in this book were commissioned by the two editors, with advice from Michael Laracy of the Annie E. Casey Foundation and Jennifer Phillips of the Joyce Foundation, and are designed to summarize what we know, five years into welfare reform, about the impacts of these legislative changes. The book opens with a series of overview chapters that set the context for the more topically focused chapters that follow.

—Thomas Gais, Richard Nathan, Irene Lurie, and Thomas Kaplan provide a broad overview of the ways in which states have chosen to implement their new TANF-funded public assistance programs.

—Rebecca Blank and Lucie Schmidt summarize the major trends in work among less-skilled women and relate these trends to changes in the economy and in policy.

—Ron Haskins indicates how these work trends translate into changes in income and poverty among less-skilled mothers.

—Charles Murray reviews the trends in nonmarital childbearing and marriage and discusses the causal factors behind these trends.

—Hugh Heclo and Larry Mead provide their interpretations of the political process that produced major welfare reform in 1996.

Following these overview chapters, a variety of topical chapters discuss the evidence on program changes and their impacts. Each of these chapters makes specific recommendations for the reauthorization process.

—Julie Strawn, Mark Greenberg, and Steve Savner discuss arguments for expanding welfare-to-work programs into work force training and retention programs.

—Ladonna Pavetti and Dan Bloom review the evidence on the impacts of sanctions and time limits.

—Charles Michalopoulos and Gordon Berlin discuss the evidence on how to most effectively provide financial work incentives for the working poor.

—Jason Turner and Thomas Main review the history of work experience programs, the role they play in welfare reform, and the role they should play in a well-designed state welfare program.

—Sheila Zedlewski and Pamela Loprest summarize the evidence on how to most effectively serve highly disadvantaged families with multiple barriers to work.

—Robert Greenstein and Jocelyn Guyer review the changing trends in food stamp and Medicaid use by families leaving welfare and discuss the factors shaping these trends.

—George Borjas discusses the use of welfare among noncitizens and the impact of the 1996 reforms on welfare use by noncitizens.

The final set of chapters focuses on a range of issues that relate to family formation and child well-being.

—Greg Duncan and Lindsay Chase-Lansdale summarize the evidence on the impact of welfare reform on child well-being.

—Wade Horn and Isabel Sawhill discuss policies that could reduce early childbearing, encourage marriage, and reinvolve fathers in their children's lives.

—Irwin Garfinkel reviews changes in the child support system and evidence on the impact of these changes.

—Douglas Besharov and Nazanin Samari discuss how states are dealing with child care issues and the impact of child care subsidies on low-income families.

—Lynn Karoly, Jacob Klerman, and Jeannette Rogowski examine the effects of changes in SSI program eligibility among children, immigrants, and the disabled.

Most of these chapters are followed by brief comments from an expert, often a person who holds views somewhat divergent from the chapter author(s). These comments help frame the debate that is likely to emerge during reauthorization.

Recommendations Regarding Reauthorization

As always happens when Congress faces the reauthorization of major legislation, members of Congress, committee staff, interest groups, and social scientists all have changes to suggest. The authors in this volume, for example, propose more than 100 changes in the 1996 legislation. In this section we concentrate on a set of policies that in our judgment meet two criteria: they will play a central role in the reauthorization debate, and they are of broad importance to child and family well-being. These recommendations reflect our particular viewpoints and are laid out only briefly. The following chapters (and their comments) provide more extensive descriptions of the evidence and the arguments behind these recommendations.

We come to this discussion with somewhat different perspectives. Haskins is a developmental psychologist and has served as a senior Republican staff member on the House Ways and Means Committee for fourteen years. Blank is an economist and recently completed a term as a member of the Council of Economic Advisers for President Clinton. Our colleagues have no trouble identifying which of us is the conservative and which the liberal. We are, however, both more centrist than many identified with either the right wing or the left wing of the welfare reform debate. And we are both committed to the idea that policy analysis and evaluation should be an important part of legislative decisionmaking. On some issues we are in agreement and speak with one voice. On other issues we disagree and speak separately. We address eleven issues that are crucial for the reauthorization debate: the funding level, floundering families, problems with Medicaid and the Food Stamps program, family issues (illegitimacy and marriage), time limits and sanctions, work programs, education and training, retention and advancement, child care, child support, and noncitizens.

Funding Level

One of the most important issues in the debate over reauthorization will be the level of funding for the TANF block grant in 2003 and beyond. The TANF block grant is currently funded at $16.5 billion per year. Congress also authorized more than $0.5 billion per year for performance bonuses and an annual supplemental payment to states that have low welfare spending per poor person and high population growth. The $16.5 billion block grant funding level is simply the sum of basic TANF funding received by each state. State block grant levels were calculated as the highest amount of federal money a state received under the old AFDC program in either 1994 or 1995, or the average of 1992, 1993, and 1994.

Given that caseloads have declined by more than half since the block grant funding level was adopted in 1996, it is a safe bet that some members of Congress, especially on the Budget Committees in the House and Senate, will want to substantially reduce the block grant. The rationale, of course, is that if TANF is primarily a cash-welfare program, a large reduction in the number of people receiving benefits means that states need less money to maintain their benefit payments. This argument is buttressed by the fact that a number of states have not spent all their TANF dollars. However, the claim that TANF can be cut because the rolls are down betrays a fundamental misunderstanding of the actual program created by Congress. TANF-funded programs in most states are increasingly work-support programs, not just cash-assistance programs. States are using TANF funds to provide child care, work training, education and retention programs, earnings disregards (which allow workers to keep some of their welfare benefits when starting in low-wage jobs), and, as discussed shortly, to address the problems of more disadvantaged women who continue to receive welfare.

The evidence in this volume suggests that most states are using their funds effectively and that there has been a sharp rise in work among less-skilled women (see Blank and Schmidt, chapter 3) and a significant drop in poverty among single mothers and their children (see Haskins, chapter 4), in part because of the 1996 reforms. Cutting TANF dollars would make it hard for states to continue these programs and would threaten the progress the nation is now making in helping single mothers work and in reducing poverty. In addition, the evidence presented by Duncan and Chase-Lansdale in chapter 15 suggests that states that fund strong work support programs have better child and family outcomes.

RECOMMENDATION: *Both of us recommend that the TANF block grant funding be maintained at its current level (Blank could even argue for increased dollars) and that an annual inflation adjustment be included.*

A major and unanswered question about TANF is how the level of funding should respond to changes in the business cycle. The block grant is a fixed amount. A small contingency fund of $2 billion is available to supplement block grant payments to states with rising need as measured by unemployment and food stamp enrollment, and there are provisions in the TANF program for federal loans to needy states. The ongoing economic expansion since 1996 has created little need for these emergency provisions, but many worry that state TANF programs may not be able to deal well with a recession. Public assistance has always been countercyclical: a one-point rise in unemployment increased the AFDC rolls by about 4 percent over the past two decades (Blank, 2000). State balanced-budget requirements limit a state's ability to deficit-finance, and a fixed block grant does nothing to offset this problem. The result is that states may have to restrict their employment and public assistance programs at exactly the point when need is rising. If the current economic expansion continues through the reauthorization debate in 2002, there is likely to be little pressure to deal with the potential problems that might arise in TANF programs during a recession. The 1996 legislation was passed at a particularly fortunate time, in that it encouraged states to build more work-oriented public assistance programs at precisely the moment when the U.S. labor market entered one of its longest and strongest expansions. But it would be unwise to develop programs that work only in an unusually strong economy. The challenge for both the federal government and the states is to develop programs that are financially and programmatically sustainable in times of both more and less rapid economic growth.

> RECOMMENDATION: *We both recommend that Congress consider ways to provide greater cyclicality in the flow of federal funds to state TANF programs. Blank would like to see the block grant amount respond to cyclical indicators (such as state unemployment rates). Haskins believes that maintaining the block grant at its current level with an inflationary adjustment, coupled with an expansion of the loan program for states that need additional funds, will allow states the needed flexibility to handle economic downturns. Both of us agree that the current Contingency Fund provisions need to be revised and strengthened.*

Floundering Families

Many women on welfare have multiple barriers to employment such as low skills, family health problems, language difficulties, addictions, histories of domestic violence, or little recent work experience (see Zedlewski and Loprest, chapter 12). If state TANF programs are to successfully encourage work, they must cope with the problems of more disadvantaged families.

Some of these families need sustained and often expensive assistance to cope with problems of domestic violence, substance abuse, or learning disabilities. Some are unlikely to ever be fully self-sufficient in the labor market, owing to health or cognitive limitations. Yet the evidence suggests that many of these women can and do work, although often at low wages and in short-term jobs. The 1996 legislation allows states to exempt 20 percent of their caseload from the federally imposed sixty-month time limit, and many states may be tempted to deal with the work barriers problem by simply exempting the most disadvantaged families from work requirements. Whether states can and want to do more than just issue exemptions is a test of how thoroughly the goal of work opportunities is pursued.

> RECOMMENDATION: *Blank believes that the current exemption rules are arbitrary and need to be reviewed and changed. Rather than basing exemptions on a rigid share of the caseload, Blank would argue for substantially expanding the exemption options for states. While women facing multiple barriers to work should have incentives and help in moving toward employment, some women may always need some level of ongoing welfare assistance in order to survive economically. Haskins believes maintaining the time limit is important and would not expand the 20 percent exemption limit unless it can be shown that lots of families that are making serious work efforts are losing benefits because states are up against the 20 percent limit. Both of us agree that too few programs address the needs of adults with multiple barriers to employment and that Congress should spend more money on research and demonstration programs to learn more about how to help these families.*

Problems with Medicaid and Food Stamps

States have worked hard to reduce caseloads in their TANF programs by moving more women into employment. At the same time, enrollment has fallen in other safety net programs that should have helped cushion the transition to employment. As Greenstein and Guyer show in chapter 13, public recognition of and research on this problem for the Food Stamp and Medicaid programs make it highly likely that enrollment of families leaving welfare in these programs will be an issue in reauthorization.

In most cases, women who leave welfare are in low-wage jobs and should retain their eligibility for food stamps. Indeed, as they replace welfare income with earnings, food stamps ought to help them maintain or improve their standard of living without TANF dollars. Food stamp rolls have fallen by nearly 40 percent since 1994, however, and the evidence shows clearly that a large share of eligible families are not receiving food stamps.

In the past, families that qualified for AFDC were automatically eligible for food stamps in every state. As the AFDC program has disappeared and been replaced with TANF, it has become clear that the Food Stamp program is not well designed to independently identify and assist eligible families. In addition, application and administrative procedures of the Food Stamp program have not been well adapted to working mothers: many offices are open only during the day, cases that have regular monthly earnings are difficult to deal with, and earnings must be verified frequently to redetermine food stamp levels. Although recently enacted legislation has improved state flexibility, the quality control system often penalizes those states with large shares of working families in their Food Stamp caseload.

> RECOMMENDATION: *We both agree that the Food Stamp program needs to undergo a major review so that it can operate independently and more effectively serve working low-income families, especially those not receiving other assistance. Haskins believes that it would be valuable to conduct rigorous evaluations of the effects of giving Food Stamp money to five or more states as a block grant on the condition that certain individuals and families be guaranteed coverage. Blank strongly opposes this recommendation and believes that the individual entitlement to food stamps must continue. But she believes that the program needs reform in order to operate effectively as a safety net for working low-income families. In particular, she would like to see the eligibility rules for working families simplified, changes in the quality control system, and greater state flexibility.*

Similar problems are occurring with the Medicaid program. Even though children in families leaving welfare continue to be eligible for Medicaid, many of them disappear from the Medicaid rolls. Similarly, many mothers seem unaware of their continuing Medicaid eligibility for up to a year (and more in some states) after leaving welfare. In 1996 and 1997, there was growing concern about falling levels of health insurance coverage among children in former welfare families. Medicaid administrations at both the state and the federal levels responded to this concern, with the result that Medicaid enrollment among low-income children has risen in many states since 1998. Health insurance among working low-income parents remains low, however. We do not make a recommendation here but urge that states and the federal government work together to find more effective ways to provide low-income working adults and children with access to health care.

Family Issues: Illegitimacy and Marriage

Congress was explicit about its concern with high out-of-wedlock birth rates and low marriage rates among low-income families. The very first section of the 1996 law states that three of the TANF program's goals are to promote marriage, prevent illegitimacy, and encourage two-parent families. The extent to which states have aggressively pursued these goals is likely to be a major issue in the reauthorization debate. Conservatives will argue that states have done too little to pursue these goals in their TANF programs, and that the federal government should put stricter mandates on the states to address these problems programmatically. They will also call for changes in the Illegitimacy Reduction Bonus and the TANF Performance Bonus to target bonus payments on states that implement strong programs and states that achieve results.

It is clear that many observers would just as soon forget about these goals from the 1996 legislation. Many liberals did not support them from the beginning. But even states with Republican governors and legislators have devoted little more than rhetorical attention to reducing illegitimacy and encouraging marriage in TANF programs. States have not been more aggressive in implementing programs to reduce illegitimacy for three principal reasons. First, out-of-wedlock birth rates have, for the first time in several decades, been steady since about 1994, so states that have done nothing programmatic can still claim success. Second, and perhaps more important for the reauthorization debate, it is not at all clear what programs are effective at reducing nonmarital births and increasing marriage (see Murray, chapter 5; Maynard, 1997). In the absence of rigorous evaluation evidence showing that specific programs can reduce out-of-wedlock births, state human service agencies often do not know what they can do to address these issues programmatically and do not want to put their agency in the midst of the political controversy that such issues often arouse. Third, there appears to be a lack of consensus among the states that the government should be fighting illegitimacy or promoting marriage.

> RECOMMENDATION: *We disagree on the appropriate federal response to family formation issues, although neither of us believes there are any magic bullet programs to reduce illegitimacy and increase marriage. Haskins is dubious about the extent to which existing programs can be effective in reducing out-of-wedlock births but strongly supports funding for demonstration projects (and their rigorous evaluation) that will help define useful*

programmatic interventions, especially interventions designed to promote marriage. In his view, the abstinence education program that was part of the 1996 reforms should be refunded and even expanded and demonstrations of ending eligibility for cash benefits for teen mothers should be encouraged. Blank believes the research literature strongly suggests that the best way to reduce illegitimacy is to expand the sense of future opportunities available to teenage girls as well as boys. Hence she thinks illegitimacy rates will fall faster if schools can do a better job and work can pay in the labor market. She would support funding demonstration projects aimed at lowering the teenage birth rates, but until the effectiveness of such programs is shown, she would oppose a federal mandate that states do more to reduce out-of-wedlock births or encourage abstinence.

Time Limits and Sanctions

Among the most controversial features of the 1996 legislation was the imposition of the five-year time limit on individuals receiving federal public assistance. Many states have chosen to impose even shorter time limits. Similarly, the legislation required that states impose sanctions on persons who refuse to engage in work or work-related activities, although it left the details about sanction design to states. As Pavetti and Bloom show in chapter 9, these two requirements have come to be viewed as interrelated because many individuals who might at some point be subject to time limits are hitting sanctions at an earlier stage.

After four years of implementation, it is now clear that states make widespread use of sanctions. Thirty-five states use full-family sanctions, meaning that the entire cash benefit can be ended for families that do not meet program requirements. In addition, nineteen states eliminate a family's food stamp benefit for failure to meet work requirements.

Although it will be the fall of 2001 before families begin hitting the federal five-year time limit, as of this writing about 60,000 families (a relatively small number) have already hit the time limit in the states that have time limits shorter than five years. Most of those who have reached the time limit have had their benefits terminated. This is an important finding because many observers doubted that states would actually terminate the benefits of families that reached the time limit. However, the research shows that most families that reach the time limit are working and therefore are not destitute. But what about families that are not working? Careful research in Connecticut (Bloom and others, 1999) and Florida (Bloom and others, 2000) shows that states have sharply different policies and practices on this question. In Connecticut, most families that were meeting all the requirements and reached the time limit without substantial income received benefit extensions. But in Florida most families that reached the time limit were carefully reviewed and determined to be noncompliant and therefore had their benefits terminated.

Blank believes that time limits are the most objectionable part of the 1996 legislation and are based on the assumption that most people can become entirely self-sufficient within a five-year period. Evidence on the instability of work and low wages available to most women—especially those with multiple barriers to work—suggests to her that this is not an accurate assumption (Edin and Lein, 1997). She would remove strict federal time limits entirely; if this is politically infeasible, she would instead try to give states much greater discretion in how they are applied.

As we noted earlier, the 20 percent caseload exemption from time limits is a somewhat arbitrary number and Blank would like to give states much more leeway in making decisions about time limit exemptions. Haskins remains strongly supportive of time limits as a way to send the message that public assistance is not a long-term entitlement for anybody. The 20 percent figure was established through a lengthy political process and should not be changed until research shows specific harm associated with the 20 percent limit.

Sanction policy is an important component of TANF-funded programs in all states, although states vary enormously in what sort of sanctions they apply. A major issue that we believe will be increasingly important in the years ahead is the due process procedures around the implementation of both sanctions and time limits. In part because of difficulties in tracking client behavior and in part because of inadequate training by caseworkers, there appear to be many complaints that sanctions and time limits are being applied in a somewhat arbitrary fashion.

RECOMMENDATION: *Blank favors abolition of the federal time limit. If this is not feasible, she recommends that states be allowed to stop the federal time-limit clock when families are working twenty-five or more hours per week and that states should have much more flexibility in offering exemptions. We both recommend that the federal government maintain close oversight on the process by which states impose and track sanctions and time limits, and that states be given strong incentives to operate fair processes. The federal government should also ensure that careful research is conducted on the characteristics and fate of families that lose benefits because of sanctions and time limits.*

Work Programs

Most states have designed and implemented strong job-placement programs for their welfare clients. All states are in compliance with the federal requirement that a specified percentage of the caseload (40 percent in 2000) must be working or participating in a work program, in large part because states can apply their percentage reduction in the TANF caseload to the work participation requirement. If, for example, a state reduced its caseload by 20 percent in relation to 1995, its work requirement in 2000 would be 40 percent minus the 20 percent caseload reduction credit, or 20 percent. Furthermore, states have been able to meet these work requirements without putting recipients into public sector jobs that states have created. At some point in the future, however, the nation will face higher unemployment rates and less job availability. Even so, public policy should continue sending the message that work is a better option than long-term welfare dependency. This will require making "jobs of last resort" available to recipients who cannot find jobs in the private sector. In addition, states need work programs to help recipients with multiple barriers prepare for the day when they will be able to get a real job outside welfare.

The vision of many of those who strongly supported work requirements during the 1996 debate was that most people on welfare would be working in exchange for their benefits. They envisioned work experience programs in which women still on welfare work, typically in publicly provided jobs. As Turner and Main show in chapter 11, few states have so far elected to use extensive work experience programs, in part because they have not needed them to meet their caseload work requirements.

RECOMMENDATION: *Haskins recommends that Congress give states either a requirement or incentives to maintain at least a modest percentage of their caseload, say 10 percent, in work experience programs. Blank would allow states to continue deciding how many mothers should be placed in work-for-your-benefit programs. We both agree that states should be given incentives to experiment with public sector job-creation programs. Congress should also encourage states to establish demonstration programs on how to provide work experience to adults with multiple barriers to employment.*

Education and Training

Most state welfare-to-work efforts focus on "work first" programs that move women into jobs as quickly as possible without any major training component. While gaining work experience is clearly important, some women may be able to benefit from additional education or training. Strawn, Greenberg, and Savner discuss this issue in more detail in chapter 8. The need for follow-up education and training is likely to become even more acute as women who have moved into work realize that they will not be able to gain access to better jobs at higher wages without more training. Many states, however, find it difficult to place women in education and training programs. These typically do not count against the work requirement, so that a woman in a full-time education program would also have to be working steadily in order to count toward the state's work requirement.

> RECOMMENDATION: *Blank recommends that states be encouraged to count approved educational or job-training programs that require a substantial time commitment as a valid fulfillment of the work requirement for welfare recipients. Haskins agrees that education and training for job advancement are important and would use the TANF Performance Bonus to reward states that can effectively help former welfare mothers get better jobs. However, he would not allow education and training to count toward fulfilling the work requirement out of fear of diluting the work requirement. He also believes states already have enough flexibility to put more recipients or workers in training.*

Retention and Advancement

Closely linked to welfare-to-work programs and education programs are retention and advancement programs. We discuss retention and advancement as a separate topic because we think it deserves more attention than it has received. Critics who have watched welfare-to-work programs evolve now say that the biggest problem is the lack of attention to follow-through issues once a woman finds a job. Many of these programs focus entirely on that first placement, without attention to retention or advancement over time. As Strawn, Greenberg, and Savner argue in their chapter, if women are to achieve long-term economic stability and independence, it may be as important to provide assistance with job retention and job advancement as it is to provide assistance with initial job placement. Most of the welfare-to-work programs that have been rigorously evaluated are not concerned with these issues, and hence there is limited information on what effective retention and advancement programs might look like and what they might accomplish.

> RECOMMENDATION: *We recommend that the federal government provide special grants to states interested in experimenting with retention and*

advancement programs for low-wage workers. These grants should include a requirement for rigorous program evaluation.

Child Care

Child care issues are likely to be highly controversial in the reauthorization debate. On the one side, conservatives tend to argue that federal and state funds available for child care have increased substantially, and that there is little evidence of any ongoing problem in this area. Given the large increase in employment among single mothers with young children, these women are obviously finding child care (see Besharov and Samari, chapter 18).

On the other side, liberals tend to argue that too little attention is being given to child care issues. The subsidies available to many mothers are quite limited, and they may not be able to use them because they cannot find affordable and conveniently located child care with available subsidies. Such mothers are forced to rely on a mixture of relatives and friends. Furthermore, the child care settings that low-wage women must use may be of very limited quality, with high children-to-staff ratios and limited early childhood education or stimulation. Increasing interest in after-school care for older children will also add to costs. As Duncan and Chase-Lansdale show in chapter 15, the importance of after-school activities for older children is underscored by the finding from several experiments that older children of mothers who leave welfare for work are more likely to engage in problem behavior such as drinking or drug use.

> RECOMMENDATION: *Blank believes the child care funding increases in the 1996 law were good but that further increases in federal money available for child care subsidies are necessary to increase the availability of child care subsidies and to help women find more stable and higher-quality care. Similarly, the enforcement of standards in child care quality must be linked to these subsidies: states must demonstrate that their subsidies are adequate to purchase care that meets certain standards. Haskins believes that the substantial increases in child care funding provide much of the money needed and is wary of further legislation in this area. He opposes federal standards.*

Child Support

The child support provisions have turned out to be among the least controversial provisions in the 1996 law. The general themes of the child support reforms were to provide access to new sources of information about noncustodial parents, to streamline and automate child support activities, and to improve enforcement in interstate cases. Above all, the reforms aimed to automate as much of child support as possible. Garfinkel discusses these issues further in chapter 17. Although there are no studies that link any of the specific 1996 reforms with improved outcomes, the steady increase in paternity establishment, collections, and other measures of program performance suggests that the child support program is improving.

However, there are at least two important issues that must be addressed during reauthorization. The first issue is the rules for distributing child support to federal and state governments, on the one hand, or to mothers and children, on the other. Under current law, states may retain child support payments while the mother is on welfare to repay taxpayers for the costs of welfare. (The AFDC program required states to pass through a minimum of $50 in child care payments to the mothers but allowed states to retain the rest.) In addition, once the mother leaves welfare, approximately half the payments on overdue child support can also be retained by the government. In the 106th Congress, the House passed, on a striking vote of 405 to 18, legislation that would have provided more of these funds to mothers and children. This legislation or similar legislation is certain to be introduced early in the 107th Congress and to become a part of the welfare reauthorization debate. The question is whether Congress wants most child support payments to go to the government or to mothers and children. We think Congress is likely to select mothers and children and to include this reform in the welfare reauthorization legislation.

A second and very serious problem that should be considered during reauthorization is that the basic financing of the child support program is in jeopardy. The average state finances about 30 percent of its program by retained collections from current or former welfare cases. However, the rapid decline in welfare rolls means that this source of income is also dropping rapidly. In the long run, if the welfare rolls remain low, nearly every state is going to have to consider new ways of financing its child support program. States are already asking for more federal funding, but federal legislators can be expected to argue that states should pick up the major burden of new financing needs.

RECOMMENDATION: *Both of us would provide federal financial incentives for states to provide more child support payments to mothers who leave welfare. In addition, Blank would mandate that states pass through at least the $50 required under the AFDC program (while the mother is still on welfare). Congress should fund studies that propose and evaluate new methods of financing child support enforcement.*

Noncitizens

The provisions that imposed substantial restrictions on welfare for noncitizens, including the ban on welfare for noncitzens who arrive in the United
States after August 22, 1996, were among the most controversial parts of the
1996 legislation. Although the Balanced Budget Act of 1997 restored some
of these benefits, the ban on assistance to new entrants to the United States is
still national policy. As a result, immigrant and child advocacy groups will
make a major effort to change the August 22, 1996, dividing line, probably
by aggressively pushing a proposal to provide Medicaid to children and pregnant women who enter the country after August 22, 1996. Borjas discusses
the evidence on the effects of the 1996 reforms on benefit use by noncitizens
in detail in chapter 14.

Like the country, we are divided on this issue. Haskins believes the ban on
welfare benefits for noncitizens, which was U.S. policy for nearly a century
after welfare restrictions were first imposed in the 1880s, is reasonable and
fair. People should come to America for opportunity and freedom, not to
participate in welfare programs. The 1996 legislation provides reasonable
exceptions to the ban on benefits. These include requiring noncitizens to
have sponsors who are legally required to provide assistance if the noncitizen
becomes destitute; allowing exceptions for medical emergencies, communica-
ble diseases, natural disasters, and child abuse; and permitting participation
in means-tested education and training programs that noncitizens can use for
self improvement. Moreover, once aliens become citizens, they become eligible for welfare benefits on the same basis as natives. In Haskins's view, the
restrictions on welfare for aliens are necessary because experience shows that
they are even more likely than citizens to use welfare if there are no restrictions; because American taxpayers should not be responsible for paying welfare benefits, except under emergency conditions, to families that come to
the United States for opportunity; and because not providing welfare to new
entrants can, in the long run, ensure that only aliens truly interested in
opportunity and personal freedom come to America.

Blank strongly disagrees with banning noncitizens who have legally
entered the country from all forms of public assistance. She agrees with the
enforcement of sponsorship agreements, so that sponsors are financially
responsible for noncitizens. But there are some forms of public assistance that
should be available to all legal U.S. residents. In particular, access to Medicaid and to food stamps should be available even to noncitizens. Access to SSI
should be available to those who become disabled after entering this country.
It is unacceptable that some U.S. residents should be hungry or unable to

receive basic medical care. Limiting access to these programs has negative consequences not only for the noncitizens, but also for the larger society.

> RECOMMENDATION: *Haskins would retain the provisions that exclude (with some exceptions) noncitizens from public assistance. Blank would change the 1996 provisions to allow noncitizens access to Medicaid and food stamps and, under some circumstances, SSI.*

Comments on Recommendations

The eleven areas outlined in this chapter are all likely to be subjects of concern within the reauthorization debate. We are struck by how many areas of agreement we have, which suggests that there may be bipartisan support for some of these recommendations. On the other hand, there are clearly some key areas of disagreement around time limits, food stamp changes, fertility and marriage provisions, child care, and noncitizen access to benefits. These will be hotly debated.

One issue that is likely to arise in the reauthorization debate is whether lower poverty rates ought to be added as an explicit goal of the 1996 legislation. Liberal groups are particularly likely to want to focus public attention on the antipoverty effects of these program changes, and to reward states for reducing poverty rather than only for reducing caseloads. Blank would strongly support these efforts.

We want to underscore that the resolution of these issues will depend on the larger political and economic environment facing Congress in 2001 and 2002. If the divisiveness of the recent presidential election continues to be played out in Congress, welfare reform may become one of the symbolic issues that Republicans and Democrats use to stake out their rhetorical ground. Under these circumstances, the reauthorization debate and vote will be much more partisan. The economic outlook in 2002 will matter as well. If states face an economic slowdown, it will be easier for Congress to maintain funding in the TANF block grant, and efforts to emphasize job retention and public sector job placement will be boosted.

Finally, we note one fundamental change in the 1996 legislation that we think will not be seriously challenged: the devolution of welfare program authority to states. Over the past five years states have made a major investment in designing and implementing their own set of TANF-funded programs. The benefits and costs of devolution should and will be discussed during reauthorization. In some states, current programs are unambiguously better than the old AFDC program. In other states, programs are too focused on removing people from welfare rather than helping them to become economically self-sufficient. Blank believes there are more of the latter states than Haskins does. But regardless of how we view the substantial devolution of power and responsibility for social programs to states, neither of us believes that returning major authority for designing cash welfare to the federal government will be on the table during reauthorization. States are not willing to give back the authority they were granted in the 1996 legislation.

Conclusion

Welfare reform has been one of the most closely watched legislative changes of recent decades. There is enormous interest in what states are doing and how well the new TANF programs are functioning. The jury is still out on the long-term impacts of these changes, but nobody doubts that they have fundamentally altered the public assistance system in this country and the expectations of those who apply for cash welfare.

This volume summarizes what we know almost five years after the 1996 legislation. The chapters describe the major program and behavioral changes that have occurred. They set the stage for the reauthorization debate and point to key areas in which further legislative changes may or may not be useful. But they go beyond a simple discussion that prepares for reauthorization. They are an assessment of where we are as a nation on the issues of welfare, poverty, and work and how we have come to this place over the past five years. As such, this volume can inform not only the reauthorization debate at the federal level, but also the much more focused programmatic debate within states, as states continue to fine-tune and experiment with their public assistance programs. We are quite confident that many of the issues raised in this chapter and in this volume are not going to be finally settled in the reauthorization debate but will continue to create controversy and program experimentation in the decades ahead.

References

Blank, Rebecca M. 2000. "What Causes Public Assistance Caseloads to Grow?" *Journal of Human Resources* 36 (Winter): 1.

Bloom, Dan, Mary Farrell, James J. Kemple, and Nandita Verma. 1999. *FTP: The Family Transition Program: Implementation and Three-Year Impacts of Florida's Initial Time-Limited Welfare Program.* New York: Manpower Demonstration Research Corporation.

Bloom, Dan, and others. 2000. *Jobs First: Implementation and Early Impacts of Connecticut's Welfare Reform Initiative.* New York: Manpower Demonstration Research Corporation.

Edin, Kathryn, and Laura Lein. 1997. *Making Ends Meet: How Single Mothers Survive Welfare and Low-Wage Work.* Russell Sage.

Maynard, Rebecca. 1997. "Paternalism, Teenage Pregnancy Prevention, and Teenage Parent Services." In *The New Paternalism: Supervisory Approaches to Poverty*, edited by Larry M. Mead. Brookings.

Murray, Charles. 1984. *Losing Ground: American Social Policy 1950–1980*. Basic Books.

Research Forum on Children, Families, and the New Federalism. 2001. *Research Perspectives: Past, Present, and Future*. New York.

U.S. General Accounting Office (GAO). 1995. *Social Security: New Functional Assessments for Children Raise Eligibility Questions*. GAO/HEHS-95-96.

U.S. House of Representatives, Committee on Ways and Means. 1998. *1998 Green Book: Background Material and Data on Programs within the Jurisdiction of the Committee on Ways and Means*. Government Printing Office.

PART II

The Biggest Issues

2

THOMAS L. GAIS
RICHARD P. NATHAN
IRENE LURIE
THOMAS KAPLAN

Implementation of the Personal Responsibility Act of 1996

IN THE FALL OF 1996, two of us attended a meeting in Washington, D.C., of research, governmental, and advocacy organizations interested in states' implementation of the recently enacted Personal Responsibility and Work Opportunity Reconciliation Act. Toward the end of the meeting, we discussed timing: when could we draw firm conclusions about how states were responding to the flexibility and responsibilities granted them under the Temporary Assistance for Needy Families (TANF) program established by the new law? Some argued that changes would follow soon after state legislatures enacted new welfare laws in early 1997. More thoughtful responses came from analysts who believed it would take the summer for most legislatures to act, and state agencies would need several months to write administrative rules and revise manuals for case managers and supervisors.

Neither of us found these estimates to be realistic, particularly since one of

We would like to thank our field research directors, who analyzed and documented the state-level changes discussed here: John Hall (Arizona); Christy Jenkins (California); Malcolm Goggin (Colorado); Robert Crew (Florida); Michael Rich (Georgia); Jocelyn Johnston (Kansas); Carol Weissert (Michigan); Thomas Luce (Minnesota); David Breaux, Christopher Duncan, Denise Keller, and John Morris (Mississippi); Lael Keiser and Peter Mueser (Missouri); Richard Roper (New Jersey); Sarah Liebschutz (New York); Deil Wright (North Carolina); Charles Adams and Miriam Wilson (Ohio); Thomas Anton (Rhode Island); John Gnuschke (Tennessee); Christopher King and Dan O'Shea (Texas); Gary Bryner (Utah); Betty Jane Narver and Janet Looney (Washington); Christopher Plein and David Williams (West Virginia); and Thomas Corbett and Thomas Kaplan (Wisconsin).

us had just reported how another attempt at reforming welfare, the Family Support Act of 1988, had still not been fully implemented years after its enactment (Hagen and Lurie, 1994). Yet our different expectations also grew out of different views of what constitutes implementation. Implementation might be viewed, at the most general level, as changing the behavior of administrative institutions to reflect the goals and tasks of the laws. To many of our colleagues at that meeting, such change follows as a matter of course from the elaboration of specific rules to guide bureaucratic behavior: a kind of downward cascade of legal interpretations. When to apply sanctions to families? Who is exempt from work requirements, and for how long? Who would perform what functions? What are the responsibilities of social service agencies and work force development boards, and how should clients be referred from one to the other?

With few exceptions, most states have succeeded in formulating specific policies under the Personal Responsibility Act. Yet the history of welfare reform suggests that writing and transmitting new instructions may not change bureaucratic behavior. Despite the enactment of work requirements several times in the history of Aid to Families with Dependent Children (AFDC), and despite their translation into specific rules, these requirements typically had little effect at the local level. One reason for their impotence was the failure to change the missions of local welfare offices—offices that focused on minimizing eligibility errors by requiring families to document extensively their income and assets, children's birth records, and other eligibility data (Kane and Bane, 1994). Implementation not only demanded new rules, it required changes in standard operating procedures and the infusion of new purposes throughout the vast structures that administered welfare and related social programs. Implementation was thus in part a problem of institutional engineering: of transforming organizations, creating new organizations, and forging linkages among organizations in order to fuse the new purposes with the required capacities.

Somewhat surprisingly to us, states have made major changes in their social service systems reflecting the employment and antidependency goals of the Personal Responsibility Act. Their successes in this regard have surely benefited from fortunate circumstances. Unlike the Family Support Act—which suffered from the unhappy coincidence of going into effect during a mild recession—the Personal Responsibility Act was implemented during a period of extraordinary economic growth that reduced unemployment, shrank caseloads, and swelled state revenues. Under these conditions, a wide range of political and bureaucratic actors found employment-related goals feasible and acceptable. To change the goals of their welfare systems, states and localities added new processes and requirements, gave greater power to institutions with strong employment missions, shifted the mix of benefits to those that support work rather than directly relieve poverty, and often devolved greater discretion down to local governments, welfare offices, and frontline workers. Much variation exists among state strategies and success in implementing these changes, and state welfare systems still face important institutional challenges. Yet the rapidity and breadth of change have been stunning. State and local human service systems may now be one of the most quickly changing components of American governmental institutions, and the 1996 Personal Responsibility Act may be a major cause.

There is, however, yet another level of implementation: a capacity to adapt program elements to changing circumstances. From this perspective, implementation does not produce closure, some final consonance between laws and administrative behavior. Instead, it demands the ability to recognize problems, devise new solutions, and put those solutions into effect. State and federal welfare reforms enacted basic goals, and it makes little sense that such goals can always be attained in the same way with a constantly shifting mixture of families and economic conditions. Thus implementation demands not only rule formulation and institutional engineering but also a capacity for governance, a capacity to alter program elements in light of new information, circumstances, and experiences. In this sense of the word, states are still in the process of implementation: adaptation has occurred, but learning has been limited by the lack of recurrent information at the state and local levels about low-income families.

Data Sources

Our chapter draws on implementation studies performed by a number of organizations, but it relies largely on data collected by the Nelson A. Rockefeller Institute of Government (of the State University of New York) in its State Capacity Study. This study has several components. We conducted intensive field research in 1997 and early 1998 on the changing institutions and management systems states were using to implement their welfare reforms. Research teams of experienced university scholars in nineteen states analyzed institutional changes and characteristics by means of a comparative field analysis method, one that relies on a common, agreed-upon "report form." These data were updated in 2000 in fifteen states. The chapter also uses financial data from a pilot study in four states of changes in spending on social services before and after the Personal Responsibility Act, a study that has since been expanded to include thirteen states (Ellwood and Boyd, 2000).

We also draw on the Frontline Management and Practice Study being conducted at the institute by Irene Lurie and Norma Riccucci of the University at Albany and Marcia Meyers of Columbia University. This project examines eleven local welfare offices and related service systems in Georgia, Michigan, New York, and Texas. The study seeks to learn how state and local policies are implemented at the ground level by directly observing face-to-face interactions between TANF applicants and recipients and frontline workers. The sample of interactions included all types of encounters, such as eligibility determination, orientation to work programs, arranging for child care, and conciliation and sanctioning.

Changing Behavior by Changing Signals

The formal purposes of the TANF block grant were to provide assistance to needy families so that children can be cared for at home; end the dependence of needy parents on government benefits by promoting job preparation, work, and marriage; prevent and reduce the incidence of out-of-wedlock pregnancies; and encourage the formation and maintenance of two-parent families. To achieve these goals, the law incorporated a distinct conception of welfare, in which time limits, work requirements, sanctions, special rules for minor parents, and expanded funding for services were expected to encourage behavioral changes with respect to employment, reproduction, and marriage. The law also expressed a theory of federalism, in which states were given flexibility in designing policies and dealing with clients in exchange for state accountability to financial penalties and bonuses attached to program goals.

Because political support for employment is widespread while debates about the means of reducing out-of-wedlock births continue, states have put more direct emphasis on the work and antidependency goals of TANF than on the goals relating to marriage and reproduction. Much of this new focus emerged as states used their new flexibility to redesign the way they handle clients and to introduce new organizations, with different missions and capacities, into welfare systems. These changes have altered the "signals" of welfare programs, that is, the basic messages about what the welfare program offers to clients as well as what it demands in return.

Processes as Signals

The strongest new signal is the "work first" message: get a job quickly or exhaust all alternatives to cash assistance. States are sending this signal about the importance of quick entry into the work force not just in words but by augmenting the processes clients go through when they apply for assistance.

Redesigning these procedures is a critical way of communicating with families. The complexity of the eligibility process, which requires extensive collection and verification of information about a family's circumstances, puts eligibility workers under time pressure in their meetings with clients. Demands for information can crowd out conversation not directly related to establishing eligibility, such as conversation about child support, mandates to work, time limits, family caps, and so forth. Although clients must sign a form saying they understand the rules and agree to comply with them, our observations suggest that they often sign after hearing little or no explanation of the form and without reading it. Furthermore, unless a client is monitored for complying with the rules, it is just a piece of paper. Unless a rule is hard wired into the eligibility process, workers apply it unevenly.

Under TANF, states can create new forms of hard-wiring. Unlike AFDC law, the new law does not require states to give everyone the opportunity to apply for aid or to provide aid with "reasonable promptness." These changes have allowed agencies to redesign the front door of the welfare system, the process that people go through when they apply for assistance. In all eleven sites in the institute's Frontline Management and Practice Study, states have adopted a variant of a work first model, which requires that individuals cooperate with work requirements while applying for welfare. In every site, applicants for welfare must go through one or more activities designed to inform them that recipients will be encouraged and assisted to work. Moreover, they must complete this process before the welfare agency approves their application for welfare.

In Texas, for example, the applicant attends a group orientation at the Texas Workforce Center before the application can be approved. The orientation explains time limits and work participation and the availability of employment services, education and training, child care, and transportation assistance. The work force agency stamps a form brought by the applicant, who returns it to the welfare agency. When the welfare agency receives this form, it can authorize assistance. In Suffolk County, New York, the welfare agency gives people an application for assistance and then, like Texas, refers them to a group orientation at the Department of Labor. Following the orientation, labor department staff interview people to gather enough information to assign them to a work activity. Everyone leaves the orientation not only with a form verifying their attendance, but also with a referral to a job readiness program, a referral to the health department, or an appointment with a job counselor at the Department of Labor.

Michigan has a longer process. After applying for assistance, all parents must attend a group orientation operated jointly by the welfare agency and the contractor providing employment services. Unless they are already employed, they then attend an individual orientation with the contractor where they are assigned to an initial work activity. Only after attending the first day of the initial work activity will the welfare agency authorize assistance.

The process in Georgia is even more rigorous. Applicants must search for a job for a specified period of time before assistance can be authorized. In both of the study sites in Fulton County (Atlanta), the Georgia Department of Labor has an office at the welfare agency where it runs a two-week group job search program. In Bibb County (Macon), where the Department of Labor has a satellite office across the street from the welfare agency, applicants must search for a job for five weeks before assistance can be authorized, making contact with four employers per day. Each morning, they come to the welfare agency to report the contacts made with employers the previous day and, if necessary, go to the Department of Labor for more job leads.

Although their efforts varied in rigor, all these sites established a norm that work is expected. They conveyed this message through an experience for the applicant, not through a verbal explanation, a video, or a piece of paper that could be ignored or misunderstood. Conveying the message through the experience of going to an employment agency reduces the likelihood that the message will fail to reach the applicant, a risk in implementing welfare reforms. The process itself conveys the signal that work is now part of the culture of welfare.

These findings reinforce conclusions from our first round of research, during which we examined intake sequences in thirty local welfare offices (Nathan and Gais, 1999). We found that eligibility determinations for TANF cash assistance were often preceded by (1) a program orientation; (2) a job search or registration for a job search; (3) child support enforcement, accomplished, for example, by establishing paternity and securing a child support order; (4) creation of a personal responsibility plan, which sometimes identifies alternatives to welfare; and, less commonly, (5) offers of diversion assistance, such as one-time cash payments, services, referrals to private charities, or entitlement benefits (such as Medicaid or food stamps) in lieu of continuing cash payments.

What is missing in many of these intake processes is also interesting: few rely on early assessments of the employability of clients. States typically require all applicant caregivers to seek jobs immediately, unless they are categorically exempt from work requirements, such as mothers of very young infants. Only if people fail to find work after a certain number of weeks, job contacts, or other measures of effort do formal assessments come into play.

This reactive, empirically based approach was evident in the fact that assessments of employability and service needs typically occurred late in the client-intake process. Rather than assume that people entering the TANF program are in need of assistance, states offer intensive services only to those who fail to find work. The importance of work is thus signaled by pushing most adults into the labor market for some direct experience with employers and then using the market to sort out which cases are problematic and which are not.

One implication of these complex, front-loaded processes is that a strategy for preventing people from becoming dependent on welfare may also prevent working families from receiving the services they need to remain independent of cash assistance. If the focus of attention at the front door of the welfare agency is diverting families from welfare, families may not receive complete information about benefits available to the working poor such as food stamps, Medicaid, and child care. This problem is compounded by the fact that welfare agencies are only beginning to develop processes for the back door of the welfare system. Some states operate programs to help recipients retain jobs and even extend job retention services to those who leave assistance. However, recruiting participants into these programs is difficult. In states with generous benefit levels and earnings disregards, where families are likely to be eligible for welfare after they find work, states can identify and recruit families that might benefit from such services. Yet because recipients often do not inform their eligibility worker that they are leaving welfare but simply fail to show up for a recertification appointment, people who leave welfare are not easy to serve. If signals are expressed through a process and there is no process, the signal that welfare agencies will support working families will not be heard.

The New Role of Employment Bureaucracies

To deliver the signal about work, states gave greater control over program operations to entities that emphasize employment goals and created quicker and stronger administrative connections. Signals are changed by adding new signalers. One of the striking characteristics of state legislative debates over welfare reform in the 1990s was the intense focus and frequent disagreement over who should control welfare programs, in contrast to a relative lack of conflict over the content of the reforms (such as time limits, the severity of sanctions, and services offered). There was a strong political reaction among legislators and some governors against giving traditional social service bureaucracies predominant control over the administration of new work-based welfare programs. In most states, this reaction led to the assignment of greater responsibilities to state work force development systems. As we wrote in our *First Look* report (Nathan and Gais, 1999), out of nineteen states, two (Utah and Wisconsin) gave nearly all responsibilities for administering their TANF programs to employment bureaucracies, nine assigned exclusive responsibility for TANF job services to labor departments, and three increased the role of labor departments in their welfare programs. Since that report, several states—including Missouri, Florida, and Ohio—have further strengthened the institutional connections between their work force development and welfare agencies.

Privatization also reduced the control exercised by traditional social service agencies. Arizona and Mississippi kept their welfare programs within their social service agencies, but both initially attempted major privatization efforts. Arizona privatized the administration of its TANF program in Phoenix, while Mississippi initially privatized not only its job services but also its case management functions (though these functions were eventually brought back under direct public control; see Breaux and others, 2000). When Florida enacted its WAGES program, it initially created a complex tripartite division of control, with its child and families services department handling eligibility, its labor department handling work first services, and its newly created local WAGES boards dealing with "deep end" services to adults who did not get jobs after several weeks of trying. These complex relationships did not work out, however, and in 2000 Florida gave complete responsibility for TANF services to the state's Workforce Development Board, a public/private entity reporting to the governor. Florida also required that services to welfare and other low-income clients be carried out by privately owned service agencies that served all Floridians. Agency realignments like these can have a powerful effect: by eliminating institutional distinctions between employment services provided to poor caregivers and all other Floridians, the state essentially said its strategy for assisting poor citizens is an employment strategy; and that "cash assistance should be viewed as one of the least desirable resources available to families and should be used only as a last resort" (Crew and Davis, 2000, p. 25).

We can see how some of these employment bureaucracies are involved in local welfare offices by looking at eight of the eleven sites in the Frontline Management and Practice Study. In each of these sites, researchers examined the offices responsible for cash assistance, work activities, and authorizing child care assistance. Some states assign all three functions to a single organization, but most divide them among specialized organizations.

The arrangements for delivering services and the configuration of staff within these institutions vary a great deal among these sites, as shown in table 2-1. Some of the variation runs along a public-private scale. At one extreme is New York, where welfare is administered by the counties. County welfare agencies may either take the lead responsibility for work activities or contract out to other agencies. The Suffolk County Department of Social Services contracted out this responsibility to the county Department of Labor, while the Albany County Department of Social Services serves as the lead work agency and contracts with multiple organizations for services. In Georgia, the state welfare agency contracts with the state Department of Labor for job search and placement services. In Michigan and Texas, work programs for welfare recipients are the responsibility of the state work force agency, which also oversees the Workforce Investment Act, Unemployment Insurance, and other work programs. The state agencies operate through local work force boards, which in turn contract out to service organizations. Texas permits the work force boards to contract with for-profit companies, as in the case of Dallas, where the board contracts with the for-profit Lockheed Martin Corporation. Although table 2-1 shows only part of the local service delivery system for TANF programs, which may involve many specialized services, it is clear even from this picture that local staff arrangements are often complex and local systems often encompass both public and private organizations. Rather than a simple trend toward privatization, we see a broader movement toward complex combinations of diverse institutions drawn from both the public and private sectors.

The Culture Change Hypothesis

An overarching question about welfare reform is the magnitude of the "culture change" taking place in local offices. Critics of AFDC have sought to transform welfare agencies from a culture focused on collecting information to ensure eligibility and compliance to a self-sufficiency culture that emphasizes finding people work (Kane and Bane, 1994).

Articulating New Goals

At the top of the welfare agencies in the Frontline Study, culture change is an often-heard theme. Most of the administrators we interviewed said they have adopted strategies aimed at shifting their agency's culture toward work and self-sufficiency. They emphasized employment or diversion from welfare in their formal statements of goals. In Georgia, they used the language of vision, mission, and empowerment: "We are changing the culture by creating a vision and empowering local agencies, not by regulating them. . . . Our mission is to assist TANF clients in becoming employed, with TANF, food stamps, and low-income Medicaid supporting the employment process." In

Table 2-1. *Institutional Arrangements and Staff in Selected Local Welfare Systems*

County/agency	Staff position[a]	Number of staff[b]
	Georgia	
Fulton County, Northwest Office (Atlanta)		
Department of Family and Children Services	Reception	4
	Intake (eligibility)	5
	Ongoing (eligibility)	16
	Child care	6
Department of Labor	Service specialist	2
Site total		33
Bibb County (Macon)		
Department of Family and Children Services	Screeners	5
	Intake (eligibility)	11
	Ongoing	12
	Employability	6
	Challenger	4
	Work Experience Program	4
	Child care	4
Department of Labor	Service specialist	4
Site total		50
	New York	
Albany County		
Department of Social Services	Reception clerks	9
	Reception examiners	10
	Reception child support enforcement	1
	Eligibility and undercare examiners	23
	Employment Unit	[6]
Contractors on site	Child care counselors	2
	Assessment for mental barriers	1
	Assessment for domestic violence	1
Site total		53
Suffolk County, Smithtown Office		
Department of Social Services	Eligibility	7
	Undercare	[10]
	Clerk/reception	3
	Suffolk Works Employment Program	9
	Child care	6
	Front-end detection system	2
Department of Labor: serves four welfare offices	Assessment	24
	Registration	4
	Job readiness training	3
	Job development/OJT	4

continued on next page

Table 2-1. *Institutional Arrangements and Staff in Selected Local Welfare Systems* (continued)

County/agency	Staff position[a]	Number of staff[b]
	Job placement	5
Site total		77
	Michigan	
Macomb County, Sterling Heights Office		
Family Independence Agency	Family independence specialist	24
	Registration support	2
Work First Agency: St. Clair Shores Born Center	Community resource specialist	1
	Job club and retention	2
	Job readiness	1
	Job search	1
	Assessment	1
Site total		32
Wayne County (Detroit), Glendale/Trumbull Office		
Family Independence Agency	Family independence specialist	49
	Registration support	2
Jewish Vocational Services	Retention specialist	4
	Case coordinator	3
Operation Help	Orientation	1
	Job developer	4
Site total		63
	Texas	
Dallas: Masters Office		
Department of Human Services	Texas works advisor	19
	Receptionist	1
Texas Workforce Center (Lockheed-Martin): serves two welfare offices	Career counselor	6
	Seminar leader	2
	Resource room monitor	1
	Child care	2
Site total		31
Denton County		
Department of Human Services	Texas works adviser	12
	Receptionist	2
North Texas Human Resource Group	Career development	2
	Workshop facilitator	1
	Counselor	1
Site total		18

Source: Frontline Management and Practice Study.
a. Includes staff providing cash assistance, employment services, and child care.
b. Staff with face-to-case contact with TANF clients. Brackets indicate infrequent contact.

Michigan: "Our goal is for all offices to have 100 percent employment." In Texas, the state welfare commissioner expressed his main goal by a phrase heard repeatedly: "Get a job, get a better job, get a career." Only in New York did we find a welfare administrator say he was not interested in changing his agency's focus on eligibility functions, as he felt that such a change would undermine its capacity to minimize eligibility errors, a goal that remains important in both the county and the state.

Welfare administrators designed physical space to communicate the importance of these goals. A big banner in the lobby of one office proclaimed "Welcome Job Seekers!" Posters in the waiting room said, "You Have A Choice, Choose a Job—Work First"; "Work First So That Your Child Is Not the Next Generation on Welfare"; "Life Works If You Work First." The message was the same in another state's welfare office: "Job Seekers Welcome!" and, in English and Spanish, "Time Is Running Out/Welcome Job Seekers, Your Independence Is Our Success."

Some welfare agencies have tried to redefine the job of frontline workers. In the self-sufficiency culture envisioned by Bane, welfare agencies would structure interactions between workers and clients around employment instead of eligibility rules and paperwork. Table 2-1, which shows the frontline staff who have face-to-face contact with TANF applicants or recipients, suggests that with the exception of one site in New York, state welfare agencies included elements of this redesign in their culture-change strategies. All states changed the titles of their frontline workers to reflect the goals of work and self-sufficiency. For example, before welfare reform, Michigan had a job title, Assistance Payment Worker, a person who dealt exclusively with AFDC, food stamps, and Medicaid. Michigan now has Family Independence Specialists, who provide not only these benefits but also child care and other support services. With the exception of Texas, the new titles entailed real changes in duties. In Georgia, for example, positions known as Family Independence Case Managers combined the responsibilities formerly split among AFDC, food stamps, Medicaid, and workers in the Jobs Opportunities and Basic Skills training program.

At the frontlines of the agencies, however, the goals of accurate eligibility determination and compliance with rules are still evident. When lower-level managers, supervisors, and especially frontline workers described the agency's goals, they talked less about self-sufficiency and more about accuracy in determining eligibility and benefits. Another frequently articulated goal was getting their work done on time, expressed as "timeliness" or "standard-of-promptness." Eliminating fraud was also important, with finger-imaging of all applicants in New York and Texas and access to an extensive database of personal information in Texas. Their most common worry was the high rate of error in the Food Stamp program. Before TANF, the federal government operated a quality-control (QC) system that imposed financial penalties on states with excessive rates of error in determining AFDC eligibility and benefits. The TANF law ended the federal QC requirement for cash welfare, but the Department of Agriculture still operates a QC program for food stamps. Because families with earnings generate more errors than those without jobs, the success of the economy and TANF in moving people into employment may have contributed to the growth of food stamp error rates since 1997. At least, states have acted as if that were true, as many have stepped up their efforts to verify eligibility for food stamps (Fossett, Gais, and Thompson, forthcoming; see also Greenstein and Guyer, chapter 13). Because welfare agencies administer the Food Stamp program together with cash assistance, often using the same forms, computer screens, and people to gather information, efforts to reduce the food stamp error rate help sustain an agency's overall emphasis on accurate benefit determinations. Just as welfare reform has affected access to food stamps, food stamp goals and processes have spilled over into the administration of welfare.

Practices at the Frontlines of Welfare Agencies

The Frontline Study did not just ask workers about their goals; we observed how welfare workers actually treat their clients. Preliminary analysis of data from the worker-client encounters indicates that much of the time is spent collecting information about the applicant, other family members, and absent parents. Workers collect documents to verify family relationships and residence, such as birth certificates, social security cards, immigration papers, driver's licenses, marriage licenses, divorce papers, and leases or other proof of residence. They collect documents to verify income and assets, such as pay stubs, letters from employers, tax returns, bank statements, and vehicle registrations. Because applicants must pursue other available sources of support, workers may require proof that the individual has applied for Social Security, Unemployment Insurance, disability insurance, or private health insurance. Workers also collect documents to verify the expenses incurred by applicants, such as a landlord's statement, mortgage bills, utility bills, or hospital bills, or to verify the crisis facing the applicant, such as an eviction letter. Finally, workers may need to obtain documents about the applicant's children, such as proof of immunizations or school registration. Because accountability is still important to welfare agencies, the eligibility/compliance culture described by Bane has not faded away with the repeal of AFDC.

At the same time, workers almost always mention an initial, required work activity during the first interview in the application process. Often, this comes early in the interview and is repeated at its end with a specific date or choice of dates for attendance. Unlike AFDC, which made referrals to work activities after eligibility was authorized, and when referrals were often to an education or training program that might not start for several months, TANF made its participation mandate immediate and a condition of eligibility. Imposing the mandate through job search programs, which operate on a short cycle or continuously, means that clients need not wait to begin. Right away, they experience the signal that work is expected. The practices of front-line workers thus reflect both the work and the accuracy/compliance goals. Change has occurred by augmenting, not transforming, the culture of local agencies.

The fact that signaling is done largely through institutional processes and structures may help account for the interesting patterns of program understanding among participants. The evidence available from client surveys and focus groups suggests that the general messages sought by policymakers have made it through to participants. A study in Boston, Chicago, and San Antonio (Cherlin and others, 2000, p. 8) indicates that "recipients by and large know that there is a time limit. In two of the three cities, a substantial majority knows how long the time limit is. Nonetheless, there exists widespread uncertainty about the details of time limits and related policies." Programs may not be fully explained to participants, but because caregivers experience processes that express the new messages, they get to know the general expectations.

Changing Services

In addition to changes in program signals, we have seen major changes in the benefits and services states provide to their low-income populations. Perhaps the most definite change has been the decline in the provision of cash assistance and a corresponding increase in the provision of services, particularly those that support work.

However, describing the shift in benefits provided to low-income families before and after the enactment of the Personal Responsibility Act is no easy task. Federal data, collected by the Administration for Children and Families through Form ACF-196, are suggestive at best. Although these data include both federal TANF and state maintenance of effort (MOE) money (that is, state spending for the goals of welfare reform, mandated under the federal block grant), they do not include other relevant funding streams, including

Figure 2-1. *Proportion of Total (Federal and State) Funds Spent on Cash Assistance, Fiscal 1999*

Number of states

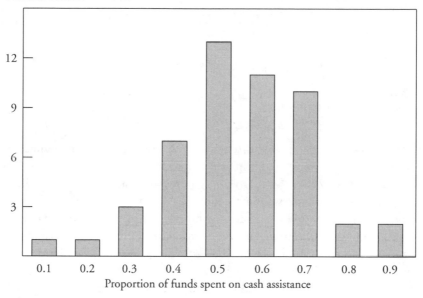

Proportion of funds spent on cash assistance

Source: U.S. Department of Health and Human Services.

the federal Child Care Development Fund, a separate block grant also enacted as part of the 1996 Personal Responsibility Act. Still, even this incomplete picture of state spending on welfare-related purposes suggests that many states are no longer spending most of their human services money on cash assistance. Figure 2-1 shows the distribution of states with respect to the proportions they devoted to cash assistance in federal fiscal year 1999. The median state spent 54 percent of its state and federal money on cash assistance, while one out of four states spent 45 percent or less. States that spent the least on cash assistance were typically those that have seen very large declines in caseloads or those that have had the most experience with welfare reform. Michigan, for example, has been reforming its welfare programs since 1992: it spent only 42 percent of its TANF/MOE funds in 1999 on cash assistance, less than the total of what it spent on work activities (15 percent) and child care (30 percent). Wisconsin, with welfare reforms that date back to the 1980s, spent 28 percent of its funds on cash benefits compared with 25 percent on work activities and 19 percent on child care.

The federal data, however, do not reflect changes in state spending priorities since the enactment of the Personal Responsibility Act. To discern those

Table 2-2. *Changes in Social Services Spending, State Fiscal Years 1995 –99*
Percent

State	Poverty relief	Child care	Employment and training	Poverty prevention	Mental health and other	Child protection	All social services
California	−29	115	52	32	39	64	4
Georgia	−51	76	56	34	4	31	−1
Missouri	−29	120	111	11	20	54	16
Wisconsin	−48	168	20	5	12	34	−8

Source: Ellwood and Boyd (2000).

changes, the Rockefeller Institute conducted pilot research on changes in social service spending in California, Georgia, Missouri, and Wisconsin (Ellwood and Boyd, 2000). So that we might compare states' spending before and after welfare reform, we examined changes in all social services, not just those directly supported by the federal block grant or state maintenance of effort spending. This comprehensive approach not only offers comparability, it also sheds light on how states shifted spending among social service categories and between federal and state budget sources and how some categories of spending, such as mental health or child welfare, might be affected indirectly by the new flexibility in spending under TANF.

When we compared expenditures in fiscal 1999 and fiscal 1995, we found major shifts in priorities in all four states. As table 2-2 demonstrates, all four states had major declines in "poverty relief," meaning direct financial assistance to households for living expenses, including cash assistance, emergency assistance, state supplementation to federal Supplemental Security Income payments, and other programs. These declines were closely correlated with falling AFDC/TANF caseloads. The largest declines in poverty relief were in Georgia and Wisconsin, where welfare caseloads fell the most.

In contrast, we found increases in all other categories of social service spending. First, spending on child care and child development programs rose in all four states more than any other category of spending. All states except Georgia at least doubled their spending on child care and child development. Second, spending on employment and training increased in each of the states, though not as much as child care expenditures. Third, spending on poverty prevention programs—such as diversion payments, pregnancy prevention programs, and substance abuse prevention and treatment—grew but at a much lower rate, as did spending on services for mental health and developmental disabilities. Fourth, child protection services, mostly spending on child welfare, increased substantially, although the reasons for growth do not seem to be related to changes in the welfare system (Ellwood and Boyd, 2000).

Except for a 16 percent increase in Missouri, states' total spending on social services did not change very much. Overall spending in California and Georgia was stable, with California's expenditures increasing by 4 percent and Georgia's decreasing by 1 percent. Wisconsin's total social service spending declined by 8 percent, perhaps because the state began its welfare reforms well before 1995. Even after the decline, Wisconsin spent more money on social services per person in poverty than the other three states.

Though spending totals were fairly stable, the distribution of expenditures across functions shifted dramatically. Child care spending ranged between 4 and 7 percent of the total social services budgets in 1995. By 1999, however, that percentage grew to between 10 and 14 percent. In contrast, the percentage of the social services budget going to poverty relief programs fell from 33 to 16 percent in Georgia, from 49 to 27 percent in Wisconsin, from 65 to 45 percent in California, and from 33 to 20 percent in Missouri.

In field research we conducted in 2000, we listed all types of services supported by states' TANF/MOE funds in fiscal 1999 and estimated, working with state officials, the rough magnitude of spending changes on these social services between 1995 and 1999. Again, to ensure comparability over time, the estimates include all state spending on these social services, not just the part funded in the latter years by TANF or designated by the state as MOE money. For each area, we estimated changes in spending according to a five-fold scale: large increase (35 percent or more between state fiscal years 1995 and 1999); significant increase (greater than 10 percent but less than 35 percent); little or no change (between a 10 percent increase and a 10 percent decrease); significant decrease (a decline greater than 10 percent and less than 35 percent); and large decrease (greater than 34 percent). We obtained usable data from fourteen states.

These data confirmed the more detailed four-state analysis. Spending for most forms of direct poverty relief fell, most dramatically for cash assistance, which declined in thirteen of the fourteen states, but spending also fell for food stamps and housing. The only widespread exception to declining spending for poverty relief was child support enforcement: eleven of fourteen states reported a significant growth in spending on efforts to secure child support payments. Direct poverty relief also grew in some states in the form of emergency assistance and a variety of small programs providing targeted in-kind supports, such as clothing vouchers.

Spending on work support and front-end job services grew vigorously. Child care spending showed large increases in ten of fourteen states and smaller increases in three other states. Transportation spending also grew in most states. Spending on job search and placement services increased, while trends for other employment and training services varied from state to state. Work experience programs grew in four states—New York, Ohio, West Virginia, and Arizona—and showed little change or declines in others. Postemployment services also showed variation: five of the eleven states responding to this question increased spending on such services, while four states did not have such programs. Only in Ohio did spending on wage subsidy programs grow, and no state spent TANF/MOE funds on public sector employment programs.

States seem to be expanding the range of services offered since the first couple of years after the 1996 reform legislation passed. Seven of thirteen responding states have increased spending on pregnancy prevention programs, though these programs generally remain small. Also, some states are responding to perceived changes in their caseloads, which administrators view as increasingly composed of families with severe obstacles to employment. Mental health expenditures increased in six of ten reporting states; in contrast, substance abuse prevention and treatment expenditures increased only in two states and otherwise remained constant.

Variations on Work First

The data on spending patterns, processes, and administrative structures are certainly consistent with the work first paradigm. Yet states also vary within the work first framework. Two important differences involve the operational goals of the program, which range between states that emphasize work participation and those that also stress caseload reduction, and the structures and services states use to achieve those goals. These structures and services reveal different ways of construing the problems of moving people into jobs and helping them achieve independence. Some states treat the problems of not working and dependence as motivational in nature; some state systems are built around the assumption that such problems stem from a lack of job-related skills; and still others have implemented eclectic, adaptive, sometimes ad hoc service systems, on the premise that many barriers may prevent families from achieving independence, depending on the specific cases and local circumstances. Given these categories, at least six variants of the work first model may be discerned.

Motivational Strategies: Work Participation as Primary Goal

States in this category try to motivate people to work by decreasing the costs of employment and increasing its gains, that is, by "making work pay." Minnesota's TANF program, which resembles its AFDC-waiver antecedent, the Minnesota Family Investment Program (MFIP), supplements earnings with services, offers high benefit levels and sufficient earnings disregards to allow families to receive cash assistance up to 120 percent of the poverty level, provides generous asset disregards (including a relatively high value for a vehicle), and augments earnings through the state's earned income tax credit. The program stresses short-term job search; it puts less emphasis on the training and education services offered under its MFIP pilot. A sliding scale child care program is available to many working families (though the program is not yet fully funded). We found some diversion activities in one of two counties studied, but the program is designed to encourage work, not minimize caseloads.

Missouri assigns greater prominence to work support services than to cash supplements, though in 1999 the state doubled its disregard, from one-third to two-thirds, for income earned while on welfare. Its reforms attempt to reduce the costs of working and searching for work, not only for families through its generous child care, transportation, and medical assistance programs but also to employers through a fast-growing wage subsidy program. To families that find jobs, the state offers an additional grant of up to $350 a year for other job-related expenses. Missouri's TANF program has extensive up-front job search requirements but no explicit diversion programs. Administration is centralized, and case managers focus on explaining state rules and service options. State administrators stress work participation rates, not caseload reduction.

Motivational Strategies: Reducing Dependence as Primary Goal

States in this group also try to motivate families to behave in certain ways. But rather than encouraging families to mix earnings and cash assistance, these states attempt to minimize families' dependence on cash. Wisconsin's W-2 program, which is organized to resemble the "real life" of work (Kaplan, 2000), is the most fully developed system of this kind. Families are paid only for hours they have clocked. Payment levels are keyed to the level of participation—more demanding work activities have higher "wages"—and family size is irrelevant to the determination of benefits. W-2 families make co-payments for child care services, but, just as in the real world of work, the state (their "employer") keeps none of their child support payments. No income or asset disregards exist, since employable caregivers receive no cash assistance (except for the state's earned income tax credit). Employment and career services are offered through the state's often impressive county job centers, where services are open to all people looking for work, not just low-income families. W-2 thus encompasses a two-pronged strategy. For parents who are employable, it offers generous work support services and an earned income tax credit to a large part of the low-income population. For parents who cannot find unsubsidized jobs, it offers employment of last resort, though entry to and use of this employment are restricted. W-2 case managers explain options, requirements, and consequences; they are not expected to find jobs for caregivers or to solve family problems. Families are expected to do that for themselves, drawing on the ample resources the state makes available to working families.

Texas's welfare program is quite different from Wisconsin's and perhaps belongs to a different category. It does not offer a rich array of services to such a wide range of working families, nor has it yet fashioned close administrative connections between the state's welfare and work force development systems. Texas, however, is like Wisconsin in trying to motivate families to avoid cash assistance. Yet rather than using a "real world of work" approach, Texas emphasizes error-minimization and antifraud activities to restrict entry onto the welfare rolls by making welfare even less attractive than it might otherwise be. The Lone Star Imaging System for detecting TANF, food stamp, and Medicaid caseload duplication requires all adults in participating households to be finger-imaged. Quality-control efforts have intensified in recent years, and investigations into anomalies may involve home visits. During interviews, eligibility specialists can look up an applicant's recent credit card purchases and balances and ask for explanations. However, once people get on the rolls, the pressures to leave do not seem great. The state recently increased earnings disregards, which can extend clients' time on assistance.

Employment Services Strategy: Work as Primary Goal

These work first systems try to move people into jobs less by offering incentives than by building job-related skills through employment, training, and education services. Such states do provide work supports and earnings disregards, but rather than assuming that barriers to independence are motivational, these programs presume that caregivers most need assistance in finding jobs or getting training, counseling, and even education for better jobs.

Michigan, like Minnesota and Wisconsin, offers generous cash benefits, child care services, and other work supports. Yet the dominant chord in the Michigan Family Independence Program is the extensive array of employment services offered to TANF clients through the state's work force development agency. Its twenty-five local agencies contract out to private organizations, called Work First agencies, which in turn "develop individual service plans to move participants into . . . unsubsidized employment as quickly as possible and increase the responsibility and amount of work the participant is able to handle over time" (Weissert, 2000, p. 152). They do this by providing employment and postemployment services, which have expanded over the years. In 1999, for example, the state liberalized its policies so that "recipients working 10 hours a week and enrolled in education programs for 10 hours can meet the state's 30-hour work requirement, which counts 10 hours of study time" (Weissert, 2000, p. 152). Emphasis is on work participation, not caseload reduction. This goal is signaled by the governor's strong interest in the state's Project Zero sites, local offices that were given administrative flexibility in exchange for accepting the goal of reducing to zero the number of persons on the welfare rolls without earnings. Michigan has no diversion program, nor does it impose time limits on cash assistance. The state is committed to supporting families with state funds when they exceed the five-year federal time limit.

Tennessee's First Families program also stresses employment services and work participation. It has no diversion program, nor does it require an immediate search for work. No policy of "banking" time on assistance exists. That is, case managers do not review cases with earnings in order to encourage recipients to get off the rolls and preserve their time on assistance, perhaps because in a low-benefit state like Tennessee, people with significant earnings quickly lose their eligibility. Families First administrators pride themselves on the program's education and training focus, but as one might expect in a low-benefit state, they have problems securing participants. To encourage participation, the state pays clients to complete education, training, and other work-related milestones; cash bonuses are awarded for getting a job, completing a general equivalency diploma or college degree, or retaining a job for six or twelve months. The state also offers strong work supports, including a First Wheels program that provides zero-interest auto loans.

A state could, theoretically, implement an employment services strategy while minimizing access to cash assistance, and that would constitute another type in our taxonomy. Florida's newly revised system, which aims to subsume "welfare" under the state's work force development system, may implement this approach, but it is too early to tell. Florida clearly tries to reserve cash assistance as a last resort: it offers at least six varieties of diversion, each serving distinct short-term needs, including help in relocating to places where jobs are plentiful.

Adaptive Services Strategies: Work as Primary Goal

These states rely on services and emphasize work participation more than caseload reduction; what distinguishes them is the range of services provided as well as the discretion given to workers and administrators. The idea is to create a large repertoire of services that case managers can use in responding to the particular needs of families. These programs take shape at the point of contact with clients and thus display "second-order devolution." They may not emit clear signals—as do the motivation-based systems—but their individualized service strategies make them more adaptable to diverse and changing circumstances.

Kansas, for example, puts little emphasis on caseload reduction. It offers no diversion benefits, and it has relaxed its applicant job search requirements for the many "recyclers" to the program. Kansas, unlike most states, conducts extensive up-front assessments. Domestic violence counselors are co-located in intake offices to screen for and provide support services, and clients are assessed for learning disabilities through a learning disability diagnostic tool. As caseloads declined and officials felt that they had to help with people who were hard to employ or who cycled in and out of jobs, our Kansas field researcher discerned a shift in strategy toward job retention for the remaining TANF adults, many of whom need intensive support services, such as enhanced transitional services, vocational rehabilitation services, remediation for the learning disabled, treatment for substance abusers, and intensive family preservation.

Adaptive Services Strategies: Reducing Dependence as Primary Goal

West Virginia and Washington, like Kansas, have formulated a variety of programs and have given local workers discretion in deciding what treatments are appropriate in specific cases. Both states, however, put greater stress than Kansas on minimizing the use of cash assistance. West Virginia's high level of unemployment, viewed by policymakers as suggesting that residents need to "bank" their time on cash assistance, and the state's concern about minimizing costs have led it to push for diversion and rapid exit from its cash assistance rolls. District offices require a waiting period before enrollment in TANF. Applicants must search for a job, document that effort, and complete a personal responsibility contract before applications can be completed. Our field researcher reported that in 2000 case managers were being encouraged to use diversion and support services to prevent initial enrollment, facilitate transition from the rolls, and prevent reenrollment. Frontline staff may dissuade families from entering the rolls by offering alternative benefits such as food stamps, emergency assistance, help in getting child support, assistance from community service organizations, or a formal diversion payment. The state also moves people off the cash assistance rolls by offering potential welfare "leavers" a wide variety of in-kind benefits: clothing vouchers, dental and vision services, vouchers to obtain tools and licenses, money for relocation, and transportation assistance.

Washington's WorkFirst program also entails a pluralistic, adaptive services strategy. Getting people off cash assistance is a primary goal. Individual responsibility plans focus on leaving cash assistance, the state offers cash diversion, and state administrators establish annual targets for caseload reduction. These goals are implemented through an informal, individualized case management model, in which the case manager serves as "a broker of services, expected to evaluate, support, coach, monitor, network, and refer clients." The program's success "rests heavily on the ability of [eligibility] and [job service] frontline service deliverers to work with individual clients, service providers, employers, and other stakeholders (Looney and Narver, 2000, pp. 86–87)." If clients and families face multiple barriers to employment, a team of workers dealing with the case may include a social worker and community providers. To give frontline workers the capacity to solve the employment-related problems of a diverse caseload, the state has generated many distinct work-related programs, devolved discretion down to case managers, and kept administrative structures flexible. Administrative regulations governing the work of case managers have been reduced from fifty-four pages under AFDC to twelve pages under WorkFirst; and rather than relying on formal agreements, such as memoranda of understanding, there is a desire to keep the relationships among implementing agencies fluid.

Compound Systems

Some states resist classification at the state level because they have devolved so many policy and administrative decisions down to counties or cities. This form of second-order devolution is itself a strategy, yet the component local welfare systems may also fit into one of the types listed above. One of the major distinctions among these states has been between those, like New York and New Jersey, that have left the basic relationships between state and county governments largely intact, and those, like Ohio and Colorado, that have restructured those relationships. Ohio, for example, drew on the private sector franchise model (after consultation with Wendy's) to refashion its welfare system and its intergovernmental relationships (Adams and Wilson, 2000). The state consolidated eight funding streams into a single block grant to counties with approved "partnership agreements" for welfare reform giving counties considerable power and flexibility. The state also created a new intergovernmental liaison called "account managers," who mediate the complex interactions between state agencies and counties.

These states show certain tendencies in signals and services. They tend to use adaptive, service-based strategies; and while Ohio stresses caseload minimization, New Jersey and New York put more emphasis on work participation. A striking fact in all these states is the enormous amount of time it takes for change to filter through these multiple levels. In Ohio, although counties submitted their community plans in 1997, partnership agreements (which allowed the consolidation of funding streams) were not approved in all counties until October 2000.

As this last point suggests, different work first systems experience different implementation problems. In states that try to motivate parents to work or avoid assistance, the primary challenge is to communicate options, rules, and potential consequences to family heads, and to maintain contact with families as their circumstances change. In states that use employment service strategies, an enormous challenge is to overcome the tensions between state welfare and work force development agencies. These tensions have become more acute in recent years as administrators' attentions focus on the hard-to-employ clients, who may soon be facing time limits. Work force development agencies have traditionally not served these clients because they are not the higher-skilled workers sought by employers, a critical constituency for most such agencies. States with adaptive, pluralistic service strategies face many management challenges. Each set of specialized services involves a distinct set of public agencies, service providers, eligibility rules, and political actors, as well as a separate information system. In addition, local welfare managers and workers may feel unprepared to handle the discretion they have been given, and concerns about equity and fairness often arise about differences in how that flexibility is handled in different localities and even for different individuals.

We should stress that the taxonomy captures differences in emphasis. Just as we stressed overall patterns in the first sections of the chapter, this section stresses distinctions. Both viewpoints are needed for a complete picture of state implementation. States may even move from one type to another, and in recent years it seems as if there has been some movement toward greater pluralism in services, partly in response to perceptions of a changing caseload, perhaps in response to the pressures to spend the TANF surpluses. Yet there are some differences that are not easily overcome and that would suggest some stability in state approaches. For example, states that offer low cash benefits seem predisposed to adopt strategies emphasizing caseload reduction, perhaps because it is easier for them to dissuade clients from applying for assistance or remaining on the rolls, or perhaps because it is harder for such states to attain high work participation rates when even low earnings make most families ineligible for benefits. In contrast, states that offer high benefits tend to put less emphasis on caseload reduction in their implementation of welfare reform and more on work participation rates. Indeed, the fact that TANF allows work participation rate targets to be achieved with caseload reduction credits permits the great range of signals and goals that our taxonomy captures.

Implementation Challenges

While we have seen considerable change in signals and services, states and localities still face common challenges in implementing work-based TANF systems. Many of these difficulties involve managing the complex human service systems states are constructing. The complexity arises from several sources. First, work first processes involve many separate contacts with clients over time, and it is no simple task to guide and track families through these processes. Second, the work first orientation has not replaced but has supplemented the older AFDC administrative culture, forcing staff to make two different orientations operate together. Third, states have shifted away from providing cash assistance and toward the delivery of multiple services, each of which may engage a different agency, set of providers, and information system. Fourth, the move to a service strategy has often led to transfers of administrative control from centralized state welfare agencies to intricate local coalitions of public and private institutions.

The complexity poses many challenges. TANF programs must (1) design information systems that help administrators and workers operate and oversee complex service systems and detect and respond to problems, (2) create and maintain bureaucratic incentives to achieve the new goals of employment and independence, and (3) adapt work first processes and structures to the needs of working families.

Welfare Information Systems

The new work-focused welfare systems require managers and workers to obtain information on how program participants are proceeding through complex intake processes and service programs. To understand the capacities of welfare information systems, our field researchers asked state officials and local administrators (in two local offices per state) whether, and how easily, they could answer forty questions about their clients and work activities. We found that welfare information systems could answer many questions at the state level about clients' eligibility for traditional benefits, the number of cases being served, some demographic information, and other basic information about the status of welfare households. However, these systems were much less capable of keeping track of work activities, work-support services (such as child care), reasons for client exemptions from work requirements, and major barriers clients were diagnosed as facing (Nathan and Gais, 1999).

The continuing weaknesses of welfare information systems have been documented in a recent study jointly conducted by the Rockefeller Institute and the U.S. General Accounting Office (GAO, 2000). The GAO report found that case managers are still often unable "to obtain data on individual TANF recipients from some of the agencies serving them, including job assistance agencies" (p. 9). Many TANF case managers cannot "arrange needed services, ensure that the services are provided, and respond quickly when problems arise," and staff find it "difficult or impossible to query automated systems to obtain information for planning service strategies for their overall TANF caseloads" (p. 9). A study by the Manpower Demonstration Research Corporation of welfare reform in four cities also cites concerns that managers and staff lack accurate and timely information concerning where clients are in their program and how they are progressing through the welfare-to-work process (Quint and others, 1999, pp. 141–42). In Miami/Dade County the evaluators noted that the system failed to clock how much time remained on a participant's time limits, and it was impossible to report data on backlogs of recipients waiting for orientation, job club, or work experience slots. This problem still exists. Our update research in 2000 found that many states are still having problems with their welfare information systems, including basic deficiencies such as the inability to count the months assistance has been received so as to inform the client how many months are left.

Bureaucratic Incentives in State Programs

In the early years of welfare reform, governors and top administrators devoted much attention to the new goals of increasing work participation and minimizing dependence. But states have found it hard to institutionalize these purposes. Under AFDC, many states created, whether intentionally or not, bureaucratic incentives that encouraged large caseloads. In Georgia, for example, the state's Department of Family and Children Services organized its 159 county offices into six tiers. Larger caseloads resulted in placement in a higher tier, which in turn generated more staff and higher administrative salaries.

Neither Georgia nor other states in our sample still explicitly tie administrators' compensation to caseloads. But states have yet to create new systems of administrative incentives fully congruent with the broad purposes of welfare reform. States still tend to base staffing and budget allocations across counties, districts, and offices on projected cash assistance caseloads. In the first years of welfare reform, governors and state executives often tried to assure employees that their success in reducing caseloads would not mean the end of their jobs. But many states have cut staff nonetheless. These competing bureaucratic incentives would appear to be easier to resolve for contractual relationships, which may be established on the basis of program performance measures. Contractors, often private organizations, can thus be required to focus on specified performance goals.

However, overseeing contractors' real (not just reported) performance is no easy task. In fact, the problems of overseeing and controlling private contractors have already led one state, Mississippi, to abandon its privatization initiative (Breaux and others, 2000). Also, creating incentives for contractors to be efficient while helping families achieve independence is especially hard to do. Wisconsin initially allowed W-2 contractors to keep a significant share of the money remaining after fulfilling their contracts. But the political fall-out from the public perception of contractors "profiting" from caseload reductions eventually led the state to implement a more complex set of performance measures and system of bonuses and penalties—and one that would seem to be even harder to oversee.

Thus, although states are collecting more performance information—including TANF's high-performance bonus criteria as well as work participation rates and caseload reduction—less progress has been made in formalizing incentives to achieve these goals. The strong focus by welfare agencies to date on increasing work participation rates, moving people into unsubsidized jobs, and reducing cash assistance caseloads has largely been a response to the personal attention and priorities of top state executives, often including the governor. The difficulties of institutionalizing performance goals may mean that state welfare systems will remain sensitive to the personal concerns and attentions of governors and top administrators, a dependence that risks drift and loss of focus if new state administrations find welfare reform to be less interesting than did the generation of governors who helped build these programs in the 1990s.

Adapting Processes and Systems to Working Families

Most states have altered their processes and requirements to encourage work, but they have not been as successful in adapting those systems to working families. Work first requirements and processes, combined with continued importance of the quality-control orientation, may encourage working families to avoid welfare offices, even if they still qualify for Medicaid, food stamps, and other benefits and services. Many policymakers view this avoidance effect as desirable, a way of encouraging independence. Yet it may create a kind of administratively induced notch, such that families who leave welfare for work are less well off than if they continued to receive cash assistance, not necessarily because their cash income has declined, but because they no longer receive noncash benefits for which they are eligible. As one of our researchers noted in an update report, "The state has extended eligibility for all transitional services (such as transportation, special service allowances, transitional Medicaid, and childcare supplements) to 12 months after employment is secured. Officials note, however, that few clients take advantage of these services." Washington State has enacted an extensive array of postemployment service programs, but finding clients willing and able to use them has not been easy. Re-Employ Washington Workers—a program designed to reduce rates of recidivism to public assistance through rapid re-employment—was eliminated soon after its implementation in 1999 owing to a lack of client response.

Part of the problem in reaching the working poor may also stem from the fact that while states and localities have integrated service delivery systems for families on cash assistance, the systems serving families not on cash assistance—and therefore not subject to time limits—have generally not changed. Our researcher in West Virginia noted:

> For those 13,000 or so families that remain on TANF, they have had the advantage of being assigned one case manager to assist them. But for those who have left the rolls, or those who are in or near poverty, the system that they must rely on continues to be disjointed and fragmented. . . . A citizen seeking assistance may be referred to any number of workers in their efforts to secure benefits.

States have still not developed the "back end" of their processes and fashioned easy-to-use, more integrated systems for assisting working families not on cash assistance.

Conclusions and Implications

State experiences in the implementation of TANF have common elements. New work-focused agencies play a larger role in nearly all state welfare systems. States have created processes front-loaded with new obligations and activities that confront families entering welfare systems, and these processes signal new expectations and opportunities regarding work for low-income families. We have found that this work-focused agency "culture" has not replaced the older AFDC agency operational goals of minimizing eligibility errors and ferreting out fraud and abuse; rather, it has been added onto the AFDC culture. The resulting hybrid is a complex set of procedures, requirements, and organizational arrangements. The focus on work also comes across as states change the mixture of benefits and services provided to families from cash assistance to benefits and services supporting work. Despite these common patterns, state systems vary a great deal. A major division among the states is between those that place special emphasis on reducing reliance on cash assistance and states that focus on work without emphasizing caseload reduction. Within these two main categories, states are evolving distinct approaches to implementing these particular goals.

States face major challenges in operating new human service systems. Their information systems remain for the most part mismatched to the new tasks and distribution of power in state welfare programs. States are only beginning to develop methods of institutionalizing the new goals of work and independence in their administrative structures. What is particularly important, states have created processes that strongly encourage work, but because those processes are often complex and burdensome, they may discourage the use of services by working families.

To us, the most striking findings from the early implementation of TANF are the size and scope of the opportunities and challenges, and the need for time and stability to allow states and localities to work them out. These systems cannot adapt well to instability with respect to money or policy. The administrative structures involved are complex, often involving hundreds, even thousands, of contracts, memoranda of understanding, and informal agreements among a wide variety of public and private agencies at all levels of government. More important than the overall movement toward greater reliance on nonprofits, for-profits, state labor departments, or some other type of institutions has been the shift toward greater dependence on all of these institutional types, often within the same state and locality. Making these systems work demands enormous investments in staff training, information systems, and contract negotiations, as well as informal adjustments and the building of trust among diverse state agencies, different levels of government, service providers, and community organizations.

To create and manage these complex local coalitions of agencies and providers requires not only time but also predictability at the top, particularly at the federal level but even at the state level. To give one example, states showed a great deal of caution in interpreting what services were subject (or not subject) to the time limits before the federal government approved final regulations that offered them considerable flexibility. Even then, states have been slow to adjust to the regulations. Uncertainty about the basic rules and the availability of funds can undermine long-term relationships, prevent participation by a variety of potential service providers, and lead to short planning horizons in addressing the needs of families. To be adaptive, effective, and innovative, these particular social service systems need a stable policy and financial environment. Devolution, in short, demands restraint at the center.

Devolution also demands accountability, and though many states are beginning to develop reporting systems that take into account a variety of performance factors that satisfy a number of political interests, there is one glaring omission. States and especially localities know very little about the growing number of poor households that are not receiving cash assistance or services. What information they have on these families is scattered and not integrated into a clear picture of how families in different communities are faring. Devolution has moved decisionmaking down to states—and many states have moved important policy and management decisions down to counties and even communities—without creating an information infrastructure that allows local administrators, policymakers, and citizens to understand the magnitude and nature of the problems confronting families in their areas. The Personal Responsibility Act requires quarterly reports regarding individuals and households receiving cash assistance under TANF. And more than half of the states have conducted "leaver studies" of various sorts, studies that examine the employment status and other measures of well-being of families leaving cash assistance. However, no systematic and timely data are collected regarding such basic questions as trends in poverty levels in American communities. Thus even though these new social service systems are responsible for, and expected to influence the behavior of, all families, not just the decreasing number who are getting or who have recently received cash assistance, the nation does not now track the status of low-income families at the level where important administrative and policy decisions are being made. Devolution not only requires predictability and stability at the top, it also needs information at the bottom. States have certainly gone a long way in implementing a particular theory of welfare and its variants, but they still have far to go before they meet the growing challenges of governance.

COMMENT BY
Susan Golonka

When the Personal Responsibility and Work Opportunity Reconciliation Act (PRWORA) was enacted in 1996, states moved quickly to adopt a series of policies that would transform welfare from a system of cash assistance to one of helping families attain the supports they need to move into employment. Indeed, many states had already begun the transformation under federally granted waivers. The decisions made by state policymakers reflected a vision of a system that would respond to the particular needs of individual families, thus requiring implementation at the local level, where an array of services—including placement services, job training, child care, transportation, and substance abuse and mental health treatment—could be offered by frontline staff that enjoyed considerable discretion.

In chapter 2, Thomas Gais and his colleagues provide a highly informative and compelling picture of state and local implementation of welfare reform. By examining the frontline practices and procedures, the increased involvement of the work force system, and shifts in state social service spending, the authors affirm that states have "made major changes in their social service systems reflecting the employment and antidependency goals of the Personal Responsibility Act." As the authors note, implementation is more than a matter of changing rules and procedures; it also requires "a capacity for governance, a capacity to alter program elements in light of new information, circumstances, and experiences." This ability to adapt will continue to be critical if states are to meet the emerging challenges of welfare reform.

Because the authors' research focused primarily on implementation efforts directed at dependency reduction and job placement, it overlooks to some degree the multiple goals and variety of activities being pursued. Taking advantage of the flexibility permitted under the law and the availability of resources previously spent on cash assistance, most states have embraced an even broader set of goals, consistent with the purposes of the Temporary Assistance for Needy Families (TANF) block grant. These include promoting employment retention and wage advancement, preventing teen pregnancy, improving family and child well-being, supporting parenting and marriage, and reducing poverty. The beneficiaries of these efforts are much broader as well. They include not only families remaining on the cash assistance rolls, but also noncustodial parents, former TANF recipients, and working poor families that have never been on welfare. These newer directions in welfare reform will increase the complexity and challenges of implementation because they require the involvement of a greater number and range of agencies and organizations and the local delivery of individualized services.

Evidence that states are supporting these broader goals is found in data on how states are spending their TANF and state maintenance of effort (MOE) funds. This spending goes far beyond that discussed by Gais and his colleagues. According to information from a survey of state TANF administrators on the use of TANF and MOE funds in forty-seven states, as of January 1, 2000, forty-one of those states are funding some type of family support services. For example, twenty-five states fund home visits to pregnant/new parents or to former recipients, nineteen states fund kinship care services or payments, and fifteen states fund housing assistance. Programs for noncustodial parents (generally employment/job search services) are funded in twenty-six states, and services to low-income families (usually child care) not receiving assistance are funded in twenty-five states. Thirty-four states fund teen-parent prevention programs, forty-seven states fund transportation assistance, and thirty-four states fund early childhood and child care programs. States are also funding an array of services for families that have left welfare. For example, thirty-seven states fund case management, thirty-three fund education/training, fourteen fund expense allowances, and thirteen fund retention bonuses (see www.info.org/spd-reports.htm).

Welfare reform has also required the capacity to take action in the face of uncertainty, without complete knowledge of whether a particular strategy will work or what elements will be key to successful implementation. State and local officials do not have the luxury of waiting for the findings of a five-year evaluation. With clients facing work requirements and ticking clocks, officials have had to base decisions on the best available information, making adjustments as they go along. States also had to make major decisions and take action before the promulgation of final regulations in April 1999, while under the shadow of punitive proposed rules.

Implementation, then, required the willingness to take risks. In TANF, the high-performance bonus, with its focus on outcomes rather than processes, rewards successful risk-taking and experimentation. Unfortunately, rules in other federal programs, such as the Food Stamp program, with its focus on error rates and compliance, discourage experimentation and risk-taking. This has meant that frontline workers must continue to spend a significant amount of time verifying eligibility and collecting data from applicants and recipients. The authors do not address whether the continued focus on accuracy and compliance in the Food Stamp program has had a harmful effect on state efforts to move families toward self-sufficiency. However, state and local officials have widely condemned Food Stamp rules and requirements for working at cross-purposes with TANF.

The fact that states do continue to change their policies and practices in light of changing circumstances and new information makes analysis of implementation like trying to hit a moving target. As the authors observe, the focus on front-end procedures had unintended consequences for the back door of the welfare system: many families either left or were diverted from welfare without receiving the food stamps and Medicaid for which they were eligible. The delinking of Medicaid and welfare eligibility in PRWORA and administrative complexities of the Food Stamp program contributed to this problem. States have, however, moved quickly to mitigate this problem by adopting a variety of new procedures, including providing up-front information on food stamps and Medicaid, simplifying application and recertification processes, extending office hours, and stationing outreach workers in community organizations (Brown, 2000).

Changes also are being made at the front door of the welfare system. While states continue to require applicants to engage in work-related activities, a number in 1999 and 2000 adopted policies to permit greater access to postsecondary education and training for TANF recipients. States have funded work-study positions, stopped the clock for full-time students, and changed the work requirement to allow more education (Strawn, Greenberg, and Savner, 2001). Confident of their ability to meet the work participation requirement, states have made changes to respond to the needs and characteristics of current recipients. These include low-skilled, long-term recipients with little work experience as well as families that are working but have low enough wages to remain eligible for cash. With further training assistance, these individuals may receive a wage boost that will enable them to leave the rolls. Whether these policy changes are being translated into options for clients who are encouraged by the messages and signals sent by frontline workers is an open question.

In my view, one of the largest implementation challenges is to coordinate systems that have different missions and performance expectations while balancing accountability with local discretion. First, states must improve coordination of the welfare, work force development, and postsecondary education systems to provide better work supports and opportunities for career advancement for former recipients and other low-wage workers. For example, one-stop centers such as those required under the Workforce Investment Act could be designed to offer universal access (and thereby reduce the stigma of welfare) and bring together in one location transitional support services, education and training providers, and employers. Coordination could be facilitated by compatible information systems, common performance measures across programs, flexible federal funding streams, and federal program rules that permit state and local flexibility.

Second, states must create effective networks of public and private providers at the local level that can respond to the needs of hard-to-serve families and those at risk of hitting the time limit. Assisting these families means conducting rigorous assessments of potential barriers to employment, developing individualized plans, and tracking recipients as they progress through a variety of services. These services might include substance abuse and mental health treatment, domestic violence services, parenting classes and family support programs, and education and training. Helping these families requires considerable discretion at the community level but raises state concerns about accountability. These issues can be partly addressed by adopting higher professional standards for staff, developing an information system that can track recipients through multiple activities, and requiring contracts with local providers to be performance driven.

Third, states must use TANF funds to assist more low-income families, not just those leaving welfare. However, enthusiasm to recraft TANF as a block grant for low-income working families must be tempered with realistic expectations about outcomes. To improve the long-term prospects of these families will require the commitment and involvement of multiple systems (including work force development, education, housing, child support, and health), as well as a reexamination of state tax policies. In addition, aggressive outreach and universal service delivery may be required to reach more low-income families.

Gais and his colleagues conclude with an important caveat: if progress in promoting individual responsibility is to continue, the policy and financial environment must be predictable. Governors could not agree more. The funding and flexibility of TANF must be maintained. States will also continue to seek the removal of barriers in other programs that make it hard to move poor families toward long-term self-sufficiency.

References

Adams, Charles F., and Miriam S. Wilson. 2000. "Welfare Reform Meets the Devolution Revolution in Ohio." In *Learning from Leaders: Welfare Reform Politics and Policy in Five Midwestern States,* edited by Carol Weissert. Albany, N.Y.: Rockefeller Institute Press.

Breaux, David A., Christopher M. Duncan, C. Denise Keller, and John C. Morris. 2000. "To Privatization and Back: Welfare Reform Implementation in Mississippi." In *Man-

aging Welfare Reform in Five States: The Challenge of Devolution, edited by Sarah F. Lieb-schutz. Albany, N.Y.: Rockefeller Institute Press.

Brown, Rebecca. 2000. *State Outreach and Enrollment Strategies to Improve Low-Income Families' Access to Medicaid.* Washington: National Governors' Association Center for Best Practices.

Cherlin, Andrew, and others. 2000. *What Welfare Recipients Know about the New Rules and What They Have to Say about Them.* Policy Brief 00-1. Johns Hopkins University.

Crew, Robert, and Belinda Creel Davis. 2000. "Florida Welfare Reform: The WAGES Program." In *Managing Welfare Reform in Five States: The Challenge of Devolution,* edited by Sarah F. Liebschutz. Albany, N.Y.: Rockefeller Institute Press.

Ellwood, Deborah A., and Donald J. Boyd. 2000. *Changes in State Spending on Social Services Since the Implementation of Welfare Reform.* Albany, N.Y.: Rockefeller Institute Press.

Fossett, James, Thomas Gais, and Frank Thompson. Forthcoming. "Federalism and Performance Management." In *Faster, Cheaper, Better? Performance Management in American Government,* edited by Dall Forsythe. Albany, N.Y.: Rockefeller Institute Press.

Hagen, Jan L., and Irene Lurie. 1994. *Implementing JOBS: Progress and Promise.* Albany, N.Y.: Rockefeller Institute Press.

Kane, Thomas J., and Mary Jo Bane. 1994. "The Context for Welfare Reform." In *Welfare Realities,* edited by Mary Jo Bane and David T. Ellwood. Harvard University Press.

Kaplan, Thomas. 2000. "Wisconsin's W-2 Program: Welfare As We Might Come to Know It?" In *Learning from Leaders: Welfare Reform Politics and Policy in Five Midwestern States,* edited by Carol S. Weissert. Albany, N.Y.: Rockefeller Institute Press.

Looney, Janet, and Betty Jane Narver. 2000. "Washington's WorkFirst Program: Key Policy Challenges." In *Managing Welfare Reform in Five States: The Challenge of Devolution,* edited by Sarah F. Liebschutz. Albany, N.Y.: Rockefeller Institute Press.

Nathan, Richard P., and Thomas L. Gais. 1999. *Implementing the Personal Responsibility Act of 1996: A First Look.* Albany, N.Y.: Rockefeller Institute Press.

Quint, Janet, and others. 1999. *Big Cities and Welfare Reform: Early Implementation and Ethnographic Findings from the Project on Devolution and Urban Change.* New York: Manpower Demonstration Research Corporation.

Strawn, Julie, Mark Greenberg, and Steve Savner. 2001. *Improving Employment Outcomes under TANF.* Washington: Center for Law and Social Policy.

U.S. General Accounting Office (GAO). 2000. *Welfare Reform: Improving State Automated Systems Requires Coordinated Federal Effort.* GAO/HEHS-00-48.

Weissert, Carol S. 2000. "Michigan's Welfare Reform: Generous But Tough." In *Learning from Leaders: Welfare Reform Politics and Policy in Five Midwestern States,* edited by Carol S. Weissert. Albany, N.Y.: Rockefeller Institute Press.

3

REBECCA M. BLANK
LUCIE SCHMIDT

Work, Wages,
and Welfare

IN 1996, AMID heated political debate, Congress passed landmark welfare
reform legislation, the Personal Responsibility and Work Opportunity
Reconciliation Act (PRWORA). This led states to drastically alter their public assistance programs by enforcing work requirements and restricting the
availability of welfare. Supporters of the legislation praised the effort to move
more women into work and toward economic self-sufficiency. Critics
claimed that there were not enough jobs available for former welfare recipients, that wages were too low to allow former recipients to achieve self-
sufficiency, and that passage of PRWORA under these conditions was equivalent to "waging war on the poor."

Nearly five years later, the labor force participation rates of less-skilled
women with children have undergone unprecedented increases. There have
been parallel and equally dramatic decreases in welfare caseloads. And preliminary evidence suggests that the families of many single mothers are experiencing increases in income and decreases in poverty. These facts, many
claim, offer evidence that PRWORA has been far more successful than even
its supporters expected.

Can PRWORA claim full responsibility for the labor market advances
made by less-skilled women? Probably not. At the same time as these changes
were being implemented, the U.S. economy was undergoing a period of sustained and very strong economic growth. Throughout the latter part of the

1990s, unemployment remained low and the demand for workers was high. This smoothed the way for states to pursue the work-oriented welfare reform encouraged by PRWORA.

Any evaluation of the behavioral changes in work and welfare usage following the 1996 legislation must take the interaction of policy and the economy into account. The more that behavioral outcomes in recent years are ascribed to a strong economy rather than to the effects of policy, the warier one might be in drawing strong conclusions about the effectiveness of welfare reform based on the evidence of the past few years. The state of the economy at the time when PRWORA is up for reauthorization is likely to significantly affect the discussion.

We present evidence on changes in labor market involvement among less-skilled workers, particularly those most likely to have been affected by welfare reform. We focus on less-skilled women as the group most directly affected by welfare reform, but for comparison we frequently show changes among less-skilled men and among more-skilled women. We place more recent changes in the context of economic changes over the past several decades. The comparison years we use most frequently are 1969, 1979, 1989, and 1999. These are all years at or near the end of sustained economic expansions.

Changes in Work and Earnings

Over the past decade, there have been stunning changes in the labor market involvement of less-skilled women. Figure 3-1 shows how labor force participation has changed among women over the past decade by marital status and the presence of children. Around 1994 labor force participation among single mothers began to rise steeply. This group's labor force participation increased 9.7 percentage points between 1994 and 2000. Participation rates among married women showed a much milder increase, while those of single women without children remained relatively constant. This suggests that the changes among single mothers cannot be attributed entirely to general labor market conditions affecting all women.

These patterns by marital status are directly related to increases in labor force participation among less-skilled women, since women with low levels of education are much more likely to become single mothers. Table 3-1 shows labor force participation rates from 1969 to 1999 among women and men by education level. Labor force participation among less-skilled men declined in the 1970s and 1980s and held constant in the 1990s, while labor force participation among more skilled men was largely constant over this period. Quite a different pattern is visible among women: labor force partici-

Figure 3-1. *Labor Force Participation Rates for Women by Marital Status and Presence of Children, 1989–2000*

Rate

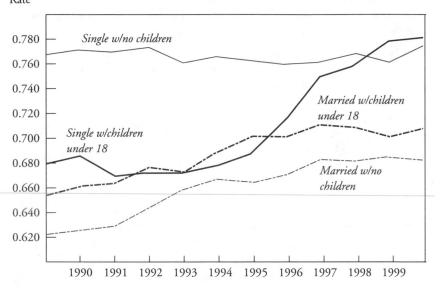

Source: Authors' tabulations of March Current Population Survey data for women aged 20–65.

Table 3-1. *Labor Force Participation Rates by Gender and Education Level, 1969–99*

Percent

Gender and education	1969	1979	1989	1999
Women				
Total	48.6	59.2	67.7	72.2
H.S. dropout	41.6	43.7	44.5	50.3
H.S. diploma	51.4	61.2	68.0	70.1
Some college	51.1	65.9	74.3	75.9
College diploma	62.0	73.3	81.1	81.9
Men				
Total	89.4	87.2	86.3	85.3
H.S. dropout	88.6	79.4	75.4	74.3
H.S. diploma	93.2	90.7	88.2	85.5
Some college	85.6	87.2	86.9	84.7
College diploma	91.2	92.8	92.3	91.5

Source: Authors' tabulations of March Current Population Survey data; based on labor force status in the week of survey; all persons aged 20–65.

Figure 3-2. *Labor Force Participation Rate in March among Single Mothers Who Received Public Assistance during the Previous Year, 1989–2000*

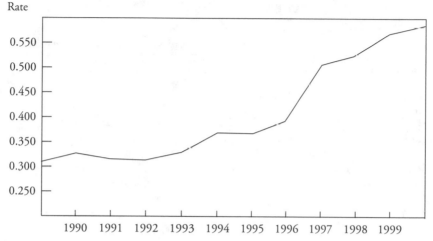

Rate

Source: Authors' tabulations of March Current Population Survey data. Includes all women aged 20–65 who report receiving public assistance in previous year.

pation among women without a high school degree was largely unchanged between 1969 and 1989 but rose six percentage points in the 1990s. Among more skilled women, labor force participation was largely unchanged in the 1990s, after substantial increases in earlier decades.

Figure 3-2 indicates the strength of these trends among women who have historically relied on the public assistance system. It plots the share of women in the labor force (in March of each year) among those women indicating that they received public assistance income in the previous year. Labor force participation rates for this group were close to 30 percent in 1989 but almost double, close to 57 percent, by 2000.

These changes appear even more dramatic when taking into account the fact that the share of the population with low educational attainment was shrinking over this time period. One might expect rapid increases in labor force participation among the least skilled to lead to overall lower levels of education among working women, but increases in education have outstripped the increases in work among less-skilled women. Forty-six percent of women in the bottom 20 percent of the wage distribution were high school dropouts in 1979. This fraction declined to 34 percent in 1989 and to 30 percent by 1999. These increases in overall education levels are promising and suggest that women's growing investment in what economists refer to as "human capital" will help raise their wages over time.

Table 3-2. *Earnings and Income Changes among Female High School Dropouts, by Marital Status and Presence of Children*[a]
1999 dollars, unless otherwise specified

Income measure and year	All	Single w/children	Married w/children	Single, no children	Married, no children
Own earnings	6,502	6,641	6,088	7,006	6,336
Change in own earnings (percent)					
1979–89	3.2	–18.5	15.4	–0.6	6.3
1989–99	22.0	42.6	13.7	14.0	24.5
Own earnings as percent of family income					
1979	25.4	56.1	14.6	71.4	17.8
1989	34.9	68.9	21.1	76.3	21.9
1999	43.3	83.8	23.4	78.4	26.1
Family income	15,000	7,924	26,000	8,932	24,282
Change in family income (percent)					
1979–89	–24.7	–33.6	–20.0	–6.9	–13.6
1989–99	–1.8	17.3	2.5	10.8	4.4

Source: Authors' tabulations of March Current Population Survey data.

a. Own earnings figures are means, while family income figures are medians because large outliers in the family income figures skew the means. Ages 20–65.

The increases in work among single mothers are reflected in a sharp increase in their annual earnings in the 1990s. Table 3-2 shows earnings and family income levels in 1999 and their changes over the previous two decades among female high school dropouts. It also presents earnings as a share of total family income. Among high school dropouts, married women's earnings increased in the 1980s, whereas earnings of single women with children fell. In the 1990s single mothers—the group with substantial increases in labor force participation—show by far the strongest earnings growth. Note, however, that annual earnings levels remain very low for all high school dropouts, at less than $8,000 in 1999.

As the earnings of these less-educated women grew, the share of family income from earnings also increased. This increase in share was greatest among single mothers, with earnings rising from 56 percent of family income in 1979 to 84 percent in 1999. The family incomes of married less-skilled women are far higher than those of single women, but the only category showing substantial growth in family income between 1989 and 1999 is less-skilled single women with children, the very group that became increasingly reliant on earnings and less upon welfare.

These data indicate an amazingly rapid shift in work behavior among less-skilled women, particularly those with children, over a relatively short period of time. The timing of these changes over the decade shows that they accelerated in the mid-1990s, exactly when major policy changes were enacted in welfare, but also when the economic boom moved into high gear. The next section discusses these underlying causal factors by looking at changes in the economy, in welfare policy, and in other policies that are likely to have affected work incentives among these women.

The Changing Environment

The economy of the 1990s showed strong declines in unemployment, substantial increases in earnings (after the mid-1990s), and some shifts in the nature of work held by women. This section reviews each of these changes.

A Changing Macroeconomy

Unemployment rates fell sluggishly at the beginning of the 1990s, following the economic slowdown of 1990–91. But by the mid-1990s, unemployment was steadily ticking downward, remaining at or below 5 percent from April 1997 onward. Figure 3-3 plots the unemployment rate among all persons, all women, and among high school dropouts (available only in more recent years). Female unemployment rates in the late 1990s were at levels comparable to those of the late 1960s. This period of low and sustained unemployment rates clearly provided new work opportunities for less-skilled women, as employers' ongoing need for labor made them more willing to hire and train new groups of workers. Even among high school dropouts, unemployment rates fell rapidly, to nearly 6 percent.[1]

As unemployment fell, wage rates began to rise. Figure 3-4 plots trends in average weekly earnings among the least-skilled groups of full-time workers aged 25 to 65, by gender, between 1979 and 1999. Adjusted for inflation, wages among male high school dropouts deteriorated from the late 1970s until the mid-1990s, falling 22.2 percent in real terms between 1979 and 1994. But they rose by 5.0 percent from 1994 to 1999. Less-skilled women

---

1. Our tabulations of Current Population Survey data suggest that unemployment rates for female high school dropouts track those of all high school dropouts closely over this time period.

Figure 3-3. *Unemployment Rates among Selected Persons, 1969–99*

Rate

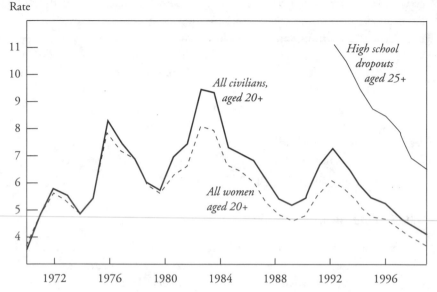

Source: Department of Labor, Bureau of Labor Statistics, historical data from "A" tables of Employment Situation News Release.

never experienced declines quite so severe, with a 7.9 percent drop in wages between 1979 and 1994. However, they experienced a 3.5 percent increase from 1994 through 1999. In contrast, wages among more-skilled workers rose strongly through this period, and continued to rise in the late 1990s. The rising wages among less-skilled workers after the mid-1990s meant a substantial slowdown in the growth of wage inequality. However, the wage growth of the past few years has not made up for the large wage declines in the 1980s and early 1990s. Real wages in 1999 were below their 1979 levels for those with the lowest levels of education.

Figure 3-4 also makes clear how badly wage opportunities have deteriorated for men in comparison with women. In contrast to the declining wages of less-skilled men, women with high school degrees experienced steady improvements in their earning opportunities over the 1990s. Although women's wages remain well below men's wages, because of falling wage opportunities for less-skilled men, the wage gap has narrowed.

Continued declines in unemployment since the mid-1990s, combined with wage increases, should have a strong effect on the incomes of less-skilled persons. Not only are people working more, but they are also earning more for every hour they work. This is in contrast to the expansion of the 1980s,

Figure 3-4. *Average Weekly Earnings among Less-Skilled Male and Female Full-Time Workers, 1979–99*

Earnings (1999 dollars)

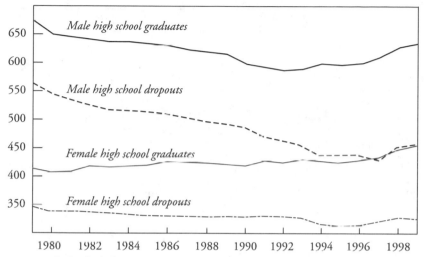

Source: Authors' tabulations of Current Population Survey Outgoing Rotation Group data for workers aged 25–65; high school graduates do not include any individuals with one or more years of college.

when unemployment fell but wages did not rise among the least skilled. The result was a very sluggish response to the expansion in terms of income growth and poverty declines in the 1980s. Income growth and poverty declines have been greater during the expansion of the 1990s (Haveman and Schwabish, 1999; Blank, 2000).

While wages have increased among even less-skilled women in recent years, it does appear that the set of wage opportunities for these workers has become more limited. Table 3-3 shows the distribution of women's wages in 1979, 1989, and 1999 by educational category. The column heads closely correspond to the quintile breaks in the overall wage distribution among all workers in 1999. In that year, 20 percent of all workers would be found in each of these groupings. The third row of table 3-3 indicates that more women (24 percent) worked at wages of less than $7/hour, and fewer (14 percent) worked at $20/hour or more in 1999. The higher proportion of women in the lower wage categories is evidence of a continuing wage gap between men and women.

Table 3-3 also indicates the increasing importance of education as a determinant of earnings. Between 1979 and 1999, women's overall probability of being in the lowest category of earnings declined from 34 percent to 24 per-

Table 3-3. *Distribution of Women's Wages by Education Category, 1979–99*
Percent

Education	Wages per hour[a]				
	< $7	$7–10	$10–13.50	$13.50–20	> $20
All women					
1979	33.8	29.5	20.2	12.5	4.0
1989	29.4	25.7	20.1	16.8	7.9
1999	24.1	21.5	21.7	18.6	14.1
H.S. dropout					
1979	61.0	24.8	9.6	3.8	0.8
1989	62.5	23.5	9.7	3.5	0.9
1999	64.4	21.2	10.0	3.3	1.1
H.S. diploma					
1979	31.3	35.1	21.0	10.5	2.2
1989	32.0	31.6	21.5	12.1	2.9
1999	27.9	28.6	24.5	14.0	5.0
Some college					
1979	26.8	31.4	23.5	14.7	3.6
1989	25.2	27.2	22.7	18.3	6.6
1999	21.6	23.9	24.9	19.7	10.0
College diploma					
1979	10.9	18.7	29.1	27.4	13.9
1989	7.9	15.0	21.7	32.4	23.1
1999	6.3	10.4	19.2	29.1	35.0

Source: Authors' tabulations of Current Population Survey Outgoing Rotation Group data.

a. Wage categories (≤ $7, > $7 and < $10, ≥ $10 and ≤ $13.50, > $13.50 and < $20, ≥ $20) are based on the quintile breaks in the overall wage distribution among all workers in 1999 ($7.06, $9.95, $13.57, and $19.80). Calculations for each year based on 1999 dollars.

cent. But among the least-skilled women, this probability actually rose, from 61 to 64 percent. These shifts partly reflect the shrinking share of less-skilled workers, so that the group remaining behind may be selectively more disadvantaged. At the same time, highly educated women have become much more likely to be in the higher wage categories.

The nature and characteristics of jobs have also changed over recent decades. There has been a notable shift away from manufacturing and toward service sector jobs. While the impact of these changes on less-skilled men is often discussed, this shift has affected less-skilled women as well. Table 3-4 shows industry and occupational location of men and women in 1979, 1989,

Table 3-4. *Industry and Occupation of Male and Female High School Dropouts, 1979–99*

Percent

Industry or occupation	Women			Men		
	1979	1989	1999	1979	1989	1999
Industry						
Construction	0.8	1.6	2.0	16.3	20.5	22.3
Durable goods	16.6	9.6	7.8	23.2	15.7	11.6
Nondurable goods	19.7	16.6	11.1	11.2	10.1	9.9
Retail trade	22.6	28.0	31.0	12.0	15.8	19.2
Finance, insurance, and real estate	2.4	2.7	2.3	1.2	1.4	1.3
Business services	2.4	5.3	5.6	1.8	2.9	4.8
Medical (including hospitals)	8.2	8.1	9.1	1.3	1.3	0.5
Legal, educational, social, and other professional services	5.9	6.8	7.2	2.1	2.7	1.4
Occupation						
Executive, administrative, and managerial	2.7	3.0	3.3	3.3	2.8	2.5
Professional	1.7	1.7	1.6	1.0	0.7	0.7
Sales	7.9	12.7	15.3	1.7	.4	3.7
Administrative support	11.9	11.5	10.8	2.6	2.3	2.5
Service	28.7	31.0	34.5	8.0	10.8	14.4
Precision production, craft, and repair	3.1	5.2	4.5	26.4	28.3	27.3
Machine operators, assemblers, and inspectors	33.4	21.9	15.6	23.1	15.0	13.1

Source: Authors' tabulations of Current Population Survey Outgoing Rotation Group data for ages 20–35.

and 1999. In 1979 one-third of women without a high school degree worked as machine operators or assemblers. By 1999 that share had fallen to 16 percent. Corresponding declines occur in the share of women in durable and nondurable goods industries. By contrast, the proportion of women in sales and service occupations and industries grew strongly over this time period.

While the influx of more women with young children into the labor market might be expected to increase part-time work, the strong economy should also have pushed firms to expand hours among their workers. The net effect over the 1990s has been virtually no change in part-time work among women. According to our tabulations of Current Population Survey (CPS) data, part-time work among women without a high school degree has declined slightly, from 29.5 percent in 1989 to 25.7 percent in 1999. Despite relative invariability in the share of women working part time, there has been a notable decline in "involuntary" part time, meaning those persons who want full-time work but work part time because they cannot find a full-time job (U.S. Bureau of Labor Statistics, 2000).

Overall, the economy since the mid-1990s has outperformed all forecasts and expectations. Employment at the end of 2000 had grown by 13.6 percent since the peak of the previous expansion. This has created new work opportunities and improved wages for all workers, but has been particularly important in increasing employment among the least skilled. Economic growth has made the country a much easier place in which to implement the policy changes discussed next.

Major Changes in Welfare Reform

The welfare reform legislation of 1996 abolished the Aid to Families with Dependent Children (AFDC) program and created the Temporary Assistance for Needy Families (TANF) block grant. States were given much greater discretion in designing their public assistance programs, and many states responded by implementing significant changes in these programs.

A key goal of the states was to create stronger incentives for work. This meant improving and expanding welfare-to-work programs in almost all states. But a variety of other programmatic changes designed to increase work incentives have also been implemented among current or potential public assistance recipients. Some of these increase the positive incentive to work, through policies such as earnings disregards that allow women to keep a higher share of their benefits as their earnings increase. Other changes are more punitive and are designed to increase the costs of not working, such as time limits or sanctions on those who do not comply with the welfare-to-work requirements. We briefly review some of the major changes across states in their public assistance programs that should have increased work among current and potential welfare recipients (for a full description of changes by states, see Gais and others, chapter 2).

WELFARE-TO-WORK PROGRAMS. States have been expanding welfare-to-work programs at least since 1988, when the Family Support Act required an increase of welfare-to-work activities within AFDC. Federal mandates in TANF required states to further increase the share of their TANF population in work programs to 35 percent by 1999, and to 50 percent by 2002, a substantial rise over 1996 participation in most states. In fiscal year 1999, all states met these federal work requirements, and the average rate of participation in work activities among TANF recipients was 38.3 percent (HHS, 2000; for a more detailed discussion of these welfare-to-work programs, see Strawn, Greenberg, and Savner, chapter 8).[2]

BENEFIT LEVELS. Analysts have long viewed the base level of public assistance support, or the amount of money one receives with no other income sources, as one measure of work disincentives. Standard models of individual decisionmaking in economics suggest that higher benefits reduce the incentive to work, and the empirical evidence supports this point. However, benefit levels have actually changed less than almost any other component of welfare programs since 1996. Fully thirty states have the same nominal benefit level in their TANF program in 2000 that they had for AFDC in 1996. Fifteen states have increased benefits between these four years, and only six have decreased benefits. On net, the median TANF benefit (adjusted for inflation) has fallen only slightly, from $399 in 1996 to $381 in 2000. This suggests that changes in benefit levels have not substantively altered work incentives.

EARNINGS DISREGARDS. The earnings disregard is the inverse of the rate at which benefits are reduced as earnings increase. Under AFDC, the earnings disregard was 33 percent, meaning that benefits were reduced 67¢ for every additional dollar in earnings. This was largely limited to the first year of AFDC receipt. After this year, the disregard went to zero, meaning benefits were reduced by a dollar for each dollar of additional earnings, so there were few incentives to work at low-wage or part-time jobs.[3] Dissatisfaction with the incentives implicit in this system caused many states to increase earnings disregards after TANF was enacted. Many states now have TANF programs with much more generous earnings disregards than AFDC.

SANCTIONS. If welfare-to-work programs attempt to use positive incentives to motivate people to find jobs, sanctions are the "stick" that enforces participation. States have adopted a wide variety of sanctioning policies, primarily reducing benefits for some period of time if a person does not comply with the work requirements (or other provisions) in TANF. Currently, nine states

2. If a state's average monthly assistance caseload decreased in the previous year in comparison with the state's average caseload in fiscal year 1995, the federal minimum participation rate standard is reduced by the number of percentage points the caseload declined. This means that some states met the federal requirements in 1998 with actual work participation rates as low as 11.2 percent (Maryland) (HHS, 2000).

3. AFDC also had a $30/month lump-sum earnings disregard, and exempted child care and work costs, up to a cap.

have a full lifetime sanction, meaning that someone who reaches the final sanctioning point will be forever ineligible for future TANF benefits. Another twenty-seven states impose a full benefit reduction but only for a temporary period of time. The remaining fifteen states have only partial and temporary benefit reductions as their ultimate sanction.

TIME LIMITS. The PRWORA legislation imposed a sixty-month federal time limit on TANF recipients, meaning that persons could not receive federally funded TANF services for more than sixty months during their lifetime. Seventeen states have imposed even stricter time limits, but nine states actually use state funds to provide some assistance past the sixty-month federal deadline (for more detail on both sanctions and time limits, see Pavetti and Bloom, chapter 9).

DIVERSION ACTIVITIES. In addition to policies designed to increase work among current welfare recipients or to move current recipients off welfare and into employment more quickly, states are also trying to prevent persons from entering public assistance in the first place by operating "diversion" programs (see Maloy and others, 1999). Many of these programs offer a one-time, lump-sum level of cash assistance, in exchange for a period of ineligibility for TANF programs. Twenty states have such cash diversion programs, thirteen of which demand three months of ineligibility following receipt of the lump sum. In fifteen states, it is also legal to impose job search requirements on public assistance applicants. Applicants seen as work-ready may have to participate in a period of job search or contact a certain number of employers before they can register for TANF.

The combined effect of all of these program changes is to vastly reduce the availability of public assistance over time to less-skilled women, and to greatly increase their incentives to work. Table 3-5 characterizes the generosity of state programs with regard to benefit levels, earnings disregards, time limits, and sanctions. States with the greatest work incentives are those with low benefits, high earnings disregards, strict sanctions, and short time limits. The last column of table 3-5 indicates states with particularly strong work incentive programs in their TANF policy, states with weak work incentives, and states with mixed policies. We characterize fourteen states as having strong work incentives, ten as having weak work incentives, while the remainder have mixed incentives across these program components.

This type of summary measure of work incentives can only be partial. For instance, we have no measures of the stringency or effectiveness of states' welfare-to-work programs. Nonetheless, as a test of how state programs are correlated with work behavior, we can compare changes in work behavior in the aftermath of PRWORA among less-skilled women across states with different types of work incentives. We find that while labor force participation rates among single mothers have increased 7.2 percent between 1996 and 1999 in states with "weak" incentives, they have increased 11.7 percent over the same time period in states with "strong" incentives. This provides at least preliminary evidence that the labor supply of less-skilled women responds to work incentives within state TANF programs.

Other programs also interact with the TANF program and affect work incentives. The growing availability of Medicaid to low-income children has reduced the incentives to remain on public assistance in order to maintain health insurance (until the mid-1980s, Medicaid eligibility was largely determined by AFDC eligibility). In spite of this "de-linking" of Medicaid and TANF eligibility, however, enrollment in the Medicaid program fell substantially after the passage of PRWORA. Also declining rapidly is participation in the Food Stamp program, which should be available to all low-income households regardless of work or welfare status. Greenstein and Guyer discuss the interaction between welfare reform and the Medicaid and Food Stamp programs in chapter 11. Finally, efforts to move disabled women from the AFDC or TANF programs into Supplemental Security Income (SSI), a cash support program for the disabled and elderly, should have reduced the share of AFDC recipients who cannot hold a job due to severe physical or mental disability (see Karoly, Klerman, and Rogowski, chapter 19).

Overall, the magnitude of change within state public assistance programs has been enormous. Most states are explicitly trying to shape public assistance programs that place work, rather than benefit receipt, at their center. While there are large differences across states in the components and design of their TANF programs, all states are increasing their efforts to move public assistance applicants and recipients into work.

Changes in Other Public Policies That Support Work

The 1996 PRWORA legislation was far from the only significant policy change affecting less-skilled workers over the 1990s. A variety of other programs also changed in ways that increased the attractiveness of work. This section summarizes some of these changes.

EARNED INCOME TAX CREDIT. The biggest policy change for less-skilled persons who worked steadily throughout the 1990s was not the 1996 welfare reform legislation, but the substantial expansions in the Earned Income Tax Credit (EITC) in the first half of the 1990s. These expansions turned the

Table 3-5. *State Rankings for Components of the TANF Program and Overall Work Incentives*

State	Benefit generosity[a]	Earnings disregards[b]	Sanctions[c]	Time limits[d]	Overall work incentives[e]
Alabama	Low	Low	Strict	Moderate	Mixed
Alaska	High	Medium	Lenient	Moderate	Weak
Arizona	Medium	Low	Moderate	Lenient	Weak
Arkansas	Low	Medium	Lenient	Strict	Mixed
California	High	High	Lenient	Lenient	Mixed
Colorado	Medium	Low	Moderate	Moderate	Weak
Connecticut	High	High	Moderate	Strict	Mixed
Delaware	Medium	Low	Strict	Strict	Mixed
District of Columbia	Medium	Medium	Lenient	Moderate	Weak
Florida	Medium	High	Strict	Strict	Strong
Georgia	Medium	Low	Strict	Strict	Mixed
Hawaii	High	High	Strict	Moderate	Mixed
Idaho	Medium	Low	Strict	Strict	Mixed
Illinois	Medium	High	Moderate	Moderate	Strong
Indiana	Medium	Low	Lenient	Lenient	Weak
Iowa	Medium	High	Strict	Moderate	Strong
Kansas	Medium	Medium	Strict	Moderate	Strong
Kentucky	Low	Low	Moderate	Moderate	Mixed
Louisiana	Low	High	Strict	Strict	Strong
Maine	Medium	High	Lenient	Lenient	Mixed
Maryland	Medium	Low	Strict	Lenient	Mixed
Massachusetts	High	High	Strict	Strict	Mixed
Michigan	Medium	Medium	Strict	Lenient	Mixed
Minnesota	High	Medium	Lenient	Moderate	Weak
Mississippi	Low	High	Strict	Moderate	Strong
Missouri	Medium	Medium	Lenient	Moderate	Weak
Montana	Medium	Medium	Lenient	Moderate	Weak
Nebraska	Medium	Low	Strict	Strict	Mixed
Nevada	Medium	Medium	Moderate	Strict	Strong
New Hampshire	High	High	Lenient	Moderate	Mixed
New Jersey	Medium	Medium	Strict	Moderate	Strong
New Mexico	Medium	High	Moderate	Moderate	Strong
New York	High	High	Lenient	Lenient	Mixed
North Carolina	Low	Medium	Moderate	Strict	Strong
North Dakota	Medium	Low	Strict	Moderate	Mixed

continued on next page

Table 3-5. *State Rankings for Components of the TANF Program and Overall Work Incentives (continued)*

State	Benefit generosity[a]	Earnings disregards[b]	Sanctions[c]	Time limits[d]	Overall work incentives[e]
Ohio	Medium	High	Strict	Strict	Strong
Oklahoma	Medium	Medium	Strict	Moderate	Strong
Oregon	Medium	Medium	Moderate	Strict	Strong
Pennsylvania	Medium	Medium	Moderate	Moderate	Mixed
Rhode Island	High	High	Lenient	Lenient	Mixed
South Carolina	Low	Low	Strict	Strict	Mixed
South Dakota	Medium	Low	Strict	Moderate	Mixed
Tennessee	Low	Low	Strict	Strict	Mixed
Texas	Low	Low	Moderate	Moderate	Mixed
Utah	Medium	High	Strict	Strict	Strong
Vermont	High	Medium	Moderate	Lenient	Weak
Virginia	Medium	Low	Strict	Strict	Mixed
Washington	High	High	Lenient	Moderate	Mixed
West Virginia	Medium	Low	Moderate	Moderate	Weak
Wisconsin	High	Low	Strict	Moderate	Mixed
Wyoming	Medium	Low	Strict	Moderate	Mixed

a. Source: State Policy Documentation Project (www.spdp.org). High = maximum benefits > $100 above the median state benefit; medium = maximum benefits within $100 of median; low = maximum benefits < $100 below the median

b. Weighted average of the amount of earnings that would be disregarded (taking breakeven points into account) in the first and twelfth months of benefit receipt for a single mother working full time at $6.00 per hour. Source: State Policy Documentation Project (www.spdp.org). High = amount of earnings disregarded > $100 above median state disregard; medium = amount of earnings disregarded within $100 of median; low = amount of earnings disregarded > $100 below the median.

c. Source: Pavetti and Bloom (chapter 9). Strict = immediate full family or gradual full family plus food stamps/Medicaid; moderate = gradual full family or partial plus food stamps/Medicaid; lenient = partial.

d. Source: Pavetti and Bloom (chapter 9). Strict = termination under 60 months; moderate = state time limit of termination after 60 months; lenient = benefit reduction or no time limit.

e. A state with unambiguously strong work incentives would have low benefit generosity, high earnings disregards, strict sanctions, and strict time limits. A state with the weakest work incentives would have high benefit generosity, low earnings disregards, lenient sanctions, and lenient time limits. Strong = at least one category has the strongest work incentives, and no other category has the weakest work incentives; weak = at least one category has the weakest work incentives, and no other category has the strongest work incentives; mixed = all others (states that mix strongest and weakest incentives, or states that are entirely in the middle).

EITC from a relatively small program into a $30 billion program in 2000, larger than TANF, Food Stamps, or SSI. More than 18 million workers were expected to receive some EITC credit on their tax bill in 2000 (U.S. House of Representatives, 2000, Section 13).

The EITC is a refundable tax credit available to low-wage workers living in low-income families. Because of this design, it is a well-targeted program, as low-wage workers who live in higher-income households are not eligible for an EITC. While many workers essentially "receive" the EITC through lower withholding and lower tax bills, the refundability of the EITC means that the poorest workers, who owe no taxes, actually get money back. In 1999, among eligible workers earning less than $9,720, for every dollar they earned they could receive another 40¢ from the EITC tax credit, essentially increasing their income by 40 percent.[4] At higher earnings, workers receive a flat credit amount, which then slowly tapers off as earnings continue to increase. For those who are out of the labor force, the EITC unambiguously increases work incentives. For those already working, the effect of the EITC on work behavior is ambiguous, although the credit will continue to increase their total earnings.

The EITC has been shown to increase work among single mothers (Eissa and Liebman, 1996; Meyer and Rosenbaum, 1999; Ellwood, 2000), the group most likely to be out of the labor market or working few hours at low wages. In contrast, its effect on the labor supply of married women, who are more likely to be in the flat or phase-out ranges, appears to be slightly negative (Eissa and Hoynes, 1999).

MINIMUM WAGE. A series of increases have occurred in the federal minimum wage, which went from $3.35 at the beginning of the 1990s to $5.15 in 1999. The minimum wage and the EITC interact in useful ways. The minimum wage provides a base to the EITC, so the credit need not be as large for very low earners. This means that the "claw-back" period for the EITC (the period when the credit is being reduced to zero) is shorter and thereby creates fewer work disincentives. Conversely, the EITC supplements the minimum wage. Without the EITC, there would be greater pressure to increase the minimum wage, which has growing disemployment effects as it rises, since it induces employers to substitute away from less-skilled labor toward other technologies.[5]

---

4. These are the numbers for an adult with two children in the family. With one child, workers who earn up to $6,920 could receive another 34¢ for each dollar earned. A much smaller credit also exists for childless workers over the age of 25.

5. Virtually all analysts agree that the disemployment effects of the minimum wage grow as the minimum wage rises. There is more disagreement about the actual magnitude of those effects.

Table 3-6. *Effects of Changing Policy on Earnings of Single Mothers,*
1989 and 1999
1999 dollars unless otherwise specified

Policy	1989	1999	Percent change
Minimum wage	4.48	5.15	15.0
Maximum EITC subsidy			
Single mother (1 child)	1,216	2,312	90.1
Single mother (2 children)	1,216	3,816	213.8
Earnings (single mother working full time at minimum wage)			
Single mother (1 child)	10,013	12,612	26.0
Single mother (2 children)	10,013	14,116	41.0
Ratio of earnings to U.S. poverty line			
Single mother (1 child)	0.89	1.10	. . .
Single mother (2 children)	0.76	1.05	. . .

Source: Authors' calculations.

At the current level of the minimum wage, the disemployment effects appear to be relatively mild. Bernstein and Schmitt (1998) indicate that the overall employment effects of the mid-1990s increases in the minimum wage were very small. Neumark (1999) finds evidence of effects on the employment of unskilled young workers, but few effects on any other group. Table 3-6 presents the growth of the minimum wage and EITC in real terms over the past decade, as well as their interactions with each other. The earnings entry shows take-home incomes have increased among single mothers who work full time at the minimum wage. With no change at all in work behavior, a mother with one child earned 26 percent more in 1999 than in 1989. A mother with two children earned 41 percent more. By the end of the decade, the minimum wage together with the EITC ensured that full-time work, even at the minimum wage, put a worker above the official U.S. poverty line. Even without any changes in the economy or in welfare policy, the increases in the minimum wage and EITC shown in table 3-6 would have increased the incentives to work for many women.

CHILD CARE SUBSIDIES. A growing share of TANF dollars is being spent on subsidies for child care for working mothers or mothers in job search programs. States can use TANF dollars for this purpose, but the same legislation that created TANF also eliminated a number of child care subsidy programs and increased dollars to the Child Care and Development Block Grant. Most states attempt to subsidize child care for women in mandatory work programs and provide at least temporary child care subsidies to women who leave public assistance for work. To the extent that child care expenditures are an important part of the incentives (or disincentives) to work, particularly among single mothers, these increases in child care subsidies should have increased work opportunities (see Besharov and Samari, chapter 18).

CHILD SUPPORT PROGRAMS. For the past two decades, the federal government and the states have worked together to increase the payment of child support from noncustodial parents to their children, particularly among public assistance recipients. If received in a reliable and steady manner, child support may reduce work incentives but improve the economic circumstances of the family. But actual values of child support received tend to be small, particularly for public assistance recipients, and are often not received every month. The legislative changes of the past two decades have increased the frequency and the level of child support collections, but not by a large amount (see Garfinkel, chapter 17).

Evaluating the Effects of These Changes

The foregoing evidence suggests dramatic changes in the environment surrounding less-skilled workers, particularly less-skilled women with children. On the one hand, employment and earnings opportunities have expanded, particularly when one takes into account both the robust macroeconomy and increases in the federal minimum wage and the EITC. On the other hand, public assistance income opportunities have declined dramatically, and the safety net programs have been redesigned to push recipients into the labor market and off public assistance as fast as possible.

All of these changes should have increased work and reduced public assistance caseloads. It is difficult to disentangle the effects of each of these factors because of the overlap and interaction among them. The strong labor market has made it possible for states to focus on implementation and design issues in public assistance, without having to worry about job availability. The changes in welfare opportunities may have directly affected the relationship of less-skilled women to the labor market. Ideally, we would like to understand the impact that each of these recent changes has had on women's work behavior and on their financial well-being. We summarize here four groups of studies that address this question.

Leavers' Studies

Perhaps one of the most obvious ways to study the impact of policy reforms is to follow people affected by them over time. Hence, a number of researchers have collected longitudinal information on persons on welfare at one point in time, and compared it to information collected at a later period. This research is particularly concerned with investigating how persons who left welfare following the 1996 reforms have fared.

Studies of this kind have a number of methodological limitations. First, by focusing only on those persons actually receiving welfare, these studies say nothing about the effects of welfare reforms on those who are deterred from ever applying for assistance. Second, these studies typically have no real control group. Because all individuals in the sample are affected by the policy changes, there is no way for these studies to differentiate between causal factors. While the data from these studies show us how many women are working after leaving welfare, it is impossible to determine how much of this increased employment would have occurred anyway, how much is due to the booming economy, and how much is due to the restructuring of welfare programs. Despite these caveats, the leavers' studies provide evidence on how women who were previously on welfare are faring under the new regime.

In general, these studies find that the majority of welfare leavers, including a majority of those who are sanctioned off welfare, are working at some future point (Parrott, 1998; Brauner and Loprest 1999; U.S. House of Representatives, 2000, appendix L). Those who remain off welfare are more likely to be employed than those who return to welfare. Many continue to use some government programs (most often Medicaid or Food Stamps) even after they leave public assistance. These studies offer only limited evidence about income. A substantial minority of leavers appear to report lower or similar incomes than they had while on welfare, although most do not count income from the EITC (see Haskins, chapter 4).

A more recent study in Wisconsin (Cancian and others, 2000) differs from the other studies in that it does try to create a control group, by comparing women who left welfare in Wisconsin in 1995 with those who left two years later (after TANF was implemented). The post-TANF leavers were more likely to be working than those who left in 1995 but had lower earnings. These later leavers were also more disadvantaged in terms of their personal and family characteristics, which is consistent with the hypothesis that the new welfare regime pushes people with fewer employment skills into the labor market. In Wisconsin, a majority of both the earlier and the later leavers appear to have lower income after leaving welfare than while on welfare.

Other recent studies also show that more disadvantaged women are less likely to leave welfare, and have poorer earnings and work performance once they do leave (Loprest, 1999; Danzinger and others, 2000). In chapter 12, Zedlewski and Loprest discuss the issues associated with employment among these women with multiple barriers such as limited education, physical or mental health problems, or drug and alcohol addictions.

State Panel Data Analysis of Caseloads and Labor Force Participation

A more aggregate evaluation of behavioral changes is provided by studies that use state panel data across a series of years to investigate changes in welfare caseloads. These studies control for long-term fixed differences between states and attempt to measure the impact of both economic and policy changes on caseload changes within a state over time. These studies have the advantage of using the entire national population rather than focusing on results from just one state. Because they often use data from the late 1970s through the mid-1990s, one is able to compare recent and past changes to see if the determinants of caseloads are different in more recent years. They also allow one to separately control for the effects of economic environment versus policy change.

The drawback of these studies is that they tend to focus on only one primary outcome, caseloads. In addition, most of these studies end in 1996 and consider the welfare waivers granted to states in the early 1990s to be their primary policy change. Because the 1996 legislation was put into place at about the same time in most states, it is difficult to identify what share of the post-1996 change is due to policy versus factors such as the economy that were changing at exactly the same time. Similarly, with this methodology it is hard to evaluate the effects of other policies implemented nationwide at about the same time, such as the EITC changes. Those changes, common to all states in the same year, cannot be separately identified. Finally, even these studies cannot fully separate economic and policy effects. If the strong economy is helping policy to function more effectively, that is difficult to measure separately.

According to these studies, about 15 percent of the caseload decline between 1990 and 1996 is related to welfare policies and 30 to 40 percent to improved labor market conditions (for a list of studies, see Blank, forthcoming). Looking directly at the post-PRWORA period, a Council of Economic Advisers study (1999) found that one-third of the decline between 1996 and 1998 was due to welfare reform and about 8 to 10 percent was due to improvements in the labor market. This is consistent with the fact that TANF focused more on moving people off welfare than did the pre-1996 reforms. A second study (Schoeni and Blank, 2000) investigates the effects of both TANF and the welfare waivers on a broader set of measures, including labor force participation, earnings, and income. The authors also find evidence that the TANF program had a particularly strong impact on caseloads, but that the labor market had a stronger effect on labor force participation in the late 1990s. The bottom line of this research appears to be that both policy and the economy have affected behavior, but that the size and nature of the impact vary over time.

Formal Randomized Evaluations

Since the early 1980s, a series of formal randomized evaluations have tried to measure the impact of welfare-to-work programs and other welfare reforms. Such evaluations offer a strong advantage. If done effectively, they provide a control group that does not receive the new program or reform but is otherwise identical to the group that does receive the program, before the program's implementation. If the control group and the treatment group have truly been randomly selected from a similar group of persons, then one can track the outcomes in both groups and attribute any differences to the explicit effect of the program. In fact, the evidence from these evaluations, which showed the effectiveness of welfare-to-work programs in increasing employment and reducing AFDC usage, was an important impetus to the 1996 legislation, as well as earlier legislation (for a summary of this research, see Gueron and Pauly, 1991).

With the evolution of more complex welfare reform efforts involving not just work programs but also a host of other changes in program parameters—such as earnings disregards, sanctions, and time limits—randomized evaluations become more complicated. In part, this is because multiple changes in the welfare environment often mean that the "control group" experiences some of these changes as well, even if it is not formally eligible for a new program. In addition, the effects of multiple changes within a randomized experiment are difficult to untangle. Given these caveats, a number of creative evaluations have tackled this very problem.

Most formal evaluations occurred in programs implemented under waivers and before TANF. The waivers requested by states to run somewhat revised AFDC programs in the early 1990s were granted only if the state agreed to an evaluation, in many cases a formal randomized evaluation. However, a growing body of evidence is becoming available from the studies that investigate the impact of TANF programs after 1996.

In general, the earlier literature suggested that welfare-to-work programs could increase employment and reduce AFDC participation. Although these effects were significant, they were often not huge. The largest recorded effects are found in the Greater Avenues to Independence (GAIN) welfare-to-work program in Riverside County, California, and are generally considered the maximal bound for the effect of these programs. This program finds a nine percentage point gain in the probability of employment and a $1,000 annual increase in earnings among GAIN participants in comparison with the control group three years afterward (Riccio, Friedlander, and Freedman, 1994).

Later evaluations of more complex welfare reform programs have also found quite substantial effects. Evaluations of eleven state TANF programs confirm that these programs increased employment and reduced welfare use (Freedman and others, 2000). Few of these effects were large, but their consistency across a host of different programs suggests that states have found effective ways to use TANF-funded programs to achieve increases in work. Despite these employment gains, net income among participants in these programs was largely unchanged, with increases in wages being offset by declines in benefits. These results reflect both the good and bad news from welfare reform: employment is up and public assistance usage is down, but few programs appear to have generated substantial gains in income or declines in poverty.

One of the most promising program evaluations comes from the Minnesota Family Investment Program (MFIP), which involved a strong work participation component as well as a big increase in the earnings disregard. Chapter 10, by Michalopoulos and Berlin, provides information on MFIP and other similar programs that appear to have had positive effects on both employment and income.

Evidence on Jobs and the Labor Market

The research cited so far has focused on individual behavior, and not on the nature of the labor market and jobs. The long-term success of welfare recipients will depend upon the labor market in which these women find themselves. Both the willingness of employers to hire welfare recipients and the wage progression that a less-skilled woman can expect over time will be critical in determining the long-term success of these women in the labor market. Recent work by Holzer and Stoll (2000) analyzes the first of these issues: the willingness of employers to hire welfare recipients. They use data from a survey of employers in four major cities in 1998 and 1999. They find that employers have filled almost 3 percent of job openings over the past year with welfare recipients. This level of overall demand is quite high, and is theoretically large enough to absorb the aggregate increase in labor supply by persons leaving welfare. However, there is some evidence of racial disparities, as the rate of hiring among minority recipients is lower than their representation in the female-headed low-income populations of these four cities. This appears at least partly related to spatial mismatch problems, with blacks more likely to reside in central cities while more of the job growth is occurring in the suburbs.

The evidence in table 3-3 suggests that, once hired, less-skilled women tend to be located in low-wage jobs and may have difficulty moving into higher-paying employment. In many cases the goal must be to get women into $8 to $10/hour jobs, earning a wage well above the federal minimum, which is essential if women must pay for child care and meet other budget demands. The strategy of moving women off public assistance and into low-wage jobs is less attractive and less effective in the long run if these women are not able to reach an earnings level that stabilizes their income and allows them to support their families without ongoing subsidies.

More recent work on wage growth over time among less-skilled women suggests that experience in the labor market does lead to real wage growth. Gladden and Taber (2000) indicate that the wages of less-skilled women grow as fast with experience as do those of more educated women, albeit from a much lower base. However, they also find that less-skilled female workers tend to acquire less experience over time, slowing their overall wage growth. This evidence suggests a potential long-term benefit of the current sustained economic expansion. If women are able to find employment and hold these jobs for longer periods of time, the increase in their work experience should result in long-term wage gains.

It is also possible that the large increase in labor supply of former and current welfare recipients has affected the overall low-skill labor market, possibly displacing other less-skilled workers or driving down wages. Bartik (2000) looks at these questions from a variety of perspectives and suggests that both displacement and lower wages are likely to have resulted from the increase in work among former welfare recipients. The magnitude of these effects is likely to be small, however, and is difficult to estimate precisely.

The evidence that is beginning to emerge in the post-PRWORA era suggests that there have been dramatic increases in the labor market participation of less-skilled women and corresponding dramatic decreases in welfare caseloads. Improvements in the financial well-being of these women are less dramatic, since decreasing benefits have offset rising earnings, but as Haskins shows in chapter 4, many women have gained in overall income. Research also suggests that both the strong economy and the policy changes are playing an important role in generating these behavioral changes among less-skilled women. However, there is an important caveat to all of the research summarized in this chapter: none of these studies are truly able to deal with the simultaneous nature of policy design and economic environment. It may be that states are designing and implementing their current configuration of programs in part because the current environment makes jobs so available. At the same time, individual responses to welfare changes are affected by perceptions of how good the alternatives to welfare (particularly the labor market alternatives) appear. It is not at all clear that the policy effects would be the same in a period of economic stagnation or recession. Hence it may be impossible to determine how many of the observed changes in behavior are due to policy and how many to the strong economic environment until more is known about how today's policies would operate in a very different economic environment.

What Does This Mean for Reauthorization?

One frequently hears two opposite interpretations of the past few years of labor market and welfare history. According to one interpretation, recent policies have been effective beyond anyone's wildest dreams. Policy changes have reduced welfare usage, increased work effort, and moved millions of women onto the road toward economic self-sufficiency. Having started down this road, things will only get better as women move into better jobs and permanently leave all forms of government assistance.

According to the other interpretation, all of these successes are entirely dependent upon the current economic boom and the ready availability of jobs. Given how atypical the economy of the last few years has been (matched only by a short period in the late 1960s), recent policy changes may well turn into headaches when the economy finally slows down. Women who have left (or been pushed off) welfare will find themselves unemployed or earning far too little to support their families. If time limits, sanctions, or other provisions prevent them from returning to public assistance, poverty and need will rise to new levels.

We suspect the truth lies somewhere between these two interpretations. These policy changes have almost surely had some real and permanent effects that would have occurred even in a weaker economy. More women would have stayed off welfare, increased their labor supply, and seen higher earnings. But we also worry a great deal about the possibilities inherent in the second interpretation. At this point it is fundamentally impossible to decide how much of the current increase in work is due to the unique economic environment. The existing estimates in the literature are most likely too low, since they do not take into account the effects of this strong economy on policy design and implementation, or on individual expectations that influence behavioral responses.

The evidence on overall income growth among women leaving welfare suggests that while increases in earnings have caused some women to experience real income growth, these increases have been partly offset by benefit reductions. In addition, studies indicate that some women who have left welfare appear to have lost income (see Haskins, chapter 4). If overall income gains are relatively small in this economy with these unprecedented increases in work behavior, it is quite possible that in a period of lower growth (or, even worse, no growth), these policies would have led to severe income declines.

All of this suggests that the debates around reauthorization will be heavily affected by the state of the economy in 2002. If the economy continues to boom, we expect that the first interpretation will dominate the political debate and that the impetus to make major changes in PRWORA will be weak. On the other hand, if the economy has slowed down significantly by 2002, with noticeably higher unemployment, then there may be demands for substantial changes in PRWORA during reauthorization.

Under the first scenario, in the absence of concern about jobs and job availability, reauthorization might focus on a number of work-related changes, such as allowing greater flexibility for states to place persons in training programs in addition to work first job-search programs, encouraging firms and/or regional alliances to provide private sector training and job mobility opportunities that help less-skilled workers increase their wages over time, making sure states are spending their child care funds most effectively, and increasing access to child care for women who need it.

If reauthorization is limited to these factors and ignores the larger cyclical issue, it will be a missed opportunity. Preparing for the next economic slowdown now would be a very wise thing to do, even if that slowdown has not yet occurred in 2002. At least four issues should be considered in preparation for the next downturn in the economy. First, states should have incentives to launch demonstration programs that place women unable to find private sector jobs into public sector employment. These programs should be set up and their management systems developed before they need to operate at a larger scale in a slower economy.

Second, the funds provided by the TANF block grant should have a cyclical component. For instance, at least some share of the block grant might be linked to changes in state unemployment rates. In a recession, the abundance of funds that states are currently spending on their welfare-to-work programs may dry up, with cuts occurring at the very time that the demand for public assistance is rising. The federal government is best able to provide counter-cyclical financing, given that most states operate under balanced-budget requirements.

Third, as more women move closer to time limits, there should be greater flexibility in the exemptions available to states. In an economy with higher unemployment, states may need to provide ongoing support to a larger share of the caseload. The current 20 percent exemption is entirely arbitrary and may make little sense in a world where the caseload is more disadvantaged, or in a world where fewer jobs are readily available.

Fourth, low-wage and part-time workers need access to standard labor market safety net programs. Among other things, this may require major reforms in the Unemployment Insurance (UI) program. Women who are working part time should be able to receive unemployment benefits if their jobs end (currently employers pay into the system for these women, but in most states they cannot collect benefits). Similarly, the qualifying period for UI benefits might be shortened, so that workers in more short-term and unstable work may have more access to UI.

In general, we do not believe that the current economic environment is sustainable over a long period of time. What goes up must come down. When employer demand weakens and unemployment rises, the current con-figuration of state TANF plans and federal regulations may create some very unpleasant situations in which single mothers are unable to locate private sector employment and are also left without a claim on public sources of sup-port. We worry about the short-term poverty effects on these mothers and their families, and we worry even more about the long-term impacts on the children.

Given the economic uncertainty and vulnerability that exist among this population, we object to unilateral legislation on the part of either state or fed-eral governments that cuts certain groups off from assistance for their entire lifetime (whether through sanctions or time limits). What may have been called "tough love" in a strong economic environment with available jobs, could create extreme hardship in a more normal economic environment with fewer work opportunities for less-skilled women. State welfare agencies will need to adapt their policies to the realities of the labor market. In a very uncertain economic world, this may mean that there are times when welfare-to-work programs must be buttressed by public sector employment, by tem-porary increases in public assistance expenditures, and by less rigid time limits.

COMMENT BY
Robert Topel

This slightly mistitled chapter summarizes the effects of the welfare reform provisions enacted in the wake of the Personal Responsibility and Work Opportunity Reconciliation Act (PRWORA) of 1996 and offers policy recommendations for the reauthorization of those reforms that will be considered by Congress in 2002. Rebecca Blank and Lucie Schmidt make several key points. First, these reforms provided strong incentives for welfare recipients to work. Their overall impact has been to increase employment, earnings, and labor force participation among less-skilled women who would otherwise qualify for welfare. Second, because the reforms came in a fairly strong labor market when the demand for less-skilled people was evidently rising, it is difficult to disentangle their effects on employment and earnings of welfare reform from the impact of a strong labor market. Blank and Schmidt seem to argue for a sort of interaction between policy and environment: welfare reform "worked" because it was enacted during a period when demand was strong; its effects would be smaller in a period of weaker demand for less-skilled people, such as the 1980s. Third, in light of the presumed interaction of policy and environment, the authors are concerned that the social safety net that has evolved since 1996 will prove inadequate when the economy slows and overall unemployment rises. They suggest various other structural remedies for this prospective problem, such as public employment, countercyclical funding of Temporary Assistance for Needy Families (TANF) block grants, and expansion of unemployment insurance (UI) to cover part-time workers.

The first two points are uncontroversial, in part because the authors do not take a strong stand on them. Welfare reform did something to increase participation, and the economy has surely played some role in increasing employment of less-skilled women. Blank and Schmidt do not seek to nail down the relative contributions, nor do they try to estimate what labor market outcomes would be for less-skilled women in a weaker overall economy. This makes their policy prescriptions—which occupy only a small section of their discussion—less compelling. And even if they are right about the interaction of welfare reform with economic conditions, they do not provide much support for the particular forms of policy that they advocate.

My comment focuses on two issues. First, how has welfare reform affected the earnings, employment, and labor force participation of women who have contact with the welfare system? Second, given recent experience, what other reforms to welfare might improve the performance of the social safety net, in terms of either lower social costs or improved economic outcomes?

The major goal of the 1996 welfare reform law was to reduce the dependence of low-income households on government support by improving work incentives while continuing to maintain a social safety net for qualified families. Within the legislation, the replacement of the Aid to Families with Dependent Children Program (AFDC) by block grants to states under TANF was the central and most prominent change. Advocates of TANF predicted that it would place welfare recipients on a path to self-sufficiency, while opponents predicted that abandoning the poor to their labor market fate would have dire consequences.

There is good reason to believe that TANF has succeeded in one of its main goals—raising employment among poor households—at least in the current economic environment. Figures 3-1 and 3-4 of the chapter speak indirectly to this issue. Figure 3-1 graphs the labor force participation rate (not the employment rate, one should note) of welfare recipients from 1989 to 2000. While participation was trending up for various reasons I will mention shortly, no one would have predicted the sharp increase that occurred between March of 1996 (before the legislation) and March of 1997. This upward surge of participation continued after 1997. Figure 3-4 shows conformable evidence for single mothers with children younger than 18. Participation increased sharply from 1995 to 1997, faster than in any other benchmark group of women. While the surge from 1995 to 1996 gives one pause, coming before the 1996 reforms, it is clear that something important happened around 1996 and that it was not simply an improvement in the labor market circumstances of women.

What of rising participation (and employment) rates before 1996? While there is surely some role for labor market effects, the evidence seems to be that improved incentives to work have played a strong role here as well. Meyer and Rosenbaum (2000) document pre-1996 changes in welfare policies, the earned income tax credit (EITC), Medicaid, and other policy variables that affect labor supply incentives for welfare-eligible households. Overall, they find that financial incentives to work increased substantially during the late 1980s and early 1990s—owing in large part to increases in the EITC—and that improved incentives were accompanied by increased labor force participation and employment among families that are traditional welfare recipients. What is important for this discussion is that they also find that little of the increase in employment can be attributed to the effects of labor demand on low-income, female-headed households. In other words, incentives to work matter.

I think the Meyer and Rosenbaum results document a broader context of welfare reform that was going on well before 1996, and that has been successful in moving low-income families away from dependence on active government programs. This as well as other evidence leads me to conclude that "welfare reform" has been successful, at least in the current economic environment.

One can still argue, as Blank and Schmidt do, that the current system would be less successful in a weaker labor market. In other words, there is an interaction between policy reforms and labor demand that allows the reforms to "work" in a strong labor market. For their purposes, this hypothesis has the unfortunate (or fortunate) property of being untestable: the current system has never operated in a recession. This allows Blank and Schmidt to advocate policy positions based on the assumption that the current system will provide substantially less of a safety net during a recession than would the old pre-1996 welfare program. I can go along with this supposition. But I cannot buy their proposals.

Blank and Schmidt are concerned that the current economic environment will affect the nature of reform, with the risk that the current system could fail to achieve its income-supporting goals in times of weaker labor demand. They advocate several policy proposals that are meant to deal with this risk, including public sector employment, countercyclical funding of TANF grants, flexible exemptions, and access to UI for part-time workers. Even absent these cyclical concerns, they also advocate increased reliance on job training programs for welfare recipients.

The most controversial (and costly) of these proposals are the provision of public sector jobs and training programs. Indeed, I think the evidence on the operation of such programs suggests that they are exceedingly bad ideas.

Consider the proposal to provide public sector jobs when private demand proves inadequate. Relief work has a long and not very bright history as a method for providing jobs. In Sweden, it has long been a part of what are known as "active" labor market policies that were, for a time, alleged to keep the Swedish unemployment rate low. These programs were studied in detail by Anders Forslund and Alan Krueger (1997), as part of a larger study of the Swedish welfare state. Looking specifically at construction sector jobs, the authors found that each publicly provided job displaced about 0.7 private sector jobs. In other words, the social cost of increasing employment by one position was about three times the public expenditure on the position. Their evidence for health-service jobs was more mixed, but it is fair to say that they found no evidence that government-funded relief work substantially increased overall employment. For the United States, other studies have found conformable results, and I know of no studies that indicate a substantial positive impact on employment.

There is another cost of public sector jobs programs that I believe is even more serious. They would not simply be employment programs for the less fortunate during times of weak labor demand. Such programs take on a life of their own and will be subject to the usual rent-seeking activities that plague all government programs, but especially redistributive ones. The programs would inevitably grow, and the activities would have little relation to the production of anything truly valuable. Better, I think, to just give people money.

Training programs seek to provide participants with marketable skills, in the hope of raising their future employability. Unfortunately, the evidence that such programs yield economically meaningful returns is weak: the programs do not justify their costs. The rate of return on a training program depends on the effect of training on future earnings and probability of employment. To be worthwhile, the rate of return should be on the order of 3 percent. But the results from a number of studies indicate that the return on such programs is substantially smaller than 3 percent. They may have no return at all. In short, participants may be better off searching for private sector employment than enrolled in public sector training programs.

Evidence from a number of sources indicates that "welfare reform," broadly defined, has increased employment, labor force participation, and earnings among targeted groups. The long-run impact of these changes on economic welfare is likely to be positive, as evidence indicates that time in the labor market improves future employability. Blank and Schmidt are correct, I think, to attribute some of the "success" of welfare reform to the economic environment. But their concern may be overstated. If wage distributions are any guide, the demand for less-skilled workers is no greater today than it was in, say, 1980, and it is weaker than in the 1970s. This tells me that current reforms would have had similar effects in other times. So I am less concerned about the future than they.

References

Bartik, Timothy J. 2000. "Displacement and Wage Effects of Welfare Reform." In *Finding Jobs: Work and Welfare Reform*, edited by David Card and Rebecca M. Blank. Russell Sage.

Bernstein, Jared, and John Schmitt. 1998. *Making Work Pay: The Impact of the 1996–97 Minimum Wage Increase.* Washington: Economic Policy Institute.

Blank, Rebecca M. 2000. "Fighting Poverty: Lessons from Recent U.S. History." *Journal of Economic Perspectives* 14 (2): 3–19.

———. Forthcoming. "Declining Caseloads/Increased Work: What Can We Conclude about the Effects of Welfare Reform?" *Economic Policy Review.*

Brauner, Sarah, and Pamela Loprest. 1999. *Where Are They Now? What States' Studies of People Who Left Welfare Tell Us.* Series A, A-32. Washington: Urban Institute.

Cancian, Maria, Robert Haveman, Daniel R. Meyer, and Barbara Wolfe. 2000. *Before and after TANF: The Economic Well-Being of Women Leaving Welfare.* Special Report 77. University of Wisconsin Institute for Research on Poverty.

Council of Economic Advisers. 1999. *Economic Expansion, Welfare Reform, and the Decline in Welfare Caseloads: An Update.* Executive Office of the President.

Danziger, Sandra, Mary Corcoran, Sheldon Danziger, and Colleen Heflin. 2000. "Work, Income, and Material Hardship after Welfare Reform." *Journal of Consumer Affairs* 34 (1): 6–30.

Eissa, Nada, and Hilary W. Hoynes. 1999. *The Earned Income Tax Credit and the Labor Supply of Married Couples.* Working Paper E99-267. University of California at Berkeley, Department of Economics.

Eissa, Nada, and Jeffrey B. Liebman. 1996. "Labor Supply Response to the Earned Income Tax Credit." *Quarterly Journal of Economics* 111 (2): 605–37.

Ellwood, David T. 2000. *The Impact of the Earned Income Tax Credit and Social Policy Reforms on Work, Marriage, and Living Arrangements.* Harvard University, Kennedy School of Government.

Forslund, Anders, and Alan B. Krueger. 1997. "An Evaluation of the Swedish Active Labor Market Policy: New and Received Wisdom." In *The Welfare State in Transition: Reforming the Swedish Model,* edited by Richard B. Freeman, Robert Topel, and Bingitta Swedenborg. University of Chicago Press.

Freedman, Stephen, Daniel Friedlander, Gayle Hamilton, JoAnn Rock, Marisa Mitchell, Jodi Nudelman, Amanda Schweder, and Laura Storto. 2000. *National Evaluation of Welfare-to-Work Strategies.* New York: Manpower Demonstration Research Corporation.

Gladden, Tricia, and Christopher Taber. 2000. "Wage Progression among Less Skilled Workers." In *Finding Jobs: Work and Welfare Reform,* edited by David Card and Rebecca M. Blank. Russell Sage.

Gueron, Judith M., and Edward Pauly. 1991. *From Welfare to Work.* Russell Sage.

Haveman, Robert, and Jonathan Schwabish. 1999. *Macroeconomic Performance and the Poverty Rate: A Return to Normalcy?* Discussion Paper 187-99. University of Wisconsin, Institute for Research on Poverty.

Holzer, Harry J., and Michael A. Stoll. 2000. "Employers and Welfare Recipients: The Effects of Welfare Reform in the Workplace." Unpublished paper. San Francisco: Public Policy Institute of California.

Loprest, Pamela. 1999. *Families Who Left Welfare: Who Are They and How Are They Doing?* Publication 99-02. Washington: Urban Institute.

Maloy, Kathleen, LaDonna Pavetti, Julie Darnell, and Peter Shin. 1999. *Diversion as a Work-Oriented Welfare Reform Strategy and Its Effect on Access to Medicaid.* Washington: U.S. Department of Health and Human Services.

Meyer, Bruce D., and Dan T. Rosenbaum. 1999. "Welfare, the Earned Income Tax Credit, and the Labor Supply of Single Mothers." Working Paper 7363. Cambridge, Mass.: National Bureau of Economic Research.

———. 2000. "Making Single Mothers Work: Recent Tax and Welfare Policy and Its Effects." *National Tax Journal* 53 (4): 1027–62.

Neumark, David. 1999. "The Employment Effects of Recent Minimum Wage Increases: Evidence from a Pre-Specified Research Design." Working Paper 7171. Cambridge, Mass.: National Bureau of Economic Research.

Parrott, Sharon. 1998. *Welfare Recipients Who Find Jobs: What Do We Know about Their Employment and Earnings?* Washington: Center on Budget and Policy Priorities.

Riccio, James, Daniel Friedlander, and Stephen Freedman. 1994. *GAIN: Benefits, Costs, and Three-Year Impacts of a Welfare-to-Work Program.* New York: Manpower Demonstration Research Corporation.

Schoeni, Robert F., and Rebecca M. Blank. 2000. "What Has Welfare Reform Accomplished? Impacts on Welfare Participation, Employment, Income, Poverty, and Family Structure." Working Paper 7627. Cambridge, Mass.: National Bureau of Economic Research.

U.S. Bureau of Labor Statistics. 2000. *Employer Costs for Employee Compensation.* News Release 00-186. Government Printing Office.

U.S. Department of Health and Human Services (HHS). 2000. *Temporary Assistance for Needy Families (TANF) Program: Third Annual Report to Congress.* Government Printing Office.

U.S. House of Representatives, Committee on Ways and Means. 2000. *2000 Green Book: Background Material and Data on Programs within the Jurisdiction of the Committee on Ways and Means.* Government Printing Office.

4

RON HASKINS

Effects of Welfare Reform on Family Income and Poverty

THE POOR ARE a perennial focus of national concern. We are concerned about their income, their work, their use of welfare, their child rearing, their sexual behavior, and their values. For most Americans, how the poor are treated is a major criterion by which the success of government programs should be judged. But as the nation and above all its social scientists have struggled to understand the poor, controversy and disagreement have abounded regarding what causes poverty and what can be done to cure it. The poor have bad genes; no, they have bad environments. The poor are shiftless; no, they are unfortunate victims of society. The poor are retarded; no, they are poorly educated. The poor should be given decent provision; no, they should be required to work for what they get. The poor have illegitimate children they cannot support; no, they have nonmarital births because their choices are constricted by an indifferent society. And so on.

These sharply differing views have been played out in the development of American social policy (Haskins, 2001a), the broad outline of which is clear enough. Until the rise of the New Deal in the 1930s, welfare was largely a matter left to private organizations and local and state governments. In truth, there were few government programs at any level. But beginning with the Social Security Act of 1935, America gradually located considerable responsibility for the poor at the federal level. As the nation's economy and the power of the federal government grew simultaneously, beginning roughly with our entry into World War II, more and more federal welfare programs were created, especially in the years after 1965, eventually growing to over 300 programs that spent about $350 billion in federal and state dollars on the eve of the welfare debate in 1994 (Rector and Lauber, 1995; Burke, 1999; Haskins, 2001a).

A little-known but interesting fact is that the creator of the American welfare state, President Franklin Roosevelt, signaled his uneasiness with welfare at the very moment he sent his proposal for cash welfare for single mothers to Congress. In arresting language, he told Congress in his 1935 message:

> The lessons of history, confirmed by the evidence immediately before me, show conclusively that continued dependence upon relief induces a spiritual and moral disintegration fundamentally destructive to the national fibre. To dole out relief in this way is to administer a narcotic, a subtle destroyer of the human spirit. It is inimical to the dictates of sound policy. It is in violation of the traditions of America. Work must be found for able-bodied but destitute workers. (Roosevelt, 1935, pp. 19–20)

I doubt that any speech given by a partisan Republican during the 1995–96 debate on welfare reform came close to the eloquence of these FDR dictums. While planting the seed that created the towering oak, Roosevelt warned against the very problem Congress addressed with the 1996 welfare reform law. That Congress was forced to reform welfare, yet again, in 1996 owes a great deal to the fact that previous Congresses had ignored FDR's wisdom and had created the blizzard of programs that, in the view of Republicans who carried the debate in 1995–96, did administer a narcotic, did violate the traditions of America, did subtly destroy the human spirit, did lead to moral disintegration, and did violate the dictates of sound policy.

Cutting through the rhetoric that was abundant in Congress during the welfare reform debate (some of which I wrote), the major issue was work. From the perspective of our brief historical overview, the 1996 welfare reform law was a return to the tradition of welfare that requires something of recipients, or to the type of individual responsibility Roosevelt (1935) had in mind when he promised, in the same 1935 message to Congress cited above, that the government "must and shall quit this business of relief" (p. 20). Of course, as Congress built the Great Society and continued creating programs and increasing spending straight up until 1994, the need for programs was usually couched in terms of work and personal responsibility. But it was not until Congress enacted the 1996 reforms that federal law actually required work and imposed financial sanctions on both states and individuals that failed to meet work requirements. Combined with ending the entitlement to cash benefits and imposing a five-year limit on cash benefits, these 1996 reforms led to pervasive changes at the state and local levels, as discussed in chapters 2 and 3.

One change was that employment by mothers formerly on welfare or demographically eligible for welfare increased dramatically. The increase in work was especially dramatic among never-married mothers, precisely the mothers most likely to go on welfare and to stay for long spells (Haskins, 2001b). This chapter examines the evidence on the financial well-being of families headed by these mothers.

Although, as always, the data available impose certain limitations on any attempt to describe the financial condition of these mothers and their children, let me begin at the end, by saying that the evidence available is diverse and mostly of decent quality, that the picture portrayed by these data is generally consistent, and that the resultant portrait of the financial status of these families seems likely to stand the test of time. Future studies will produce lots of new details, but the general picture drawn in this chapter is likely to stand, at least until the next recession.

The portrait can be summarized in three statements. First, most mothers and children who have left welfare have more money than they had when they were on welfare. They have more money because their earnings are much greater than in the past and because the nation has developed a set of work support programs—including Food Stamps, Medicaid, child care, and above all the Earned Income Tax Credit (EITC)—that provide substantial public benefits to low-income workers. Second, child poverty has declined substantially since the enactment of welfare reform. Third, there is a small to moderate-sized group of mother-headed families that are worse off than they were before welfare reform. Again, these generalizations capture what has happened in a strong economy; what will happen when the economy goes sour remains to be learned.

Income

The floor debate on welfare reform in the U.S. House of Representatives was not one of the friendlier debates of recent years. Because President Bill Clinton vetoed the Republican bill twice (once in December of 1995 and once in January of 1996), the House had many opportunities to debate the legislation.

What Welfare Reformers Expected

During the course of the debates, Republicans and Democrats disagreed sharply over the fate of mothers who took low-wage jobs. On the one hand, Democrats held that mothers would be stuck in lousy, dead-end, hamburger-flipping jobs that would leave them and their children destitute. Republicans argued that there was no such thing as a lousy job and that any job was preferable to welfare. Republicans also argued that even low-wage jobs would provide families with more money than welfare. In the heat of debate, Republicans actually resorted to bringing charts to the floor of the House of Representatives that compared welfare income with work income. One of their charts looked something like this:

Welfare	Dollars	Work	Dollars
Cash	4,400	Minimum wage	10,000
Food stamps	3,500	Food stamps	2,000
		EITC	3,500
Total	7,900		15,500

This chart stands as a fair representation of what most of those who supported welfare reform expected from a work-based welfare system. The mathematics of the comparison between welfare and work made it clear that, in large part because of the nation's work support system, which provides benefits such as food stamps and the EITC to working families, even those working at the minimum wage would have more money than when they were on welfare. Although working families would have additional expenses such as child care and transportation, the Republican chart failed to list many billions of dollars of benefits such as housing, child care, education and training assistance, and child nutrition that also went to working families.

The nice thing about mathematics is that it generally produces the same results for the same problem regardless of the political context. Despite the faint odor of politics in the Republican accounting of welfare and work benefits, researchers at the nonpartisan Urban Institute recently published a detailed study of welfare reform in twelve states that included a comparison of the income of families on welfare with the income of families working half time at minimum wage (Coe, Acs, and Watson, 1998). As far as I know, the Urban Institute researchers had not been overly influenced by the charts Republicans used during the floor debate on welfare reform. Even so, their analysis produced the conclusion that mothers working half time at minimum wage would be financially better off than mothers on welfare, even in high-benefit states like California. Republicans never made a claim that radical.

Of course, mathematics can only take one so far. The cleanness of the above analysis obscures much of the messiness of events in the real world. For one thing, most workers have expenses, such as clothing and transportation, that nonworkers do not have. Even daily public transportation can cost as much as $100 or $150 per month. Child care is another and even bigger issue. Indeed, child care was a major part of the welfare reform debate. By the end of the debate, two major improvements had been made in the nation's child care programs. First, the new law ended several overlapping and redundant programs and provided states with one primary source of authority and funds to pay for child care. This source, the Child Care and Development Block grant, provided states with great flexibility in who received child care support and in what form. Second, funding in the block grant was increased by about $4.5 billion over six years as compared with child care funding under previous law. The child care issue is pursued in detail elsewhere in this volume by Besharov and Samari, but here it is sufficient to note that according to recent data fewer than a quarter of the mothers leaving welfare for work even use subsidized care and there is little evidence that mothers are being held back by the lack of availability or cost of child care.

Another major issue, which is addressed by Greenstein and Guyer (chapter 13), is that families leaving welfare might not receive all the work support benefits to which they are entitled (Zedlewski and Brauner, 1999). The problem here, largely unsuspected at the time of the welfare reform debate, is that as states converted welfare to a work-oriented program, the administrative requirements of ensuring that families would continue receiving food stamps and Medicaid even when they no longer receive cash welfare proved too difficult for states to handle well.

Despite these issues, there is no question that the members of Congress who wrote the welfare reform law and developed the various arguments to defend it believed that mothers leaving welfare would have more money than while they were on welfare. Now let us see if they were correct.

What Is the Baseline?

The welfare reform law was enacted in 1996. All states were required to have approved reform plans consistent with the new federal law by July 1, 1997. Given the dramatic flexibility states had to design their reform programs, conducting a national random assignment experiment to study the impacts of welfare reform is impossible. Thus one approach to studying the outcomes of welfare reform is to compare measures of work, income, and poverty before welfare reform began with such measures after welfare reform was implemented. Just on the basis of the dates of enactment and state implementation, it would seem that data for 1995 or 1996 would be a good baseline year and that data for 1997 and later years could be compared with 1995 or 1996 to study changes associated with welfare reform. However, in addition to the substantial variability in the speed of state implementation of welfare reform (Gais and others, chapter 2; Nathan and Gais, 1999), thereby raising questions about what year is "after" welfare reform, the selection of 1995 or 1996 as the baseline year is complicated by the fact that many states were already implementing their own versions of welfare reform by the time national legislation was passed in 1996.

Since the Reagan presidency in the 1980s, the White House and the Department of Health and Human Services (HHS) had been emphasizing state experimentation with welfare reform. Section 1115 of the Social Security Act permitted the Secretary of HHS to grant waivers of most provisions of the old Aid to Families with Dependent Children (AFDC) program (and a number of other programs in the Social Security Act, including Medicaid) if "in the judgment of the Secretary" a state waiver demonstration project would promote the objectives of the AFDC program (U.S. House of Representatives, 1999, pp. 548–49). To his credit, President Clinton continued the emphasis on using waivers to experiment with welfare reform and, in truth, expanded the waiver process substantially. Although states frequently complained about the difficulty and rigor of the process of getting a waiver application approved, by the time welfare reform was enacted in 1996 nearly forty states had approved waivers and were at various stages in the process of implementation. Because these waivers were so pervasive, and because most involved the same types of welfare-to-work provisions embodied in the 1996 legislation, using 1995 or 1996 as the baseline year would actually capture some of the effects of welfare reform in the baseline, thereby confounding conclusions about reform's true effects.

By 1994 more than half of the states were implementing waivers. Furthermore, in 1994 the decline in welfare rolls began, albeit slowly at first. To the extent that the decline in rolls is an indicator of reform implementation at the state and local levels, a baseline year before the decline is desirable. Thus in most comparisons here I use 1993 as the baseline year. However, I also typically include data for all the years between 1993 and 1999, the latest year for which data are available. Thus readers may examine changes across the entire period and draw their own conclusions about the appropriate baseline year.

Leavers Studies

The task of describing the effect of welfare reform on mothers' incomes requires information both on mothers who have left welfare and on poor and low-income mothers who are eligible for welfare but never joined up. Some in this latter group do not know much about welfare, some regard welfare as stigmatized, and some have been persuaded by the new state welfare programs that they should try to avoid welfare (so-called "welfare diversion" policies). In any case, a narrow view of our problem requires describing the financial status of mothers and children who leave welfare; a broader view requires describing the financial status of all mother-headed families in the lower part of the income distribution, some of which will be or have been on welfare.

As of this writing, mothers who left welfare are the subject of forty-three state studies, often referred to as "leavers" studies (GAO, 1999; Congressional Research Service, 2000; Devere, Falk, and Burke, 2000). These studies vary greatly in quality. Devere and her colleagues, in their thorough review of welfare reform studies of both waivers granted by HHS in the years leading up to the 1996 reforms and the effects of the 1996 reforms themselves, included information on all forty-three studies. Here I ignore quality and include every study that reported data on the particular measure of interest (all data are from Congressional Research Service, 2000, table L-11).

Of these forty-three studies, thirty are based on state surveys of adults who left welfare and thirteen on income information from the quarterly wage reports on employees that employers are required to submit to state unemployment insurance agencies. Both types of studies provide valuable information on the income of mothers leaving welfare. Of the thirty survey studies, thirteen provide a point estimate of the average number of hours mothers who left welfare were working at the time of the survey. An additional eleven studies provide information on hours worked, but the data were grouped by the percentage of mothers who worked a certain number of hours, thereby making it impossible to compute an average. According to just the thirteen states that provide point estimates, the average number of hours worked per week was 34.2. By comparison, the U.S. General Accounting Office review, based on the seven best studies available in 1998, reported a mean of 35.2 hours worked per week (see GAO, 1999, table 2, p. 18).

Information on average wages was reported by twenty of the thirty states that conducted surveys, although some of them reported a range of salaries. If the midpoint of the range for these states is used as the best point estimate, the average wage rate across these twenty states was $6.71 per hour. The range was $5.50 to $8.16, with fifteen of the twenty states reporting rates between $6.00 and $7.99 per hour.

Yielding to a certain boldness of extrapolation, one might compute the annual earnings of the mothers in these twenty states by multiplying the average number of hours worked from the thirteen states reported above by the $6.71 per hour wage rate. Then the average annual income would be about $11,900. This estimate, of course, is suspect because of the flaws in the various studies, some inexactness in the point estimates for each state, and the fact that hours worked and wage rates were calculated for different states. Even so, it seems reasonable to offer the tentative generalization that the typical mother leaving welfare would earn about $11,900 per year if she worked year-round. However, the state leavers studies as well as a host of other studies (Devere, Falk, and Burk, 2000) show that many working low-income and former welfare mothers do not work year-round.

This problem is somewhat mitigated by weekly, monthly, or quarterly income data reported by the state survey studies. Converting all fourteen of the studies of this type to annualized earnings yields an average income of $10,684, which is about $1,000 less than the estimate yielded by multiplying average hours worked by average wage rates in the state leavers studies.

These estimates—$11,900 based on self-reported hourly earnings and hours of work and $10,570 based on quarterly earnings reported by employers to the unemployment insurance systems of the respective states—are quite similar, thereby providing some confidence that they are at least moderately accurate. However, there are flaws in the studies. First, as already mentioned, many of the mothers leaving welfare do not work year-round. Second, the individual estimates from states are inevitably based on less than 100 percent reporting. The response rate averaged across the twenty-six (of thirty) survey states that reported this information was 57 percent, with a range of 16 to 87 percent. Although there are no firm guidelines for acceptable response rates in surveys, anything below 60 percent for nonlongitudinal studies seems suspect.

The third problem with these estimates is that less than 100 percent of the mothers are actually working. Of the forty-three studies, thirty-eight reported an estimate of the average number of mothers working at the time of the survey or administrative report. Averaging across these thirty-eight studies indicates that 56.8 percent (range: 33.6 percent in Mississippi to 83 percent in Connecticut) of the mothers were working at the time of the study. By comparison, the GAO study (1999, table 2, p. 18) reported an average of 64.1 percent employed at the time of the survey. A total of twenty-four of the forty-three studies reported whether mothers had ever been employed between the time they left welfare and the time of the survey or report (an average of about ten months). The ever-employed average was 74.7 percent (range: 47 percent in Mississippi to 89 percent in Colorado). The upshot of these figures is that at any given moment perhaps a little more than 40 percent of mothers leaving welfare are not employed; over a period of about ten months, this figures falls to about 20 percent. That 40 percent of mothers leaving welfare are not working at any given moment and a little over 20 percent do not work for long periods of time must play some role in the accounting of welfare reform's success or failure. Here is an issue that bears careful examination during reauthorization and funding for careful intervention research on ways to avoid the stark policy choice of welfare dependency or destitution.

A fourth problem with the data from the leavers studies is that not all income is reported. It seems useful to think of two types of underreporting. First, as Edin and Lein (1997) have shown, nearly all mothers on welfare have income they do not report to public officials. Of course, the Edin and Lein study was conducted with mothers still on welfare. Once mothers leave welfare, there is much less reason for them to underreport income. Even so, some mothers may have income from illicit activities that they do not report. Furthermore, relying on data reported from employers to the unemployment insurance system is problematic. One problem is that some mothers leaving welfare are self-employed and many of the self-employed fail to report their earnings, even when the earnings are entirely legitimate. Another and perhaps bigger problem is that the state leavers studies that used unemployment data obtained wage reports only from their own state unemployment insurance system. This approach is flawed because, especially near the borders of many states, mothers may live in one state but work in an adjacent state. In all these cases, the mother's income will be missed.

While acknowledging these problems with the initial estimates of annual earnings for mothers leaving welfare, let me return to the charts used by Republicans during welfare reform to see whether their expectations for mothers leaving welfare for work are being fulfilled. To conduct this exercise, I use the average of the two estimates ($11,900 and $10,570) reached above; the average is $11,235. Call it $11,000.

With the standard deduction, the earnings disregard, no child care expenses, and no shelter expense disregard, the food stamp benefit for a mother earning $11,000 would be about $2,200. In addition, if the mother had one child, she would qualify for an EITC of about $2,400 in 2000; if she had two children, she would qualify for about $3,900. Thus, including income from the work support system, a mother with earnings of $11,000 would have total cash and near-cash income of $15,600 if she had one child and $17,100 if she had two children. Moreover, the mother's children would be covered by Medicaid in every state as long as her income did not change substantially, and the mother herself would be covered for a year in every state and longer in some states.

By way of comparison with the income and benefits of mothers leaving welfare for low-wage jobs, the maximum cash welfare and food stamp benefits in Mississippi (a low-benefit state), Pennsylvania (a moderate-benefit state), and Connecticut (a high-benefit state) for a family of three in 1999 were $5,220, $8,700, and $10,500, respectively. Furthermore, the 2000 poverty levels for families of two (mother and child) and three (mother and two children) were about $11,250 and $14,150, respectively. Thus keeping the caveats reviewed above in mind, the expectations of those supporting the 1996 welfare legislation are being met and even exceeded for many of the mothers leaving welfare, assuming the mothers actually receive the food stamp and EITC benefits to which they are entitled (but see Greenstein and Guyer, chapter 13).

The conclusion that the combination of low-wage work and benefits from the national work support system is producing incomes in excess of both welfare and poverty could be subjected to more rigorous tests if one had information on what low-income working mothers with various levels of income actually receive from the work support system. Fortunately, the Census Bureau publishes information of exactly this type.

National Data on Family Income

The two most important shortcomings of data from leavers studies are that they do not provide information on all poor and low-income mothers and they generally report data only on earnings. Happily, the information on income necessary to address these shortcomings of the leavers studies is collected by the Census Bureau in its March supplement to the Current Population Survey (CPS).

CURRENT POPULATION SURVEY. On the basis of a random sample of 50,000 households selected to be representative of the nation, Census Bureau interviewers ask about sources of income, welfare use, employment, and a host of other measures. As a result, the CPS lends itself nicely to examining changes in total income and income from various sources among all poor and low-income mothers over time.

Figures 4-1 and 4-2 present income data in constant 1999 dollars for female-headed families with children; figure 4-1 is income for the fifth of these families at the bottom of the income distribution of the category; figure 4-2 is income for such families in the second fifth of that income distribution. Together these two groups represent mothers in the bottom 40 percent of the distribution of income for all single mothers with children (U.S. Bureau of the Census, 2000a). Several points are apparent. First, for families

Figure 4-1. *Average Income of Female Family Heads with Children in the Bottom Fifth of Post-Tax Income, 1993–99*

Total income after taxes
and transfers (1999 dollars)

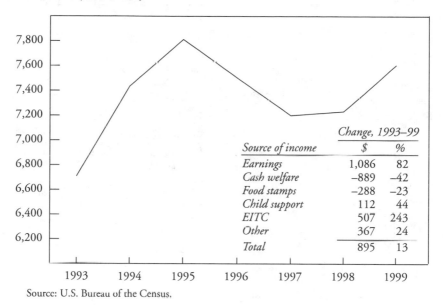

Source of income	Change, 1993–99	
	$	%
Earnings	1,086	82
Cash welfare	–889	–42
Food stamps	–288	–23
Child support	112	44
EITC	507	243
Other	367	24
Total	895	13

Source: U.S. Bureau of the Census.

in both the bottom and second fifths, income over the 1993–99 period increased. The rise for families in the bottom fifth was modest, about $900, or 13 percent; the rise for families in the second fifth was more substantial, about $2,800, or 21 percent. Second, the rise in income over the entire period, especially for the bottom fifth, masks years in which the increase in total income was stagnant or actually declined. In both 1994 and 1995, income rose sharply for both groups, by about $1,200 for the bottom fifth and $2,000 for the second fifth. However, this rapid increase in income was followed by two years of decline (1996 and 1997) for the bottom fifth and one year of decline (1996) for the second fifth. The total income of mothers in the bottom fifth resumed its rise in 1998 and 1999, although the rise in 1998 was very modest. The second fifth had a modest increase in 1997 and then more substantial increases in 1998 and 1999.

It is also instructive to look at changes in the constituent sources of income that produce the broad patterns seen in figures 4-1 and 4-2. As table 4-1 shows, the trend in earnings over the entire 1993–99 period is unambiguously up in both the bottom and second fifths of families. These single mothers earned more money almost every year than they had earned the year

Figure 4-2. *Average Income of Female Family Heads with Children in the Second Fifth of Post-Tax Income, 1993–99*

1999 dollars

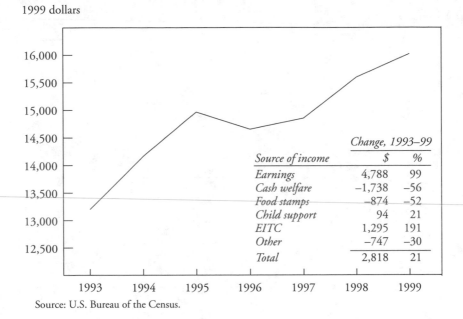

Source of income	Change, 1993–99	
	$	%
Earnings	4,788	99
Cash welfare	−1,738	−56
Food stamps	−874	−52
Child support	94	21
EITC	1,295	191
Other	−747	−30
Total	2,818	21

Source: U.S. Bureau of the Census.

before. In the case of the bottom fifth, earnings increased over 80 percent during the 1993–99 period; in the case of the second fifth, earnings increased nearly 100 percent (see inserts in figures 4-1 and 4-2). By any criterion, these are substantial and impressive changes, and they reflect the dramatic increase in work by these mothers discussed in detail by Blank and Schmidt in chapter 3. As might be expected, these gains in earnings are paralleled by increased income from the EITC. For the bottom fifth, the gain from 1993 to 1999 was over $500 dollars or more than 240 percent; for the second fifth, the gain was nearly $1,300, or 190 percent. Again, especially in percentage terms, these are sizable gains.

The second notable change in table 4-1, and again a change that is remarkably consistent across years, is the drop in welfare income. With only a few exceptions, families received less income from both cash welfare and food stamps every year (see also Zedlewski and Brauner, 1999). The combined cash and food stamp declines in both cases were substantial, amounting to $1,177 in the bottom fifth and $2,612 in the second fifth.

Putting these pieces of data together yields a remarkably straightforward story. In both the bottom fifth and the second fifth of female-headed families

Table 4-1. *Income by Source for Female-Headed Families with Children in Bottom Two Fifths of Post-Tax Income, 1993–99*[a]
Dollars

Category	1993	1994	1995	1996	1997	1998	1999
Bottom fifth							
Total	6,711	7,436	7,813	7,502	7,201	7,233	7,606
Earnings	1,331	1,555	1,715	1,843	1,827	1,932	2,417
CSE	253	290	333	382	318	268	365
Means-tested cash	2,107	1,408	1,419	1,821	1,504	1,478	1,218
Food stamps	1,276	1,408	1,419	1,222	1,199	1,010	988
EITC	209	382	479	562	552	578	716
Second fifth							
Total	13,201	14,164	14,964	14,653	14,851	15,592	16,019
Earnings	4,815	5,520	6,669	6,454	6,836	8,384	9,603
CSE	446	490	467	509	617	485	540
Means-tested cash	3,099	2,999	2,840	2,566	2,158	1,634	1,361
Food stamps	1,684	1,774	1,454	1,483	1,330	1,126	810
EITC	678	1,084	1,305	1,374	1,561	1,878	1,973

Source: Bavier, U.S. Office of Management and Budget.

a. Income fifths are based on post-tax, post-transfer income; female heads of primary families and unrelated subfamilies with children.

with children, earnings and EITC income are up and income from cash welfare and food stamps is down. This pattern is so consistent across the two groups and across years that it can stand as a hallmark of the post-welfare reform landscape. More mothers work and therefore have more earnings and EITC income. To determine whether they are financially better off, compare the increase in earnings and EITC with the decrease in welfare income. If the former is larger, they have higher incomes; if the latter is larger, they have lower incomes. I will return to this story shortly.

A final and somewhat disappointing change portrayed in table 4-1 is the modest level of child support income. Virtually all these mothers are eligible for child support because nearly all of them have children with living but absent fathers. Moreover, throughout this period states were implementing major child support reforms enacted by Congress in 1988 and 1996. And yet the bottom fifth received only $253 on average from child support in 1993. Although this amount increased modestly over the next three years, it fell in both 1997 and 1998 before ending with a strong increase in 1999. Over the entire period, child support increased $112, or 44 percent, but from a some-what paltry base of $253. The second fifth did not fare much better, increasing from only $446 in 1993 to $540 in 1999 or a little over 20 percent. The second fifth also experienced a drop in child support in two of the six years (1995 and 1997). Both the absolute level of child support received by these families and the pattern of change between 1993 and 1999 reflect discouraging results, especially in view of the fact that states were implementing the major 1996 child support reforms in the last two or three years of this period. This means much more must be done if child support payments are to increase the income of poor and low-income single mothers in anything more than a modest way and thereby contribute to the national agenda of increasing personal responsibility (Garfinkel, chapter 17). A cynic might question whether child support will ever do much to raise the average income of poor and low-income single mothers.

CONSUMER EXPENDITURE SURVEY. Another source of information about the financial well-being of single mothers and their children is the Consumer Expenditure Survey (CEX) conducted by the Census Bureau in cooperation with the Bureau of Labor Statistics. It is somewhat curious that so much of our national debate about the poor relies on income statistics and poverty statistics based on income. Common sense leads to the view that the most direct measure of financial well-being is consumption, not income. After all, people's consumption and income over a given period often do not match. Individuals and families can borrow money, they can spend from savings, and they often have access to the money of relatives and friends. And the goods and services they actually consume are, at least conceptually, the heart of well-being. Of course, people who borrow too much for consumption purposes could be judged to have more well-being than more frugal consumers, a conclusion that many Americans would reject, especially in the long run.

The CEX is a panel-based interview study that involves about 5,000 households (although beginning in 1999 the sample size has been increased by about 50 percent). Compared with the nearly 50,000 households in the CPS, the CEX is very small and therefore less reliable; this fact should be kept in mind as differences between the CPS and CEX are considered. CEX interviewers ask families to provide details of their consumption expenditures for the previous quarter. The estimate of the family's total consumption is the sum of outlays on food, housing, transportation, medical services, entertainment, reading materials, education, tobacco products, alcohol, retirement contributions and insurance premiums, and "other" expenditures. Federal (except Social Security FICA), state, and local taxes are not included.

Figure 4-3. *Spending by Unmarried Female Unit Heads with Children in Second and Bottom Spending Fifths, 1993–98*

1997 dollars

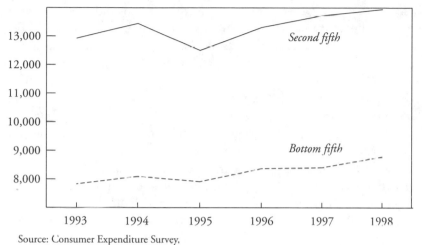

Source: Consumer Expenditure Survey.

Figure 4-3 presents annual estimates of spending based on quarterly data reported by the CEX for the bottom two fifths of the spending distribution (the distribution in Figure 4-3 is based on spending, not income; Bavier, 1999). The first point to note about the spending patterns of mothers in both of the bottom fifths of income is that like many Americans, these mothers spent at a level well above their income, as measured by the CPS. In fact, their CEX spending exceeded their CPS income in every year, by between $400 and $1,700. This pattern, however, does not apply to the second fifth of consumers. These mothers spent more than their income only in 1993. Thereafter their income always exceeded their spending; in 1995 and 1998 the excess income was about $1,950 and $1,300, respectively.

A second point is that the decline in well-being as measured by CPS income data for mothers in the bottom fifth is much less evident in the CEX. There is a slight dip in consumption in 1995, as there was in income, but the dip is small and every other year shows increased spending on consumption. Over the 1993–98 period, spending increased $840, or 11 percent, in constant dollars. The second fifth of consumers showed the same pattern of a decline in 1995 but an increase in every other year. However, in percentage terms the increase in spending in the second fifth over the entire period was only about 6 percent, a little more than half the increase for the bottom fifth.

Richard Bavier (1999), in trying to explain differences between income data as reported by the CPS and spending data as reported by the CEX, shows that although the characteristics of all mothers in the two surveys are very similar, the bottom fifth in the CEX has many more black mothers than the CPS. The two surveys also count housing subsidies differently. Even so, these factors do not go very far in explaining the striking differences between income and both the level and pattern of spending in the bottom fifth in the two surveys. Unreported income, income sharing, and credit in all likelihood play a role, but detailed information about these and other factors is not available.

A recent analysis of CEX data from 1994 through 1997 by Gene Falk (2000) of the Congressional Research Service provides a somewhat different perspective on spending in the two bottom fifths of the distribution (the Falk analysis ignores inflation). Unlike Bavier, Falk divides the distribution on the basis of income, not spending, and then examines consumption in the bottom two fifths of income. This approach produces some surprises. First, Falk shows that consumption expenditures among female-headed families with children increased by 18 percent between 1994 and 1997, a rate almost one-half higher than the rate for all families with children. Second, like Bavier, Falk finds that spending by low-income mothers greatly exceeds their income. However, whereas Bavier found the income-spending discrepancy only in the bottom fifth of earners, Falk finds it in both of the two bottom fifths of the distribution based on spending.

For the purposes of this discussion, the most pertinent points Falk makes concern spending trends at the bottom of the distribution. Whereas Bavier had found a slight decline in spending in 1995 and increases in the other years, Falk finds increased expenditures in the bottom fifth every year between 1994 and 1997. Over the 1994–97 period, spending increased from $11,391 to $14,171, an increase of nearly 25 percent in just three years. Moreover, the difference between spending by female heads with children in the bottom fifth of income is surprisingly similar to spending by female heads with children in the second fifth. Thus even though mothers in the bottom fifth had incomes that averaged just $5,091 over the four years as compared with incomes that averaged $9,698 among mothers in the second fifth, the mean difference in spending between the two groups was only $1,754.

If one takes the CEX consumption data seriously, the news about well-being in both the bottom and second fifths is even better than the news based on income as measured by the CPS. With one modest exception in the two studies reviewed here, mothers and children in both of the bottom fifths are better off each year than the year before if consumption is used as the measure of well-being. In drawing conclusions from CEX data in relation to

CPS data, however, one must bear in mind that the CPS data are much more reliable. Fortunately, both surveys yield the same general picture of increased well-being for poor and low-income female-headed families with children over the period from 1993 or 1994 to the late 1990s. The major difference between the findings of the two surveys is that the poorest of these families appears to be somewhat better off as measured by consumption than income.

Poverty

During the nearly two-year debate on the welfare reform law in 1995 and 1996, a major argument against the Republican bill was that its harshness would throw many children into poverty. Senator Daniel Patrick Moynihan even argued that many families would wind up homeless and destitute:

> In a very little while as the time limits come into effect, I estimate a 5-year time [limit] might put half a million children on the streets of New York City in 10 years' time, and we will wonder where they came from. We will say, "Why are these children sleeping on grates? Why are they being picked up in the morning frozen? Why are they scrambling? Why are they horrible to each other, a menace to all, most importantly to themselves?" (Moynihan, 1995, p. S12682)

Similarly, Wendell Primus and others, first at the Department of Health and Human Services and then at the Urban Institute in Washington, D.C., produced an econometric report claiming that the Republican bill would cast a million children into poverty (Zedlewski and others, 1996).

The claims of many Democrats, especially Senator Moynihan, that welfare reform would lead to dramatic increases in poverty and worse, as well as the million-kids-in-poverty claim of the Urban Institute report, have served to further politicize the already raucous issue of poverty that was such a central part of the 1995–96 debate. Even so, the effect of welfare reform on children's poverty is an issue of great importance. Data on progress against poverty must be taken as one of the important indicators of the success or failure of welfare reform. Four years after passage of the legislation and three years after implementation by every state, a substantial amount of information about poverty is available to assess the claim that child poverty would grow.

For their part, Republicans have often been reluctant to agree that poverty should be an important outcome measure of welfare reform. The key to understanding Republican thinking on this issue penetrates to a major differ-

Figure 4-4. *Simultaneous Decline of Welfare Caseloads and Children's Poverty, 1995–99*

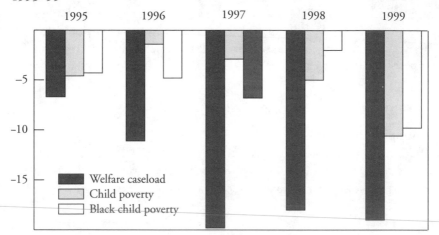

Percentage decline

Source: Caseload data from Congressional Research Service; poverty data from U.S. Bureau of the Census.

ence between conservatives and liberals on social policy. The goal of liberal social policy is to use government welfare payments to make the poor better off, especially by raising them above some defined but constantly rising cut-off such as the poverty line or by decreasing the difference in income between the rich and poor. Conservatives utterly reject the goal of redistributing income to bring the poor closer to the rich and focus attention instead on how people get their money, not how much of it they have. Starkly put, many conservatives think welfare reform would be a great success if every poor person in the nation had exactly as much money after as before welfare reform on the single condition that after reform the poor earned most of their own money rather than getting it from taxpayers through government transfers.

Figure 4-4 compares the percentage annual changes in the welfare rolls with percentage annual changes in overall child poverty and poverty among black children for the years between 1995 and 1999 (U.S. Bureau of the Census, 2000b). All three measures decline every year. The decline in welfare rolls for all five years is greater in percentage terms than the decline in welfare rolls during any other year since 1950. Simultaneous with these historic declines in welfare rolls, both overall child poverty and black child poverty decline substantially. In fact, declines among black children in 1997 and

Figure 4-5. *Decline in Children's Poverty by Broad Definition,*
1983–89 and 1993–99

Percent

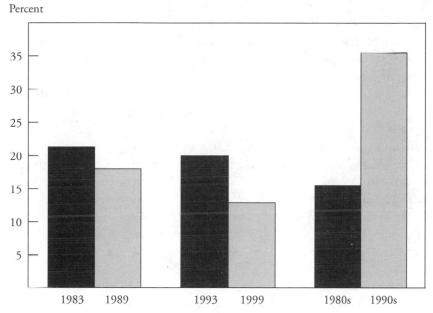

| | 1983 | 1989 | | 1993 | 1999 | | 1980s | 1990s |

Source: U.S. Bureau of the Census.

1999 are the biggest single-year declines on record and the 1999 level of
black child poverty is the lowest ever. Similarly, the overall child poverty rate
in 1999 is lower than in any year since 1979.

One problem with the official Census Bureau measure of poverty is that it
fails to take into account billions of dollars of government transfer payments
that, in effect, increase the income of poor and low-income families, especially working families. As table 4-1 demonstrates, single mothers in both the
bottom and second fifths of income receive about 20 percent of their income
from food stamps and the EITC, neither of which is included in the official
poverty measure.

Fortunately, the U.S. Bureau of the Census (2000b, p. 28ff., definition
14) publishes an experimental poverty measure that takes both food stamps
and the EITC, as well as a few other noncash welfare payments, into account
in computing poverty. Figure 4-5 compares progress against poverty using
this broader Census Bureau measure during the economic expansions of the
1980s and the 1990s. For both decades, the first year (dark bar graphs) for
the comparison is the year (1983 and 1993, respectively) of peak poverty
during the recession that preceded the recovery. In the case of the 1980s, the

last year for the comparison (1989) is the last year during which poverty declined before it began increasing during the mild recession of the early 1990s. In the case of the 1990s, the last year for the comparison (1999) is the last year for which poverty data are available.

Both decades saw substantial progress against poverty. However, the drop in poverty during the six-year economic expansion of the 1990s is more than twice as great as the drop during the six-year expansion of the 1980s. The explanation for this remarkable difference cannot be greater job growth during the 1990s because the net increase in employment was about 20 million during both periods (Executive Office of the President, 1999, p. 380). Although strong scientific evidence cannot be adduced to explain this striking difference, a two-part explanation is consistent with the available evidence.

First, as I noted earlier, during the 1990s welfare reform was associated with a huge reduction in the welfare rolls and, as Blank and Schmidt (chapter 3) show, historic increases in employment by single mothers. By contrast, employment among single mothers was virtually flat during the economic expansion of the 1980s, and the welfare rolls actually grew by well over 10 percent.

Second, when mothers entered the work force in such impressive numbers during the 1990s, they encountered a friendly system of public work supports that augmented their earnings. This system of work supports had grown dramatically since the 1980s. Administrative data for the EITC show that between 1993 and 1999 the number of families receiving EITC cash jumped from 15.1 million to over 20 million (about 30 percent), the average EITC benefit increased from $1,028 to $1,541 (50 percent), and total spending on the EITC grew from $15.5 billion to $30.0 billion (over 90 percent; see U.S. House of Representatives, 2000, p. 813).

Additional evidence on recent progress against poverty can be obtained by examining changes in the impact of economic activity and government transfer programs on two measures of poverty among children over selected years between 1979 and 1999. Table 4-2, based on the Census Bureau's CPS data and adapted from the *2000 Green Book* (U.S. House of Representatives, 2000, pp. 1318–27), provides estimates of the impacts of four types of federal programs on children's poverty rates and the children's poverty gap (the amount of money that would be needed to lift every poor child to the poverty line). The four types of government programs are social insurance (Social Security, unemployment compensation, and workers' compensation), means-tested cash (TANF/AFDC, Supplemental Security Income, and General Assistance), means-tested noncash (food stamps, housing benefits, and school lunch), and federal payroll and income taxes, including the EITC. Note the "cash income

Table 4-2. *Impact of Government Programs on Children's Poverty and Poverty Gap*[a]

Measure	1979	1983	1989	1993	1999
Number of children (thousands)	63,375	62,337	65,602	69,292	71,731
Poverty rate (percent)					
Cash income before transfers	20.1	25.9	22.8	26.3	19.6
Plus social insurance	17.9	23.1	21.1	24.1	17.9
Plus means-tested cash	16.4	22.3	20.1	22.7	16.9
Plus means-tested noncash	13.3	20.0	17.4	20.0	14.9
Plus federal taxes	13.6	21.0	18.0	20.0	13.9
Percentage-point reduction in poverty					
Social insurance	10.9	10.8	7.4	8.3	8.7
Means-tested cash	7.7	3.1	4.6	5.3	5.1
Means-tested noncash	15.3	9.0	11.7	10.2	10.1
Federal taxes	−1.6	−5.1	−2.7	0.1	10.0
Total	32.5	17.7	21.0	23.9	34.0
Poverty gap (billions of 1999 dollars)					
Cash income before transfers	33.9	45.0	41.2	51.7	34.8
Plus Social Insurance	28.5	37.9	35.8	44.7	29.5
Plus means-tested cash	18.7	27.1	25.6	32.1	24.3
Plus means-tested noncash	12.7	18.8	17.2	21.3	17.6
Plus federal taxes	12.8	19.4	17.2	20.8	15.2
Percentage-point reduction in poverty gap					
Social insurance	16.1	15.8	13.1	13.6	15.1
Plus means-tested cash	28.8	24.0	24.8	24.3	14.9
Plus means-tested noncash	17.5	18.4	20.5	20.9	19.4
Federal taxes	0.0	−1.2	0.0	1.1	6.8
Total	62.4	56.9	58.4	59.8	56.3

Source: Computations performed by the Department of Health and Human Services and the Congressional Budget Office, based on Current Population Survey data (U.S. House of Representatives, 2000, appendix H).

a. Poverty gap is the amount of money that would be required to lift every poor child exactly to the poverty line.

before transfers" (that is, the poverty level after earnings and other private income but before government transfers) listed under the poverty rate and poverty gap. This measure reflects the ability of families to avoid poverty using their own resources and without any help from the government.

The poverty rate for children is calculated before any transfers and then after each of the four types of government transfers is counted. The poverty rate before transfers was 19.6 percent in 1999, its lowest level since 1979 and nearly 25 percent lower than in 1993. Similarly, the 1999 child poverty rate after all transfers are taken into account was 13.9 percent, its lowest level since 1979 and more than 35 percent below its level in 1993. Like the poverty data examined above, these figures show substantial progress against children's poverty, both before and after government transfers. Table 4-2 clearly shows that the pretransfer poverty level was low in 1999 and that it has been declining rapidly since 1993. Thus once again the dramatic increase in work by former welfare mothers starting in roughly 1994 seems to be playing a vital role in poverty reduction among children.

The role of increased work by mothers is also suggested by the data on percentage of children removed from poverty owing to federal taxes. All the figures for "federal taxes" indicate that federal tax policy, especially the EITC, is having a major and growing effect on reducing poverty. In 1983, when the EITC was still very modest and before the tax reforms of 1986 dropped nearly 8 million low-income families from the income tax rolls, federal taxes actually increased the poverty level among children by 5.1 percent. However, as the federal government reduced the personal income taxes of poor and low-income families and expanded the EITC, the impact of taxes actually became positive. By 1999, 10 percent of children were removed from poverty by federal taxes, especially the EITC.

Data on the poverty gap for children are also positive even though means-tested government programs have lost some of their effectiveness in reducing children's poverty. As was the case with the child poverty rate, data on the pretransfer poverty gap are uniformly positive. Despite the fact that the number of children grew by nearly 9.4 million, or 15 percent, between 1983 and 1999, the poverty gap before transfers nonetheless fell from $45 billion in 1983 to $34.8 billion in 1999, a decline of 23 percent. There was a steady and especially steep decline after 1993, from $51.7 billion to $34.8 billion, or 33 percent in just six years. However, means-tested cash transfers and means-tested noncash transfers became generally less effective in reducing the poverty gap in the late 1990s as compared with previous periods. As can be seen by adding together these two categories of government transfers, their combined impact reduced the poverty gap by only 34.3 percent in 1999 as compared with 46.3 percent in 1979, 42.4 percent in 1983, 45.3 percent in 1989, and 45.2 percent in 1993.

As in previous analyses, the effect of the EITC and other federal taxes on reducing the poverty gap remained potent; in fact, at 6.8 percent in 1999 it was greater than in any previous year. Despite the effectiveness of the EITC and other taxes, the overall impact of government programs in 1999 reduced the poverty gap by only 56.3 percent, much less than in any previous year except 1983 and well below the 62.4 percent reduction of 1979. The major reason for the decreased effectiveness of government programs in reducing the poverty gap is a decline in the impact of means-tested cash benefits. In 1979 these benefits reduced the poverty gap by 28.8 percent. By contrast, in 1999 they reduced the gap by only 14.9 percent.

The data in table 4-2 are generally consistent with previous analyses. First, they show that families are able to keep themselves out of poverty more effectively and to reduce the poverty gap more than at any time since 1979. The high level of work by single mothers undoubtedly plays a major role here. Second, federal taxes and especially the EITC are becoming ever more effective in removing children from poverty and reducing the poverty gap. Again, the high level of work by single mothers is crucial in producing this effect because EITC payments are contingent on work. Third, nontax government transfer programs, especially means-tested cash, are less effective than previously in reducing the poverty gap. As noted in the analysis of CPS data, welfare cash income is declining among single mothers in the bottom two-fifths of income, in large part because so many of them have left welfare for work. Thus it is not surprising that means-tested cash removes fewer families from poverty.

If the overriding goal of social policy is to reduce child poverty, one should count as a success the fact that the combination of earnings and the EITC is producing a lower child poverty level in female-headed families than the combination of less earnings but more means-tested cash and noncash transfers. And who can object to families making a bigger contribution to their children's welfare while welfare makes a smaller contribution, especially since the increased effectiveness of government tax policy partly offsets the declining effects of means-tested spending programs?

The remarkable progress against children's poverty is also reflected in progress against children's deep poverty, defined as the percentage of children living in families with incomes below one-half the poverty level (about $7,000 for a family of three in 2000; see Duncan and Chase-Lansdale, chapter 15). The trend in children's deep poverty is somewhat surprising. After declining in both 1994 and 1995 as more and more single mothers took jobs, the deep poverty rate for children actually increased in 1996 and showed no improvement in 1997. Understandably, the Children's Defense Fund (Sherman and others, 1998) used these data to caution that welfare reform was leading to increases in deep poverty. However, both 1998 and 1999 saw steep declines in deep poverty. Indeed, during these two years children's deep poverty declined from 9.0 percent to 6.9 percent, a drop of nearly 25 percent in just two years. On balance, these trends seem to support the claim that in the years following welfare reform, the employment of low-income mothers increased greatly and both children's poverty and children's deep poverty declined substantially. In fact, if 1993 is taken as the baseline year, children's deep poverty has declined from 10.1 percent to 6.9 percent, or nearly a third over the entire period.

How to Maintain Income Gains and Help Families at the Bottom

The foregoing review yields a fairly consistent portrait of the financial status of families leaving welfare since the enactment of welfare reform. Without making any claims about causality, or about the relative impacts of block grants, time limits, work requirements, the EITC, or the economy, it seems that most families leaving welfare have done well. The information on income from the leavers studies and the Current Population Survey is mostly good; information from the Consumer Expenditure Survey is unambiguously good; and poverty data from the Census Bureau, especially using a broad definition of poverty, are also unambiguously good.

All in all, the strong requirements of the 1996 legislation provided a "push" to encourage and, where necessary, force mothers off welfare and into jobs. Although the welfare caseload has always been characterized by lots of turnover as mothers enter and leave, exit rates now exceed entrance rates and mothers are now more likely to work while still receiving welfare. In addition, mothers in the bottom two-fifths of income are more likely to work than in the past. Simultaneously, the strong economy and the work support system, especially the EITC, have combined to greatly increase the attractiveness of the low-wage jobs that have been plentiful and for which former welfare mothers can qualify. On paper, leaving welfare for work can substantially increase mothers' income if they work anywhere close to full time and year-round and if they receive the food stamps and EITC to which they are entitled. Leavers studies demonstrate that most mothers are working and most working mothers are working close to full time.

Nationally representative data on poor and low-income mothers with children support and extend these facts and, taken together, yield a coherent picture of these mothers' income. Throughout the 1993–99 period, the welfare income of mothers in the bottom two-fifths of earners declined as more and more mothers left cash welfare. Simultaneously, income from earnings and the EITC increased.

These CPS data can be taken to establish something like the first law of welfare reform: when mothers leave welfare, their welfare income as a group will decline and their earnings and EITC income will increase. If the former exceeds the latter, they will have less income; if the latter exceeds the former, they will have more income. Like other American families, over a million previously welfare-dependent families now rely in large part on their own efforts.

At this point, it seems useful to recall spending data from the Consumer Expenditure Survey. Although the CEX reported income declines in a few years similar to those in the CPS, mothers in the bottom fifth continued to consume at a rate well above their income and with only a slight dip in 1995. Exactly how mothers pull off this feat is still unclear, but it appears that they are able to borrow or otherwise have the use of funds that allow them to maintain purchasing power far in excess of that dictated by their income. An optimist might conclude that, at least in the short run, mothers in the bottom fifth can avoid destitution by drawing on credit, relatives, and friends. In any case, the CEX seems to show that many, perhaps most, mothers and children in the bottom fifth do not suffer the fate that is implied by their income.

Perhaps the strongest evidence supporting the effectiveness of the new system of low-wage work supplemented by the EITC is the data on poverty. In 1999 the nation enjoyed the lowest rate of child poverty since 1979. The comparison of poverty declines under a definition that includes noncash benefits and the EITC shows that the decline in children's poverty in the 1990s has been substantially greater than the decline during the 1980s, when work was not as common among mothers in the bottom two-fifths of income. Similarly, the comparison of the impacts of family earnings and government programs on poverty since 1979 shows clearly that the poverty level produced by the market before any government transfers was lower in 1999 than in any year since 1979 and has been declining steadily and rapidly since 1993. Moreover, although government welfare programs are less effective in reducing poverty than in the past, probably because, as shown clearly by the CPS data, fewer mothers are receiving cash welfare and food stamps, the EITC reduces children's poverty more and more every year. In short, at least for fighting poverty, the lowered effectiveness of welfare payments is more than offset by the increased effectiveness of earnings and the EITC.

Finally, it is worth emphasizing that the portrait I have drawn in this chapter does not differ in any serious way from that drawn by notable scholars who are long on academic and short on conservative credentials, namely, Becky Blank (Schoeni and Blank, 2000) and Wendell Primus (Primus and others, 1999).

I am led to conclude that there is much to conserve in the 1996 welfare reform law—and in the 1990s economy—if only Congress could ensure continuing economic growth. The data on income, consumption, and poverty show that the nation is making more progress in reducing poverty than in recent decades. Moreover, many more low-income mothers are earning a steadily increasing share of their income.

However, the portrait has some blemishes. The evidence also shows a group of mothers and children in the bottom fifth who have less income when they leave welfare. For these mothers, the new system of low-wage work and the EITC is not working well. In this regard, the data on increased numbers of mothers and children below half the poverty level are especially compelling, notwithstanding the data on consumption showing that even these mothers maintain a surprisingly high level of spending.

Logic points to two paths out of the problem of very low income: more work or more welfare. In my view, the results of the increased work by mothers formerly on welfare speak for themselves. On paper, nearly all mothers on welfare would be better off if they work even close to full time at low wages and get the EITC. The problem of very low income occurs when mothers leave welfare and experience a loss of welfare income but do not replace lost welfare income with earnings through work. Given the proven effectiveness of work in increasing income and reducing poverty, I believe it would be unwise to help this group of mothers by loosening welfare's emphasis on work. Rather, policymakers should emphasize the importance of state and local programs finding ways to help these mothers increase their income through work. Happily, the Department of Health and Human Services has already awarded several research contracts to pursue exactly this policy.

More welfare is a second path away from very low income. Here there are two categories of solution. The first would be to make it easier for mothers to stay on welfare. As already indicated, I think this path is fraught with danger and should not be taken. States already have enough flexibility in their use of federal and state funds to permit many of these mothers to remain on welfare indefinitely. There is a 20 percent exemption in the five-year time limit, and states, at least for the foreseeable future, have plenty of money to pay welfare benefits to mothers who, because of personality problems, mental problems, addictions, and similar afflictions, prove themselves to be incapable of supporting themselves and their children. If certain states think they need to provide the time-limit exemption to more than 20 percent of their caseload, they can spend their own money, which they are required to spend anyway under the federal law's maintenance-of-effort requirements. At the very least, before anyone seriously considers relaxing the federal time limit, there should be strong evidence that some states are not able to maintain all the mothers they believe need cash welfare beyond the time limit. So far, there is no evidence of this type.

The second welfare-based solution is to change administration of the Food Stamp program so that more qualified mothers who are not receiving cash welfare receive food stamps. Virtually all the mothers in both of the bottom two-fifths of income are eligible for food stamps. Because food stamps are an entitlement, if these mothers fulfill the application requirements, they will receive the benefits. In 1999 mothers in the bottom fifth of income received on average less than $800 in food stamps (see table 4-1). They are eligible for an average of at least $3,000 in food stamps. If they received all the food stamps for which they are qualified, their income losses over the 1995–96 period would be eliminated and many would even move into the second fifth of income.

There is a problem here, however. Food stamps are welfare and are highly stigmatized both among those who receive them and among those who do not. Anecdotal evidence indicates that many people do not take food stamps because of the hassle involved and because they want to be free of welfare. To solve this problem, advocates and others who want to provide more money to working poor families should figure out new ways to give them money that are not as stigmatized as food stamps. For example, a few states could experiment with using Food Stamp money to provide an equivalent amount of income to families eligible for food stamps. Meanwhile, states should take strong administrative action to let mothers leaving or avoiding welfare know they are eligible for food stamps and to make it as easy as possible for them to apply for and maintain their eligibility, especially through the use of phone applications.

Although I have not addressed Medicaid benefits in this paper, several studies show that many mothers and children leaving cash welfare are not receiving Medicaid (Greenstein and Guyer, chapter 13; Smith and others, 1998). As was the case with food stamps, the federal Medicaid statutes make it clear that nearly all these mothers and children are eligible and that the benefits are an entitlement. Evidence again points to a role for hassle and stigma in preventing families from maintaining their Medicaid eligibility. A recent hearing by the Committee on Ways and Means, however, showed that some states have revamped their procedures for taking applications and for maintaining Medicaid eligibility and have had substantial success in maintaining Medicaid enrollment even after families leave welfare. Moreover, recent national data show that since declining in 1995, 1996, and 1997 as the welfare rolls shrank, the number of children receiving Medicaid increased substantially in 1998 and 1999 (U.S. House of Representatives, 2000, p. 914). Nonetheless, this issue should receive close attention during the welfare reauthorization debate.

The low level of income from child support for mothers in the bottom two-fifths of income is disappointing. Much more needs to be done to strengthen child support enforcement and to provide more of the collections to mothers leaving welfare. In a little-noticed section of the 1996 welfare reform law, states were required to pay to former welfare mothers approximately half of the fathers' payments on past-due child support. Previous law had allowed the state and federal governments to retain these payments. The 1996 reform provision is now providing mothers leaving welfare with approximately $800 million per year in cash paid by fathers. Legislation that passed the House of Representatives overwhelmingly in 2000, but was never taken up by the Senate, would have given mothers the other half of this money and would have improved the financial well-being of mothers and children leaving welfare by another $900 million per year. This provision should be taken up and passed by Congress as part of reauthorization.

The agenda of personal responsibility and work was given an immense boost by the 1996 welfare reform law. Welfare rolls and child poverty are down; work and earnings and income are up. If these results can be achieved in five years, further improvements in family earnings and income seem within reach. The outcome of welfare reauthorization should be conservation of the basic structure and major features of the 1996 legislation, including its funding level, with only minor adjustments such as improvements in food stamp and Medicaid administration by states, experimentation with new ways of paying Food Stamp benefits, and payment of certain child support collections to mothers. The combination of work requirements and generous work supports is working.

COMMENT BY
Wendell Primus

This engaging chapter by the former primary welfare adviser to the Republican majority in Congress carefully documents and analyzes family income and poverty trends in the 1990s. I find myself in agreement with its conclusions to a large extent. Ron Haskins recognizes that some families are floundering economically, that both the Food Stamp and the Medicaid programs should be thought of as work supports, that in both of these programs participation has fallen, and that the strong economy, the earned income tax credit (EITC), and expanded child care funding are all important factors in explaining why the earnings of single mothers have increased so dramatically.

To my mind, Haskins overstates positive findings regarding income and poverty trends while casting doubt on some of the more negative findings, though he does acknowledge that some families are floundering. Let me describe five instances in which the spin given to the evidence is too positive.

First, when reviewing state surveys of recipients who have left welfare ("leavers"), the author carefully examines the evidence on employment but not on income or poverty trends. This is a serious omission. Most of the state studies of leavers conclude that they cannot determine whether families are better off financially after they leave the welfare rolls. Yet the author states that "most mothers and children who have left welfare have more money than they had when they were on welfare." Two studies that have directly addressed the question of whether leavers are "better off" come to a different conclusion, albeit with various caveats. One study of Wisconsin's welfare program shows that one year after leaving welfare, between 55 percent (for the 1997 cohort) and 60 percent (for the 1995 cohort) of leavers had incomes that were at least $1,000 lower than the previous year. Only about 30 percent of the leavers had at least $1,000 more in income (Cancian and others, 2000). Income, as measured in this study, included earnings, cash assistance, food stamps, the EITC, and payroll and income taxes. A study conducted by Richard Bavier (2000) using data from the Survey on Income and Program Participation (SIPP) reaches similar conclusions. The evidence from both studies calls into question whether "most" households are indeed better off when they leave welfare. Both of these studies suggest that only about one half of the "leaver" population is "better off."

Second, to his credit, Haskins readily admits that "there is a small to moderate-sized group of mother-headed families that are worse off than they were before welfare reform." Given the very strong economy, increased child care resources, and the EITC, why should there be any significant number of families that are worse off? According to the best estimate, 700,000 families are worse off. This estimate is obtained using data from the Current Population Survey (CPS) and arraying single-mother families by the ratio of income to poverty and counting the number of families in 1999 that have significantly less income (about $300 annually) than their counterparts in 1995. Unfortunately, the number of single-mother families with less income is not insignificant.

Haskins also minimizes this problem by turning to consumption data (CEX), which he argues are conceptually a better measure of well-being. Haskins points out that the consumption of the poorest families has not declined. Until there is a better explanation of why consumption can increase while income is falling, however, one should put more faith in the income

Table 4-3. *Poverty Gap for Families with Children*
Billions of 1999 dollars

Before or after taxes and transfers	Gap in selected years			Reduction in gap	
	1993	*1995*	*1999*	*1993–95*	*1995–99*
Before	85.0	73.0	55.9	12.0	17.1
After	32.0	24.8	22.5	7.2	2.3

Source: Author's tabulations from Current Population Survey data.

data from the leavers studies, the SIPP, and the CPS and not place too much weight on the much smaller and less reliable CEX.

Third, given the strong economy and "make work pay" policies, one would expect earnings to increase and child poverty to decline significantly. Haskins acknowledges that government programs were "generally less effective in reducing the poverty gap in the late 1990s as compared with previous periods." The poverty gap measures the total number of dollars that would be required to bring all people with incomes below the poverty line up to the poverty line; thus it takes into account not only the breadth of poverty, but also its depth. As shown in table 4-3, between 1995 and 1999 the increased earnings of low-income families with children reduced the pretransfer poverty gap (the poverty gap before government transfers and taxes) by an impressive $17.1 billion. Yet the reduction in the poverty gap after all government benefits and taxes are included was only about $2.3 billion. This latter reduction is only one-third of the reduction that occurred between 1993 and 1995, despite the fact that the pretransfer poverty gap was reduced by a considerably smaller amount in those years. These two numbers summarize the overall impact of welfare reform thus far: very large gains in earnings but much less movement in disposable income. Why did the improvements in the posttransfer poverty gap between 1995 and 1999 not mirror the improvements between 1993 and 1995?

This question can be answered by examining the income of single-mother families. Between 1995 and 1999, the poorest 40 percent of single-mother families increased their earnings by about $2,300 per family on average after adjustment for inflation. However, their disposable income increased on average by only $292. The increase in disposable income was very modest in large part because many of these families stopped receiving cash assistance and food stamps even though they generally remained eligible. It is important to strengthen the work supports of food stamps, child care, and Medicaid for these families so that more eligible families, especially those that are working, receive these benefits (see Greenstein and Guyer, chapter 13). In reality, these working single parents are probably worse off than these statistics indicate because they are incurring additional expenses for child care, transportation, and clothing that are not reflected in these data.

Fourth, while Haskins agrees that government programs excluding the EITC have been less effective in combating poverty, he argues that the 1995 and 1996 analyses predicting increased poverty as a result of welfare reform are wrong. Haskins argues that declines in child poverty since welfare reform was implemented prove that the prediction that 1 million children would be made poor by the legislation was a gross overstatement that will never come true. This conclusion is premature and therefore is unwarranted. Some welfare reform changes have yet to be implemented. At the present time, the impacts of the five-year time limits and an economic downturn on poverty levels under the 1996 welfare law remain unknown. Of particular importance, it should be noted that the analysis conducted in 1995 and 1996 predicted there would be an increase of 1 million poor children compared with the number of poor children in the absence of welfare reform.

Changes in the Food Stamp program and in safety net programs for legal immigrants were the main factors driving the 1995 study result that predicted that more than 1 million children would be cast into poverty by welfare reform. According to Congressional Budget Office estimates at the time of enactment, the welfare reform bill would reduce outlays by $55 billion between fiscal years 1997 and 2002. The primary savings in the bill were reductions in Food Stamp spending (about $27.4 billion) and benefits for legal immigrants in other programs. Haskins never acknowledges the substantial reductions in Food Stamp program benefits, which were motivated primarily by budget deficit concerns, not welfare policy goals.

How would poverty trends look today if Congress had legislated only the changes in the Aid to Families with Dependent Children program without making the Food Stamp and immigrant reductions that remain in effect? I believe that child poverty would be substantially lower than it is. The funding reductions in the Food Stamp program, the emphasis on reducing caseloads, the declining participation rates in both food stamps and TANF, and the immigrant restrictions are all having a negative impact on children's financial well-being. If the antipoverty effectiveness of means-tested cash assistance and the Food Stamp program had not declined between 1995 and 1999, for example, about 400,000 fewer children would be poor today, and the poverty gap among families with children would be about $6.7 billion lower.

Fifth, in describing data about poverty trends among the bottom quintiles of single-mother families, Haskins could have profitably discussed the sensitivity of these results to methodological issues surrounding what population is included in the analysis, how the comparisons in well-being are made across time, and what measure of income is used in the analysis. Additional analyses using household income, different years, and different measures of income reveal that Haskins's results, and therefore his conclusions, are not robust to different analytic approaches. For example, if the effects of welfare reform are measured beginning in 1995, the year before the reform legislation became law, rather than beginning in 1993, the bottom income quintile of single mothers loses income between 1995 and 1997. Indeed, if one examines the income of single mothers who lived in a household with no other adults, income continued to decline between 1997 and 1999. This picture of income is very different from the one portrayed by Haskins.

Two additional issues should be mentioned. The author spends a page bemoaning the lack of results on child support and questions whether child support will ever play more than a minor role in raising the income of single-mother families. This conclusion is again premature. The author bases his analysis on data from the Current Population Survey, which substantially underreports child support income. Even more important, the 1996 child support reforms have not yet had time to produce their full effect. Judgment on the impact of the 1996 child support changes needs to be deferred and based on data other than the CPS.

Finally, Haskins mentions that the nation is spending a very large sum of money—$300 billion—on programs for low-income individuals. From this fact, he moves to a discussion of low-income single-parent families. The impression that may be left in the minds of many readers is that single mothers with children are the primary reason so much money is spent on low-income families. Yet nothing could be further from the truth; most of these dollars are spent on the elderly and disabled and on medical assistance.

If one looks at all families with children that have earnings equal to or less than the poverty line (including families with no earnings) and adds up all of the means-tested cash assistance, school lunch, housing, food stamps, and EITC income these families receive (and adjusts for underreporting of these benefits), it amounts to $2,500 per child, or $40 billion annually. This is substantially less than $300 billion. Moreover, middle-income taxpayers also receive a significant amount of income support per child: $912 per child from the child tax credit and the value of the personal exemption. Consequently, poor families receive only about $1,600 more per child in income support assistance than middle-income families receive. In many instances, the disparity in federal funding for various kinds of income support between poor children in our society and children of middle-income families is less than the disparity in education funding per child between inner cities and wealthier suburbs. The Bush tax cut passed in spring 2001 will narrow the gap in support per child even further when provisions to double the child tax credit to $1,000 and make it partially refundable are implemented.

The employment gains by single-mother families during the last two-thirds of the 1990s have truly been impressive, and as a result poverty has declined. In addition, the EITC is moving more children (2.6 million in 1999) out of poverty than it did in 1993 (1.1 million). Given these gains in earnings and the improvements in the EITC, the remaining income and poverty trends have been disappointing. The reason income has not increased more with gains in earnings is that the increase in earnings has been offset in large part by declines in cash assistance and food stamps. And in the bottom quintile of single-mother families, average income was, in 1999, still below 1995 levels. Income among the poorest single-mother families declined despite the fact that the economy has been extremely strong, that there have been real wage gains at the bottom of the wage rate distribution, and that one of the primary features of the 1996 law—time limits—has not yet affected very many families. All of this suggests that in the next round of welfare reform, policy needs to focus squarely on increasing the income of these families.

References

Bavier, Richard. 1999. "A Second Look at the Effects of Welfare Reform." Paper presented at the American Enterprise Institute conference on Welfare Reform and Child Outcomes, Washington, December 8–9.

———. 2000. "A Look at Welfare Reform in the Survey of Income and Program Participation." Unpublished paper.

Burke, Vee. 1999. *Cash and Noncash Benefits for Persons with Limited Income: Eligibility Rules, Recipient and Expenditure Data, FY1996–FY1998*. RL30401. Congressional Research Service.

Cancian, Maria, Robert Haveman, Daniel R. Meyer, and Barbara Wolfe. 2000. *Before and after TANF: The Economic Well-Being of Women Leaving Welfare*. Special Report 77. University of Wisconsin-Madison, Institute for Research on Poverty.

Coe, Norma B., Gregory Acs, and Keith Watson. 1998. *Does Work Pay? A Summary of the Work Incentives under TANF*. Series A, no. A-28. Washington: Urban Institute.

Congressional Research Service. 2000. "Monitoring the Effects of Pre- and Post-TANF Welfare Reform Initiatives." In U.S. House of Representatives, Committee on Ways and Means, *2000 Green Book*. WMCP: 106-14, appendix L. Government Printing Office.

Devere, Christine, Gene Falk, and Vee Burke. 2000. *Welfare Reform Research: What Have We Learned since the Family Support Act of 2000?* RL30724. Congressional Research Service.

Edin, Kathryn, and Laura Lein. 1997. *Making Ends Meet: How Single Mothers Survive Welfare and Low-wage Work*. Russell Sage.

Executive Office of the President. 1999. *Economic Report of the President.* Government Printing Office.

Falk, Gene. 2000. "Consumption Expenditures for Families with Children." Unpublished memorandum, July 12. Congressional Research Service.

Haskins, Ron. 2001a. "Liberal and Conservative Influences on the Welfare Reform Legislation of 1996." In *For Better and for Worse: State Welfare Reform and the Well-Being of Low-Income Families and Children,* edited by Lindsay Chase-Lansdale and Greg Duncan. Russell Sage.

————. 2001b. "Effects of Welfare Reform at Four Years." In *For Better and for Worse: State Welfare Reform and the Well-Being of Low-Income Families and Children,* edited by Lindsay Chase-Lansdale and Greg Duncan. Russell Sage.

Moynihan, Daniel P. 1995. Family Self-Sufficiency Act. *Congressional Record 141:*S12682.

Nathan, Richard, and Tom Gais. 1999. *Implementing the Personal Responsibility Act of 1996: A First Look.* Albany, N.Y.: Rockefeller Institute.

Primus, Wendell, Lynette Rawlings, Kathy Larin, and Kathy Porter. 1999. *The Initial Impacts of Welfare Reform on the Incomes of Single-Mother Families.* Washington: Center on Budget and Policy Priorities.

Rector, Robert, and W. F. Lauber. 1995. *America's Failed $5.4 Trillion War on Poverty.* Washington: Heritage Foundation.

Roosevelt, Franklin D. 1935. *The Public Addresses of Franklin D. Roosevelt.* Vol. 4. Random House.

Schoeni, Robert, and Rebecca Blank. 2000. "What Has Welfare Reform Accomplished? Impacts on Welfare Participation, Employment, Income, Poverty, and Family Structure." Unpublished manuscript. University of Michigan, Gerald R. Ford School of Public Policy.

Sherman, Arloch, and others. 1998. *Welfare to What? Early Findings on Family Hardship and Well-Being.* Washington: Children's Defense Fund.

Smith, Victor, Robert G. Lovell, Karin A. Peterson, and Mary Jo O'Brien. 1998. *The Dynamics of Current Medicaid Enrollment Changes.* Ann Arbor, Mich.: Health Management Associates.

U.S. Bureau of the Census. 2000a. "Money Income in the United States: 1999." *Current Population Reports.* Series P60-209. Government Printing Office.

————. 2000b. "Poverty in the United States: 1999." *Current Population Reports.* Series P60-210. Government Printing Office.

U.S. General Accounting Office (GAO). 1999. *Welfare Reform: Information on Former Recipients' Status.* GAO/HEHS-99-48.

U.S. House of Representatives, Committee on Ways and Means. 1999. *Compilation of the Social Security Laws.* WMCP: 106-2. Government Printing Office.

————. 2000. *2000 Green Book.* WMCP: 106-14. U.S. Government Printing Office.

Zedlewski, Sheila, and S. Brauner. 1999. *Are the Steep Declines in Food Stamp Participation Linked to Falling Welfare Caseloads?* Series B, No. B-3. Washington: Urban Institute.

Zedlewski, Sheila, Sandra Clark, Eric Meier, and Keith Watson. 1996. *Potential Effects of Congressional Welfare Reform Legislation on Family Incomes.* Washington: Urban Institute.

5

CHARLES MURRAY

Family Formation

SOME ISSUES REGARDING welfare policy in the wake of Aid to Families with Dependent Children (AFDC) lend themselves to straightforward analysis. What has happened to the size of the welfare rolls? Do former welfare recipients get and hold jobs? What is their income? In each case, which way is up is reasonably clear and not the subject of much controversy. Employed is better than unemployed. More income is better than less. But complications remain. Is somewhat more income from a welfare check better than somewhat less income from gainful employment? These complications, however, seldom divide observers into hostile camps.

For measures of family formation, "up" and "down" are more ambiguous. The word "illegitimacy" is an example. Is it a mean-spirited anachronism or a sociologically accurate label for births out of wedlock? Is marriage necessarily a good thing? Suppose it were to be shown that the threat of losing welfare leads a significant number of women to stay in marriages that they would otherwise have left. Is this good or bad? Would a return of the shotgun marriage be good or bad?

The different positions that people take on such issues lead to radically different views of what constitutes success in the domain of welfare reform

My thanks go to Douglas Besharov, Peter Germanis, Steve Whipple, and Rebecca Maynard for providing answers to various questions, and to David Ellwood, Rebecca Blank, Ron Haskins, and Lawrence Mead for helpful critiques.

known as "family formation." Yet Congress in 1996 passed an act that treated the reduction of nonmarital births as a major objective. Why?

For members of Congress and for scholars alike, the question has soft and hard answers. The soft answer is that single parenthood is, on average, bad for children. After taking the relevant socioeconomic and cultural/ethnic variables into account, children fare best in two-parent families, next best in divorced families (with remarriage doing little to improve the situation), and worst in families where the mother has never married (McLanahan, 1998). This generalization appears to hold true across a wide variety of outcomes, including their home environment (Demo and Acock, 1996; Brown and others, 1998), educational performance (Luster and McAdoo, 1994; Shumow, Vandell, and Posner, 1999), cognitive functioning (Bacharach and Baumeister, 1998), physical health (Scholer, Mitchel, and Ray, 1997), emotional development (Kendel, Rosenbaum, and Chen, 1994; Beatty, 1995; Florsheim, Tolan, and Gorman-Smith, 1998; Harris, Furstenberg, and Marmer, 1998), substance abuse (Denton and Kampfe 1994), criminality (Dahlberg, 1998; Darby and others, 1998), and adult success (Cook and others, 1996). The degree to which these generalizations have gained broad acceptance across the political spectrum helps explain why Congress could muster a bipartisan majority to pass legislative measures to reduce nonmarital births and why a Democratic president signed them.

The soft answer goes only to the point of agreeing that the effects of nonmarital birth tend to be negative, in the usual statistical sense of "tend": that is, the means for populations of children of two-parent families are different from the means for populations of children of never-married mothers, but the overlap in the distributions is large. In terms of policy, the appropriate conclusion is that it would be desirable if somehow a larger proportion of children could grow up with two parents, just as it would be desirable if a smaller proportion of children could grow up in families below the poverty line. Reducing nonmarital births is one of many policy objectives regarding children, but no more than that.

The hard answer is more ambitious, holding that high-density nonmarital parenthood is the driving force behind the creation and persistence of an underclass. I am a proponent of this position. The logic of the argument goes like this:

Where single parenthood is scattered, it poses a statistically higher risk for children, but a manageably higher risk. If a boy grows up without a father but in a neighborhood filled with fathers, he has a high probability of reaching adulthood socialized to the norms of a responsible adult male, even though he has had no father to teach him those lessons personally. If a girl grows up without a father but in a neighborhood filled with fathers, she has a high probability of reaching adulthood with appropriate expectations of men as partners and parents. If the single parenthood is caused by divorce, but the divorce occurred after the child's most formative years, the effects of single parenthood are attenuated. If a divorced or never-married father remains a close and loving presence throughout the child's developmental years, the effects of single parenthood are attenuated.

Take away all of those attenuating factors, the hard position argues, and the consequences are more than additive. In communities where the illegitimacy ratio is so high that most children grow up without seeing men act as responsible parents and spouses, essential transmission lines of socialization have been severed. The increased level of risk is not manageable. The next generation will grow up with a high proportion of both men and women who are unable to function in mainstream American society. That community can exist only as a custodial community, kept habitable only by a high level of police presence, subsidy of the incompetent, and incarceration of the criminal.

The hard position on nonmarital births rests on hypotheses that are still empirically open, but it is also consistent with recent trends. Two benchmarks with strong rationales as indicators of an underclass are criminality and male dropout from the labor force (Murray, 1999). Throughout the 1990s, despite falling crime rates and the lowest unemployment rates in decades, both indicators suggest that the underclass has not shrunk and has probably continued to grow. The percentage of both white and black males under correctional supervision (unlike imprisonment rates, a reasonably consistent measure over time) grew by 20 percent from 1991 to 1996, the most recent year with breakdowns by age and race. The percentage growth was about equal for blacks and whites. The magnitude of the black figure is extraordinary: 29 percent of black males aged 20–29 were under correctional supervision in 1996 (Beck, 1999). In the labor market, youth unemployment fell for both black and white males, but the percentage of young males not in the labor market (and therefore not part of the calculation of the unemployment rate) continued to grow among both blacks and whites, but most markedly for blacks (Murray, 1999). Consider, for example, the population of young black males who are beyond their high school years but are neither in school nor seeking work. In the 1970s and 1980s, it was widely held that these young men consisted in large part of discouraged workers who would return to the labor market if a full employment economy continued long enough (see, for example, Wilson, 1987; Haveman, 1988; Hacker, 1992). This expectation has been confounded by the experience of the 1990s.

Despite tight labor markets, the proportion of black males aged 20–24 who are neither in school nor in the labor market did not fall from 1990 to 2000. It actually grew slightly (11.5–13.6 percent). Among black males 18–19 years old (according to my calculations using pooled data for school months in 1990 and 2000), this population increased by more than half, from 8.8. to 14.1 percent.[1]

Crime down, but criminality up; unemployment down, but male labor force dropout up—these are the signs, argue partisans of the hard position, of an unsocialized generation of young males produced by communities with a high density of nonmarital births.

Soft or hard, concern about the effects of nonmarital childbearing provided much of the impetus behind the welfare reform movement of the 1990s in general and the 1996 act in particular. It is in that context that I examine what is currently known about the effects of welfare reform on family formation. I have three objectives. The first is to review the project-by-project findings regarding effects on family formation. The second is to present long-term trends in the basic family formation variables since 1960, comparing events of the last few years with a broader context to help evaluate the plausibility of national effects that the welfare reform movement might have generated. The third objective is to consider what is yet to be learned from the as yet unevaluated aspects of welfare reform. I conclude with a personal assessment of what most needs to be learned.

Project-by-Project Effects of Welfare Reforms in the 1990s

If welfare reform had started with the Personal Responsibility and Work Opportunity Reconciliation Act (PRWORA) in 1996, there would be nothing at all worth saying about the effects of welfare reform on family formation. Many states have undertaken many initiatives to reduce nonmarital births and increase marriage under the provisions of PRWORA (GAO, 1998), but the time required to mount major reforms combined with the lag time before effects can be observed and measured would preclude any meaningful results as of 2000. Welfare reform did not begin in 1996, however. PRWORA was as much a ratification of ongoing welfare reform as it was the instigator of reform. By the time the act was passed, forty-two states had applied for waivers of federal welfare regulations so that they could implement reforms, and 452 such waivers had already been approved (Maynard

---

1. It should be noted that this figure is not confounded with increased imprisonment during the 1990s. The calculation of labor force participation is based on the civilian noninstitutional population.

and others, 1998). Some of these reforms date back to the late 1980s and provide a handful of useful evaluation results.

The Research Forum on Children, Families, and the New Federalism, part of the National Center for Children in Poverty at the Columbia School of Public Health, provides the most comprehensive catalog of recent and ongoing welfare evaluation efforts. As of December 2000, its database included 47 reviewed and 140 unreviewed research projects. Of the reviewed projects, 27 measured variables on family formation. A subset of 22 of these projects also collected data on births and pregnancies. Eleven of the 27 projects have not yet produced any results, however, and the reports of another 11 projects contain no information on the family or births variables that were said to have been included in the evaluation design. This leaves 5 projects with some information. The results for these projects and the conclusions of the evaluators are summarized in the following sections, along with two other assessments of welfare reforms bearing on questions of family formation.

New Chance

New Chance offered assistance to teenage mothers in acquiring educational and vocational credentials and skills intended to lead to increased employment and decreased welfare dependency (Quint, Musick, and Ladner, 1994; Quint, and others, 1994). Eligibility was limited to mothers 16–22 years of age on AFDC who had had their first child as a teen and lacked a high school diploma or its equivalent. Family planning counseling was an integral part of the program. The evaluation found that, contrary to the program's intentions, the pregnancy rate in the experimental group was higher than in the control group (by 8 percent, $p < .05$).

Delaware's A Better Chance (ABC) Program

The ABC had a time limit of twenty-four months for families headed by employable adults but offered an additional twenty-four months of benefits for those working in an unsubsidized job or participating in a work-experience program. The program also called for progressive grant reductions for failure to meet program requirements, a family cap for children born more than ten months after becoming subject to ABC, retention of 50 percent of the grant amount they would have lost while working under AFDC's rules, mandatory participation in job search and placement activities, expanded child care and other work supports, mandatory attendance at parenting education classes, and mandatory consultation with a family planning provider (Fein, 1999).

The ABC randomly assigned recipients and applicants in five pilot offices to a treatment group fully subject to ABC policies or to a control group that continued under traditional AFDC policies. Data were obtained from 1,547 women through telephone interviews in April 1997, capturing an average of twelve months of follow-up. The results showed little evidence of any impacts on marriage, marriage expectations, or nonmarital cohabitation across the entire sample. Within subgroups, a statistically significant ($p < .05$) positive effect on marital cohabitation was observed among women under the age of 25 and among those with less than twelve years of school. ABC had no samplewide impact on actual fertility and a small, statistically insignificant impact on stated desire to have more children. One subgroup, those with intermediate-duration welfare histories, showed a statistically significant reduction in actual fertility. Statistically significant effects on reduced expressed desire to have more children were observed among women aged 25 or older, women who had been married, and women with intermediate welfare histories.

Minnesota Family Investment Program (MFIP)

The MFIP provided for welfare benefits until income reached 140 percent of the poverty line; child care subsidies paid directly to the provider if the recipient worked while receiving welfare; mandatory participation in employment and training activities; cashing out of Food Stamps benefits, which were then included in the MFIP grant; and elimination of the work history requirement and 100-hour rule for two-parent families (Knox, Miller, and Gennetian, 2000). The evaluation was based on random assignment to MFIP or AFDC of more than 14,000 recipients between April 1994 and March 1996. The final report, issued in June 2000, represents a three-year follow-up.

The family formation variable included in the evaluation report was incidence of marriage: 10.6 percent of the MFIP unmarried parents were married by the end of the third year, compared with 7.0 percent of AFDC single parents ($p < .05$). MFIP also had a substantial effect on marital stability. Among two-parent families receiving assistance at the beginning of the program, 67.0 percent of the MFIP families were married at the end of the three-year follow-up compared with 48.5 percent of the AFDC families ($p < .01$).

Teenage Parent Demonstration Program

This demonstration program was in effect in New Jersey and Illinois from 1987 to 1991. It required first-time teenage mothers to participate in education, job training, or employment activities and offered them support services including enhanced case management, child care, and transportation (Kisker, Rangarajan, and Boller, 1998). The evaluation report, which took the program participants through a three- to four-year post-program follow-up, concluded that "exposure to the demonstration welfare policies and programs did not substantially reduce subsequent pregnancies and births."

Prenatal and Infancy Home Visitation by Nurses

This Memphis, Tennessee, project replicated a home visitation approach implemented with a sample of young white mothers in the early 1980s in Elmira, New York (Kitzman and others, 2000; results are not yet available for the second replication site in Denver). The Elmira program consisted of a series of visits by registered nurses to young women pregnant with their first child. The visits continued for the first two years after birth to monitor the well-being of mother and child and to counsel and help the mother complete high school, gain employment, and avoid unplanned subsequent births. Unlike other strategies reviewed here, the visitation approach had nothing to do with the amount, duration, or eligibility rules for welfare, but it could be funded through Temporary Assistance for Needy Families (TANF) and in that sense is relevant to welfare reform.

An evaluation of the Elmira demonstration using randomized treatment and comparison groups (n = 184 for the comparison group, 116 for the treatment group) found a large (43 percent) and statistically significant reduction in subsequent pregnancies among the poor unmarried women in the sample at forty-six months postpartum, and delay of the birth of a second child by an average of twelve months (Olds and others, 1988). No effects on family formation were reported. A fifteen-year follow up found that many of the positive effects of the initial evaluation were sustained (Olds and others, 1997).

The replication in Memphis in the early 1990s was implemented for a randomized sample of primarily black (92 percent) disadvantaged young women with 515 in the comparison group and 228 in the treatment group. Effects at the fifty-fourth postpartum month were statistically significant but considerably smaller than the Elmira effects: subsequent pregnancies decreased by 14 percent ($p = .03$) and the delay in the second pregnancy was four months greater ($p = .004$). Nineteen percent of the women in the treatment group were living with the father of the child at the end of the follow-up compared with 13 percent of women in the comparison sample ($p = .03$).

California Work Pays Demonstration Project (CalWorks)

CalWorks (Hu, 2000), begun in December 1992, decreased maximum benefit levels for AFDC recipients. For a family of four, the maximum benefit was reduced from $788 to $743 in the first year and to $723 in the remaining three years of the demonstration. The reforms also reduced the benefit reduction rate from 100 percent to 67 percent in spells lasting longer than four months. The $30 income disregard was extended past the initial twelve months of AFDC receipt. One-third of the 15,000 cases in the demonstration were randomly assigned to a control group. A regime of lower benefits and higher work incentives was found to have sizable and statistically significant effects on marriage behavior, consisting of a treatment-control difference of seven percentage points in marriage rates. This effect was observed in the decision to remain married, with little effect observed on the probability that single-parent recipients would marry. The effects on married recipients became larger over time, suggesting the possibility of long-run effects.

New Jersey's Family Development Program (FDP)

The FDP package included elimination of some of the financial penalties for marriage, an income disregard for up to 50 percent of cash benefits, extended Medicare eligibility after the recipient left welfare, and a "family cap" that denied additional benefits for children conceived after the program began (Camasso and others, 1998a, 1998b). An initial evaluation using a quasi-experimental design revealed significant effects of the marriage cap on subsequent fertility; this finding led to much media attention and controversy. New Jersey commissioned another quasi-experimental study by a team from Rutgers University, completed in 1998. The team reported that members of the experimental group had about a 9 percent lower birthrate than the control group, used family planning services about 10 percent more often, and had about 28 percent more sterilizations. There were no statistically significant differences in abortions. For new cases, the birthrate of the experimental group was 12 percent lower than for the control group, the abortion rate was 14 percent higher, and contraceptive drugs and devices were used 21 percent more often. There were no statistically significant differences in family planning use or sterilization.

Other Research Programs and Reviews

Four additional demonstration programs have used quasi-experimental designs (see Maynard and others, 1998): Job Start, a general employment and job training program; Project Redirection, a comprehensive educational and training program targeted specifically at teen mothers; Ohio Learnfare, a mandatory program that required teenage welfare recipients to participate in educational or training opportunities; and the Teenage Parent Welfare Demonstration, which was similar to the Elmira and Memphis home visitation programs discussed earlier.

The one success story was the home visitation program. Like the Elmira demonstration, it reported a large (57 percent) reduction in subsequent pregnancies. In the other three programs, the experimental groups experienced more births than the control group, not fewer as hoped.

The nature of these results will be familiar to all who work in the field of program evaluation: many cases of "no effect," a scattering of statistically significant effects that are generally modest in size and subject to controversy in their interpretation, and an occasional large effect. Discerning a theme in this pudding is problematic. A quantitative analysis of the whole range of programs begun under welfare waivers (Horvath-Rose and Peters, 2000) concluded that family cap provisions provide the most consistent evidence for such downward pressure on nonmarital birth ratios. Time limits and work requirements appear to have little impact on nonmarital fertility here. Most surprising, the minor parent provision, which makes welfare benefits for an unmarried teen mother contingent on staying in school and living in a supervised setting (usually with parent or parents), is associated with increases in nonmarital birth ratios. In the larger context, however, none of the waiver programs have had a large effect and are responsible for only a small portion of the overall downward pressure on the illegitimacy ratio.

Broad analyses such as the foregoing involve complex modeling decisions that leave them open to as many technical disputes as program-specific evaluations. Even taken at face value, the results are open to alternative interpretations on which reasonable people will differ. My own reading of the data is that educational and training programs are not a promising strategy for affecting fertility behavior. Home-visitation strategies certainly warrant exploration, as the Elmira and Teenage Parent Welfare Demonstration programs demonstrate, but the Memphis replication warns against assuming that large effects can be consistently achieved. The results of the Denver replication may clarify that story. I will return to the topic of more specific welfare reform strategies—family caps, overall benefit reductions, and time limits—later in this chapter, but for now it may be said that the results are at best spotty. Even when effects have been positive, they have generally been small.

Trends in Family Formation: 1960–90 versus 1990–99

Another way to assess the impact of welfare reform on family formation and fertility is to view such reform not as discrete policies but as a change in the national zeitgeist. Until the end of the 1980s, two wisdoms existed about welfare. The popular conventional wisdom, reflected in opinion polls and focus groups, was that welfare encouraged freeloading, created welfare dependency, and caused single women to have babies (Gilens, 1999). The elite conventional wisdom, reflected in the academic journals and the editorial columns of the nation's leading newspapers, was that most welfare was used for only a short time, provided modest and usually inadequate support, had been proved to have no causal effect on fertility and family formation, and, overall, was an essential response to need in a postindustrial society.

This difference of opinion was reinforced by a parallel split about the traditional two-parent family. Earlier, I referred to the soft and hard positions on the importance of nonmarital births. Even the modest consensus represented by the soft position is a recent development. In the public mind, the two-parent family may have remained the unquestioned ideal. In academia and policy circles, however, the merits of the two-parent family had come under intense assault during the 1970s. By the 1980s, the two-parent family was not considered to be of much interest when analyzing the nature of social ills. It was rare during those years to find marital status treated as an important independent variable, let alone the single-parent family as a seriously deficient structure for raising children or organizing communities. Attempts to promote the two-parent family were typically characterized as political conservatism.

As the 1980s came to a close, these divisions of popular-elite and right-left began to blur. Academicians became more interested in the problematic aspects of the welfare system and in the independent effect of the single-parent household. Democratic politicians became more critical of welfare. The change was rapid. By 1992 the Democratic presidential candidate had made a promise to "end welfare as we know it," the most politically powerful single theme of his campaign. Each new issue of journals such as *Child Development* or *Journal of Marriage and the Family* seemed to contain an article about negative effects associated with welfare or single-parent families.

Left-right and popular-elite distinctions remained. President Bill Clinton's welfare plan focused on reducing welfare dependency, not reducing illegitimacy, and large segments of academia remained hostile to the idea that the single-parent family was an inherently inferior structure for raising children. But the center of gravity on these issues had shifted perceptibly.

The impact of this shift is as yet unclear. It is one thing to try to institute a workfare reform when policy analysts and welfare administrators are adamantly opposed to it on principle; quite another when many respected professionals hold that it is a good idea. Similarly, changes in the elite wisdom percolate into the popular culture: Ally McBeal in the early 2000s is unlikely to be as cavalier about having a baby without a husband as Murphy Brown was in the late 1980s. Changes in the zeitgeist happen without announcement and alter perspectives in ways that are difficult to measure. Such was the nature of the change regarding welfare and the single-parent family.

The long-range time series on family formation and fertility variables provide some insight into national behavior since the welfare reform movement gathered force. Changes in that behavior are not necessarily causally linked to welfare reform, but the trendlines can at least provide a framework for thinking about the scattered and inconsistent effects of individual welfare reform projects.

Figures 5-1 to 5-6 show year-by-year data along with a pair of fitted linear trendlines: one for 1960–90, and another for 1990–99. It must be emphasized that the trendline for 1960–90 is inserted only as a visual aid for estimating the degree to which the experience of the 1990s is consistent with or diverges from that of the previous thirty years. It is not intended to suggest that the experience during 1960–90 was in fact a single, linear trend. Nor is there anything uniquely significant about the year 1990 as a beginning for the second trendline. It is a round number and signifies a time when welfare reform activity was getting under way.

All calculations are restricted to women of childbearing age, operationally defined as aged 15–44. All trends are presented separately for blacks and whites. From 1960 to 1968, data for blacks refer to all non-whites; from 1969, blacks only. Parallel analyses separating non-Hispanic white and Hispanic trendlines for 1990–99 were conducted, but they did not materially add to the generalizations presented in the text. The source for the data is the annual advance report on natality statistics of the National Center for Health Statistics (Ventura and others, 2000) and comparable volumes in earlier years. As of this writing, data on marriage and fertility were available through 1998; data on the illegitimacy ratio were available through 1999.

Marriage

The most basic family formation variable is marriage. The percentage of women who are married is shown for 1960–98 (figure 5-1). The last half of the twentieth century saw an extraordinary change in this basic demographic variable, with the white marriage ratio dropping by a quarter, from 72 to 54 percent, and the black marriage ratio dropping by more than half, from 66 to 32 percent. The 1990s did not see any obvious change for whites. The white trendline flattened in the last half of the 1980s but resumed its downward slide in the last half of the 1990s. For blacks, the steep downhill slide became shallower in the last half of the 1980s.

Figure 5-1. *Marriage among Women of Childbearing Age by Race, 1960–98*[a]

Married women per 100, aged 15–44

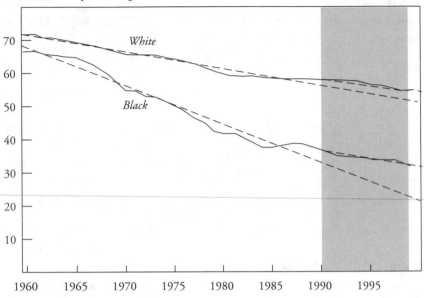

Source: Ventura and others (2000 and earlier editions)
a. Trendlines (broken lines) are calculated separately from 1960–90 and from 1990–98.

Nonmarital Births

Trends in nonmarital births can easily be confusing. When a newspaper reports that illegitimacy is rising or falling, it may be referring to one of two measures: the proportion of babies that are being born out of wedlock (the ratio), or the number of babies being born out of wedlock per some unit of population (the rate). Often it is not made clear which of these measures is being used. To further confuse matters, trends in these two measures do not necessarily track with each other. They are computationally independent and can go in opposite directions at the same time, as indeed they have done in the course of recent American history.

I begin with the measure most commonly used in the technical literature to characterize trends in nonmarital births: the illegitimacy *ratio*, or percentage of live births that occur out of wedlock. Figure 5-2 shows the trendlines since 1960. The 1990s saw something resembling an inflection point for both blacks and whites in 1994. There is an element of artifact in it, because improvements in reporting for both Texas and Michigan in 1994 exaggerate the steepness of the one-year rise from 1993 to 1994. But it remains true that

Figure 5-2. *The Illegitimacy Ratio by Race, 1960–99*[a]

Illegitimate births as a
percentage of all live births

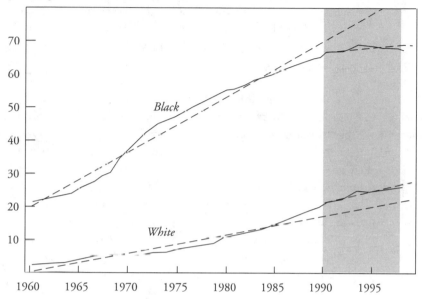

Source: Ventura and others (2000 and earlier editions)
a. Trendlines (broken lines) are calculated separately from 1960–85 and from 1990–99.

the black ratio had been rising continuously for decades and declined slightly after 1994. Less dramatically, whites show a shallower slope after 1994, though slight increases have continued through the most recent data.

The complications arise in the trends in the *rate* of nonmarital births. The standard method of presenting data on this rate—the measure of "how many?"—is what I call nonmarital fertility among unmarried women, measured as the number of nonmarital births divided by the number of unmarried women aged 15–44. This is the measure used by the National Center for Health Statistics and by the media when referring to changes in the rate of nonmarital births. On this measure, the secular trend during 1960–98 rose steeply upward for whites, from nine births per 1,000 unmarried white women in 1960 to thirty-eight in 1998. For blacks, the picture is radically different. In 1960 blacks experienced ninety-eight births per 1,000 unmarried women. By 1998, that figure had fallen to seventy-three, after the same thirty-eight years that saw the black illegitimacy ratio rise from 22 percent to 69 percent.

The problem with using nonmarital fertility as a measure is that it begs to be misunderstood when presented as a trend over a period in which marriage rates have been changing. To a casual reader, the data just presented for blacks might understandably imply that, after controlling for changes in population, fewer black babies were being born out of wedlock in 1998 than in 1960. But that is not what the statistic really means. Fewer babies were born out of wedlock per 1,000 unmarried black women. As figure 5-1 showed, the proportion of black women who are married plummeted from 1960 to 1998. This creates a paradox: in 1960 about 141,800 black children were born out of wedlock compared with 417,400 in 1998, a raw increase of 194 percent. During the same period, the African American resident population grew from 19.0 million to 34.7 million, a raw increase of 83 percent. In other words, not only did the raw number of nonmarital black births increase from 1960 to 1998, so did the number of nonmarital black births after controlling for changes in the black population. Yet nonmarital fertility for blacks went down.

The nonmarital fertility measure also poses a more subtle problem of interpretation. When the marriage ratio changes drastically, it is prudent to assume that the distributions of personal characteristics in the pool of unmarried women have changed as well. To be an unmarried 30-year-old in 1960 was unusual, and the reasons for being unmarried were likely to be associated with unusual personality characteristics (or simply physical unattractiveness). To be an unmarried 30-year-old in 1998 was not unusual. On the contrary, it is the population of women married at age 20 who were more likely to exhibit profiles outside the norm. To compare the fertility of single women in 1960 and 1998 without considering the change in the pool of unmarried women is like comparing the mean SAT scores of college-bound seniors in 1960 and 1998 without considering the change in the pool of high school seniors who go to college.

Thus a second measure of "how many" nonmarital births is appropriate. I call this measure the nonmarital birthrate. It uses the entire population of women aged 15–44 as the denominator rather than the population of single women.[2] In effect, it represents the production of nonmarital babies per unit population capable of bearing children. As trends for the two measures in the black population (figure 5-3) indicate, the choice of measure is not a trivial one.

Figure 5-3 could serve as a case study in the confusion that can be caused by apparently innocuous changes in statistical definitions. Changing the

2. Using the entire racial population, male and female combined, rather than women aged 15–44 would be a closer parallel to the usual calculation of the birthrate, but it would also fail to control for changes in the age distribution of women over the period 1960–99, which remains pertinent to the issue in question. As it happens, using the entire racial population produces results substantively indistinguishable from those produced by using women aged 15–44.

Figure 5-3. *Two Measures of the Rate of Black Nonmarital Births, 1960–98*[a]

Births per 1,000
black women aged 15–44

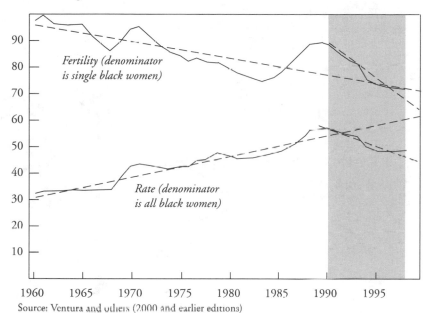

Source: Ventura and others (2000 and earlier editions)

a. Trendlines (broken lines) are calculated separately from 1960–90 and from 1990–98.

denominator from unmarried black women to all black women produces contradictory trendlines for 1960–90. The main substantive result of this analysis is to show the decline of the 1990s in a different light. Suppose that figure 5-3 showed only the nonmarital fertility trendline. One would then be justified in concluding that no significance can be attached to the reductions during the 1990s. One would merely be observing a regression to the long-term mean after a short spike in nonmarital fertility in the last half of the 1980s. The actual fertility figure for 1998 is exactly where the trendline for 1960–90 would have predicted. But if one instead uses the nonmarital birthrate as the measure, the turnaround in 1990 is more persuasive. In the 1990s, for the first time during the period covered in figure 5-3, black non-marital births per unit population began a sustained decline.

For whites, the difference between the two measures of production of nonmarital births is one of degree, not direction (figure 5-4). The incidence of white nonmarital birth increased from 1960 to 1998 under both mea-sures. Even so, the interpretation of the white experience in the 1990s varies

Figure 5-4. *Two Measures of the Incidence of White Nonmarital Births,*
1960–98[a]

Births per 1,000
white women aged 15–44

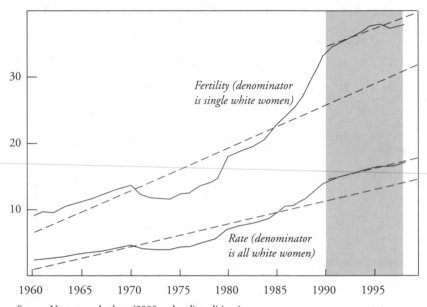

Source: Ventura and others (2000 and earlier editions)
a. Trendlines (broken lines) are calculated separately from 1960–90 and from 1990–98.

by measure. The nonmarital fertility rate declined slightly from 1996 to
1998; the nonmarital birthrate continued to increase slightly.

Because the media have given so much attention to the reduction in the
incidence of teen births (operationally defined as births to women aged
15–19) during the 1990s, it is appropriate to conclude the discussion of birth
trendlines with the figures limited to teenagers. Once again, the numbers
have been presented without regard to changes in marital behavior among
teens, and, once again, this omission makes a major difference. As of 1960,
only 7 percent of white teen births were nonmarital; by 1998, 72 percent of
them were nonmarital. During the same period, the illegitimacy ratio for
black teen births went from 42 percent to 96 percent. The next two figures
therefore repeat the procedure used earlier, showing nonmarital fertility for
women aged 15–19 alongside the nonmarital birthrate for the same group.
Figure 5-5, which shows the story for black teens, is a replay of the story for
black nonmarital births in general. When the commonly reported measure,
nonmarital fertility, is used, black teen births show a pronounced secular

Figure 5-5. *Two Measures of the Incidence of Black Teen Births, 1960–98*[a]

Births per 1,000
black women aged 15–19

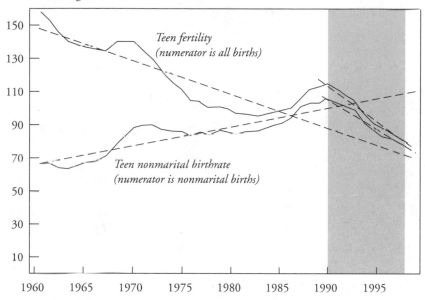

Source: Ventura and others (2000 and earlier editions)
a. Trendlines (broken lines) are calculated separately from 1960–90 and from 1990–98.

decline from the beginning of the period through the mid-1980s, then a sharp rise followed by a decline in the 1990s. As of 1998 the black figure remains modestly above the one that would have been predicted on the basis of the trend from 1960 to 1990. When the nonmarital birthrate among teens is the measure, however, a secular increase occurs from 1960 to 1991, followed by a decade of decline. The decline in the teen nonmarital birthrate in the 1990s represents an authentic change in a long-term trend, whereas the reduction in the teen fertility rate appears to be no more than a regression to the mean, not yet complete, from the anomalous late 1980s.

Figure 5-6 shows the parallel story for white teenagers. With nonmarital fertility as the measure, white teen births, like black teen births, fell steeply from 1960 to 1985, increased sharply over the rest of the decade, then resumed a decline in the 1990s, leaving the 1998 rate far above the one that would have been predicted on the basis of the period from 1960 to 1990. But with the nonmarital birthrate, there was no decline at all in the 1960s and 1970s; rather, there was a nearly continuous increase from 1960 until 1994. Since 1994 the nonmarital birthrate has declined slightly. The rate in

Figure 5-6. *Two Measures of the Incidence of White Teen Births, 1960–98*[a]

Births per 1,000
white women aged 15–19

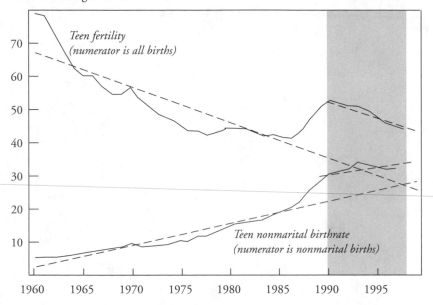

Source: Ventura and others (2000 and earlier editions)
a. Trendlines (broken lines) are calculated separately from 1960–90 and from 1990–98.

1998 nonetheless remained elevated in relation to the trend in the period 1960–90.

Cohabitation

These trendlines raise an obvious question. How would these profiles change if cohabitation was taken into account? Suppose that instead of counting marital and nonmarital births one counted births that did and did not occur to a mother and father who were in a stable relationship throughout the child's formative years? Cohabitation clearly began to rise steeply around 1970 (Bumpass and Sweet, 1989) and by now is a common feature of American life. But it also appears that cohabitation in the United States is characteristically short and unstable (Bumpass and Sweet, 1989; Huffman and others, 1994; Forste and Tanfer, 1996), which implies that only a small percentage of children born to cohabiting couples have an experience similar to those of children born to married couples. Presumably some do, however, just as some children born to formally married but estranged parents do not enjoy the benefits of a genuine two-parent family. Knowing the magnitude of the proportion of cohabiting couples who are in stable relationships would be useful in interpreting trends in marriage and nonmarital births. As yet, however, national data sources do not permit such interpretation for any point in time, let alone an estimation of how this proportion might have changed over time.

Assigning Causes

To what extent has welfare in general or PRWORA in particular affected family formation? The question has no clear answer. The scattered findings from the demonstration projects suggest that reforms can increase the probability that women who are already married stay married, that a family cap may reduce the number of subsequent births, and that home visitation can reduce second births to poor teenagers. Such findings are not inconsistent with other research on the relationship of welfare to family formation and births (reviewed in Moffitt, 1998), but that record is itself so inconsistent that it is difficult to say more than that an effect of some magnitude is probably real. There remains no way of estimating the magnitude of effect that might be expected from national implementation of any specific reform.

The trendlines are in many ways more provocative than the results from the demonstration projects. Something seems to have happened during the 1990s to alter past trends in nonmarital births, whether measured by rate or by ratio. The problem with interpreting that "something" is that all of the good changes in the 1990s must be balanced against the spike in births that immediately preceded them. Here is the case that advocates for either extreme might make.

The Optimistic Case

A number of trends in the data can be interpreted as a reflection of improvements in the environment for family formation.

For blacks:

—The marriage ratio was substantially higher in 1998 than the trendline for 1960–90 would have led one to predict.

—The overall nonmarital birthrate and the teen nonmarital birthrate both declined almost continuously from 1991 to 1998, the first sustained decline in either measure since the beginning of the 1960–98 period.

—The illegitimacy ratio peaked in 1994 and has since declined every year through 1999, albeit by small amounts.

For whites:

—The teen nonmarital birthrate fell slightly in the last half of the 1990s.

—The white illegitimacy ratio increased much more slowly in the last half of the 1990s than in the preceding five years.

There remains another perspective on the white illegitimacy numbers that may warrant an optimistic assessment. As the United States entered the 1990s, the white illegitimacy ratio stood at 20 percent after increasing at the rate of almost a percentage point a year during the preceding decade. Unlike the black ratio, the white ratio had lots of room for an increase. During the past two decades, Western European countries have been demonstrating that increases in the white illegitimacy ratio do not necessarily slow down after passing the 20 percent mark. This is true not only of the well-publicized Scandinavian cases, but of countries such as Britain and France, which had known very low illegitimacy ratios well into the 1970s. In Britain, the illegitimacy ratio (which is overwhelmingly determined by white women) reached 20 percent in 1986. During the next five years, the ratio went to 30 percent. By 1999 it had reached 39 percent (Office of Population Censuses and Surveys, 2000, and comparable earlier volumes). In the United States, the increase in white illegitimacy after 20 percent slowed to a crawl. This divergence with the trendlines of other Western countries is a phenomenon with many possible explanations, but it is nonetheless worth keeping in mind when appraising the extent to which the trends in U.S. white nonmarital births may have shifted.

The Pessimistic Case

Rubbish, the pessimists may plausibly say of the optimists:

—For whites, the apparently good things about the 1990s are a recovery from an aberrant period during the late 1980s. All of the measures of white nonmarital births were higher as of the most recent figures than the trendline for 1960–90 would have led one to expect.

—The black marriage ratio may have been higher than predicted from the 1960–90 trendline, but it nonetheless continued to fall throughout the 1990s, as did the white marriage ratio.

—The drop in the black nonmarital birthrate had nothing to do with welfare reform. The black nonmarital birthrate began falling in 1991, with a 15.3 percent reduction through 1998. During the same period, the nonmarital black birthrate fell by even more, 19.7 percent.

—A black illegitimacy ratio in excess of two-thirds had almost no room to increase. The slight reduction from 1994 to 1999 (from a high of 70.5 percent in 1994 to 69.1 percent in 1999) is parsimoniously interpreted as stabilization at an asymptote, not an authentic reduction.

Presumably the optimistic version is too optimistic and the pessimistic version too pessimistic, leaving the truth somewhere in between. My own reading of the data is that the turnaround in the black nonmarital birthrates, overall and among teens, is the best evidence of a positive change. I also consider the contrast between the slowdown in white American illegitimacy and the lack of a slowdown in Europe to be a phenomenon worth exploring.

In other respects, I find the pessimistic points easier to defend than the optimistic ones. In particular, it is very difficult to attribute the leveling off of the black illegitimacy ratio to welfare reform. Among urban low-income blacks most affected by welfare—where, depending on locale, the ratio has been in the 80 to 90+ range for some years—there was almost no room for the ratio to increase. Perhaps most disturbing is the quietly deteriorating situation in white nonmarital births. After nearly a decade of a changed welfare environment, the indicators for white nonmarital births as of the late 1990s were nonetheless worse than a linear extrapolation of the preceding thirty years would have suggested. That the American white illegitimacy ratio is climbing more slowly than European white ratios may be significant, but it is hard to interpret the overall trends as good news.

The Prospects for Effects Yet to Come

Virtually nothing is still known about many aspects of PRWORA's effects on family formation. Evaluations of both abstinence and sex-education approaches have yet to be completed. The New Jersey analysis discussed earlier is one of the few studies of the family cap, with twenty such provisions on the books in other states yet to be assessed (Maynard and others, 1998). But in terms of the possible effects on births and marriages, the most obvious untold story involves time limits on welfare.

It is already clear that the effects of time limits in practice will not represent a test of what happens when welfare benefits stop. States are permitted to exempt recipients from the time limits, and the flexibility in those rules means that no state must deny benefits to large numbers of persons if it wishes to avoid doing so. More important, by the time PRWORA was passed the cash payment had become only one part, often a minor part, of the package of benefits to which a low-income single mother has access. Food Stamps, Medicaid, and housing, plus a variety of state-specific or city-specific benefits, remain even after the cash grant goes. In aggregate, they are much more valuable than the cash payment. People who have left the welfare rolls to date have made up the loss of the cash payment in a variety of ways: often through work, but also through coresidency with a parent, a boyfriend, a friend, or through monetary support from one of those sources (Besharov and Germanis, 2000).

Nor have any of the states implemented a strategy that would permit assessment of what happens when even the cash portion of the package disappears immediately, for example, by denying any cash benefits to minors. Instead, according to state plans now in place, welfare recipients in the post-TANF world will de facto be subject to a percentage reduction in the benefit package. Researchers will be limited to examining a familiar research issue, the relationship between the amount of welfare—not the existence of welfare—and fertility and marital behavior. What results might that experience produce?

The state of knowledge about the relationship among fertility, marital behavior, and the amount of welfare offers another example of a recent shift in the received wisdom. Throughout the 1980s, it was commonly accepted that no significant relationship existed (as argued by Ellwood and Bane, 1985). By the early 1990s, that conclusion had been called into question, but whatever relationship existed was still seen as inconsequential (Moffitt, 1992). During the 1990s, many additional studies have been published (most recently reviewed in Moffitt, 1998). Seen from one perspective, the findings continue to be inconsistent. A simple majority of them show a significant correlation between welfare benefits and marriage or fertility, but the magnitude of the relationship is sensitive to the methodology and specifications used. From another perspective, a major change has occurred, with the professional consensus moving in the last decade from "There's no relationship worth worrying about" to "There appears to be a significant relationship, but we still have much to learn."

A similar shift seems appropriate for the magnitude of the relationship. Some findings (Rosenzweig, 1995) imply that a 25 percent reduction in welfare benefits would produce about a 30 percent reduction in the probability of a nonmarital birth. Others imply comparably large reductions (Bernstam, 1988; Fossett and Kiecolt, 1993; Hill and O'Neill, 1993; Winegarden and Bracy, 1997). At the other extreme are statistically significant but very small effects (Danziger and others, 1982; Duncan and Hoffman 1990; Lichter, McLaughlin, and Ribar, 1997). A reasonable conclusion is that analysts need to learn more. But imagine that several careful studies had found that a 25 percent increase in per-child expenditures on Head Start would reduce the probability of subsequent criminal behavior by 30 percent but some other studies had found much smaller effects. The headlines would not read "Head Start May Not Work." Nor should they. In policy research, inconsistent findings across studies must be expected. When several solid analyses suggest that a substantial effect is out there, that finding should be the center of attention. In the case of welfare and nonmarital births, it has not been.

Recommendations for TANF Reauthorization

The media attention devoted to the dramatic reduction in the welfare rolls is understandable, but it has diverted attention from the problem represented by high illegitimacy ratios in both the black and white populations. The question must be faced squarely. If the issue is how the next generation of low-income children will be raised, is a community without fathers in which the women are working really that much different from a community without fathers in which the women are on welfare? The literature on the effects of single parenthood gives little reason to think so. Thus my chief recommendation is that reducing illegitimacy must be restored to the central position it held during the deliberations that led to the passage of the 1996 welfare reform legislation. Everything learned in the interim gives one reason to think that high-density nonmarital births are at least as damaging to the prospects of individual children and to the socialization of the next generation as people thought in 1996.

If Americans are serious about making major inroads on illegitimacy, the most important unanswered policy question is this: What would be the effect of eliminating welfare for unmarried mothers altogether, not just the TANF cash payment, but the entire package of benefits?

The present ability to estimate the effect is severely limited. Suppose for purposes of argument that a percentage point reduction in the welfare package is associated with a half percentage point reduction in the nonmarital birthrate (a magnitude consistent with the set of studies finding a substantial relationship). The observed values of changes in benefits in the real world that produce these estimates are highly truncated, usually representing a small percentage of the value of the welfare package. They provide no adequate basis for assessing whether the observed effect would be linear across the range. If it is linear, the implication is that a 100 percent reduction would produce a 50 percent drop in the nonmarital birthrate. But if the relationship of welfare to nonmarital fertility is an enabling relationship with a threshold of "enough" that permits an unmarried woman to think she can support a child without a husband (Murray, 1993), then it is plausible that the function will be nonlinear, with a 100 percent reduction in benefits producing considerably more than a 50 percent reduction in nonmarital births.

Presumably others can think of hypotheses that predict nonlinearity in the opposite direction, with a larger effect from the first dollar of reduction than from later ones. The point is that people do not know, and cannot know, what the real shape of the reductions in fertility might be across the whole range of reductions in the welfare package unless some state cuts off all benefits (or something approaching that ideal) to some subset of women. A plausible test case would be for a state with a relatively small caseload and a history of effective nongovernmental social welfare—the Western plains and mountain states offer several possibilities—to cut off all benefits for girls under the age of 21. Under the terms of the current legislation, this would not be possible. Only the cash benefit could be eliminated. The provisions of the TANF reauthorization should do everything possible to see that such a test case occurs.

Using terms like "response curve" and "important additional data" to talk about the effects of eliminating welfare seems cold-blooded. What if this social experiment should cause terrible deprivation for mothers and their babies? That worry is one good reason for finding a limited niche (small caseload, minors) where there is reason to be confident that alternative resources will be available. But whether it is worth trying to mount such an experiment also depends crucially on whether one takes the soft or hard position toward the importance of nonmarital births in creating the underclass. For partisans of the soft position, the risk is not worth the potential gain; for partisans of the hard position, almost any risk is appropriate. In this sense, the first step toward a productive policy debate about family formation in the post-TANF era is not better estimates of the effects of the welfare reforms that have been enacted, but a realistic appreciation of the amount of damage that continues to be caused by high-density nonmarital births.

COMMENT BY
Rebecca A. Maynard

Charles Murray makes four major points in his chapter: (1) none of the major welfare reform initiatives has had more than a modest impact on fertility patterns and family formation; (2) fertility trends in the 1990s send mixed signals about whether the situation is improving; (3) high-density out-of-wedlock childbearing is especially problematic for its contagion effects; and (4) the extent to which welfare is adversely or favorably affecting trends is uncertain. Murray presents convincing statistics documenting the demise of marriage as a core institution in this country, the adverse consequences for children of growing up in a single-parent household, and some of the complications in understanding the causes of the differences in trends across population subgroups. Murray's provocative recommendation is that we rigorously assess the consequences for family formation of withholding all welfare from girls under 18 who have children.

I am going to take a somewhat "softer" approach to examining the precipitating forces behind the incredibly high rate of out-of-wedlock childbearing and propose a "softer" strategy for better understanding and promoting the more favorable trends that have begun to emerge. The key objectives of my recommendation are to clearly communicate social values through government policies and the media, to provide generous transitional support, and to provide ongoing support for those with chronic disabilities that impede their ability to adequately care for themselves and their families.

Murray observed four important trends: a consistent decline in the marriage ratio since 1960—a trend that is nearly linear through 1985, after which the rate of decline slows; a steady increase in the illegitimacy ratio (illegitimate births divided by total births) since 1960, which began to level off in the late 1980s and early 1990s, particularly for blacks; a steady increase in the out-of-wedlock birthrates of all women through the mid-1990s and for white women continuing through the present; and a decline in overall teen fertility rates at the same time out-of-wedlock birthrates among teens continually increase. Overlying these trends, there seem to be three turning points in the data: first, the mid- to late 1960s, when the out-of-wedlock birthrate crept past the 20 percent mark; second, the mid- to late 1980s, when rates of sexual experience among school-age teens passed the 50 percent mark and the out-of-wedlock birthrate exceeded 33 percent; and third, the early to mid-1990s, when trends in teen sexual activity, out-of-wedlock birthrates, and welfare dependence all leveled off or showed improvements.

Over the period from 1980 through the present, there have been parallel trends in welfare caseloads, in teenage birthrates, in nonmarital birthrates, and in abortion rates for teens (figure 5-7). The correlations among these trend lines range from 0.73 (welfare caseloads and the total teen birthrate) to 0.98 (the teen and the total nonmarital birthrate). However, there is no similar link between these trends and the economy, nor have researchers found strong links between factors such as the generosity of welfare benefits and these trends (O'Neil, 1994).

What changed dramatically over the late 1960s and 1970s was the nature and goal of social services and the resulting messages they conveyed to the American public regarding expectations and values about sexual activity, childbearing, and family structure. Beginning in the 1970s, public assistance became more widely available and social service providers worked to empower women, particularly poor single mothers. The pill was gaining

Figure 5-7. *Trends in Welfare Caseloads, Total Nonmarital Births, Teen Nonmarital Births, and Teen Abortions, 1980–98*
Number

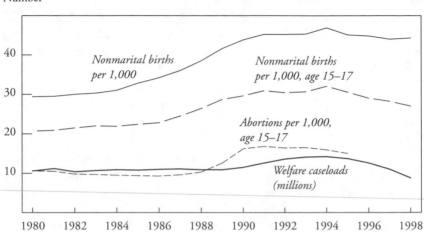

Sources: U.S. Department of Health and Human Services (2000); U.S. House of Representatives (1998, appendix F).

widespread acceptability as an effective contraceptive. Increasing proportions of women attended college and delayed marriage in favor of careers; as a result, there was a modest decline in the overall marriage rate, but a continuation of a trend begun in the 1960s of a significant decline in the marriage rates among 18- to 19-year-olds concurrent with a rise in the rates of sexual activity among school-age teens. The 1970s also saw the start of the sexual revolution. One notable marker of this revolution was the liberalization of policies on college campuses, such as the opening of dorms to coed visitation, and, subsequently, to coed living and the end of curfews.

This era was followed in the 1980s by an explosion of programs serving reproductive health needs, particularly of adolescents, through school and neighborhood health clinics. In addition, school-based programs for teenage parents and, often, their children were introduced. By the late 1980s, these special programs to support unmarried young mothers and their children had become integral parts of state and local welfare programs. For example, between 1984 and 1991 funding for family planning services increased by 41 percent, while the client caseload increased by only about 30 percent (Brown and Eisenberg, 1995). The Family Support Act of 1988 mandated that states serve teenage parents who had not completed high school as a priority group in their state welfare-to-work programs. By the early 1990s, the nation had entered a period of public policy and reproductive behavior that clinical psychologists might label as codependency. Men could father children with little legal or moral obligation to support them; women could bear children with few social or economic sanctions (Hotz, McElroy, and Sanders, 1997); only the children and taxpayers faced significant measurable consequences (McLanahan and Sandefur, 1994).

As Murray notes in his review, the various programs of the mid-1980s to mid-1990s intended to improve outcomes for single mothers and their children produced at best modest improvements in economic and social well-being. Moreover, several efforts to promote greater involvement in the social, emotional, and economic support of children by noncustodial fathers failed to generate meaningful changes in behavior. The few promising programs that have been evaluated share three seemingly important features. First, they have very specific goals that are communicated clearly to program staff who, in turn, communicate them to clients. Second, they emphasize responsibility and link program benefits to meeting those responsibilities. Third, they provide supports to enable clients to meet their personal and family responsibilities (Maynard, 1997).

The 1990s was a decade of major shifts in medium and messages: shifts in the medium for providing support to poor families and to teenage parents and changes in the messages regarding parental responsibilities, out-of-wedlock childbearing, and teenage and out-of-wedlock sex. The 1992 presidential campaign introduced bipartisan support for "ending welfare as we know it," a key aspect of which was establishing time limits on cash assistance. The disagreements were over how and when to call an end to the old system. There was widespread support for strengthening the messages to teenagers regarding the responsibilities they would shoulder: namely, to complete their education and to contribute to the support of any children they had. For adults and teen parents alike, there was widespread support for ending the open-ended entitlement to cash assistance. The major disagreements were over issues such as exemption policies and the support systems to promote economic self-sufficiency. These differences were addressed by devolving welfare authority to states.

In addition to the major shifts in welfare policies, the 1990s witnessed a retrenchment in the sex education policies and practices of many communities. Between 1988 and 1999, for example, the proportion of school districts that had programs devoted exclusively to teaching abstinence rather than birth control increased from 2 percent to 23 percent, with a corresponding reduction in the proportion of districts offering comprehensive sex education programs (Warren and others, 1998). Similarly, the proportion of school districts that addressed issues of sexually transmitted diseases, whether in the context of comprehensive sex education or abstinence-only education, increased over this period, with the result that the proportion of adolescents using condoms increased (from 38 to 48 percent for females at last intercourse and from 55 to 61 percent for males). However, this increase in condom use has been accompanied by a sizable reduction in the use of oral contraceptives (from 14 to 11 percent for males and from 23 to 18 percent for females). The overall proportion of females aged 15 to 19 having had sexual intercourse peaked in 1995 at 55 percent before starting on a slow decline (Moore, Driscoll, and Lindberg, 1998). The nation needs more public discourse over the role of abstinence messages in these trends.

Present trends in sexual activity and nonmarital births are in the right direction. Fewer teens are having sex, there are fewer teen births, and the incidence of out-of-wedlock childbearing is declining. Rather than engage in a radical experiment on even a small portion of the population, as Murray recommends, the nation should experiment and systematically evaluate the impacts of strengthening the messages regarding the value Americans place on parental responsibility and on the institution of marriage. These messages should be transmitted through both the media and public policies and should be combined with strong messages for adolescents regarding standards of behavior and responsibility. Simultaneously, policymakers should implement programs to promote positive youth development, perhaps examining these strategies both in a context of abstinence-only education and in a context of comprehensive sex education. Conducting such experiments in a variety of states with contrasting welfare policies, social contexts, and economic conditions should contribute enormously to the general understanding of why there are still so many children being born and reared in single parent homes and how Americans might preserve and even strengthen the favorable downward trends in these rates.

References

Bacharach, Verne R., and Alfred A. Baumeister. 1998. "Effects of Maternal Intelligence, Marital Status, Income, and Home Environment on Cognitive Development of Low Birthweight Infants." *Journal of Pediatric Psychology* 23: 197–205.

Beatty, Lee A. 1995. "Effects of Paternal Absence on Male Adolescents' Peer Relations and Self-Image." *Adolescence* 30: 873–80.

Beck, Allen J. 1999. "Trends in U.S. Correctional Populations." In *The Dilemmas of Corrections: Contemporary Readings,* 4th ed., edited by K. C. Haas and G. P. Alpert. Prospect Heights, Ill.: Waveland Press.

Bernstam, Mikhail S. 1988. "Malthus and the Evolution of the Welfare State: An Essay on the Second Invisible Hand." Parts I and II. Working Papers E-88-41 and E-88-42. Palo Alto, Calif.: Hoover Institution.

Besharov, Douglas J., and Peter Germanis. 2000. "Welfare Reform—Four Years Later." *Public Interest* no. 140 (Summer): 17–35.

Brown, Jocelyn, and others. 1998. "A Longitudinal Analysis of Risk Factors for Child Maltreatment: Findings of a 17-Year Prospective Study of Officially Recorded and Self-reported Child Abuse and Neglect." *Child Abuse and Neglect* 22: 1065–68.

Brown, Sarah, and Leon Eisenberg, eds. 1995. *The Best Intentions: Unintended Pregnancy and the Well-Being of Children and Families.* Washington: National Academy Press.

Bumpass, Larry L., and James A. Sweet. 1989. "National Estimates of Cohabitation." *Demography* 26 (4): 615–25.

Camasso, Michael J., Carol Harvey, Radha Jagannathan, and Mark Killingsworth. 1998a. *A Final Report on the Impact of New Jersey's Family Development Program: Results from a Pre-Post Analysis of AFDC Case Heads from 1990–1996.* Trenton: New Jersey Department of Family Services.

———. 1998b. *A Final Report on the Impact of New Jersey's Family Development Program: Experimental-Control Group Analysis.* Trenton: New Jersey Department of Family Services.

Cook, Thomas, and others. 1996. "The Development of Occupational Aspirations and Expectations among Inner-city Boys." *Child Development* 67: 3368–85.

Dahlberg, Linda L. 1998. "Youth Violence in the United States: Major Trends, Risk Factors, and Preventive Approaches." *American Journal of Preventive Medicine* 14: 259–72.

Danziger, Sheldon, George Jakubson, Saul Schwartz, and Eugene Smolensky. 1982. "Work and Welfare as Determinants of Female Poverty and Household Headship." *Quarterly Journal of Economics* 97 (August): 519–34.

Darby, Patrick J., and others. 1998. "Analysis of 112 Juveniles Who Committed Suicide: Characteristics and a Closer Look at Family Abuse." *Journal of Family Violence* 13: 365–74.

Demo, David H., and Alan C. Acock. 1996. "Family Structure, Family Process, and Adolescent Well-Being." *Research on Adolescence* 6: 457–88.

Denton, Rhonda E., and Charlene M. Kampfe. 1994. "The Relationship between Family Variables and Adolescent Substance Abuse: A Literature Review." *Adolescence* 114: 475–95.

Duncan, Greg J., and Saul D. Hoffman. 1990. "Welfare Benefits, Economic Opportunities, and Out-of-Wedlock Births among Black Teenage Girls." *Demography* 27 (4): 519–35.

Ellwood, David, and Mary Jo Bane. 1985. "The Impact of AFDC on Family Structure and Living Arrangements." In *Research in Labor Economics,* vol. 7, edited by R. G. Ehrenberg. Greenwich, Conn.: JAI Press.

Fein, David J. 1999. *Will Welfare Reform Influence Marriage and Fertility? Early Evidence from the ABC Demonstration.* Bethesda, Md.: Abt.

Florsheim, Paul, Patrick Tolan, and Deborah Gorman-Smith. 1998. "Family Relationships, Parenting Practices, the Availability of Male Family Members, and the Behavior of Inner-City Boys in Single-Mother and Two-Parent Families." *Child Development* 69: 1437–47.

Forste, Renata, and Koray Tanfer. 1996. "Sexual Exclusivity among Dating, Cohabiting and Married Women." *Journal of Marriage and the Family* 58: 33–47.

Fossett, Mark A., and K. Jill Kiecolt. 1993. "Mate Availability and Family Structure among African Americans in U.S. Metropolitan Areas." *Journal of Marriage and the Family* 55 (May): 288–302.

Gilens, Martin. 1999. *Why American Hate Welfare: Race, Media, and the Politics of Anti-Poverty Policy.* University of Chicago Press.

Hacker, Andrew. 1992. *Two Nations: Black and White, Separate, Hostile, Unequal.* Scribner.

Harris, Kathleen Mullan, Frank F. Furstenberg Jr., and Jeremy K. Marmer, 1998. "Paternal Involvement with Adolescents in Intact Families: The Influence of Fathers over the Life Course." *Demography* 35 (May): 201–16.

Haveman, Robert. 1988. *Starting Even: An Equal Opportunity Program to Combat the Nation's New Poverty.* Simon and Schuster.

Hill, M. Anne, and June O'Neill. 1993. *Underclass Behaviors in the United States: Measurement and Analysis of Determinants.* City University of New York, Baruch College.

Horvath-Rose, Ann, and H. Elizabeth Peters. 2000. "Welfare Waivers and Non-marital Childbearing." Cornell University. Mimeo.

Hotz, V. Joseph, Susan Williams McElroy, and Seth G. Sanders. 1997. "The Impacts of Teenage Childbearing on the Mothers and the Consequences of Those Impacts for Government." In *Kids Having Kids, the Economic and Social Consequences of Teen Childbearing,* edited by Rebecca A. Maynard. Washington: Urban Institute.

Hu, W. 2000. "Marriage and Economic Incentives: Evidence from a Welfare Experiment." University of California at Los Angeles. Mimeo.

Huffman, Terry, and others. 1994. "Gender Differences and Factors Related to the Disposition toward Cohabitation." *Family Therapy* 21: 171–84.

Kendel, Denise B., Emily Rosenbaum, and Kevin Chen. 1994. "Impact of Maternal Drug Use and Life Experiences on Preadolescent Children Born to Teenage Mothers." *Journal of Marriage and the Family* 56: 325–40.

Kisker, Ellen Eliason, Anu Rangarajan, and Kimberly Boller. 1998. *Moving into Adulthood: Were the Impacts of Mandatory Programs for Welfare-dependent Teenaged Parents Sustained after the Programs Ended?* Princeton, N.J.: Mathematica.

Kitzman, Harriet, and others. 2000. "Enduring Effects of Nurse Home Visitation on Maternal Life Courses: A 3-Year Follow-up of a Randomized Trial." *Journal of the American Medical Association* 283 (15): 1983–89.

Knox, Virginia, Cynthia Miller, and Lisa A. Gennetian. 2000. *Reforming Welfare and Rewarding Work: A Summary of the Final Report on the Minnesota Family Investment Program.* New York: Manpower Demonstration Research Corporation.

Lichter, Daniel T., Diane K. McLaughlin, and David C. Ribar. 1997. "Welfare and the Rise in Female-Headed Families." *American Journal of Sociology* 103 (1): 112–43.

Luster, Tom, and Harriette Pipes McAdoo. 1994. "Factors Related to the Achievement and Adjustment of Young African-American Children." *Child Development* 65: 1080–94.

Maynard, Rebecca A. 1997. "Paternalism, Teenage Pregnancy Prevention, and Teenage Parent Services." In *The New Paternalism: Supervisory Approaches to Poverty,* edited by Larry M. Mead. Brookings.

Maynard, Rebecca, Elisabeth Boehnen, Tom Corbett, Gary Sandefur, and Jame Mosley. 1998. "Changing Family Formation Behavior through Welfare Reform." In *Welfare, the Family, and Reproductive Behavior,* edited by R. A. Moffitt. Washington: National Academy Press.

McLanahan, Sara. 1998. "The Consequences of Father Absence." In *Parenting and Child Development in Nontraditional Families,* edited by M. Lamb. Mahwah, N.J.: Erlbaum.

McLanahan, Sara, and Gary Sandefur. 1994. *Growing Up with a Single Parent.* Harvard University Press.

Moffitt, Robert. A. 1992. "Incentive Effects of the U. S. Welfare System: A Review." *Journal of Economic Literature* 30 (March): 1–61.

———. 1998. "The Effect of Welfare on Marriage and Fertility." In *Welfare, the Family, and Reproductive Behavior*, edited by Robert A. Moffitt. Washington: National Academy Press.

Moore, Kristin Anderson, Anne K. Driscoll, and Laura Duberstein Lindberg. 1998. *A Statistical Portrait of Adolescent Sex, Contraception, and Childbearing*. Washington: National Campaign to Prevent Teen Pregnancy.

———. 1998. "The Effect of Welfare on Marriage and Fertility." In *Welfare, the Family, and Reproductive Behavior*, edited by Robert A. Moffitt. Washington: National Academy Press.

Murray, Charles. 1993. "Welfare and the Family: The American Experience." *Journal of Labor Economics* 11 (1): 224–62.

———. 1999. *The Underclass Revisited*. Washington: American Enterprise Institute.

Office of Population Censuses and Surveys. 2000. "Birth Statistics: England and Wales." London.

Olds, David L. 1988. "Improving the Life-Course Development of Socially Disadvantaged Mothers: A Randomized Trial of Nurse Home Visitation." *American Journal of Public Health* 78 (11): 1436–45.

Olds, David L., and others. 1997. "Long-Term Effects of Home Visitation on Maternal Life Course and Child Abuse and Neglect: 15-Year Follow-up of a Randomized Trial." *Journal of the American Medical Association* 278: 637–43.

O'Neil, June. 1994. *Expert Testimony in* C.K. *v.* Shalala. United States District Court for the District of New Jersey, Civil Action no. 3-5354.

Quint, Janet C., Judith Musick, and Joyce Ladner. 1994. *Lives of Promise, Lives of Pain: Young Mothers after New Chance*. New York: Manpower Demonstration Research Corporation.

Quint, Janet C., Denise F. Polit, Johannes M. Bos, and George Cave. 1994. *New Chance: Interim Findings on a Comprehensive Program for Disadvantaged Young Women and Their Children*. New York: Manpower Demonstration Research Corporation.

Rosenzweig, Mark. 1995. "Welfare, Marital Prospects and Nonmarital Childbearing." University of Pennsylvania. Mimeo.

Scholer, Seth J., Edward F. Mitchel, and Wayne A. Ray. 1997. "Predictors of Injury Mortality in Early Childhood." *Pediatrics* 100 (3): 342–47.

Shumow, Lee, Deborah Lowe Vandell, and Jill Posner. 1999. "Risk and Resilience in the Urban Neighborhood: Predictors of Academic Performance among Low-Income Elementary School Children." *Merill-Palmer Quarterly* 45: 309–31.

U.S. Department of Health and Human Services. 2000. *Vital Statistics*. Vol. 48, no. 16, table 3; ser. 21, no. 56, table 3; and vol. 47, no. 26, table 3.

U.S. General Accounting Office (GAO). 1998. *Teen Pregnancy: State and Federal Efforts to Implement Prevention Programs and Measure Their Effectiveness*. GAO/HEHS-99-4.

U.S. House of Representatives, Committee on Ways and Means. 1998. *1998 Green Book*. Government Printing Office.

Ventura, S. J., S. C. Curtin, T. J. Mathews, and M. M. Park. 2000. *Births: Final Data for 1998*, 48 (3). Hyattsville, Md.: National Center for Health Statistics.

Warren, Charles W., and others. 1998. "Sexual Behavior among U.S. High School Students, 1990–1995." *Family Planning Perspectives* 30 (4): 170–72, 200.

Wilson, William Julius. 1987. *The Truly Disadvantaged: The Inner City, the Underclass, and Public Policy.* University of Chicago Press.

Winegarden, C. R., and Paula Bracy. 1997. "Welfare Benefits and Illegitimacy in the U.S.: Reconciling Contradictory Trends." *Southern Economic Journal* 64 (1): 167–79.

6

HUGH HECLO

The Politics of Welfare Reform

For the last third of the twentieth century, in fits and starts, America's political class struggled to enact comprehensive changes in national welfare policy. In 1996 it finally happened. Long-standing rhetorical promises about making welfare a transition-to-work program were crystallized in the statutory language of federal law. Simultaneously, the promise to underwrite state income support for poor mothers and children disappeared from federal law, as Washington's sixty-year-old Aid to Families with Dependent Children (AFDC) program was summarily abolished. Rather than provoking a strong reaction, this all seemed to happen with relative ease. There was an almost audible public yawn as, for the first time in living memory, a major federal entitlement program was eliminated. Polls taken in the days immediately after passage of the new welfare law showed that a large majority of Americans approved of the reform legislation. When probed, however, almost half of the public had not heard about it or did not know enough to have an opinion (Weaver, 2000, p. 338).

The political forces underlying the 1996 transformation carry important implications for welfare policy in the early twenty-first century. To appreciate these implications, it is worth taking stock of how, politically speaking, the choices of the 1990s occurred. The "new world of welfare" did not emerge suddenly in 1996. In this chapter, I first consider the policy history shaping the nation's welfare debate in the 1990s. This long-term legacy has been the

decisive point of departure within which policymakers of all political persua-
sions must maneuver. I then assess the three political forces that converged to
produce the new welfare system formally enacted into federal law during
1996. The nation's AFDC welfare entitlement was destroyed by a confluence
of events that individually may not have posed an insurmountable threat but
collectively were devastating. Conversely, the initial years of operating the
new welfare system have enjoyed a no less remarkable confluence of favorable
conditions, in other words, perfect sailing weather following the perfect
storm. I conclude by identifying political factors that are likely to give direction to public deliberation on welfare policy during the next few years.

It is no wonder many longtime observers of U.S. welfare policy were surprised by the sweeping legislative change of 1996. By the 1990s those who
paid serious attention to this policy area had lived through three decades of
false starts in welfare reform. In general, politicians of both parties demonstrated that more was gained by proposing than by actually carrying through
with the unglamorous task of reforming welfare programs.

Meanwhile, a complicated series of incremental adjustments to national
welfare policy continued from one administration to the next. "Tireless tin-
kering" was the phrase one leading scholar used in 1971, and the same term
aptly applied throughout the thirty-year period from Presidents John
Kennedy to Bill Clinton. The various adaptations were complex and usually
attracted little notice outside a small circle of advocacy groups, administrators, academic policy experts, and the very few politicians who paid serious
attention to welfare programs from one year to the next. Taken together,
these incremental changes were the essential prologue to what happened to
welfare policy in the 1990s. Indeed, today's politics of welfare reform is
shaped more by this history than by any research findings, interest group
agendas, or political party platforms. Since this inherited policy legacy is crucial for understanding the transformation of the federal government's welfare
entitlement program, AFDC, into Transitional Assistance for Needy Families
(TANF), it is here that I begin.

Creating Washington's Most Unloved Program

What became known as federal "welfare" policy began during the depression
of the 1930s and President Franklin Roosevelt's New Deal policies. Active,
experimental use of government was the dominant mood in Washington,
and the New Deal eventually embraced several distinct approaches that were
perceived and administered as separate policy domains.

In the first place, the federal government launched a series of emergency relief measures to confront the immediate problem of massive unemployment. These initiatives involved some form of publicly supported jobs ("work relief"), but federal direct involvement with employment programs and the labor market more generally was treated as a temporary, emergency activity. Federal work-based relief policies eventually faded away with the passing of the depression and the onset of World War II.

Second, the New Deal also instituted a series of structural changes. Most important for welfare policy was the 1935 creation of the Social Security system. Contributory social insurance promised a future in which breadwinners—usually assumed to be males—and their families could find security against income loss produced by old age, unemployment, and widowhood (health insurance was deliberately excluded from the plans as too politically risky). Within a few years, disability and other benefits were added to the system, and rules were adapted to give better financial returns to lower-paid workers. However, the central focus of this remarkably successful system of social insurance remained on those who enjoyed a stable full-time attachment to the work force.

The policy legacy from the 1930s contained a third element that would eventually dominate discussion of "welfare" policy during the last third of the twentieth century. The 1935 legislation creating the Social Security system also initiated a federal financial aid program for three categories of needy persons: destitute elderly people, blind persons, and mothers left alone with children (which became known as Aid for Dependent Children). The three categories covered people who were presumed to be not employed but especially deserving of public assistance. This welfare initiative came from federal policymakers, most of whom had begun their political careers in state-level reform movements of the Progressive Era. The Aid for Dependent Children program was designed to strengthen and systematize the existing patchwork of "mothers' pensions" that had been enacted by Progressive reformers in various states. The aim of these mothers' pensions had been to help impoverished, deserving widows remain at home caring for their children rather than be forced to enter a Dickensian job market or send their children to work (and thus undermine state compulsory public education laws that were becoming more prominent in the early twentieth century). This New Dealers' Aid for Dependent Children program essentially nationalized much of the funding and a few of the rules for mainly widowed mothers' cash relief. This mother-child income support program would grow into the preoccupying focus of welfare reform after the 1950s.

The Ambivalent Entitlement

Since the "entitlement" nature of the federal welfare program created in 1935—and its abandonment in 1996—came to assume great political significance in the politics of welfare reform, it is important to be clear about the legal versus political and symbolic meaning of this term. The 1935 law enacted a legal promise for the federal government to provide such matching funds as might be required for states to pay benefits to all persons eligible under prevailing law. The "legal" entitlement in this sense did not imply that people have a right to income support. In theory, a state could refuse the federal matching funds and operate no AFDC program at all. Alternatively, the technical term "entitlement" came into use after the 1974 Congressional Budget and Impoundment Act employed it for classifying different types of federal spending. Like Medicare or Social Security, AFDC funds flowed from Washington outside the annual appropriation process in Congress and could not be adjusted up or down as part of the budget-making process.

That AFDC represented a federal open-ended entitlement for states was clear. That it might have the aura of an entitlement to individuals became evident only through court and administrative decisions in the 1960s. Still, the 1935 program was a major policy breakthrough inasmuch as it represented widespread acceptance of the federal government's legal and political obligation to provide funds that would match whatever state AFDC programs might require. Under the New Deal, demands for an active, national government had only partially prevailed in welfare policy. The new federal program produced more uniformity of standards and continuity of financing than would ever have been possible under forty-eight separate state arrangements. At the same time, the AFDC program allowed much greater diversity in state operations, benefit levels, and eligibility conditions than one would have ever found in a unitary, nationally administered welfare program. So long as there was a statewide program, a residency requirement of no more than one year for benefits, and some administrative appeals process, state governments could do pretty much as they wanted. Especially in the South, this state-level discretionary power meant using various tests of a claimant's "morality" to exclude non-white Americans from welfare programs.

Therefore two key features were embedded in the deep structure of federal welfare policy erected in the 1930s and carried on into the 1960s and beyond:

—A dual system divided between social insurance (to protect workers against income loss from retirement, disability, unemployment, death of a breadwinner) and means-tested public assistance ("welfare"), which transferred income to certain deserving categories of destitute nonworkers. This meant a de facto separation of the welfare income transfer program from the world of work and labor market policies.

—Joint management of this federal welfare program between Washington officials making rules and dispersing funds, on the one hand, and state-level bureaucracies with substantial administrative discretion, on the other.

Probably the most important force sustaining federal welfare policy for the next five decades was the sheer inertia of this basic policy framework. During the 1940s and 1950s Washington's AFDC program aroused little public attention or political controversy. However, a program that stays the same while the society around it is changing can actually amount to a transformed policy. Such policy morphing is essentially what happened to Washington's welfare program as the American society and economy evolved around it in the post–World War II years. In this postwar world, other developed countries have also had to substantially modify, if not abandon, the older male-breadwinner vision of income security, but in the United States the path to doing so has been uniquely contentious and socially divisive (Sainsbury, 1996).

The Watershed of the 1960s

By the 1960s, social changes were coming at a furious rate and these were followed by equally far-reaching economic changes in the 1970s and beyond. For one thing, widowed mothers were being replaced in the AFDC system with expanding rolls of divorced, deserted, and—more than ever over time—unmarried young mothers. For another thing, a new feminist consciousness combined with rapidly growing educational and job opportunities for women brought a growing proportion of women, including mothers with children, into the work force. The "male breadwinner" model of income security was breaking down. All these changes eroded public acceptance of single AFDC mothers staying at home to collect welfare checks.

Most ominously for the political support of federal welfare policy, the 1960s ushered in a widespread perception of welfare as a problem with black people. This changing perception occurred against the background of the great black migration to northern cities during the middle of the twentieth century. However, much more than demographic change was at work. The hard-won successes of the Civil Rights movement in the 1960s brought black Americans' voices into the public arena as never before. This produced legal challenges to welfare rules as well as a grass roots, poor people's movement for welfare rights. The major social legislation of the 1930s had implicitly respected and often reinforced racial discrimination in American society (Lieberman, 1998). Nowhere was this truer than in the racist administration of the AFDC program throughout the South. Liberalizations of the Social Security program did improve the economic returns to tens of thousands of lower-income persons, including many blacks, but federal program executives had advanced such redistribution in the 1940s and 1950s with a minimum of political fanfare in order to ensure state acceptance and ease of passage in Congress.

The 1960s brought the racial politics of welfare into the open precisely because blacks were willing to publicly contest racism and push government policies to redress their grievances. At the same time, critical media coverage of President Lyndon Johnson's War on Poverty and urban disturbances were a powerful force stamping the racialization of welfare and poverty images onto public thinking. Despite declining poverty rates, media stories on poverty shot up in the mid-1960s and concentrated on poor blacks, a fraction of the poverty and welfare population that had been largely ignored until then. From the Johnson years onward, the tendency in public coverage was to associate African Americans with the most objectionable aspects of poverty and welfare, while non-blacks dominated the more sympathetic coverage during periods of economic downturns (Gilens, 1999, chap. 6). Adding fuel to the fire was the fact that the issue of work was introduced into the national debate on welfare reform by the overt racist George Wallace in his 1967–68 presidential campaign. Other Southern Democratic segregationists such as Russell Long, Wilber Mills, and Strom Thurmond soon followed suit. In short, the 1960s were a watershed; the political meaning of welfare policy became explicitly infused with issues of race (although blacks never made up more than about one-third of the nation's welfare rolls).

Early signs of trouble for federal welfare policy appeared in local efforts to tighten administrative reins on what local politicians characterized as permissive welfare spending. In 1960 Louisiana cut off benefits to AFDC families where the mother gave birth to another child (eventually to be overruled by federal officials). The next year the city of Newburgh, New York, attracted national attention by adopting stringent welfare rules. Benefits were to be cut for unwed mothers bearing another child, welfare for the able-bodied would be limited to three months, and adult males would be required to work, if necessary at menial community jobs. Similar themes would reappear far more powerfully in the late 1980s and 1990s.

One of President Kennedy's few legislative accomplishments in the Democratic Congress was to obtain passage of the 1962 Public Welfare Amendments, which sought to reverse "the whole approach to welfare from a straight cash handout operation to one in which the emphasis is on rehabilitation of those on relief and prevention ahead of time" (Patterson, 1981, p. 13). Very soon, however, this effort to combat poverty with social services broke apart against a wholly unexpected surge of new radical demands. Social scientists themselves were divided deeply between those who saw poverty in terms of personal pathologies and those who concentrated on its structural, institutional sources. Daniel Patrick Moynihan (1965), then a young academic appointed to Johnson's Labor Department, aroused a storm of protest by publishing a report that documented a collapsing black family structure associated with illegitimacy and desertion. Intimidated by charges of racism and "blaming the victim," supporters of the pathology interpretation tended to fall silent, while the structuralists were emboldened. Soon the latter joined antipoverty activists working to mobilize largely urban poor minorities to "challenge the system." The result was that by the late 1960s the loudest claim was for "welfare rights." What the poor needed was not to be somehow "fixed" by services but empowered with money, participation, and other resources.

As Kennedy's successor, Lyndon Johnson promised a much bolder national War on Poverty. Bypassing the traditional welfare system, Johnson's Great Society legislation sought to attack the structures of poverty and unequal opportunity and enhance poor people's capacity to take advantage of new opportunities. Unfortunately, changing communities and people's lives through government programs turned out to be a slow and complex process. As intellectual critics from within the older liberal ranks (now known as neoconservatives) began arguing, such social engineering was rife with unintended consequences. When quick fixes to deep-seated social ills were not forthcoming, many politicians, group advocates, and policy experts lost patience. Even more unpopular was the emphasis on community action and participation, which became readily translated into black empowerment (Aaron, 1978).

Although Great Society programs themselves (such as Head Start, community action, education grants, Model Cities projects) were more than mere income support to the poor, forces had been unleashed that pushed for just such a focus in welfare policy. All of these tendencies, in turn, reinforced the traditional idea of the federal welfare program as a system of income maintenance separated from work. It is worth considering how this policy legacy for welfare reform was created.

At the grass roots level, community activists of the 1960s began with no interest in welfare but soon discovered the AFDC system was an expedient tool to advance a political agenda. Leaders in the movement such as Richard Cloward had first been concerned with the problem of urban gangs in the 1950s. Through the personal interest of Attorney General Robert Kennedy, these social scientists' antigang approaches to structural community problems became a modest federal initiative in the Kennedy administration. This program in turn had barely gotten under way when President Johnson and his policy advisers seized on the approach to make structural empowerment a centerpiece in its War on Poverty at the new Office of Economic Opportunity and its Community Action organizations. Unfortunately, antigang experts who had now become antipoverty warriors lacked the knowledge, power, or finances to effectively change social structures. Meanwhile demands from angry, largely black, inner-city residents escalated. In this situation, the antipoverty activists increasingly promoted more welfare payments to those needing income. For leading activists, the longer-term hope was that a fiscal breakdown and racial crisis in the cities would force the Democratic party to nationalize AFDC and provide a more generous welfare system (Cloward, 2000).

At the same time, these newly mobilized advocates for the poor found the courts receptive to their push for a more accessible, uniform program of pure income support (Melnick, 1994). Lawyers from the welfare rights movement and Great Society's Office of Economic Opportunity challenged state laws restricting welfare eligibility, finding ample ammunition in the history of racial discrimination carried out by state administrators of the AFDC program. The result was a series of court decisions during the 1960s and 1970s that struck down many state welfare restrictions and moved cash assistance more in the direction of a strictly individual entitlement. The AFDC rolls more than tripled from 3 million persons in 1960 to 10.2 million by 1971, with the proportion of those eligible and actually receiving benefits rising from 33 percent to 90 percent between those years.

A compatible development was under way in academic studies far removed from the grimy world of welfare offices. Under the influence of economists, a new emphasis inside and outside government focused on the measurement of poverty in terms of an officially designated level of income. The influence of the poverty-measuring mentality was important in teaching everyone to think of welfare problems as a matter of income poverty. Hereafter, policy debates could never escape framing welfare in terms of those above or below a rather arbitrary poverty income line. Some economists now began proposing negative income tax schemes (government grants to those at income levels too low to incur tax liabilities) as a more efficient way to redistribute income than the clumsy AFDC system. At roughly the same time, social scientists who were not economists were producing influential research findings that showed spending on services was irrelevant to individual achievement. Thus on several fronts, the idea of fighting poverty with direct cash grants gained in intellectual respectability. In the 1966 Senate hearings on the ongoing urban riots, the now Harvard professor Moynihan and Martin Luther King Jr., as well as others, used such social science findings to advocate a guaranteed income policy for America's poor.

In response to growing claims of entitlement, income guarantees, and white backlash in and outside their party, the Democratic Congress in 1967 enacted the so-called WIN (Work Incentive) amendments to the nation's welfare law (Edsall and Edsall, 1991). These amendments imposed the first modest work and training requirements on some welfare recipients and froze federal funds for AFDC cases caused by illegitimate births or desertion. In practice, the work and training requirements were rarely enforced and in 1969 Congress repealed the funding freeze. Still, Moynihan, chastened perhaps by hostile reactions to his earlier work on the black family, declared the WIN amendment to be "the first purposively punitive welfare legislation in the history of American national government" (Melnick, 1994, p. 217). Other critics called the work requirements "slavefare." The racially charged atmosphere of the time meant that any such welfare policy restrictions were vulnerable to charges of being racist and anti-poor. Racist abuses of the past had now become a decisive barrier to any open and serious policy deliberation on welfare programs and problems of family stability, illegitimacy, or work expectations.

The upshot of the experience of the 1960s was that certain important political participants found existing welfare policy useful. They "wanted" AFDC in the sense that the program was politically profitable for the conservative right as a marker of the excesses of liberalism and for the left as a foil for charges of racism and hostility toward the poor. The deeper truth was this: almost no one by the end of the 1960s thought AFDC in itself was a particularly desirable program, certainly not in the sense that many people regarded food stamps, Medicaid, or (in an earlier era) mothers' pensions as intrinsically worthwhile. AFDC was becoming a program that some people wanted but no one really believed in.

Keeping AFDC Afloat

The 1960s provide the essential political context for understanding the next two decades of bold political pronouncements about sweeping welfare reform and timid, incremental adjustments to try to prevent Washington's AFDC program from being overwhelmed by its unpopularity with the American public. With former professor and Johnson administration appointee Daniel Patrick Moynihan now serving as domestic policy adviser to the president, the new Nixon administration proposed its own bold initiative to reform the welfare system with a guaranteed annual income for poor families with children. This Family Assistance Plan (FAP) was defeated in the Senate Finance Committee during 1970 and did even less well in Congress the next year. Two obscure pieces of consolation legislation were little noticed at the time but pregnant with possibilities. A new Supplemental Security Income program nationalized means-tested welfare payments for impoverished aged, blind, and disabled persons. This left AFDC mothers even more exposed and politically vulnerable. Of still greater long-term significance, Louisiana Democrat Russell Long as chairman of the Senate Finance Committee won passage of a new device called the Earned Income Tax Credit. Cash payments would now be made through the Internal Revenue Service to extremely low-paid *working* families with children. Long's rationale was that FAP-style stipends to nonworkers could threaten democracy with popular demands for ever-larger handouts (Nixon's plan would have entitled one-quarter of Louisiana's population to FAP benefits).

Reform of the social welfare system continued on its path of frustration. In 1973 the Comprehensive Employment and Training Act (CETA) began with an emphasis on training to help the disadvantaged with structural unemployment. But very quickly, economic hard times produced a shift to public jobs to cope with rising cyclical unemployment and to bail out worried urban politicians. Riddled with inefficiency, fraud, political pork barrel projects, and public scandals, CETA's public service employment program was one of the few social welfare programs the new Reagan administration was able to abolish quickly in 1981. Meanwhile, the new Carter administration tried its hand at welfare reform. The resulting Program for Better Jobs and Incomes proposed a two-tier system of income guarantees for those welfare clients expected to work and those not expected to work, the latter to include single parents with children under 14. A year after it was proposed, the congressional Democratic leadership allowed the Carter welfare reform bill to die without a floor vote in either house.

During the 1970s the U.S. economy sputtered, stalled, and then resumed a form of slow growth that no longer carried along less-skilled persons in the lower parts of the income distribution. With this new economic reality came a political awareness of the "working poor," which put the federal welfare system oriented to nonworkers in an increasingly unfavorable light. In ways large and small, welfare reformers were trying to nudge the system toward employment activities that would break with the long-standing administrative inertia separating welfare and work, all the while trying also to avoid charges of racism and victim-blaming.

All these previous incremental adjustments to federal welfare policy culminated with the passage of the 1988 Family Support Act. With the Reagan

administration coming to an end and congressional Democrats eager to show
major accomplishments, a coalition for comprehensive welfare reform
patiently developed a finely tuned remodeling of the existing welfare structure. Preparation of this 1988 legislation drew on the very best social science
research findings, based on years of state-level demonstrations, experiments,
and pilot projects. Now New York's Democratic senator and that chamber's
acknowledged expert on welfare policy, Daniel Patrick Moynihan, led the
successful congressional battle for the new legislation.

Above all, the new welfare reform measures carefully constructed a balance
of competing demands and political values. Welfare dependency would be
combated, but the vulnerable would be protected. The Family Support Act
made relatively generous provisions for education, job training, and medical
and child care services for welfare recipients needing help in the transition to
work. At the same time there would be mandatory work obligations. Moynihan led the congressional sponsors in breaking ranks with more liberal supporters (such as the Children's Defense Fund) and accepting Republican
demands for work requirements. The final compromise enacted the rather
weak federal requirement that states should have one-fifth of employable welfare clients in work, education, or training programs by fiscal 1995. Still, this
was a sign that unlike welfare reform efforts of the Nixon and Carter years,
there was now a growing agreement among national policymakers on the
need to bring welfare recipients into the work force. It was becoming possible
to mention work demands and welfare in the same sentence without being
perceived as a racist.

By 1988 it seemed that—at last—something approaching a bipartisan
approach had been achieved. National welfare policy for poor mothers and
children appeared set for a period of relative stability in the years ahead. Federal welfare policy had withstood the conservative onslaught of the Reagan
revolution. In fact, public opinion about helping the poor had grown more
rather than less favorable during the Reagan years. However, less than eight
years after its passage, the Family Support Act lay in political ruins, and a
new welfare reform that the retiring Senator Moynihan characterized as
"boob bait for the bubbas" was on its way to passage by a fervently partisan
Republican Congress and approval by the Democratic President Bill Clinton.

How It Happened

The bipartisan consensus underlying the 1988 welfare act had shallow roots
and was swept aside in the 1990s by much larger political forces. Politically
speaking, comprehensive welfare reform emerged in 1996, not out of biparti-

sanship, but through a convergence of partisanships. The converging forces can be conveniently grouped into three major categories, one having to do with policy intellectuals in an energized social conservative movement, a second with Republican resurgence in state governorships amid a sharp recession, and the third with electoral strategies at both the presidential and congressional levels. Although these features must necessarily be discussed sequentially, all three were in fact under way at the same time. After the stunning Republican takeover of Congress in 1994, these forces had ample strength to overturn a policy status quo that by then had essentially no effective political defenders.

It is important to recognize that while public opinion was a pervasive background factor to the events of the 1990s, it was hardly a moving force causing the particular policy change that occurred. From 1960 to the 1990s, public opinion regarding welfare policy remained quite stable. Americans' attitudes have long been structured like a cat's cradle of strings tensioned among competing values, any one of which can resonate as politicians pluck at them in various places. This is reflected in the public's acute sensitivity to how questions about poverty and welfare are phrased. Questions about "welfare" or "the welfare system" evoke negative responses to ideas of dependence, while Americans respond positively to questions about helping "the poor" and those in need. Even in the midst of the heated 1996 debate, both critics and supporters of activist government remained essentially ambivalent about individual versus societal causes and responsibility for poverty (Cantril and Cantril, 1999, pp. 52–54). On vital issues in dispute—such as ending welfare's entitlement status—public opinion passed beyond mere ambivalence to ignorance. Superficial media discussions of superficial poll results produced what two students of public preferences called "the journalistic equivalent of a drive-by shooting" (Jacobs and Shapiro, 2000, p. 335).

Until the mid-1970s, public opposition to welfare spending seems to have varied more or less directly with overall conditions of economic prosperity. After that time, however, the shape of American prosperity began changing. Economic growth in the 1980s ceased to bring along those in the lower portions of the income distribution. By 1992 public opposition had again begun its normal tracking with the upturn in the economy. However, the structural dislocations in the economy had been severe enough long enough so that economic insecurity was a growing public concern. One sign of concern about the insecurity of even white-collar workers was the unexpected revival of national health insurance as a major issue, first in a 1990 Pennsylvania Senate race and then in the 1992 presidential primaries. Another sign was the willingness of both political parties to embrace a quiet revolution in federal income support for low-income working families with children. Owing to changes in the Earned Income Tax Credit, Medicaid, and other programs, federal spending for working families who were not on welfare mushroomed from under $6 billion in 1984 to a projected $51.7 billion by 1999 (Ellwood, 1999). Gradually, an emergent consensus was erecting a low-wage worker-with-child welfare state.

It was against this background of public worries about both work and economic insecurity that the political maneuvering in Washington eventually produced the new system of work-centered welfare policy that is in place today. I turn, therefore, to the three political forces that produced this unexpected outcome in the 1990s.

Attack of the Conservative Policy Intellectuals

By the time Ronald Reagan arrived in Washington, the conservative movement could boast a rich and expanding network of intellectual resources to answer the liberalism of the 1960s. The neoconservative critics of Great Society programs had been joined by an array of conservative think tanks, foundations, and academic researchers. Some of these, such as Martin Anderson and Jeanne Kirkpatrick, enlisted in the Reagan administration, while many more remained outside, contributing books, articles, and media interviews in the battle for opinion.

The work of conservative policy intellectuals was informally interwoven with an impressive and growing body of conservative grass roots membership organizations. The most prominent of these were politically active Christian groups who saw welfare reform largely in terms of combating illegitimacy, family breakup, and the retreat from traditional family values. The importance of these interconnections among policy intellectuals and conservative social groups was poorly recognized at the time by their opponents, in large part because Washington-based liberal advocacy groups had little difficulty in gaining access to a Congress that seemed to be under permanent control by the Democratic party. When Democrats did finally lose control of Congress in 1994, pro-AFDC advocacy groups such as the Children's Defense Fund had no organized grass roots resources with which to pressure Republican members of Congress in their home districts. By contrast, the Family Research Council had 300,000 subscriber members in its communication bank, the Eagle Form had 80,000 members, and the Christian Coalition could marshal 1.7 million donors and activists. A great many of these politically active people had at least a passing acquaintance with conservative policy critiques of federal welfare policy and could explain why the criticisms were more than tight-fisted hostility to poor people, why in fact the existing AFDC system was an unmitigated disaster for families, women, and children.

One of the first fruits of conservative thinking on welfare policy was the decision early in the Reagan administration to simply drop the system of financial "work incentives." Work incentives allowed certain amounts of earned income to be excluded when calculating the allowable income for entitlement to welfare benefits. The new conservative thinking contended that work would be considered a behavior norm to be expected of claimants and enforced by administrations. Period. The formula for work incentives disappeared and removed some 400,000 cases of mainly working poor persons from the AFDC rolls. However, contrary to predictions of conventional antipoverty opinion, welfare recipients' rates of employment scarcely changed.

The landmark work by conservative intellectuals on welfare policy was Charles Murray's *Losing Ground,* published in 1984. Murray argued that the welfare policy apparatus ostensibly established to help people was in fact the major cause of their misery. Better, he said, that the whole system be abolished, an ominous precursor to what would be candidate Bill Clinton's new Democrat promise "to end welfare as we know it." Liberal critics chipped away at Murray's case, but his basic message resonated and pushed even his opponents to the right. Thus a young David Ellwood debated Murray and found himself drawn to accepting the depiction of an essentially dysfunctional welfare policy. As Ellwood later put it, "There are very few experiences less pleasant in life than defending the welfare system. If you went on talk shows, the welfare recipients would call you and say, 'You're drunk, this system is awful'" (Shear, 1994, p. 1287; see also Ellwood, 1988). Ellwood went on to become a leading framer of the Clinton administration's welfare proposal in 1994.

Other major works deepened social conservatives' intellectual onslaught against the AFDC program. Perhaps the most prominent was Lawrence Mead's sustained argument on the need to abandon an entitlement mentality and to institute policy expectations of work and personal responsibility from welfare recipients (Mead, 1986, 1992). The essential point is that the work of conservative policy intellectuals brought unprecedented credibility and political appeal to Republicans as potential architects of welfare policy. What had once been the conservative Republicans' Achilles heel in political debates on welfare policy—that they were indifferent or hostile to the poor and minorities—could now increasingly be countered by arguing that true compassion lay in saving people from a demoralizing and dysfunctional federal program of welfare dependency. To be able to co-opt the issue of "compassion" as their own was a major coup for Republicans as the 1980s ended.

By the early 1990s, conservative policy intellectuals had come a long way in challenging the terms of debate once dominated by liberals and antipoverty experts. Over against the latter's conventional focus on measures of income poverty, economic incentives, and rehabilitative services, there were now sections of the intellectual elite emphasizing behavioral norms and welfare clients' personal responsibility. Until the end of the 1980s, however, these were often only abstract battle lines. Recession and state budget stress provided the opening for conservative policy ideas to assume concrete form in various parts of the federal system.

Waivering toward Welfare Reform

Ever since Johnson's Great Society programs of the 1960s, Republicans had argued against the overcentralization in Washington and pressed for devolving power over welfare programs to state governments. Both Presidents Reagan and Nixon advanced ambitious "new federalism" proposals. In each case, the macro politics of new federalism produced only a stalemate. Liberals and civil rights activists vigorously opposed what they saw as a return to the bad old days of state discrimination against the poor in general and blacks in particular. In addition, any major reallocation of functions was consistently blocked by governors and state lobbies afraid of losing federal financial support. Block grants were established in certain policy areas during the 1970s and 1980s, but proposals for any comprehensive reform of federalism went nowhere.

Nevertheless, behind the political headlines, a micro politics of federalism was gradually pushing welfare policy toward greater decentralization. The mechanism by which this occurred in AFDC was not through block grants, which would have contravened the entitlement provisions legally enshrined since 1935. Instead, Washington started granting "waivers" from federal welfare rules to one state government at a time.

Welfare waivers gained acceptance in the 1980s through a kind of inadvertent bipartisanship. Before the 1980s, it was conservative Republicans who argued for giving states more discretionary control over welfare programs. Mistrust about Republican hostility to social spending and memories of racial discrimination produced little support for this idea in the Democratic-controlled Congress. With the election of Ronald Reagan and Republican gains in Congress in 1980, the political incentives of the situation were reversed. Now it was Republicans in Washington who were seeking to mandate eligibility requirements for welfare and Democrats who were objecting. Waivers grew correspondingly more attractive to Democrats. Eventually a series of compromises allowed increased state experimentation in administering welfare programs. As a result, the number of welfare waivers granted began to grow throughout the 1980s. The Bush administration was content to encourage this state waiver process, especially as more state governorships and legislatures fell into Republican hands. Well-publicized granting of "presidential" waivers to states such as Wisconsin and Michigan became a standard White House device for demonstrating Republican concern for welfare reform to the public.

It was not the waiver process itself but what state governors did with their waivers that created the crucial precedents for welfare reform in 1996. There were, of course, many differences among the various state initiatives. However, almost all fell into at least one of three categories. First, state-centered welfare reform was work-focused: welfare recipients were not simply to be getting ready for work; they were to get into jobs, and quickly. Second, it was behaviorally directive. Benefits were to be linked to responsible personal action such as staying in school, not having additional children, getting married, and (for unmarried teenagers) staying with parents. Finally, state-centered welfare support was time-limited. The first message upon entering the welfare office—"get a job"—could acquire a certain pointedness when the last message upon leaving was "and hurry up because welfare is going to end."

The result was that while conservative intellectuals were attacking AFDC's assumptions, state officials in dozens of localities were challenging conventional expectations about how welfare policy might operate. There was little serious policy research to illuminate the successes or failures of the state programs. Far more important was their political success. New state-level initiatives broke through powerful taboos that had prevailed since the 1960s. State politicians showed they could openly address issues of work requirements, illegitimacy, and time-limited welfare and not be overcome by charges of racism or hostility toward poor people. Republican governors were increasingly perceived by conservative strategists in Congress to be showing their party the way forward. All of this reflected the larger and immensely important political fact that by the 1990s, state governments had gone a long way in living down assumptions of racism in whatever they might do. Demands for work and personal responsibility among welfare recipients were now coming, not from a George Wallace or Russell Long, but from governors led by Tommy Thompson in Wisconsin, John Engler in Michigan, and William Weld in Massachusetts.

Even under the best of circumstances, the political appeal of these governors' energetic, no-nonsense measures would have put implementation of the much more slow-moving, training-oriented Family Support Act at a competitive disadvantage. The economic circumstances quickly became anything but the best. The ink was scarcely dry on the 1988 act before the fiscal condition of state budgets began to deteriorate badly. The years 1989–92 witnessed a sharp recession and faltering economic recovery. From one side, state budgets were already suffering from years of spending cuts in federal aid to states and cities instituted in the Reagan years. From another side, the recession brought new spending pressures to deal with unemployment and growing welfare caseloads. From yet another side, mandates from a federal government with its own budget problems were forcing states to spend more of their own resources on programs such as Medicaid. This financial squeeze on state budgets produced powerful incentives for state political leaders to make aggressive use of welfare waivers to achieve spending cuts. By the early 1990s, only eleven states had used their full allotment of federal funds to operate the Family Support Act's program for training and employing welfare recipients. Thus as the 1992 election season approached, the Family Support Act fell far short of the comprehensive, long-term attack on welfare dependency that its advocates hoped for. Bold, waiver-based welfare reform at the state level was displacing the cautious incrementalism favored by the national network of antipoverty experts who had created the 1988 act.

Welfare Enters the Electoral Arena

Welfare has always been an attractive symbolic issue for individual politicians in their appeals to voters. Unfortunately for those who hoped for a period of stable progress following passage of the Family Support Act, welfare reform became much more than an isolated campaign issue after 1988. It became a central focus in the strategic maneuvers of party warfare that dominated Washington's acrid partisan atmosphere in the early 1990s. Never before had the politics of welfare reform been played out at this supremely high-stakes, electoral level.

For conservative Republicans eager to carry forward the successes of the Reagan years, welfare was a powerful "wedge issue," a term Republican strategists used to identify initiatives that could split off pieces of the Democrats' political coalition. Appeals to work, family values, and compassion for the dependent poor locked in the welfare system could be expected to do their wedge work in an era when ordinary Americans were working harder and feeling more disturbed by perceptions of declining family values. Furthermore, drawing on the work of policy intellectuals such as Charles Murray and Robert Rector, Republican politicians and socially conservative religious groups increasingly highlighted a new theme: the harm done by AFDC to welfare recipients themselves. Members of the religious right, which became increasingly active in politics after the 1970s, now championed the moral claims for conservative welfare reform. Discouraging out-of-wedlock births, teen pregnancy, and separate household formation was emerging as a powerful impulse for welfare reform in the 1990s. Deterrence could mean, not bigotry, but compassion.

For Democrats stunned into self-examination by defeats at the hands of Reagan and Bush, welfare reform became a vehicle for rethinking what it might mean to be a "new Democrat." Such a Democrat would be immune to election charges of being a tax-and-spend, big-government apologist who was soft on American values. Spearheading this effort was the Democratic Leadership Council (DLC), formed in 1985 by moderate and conservative Democratic politicians and activists. By 1992 the DLC was using welfare reform proposals to trump anything then offered by Republicans in the politics of values: welfare clients would be required to work after two years, job placement rather than education and training would be the priority, health and income benefits would go to the working poor, and an intense media campaign would be launched against illegitimacy and teen pregnancy. As the 1992 political campaign got under way, welfare reform became a defining issue for what it meant to be a "new Democrat."

Thus while Republicans were refashioning themselves as compassionate in social policy, emerging Democratic leaders were seeking to show that they were tough. The defeat of the "too soft" Dukakis and emergence of the "kinder and gentler" George Bush inaugurated a kind of two-step minuet between the parties, a dance of maneuver that tended to present voters with a choice between tough liberals and compassionate conservatives. After 1988 political debate gradually dragged the existing AFDC welfare entitlement system into the middle of a devastating no-man's-land between new Democrats and socially concerned conservatives. It became the intolerable status quo against which almost any change could be seen as an improvement. Such was the strategic context in which events of the 1992 election campaign brought welfare reform back onto the political agenda.

THE CLINTON PLEDGE. The "electoralizing" of welfare reform surprised poverty experts because it occurred at the hands of pro-government Democrats rather than antigovernment Republicans. With President Bush largely silent on domestic policy as the 1992 election approached, congressional Republicans were content to sporadically borrow ideas and language from the many welfare reform initiatives that were taking place among state governments experimenting with waivers. Various Republican members of Congress who had taken little interest in the Family Support Act and its rather modest claims sought the political credit to be gained by promising to rescue the poor from welfare dependency. In April 1992 the conservative wing of House Republicans led by Newt Gingrich proposed "tough love" measures as a "first step to replace the welfare state" (Hallow, 1992). Among other things, welfare benefits would be limited to four years and recipients would be required to work or enroll in education programs after one year on the rolls. Many GOP congressional candidates quickly endorsed this platform. While Gingrich pushed welfare reform as a historic marker in his much larger ideological crusade to replace the welfare state, the public response was meager, and Republicans said nothing about abolishing the welfare entitlement program as such.

The truly significant developments for the future of welfare reform occurred on the Democratic side of the 1992 presidential election campaign. In an era of energized state governments, there were only a few bright spots to give the Democrats hope. Above all there was New York governor Mario Cuomo, whose speeches and actions stirred many Democrats' spirits. A liberalism that was not afraid to use government for social justice seemed to have found a spokesman. But Cuomo hesitated and then withdrew from the presidential campaign, opening an opportunity for another, more obscure Democratic governor to push himself forward. As governor of Arkansas, Bill Clinton had played a prominent role both in promoting innovation through the National Governors Association and supporting passage of the 1988 Family Support Act. However, for underdog presidential candidate Clinton it was not politically expedient to give the Family Support Act a chance. In a sense, Clinton faced a situation similar to that of his hero John Kennedy. It was Republican charges of Democratic softness on communism that Kennedy had to combat. By the 1990s Clinton's and the Democrats' problem was strategically comparable but domestically focused. Now, in the afterglow of Reagan and the end of the cold war, it was the perceptions of softness on big government and 1960s-style permissiveness that had to be countered. And it was here that welfare reform as a campaign issue could be called on to help. Kennedy's defense of his credentials as a cold war hawk took the Democrats to Vietnam. Clinton's defense of his tough love toward welfare took the Democrats to abandonment of the AFDC welfare entitlement program.

On paper, candidate Clinton's welfare reform proposals looked like an activist social policy that could warm the heart of any big-government liberal Democrat. There was to be full national health insurance as well as training, education, and child care support for welfare mothers to enter the labor market. Increases in the minimum wage and Earned Income Tax Credit would mean that no one getting a job would fall below the poverty level ("If you work you shouldn't be poor"). There would be time limits on welfare, a crucial indicator of being a new-style Democrat. If recipients reaching those limits could not find work in the private sector, however, Clinton's policy papers suggested an ambitious employment program of public service jobs, implying billions of dollars in federal spending far into the future.

Nevertheless, what Clinton selectively emphasized from his plan as he campaigned throughout 1991 and 1992 was something quite different. Campaign polls found a strongly favorable public response to the candidate's promise to "end welfare as we know it." The phrase itself came from Clinton's deputy campaign manager for policy, Bruce Reed, and reflected the importance of the Democratic Leadership Council's "new Democrat" appeals, where Reed had served as policy director. Also resonant with the public were time limits on the receipt of welfare, which Clinton's campaign speeches translated into the slogan "two years and you're off." Campaign strategists found that when political commercials offering these welfare reform promises were aired, the invariable result was a healthy spike upward in Clinton's poll numbers. Word went out to boost campaign resources to publicize Clinton as a wholesale reformer of the existing welfare system. Two years later, White House pollsters would advise experts planning the Clinton administration's welfare reform plan that "two" was the single most memorable number of the 1992 campaign (Ellwood, 1996, p. 26).

Within liberal Democratic circles, there was a widespread assumption that even if welfare reform was in the electoral arena, it would be another occasion for talking Right and governing Left. At least that was the hope as Clinton advanced toward the nomination and repeatedly voiced the slogans promising "to end welfare as we know it" and "two years and you're off." At one level it made sense for child advocacy groups and other Democratic supporters of the more traditional Family Support Act to remain silent while new Democrats excoriated the existing welfare system. A Democratic candidate in 1992 would need all the help he could get to unseat an ostensibly unbeatable Republican president basking in Gulf War glory. Later, liberal Democrats would justify the same calculation as the newly elected president fought his budget and health insurance battles in Congress.

At another level, however, these strategies ceded an immense advantage in all subsequent policy debates to congressional and state opponents of the existing welfare system. "Ending welfare as we know it" presumed an irredeemable federal policy. It gave immense advantage to all future political bids to abolish AFDC, since doing almost anything could now be presented as preferable to maintaining the entitlement program inherited from the 1930s. Likewise, focusing so exclusively on time limits—two years and off—legitimized the idea that viable welfare reform could entail abandoning persons who passed the time limit without being able to find sustainable employment income. It is not too much to say that—in terms of framing assumptions for Washington's later debate on welfare policy—by the end of the 1992 election the AFDC welfare system was in effect dead.

THE PRESIDENT PROPOSES AND CONGRESS DISPOSES. There were powerful political reasons why the new Clinton administration should give priority to health insurance over welfare reform in its first year. With recession and longer-term structural changes in the economy producing greater insecurity in employer-based plans, health insurance was a "middle-class" issue that could rally the country. After winning with the middle-class appeal of health insurance and revitalizing his broader Democratic coalition, President Clinton could then turn to satisfy his right flank with "new Democrat" welfare proposals. Welfare reform would at best benefit only the minority of poor persons and without doubt would strain coalition relations with liberal Democrats and the congressional Black Caucus. Besides, postelection White House polling showed the public ranked welfare reform as only third in importance as a campaign promise, after job creation and health insurance. Technical policy considerations for phasing welfare programs into a new structure of national health insurance further reinforced such calculations.

Delay became even more attractive once it was clear that the politics of financing welfare reform made it impossible to keep Clinton's sweeping campaign promises. Economic advisers won the argument that revenues from the new president's 1993 budget package would have to be devoted to immediate deficit reduction and not to the administration's still formless legislative ideas for welfare reform. Since any tax increase for antipoverty programs was considered a political nonstarter, President Clinton's welfare proposal would have to be designed within the other constraints of the 1990 Budget Enforcement Act. This meant the added costs of a reformed program for moving AFDC recipients into work (training, day care, subsidized jobs) would have to be paid for by equivalent cuts in other parts of the welfare program or—even more politically unthinkable—in middle-class entitlements such as Social Security or Medicare. These budget realities would eventually force the Clinton plan to phase in work requirements only for young mothers born after 1971, thereby throwing most new costs into future years not counted under the Budget Enforcement Act.

Not surprisingly, internal deliberations dragged on among administration policy planners, who were themselves split on basic social policy values. For some such as Bruce Reed, now a White House domestic policy adviser, it was politically unacceptable that President Clinton should not deliver—at least by proposing—what Candidate Clinton had promised; the plan would have to look like something that could be said to "end welfare as we know it." Others, centered in the Department of Health and Social Services, were committed to maintaining vestiges of a welfare safety net; for them, it would be better to do nothing than to end the Democratic party's social conscience as we know it. Little clear guidance came from Clinton himself, and internal administration negotiations dragged on.

With the president's political capital depleted by the defeat of his prized health insurance crusade, Clinton's welfare reform proposal finally emerged in June 1994. By now, fifteen months after his taking office and only four months before the congressional elections, the president's proposal seemed more an act of policymaking exhaustion rather than the urgent priority of an energetic new administration. Seven months earlier, congressional Republicans had already seized the welfare reform initiative with their own proposals. The Clinton administration's bid at welfare "end-ism" now seemed a pale reflection of the Republicans' proposals. Under the president's plan, welfare applicants would have to agree to participate in education and job readiness services, and if not working after two years on welfare they would be required to take community service jobs lasting up to a year. Clinton's welfare proposal envisioned spending slightly more taxpayer dollars to reduce welfare dependency. The price tag would be a little more than $9 billion over five years, paid for largely by cutting both entitlement benefits to unpopular clientele groups (immigrants, drug and alcohol addicts) as well as emergency state relief to potential welfare claimants. By contrast, congressional Republican initiatives on welfare reform were projected to save $40 billion to $66 billion in net budget costs over the status quo. In general, Republicans boasted stronger work requirements, stricter time limits, fewer services, and firm prohibitions against supporting teenage mothers and women who had additional children while on welfare. Fearing voters' reaction in their districts from whatever they did, Democratic leaders prepared for the 1994 election by allowing Clinton's proposal to die in the House Ways and Means Committee.

As the dynamic new conservative leader of House Republicans, Newt Gingrich had created the rare spectacle of a single congressional campaign document promising a specific policy agenda. The 1994 Contract with America bypassed controversial items favored by social conservatives (for example, abortion restrictions, school prayer) in favor of ten antigovernment measures (such as term limits, balanced-budget amendment, tax cuts) tailored to the preferences of what might have been the median Perot voter in 1992. Subsequent studies indicated that in almost no congressional races were Americans sufficiently aware of the Contract to affect the vote outcome. Still, the Contract was important symbolically in reflecting the public's political anger, and Republican leaders succeeded in claiming the results to be a mandate for a thoroughgoing attack on the status quo. Stalemated welfare reform was a prominent piece of that status quo, and action on this front became one of the Contract's promised priorities for House Republicans' first 100 days in power. The Contract envisioned allowing states to opt out of the AFDC program and receive block grants instead. There would be a five-year lifetime limit on benefits, with work activities required after two years on assistance. Every state would be prohibited from paying benefits for additional children born to welfare mothers or to any unmarried mothers under 18.

The stunning 1994 election results gave Republicans control of the entire Congress for the first time in almost half a century and sealed the fate of the AFDC entitlement program. Although it took almost two years of complicated maneuvers and countermaneuvers to finally finish the job, the underlying political dynamic of those two years was clear. With a conservative-led Republican majority dominant, the center of gravity for all other participants now shifted decisively to the right in the ongoing bargaining among House, Senate, and Clinton policymakers (Weaver, 2000, pp. 375–80). Conservatives were strongest and most disciplined in the House of Representatives, and their bitterly contested welfare reform bill did indeed pass on a party line vote in the first 100 days of the new Congress. Lest they be seen as endorsing the now widely condemned status quo, congressional Democrats unsuccessfully rallied around counterproposals for work obligations, time limits, and illegitimacy deterrence measures that they would have rejected out of hand two years earlier at the outset of the Clinton administration. A third and conventionally liberal bill for reforming AFDC entitlements received little attention, even from most Democrats. Despite the intense partisan clashes, there was an emergent consensus that legislating a new world of welfare meant two things: work requirements in exchange for welfare benefits and time limits on how long welfare could be received. Indicative of the new atmosphere, the Democratic Leadership Council now publicized revised proposals that would outdo the original 1994 Republican proposals to get "tough on welfare." Instead of a two-year limit on benefits before work, some form of work activity would be required immediately upon application for welfare; Republican exclusion of teen mothers and additional children from cash benefits would be replaced with adult-supervised group homes for young mothers.

The Senate proved a more time-consuming, and civil, arena for bargaining over welfare reform. As in the House, preliminary Senate action showed overwhelming Republican support for replacing the AFDC entitlement program with fixed-sum block grants, work requirements after two years, and a five-year lifetime limit for individuals on welfare. Unlike the House Republicans, Senate leaders responded to appeals from the GOP's leading reform governors and offered states maximum flexibility in deciding on illegitimacy, family, and work issues. The White House signaled that Clinton would not veto such a bill. By now liberal child advocacy groups concluded the AFDC entitlement cause was hopeless. They therefore switched to lobbying for federal rules that would require states to maintain block-granted spending at a fixed, high percentage of their previous spending on AFDC. The Democrats' leading welfare expert, Senator Moynihan, remained as an isolated voice protesting against abandonment of the AFDC entitlement and his half-implemented Family Support Act. However, at this point Republican forces split when a strong social conservative faction insisted on the "pro-family" mandates passed by their House allies, particularly measures to combat illegitimacy (such as bans on cash benefits to unmarried teens and for additional children born to mothers on welfare). Such welfare policy issues were further politicized by the competing presidential ambitions of Senate leader Bob Dole and Senator Phil Gramm on his right. After further delay and protracted debate, Dole's legislative skills produced a compromise backed by Clinton that isolated and defeated both the most conservative and most liberal factions in the Senate. The Senate's proposal would replace the AFDC entitlement with block grants, strong work requirements, time limits, more child care funds, and rules to maintain prior levels of state spending; illegitimacy measures would be left as state options rather than federal mandates.

By the time the Senate finally acted, however, welfare reform was entangled in a far larger political contest that preoccupied Washington from September to the end of 1995 and eventually produced an immensely unpopular government shutdown. The media covered the contest as a largely personal struggle between an embattled Clinton presidency and House Speaker Gingrich's resurgent Republican forces. In reality, behind the imbroglio over balancing budgets and tax cuts the contest was a more fundamental matter of challenging and defending America's middle-class welfare state. In the spring of 1995, President Clinton had begun abandoning a political strategy that simply echoed congressional Democrats' strident complaints about the Republicans' initiatives to cut taxes and social programs. Instead, the president and his senior strategists began to deploy a "triangulating" offensive—melding popular features of both Republican and Democratic congressional partisans to advance his own positive, centrist appeals that had been pretested by White House polls and focus groups.

For welfare reform, triangulation meant tacitly agreeing to see the AFDC entitlement program replaced with block grants to the states, while vigorously attacking unpopular features such as inadequate funding for child care and bans on cash assistance to teenage mothers. By January 1996 Clinton had twice vetoed Republican welfare reform bills. The first was a welfare reform contained in an omnibus reconciliation bill, where the president focused on unpopular cuts in Medicare and Medicaid. The second was a separate welfare package in which the president's veto highlighted unpopular changes in the school lunch and Food Stamp programs. In the end, the conservative leadership in Congress overreached and had to retreat, not at all because of attacking the AFDC welfare system, but because Clinton could effectively portray Republicans as attacking middle America's broader social safety net such as Medicaid and school lunches. The Gingrich vision of "replacing the welfare state" turned out to be a delusional political nightmare for his party.

In the context of budget battles defending middle America's welfare state, Clinton's vetoes of legislation containing the new welfare reforms were a political asset, not a liability. A few months later, as the 1996 election campaign intensified, the political context was quite different. By the summer of 1996, a majority of Americans polled considered the nation's moral decline more serious than any economic problems facing the country. This general atmosphere served the congressional Republicans well, as they identified the existing AFDC system with a morally corrupted status quo. When, in June 1996, child advocacy groups in Washington sought to stir 1960s-style liberal outrage against the pending welfare reform as an attack on children and the poor, the impact of their march on Washington appeared slight on public and politicians alike (Weaver, 2000, p. 327). The final maneuver in legislating welfare reform flowed from the converging electoral interest between a Democratic president seeking a second term and congressional Republican leaders struggling to retain control of Congress after only two years at the helm. For one of the rare moments in modern American politics, politicians' reelection calculus made it better to have welfare reform as a law than as an issue.

With the departure of presidential candidate Dole, Trent Lott had become Senate majority leader for the Republicans, and by the midsummer of 1996 the party's election prospects were deteriorating ominously amid Dole's lackluster run for the White House. Lott, who had been something of a mentor to Speaker Gingrich when both were young congressmen, was now in a position to lead an attempt to salvage congressional Republicans' election prospects. This meant seeking compromises to produce legislative achievements on the numerous important pieces of stalled domestic legislation derailed by the year of political warfare between Gingrich and Clinton. Back-channel communications between Lott and Clinton yielded an implicit reelection compact that left the mournful Republican presidential candidate to fend for himself. For welfare reform, this compact meant decoupling the issue from previously proposed cuts in some Medicaid entitlements. Lott then accommodated Clinton's desires for improvements in child care funding; a $1 billion loan fund for states became a $2 billion contingency grant fund and a $1.7 billion loan fund in case of a recession; illegitimacy measures would be optional, not federally mandated.

Lobbied heavily by liberal child advocacy groups and friends, Clinton anguished about signing the Republican welfare reform bill. His polling strategists and political advisers urged signing now and fighting later to improve unacceptable items, such as the ban on most means-tested benefits to legal immigrants. More than that, the president's political advisers encouraged Clinton's expectation that his reelection would bring with it a Democratic majority to regain control of Congress. The president could then resurrect the opportunity side of welfare reform, reassured by polls that once the popular work requirements and time limits of welfare reform were in place, the public would be much more willing to back new spending on jobs, education, and other benefits for welfare recipients and other inner-city Americans (Morris, 1999, pp. 300–04). Over against such hopes, the immediate political implications of not signing the Republican Congress's welfare reform bill were unambiguous. White House poll models revealed that, having promised to end welfare as we know it, the only event as devastating to Clinton's 1996 reelection prospects as vetoing the welfare reform bill would be if Dole acquired Colin Powell as his vice presidential running mate. Clinton's projected fifteen-point winning margin would be turned into a three-point loss. The bill was signed.

Prospects

Political history teaches that welfare reform is both a law and a process. The 1996 law is necessarily the point of departure for the next turn in a process that can have no ultimate closure. Major dilemmas of welfare policy—adequate help for the deserving but deterrence for the undeserving, common standards but local flexibility, compassion for suffering but realism about human nature—are never settled by any one particular law or administrative reform because they really *are* dilemmas. Policymakers usually seem to cope by changing the subject from one horn of a given dilemma to the other. However, it is possible to cope in better or worse ways, and a broader political understanding can help improve the chances of doing the former rather than the latter.

Political Realities

First, it is important to recognize that the reformed welfare system began with a charmed life, enjoying a set of unusually favorable circumstances that may be deceiving. The phased-in nature of work requirements and hard time limits meant that the appearance of any negative policy consequences has been delayed. At the same time, implementation of the new world of welfare occurred not only in an extremely robust economy but also in the later stages of an economic expansion when jobs and income gains were finally, after many years of stagnation, benefiting those in the lower reaches of the income distribution. Already declining welfare caseloads declined even faster after 1996 as the most employable members of the welfare caseload sought and found work in an abundant job market. Likewise, already healthy state budgets gained even more federal funds than they would have under AFDC because, despite declining caseloads, Washington's new TANF block grant remained fixed for five years at pre-reform levels of individual state AFDC allocations. All in all, the years 1997–2000 were unusually sunny times for the new welfare policy.

Second, it follows that greater difficulties should be expected as the new world of welfare faces inevitable stress from economic conditions that do not match the good times of the last half of the 1990s. The debate on welfare reform favored short-term thinking about so-called rainy-day funds (that is, grants or loans available to states in the event of a recession). Little serious attention was paid to the fact that a countercyclical policy tool (the federal AFDC entitlement helped ensure that public spending rose when economic conditions declined) was being replaced with a pro-cyclical spending system that would accelerate and brake spending roughly in line with cycles in the economy. In general, the varied proposals for a federal contingency fund amounted to so many political bargaining chips in the fitful 1995–96 contest to gain passage of a welfare bill. However, as conditions during 2001 showed, future economic downturns must be expected and prepared for. A more carefully designed contingency fund that enhances the countercyclical capacities of the varied state programs will be immensely important in maintaining political support over the long term for the new welfare system. That, in turn, implies that the question of the interstate and intrastate distribution of funds will have to be reopened so as to consider not simply what states spent on AFDC in the past but where those Americans in greatest need are geographically located.

Third, it follows from the prior two points that the process of welfare reform will face renewed challenges in dealing with a core of poor Americans who are far less employable than those who left the rolls in the sunny early

years of welfare reform. Any realistic political response requires understanding that these are individuals and families whose multiple problems will not
be addressed by simply pointing to requirements for work, time limits, and
caseload reduction. Like many who have been "reformed" off the welfare rolls
without working—it seems 40 to 50 percent of mothers who have left and
stayed off welfare are not working regularly—these are the least skilled and
poorest educated in America. We can expect to live in a twenty-first-century
society that will continue to shrink the life chances of such people and the
children dependent on them. The political temptation will be to give up on
the hard cases of welfare policy, especially since these are people with little
voting power and even less capacity for political fund-raising.

Finally, political prudence has to be enhanced by better social intelligence.
In the 1930s, the new AFDC policy had sought to systematize the state
patchwork of mothers' pensions. Thereafter bureaucratic inertia took over.
With little monitoring of what was actually happening to people and programs, the emergent policy reality at street level was eventually a monstrosity
of perverse incentives and irresponsibility. Similarly, the 1996 welfare reform
sought to generalize state-level experiments by imposing work requirements
and time limits, deterring illegitimacy, and building personal responsibility.
While the 1996 law institutionalized features of various state experiments,
there was very little opportunity to weigh actual state experiences with welfare reform. Many, if not most, states remain unable to evaluate the work,
education, family, and other experiences of people moving in and out of
today's fifty different state welfare systems. The past lack of such trustworthy,
understandable information has poisoned both public understanding and the
politics of welfare. If this history is not to be repeated, there needs to be a
major bipartisan effort to improve federal capacities to objectively gather,
evaluate, and publicize social intelligence about what is actually happening to
poor Americans in the new world of welfare and work.

Political Hopes

Given that welfare reform is an ongoing process and not just a law, there are
good reasons to think that with the 1996 legislation in operation the nation
can now do better at debating the next steps in that process than it did for
the last thirty years of the twentieth century. Out of the clashes of the 1960s
came two strongly contrasting worldviews about welfare reform. For liberals,
it was about compassion and equality, which often translated into concerns
for entitlement and racial justice. For conservatives, welfare reform was about
personal responsibility and social order, which no less often translated into
concerns for nondependency and family values. These were and are real dif-

ferences, but they are not eternal contradictions without possibilities of overlap. It was a vigorous contest of intellectual and political partisanship, not bipartisanship, that eventually produced supervening results in 1996 that neither side might have expected.

The centerpiece in that convergence has been expectations for work. Such expectations have included, but also gone well beyond, the narrow issue of reforming AFDC legislation. On one side, it came to be acknowledged that assistance checks were not necessarily compassionate or equality-enhancing, that expectations of work—with help in meeting those expectations—could be giving welfare recipients the equal respect citizens deserve. On the other side, an immense structure of income support for working Americans was incrementally constructed after the 1960s through the Earned Income Tax Credit and other policy devices. From 1993 to 1999, total aid for this welfare state of the child-endowed working poor rose from about $25 billion to $65 billion (in 1999 dollars), while all government spending (federal and state) on AFDC never exceeded $30 billion (Besharov and Germanis, 2000). Whether part of the working poor who got off welfare or who had never been on it in the first place, millions of lower-paid Americans have become dependent on federal policies to "make work pay" as it would never do otherwise. Thus by the onset of the twenty-first century a broad centrist coalition was standing behind the new world of welfare, and it included at least some liberals who had accepted work as well as some conservatives who had accepted dependency.

Underpinning this de facto coalition is extensive public support for the new foundation of welfare policy: work requirements and time limits. Having these assumptions in place—not theoretically but as a functioning reality in local welfare offices—offers the prospect of greater public acceptance for efforts to improve the lot of the most disadvantaged Americans. The more such offices become employment-focused centers, not centers administering welfare checks, the firmer the political base for doing more to help those in the nation's inner cities for whom "work" may be only a small part of the problem. This will entail providing resources for major improvements in education, day care, and labor market services. Welfare reform will have succeeded politically when "welfare reform" has been recognized as an insufficient, though necessary, condition for effective welfare policy.

For the hard cases, where welfare needs go well beyond work and economics, the 1996 law opened up new opportunities for constructive engagement with religious organizations, the one institution of civil society found even in America's most distressed communities. More than that, local faith-based organizations tend to be served by highly motivated volunteers, people with the long-term dedication required to personally touch troubled lives. With little political fanfare, Republican John Ashcroft succeeded in introducing a provision in the Senate welfare reform bill that had been crafted and promoted by several members of the evangelical Protestant community. This "charitable choice" proviso (section 104) of the 1996 legislation requires state and local governments to open the door to faith-based organizations when buying services from nongovernmental sources. With this, national policy began to re-create a new form of partnership between religion and public welfare (Carlson-Thies, 2001). Local church groups would no longer be denied direct access to government funds simply because of their association with religious activities.

As of 2001, a number of states have not effectively changed their rules of engagement with faith-based organizations. At the same time, most state politicians have been reluctant to use their new discretionary powers in welfare policy to focus on controversial matters of family formation, even though concerns over teenage childbearing and one-parent families provided a major impetus for welfare reform in the 1990s. Charitable choice offers a possibility to reduce mistrust and find at least some common ground between liberal and conservative partisans when it comes to issues such as illegitimacy, marriage, and personal responsibility for moral choices in life. While some advocacy groups will object, most people seem to agree that America's children will be better off if out-of-wedlock births are discouraged and marriage and committed fatherhood are encouraged. However, a re-engagement of religion and welfare policy will not be politically sustainable unless allocations of taxpayer dollars to religious groups are based on rigorous, trustworthy evaluations of which programs work better than others in accomplishing secular objectives. Otherwise, faith-based pork barrel may be the worst kind of pork of all. Solid evaluation of their actual performance should be rightly regarded as an essential part of good "stewardship" in such religious bodies. At the same time, government oversight and First Amendment concerns can threaten to emasculate the religious quality of welfare assistance that makes faith-based organizations valuable to distressed clients in the first place. Protecting religious organizations against undue government controls will probably require relying more on funding through individual tax credits, deductions, and vouchers rather than direct government subsidies.

In the immediate aftermath of the 2000 election, national leadership for the welfare agenda has passed to George W. Bush and an experienced collection of former state-level Republican reformers. They seem to bear a strong family resemblance to an earlier generation of Republican Progressives, people for whom the federal government is neither the enemy nor the caretaker of the American people but the instrument of their national purpose and promise. If that is so, then the political prospects for further constructive developments in welfare reform may be better than at any time since the 1960s (and that decade's echo in the Clinton-Gingrich wars).

This is not to say that bipartisanship is likely to prevail in debating and reauthorizing the welfare reform act of 1996. We can expect that those marginalized in the grand work consensus of the 1990s—liberal egalitarians and social conservatives—will have much to criticize and propose. Social conservatives will have good grounds to complain about the lost focus on issues of illegitimacy, family formation, and other cultural values that they have associated with welfare reform. Devolution of power to the states fell far short of satisfying those objectives. Egalitarians will have good cause to reopen issues concerning the interstate distribution of funds. This distribution was frozen in place in 1996 by a short-sighted but understandable political need of the time, namely, the need that summer to avoid identifying winners and losers and thus avoid derailing final passage of a House/Senate conference bill. What is at stake five years later is not simply a matter of funding formulas or bans on cash benefits to teenage mothers. Interstate disparities of treatment for people in need are an appropriate national concern, a concern that should become even more politically salient when economic conditions worsen.

Political partisanship is an unattractive sight to many Americans, but it is how democratic politics does most of its work. That, and the free clash of ideas. As history has shown, there is certainly more than one way to think about "welfare." However, there is also one unchanging political truth about welfare dependency. It is that poor people are desperately dependent on what is in the minds and hearts of America's privileged political class. They, and not just the poor, need to behave like responsible adults.

References

Aaron, Henry J. 1978. *Politics and the Professors.* Brookings.

Besharov, Douglas J., and Peter Germanis. 2000. "Welfare Reform—Four Years Later." *Public Interest* 140 (Summer): 17–35.

Cantril, Albert H., and Susan Davis Cantril. 1999. *Reading Mixed Signals.* Johns Hopkins University Press.

Carlson-Thies, Stanley W. 2001. "Charitable Choice: Bringing Religion Back into American Welfare." *Journal of Policy History* 13 (Winter): 1.

Cloward, Richard A. 2000. "The New Politics of Participatory Democracy." Panel Discussion at the Conference on the Great Society, Miller Center of Public Affairs, University of Virginia, Charlottesville, November 18.

Edsall, Thomas B., and Mary E. Edsall. 1991. *Chain Reaction: The Impact of Race, Rights and Taxes on American Politics.* Norton.

Ellwood, David T. 1988. *Poor Support: Poverty in the American Family.* Basic Books.

———. 1996. "Welfare Reform As I Knew It." *American Prospect* 26 (May–June): 22–29.

———. 1999. *The Plight of the Working Poor.* Children's Roundtable Report 2 (November). Brookings.

Gilens, Martin. 1999. *Why Americans Hate Welfare: Race, Media, and the Politics of Antipoverty Policy.* University of Chicago Press.

Hallow, Ralph Z. 1992. "GOP Lawmakers Push 'Tough Love' Welfare Plan." *Washington Times,* April 29, p. A3.

Jacobs, Lawrence R., and Robert Y. Shapiro. 2000. *Politicians Don't Pander: Political Manipulation and the Loss of Democratic Responsiveness.* University of Chicago Press.

Lieberman, Robert C. 1998. *Shifting the Color Line: Race and the American Welfare State.* Harvard University Press.

Mead, Lawrence M. 1986. *Beyond Entitlement.* Free Press.

———. 1992. *The New Politics of Poverty.* Basic Books.

Melnick, R. Shep. 1994. *Between the Lines.* Brookings.

Morris, Dick. 1999. *Behind the Oval Office.* Los Angeles: Renaissance Books.

Moynihan, Daniel P. 1965. *The Negro Family: The Case for National Action.* U.S. Department of Labor.

Murray, Charles. 1984. *Losing Ground: American Social Policy, 1950–1980.* Basic Books.

Patterson, James. 1981. *America's Struggle against Poverty, 1900–1980.* Harvard University Press.

Sainsbury, Diane. 1996. *Gender, Equality and Welfare States.* Cambridge University Press.

Shear, Jeff. 1994. "Pulling in the Harness." *National Journal* 26 (23): 1286–90.

Weaver, R. Kent. 2000. *Ending Welfare As We Know It.* Brookings.

7

LAWRENCE M. MEAD

The Politics of Conservative Welfare Reform

A LEADING ISSUE IN American politics for forty years has been how to reform America's controversial family aid program, once called Aid to Families with Dependent Children (AFDC) and, since 1996, Temporary Assistance for Needy Families (TANF). Yet welfare politics has received surprisingly little attention from scholars. Inquiry has centered mostly on the liberal period of reform controversy of the 1960s and 1970s, when the leading question was whether to raise benefits and extend welfare coverage from single-parent to two-parent families. This was the entitlement approach to welfare, giving aid to the poor on the basis of need, without stipulations about how they should live.

Much less has been written about the conservative period, in the 1980s and 1990s, when the agenda shifted to making welfare mothers work and restraining dependency. To the extent that these changes were implemented, entitlement ended. Aid was still given to needy families, but now with presuppositions about behavior. That change is still controversial, but the politics behind it may shed some light on how to go about improving the welfare system. In the past, welfare satisfied virtually nobody, on the left or right. It provided needy families only meager support while fomenting, or at least condoning, social problems among the poor, particularly unwed pregnancy and nonwork. Recent reforms—by enforcing work, restraining dependency, and making work pay—have made welfare more legitimate and improved its capacity to support families. But the job is far from finished. The United States still needs to do more to help the poor, and also to get them to help themselves. In that struggle, welfare politics is bound to be a lion in the path.

It is especially important to understand the politics behind the Personal Responsibility and Work Opportunity Reconciliation Act (PRWORA) of 1996, the act that created TANF. PRWORA was the first truly radical welfare reform. It intensified past efforts to enforce work and child support, but it also capped federal funding, limited families to five years on the rolls, and took steps to restrain unwed pregnancy, a problem Congress had not confronted before. It required that most families satisfy a work test through actual employment in available jobs, rather than through education and training designed to get better jobs later, as allowed under earlier law. And while imposing new mandates on the states in these areas, the act also gave them unprecedented control over eligibility for aid and work incentives as well as benefit levels. Those changes, coupled with earlier reforms, superb economic conditions, and new benefits for the working poor, have driven the welfare rolls down by more than half since 1994.

Where did this conservative explosion come from? How might those passions be harnessed to the crafting of a new welfare order? To address these questions, I consider why radical change came from the right rather than the left, why it came when it did, and what accounts for the unusual complexity of PRWORA, which reforms welfare in several directions at once. For the first answer, I look largely to public opinion; for the second, to decisionmaking within the government; and for the third, to the elite politics surrounding welfare. Radical reform, in short, reflected the public will and the need to solve long-standing problems in welfare, but it also reflected the proclivities of the politicians and experts who speak for the public in Washington. Their ideas drive change but pose dangers to effective policymaking. I end with some implications for the reauthorization of TANF.

The Conservatism of Reform

What accounts for the conservatism of recent welfare reform? I refer here not simply to PRWORA but to reforms of the 1980s, whose main objective was to curb dependency, promote employment by welfare adults, and force more absent fathers to support welfare families. Changes passed in 1981 under President Ronald Reagan excluded most higher-income families from the rolls and allowed states to impose workfare (unpaid labor in government jobs) on adult recipients. The Family Support Act of 1988 toughened work and child support rules while also requiring states to aid two-parent families.

These changes contrasted with the proposals that Congress rejected during the liberal period, which would have raised coverage and benefits and given recipients more incentives to work, but without making work a condition of aid.

The long-run explanation for the shift lies with public opinion. AFDC, established by the Social Security Act of 1935, attracted little attention in its early years. In the 1960s, however, it assumed a form that the public opposed. The rolls grew sharply, exceeding 11 million people by the early 1970s. This increase was due in part to Supreme Court decisions that disallowed some earlier restrictions on welfare. The nature of the adults on the rolls also changed, so as to appear less deserving. Most welfare mothers were now unwed, rather than widowed or divorced. Above all, few worked, at a time when employment was becoming usual for American mothers not on welfare, including single mothers.

Public opinion studies consistently show that voters have humanitarian feelings toward the poor; they want the government to assist needy families. But they also want those receiving aid to help themselves. Recipients should not make themselves poor. In particular, adult recipients should work alongside the taxpayers, to whom they look for support. Since AFDC traditionally did not enforce good behavior, welfare became intensely unpopular even though programs to help the poor were endorsed. These views are surprisingly strong and uniform across all subgroups, including the poor themselves and racial minorities, who have been the most reliant on welfare. They are also long-standing. The combination of willingness to help and the demand for work is found in polls as early as the 1930s (Schiltz, 1970). The only important change since then is that in the 1960s the public gave up the notion, originally enshrined in AFDC, that welfare mothers should be exempted from working so that they could raise their children full time. Since by that time most other mothers worked, most Americans felt welfare mothers should also (Teles, 1996, chap. 3).

Besides nonwork, the other important behavior that precipitates welfare dependency is unwed pregnancy, and here public attitudes are less resolute. Americans continue to affirm the value of marriage, and most disapprove of unwed pregnancy among teenagers. But they have become more accepting of unwed sexual activity, divorce, and single parenthood than was true a generation or two ago, especially among younger Americans. This makes the public uneasy about such recent conservative reform ideas as firm time limits on aid or denying coverage to teen mothers (Thornton, 1995; Weaver, 2000, pp. 177–86). People are much less willing to enforce marriage or abstinence than work as a condition of aid.

Given these views, it was inevitable that at some point welfare would be changed to enforce work and child support, if not to support marriage. The mystery is why it took thirty years for this to occur, a question I address in the next section. Several objections may be raised, however, to the notion that public opinion explains the shift and that policymakers should defer to that opinion.

Is Public Opinion Independent?

One problem is that public opinion may not reflect an independent consensus, but only the views of elites. In a representative political system, much that is called public opinion reflects back to politicians their own proposals. Public opinion about poverty or welfare can be affected by the way leaders "frame" those issues to the voters. If news stories about these problems emphasize social causes, such as the economy or failed public policies, the public will tend to do likewise. Conversely, if the media focus on the problems of individual poor families, the public will tend to hold the poor responsible for their fate (Iyengar 1987, 1989, 1990; Bobo and Smith, 1994).

Some would suggest that in recent decades conservative politicians and intellectuals have undermined public support for aid by focusing on the personal shortcomings of welfare families and otherwise demonizing the poor. Martin Gilens (1999) finds it suspicious that pictures of the poor in the media depict a higher proportion of them as black than is suggested by government statistics. Thus even journalists who are more liberal than the average citizen end up undermining support for welfare. Public views of welfare did turn more hostile in the early 1990s, a development that helped trigger PRWORA. One explanation for this change was the fierce new attacks on the unreformed system launched by politicians, particularly from the right (Teles, 1996, pp. 45–46; Weaver, 2000, pp. 171–72, 194).

But it is implausible to argue that the public's hostility to traditional welfare is to any important extent the creation of elites. Framing effects are only one of several influences on opinion. The public insists on taking a far more systemic view of unemployment than it does of poverty because joblessness is seen as more involuntary than poverty (Iyengar, 1987). And since most people assert both a social and an individual responsibility for poverty, it is hard to argue that conservatives have persuaded the public to assign all the onus for need to the poor. The public is likeliest to defer to elites in areas of policy that are technical or remote from everyday experience, such as economic regulation or arms control. In contrast, people respond to social problems out of their own lives, and elites or the media have only limited influence.

Is Public Opinion Hostile to Government?

Another question is whether the public is simply hostile to the poor or to government effort on their behalf. Some critics believe that voters respond to the welfare problem out of self-interest rather than moral concern. People want to reduce the cost of dependency so as to spend more money on themselves. This perspective, it is argued, reflects the individualism of Americans, who believe in fending for themselves and accept only limited collective responsibility for social problems. In any simple form, this interpretation is clearly wrong. The public expresses too much concern that the government aid the needy. If Americans were driven only by self-interest, one could not explain why a welfare state even exists in the United States. Indeed, there is substantial support not only for programs like Social Security that serve the bulk of the population, but also for means-tested programs, including AFDC (Cook and Barrett, 1992). Public criticism of welfare is indeed potent, but it is aimed not at the principle of aid, but at the perceived abuses of the system, particularly the apparent undeservedness of many of the adult recipients (Gilens, 1999).

In his essay in this volume, and in other work, Hugh Heclo develops the subtler position that public commitment to overcoming poverty is real but limited. People do want the government to help the needy, but they are impatient with the difficulties of doing so. Politicians oscillate between ignoring the social problem and overselling new social programs. They fail to teach the public that the struggle against poverty must be long, difficult, and costly. Without a strong political base, initiatives such as the War on Poverty tend to wither once people think they are failing. While social programs may take the edge off need, they cannot accomplish the radical redistribution and social reconstruction that are really needed to integrate the poor. Above all, welfare has been losing support ever since it became linked to black poverty and the inner city in the 1960s (Heclo, 1986b, 1994, 1995).

This view is not unrealistic, but I believe it is too pessimistic. It tends to conflate the views of voters with those of political leaders. Ideological differences about how much the government should do for the poor are much clearer among politicians than the public. In chapter 6, Heclo argues that conservative intellectuals paved the way for PRWORA by undermining support for welfare. But it is equally true that few voters followed them. The passions that ordinary Americans express about poverty do not suggest a limited commitment to overcoming the problem but rather intense frustration at past failures. The steady succession of new antipoverty approaches in Washington suggests not shallow, symbolic policymaking, but rather an ongoing search for answers that both voters and policymakers take seriously.

The current rebuilding of welfare around work, which goes back at least two decades, is just the sort of long-term endeavor that Heclo suggests is beyond the United States. The public, I would say, is not impatient with antipoverty effort in general, but rather with the permissiveness of traditional welfare. It wants to see aid policy vindicate conventional values such as work rather than tacitly abandon them. But once that is done and progress is apparent, it is willing to spend money and hang in there for the long haul. The evidence for this view is that, as the welfare rolls plummet, spending on antipoverty programs has not fallen. The nation is spending less on TANF but more on wage subsidies, health care, and child care aimed at former welfare mothers who are now working. The war on poverty continues.

Heclo also suggests that support for helping the poor varies with the times. Americans esteem welfare both in the sense of self-sufficiency and in the sense of mutual dependence. On one hand, they value buccaneering self-reliance and the independence of the marketplace; on the other hand, they believe in collective support for the vulnerable. First one view, then the other dominates our public counsels. While the New Deal and the Great Society were eras of collective endeavor, the Reagan era reasserted self-reliance, even in a society experiencing increased interdependence (Heclo, 1986a). Again, this view conflates political trends with public opinion. Certainly, the Reagan period brought to power some aggressive critics of the welfare state. But all along, the voters maintained their commitment to a humanitarian social policy. They voted for Reagan mostly because he was seen as a stronger leader than his opponents, not because they endorsed his conservative economic and social policies (Shanks and Miller, 1990).

On my reading, the American creed does not mandate self-reliance, in the sense of avoiding all dependence on the government. Otherwise, the 45 million Americans who live on Social Security could not feel good about themselves. Rather, it demands that citizens observe certain civilities, such as working and obeying the law. If they do and remain needy, the government will gladly help them. Despite living off the government, pensioners claim independence because their benefits are contributory. By contrast, welfare recipients are seen as dependent in an invidious sense, precisely because their benefits are unearned. Americans emphasize reciprocity, or balancing claims with desserts, much more than limiting claims on government. As political scientist Kent Weaver says, "The American people are much less concerned with getting people off welfare and reducing the costs of the system than they are with having recipients make an effort to help themselves" (Weaver, 2000, p. 186).

A complementary view is that public opinion has become more conservative, but this does not mean a shift to the right in the usual partisan sense, oriented mostly toward economics, of belief in smaller government, less taxing and spending, and less intervention in the marketplace. Rather, in the 1960s, in response to growing urban problems, national politics underwent a partial realignment to a different political spectrum, one concerned with good citizenship and social order. The central issue then became how demanding the government should be about enforcing mores such as "law-abidingness," the work ethic, or educational standards. The more severe conservative position enjoys stronger support than the more tolerant liberal view. That largely explains the dominance of conservatives and Republicans in national politics after Richard Nixon's election to the White House in 1968. Later Democratic presidents—Jimmy Carter and Bill Clinton—were elected only after they took more conservative positions on crime and welfare.

Conservatives, however, gained a mandate mainly to restore order to American cities, not to pursue their traditional small-government economic agenda. Ronald Reagan and, later, Newt Gingrich succeeded in reforming welfare and promoting tougher law enforcement, but not in reducing federal spending or economic controls more than marginally. And the more that order is restored, the more the older, more economic axis of national politics reasserts itself. On that spectrum, liberals and Democrats have a much stronger position than they do on social order. Big government remains popular, and politics is bound to shift to the left.

Indeed, ever since the fall in welfare began in 1994, it has done that. Today antigovernment extremism is in eclipse in the Republican party and President George W. Bush speaks of "compassionate conservatism." Far from dying with PRWORA, welfare has found a second life in the form of growing spending on the working poor. Karl Marx described the bourgeoisie as its own grave-diggers. There will never be socialism in America. But by reforming welfare, law enforcement, and the schools, conservatives may work themselves out of power.

Is Opinion Racist?

Survey analysts find that opposition to welfare runs stronger among respondents who also have negative views of blacks. Some conclude that the public's strong antipathy to welfare reflects racism, which I take to mean opposition to blacks as such (Bobo and Smith, 1994; Gilens, 1999). That might suggest that it would be wrong to base social policy on this opinion.

Since the 1960s, however, large majorities of whites say they no longer consider blacks inferior, and they accept equal opportunity and integration in principle. It is true that majorities still resist affirmative action and school busing, and some argue on that basis that the white conversion is insincere. I prefer the view that white misgiving no longer reflects traditional racism but rather the fear that blacks threaten important values, such as self-reliance and the work ethic, that all races share (Sniderman and Piazza, 1993; Sniderman and Carmines, 1997). While research cannot strictly resolve this issue, the view that whites remain racists is difficult to square with civil rights and other actions the government has taken on behalf of blacks.

A similar interpretation is that whites do not oppose welfare because it disproportionately serves blacks. Rather, they oppose nonwork and unwed pregnancy among the black poor because it promotes dependency. That is, welfare is not tarred with the brush of race; rather, blacks are tarred with the brush of welfare. Rather than racism driving opposition to welfare, opposition to welfare exacerbates racism. On this view, to reform welfare and enforce work would not harm blacks. Rather, it would serve them by reducing black reliance on welfare, raising black work levels, and thus undercutting racism. The current reform clearly is accomplishing at least the first two of those goals.

What the Public Wants

The sort of welfare that the public desires is best represented by the system that Wisconsin developed between 1986 and 1997. Wisconsin Works, or W-2, combines generosity with work demands, just as Americans want. Virtually all aid to families is conditioned on employment. Parents who can work must do so immediately, either in private or government jobs. Those who cannot work must attend remediation programs. At the same time, Wisconsin spent lavishly on the bureaucracy and services needed to achieve reform. It maintained generous benefits, and it extended subsidized child and health care to the entire low-wage working population. It is a system of almost Scandinavian generosity but, unlike most European welfare, is based on the principle of serious self-help. Some other pioneer states—for instance, Michigan, Oregon, and Iowa—have moved toward a similar policy.

The Timing of Reform

Just because it has been by and large constant, public opinion alone cannot account for the timing of welfare reform in 1996. One has to explain why the unreformed system endured for decades even after a popular consensus had crystallized against it. And if it lasted so long, why did it crumble in the 1990s? Even when a problem is serious, the timing of action depends on how the problem works its way through the governmental system. For the government to take action, a problem must be widely recognized, politicians must be committed to solving it, and policies must be available that plausibly would solve it. Only then does the issue tend to get on the governmental agenda (Kingdon, 1995). In America's complicated federal system, none of these steps is automatic.

AFDC may have been unpopular since at least the early 1960s, but for decades after that, elections did not generate leaders with a clear-cut will to change welfare. That was partly because, at the level of public opinion, welfare was usually a chronic rather than an acute concern. Issues of social order became more prominent from the 1960s on, but in most national elections they were outweighed by civil rights struggles, foreign policy crises (Vietnam, Iran), or—most frequently—economic concerns. Between 1989 and 1994, however, the AFDC rolls soared 30 percent, reaching an all-time high of over 14 million people. The jump, occurring at a time when other problems were quiescent, helps explain why public opinion hardened against welfare in the 1990s.

Within the government, the first institution to embrace welfare reform was the presidency. Once in office, presidents tend to focus on solving recognized national problems, regardless of party platforms, in order to secure their place in history. From Nixon on, every president except Gerald Ford launched some serious initiative to reform AFDC. But virtually all these were defeated in Congress. The liberalization proposals of Nixon and Carter foundered because they failed to address work and cost issues seriously. Ronald Reagan's conservative proposals to mandate workfare or turn welfare over to the states failed because Republicans lacked a majority in Congress. Reagan obtained only tightened eligibility limits and optional workfare, both in 1981. In 1988 the Family Support Act (FSA) strengthened work requirements somewhat, but it also extended welfare benefits to the two-parent poor and raised spending on training and child care. It did not bring fundamental change.

Politics shifted to focus decisively on welfare only in the early 1990s. This was when antiwelfare opinion strengthened and when leaders of both parties became committed to major change for the first time. In his effort to win the presidency and reposition his party on social issues, Bill Clinton in the 1992 campaign promised to "end welfare as we know it." And in 1994 House Republicans made radical conservative reform of welfare a key plank of their Contract with America. The GOP takeover of Congress in that year removed the Democratic control that had long blocked fundamental change from the right. Clinton proposed a moderate reform but felt bound to sign the more radical PRWORA when the Republicans put the bill to him. Otherwise, his chances of reelection in 1996 might have been threatened (Weaver, 2000).

Another force that held up change was the government's long inability to reform welfare in tune with public preferences. The voters demanded that the government somehow make welfare adults work while continuing to aid needy families. But how can one enforce work without denying aid and putting children at risk? Conversely, to guarantee aid means in practice to support parents without work. As long as the issue was seen as doing more for the poor versus doing less, a conflict between promoting self-reliance and helping people was unavoidable.

That dilemma could be transcended only if a way were found to raise work levels without abandoning the principle of aid. The solution must be to promote work from within the welfare system, rather than substitute work for aid. Liberal planners in the 1960s and 1970s hoped to accomplish this with work incentives, and, when these showed little effect, both liberals and conservatives turned to welfare work programs. Evaluations of the 1980s and 1990s established that mandatory work requirements had a potential to square the welfare circle. If well funded and implemented—a big if—they might raise work rates on welfare by as much as a quarter and earnings by as much as a half (Gueron, 1996). Gains were greatest if programs enforced participation firmly and emphasized actual work in available jobs rather than—as FSA had done—education and training for better jobs.

While only the best programs achieved this much, the promise was enough to make work enforcement the main basis of conservative reform proposals from the late 1980s on, although PRWORA, as I note shortly, was to contain other approaches too. In sum, it was the maturing of the work strategy, coupled with a more negative public feeling about AFDC and the political commitments to change made in the early 1990s, that chiefly explains the timing of PRWORA.

The timing can also be seen as the culmination of an attack on AFDC that grew over several decades. When the government first undertakes a purpose, it enacts a new program, surrounds it with edifying images, and vests control in agencies and oversight bodies likely to be supportive. But later, if problems develop, the difficulties will be publicized by experts, then by the media, and finally by politicians who see a political opportunity in offering alternatives. That can adversely change a program's reputation and shift control, exposing the program to reform and even abolition. Thus a gathering storm of opposition can dismantle a structure that earlier seemed unassailable (Baumgartner and Jones, 1993).

In the welfare case, AFDC in its early decades was shielded by a powerful ideology of entitlement, the idea that it existed to support poor mothers and children outside the labor force. Just as important, the program fell under the control of Congress's tax committees, perhaps the most powerful in Washington. Through their control of tax and budget legislation, Ways and Means in the House and Finance in the Senate could often make changes in AFDC with little detailed scrutiny in Congress. One reason why the liberal reform plans of the 1960s and 1970s failed was that the committees were then more conservative than Congress or the presidency. Finance Chairman Russell Long's opposition to the Nixon Family Assistance Plan was the main reason it never passed the Senate. Later, during the conservative 1980s and 1990s, the committees were often more liberal than the conservative presidents then proposing changes. Democrats on Ways and Means resisted the Clinton reform plan as excessively severe, even though it was more measured than the changes Republicans were later to impose (Ellwood, 1996, pp. 27, 29; Weaver, 2000, pp. 247–48). Again, fundamental change was defeated.

On the floor of Congress, as long as Democrats controlled Capitol Hill, there was a secure majority against fundamental reform from either left or right. There were too few committed liberals to enact the guaranteed income that the Nixon or Carter planners wanted, but there were too many Democrats to enact serious work tests or the devolution of AFDC to the states, as Reagan demanded. The Democratic block against conservative change grew stronger in the 1970s and 1980s as the party became more liberal, chiefly because of the enfranchisement of blacks in the South and, hence, the movement of Southern Democrats in Congress to the left.

The policy monopoly was broken only when outside criticism of welfare became overwhelming. In this analysis, the development of welfare work programs probably carried less weight than the broader criticism of conservative intellectuals that the old system was permissive and counterproductive. The cure for entitlement, these critics urged, must be individual responsibility, reciprocity, and social contract. Such rhetoric threw the defenders of entitlement on the defensive and moved the agenda for reform to the right. The Republican victory of 1994 finally broke the block on change both in the committees and on the floor of Congress. PRWORA not only changed welfare but shifted future control of it sharply to the state and local levels, which Republicans judged to be more conservative than Washington.

Indeed, policymaking at the state level played a key role, as Hugh Heclo notes earlier in this volume. Going back to the 1980s, many states gained the freedom to develop experimental welfare reform programs under waivers of normal federal rules granted by Washington. Presidents Reagan, George Bush, and Clinton all encouraged this move. Most of the initiatives aimed to enforce work more toughly than was allowed under federal law before PRWORA. Governors such as Tommy Thompson in Wisconsin and John

Engler in Michigan showed that it was possible to impose serious work requirements and thereby produce higher work levels and lower dependency without causing the widespread hardship predicted by liberal critics (Teles, 1996, chap. 7).

Wisconsin not only rebuilt its aid system entirely around work, but it did so without the prolonged paralysis seen at the federal level. A political consensus around a work-based reform gelled in Wisconsin in the mid-1980s, a decade before PRWORA. Thompson and a bipartisan coalition of legislators provided political direction while talented administrators implemented waves of reform programs (Mead, 2000). Wisconsin's government performed as impressively as its programs. Other pioneer states also acted before the nation. The effect, one might say, was to shame Washington into action.

The Complexity of PRWORA

The last mystery is the extraordinary complexity of PRWORA. The act claims to devolve responsibility for welfare to the states, but it also levies on them unprecedented mandates to raise participation in work activities and toughen child support enforcement. It also creates incentives for them to reduce unwed pregnancy. And while the act capped federal spending and ended the federal entitlement to aid, it raised spending for welfare and child care by nearly $4 billion over five years. Overall the act saved $54 billion, but this was due to cuts in programs outside TANF, some of which Congress later reversed (Weaver, 2000, p. 335). In short, some dimensions of the act weaken federal mandates and funding, whereas others strengthen them. What ties it all together is a determination to hold both states and recipients responsible for good outcomes.

The fundamental reason for this complexity is the long-standing elitism of federal policymaking in the area of welfare. People usually think of the American government as democratic. That means welfare must ultimately respect public opinion, which favors helping the needy while enforcing work. But because the system is representative, the people do not rule directly. Rather, they commission elites to govern on their behalf. The leaders who compete for that mandate typically are more extreme and more coherent in their views than are most voters.

American political parties have a reputation for being less ideological than parties in Europe, but they have become more polarized in the past thirty years. The main reason is a realignment that has made the parties in every area of the country broadly similar. Fewer Democrats are elected in the conservative South, fewer Republicans in the liberal Northeast, so both parties are more consistent ideologically than they once were. In presidential politics, would-be nominees must placate activists of the right or left in order to be nominated, before they ever get to appeal to the moderate middle of the electorate. In Congress, the parties have polarized to the point where conflicts over the budget and other salient issues can approach the ideological standoffs of Europe. That is especially true in the House, where a form of party government has taken hold. Armed with strong procedures to control debate, House leaders of the majority can more or less dictate outcomes on issues where their party is united, much as in a parliamentary system. What was true under Democratic control in the 1980s is true under Republican control since 1994.

The political conflict surrounding PRWORA was much sharper in the House than the Senate because these partisan and procedural trends were more developed there. House members are freer to be ideological than senators, because they sit for more cohesive districts. Led by the conspicuously ideological Newt Gingrich, House Republicans campaigned on the programmatic Contract with America in 1994. And once in power, they forced through much of their agenda (at least what they themselves could agree on) with minimal deference to opponents. In the Senate, procedures allow minorities to hold up action, so a more bipartisan style prevails. Yet the Republican majority in the Senate essentially endorsed the radical PRWORA.

Not only are politicians often more ideological than they are perceived to be, but they are surrounded by intellectuals whose concerns may be even more remote from those of the public. Every major policy issue in Washington is encrusted with opposing views of how to handle it developed by elected officeholders, appointive officials, lobby representatives, public interest spokespersons, and experts drawn from universities and think tanks. For the most part, these networks define the options placed before elected leaders. They can do this in part because political officials need outside advice to master their briefs and because they constantly need new ideas (Heclo, 1978).

Expert sway has been conspicuous in the areas of poverty and welfare. Lyndon Johnson's War on Poverty was strongly shaped by the sociologists of his day, while the Nixon and Carter welfare reform plans bore the mark of economists who believed a negative income tax could reconcile supporting the poor with motivating them to work. In the conservative era, evaluations by the Manpower Demonstration Research Corporation helped establish welfare work programs as a dominant approach to reform. Prescriptions further to the right, which called for narrowing welfare coverage in order to discourage unwed pregnancy, came from Charles Murray, Robert Rector, and other experts from conservative think tanks (Weaver, 2000, pp. 211–17).

The stronger the political position of a party, the more play is given to its more extreme tendencies. When Democratic majorities controlled the White House and Congress during the 1960s, their liberal wings, under the guidance of economists, had more power to shape the welfare agenda. The bureaucracy expanded in that era to pursue ambitious social programming. Some economists gained civil service positions and so retained much of their influence even after the White House turned conservative. Nixon and Reagan struggled to control these officials by downsizing the bureaucracy and supervising it with political appointees. Even under Reagan and Bush, as long as Democrats controlled Congress, liberal experts still influenced policy. Clinton could not sign PRWORA without causing several prominent welfare experts to resign from his administration.

When the GOP gained control of Congress in 1994, it curbed liberal intellectual influence but brought a new surge of elitism from the right. Republican reformers were more divided than their liberal counterparts. They included, alongside work enforcers and budget cutters, others who wanted to "get welfare out of Washington" and still others who wanted to use welfare to halt the decline of the family. These more antigovernment tendencies had never gained sway over national policy before. They aimed to reverse not just a permissive welfare policy, but other liberal policies going back to the Great Society. All strains agreed on the need to promote individual responsibility, but they did not agree on how this should be done. The budget cutters and devolvers wanted to reduce the federal presence, while the work enforcers and the family conservatives wanted to use it to uphold traditional mores. The conflicting tendencies explain the complexity seen in the Contract with America and, later, in PRWORA (Weaver, 2000, pp. 117–23, 255–93).

What is worrisome about these patterns is that neither side seems very accountable to the other, or to the facts. John Stuart Mill's argument for the free market of ideas is that it promotes the truth by forcing the proponents of any position to come to terms with opponents. Similarly, James Madison's image of the American political arena, set out in *Federalist* No. 10, aimed to force factions to adjust to each other, thus promoting a broader conception of the public interest. But scholars find that not much direct debate actually occurs in American government. Policy in each area is made mostly by separate agencies and congressional committees in which the basics about what to do are largely agreed. Only at long intervals are the fundamental choices forced onto the table.

In Congress, lack of accountability is promoted by strong incumbency. Sitting members have such an advantage over their challengers at election time that over 90 percent of House members have been routinely reelected in recent years. They can win their districts through name recognition and service to constituents, without a serious need to come to terms with opponents or voters on policy matters. For these reasons, it seemed for decades that the Democratic majority in Congress might never be broken, particularly in the House. That in turn made fundamental rethinking in social policy less likely. The elections of 1992 and 1994 did bring much greater turnover and Republican control, with radical welfare change as one result. This clearly was exceptional. The evenly divided Congress elected in 2000 is unlikely to be so resolute.

There is also unaccountability among the issue networks that surround politicians. Most liberal experts who advise Democrats on antipoverty policy believe that social barriers, such as racial bias or lack of good jobs or child care, make it unrealistic for most of the needy to support themselves. They regret the efforts to enforce work that animate the welfare initiatives of the past twenty years. Many also believe that the motivation behind reform is to save money, and that PRWORA will generate a "race to the bottom" as states compete to deny coverage to the poor.

On the other side, the conservative intellectuals who advise Republicans believe that traditional welfare is the main source of unwed pregnancy and other social ills. These experts thought that work programs by themselves could not reduce dependency by much. They wanted to deny coverage to unwed teen mothers and children born on the rolls, provisions PRWORA made optional for states. Some also wanted to devolve welfare to localities or, even better, to churches and the private sector (Weaver, 2000, chaps. 5–6).

Hard evidence raises questions about both of these viewpoints. Social barriers do not explain well why poor adults seldom work steadily. The fact that the welfare rolls have fallen by over half in the last five years, with most of the leavers working and without much hardship, confirms that many more of the poor can work than most academics believed. Work enforcement appears to be the main reason for the decline in welfare, although economic conditions and wage subsidies also mattered (Ellwood, 1999). Nor have Washington or the states cut back spending on aid. Rather, by addressing concerns about deservedness, welfare reform seems likely to usher in a more liberal period of programming for the poor.

On the other hand, there is little evidence to suggest that welfare incentives explain illegitimacy or other social evils. The recent reduction in the caseload has not caused dramatic improvements in family problems; rather, positive trends that predate PRWORA continue (Haskins, 1999, pp. 32–35). States are instituting work requirements, but they are cautious about enforcing time limits on recipients who are trying to work (Haveman and Vobejda, 1998). They have taken no serious steps to deter unwed pregnancies. This is because, as noted earlier, the public is much more ambivalent about family issues than it is about work and—more fundamentally—because programs able to prevent illegitimacy have not yet appeared (Nathan and Gais, 1999; Weaver, 2000, pp. 344–47). Meanwhile, coupled with a good economy and wage subsidies, stronger work requirements have proven quite sufficient to transform welfare. Along the way, they may have brought some positive effects on the family as well (Knox, Miller, and Gennetian, 2000). Time limits and antipregnancy efforts have played a minor role.

These trends have forced opposing camps to reach some convergence in the past decade. Some liberal politicians and experts now accept that cash aid to families must be time-limited, and that work expectations of some kind must be attached to it. Many conservatives accept that welfare cannot simply be abolished and that enforcing work implies an ongoing commitment to help the poor. Both sides have agreed on much tougher enforcement of child support, with little dissent.

The two sides continue to differ, however, over entitlement and the family. Liberals would still like some kind of ultimate safety net to be available to families regardless of behavior, and they would like education and training to count toward fulfilling work requirements, positions unacceptable to the architects of PRWORA. For their part, some conservatives would still curb welfare in order to promote marriage and deter illegitimacy, purposes that are anathema to the left. The chance to resolve these differences is perhaps greatest in Congress, where the two sides debate openly. Among experts there is less engagement; liberals tend to be based in the universities, conservatives in think tanks.

Most elite networks control policy because they know more about the issues than the ignorant public. That would certainly be true of health or foreign policy, for example. But in the case of welfare, the public has proven wiser than most experts. Elites on either the left or right continue to understand the welfare problem largely in terms of the scale of government. One side would do more for the poor, the other less. The public, however, has focused on changing the nature of welfare, on attaching work tests to existing benefits. That is by and large what PRWORA and earlier conservative reforms did. That is the step that has broken the mold of the old welfare and shown a new way forward.

As yet nothing at the national level approaches the meeting of minds that occurred in Wisconsin. There the two sides came to terms with each other's chief concerns more fully than has ever happened in Washington. Most Democrats accepted that welfare had to be refounded on work requirements, thus abandoning entitlement. Most Republicans accepted that the government's commitment to the poor should not be questioned; merely, the form of it would change. Under W-2, the government is smaller in the sense that dependency is reduced, but the government's mission—to support the low-income population in and through work—is even broader than when the goal was only to aid the needy. Family issues were avoided. The reform was based squarely on public opinion and the experience of administrators. The influence of intellectuals, either left or right, was minimized. This was the concordat that gave a new mandate for the welfare state (Mead, 2000).

Implications for Reauthorization

The clearest implication of past politics is that the reauthorization of TANF should be based more on public opinion than the original enactment was. Not only is this politic and proper on democratic grounds, but the voters have a better track record in dealing with welfare than experts of any persuasion.

TANF should be amended to ensure that it really enforces work. PRWORA told states to raise the share of adult recipients involved in work activities in steps, reaching half or more by 2002. But the states were also allowed to count against those targets any percent by which their caseloads have fallen since 1995. Because the decline in caseloads was unexpectedly sharp, the effect was to knock the bottom out of the work standards. All states now meet them, usually easily. While work requirements are strengthening at the local level, that appears to be due more to their earlier momentum, stemming from the Family Support Act and state decisions, than to current federal requirements. The caseload reduction credit should be withdrawn so that the laggard states, which typically have the largest caseloads, will once more feel pressure to rebuild the administration of aid around work. A way must also be found to bring child-only cases—in which the caretaker is not on the grant, usually because she is an alien—under the work requirement.

At the same time, the public expects that welfare will continue to be generous to needy families. Recent steps to make work pay, such as raising the minimum wage and the Earned Income Tax Credit (EITC) and expanding Medicaid, help to meet that demand. But whether they are off welfare or on, single mothers remain poor principally because they do not work normal hours. This means that work-connected benefits do them little good. The main need may now be for services to help former recipients keep jobs and move up to better ones. This cost implies that TANF funding should not be cut by as much as the caseload decline might suggest. To promote higher work levels, perhaps EITC eligibility should be conditioned on some minimum of working hours, as benefits have been in some recent successful work incentive programs (Michalopoulos and others, 1999; Knox, Miller, and Gennetian, 2000).

In the reauthorization, Congress should resist calls by liberal members and their academic supporters for new benefits unconnected to work effort, such as a return to the education and training strategy of the Family Support Act. That would be a step back toward the philosophy of entitlement—helping people simply because they are poor—that the public and events have rejected. At the same time, Congress should think more carefully about how to deter unwed pregnancy, rather than rush to enact new programs in this area. A direct assault on family problems must await a clearer public mandate and the development of more effective programs. The best way to help children and strengthen marriage at present is simply to enforce work on welfare mothers, and also on fathers owing child support, and then to provide support to working families.

The goal is a new welfare state in which families get several kinds of help to raise children, provided they work seriously. That is the combination the public has longed for ever since welfare erupted as a national issue in the 1960s. Wisconsin and the other leading states show that such a system is indeed within reach. To achieve it, however, will take more resolute, and less elitist, welfare politics than Washington has yet seen.

References

Baumgartner, Frank R., and Bryan D. Jones. 1993. *Agendas and Instability in American Politics.* University of Chicago Press.

Bobo, Lawrence, and Ryan A. Smith. 1994. "Antipoverty Policy, Affirmative Action, and Racial Attitudes." In *Confronting Poverty: Prescriptions for Change,* edited by Sheldon H. Danziger, Gary D. Sandefur, and Daniel H. Weinberg. Russell Sage.

Cook, Fay Lomax, and Edith J. Barrett. 1992. *Support for the American Welfare State: The Views of Congress and the Public.* Columbia University Press.

Ellwood, David T. 1996. "Welfare Reform As I Knew It: When Bad Things Happen to Good Policies." *American Prospect* 7 (May–June): 22–27.

———. 1999. "The Impact of the Earned Income Tax Credit and Social Policy Reforms on Work, Marriage, and Living Arrangements." Unpublished manuscript. Harvard University, Kennedy School of Government.

Gilens, Martin. 1999. *Why Americans Hate Welfare: Race, Media, and the Politics of Antipoverty Policy.* University of Chicago Press.

Gueron, Judith M. 1996. "A Research Context for Welfare Reform." *Journal of Policy Analysis and Management* 15 (Fall): 547–61.

Haskins, Ron. 1999. *Welfare in a Society of Permanent Work.* Washington: U.S. House of Representatives, Committee on Ways and Means.

Havemann, Judith, and Barbara Vobejda. 1998. "The Welfare Alarm That Didn't Go Off," *Washington Post,* October 1, p. A1.

Heclo, Hugh. 1978. "Issue Networks and the Executive Establishment." In *The New American Political System,* edited by Anthony King. Washington: American Enterprise Institute.

———. 1986a. "General Welfare and Two American Political Traditions." *Political Science Quarterly* 101 (2): 179–96.

———. 1986b. "The Political Foundations of Antipoverty Policy." In *Fighting Poverty: What Works and What Doesn't,* edited by Sheldon H. Danziger and Daniel H. Weinberg. Harvard University Press.

———. 1994. "Poverty Politics." In *Confronting Poverty: Prescriptions for Change,* edited by Sheldon H. Danziger, Gary D. Sandefur, and Daniel H. Weinberg. Russell Sage.

———. 1995. "The Social Question." In *Poverty, Inequality, and the Future of Social Policy,* edited by Katherine McFate, Roger Lawson, and William Julius Wilson. Russell Sage.

Iyengar, Shanto. 1987. "Television News and Citizens' Explanations of National Affairs." *American Political Science Review* 81 (September): 815–32.

———. 1989. "How Citizens Think about Issues: A Matter of Responsibility." *American Journal of Political Science* 33 (November): 878–900.

———. 1990. "Framing Responsibility for Political Issues: The Case of Poverty." *Political Behavior* 12 (March): 19–40.

Kingdon, John W. 1995 *Agendas, Alternatives, and Public Policies,* 2d ed. HarperCollins.

Knox, Virginia, Cynthia Miller, and Lisa A. Gennetian. 2000. *Reforming Welfare and Rewarding Work: A Summary of the Final Report on the Minnesota Family Investment Program.* New York: Manpower Demonstration Research Corporation.

Mead, Lawrence M. 2000. "The Politics of Welfare Reform in Wisconsin." *Polity* 32 (Summer): 533–59.

Michalopoulos, Charles, Philip K. Robins, David E. Card, and Gordon Berlin, 1999. "When Financial Incentives Encourage Work: The Canadian Self-Sufficiency Project." *Focus* 20 (Fall): 37–43.

Nathan, Richard P., and Thomas L. Gais. 1999. *Implementing the Personal Responsibility Act of 1996: A First Look.* State University of New York at Albany, Rockefeller Institute of Government.

Schiltz, Michael E. 1970. *Public Attitudes Toward Social Security, 1935-1965.* Research Report 33. U.S. Government Printing Office.

Shanks, J. Merrill, and Warren E. Miller. 1990. "Policy Direction and Performance Evaluation: Complementary Explanations of the Reagan Elections." *British Journal of Political Science* 20 (part 2, April): 143–79.

Sniderman, Paul M., and Edward G. Carmines. 1997. "Reaching beyond Race." *PS* 30 (September): 466–71.

Sniderman, Paul M., and Thomas Piazza. 1993. *The Scar of Race.* Harvard University Press.

Teles, Steven M. 1996. *Whose Welfare? AFDC and Elite Politics.* University Press of Kansas.

Thornton, Arland. 1995. "Attitudes, Values, and Norms Related to Nonmarital Fertility."
    In *Report to Congress on Out-of-Wedlock Childbearing,* edited by U.S. Department of
    Health and Human Services. U.S. Government Printing Office.
Weaver, R. Kent. 2000. *Ending Welfare As We Know It.* Brookings.

PART **III**

*Specific Issues
and Policies*

8

JULIE STRAWN
MARK GREENBERG
STEVE SAVNER

Improving Employment Outcomes under TANF

A SET OF IDEAS often called "work first" has played an important role in shaping state approaches to implementing the 1996 welfare law. The key beliefs of this perspective are that education and job training are not effective for unemployed parents; that the best way to promote employment is to focus on immediate job placement, regardless of job quality; and that the best way for individuals to advance in the labor force is to build a work history or participate in education and training activities while working.

A review of the experience since 1996 suggests both the strengths and limits of this approach. Since 1996 the nation has seen an unprecedented decline in welfare caseloads, much of which has been attributable to employment. However, most of the newly employed are in low-wage jobs, and the evidence to date suggests that welfare leavers frequently lose their jobs and have limited upward mobility. Research findings since 1996 support the premise that Temporary Assistance for Needy Families (TANF) programs can do much more to address job quality while maintaining a strong focus on rapid employment entry, through a range of approaches including improved job matching, better use of labor market information, closer links to employers, and increased access to skill-building activities.

This chapter summarizes the reasons behind the shift to a work first philosophy, the initial experiences and outcomes, state responses, and key research findings relevant to thinking about next steps. It concludes with recommendations for TANF reauthorization that would make improved labor market outcomes for low-income parents an explicit purpose of the law and provide for broad state flexibility and meaningful accountability in reaching that objective.

The Work First Philosophy and TANF Framework

The shift toward work first began before 1996. Under the 1988 Family Support Act, states had broad discretion in determining the mix of education and training, job search, work experience, and other components in their welfare reform efforts. However, the law required states to include basic education as a mandatory activity for individuals without high school diplomas or with weak basic skills, and many states strongly emphasized basic education.

Early in the 1990s, the beginnings of a new direction became evident. Implementation of the Family Support Act coincided with an economic downturn and rapid caseload growth; the rapid caseload growth led many to question the approach states had taken. At the same time, evaluations of programs' short-term impacts suggested that stand-alone basic education programs were having little or no effect on employment. Findings from California's GAIN program, particularly in Riverside County, suggested that programs requiring participants to take any job quickly could help them join the work force and reduce caseloads more rapidly than could basic education. (In fact, Riverside allowed substantial participation in education, but that was not widely understood.) This short-term evidence coincided with the observations of many state officials, and a general reorientation toward a work first philosophy was apparent in numerous state waiver proposals before the enactment of the 1996 law.

The 1996 law consolidated and accelerated the work first trend through a set of key features. First, the fiscal structure of the block grant placed a premium on caseload reduction because a state's federal funding stayed constant whether the caseload grew or shrank. Caseload reduction was seen as necessary to manage within the framework. Further, states had a strong incentive to reduce caseloads because they could keep any federal funds saved.

Second, the law established "participation rates" for families receiving TANF and fiscal penalties for states that failed to meet the required rates. To count as a participant, an individual must be involved in one of a listed set of work-related activities for a specified number of hours each week. Education and training activities count to only a very limited extent and generally cannot count for more than twelve months for individuals working fewer than twenty hours a week. As a technical matter, states were free to allow, pay for, and support an activity regardless of whether the activity counted toward participation rates. Nevertheless, the federal listing of countable activities strongly influenced which activities were allowed. In addition, states received a "caseload reduction credit," which lowered the state's participation rate, if the state's caseload declined for reasons other than changes in eligibility rules; this created a strong additional incentive for caseload reduction.

The 1996 law further encouraged work first by imposing time limits on the use of federal funds to provide assistance, eliminating all prior federal exemptions from work-related requirements, and broadening state authority to impose sanctions (grant reductions or terminations).

TANF Implementation and Labor Market Outcomes

The initial implementation of TANF in most states solidified a set of work first policies. By 1997–98 most states had developed programs that reduced or eliminated exemptions from work activities; increased penalties for failure to comply with work requirements; increased financial supports for families in which an adult became employed; and imposed time limits on cash assistance (State Policy Documentation Project, 2000). A handful of states adopted policies providing for universal or near-universal participation coupled with broad flexibility about the nature of activities in which an individual was required to participate. More commonly, however, state policies narrowed the range of allowable activities to restrict access to education and training and to achieve a focus on rapid job entry. Common state policies included:

—Applicant diversion policies and practices: In October 1999, twenty states required participants to look for a job while an application for assistance was pending, and twenty-three states offered lump-sum cash payments to families who agreed not to apply for assistance (State Policy Documentation Project, 2000). Many states also employed less formal policies of discouraging application until other avenues were exhausted.

—Requiring job search for many applicants and recipients: Twenty-eight states required a job search as the first work-related activity for all nonexempt or "job ready" adults.

—Increased use of unpaid work experience and community service: Though not used as broadly as some had predicted, unpaid work experience gained increasing favor as states implemented TANF. The absolute numbers of participants in unpaid work experience programs still reflect a small share of the caseload—about 5.2 percent of adult TANF recipients in 1999. However, excluding individuals in unsubsidized employment, the majority of people (51 percent) who counted toward participation rates in 1999 were in unpaid work experience programs or doing community service. By contrast, in fiscal year 1995 only 0.9 percent of adults receiving Aid to Families with Dependent Children (AFDC) participated in community work experience or other unpaid work activities, and only 6.2 percent of those counted toward the Job Opportunities and Basic Skills Training (JOBS) participation rate (see Turner and Main, chapter 11).

—Decreased use of education and training: The percentage of AFDC and TANF adults participating in education and training activities fell sharply between 1996 and 1997.

Of course, not every state adopted a work first philosophy, and not every state in which the predominant focus had been work first adopted all of these policy initiatives. However, the fundamental shift to emphasizing job search and work experience and curtailing access to education and training was clear and unmistakable as states implemented TANF.

Implementing TANF, states saw a historically unprecedented decline in the number of families receiving assistance. Studies have consistently found that most families who leave welfare have found work (Loprest, 1999) and that labor force participation has increased among female-headed families. In addition, an increasing share of TANF adults are employed while receiving assistance: 28 percent in fiscal year 1999, as compared with only 8 percent in fiscal year 1994.

Most employed welfare leavers are in low-paying jobs that provide limited or no employment benefits. According to the Urban Institute's nationally representative study, the median wage for working TANF leavers in 1997 was $6.61 per hour. Moreover, employed leavers were unlikely to receive employer-provided health care coverage or paid sick or vacation leave; the Urban Institute study found that 23 percent of employed leavers had been receiving employer-provided health care coverage (Loprest, 1999). Studies in individual states have produced similar findings (Devere, Falk, and Burk, 2000).

Prior research had found that employment loss was a significant problem for welfare parents entering employment and that the small earnings growth for those entering employment was primarily a result of working more hours or weeks in a year rather than higher wages (Strawn and Martinson, 2000). State studies provide little information about employment retention and advancement; the studies with longitudinal data usually found some earnings growth over time, but median annual earnings for adults who have left assistance are probably in the range of $8,000 to $12,000 (HHS, 2000; Cancian and others, 2000).

Can We Do Better? Lessons from Recent Research

The outcomes found by studies of TANF leavers are generally consistent with findings from earlier research on the impacts of welfare-to-work programs, which typically emphasized either job search or adult basic education services. Recent evaluations and labor market research suggest more effective welfare-to-work strategies that have the potential to help low-income parents find better jobs than they typically find on their own.

The Limits of Job Search and Basic Education

Rigorous research finds that job search–focused programs have consistently increased employment rates among low-income parents in the near term but that these results are often not sustained over the long term. For example, the National Evaluation of Welfare-to-Work Strategies (NEWWS) studied eleven welfare-to-work programs and found that those focused primarily on job search activities produced larger gains in employment and total earnings over a two-year period than adult education–focused programs. However, earnings gains in two of the three programs that focused on job search declined by the end of two years, while earnings gains in five of the seven education-focused programs grew to equal or slightly surpass them. Longer follow-up is needed to determine which approaches are ultimately most effective and for which groups (Freedman and others, 2000). Other studies have shown that the earnings gains initially shown by job search–focused programs often fade entirely within five years (Friedlander and Burtless, 1995; Strawn, 1998). Two notable exceptions were the GAIN programs in Riverside and San Diego Counties, each of which made substantial use of education and training in addition to job search (Freedman and others, 1996). Moreover, earnings gains from programs emphasizing job search generally resulted from welfare recipients' working more hours, not from attaining better jobs.

This is not to suggest that TANF would get better results if it used the approach of the Family Support Act and focused on basic education rather than job search. Despite the prevalence of low basic skills among welfare recipients, basic education–focused programs in the past have also failed to help recipients find higher-paying jobs than they would have on their own and were not as consistently successful as job search in increasing employment rates and earnings (Freedman and others, 2000; Strawn, 1998). At best, basic education programs achieve employment and earnings effects that are similar to job search, while taking longer and costing more. The programs that have been most successful with nongraduates have not relied primarily on either education or job search, but have used both as well as other services (Michalopoulos, Schwartz, and Adams-Ciardullo, 2000).

In general, the most effective welfare-to-work programs have had a "mixed strategy," using a flexible, balanced approach that offers a mix of job search, education, job training, and work activities (Freedman and others, 2000). Successful employment programs more generally provide individualized services; have a central focus on employment; have close ties to local employers; and are intensive, setting high expectations of participants (Strawn, 1998).

Some of the mixed-strategy programs have not only increased employment but have also helped welfare recipients find better jobs than they would have on their own. The best recent example is the Steps to Success program in Portland, Oregon, which is described in the NEWWS evaluation (for other examples, see Cave and others, 1993; Friedlander and Burtless, 1995; Zambrowski and Gordon, 1993). Portland provided a mix of services, including job search, life skills, work-focused basic education, and occupational training. Of the eleven NEWWS sites, Portland participants worked and earned more than participants in the three work first programs and increased their receipt of occupational licenses, certificates, and general equivalency diplomas (GEDs) by as much as the participants in the seven education-focused sites. Portland increased stable employment, hourly wages, and access to full-time work and employer-provided benefits for both high school graduates and those who entered the program without a high school diploma (Freedman and others, 2000).

How did Portland achieve its results? The evaluation design makes the answer difficult to pinpoint, but the general strategy is clear. The program helped high school graduates with solid basic skills and some work experience find better jobs primarily through careful job matching and job development. For those who entered the program with low skills or had not graduated from high school, Portland taught life skills, work-focused adult education, and occupational training. Parents were expected to participate full time, and program participation and employment were supported by a strong system for connecting parents with supports such as child care and specialized services to address specific barriers.

In addition, for those without high school diplomas or GEDs, access to occupational training may have been a key to Portland's success. The three NEWWS sites that most increased hourly pay for high school dropouts— Columbus, Detroit, and Portland—also boosted participation by this group in postsecondary education or occupational training. Only Portland, however, substantially increased their receipt of occupational licenses and certificates, an unusual achievement among welfare-to-work programs (Freedman and others, 2000).

The Importance of Initial Job Quality in Labor Market Outcomes

Evaluation research shows that it is possible to help welfare recipients find better jobs, and several recent labor market studies underscore the importance of doing so. These studies use national survey data to identify and disaggregate the personal, family, and job factors that predict how welfare recipients fare in the labor market over the long term. Although this research controls for many observable differences among those studied (such as skills, education, work history, and wages), unobservable differences (such as motivation, interpersonal skills, and family support) are likely important and are not accounted for in these analyses.

Factors Linked to Steady Work

Working steadily initially is linked to sustaining employment over time. Women who worked more in the first year after leaving welfare were more likely to be employed four and five years after leaving welfare, particularly if they worked full-time, all year (Cancian and Meyer, 2000).

Controlling for individual characteristics, the quality of an initial job as measured by wages and benefits is linked to the likelihood of maintaining employment over time. Rangarajan, Schochet, and Chu (1998) find that women who began working at higher wages worked more weeks over a five-year period. Rangarajan, Meckstroth, and Novak's 1998 study of women in four cities who left welfare for work found that those with higher wages were more likely to stay employed. This is consistent with earlier studies (Strawn and Martinson, 2000). Rangarajan and her colleagues also found that those who began jobs that offered paid vacation stayed employed for an average of twelve months at a time; in contrast, those without paid vacation stayed employed for only seven months. Similarly, those who began working in jobs that offered health insurance worked 77 percent of the following two years; those without insurance worked 56 percent of the time.

Some studies find that starting in certain occupations is linked to sustaining employment over time. Cancian and Meyer (2000) found that women who began working in sales were less likely to work in the fourth and fifth years after leaving welfare than women who started in other common occupations, such as private housekeeping, building cleaning or maintenance, clerical, and private sector care (including health care and formal child care). Two other studies also found a relationship between initial occupations and future employment; a third study did not (Strawn and Martinson, 2000).

Factors Linked to Better Jobs

One set of studies looked at factors associated with higher wages over time for women who received welfare (again holding many observable job and personal factors equal). Most studies have concluded that wages grow very modestly—by about 1 percent annually—for women who have received welfare (Strawn and Martinson, 2000), even when they work steadily (Cancian and Meyer, 2000; Rangarajan, Meckstroth, and Novak, 1998). Research by Corcoran and Loeb (1999) found a higher average rate of wage growth for each year worked by welfare recipients, though the rate was lower for those with lower basic skills, those working part-time, and those with additional children. This latter study is consistent with Gladden and Taber's (2000a) research, which showed similar rates of wage growth for lower-skilled workers as for other workers—about 4 percent for each full year of work. However, these researchers point out that given their initially low wages, even rates of wage growth as high as 4 percent are unlikely to make a substantial difference in whether families leaving welfare escape poverty (Gladden and Taber, 2000a; 2000b).

Several studies have found that changing jobs can be a path to higher wages for women who have received welfare (Cancian and Meyer, 2000; Rangarajan, 1998). However, involuntary job changes and more than one voluntary job change a year are associated with lower wages (Gladden and Taber, 2000a).

For women leaving welfare, higher initial wages are linked to greater wage growth over time. Cancian and Meyer (2000), like earlier researchers (see Strawn and Martinson, 2000), found that the initial wages of women leaving welfare are strongly linked to future wages (four or five years later), even after controlling for other work history and job and personal factors. However, Gladden and Taber (2000b), in looking at lower-skilled workers more generally, did not find lower rates of wage growth at the bottom of the wage distribution.

Starting in certain occupations is linked to subsequent higher wages. Cancian and Meyer (1997) found that, in comparison with those who began working in sales, women who started in clerical positions earned 22 percent more per hour five years later, those who began in production and manufacturing or building cleaning and maintenance earned 17 percent more per hour, and those in private care (including health care and formal child care) earned 15 percent more per hour.

Higher basic skills, and especially education beyond high school, are strongly linked to subsequent higher wages. Cancian and Meyer (1997) found that women leaving welfare whose initial basic skills scores were in the top three-fourths of all scores earned about 8 percent more per hour in the fourth and fifth years than those with scores in the bottom fourth. Having a high school diploma mattered little for wage growth after controlling for factors such as basic skills level, how much individuals worked, and at what kinds of jobs, but post–high school education or training was strongly linked to subsequent higher wages. Corcoran and Loeb (1999) found similar results. This is consistent with other research on the returns to cognitive skills and educational attainment in the labor market (Tyler, Murnane, and Willett, 2000).

The above research suggests some important policy implications:

—Helping welfare recipients and other low-skilled parents retain their jobs or quickly become reemployed after losing a job may promote steady work in later years.

—Steady work alone is unlikely to lead to significantly higher-paying jobs for many welfare recipients and other low-skilled parents.

—Changing jobs strategically can lead to higher-paying jobs.

—Helping welfare recipients and other low-skilled parents find jobs with higher pay or benefits may promote both steady work and further job advancement in later years.

—Over the long term, better access to postsecondary education or training is likely to be an important piece of the solution to promoting access to better jobs.

Increasing Access to Better Jobs

The research described above suggests that it is possible and important to help low-income parents enter better jobs—with higher wages and benefits—while still focusing on rapid employment.

The optimal approach includes three key elements: (1) better job matching to place low-income parents in the best possible jobs initially and to help them advance after they are working; (2) targeted skill upgrading on basic and job skills in demand in the local labor market for low-income parents while they are working, preferably during work hours, at or near the work site; and (3) investments in skill upgrading for low-income parents during periods of unemployment. These job advancement services should be provided as part of a comprehensive program that includes supportive services, income supplements, and initiatives for the harder-to-employ (see Zedlewski and Loprest, chapter 12).

How does such a strategy compare with the actual response of states to evidence of low earnings, few job benefits, and frequent job loss by TANF leavers? First, states appear to be focusing primarily on helping low-income parents sustain employment; there has been less attention to helping them get better jobs. For example, many states have developed postemployment retention services and have been paying more attention to "work supports" such as Medicaid, food stamps, child care, and the earned income tax credit for families leaving TANF and other low-wage workers. Second, some states have developed postemployment advancement services for families leaving TANF assistance. Third, some states have begun to reexamine services for low-income parents who are not yet working or are between jobs and to explore policies that combine a strong employment focus with greater attention to job quality.

Postemployment Retention Services

As of October 1999, thirty-four states were providing case management for at least some recipients who had found jobs or no longer received cash assistance. Thirty-two states were providing supportive services aimed at employment retention other than health care, child care, and financial help or incentives. Postemployment supportive services most commonly include transportation aid, the purchase of work clothing or tools, and the payment of work-related fees. Half a dozen states were providing short-term cash payments to help cover work expenses, several offered cash bonuses for keeping or finding jobs or leaving TANF, and several provided cash payments to cover emergencies (State Policy Documentation Project, 2000). Many of these postemployment benefits and services are new, and little information about utilization exists.

Some working families will undoubtedly be helped by postemployment retention services, but it is unclear whether the new policies will increase steady work among low-income parents. A rigorous evaluation of postemployment services (case management combined with cash payments for employment-related expenses and emergency expenses) in four cities found that the services had no impact on how long welfare recipients kept jobs or how much they earned (Rangarajan and Novak, 1999). An earlier evaluation of similar services also found no impacts (Strawn and Martinson, 2000). Case studies of retention services provided by small private agencies suggest ways to improve outcomes for those receiving postemployment case management, but no rigorous, independent evaluations of these programs have been done. Such programs are also very small. It would be prohibitively expensive to replicate their low client-to-caseworker ratios for all women leaving welfare, and to date it has been difficult to predict which women are at highest risk of job loss. The programs differ significantly from the typical state approach by pairing postemployment retention services either with months of preemployment training in job readiness, basic skills, and jobs skills or by screening out the least-employable initial participants before trying to find the others jobs (Strawn and Martinson, 2000).

There is no rigorous research concerning work expense allowances or employment and retention bonuses for women who have received welfare. Recent research on two programs that provided substantial ongoing financial assistance for working families, the Minnesota Family Investment Program (MFIP) and Canada's Self-Sufficiency Program (SSP), does show increases in stable employment for participants (see Michalopoulos and Berlin, chapter 10). Whether smaller, shorter-term financial help will produce the same results is unknown. Expanded child care subsidy assistance may also help parents better sustain employment, but little research is available.

Postemployment Job Advancement Services

As of October 1999, sixteen states had policies to provide post-TANF services aimed at job advancement. These included contracting directly for education, training, employment, and career counseling services; tuition assistance; and individual training accounts. A small but growing number of states—about half a dozen—are creating broader initiatives that are designed to serve working, low-income families generally (State Policy Documentation Project, 2000). In some cases, education and training are provided at the work site, with services customized to employer needs. As with postemployment retention services, it is unclear how many families are actually involved in these initiatives, but the number appears to be small.

There is little research on what postemployment advancement policies can achieve. On-the-job training produced increases in earnings for welfare recipients in sixteen programs funded by the Job Training Partnership Act and in demonstrations in Maine and New Jersey. Both higher wages and more hours of work contributed to the higher earnings of the program groups (Gueron and Pauly, 1991; Orr and others, 1996). On-the-job training has typically operated on a small scale and has been reserved for the most employable welfare recipients. Nonexperimental evidence on customized training programs suggests they can increase wages and job retention. Until recently, however, these programs have rarely included low-income parents (Strawn and Martinson, 2000).

Little information exists on the results of current postemployment job advancement efforts. In the handful of states, such as Florida and Utah, with some years of experience in offering financial assistance and support services to former recipients who enrolled in education or training, few people appear to have used these benefits. Participation appears somewhat higher in states with more proactive efforts, such as Oregon and Washington, to recruit and directly provide former recipients with education, training, and other advancement services, but the number of families served remains a small proportion of the target population. Participation in advancement services appears to be highest where services are provided at the work site and during work hours, but such employer-based initiatives are rare and on a small scale. State and local staff involved in such efforts typically say it is difficult to find employers interested in partnering in workplace training for the least-skilled workers. Some projects address this issue by combining TANF money with other funding so that training can be given both to newly employed welfare recipients and to incumbent workers at the same workplace. Nevertheless, scale remains an enormous barrier for these types of efforts (Strawn and Martinson, 2000).

Changes in Strategies for the Unemployed

Another state response to the problems of low wages and job loss has been to put more effort into helping unemployed parents find better jobs. Most commonly, states are increasing access to postsecondary education or training. In addition, some states are creating incentives for localities to match parents with higher-paying jobs rather than just any job.

In 1999 and 2000 a number of states expanded access to postsecondary education and training for TANF recipients. Some changed work requirements to allow participation in postsecondary education or training to meet all or most of a parent's work requirement beyond the twelve months that could count toward federal participation rates; some used TANF funds to create additional work-study positions; others created separate state student aid programs for low-income parents funded with state maintenance of effort (MOE) dollars; and some stopped the federal or state time-limit clock for recipients who were full-time students (State Policy Documentation Project, 2000; Wamhoff and Strawn, 2001). Although these state actions may suggest an emerging trend, most states still place substantial limits on access to education and training for TANF recipients.

Some states are using performance measures to encourage localities to match low-income parents with higher-paying and more stable jobs. TANF performance measures set by Alaska and Washington, for example, include wage growth and employment retention (Clymer, Roberts, and Strawn, 2001). It is worth noting that when Portland's program was evaluated in NEWWS, the Oregon TANF agency set targets for wages at placement that were substantially above the minimum wage (Scrivener and others, 1998).

Successful efforts to link unemployed parents to better jobs have achieved larger scale and higher participation than has been seen in postemployment initiatives to date. Given these practical advantages, states are more likely to help low-income parents find better jobs if their job matching and skill upgrading efforts are directed not just at low-income parents who are working but also those who are not yet employed or who are between jobs.

States and localities may find it difficult to replicate the success of a program like Portland's, however, without significant changes in policy and service delivery. Probably the most critical tasks are to involve employers directly in the design and delivery of services, to make occupational training more immediately accessible to those with low skills and to those who are working, and to supplement shorter-term training with opportunities to earn postsecondary degrees. One important step would be to integrate adult basic education and English as a Second Language services into occupational training whenever possible, or at least to provide them concurrently whenever possible (Strawn and Martinson, 2000).

Finally, despite job advancement efforts, it is likely that most former recipients and other low-skilled parents will continue to work at low-wage jobs; if increasing family income is a goal, then wage supplements and other antipoverty policies beyond welfare-to-work services will be needed.

Next Steps: Recommendations for TANF Reauthorization

TANF reauthorization will involve many issues (see Greenberg and others, 2000), but our recommendations here focus on job quality and employment retention and advancement. Some decisions about TANF could have large but indirect effects on state efforts. For example, a cut in block grant funding or MOE obligations could lead to smaller investments in new services and the curtailment of existing ones. Our discussion here, though, is limited to changes in TANF that could directly foster greater attention to job quality.

States are not prohibited from emphasizing job quality in the current TANF structure, but there is little to encourage or support it. Though the law emphasizes caseload reduction, it has no comparable emphasis on increasing family incomes; and though the law emphasizes work, it places little emphasis on wages, benefits, or other measures of job quality. We think that the federal role in TANF should not be to impose detailed prescriptions for state approaches, but rather to establish national goals and hoped-for outcomes, and to hold states accountable for making progress toward those goals and outcomes. Accordingly, our recommendations concern modifications to the goals of TANF, the state plan requirements, the high performance and accountability structure, and the participation rate provisions of the law.

First, the purposes of TANF should be revised to include the goal of reducing family poverty and promoting family economic well-being, and to make explicit that the goal of promoting work includes supporting employment retention and workforce advancement for needy families. The purposes of TANF affect whether particular expenditures are possible and signal congressional expectations. Modifying the purposes would provide a powerful statement that the next stage of TANF implementation envisions higher goals than caseload reduction.

Second, states should be required to describe in their state plans how TANF and other resources will be used and coordinated to promote employment retention and advancement and enhance family economic well-being. This would reinforce the signaling effects and perhaps help foster coordination. Although the federal government should not mandate a single strategy, states should be expected to articulate the strategies that they intend to use.

Third, the measures of state performance in TANF should strongly emphasize poverty reduction, sustained employment, earnings growth, and higher wages. The law currently provides for $200 million per year for high-performance bonuses, and the Department of Health and Human Services bases its allocation of that money on state outcomes, including employment entries, retention, and earnings gains. In the context of the overall block grant structure, the existing high-performance bonus involves a small amount of money, generates relatively little attention, does not measure poverty reduction, and has technical problems that make it an inadequate measure of sustained employment or earnings growth (Center for Law and Social Policy, 2000).

It is possible to improve the measures in the high-performance bonus structure, but efforts to promote accountability for outcomes need to go further. In the current structure, states can elect not to compete for the high-performance bonus. Moreover, each state seeking to win the bonus "competes" against every other state, and since there is no way to know in advance how other states will perform (or report performance), a state has little incentive to set clear benchmarks for its own performance. So, if a goal is to encourage states to place stronger emphasis on a set of employment outcomes, it may be more effective to ask each state, as part of preparing its state plan, to specify outcome goals and to incorporate mechanisms that would allow their performance to be measured. States could then be rewarded or penalized according to how well each met its goals. We recognize that this recommendation raises challenges as to how goals would be set and how performance would be measured; at the same time, we think it is fundamental that in a context of broad flexibility in use of resources, the federal focus should be on measuring and seeking accountability for key outcomes.

In any case, performance standards should measure outcomes for families receiving TANF assistance and for a broader group of low-income families. Many states now use TANF resources to build supports outside the welfare system so that families need not seek TANF assistance. TANF recipients are receiving a smaller share of federal block grant money, and measuring state performance should consider labor market participation and the poverty status of all low-income families, not just those in the cash assistance system.

Fourth, if participation rates are to be measured, the current approach to counting and measuring participation should be altered. Congress will need to revisit participation rules in 2002, and not solely because of the reasons discussed in this chapter. We have highlighted the restrictions on counting education and training and the caseload reduction incentives flowing from the caseload reduction credit. More broadly, in a context of a smaller caseload with more significant employment barriers, the restrictive listing of countable activities conflicts with the need to structure service strategies and individualized plans for people with multiple barriers and severe basic skills deficits. Because of the caseload reduction credit, many states now have effective rates at or near zero. The first impulse for some will be to raise rates, but simply raising rates without considering what counts and without addressing the perverse incentives created by the caseload reduction credit would only increase the likelihood that states would not develop effective service strategies for families with multiple barriers.

One problem with any participation rate approach is that it measures process, not outcomes. Thus one alternative to participation rates would be to develop results-oriented performance standards (as suggested earlier) and to substitute such performance standards for current participation rate rules. Another alternative might be to develop a broad expectation that all TANF recipients be engaged in employment, employment-related activities, or other state-approved activities, while allowing states broad flexibility in determining the nature of the activities.

If Congress maintains the participation rate approach, the rates should be revised to broaden what counts and end the "reward" for caseload reduction without regard to whether families have entered employment. For example, the law could be revised to allow states to count the time spent in approved activities identified in individualized plans. In addition, there should be no downward adjustment to participation rates for caseload decline; Congress may want to provide adjustments to reflect families that have left assistance for employment, but not for mere caseload decline itself.

TANF and Beyond

In this chapter, our discussion of job quality, retention, and advancement has been confined to the TANF framework. We have not addressed important questions about the relationship between TANF and state workforce development efforts under the Workforce Investment Act (WIA). And some of our discussion of needed changes in the delivery of employment and training services has implications both for WIA implementation and for the structure of and access to services under the Higher Education and Adult Education Acts. Moreover, the need for better access to targeted training between periods of employment should be relevant to discussions of unemployment insurance reforms. While a discussion of each of these systems is outside the scope of this chapter, it is important to consider changes in systems other than TANF that could enhance the labor market outcomes for low-income and low-skilled workers.

TANF reauthorization will provide an opportunity to set the framework for the next round of national and state efforts. In 1996 much of the focus was on the need to reduce caseloads and increase work among recipients, and both results occurred. In 2002 discussion should focus on the results that the nation hopes to see from the next round of efforts. If the desired results are sustained employment, earnings growth, and reduced poverty, it will be important to ensure that the TANF structure directly and indirectly communicates those goals.

COMMENT BY

Eloise Anderson

The chapter by Julie Strawn, Mark Greenberg, and Steve Savner states that the federal role in the Temporary Assistance for Needy Families (TANF) program should be to establish new national goals to reduce family poverty and promote family economic well-being. These goals, the authors believe, can be met by providing state assistance that supports employment retention and work advancement among welfare parents. Over the past forty years the federal government has invested billions in trying to reduce poverty. What seems to be missing from this and past discussions of poverty is an acknowledgment that those living in poverty need to make life changes in order to leave poverty. The notion that government—federal, state, or local—can keep people on the job or advance them in a job seems to be a prescription for failure for both the individual and the government. In addition, Strawn Greenberg, and Savner do not consider that there are two distinct recipient populations with very different service needs: those who are ready to work and those who need traditional social services.

Healthy adults in America who live in poverty need to be thought of as individuals who have made life choices that have contributed to their present circumstance. Welfare parents are not helpless children unable to make choices consistent with their wishes and desires. Policymakers and advocates often believe they can impose their will and goals on poor families. Welfare parents, mostly women, are seen as operating in a world without relationships. Their relationships, especially their intimates ones, influence how they respond to various government "incentives." In 1970, Edward Banfield observed that some poor people were not willing to regulate or change their present behavior for long-term benefits. Advocates for the poor who want them to change their behavior in order to achieve future benefits should consider Banfield's observation.

The authors' viewpoint seems to be that government can solve the problem of poverty and change life-styles and personal behavior. Their four recommendations would move government back to being responsible for the poor rather than making the poor personally responsible for their own lives. The recommendations would expand the role of the state, causing the state to intrude into the lives of the working poor until they reach some income level that satisfies federal policymakers and welfare advocates. Also, there seems to be a misconception about employment outside the nonprofit and government sectors. People who take jobs in the private sector must produce goods or services that at least equal their wages. An employee whose skills, knowledge, abilities, and reliability do not add to a business's bottom line is of little or negative value to the business and cannot be kept on the payroll for very long. Unless taxpayers are willing to subsidize employers for their losses when individuals are maintained in a job in which they are not productive, government efforts to promote job maintenance seem unlikely to work.

Reauthorization of TANF should not focus on changing the goals of TANF or requiring states to expand services. TANF goals and emphases are not a problem; there is, however, a problem with program location, structure, and mission.

TANF programs for the ready-to-work should be moved to the Department of Labor, where they would fit with other work force development and labor-oriented programs. The Department of Health and Human Services should focus attention on psychosocial and health issues. Welfare parents who have problems such as depression, substance abuse, or disability ought to be referred to mental health, alcohol, and other drug rehabilitation and disability programs. Conflicting organizational missions and goals hamper an organization's ability to be successful. Focusing primarily on labor market issues is not what social service agencies were organized to do. Their primary focus should be addressing the needs of those who are not ready to work. Work in this setting should be used as a therapeutic tool to move the recipient toward health.

Strawn, Greenberg, and Savner name several factors that lead welfare recipients to retain jobs. According to the research cited, welfare recipients stay in and advance in a job for the same reasons that other working persons do. In order to do reasonably well, a worker must enter the labor force with skills, knowledge, and abilities or be involved in skill development activities that will at some future date bring advancement. Equally important are the worker's motivation, interpersonal skills, and family supports. Yet these critical characteristics are not addressed in the chapter; they are simply mentioned as "likely important." Because these characteristics and having more than basic skills are important for holding a "quality" job, it is important that state and local social services agencies focus on psychosocial and physical health issues. Perhaps the most important task is program development for aid recipients who have never married and never worked.

The TANF program provides assistance to families with children. TANF reauthorization discussions should consider what is important for children's growth and development. Parental behavior and how parents fare in the work force must be considered an important influence on children. Therefore, it seems important to regard work not only as a means of gaining material resources but also as modeling behavior. Haveman, Wolfe, and Spaulding (1991) noted that parents being on welfare has a negative effect on children, especially adolescents. The viewpoint that poverty is an effect—not the cause—of the problems some welfare families face should be considered when forming policy. The problems some TANF families face are the leading cause of their poverty, not the other way around. However, many problems stem from conditions that occurred in their early childhood: health issues, including sexual and physical abuse; the absence of a father; and parental separation and divorce. Many cognitive disabilities are also the result of early experiences. These conditions and their many variations have placed some families in fragile economic conditions that in turn have jeopardized their children's well-being.

Welfare parents who enter the work force with few or limited skills are often parents who had their first child as an adolescent, did not complete high school, and have never worked. Women who were teenagers at the birth of their first child and have never been employed often enter the work force with many challenges. Their success in the world of work can occur, but it takes time; deficit reduction is a long-term proposition. For these parents, work should be seen as developmental. Their lack of skills, knowledge, and appropriate interpersonal relations, all of which can create problems in the workplace, can be viewed as adolescent deficiencies that can be overcome with training and education. Initially, low pay and multiple setbacks should be expected; over time, workplace "soft" skills will develop. For this group, job loss should not be seen as failure but as a constructive learning opportunity from which development can occur. The needs of these parents' children are paramount; therefore, early work experiences would best be focused on parenting and education. Work experience in a school classroom setting would introduce the routine of school and its expectations. Work experience in a child care setting would assist in the development of parenting skills. When soft skills, parenting skills, and the ability to maintain a job have been developed, further educational opportunities may be more readily accepted and utilized. This is a skills development approach.

The chapter states that educational programs for many welfare recipients do not work. Perhaps the recipients have not developed the skills required to be successful in the educational setting. The skills development approach introduces work, anticipates and corrects setbacks, and develops skills that are necessary for educational and child rearing success.

The impact of early childbearing on development has not been addressed for the adult parent in welfare programs. A strategy that helps develop the emotional and cognitive skills that very young mothers never acquired would rectify this oversight and put the emphasis back on personal responsibility.

Much of the research suggests that high school completion is important. A parent who completes high school has a high probability of getting a job with a salary above minimum wage and with benefits. Parents who have completed high school are also more likely to spend less time on welfare. Welfare parents are less educated than other adults. Therefore a state's prevention strategies should be focused on high school completion for the daughters of welfare recipients and girls from families in which the mother has not completed high school. Elementary and secondary schools must ensure that children have basic skills, and high schools must provide opportunities for work and vocational exploration that lead to work and technical and vocational training.

Barriers to employment that many recipients experience can be addressed by focusing on the other TANF goals. Danziger and her colleagues (1999) indicate that mental and physical health problems are important issues and that children's health problems and severe physical abuse are found in the welfare population in numbers disproportionate to those in the general population. Many recipients experience multiple barriers that make work and parenting more difficult. States should put more emphasis on the other TANF goals of keeping children with their families, decreasing out-of-wedlock births, and establishing, maintaining, and supporting marriage and two-parent families. Emphasizing these goals would help families more than would putting resources into workplace strategies. Welfare recipients have relationships with family, friends, and intimates. These relationships should be included in any attempt to eliminate employment barriers.

Some welfare families have family and personal issues that can best be addressed through the mental health system. Some TANF funds should be used to support the mental health system to provide services to these families. The work requirements for these families should be seen as part of the treatment program.

Rangarajan, Schochet, and Chu (1998) note that some of the difficulties TANF parents have are related to cognitive disabilities. Parents with persistent difficulties keeping a job should be assessed for possible cognitive disability. These families should be brought into the developmental disabilities (DD) system. The DD work programs, both sheltered and supportive, may be appropriate for many TANF recipients who are unable to keep a job. In addition, the DD system would help TANF recipients develop their parenting skills. The benefits of this network of resources will be realized over the long term, when the children become adolescents and their cognitive capacity is greater than their parents'.

Assisting families that are struggling with work demands a different way of thinking about the structure of services and the reality of these families' conditions, not placing a new requirement on the states.

References

Banfield, Edward. 1970. *The Unheavenly City Revisited.* Boston: Little, Brown.

Cancian, Maria, and Daniel R. Meyer. 1997. "Work after Welfare: Work Effort, Occupation, and Economic Well-Being." Paper prepared for the Annual Meeting of the Association for Public Policy Analysis and Management, Washington, October.

———. 2000. "Work after Welfare: Women's Work Effort, Occupation, and Economic Well-Being." *Social Work Research* 24 (2): 69–86.

Cancian, Maria, Robert Haveman, Daniel Meyer, and Barbara Wolfe. 2000. *Before and after TANF: The Economic Well-Being of Women Leaving Welfare.* Madison, Wisc.: Institute for Research on Poverty.

Cave, George, Hans Bos, Fred Doolittle, and Cyril Toussaint. 1993. *JOBSTART: Final Report on a Program for School Dropouts.* New York: Manpower Demonstration Research Corporation.

Center for Law and Social Policy and Center on Budget and Policy Priorities. 2000. *Comments on the Proposed Rule for the Bonus to Reward States for High Performance.* Washington.

Clymer, Carol, Brandon Roberts, and Julie Strawn. 2001. *Stepping Up: State Policies and Programs to Promote Low-Wage Workers' Steady Employment and Advancement.* Boston: Jobs for the Future.

Corcoran, Mary, and Susanna Loeb. 1999. "Will Wages Grow with Experience for Welfare Mothers? *Focus* (Institute for Research on Poverty, Madison, Wisc.) 20 (2): 20–21.

Danziger, Sandra, and others. 1999. "Barriers to the Employment of Welfare Recipients." Unpublished manuscript. University of Michigan.

Devere, Christine, Gene Falk, and Vee Burke. 2000. *Welfare Reform Research: What Have We Learned since the Family Support Act of 1988.* RL30724. Washington: Congressional Research Service.

Freedman, Stephen, Daniel Friedlander, Gayle Hamilton, JoAnn Rock, Marisa Mitchell, Jodi Nudelman, Amanda Schweder, and Laura Storto. 2000. *Evaluating Alternative Welfare-to-Work Approaches: Two-Year Impacts for Eleven Programs.* U.S. Department of Health and Human Services and U.S. Department of Education.

Freedman, Stephen, Daniel Friedlander, Winston Lin, and Amanda Schweder. 1996. "The GAIN Evaluation: Five-Year Impacts on Employment, Earnings and AFDC Receipt." Working Paper 96.1. New York: Manpower Demonstration Research Corporation.

Friedlander, Daniel, and Gary Burtless. 1995. *Five Years After: The Long-Term Effects of Welfare to Work Programs.* Russell Sage.

Gladden, Tricia, and Christopher Taber. 2000a. Wage Progression among Less Skilled Workers. In *Finding Jobs: Work and Welfare Reform,* edited by David Card and Rebecca M. Blank. Russell Sage.

———. 2000b. "The Relationship between Wage Growth and Wage Levels." Working Paper 173. Chicago: Joint Center for Poverty Research.

Greenberg, Mark, Jodie Levin-Epstein, Rutledge Hutson, Theodora Ooms, Rachel Schumacher, Vicki Turetsky, and David Engstrom. 2000. *The 1996 Welfare Law: Key Elements and Emerging Reauthorization Issues.* Washington: Center for Law and Social Policy.

Gueron, Judith, and Edward Pauley. 1991. *From Welfare to Work.* Russell Sage.

Haveman, Robert, Barbara Wolfe, and James Spaulding. 1991. "Childhood Events and Circumstances Influencing High School Completion." *Demography* 28 (1): 133–50.

Loprest, Patricia. 1999. *Families Who Left Welfare: Who Are They and How Are They Doing?* Washington: Urban Institute.

Michalopoulos, Charles, Christine Schwartz, and Diana Adams-Ciardullo. 2000. *What Works Best for Whom: Impacts of 20 Welfare-to-Work Programs by Subgroup.* U.S. Department of Health and Human Services and U.S. Department of Education.

Orr, Larry L., Howard S. Bloom, Stephen H. Bell, Fred Doolittle, Winston Lin, and George Cave. 1996. *Does Training for the Disadvantaged Work? Evidence from the National JTPA Study.* Washington: Urban Institute.

Rangarajan, Anu. 1998. *Keeping Welfare Recipients Employed: A Guide for States Designing Job Retention Services.* Princeton, N.J.: Mathematica.

Rangarajan, Anu, Alicia Meckstroth, and Tim Novak. 1998. *The Effectiveness of the Postemployment Services Demonstration: Preliminary Findings.* Princeton, N.J.: Mathematica.

Rangarajan, Anu, and Tim Novak. 1999. *The Struggle to Sustain Employment: The Effectiveness of the Postemployment Services Demonstration.* MPR Reference 8194-620. Princeton, N.J.: Mathematica.

Rangarajan, Anu, Peter Schochet, and Dexter Chu. 1998. *Employment Experiences of Welfare Recipients Who Find Jobs: Is Targeting Possible?* Princeton, N.J.: Mathematica.

Scrivener, Susan, Gayle Hamilton, Mary Farrell, Stephen Freedman, Daniel Friedlander, Marisa Mitchell, Jodi Nudelman, and Christine Schwartz. 1998. *The National Evaluation of Welfare-to-Work Strategies: Implementation, Participation Patterns, Costs, and Two-Year Impacts of the Portland (Oregon) Welfare-to-Work Program.* U.S. Department of Health and Human Services and U.S. Department of Education.

State Policy Documentation Project. 2000. www.spdg.org (website administered for the Center on Budget and Policy Priorities and the Center on Law and Social Policy).

Strawn, Julie. 1998. *Beyond Job Search or Basic Education: Rethinking the Role of Skills in Welfare Reform.* Washington: Center for Law and Social Policy.

Strawn, Julie, and Karin Martinson. 2000. *Steady Work and Better Jobs: How to Help Low-Income Parents Sustain Employment and Advance in the Workforce.* New York: Manpower Demonstration Research Corporation.

Tyler, John H., Richard Murnane, and John B. Willett. 2000. "Cognitive Skills Matter in the U.S. Labor Market, Even for School Dropouts." Report 15. Cambridge, Mass.: National Center for the Study of Adult Learning and Literacy.

U.S. Department of Health and Human Services (HHS). 2000. *Indicators of Welfare Dependence,* Annual Report.

Wamhoff, Steve, and Julie Strawn. 2001. *Increasing Access to Postsecondary Education for TANF Recipients: An Update on State and Local Initiatives.* Washington: Center for Law and Social Policy.

Zambrowski, Amy, and Ann Gordon. 1993. *Evaluation of the Minority Female Single Parent Demonstration: Fifth Year Impacts at CET.* Princeton, N.J.: Mathematica.

9

LADONNA PAVETTI
DAN BLOOM

State Sanctions
and Time Limits

THE WELFARE REFORMS of the 1990s dramatically expanded the range
of circumstances in which families can have their welfare benefits
reduced or canceled. In particular, sanctions (financial penalties for noncompliance with program requirements) and time limits on benefit receipt have
become central features of most state Temporary Assistance for Needy Families (TANF) programs. While sanctions have long been used to enforce program requirements, those under TANF have taken on much greater significance than in the past, in part owing to the emergence of "full family
sanctions" that remove all, rather than part, of a family's cash grant. Time
limits, on the other hand, are more recent and have set the reforms of the
1990s apart from previous efforts. Since both policies potentially involve the
loss of all cash assistance, they warrant careful monitoring to understand
both their implementation and their effects on the behavior and well-being
of families.

Although sanctions and time limits are both being used to restructure the
social contract for poor families, they operate differently. Sanctions are tied to
specific expectations and are imposed only when clients fail to meet those
expectations. A key goal of sanctions, then, is to instill in clients a realization
that the choices they make have consequences. Rather than being tied directly
to a client's behavior, time limits rely on the passage of time. Consequently,
effective implementation of time limits requires instilling in clients a realiza-

tion that their current choices may have profound consequences on their well-being in the future. Sanctions and time limits operate differently, but understanding their implementation and outcomes presents similar analytic challenges. In the current environment, states and localities make the critical decisions about sanction and time-limit policies. Thus it is difficult to document and assess their implementation. In addition, although a few rigorous evaluations have focused on welfare reforms that included sanctions or time limits, and other studies have examined the circumstances of families that were sanctioned or reached time limits, none of these studies were designed to isolate the impact of sanctions or time limits. As a result, relatively little is known with certainty about the effects of these two critical policies.

This chapter describes states' policy choices regarding sanctions and time limits, examines some of the issues involved in implementing the policies, and reviews the available research on how sanctions and time limits are affecting recipients' behavior and well-being. The final section draws some policy conclusions and identifies areas for consideration during reauthorization.

Sanction and Time-Limit Policies: Federal Framework and State Choices

State sanction and time-limit policies are influenced by federal TANF rules, but the block grant structure leaves states with great flexibility, leading to a wide variety of state approaches.

Sanction Policies

Federal law requires states to impose at least a pro rata (partial) benefit reduction on families that do not satisfy work and child support compliance requirements. The sanction must remain in place until the family complies with the requirement. States may impose more stringent penalties and can expand the penalties to program requirements other than work and child support enforcement. In addition, TANF sanctions can, under certain circumstances, affect Food Stamp benefits for the entire family and Medicaid coverage for noncompliant adults.

Most states have chosen to implement sanction policies that are much stricter than those that existed under the Job Opportunities and Basic Skills (JOBS) program and stricter than those required by federal law. In particular, thirty-seven states have adopted full family sanctions under which the penalty for noncompliance with work or other requirements is the loss of all cash assistance. In fifteen of these thirty-seven states, a full family sanction is imposed immediately, while in the remaining twenty-two, the grant is initially reduced to send a warning signal. In seven states (Delaware, Georgia, Idaho, Mississippi, Nevada, Pennsylvania, and Wisconsin), continued or repeated noncompliance may result in a lifetime bar from receiving cash assistance (Goldberg and Schott, 2000).

Only six states still use the sanctions that were in place under JOBS and that eliminate the noncompliant adult from the grant. The remaining eight states have increased the penalty for noncompliance but do not completely eliminate the cash grant. Some of these states only provide assistance in the form of vendor payments (that is, they pay some of the family's bills).

Time-Limit Policies

Federal law restricts states from using federal TANF funds to provide assistance to most families for more than sixty cumulative months, starting from the date of implementation of the state's TANF program ("assistance" is generally defined as payments designed to meet a family's ongoing basic needs). States are free to set time limits of less than sixty months but also may use TANF funds to assist families beyond the sixty-month point, as long as those families do not constitute more than 20 percent of the average monthly state caseload (calculated *after* families begin reaching the sixty-month limit— 2001 at the earliest). States also may use their maintenance of effort funds to assist families that have reached the sixty-month point. For the most part, federal law does not specify particular categories of families that are exempt from the sixty-month limit, other than child-only cases that do not include any adult recipients.

As with sanction policies, there is great variation in state time-limit policies. Nearly all states have imposed time limits, but relatively few have developed limits that are more stringent than the federal limit. Forty-three states (including the District of Columbia) have imposed a "termination" time limit that can result in the cancellation of a family's entire welfare grant. Twenty-six of these states have imposed a sixty-month termination limit. The other seventeen—accounting for about one-fourth of the national caseload— have imposed termination time limits of less than sixty months. Six of these states have imposed a lifetime limit of less than sixty months; the others have imposed "fixed-period" time limits: for example, a limit of twenty-four months of benefit receipt in any sixty-month period.

At the other end of the spectrum, eight states—including California— have not imposed termination time limits. Six of the eight have "reduction" time limits that eliminate benefits for adults but maintain benefits for children, and the other two (Michigan and Vermont) have no time limits. States are free to pursue such policies, although all states will need to use state funds if they want to assist families that pass the federal time limit and exceed the cap on exemptions.

Relationship between State Sanction and Time-Limit Policies

Table 9-1 compares state approaches to sanctions and time limits in terms of whether they are stringent, moderate, or lenient. The largest number of states (twelve) have both stringent time limits and sanctions in place. Seven states use a moderate approach for both policies. The largest concentration of TANF cases (40.4 percent), however, can be found in the five states with both lenient sanctions and time limits.

It is critical to understand the interaction between sanctions and time limits. When full family sanctions are in place, families that do not comply with program requirements are removed from the rolls. The families that remain—and that are likely to reach a time limit—are those that are employed but not earning enough to leave welfare and those that have been unable to find jobs: these are families that have "played by the rules." In states that do not have full family sanctions (or rarely impose them), time limits will affect both families that play by the rules and those that do not.

Implementing Sanctions and Time Limits

Sanctions and time limits can provide administrators and line staff with potent tools for changing expectations about the receipt of welfare, but putting the policies into practice is a complex endeavor. To impose sanctions or time limits in a meaningful way, states need to create the foundation for a mandatory employment program; they must determine which activities recipients will be assigned to, ensure that slots are available, and develop systems for monitoring recipients' compliance. Within this framework, key implementation challenges include (1) deciding who should be subject to work requirements and the sanctions and time limits that accompany them, (2) communicating sanction and time-limit policies to recipients, (3) encouraging and supporting compliance with program mandates, and (4) deciding whether and how to support families that lose cash benefits owing to sanctions and time limits.

Deciding Who Is Subject to Sanctions and Time Limits

The Personal Responsibility and Work Opportunity Reconciliation Act (PRWORA) does not explicitly define which families should be subject to work requirements (and therefore sanctions) or time limits. States are, however, required to meet work participation rates that are based on the work

Table 9-1. *Comparison of State Sanction and Time-Limit Policies*[a]

Sanction policy	Time-limit policy		
	Stringent	*Moderate*	*Lenient*
Stringent	Delaware Ohio South Carolina Tennessee Utah Virginia Massachusetts Nebraska Florida Georgia Idaho Louisiana (12 states; 17.2 percent of caseload)	Alabama Oklahoma South Dakota Wisconsin Wyoming New Jersey North Dakota Hawaii Iowa Kansas Mississippi (11 states; 6.8 percent of caseload)	Maryland Michigan (2 states; 4.8 percent of caseload)
Moderate	Connecticut Nevada North Carolina Oregon (4 states; 3.8 percent of caseload)	Colorado Illinois Kentucky New Mexico Pennsylvania West Virginia Texas (7 states; 17.1 percent of caseload)	Arizona Vermont (2 states; 1.7 percent of caseload)
Lenient	Arkansas (1 state; 0.5 percent of caseload)	Alaska Minnesota Missouri Montana New Hampshire Washington District of Columbia (7 states; 7.7 percent of caseload)	California Indiana Maine New York[b] Rhode Island (5 states; 40.4 percent of caseload)

a. For time limits, stringent = termination time limits (fixed period or lifetime) of less than sixty months; moderate = a sixty-month termination time limit; and lenient = a benefit reduction limit or no time limit. Stringent sanctions = immediate full family sanctions and gradual full family sanctions with an immediate 100 percent reduction in Food Stamp benefits or elimination of Medicaid; moderate = gradual full family sanctions with no sanction of Food Stamp benefits or Medicaid and a partial sanction with a 100 percent sanction on Food Stamp benefits; and lenient = partial sanctions with no 100 percent sanction on Food Stamp benefits.

b. New York has a sixty-month termination time limit. However, because New York has already indicated it will provide benefits through a safety net voucher program for all families who reach the time limit, we have classified its time-limit policy as lenient.

activities of all families headed by an adult, except those with a child under the age of one if a state chooses to exclude them. States are also subject to the sixty-month TANF time limit, as described earlier.

Most states exempt some families from work requirements or time limits. For example, forty-four states exempt from work requirements adult recipients who are caring for a very young child, although these exemptions are typically narrower than those under the JOBS program. Thirty-four states exempt disabled or incapacitated recipients from work requirements, many of them following or modifying exemption policies that were in place under JOBS (Thompson and others, 1998; State Policy Documentation Project, 2000).

In many states, families exempt from work requirements are also exempt from time limits, but eighteen states exempt no families from time limits. These states—most of which have sixty-month time limits—presumably plan to wait until families begin reaching the time limit to decide which families, if any, should receive extensions. States may avoid defining time-limit exemptions in advance because they want to maintain a sense of urgency for all families.

Defining and implementing exemption policies, particularly those that target disabled parents or household members, is challenging. Although many TANF recipients face personal and family challenges, some of the problems are not so severe that they make work totally unfeasible (Olson and Pavetti, 1996). These recipients may, however, need more assistance to find and maintain work than most TANF work programs provide. When this is the case, exemptions protect vulnerable families from the negative consequences of sanctions and time limits but also may keep them from receiving services they need to become self-sufficient.

The small number of states that exempt few or no TANF recipients from work requirements define allowable work activities broadly, to include such activities as substance abuse and mental health treatment (Thompson and others, 1998). However, most states are only beginning to integrate such strategies for the hard-to-employ into their TANF employment programs. Other issues that make the implementation of exemption policies complex are caseworker's level of skill and workloads. Most caseworkers have limited training or skills to identify families that may be unable to comply with work requirements. In urban areas where caseloads tend to be especially high, unless a family explicitly requests that they be exempt from program requirements, caseworkers often do not have the time to conduct a thorough assessment to determine whether a family may have difficulty meeting the program requirements.

Communicating Sanctions and Time Limits to Clients

Although sanctions and time limits can reduce the number of families receiving welfare, that is not their main goal. Rather, the policies aim to encourage TANF recipients to go to work sooner than they would in the absence of the policies. For this to happen, recipients must know what is expected of them, understand the consequences associated with those expectations, and believe that they will be adversely affected by negative actions resulting from their behavior.

In the case of sanctions, the main message that workers aim to communicate is that participation in work activities is required in order to receive full benefits. For time limits, the message is more complicated; states hope to use time limits to motivate clients to move toward self-sufficiency long before they exhaust their months. Depending on the state, or sometimes local office, clients may be encouraged to leave welfare to "bank" their months for use in emergencies, or they may be encouraged to stay on assistance, combining work and welfare, in order to benefit from earned income disregards, which have been expanded in about forty states.

Some welfare offices have problems with the most basic tasks, such as informing recipients about sanctions and time limits and explaining how they work. Often these messages are given along with other technical information regarding receipt of benefits. This makes it easy for key messages to get lost amid the masses of information that clients receive.

In the case of time limits, some offices have developed ways to inform and remind recipients about limits—they may send reminder letters showing the number of months remaining, ask recipients to cross months off on a calendar during interviews—but have found that many recipients are not strongly motivated by a time limit until they are close to reaching it (Brown, Bloom, and Butler, 1997).

Because sanctions are tied so directly to specific program requirements, one might expect fewer difficulties communicating sanctions to clients. However, a recent Inspector General's report found that even though local offices explained sanctions to clients repeatedly, TANF clients did not fully understand them (HHS, 1999). A study of sanctioned families in Tennessee found that 34 percent of families did not understand what they were required to do (Overby, 1998).

The importance of communicating expectations to clients cannot be overstated. According to some studies, work programs that sanctioned many cases tended to perform poorly in terms of job placements and other performance measures. Mead (1997) speculates that these offices did a poor job of making program expectations clear. The offices that performed well made work expectations clear; they threatened sanctions but rarely needed to impose them.

Encouraging and Supporting Compliance with Program Requirements

The way in which sanctions and time limits are enforced is likely to determine what role the policies play in creating a work-oriented assistance system and who is adversely affected by them. In the case of both sanctions and time limits, welfare offices face critical choices about how to create a balance between enforcing sanction and time-limit policies and engaging in efforts to promote compliance with program requirements. If sanction and time-limit policies are not enforced, no one will take them seriously, and their effect will be nullified. Efforts to promote compliance are likely to reduce the number of families that lose benefits because of sanctions or time limits and increase the number of families that take appropriate steps to achieve self-sufficiency.

Balancing enforcement and engagement is especially important in implementing sanctions. Since many families that are sanctioned never appear in the welfare office, it is difficult to know whether they failed to comply because they are unwilling to do so or because they do not understand what is expected of them or are experiencing problems that make compliance difficult. In the latter case, extra efforts may be required to ensure that such families understand what they are required to do and that they are capable of meeting the requirements.

In an effort to encourage workers to impose sanctions when clients do not comply with program requirements, but also ensure that sanctions are not imposed inappropriately, some states have adopted strict review procedures that must be followed before a sanction can be levied. For example, Utah requires a "case staffing" in which the case manager, client, and key service providers meet to develop a plan to avoid the sanction. In Tennessee, a customer review required before the termination of benefits reduced the number of cases sanctioned incorrectly by 30 percent (Overby, 1998). Virtually all states have maintained some form of a grievance procedure in which clients can appeal sanctions they believe to be imposed in error.

The majority of states have not had any clients reach time limits yet, so information on how states are likely to balance enforcing time limits and promoting compliance is limited. As states near time limits, some are developing more intensive job search programs for families that are nearing the time limit and have not yet found employment; the goal of these programs is to reduce the number of families that reach the time limit without employment.

The more critical decision that states face is when to grant extensions. In states where families have reached time limits, recipients who were employed when they reached the limits have usually had their benefits terminated. Canceling these families' welfare grants is sometimes seen as uncontroversial because they have a means of support and, in many cases, would have lost their benefits earlier if earnings disregards had not been enhanced (although such families may face difficulties if they lose their jobs and are unable to return to assistance).

There is greater variation and concern over canceling benefits of families that reach time limits without jobs. Presumably many of these recipients looked for but were unsuccessful in finding jobs; otherwise, in many states they would have lost benefits owing to full family sanctions. In Connecticut, nearly all recipients who reach the time limit with income below the welfare payment standard are deemed to have played by the rules and are granted at least one six-month extension. In contrast, Massachusetts, Virginia, and Florida's pilot Family Transition Program (FTP) have granted relatively few extensions, although many of those who reached the limits in those programs were employed. Some of the variation relates to the way states define "playing by the rules" and how they review cases approaching the limits. Connecticut's definition of compliance is based on the client's sanction history and leaves little discretion to the line workers who review cases, and the usual result is an extension. Other states have left the definition of playing by the rules more open, an approach that may allow for more consideration of individual circumstances but also may be more difficult to implement equitably. (It is not clear whether states will react differently when families begin reaching the federal time limit and may need to be supported with state funds if an extension is granted.)

Providing Assistance after Sanctions or Time Limits Are Imposed

States have considerable flexibility in designing programs to assist families after they have been sanctioned or reached a time limit. For sanctioned families, these programs aim to help families come into compliance with requirements and return to welfare. For families affected by time limits, the programs aim to provide alternatives for meeting basic needs.

The Cuyahoga County Safety Net program in Ohio provides an example of the kinds of programs that are being developed to help sanctioned families. Families that have been sanctioned are contacted by community agencies through phone calls and home visits in an effort to re-engage them in work activities. During the first ten months of implementation, 46 percent of sanctioned families referred to the program were assessed and provided with information and services. Almost all of these families were able to participate in work activities and have their cases reopened as a result of the program (Goldberg and Schott, 2000).

In Connecticut, the state where the largest number of families have reached a time limit, families that are terminated from assistance with income below the payment standard are referred to the Safety Net, a program run by nonprofit organizations that assists these families in finding jobs and meeting their basic needs. Those that are terminated with income above the payment standard can receive temporary rental assistance and, in some cases, are allowed to return to cash assistance if they lose their job. Although families in New York will not reach a time limit for some time, the state has indicated that it intends to provide vouchers to families that reach the limit to cover their basic needs.

Another way to assist families that reach a time limit is to provide them with a publicly funded job. Cuyahoga County, Ohio, where several thousand families were scheduled to reach a time limit in late 2000, announced that subsidized transitional jobs will be provided to able-bodied recipients who reach the limit and are unable to find unsubsidized jobs. Vermont has, since 1994, implemented a "work trigger" time limit in which recipients are required to work after thirty months on welfare, and the state provides community service jobs to those who cannot find regular jobs. With the strong economy (and a part-time work requirement for many recipients), few community service positions have been needed. Depending on the type of support that is provided, states may need to use their own funds to assist families that pass the federal sixty-month limit and exceed the cap on exemptions.

How Are Sanctions and Time Limits Affecting TANF Recipients?

Sanctions and time limits may affect recipients in a variety of ways. When individuals are sanctioned or reach a time limit, the removal of their benefits may lead to changes in their behavior or well-being. The policies may also affect recipients through deterrence: individuals may change their behavior to avoid being sanctioned or in anticipation of reaching a time limit.

Such effects are difficult to measure. Several states have surveyed individuals who left welfare owing to sanctions or time limits, but it is impossible to tell how they would have fared if they had been allowed to remain on welfare. A few rigorous random assignment studies have examined welfare reforms that included full family sanctions or time limits, but all of the reforms also included other elements (for example, expanded earnings disregards), and the studies were not designed to isolate the impact of sanctions or time limits per se.

With these limitations in mind, we now discuss what is known about how sanctions and time limits affect recipient behavior. We then look at the numbers of families that have lost benefits because of sanctions and time limits and draw some observations from the surveys of individuals who left welfare because of sanctions or time limits.

Effects on Recipient Behavior

Sanctions and time limits can clearly reduce welfare caseloads and spending when they are imposed, but both policies are designed to generate changes in behavior, to motivate recipients to find jobs, to participate in employment-related services, and so forth.

EFFECTS OF SANCTIONS. Information on the effects of sanctions that have been implemented under TANF is limited. However, comparative information from earlier studies provides some insight into their impact. Findings from the eleven programs in the National Evaluation of Welfare-to-Work Strategies (NEWWS) suggest that programs need to enforce work-related mandates in order to achieve high rates of participation in employment activities. In programs that did not closely monitor attendance and rarely imposed sanctions, participation rates were only slightly higher for those subject to the program than for those in a control group that faced no mandates. Among the programs that enforced mandates, however, higher sanctioning rates were not associated with higher participation rates (Hamilton and Scrivener, 1999).

Another means of obtaining some evidence on the impact of sanctions is to look at the way individuals respond when sanctioned. (Of course, this approach ignores those that comply with program mandates due to the threat of a sanction, the deterrent effect mentioned earlier.) According to caseworkers, recipients often do not take a sanction seriously until it is imposed. However, the available data suggest that most people do not comply with program requirements even after a sanction is imposed. In Iowa, half of all sanctions were canceled because families complied with the requirements, but most studies of the rates of compliance find them closer to 30 percent (GAO, 2000).

Another important question is whether more severe sanctions—and, in particular, full family sanctions—generate larger impacts on behavior. Under the JOBS program, staff often complained that partial sanctions were not severe enough to affect most recipients (especially because, at the time, Food Stamp benefits generally rose to partly offset the cash sanction). Three studies of this issue conclude that more stringent sanctions do lead to lower caseloads or increased employment exits. However, a closer look at individual state performance suggests that full family sanctions may not be necessary to produce these outcomes.

According to a study of the impact of waiver policies on welfare exits, more stringent sanction policies are associated with increased employment exits (Hofferth, Stanhope, and Harris, 2000). A second study estimates that the rate of caseload reduction in states with an initial full family sanction will be twenty-five percentage points higher than in states with weak sanctions (Rector and Youssef, 1999). A third study that examined the relationship between welfare reform policies, governmental quality, and caseloads found qualitatively similar results (Mead, 2000a).

Indiana's and Vermont's experiences, however, suggest that full family sanctions may not be necessary to promote high levels of employment. Indiana is one of only a few states that continue to use the JOBS sanction. Yet in 1998 the state outperformed all other states in its rate of job placements as measured for consideration for the federal high performance bonus. In 1999 and 2000, Indiana ranked thirteenth among the fifty states in its placement rate. In Vermont, a random assignment study found that a work requirement that was enforced without financial sanctions nevertheless generated substantial increases in employment (Bloom and others, 1998).

Taken as a whole, these data suggest that sanctions are influencing the behavior of many TANF recipients, but that many others have not responded even to the loss of all of their cash assistance. Families may not come into compliance with program requirements because they are unclear about what they must do in order to come into compliance or because they are unable to comply owing to personal or family circumstances. They may also find employment on their own rather than return to the welfare system for support. Some, such as those who are attending college, may choose to pursue their current activities rather than look for work.

EFFECTS OF TIME LIMITS. One could hypothesize that time limits might change behavior in several ways. Some people might stay off welfare to avoid starting their clock. Those on assistance might try to get off faster to "bank" some of their months. Those cut off at a time limit might start working or otherwise change their behavior to replace the lost income.

Some believe that the "anticipatory" impacts of time limits are quite large: that many people have resisted going onto welfare or left more quickly to avoid using up their scarce months of assistance. Most of the evidence is anecdotal, but one study using Current Population Survey (CPS) data estimated that time limits may account for 16 to 18 percent of the recent caseload decline, even though few people have actually reached a time limit (Grogger, 2000).

The evidence from random assignment studies tells a somewhat different story. In evaluations of welfare reform waiver programs in Connecticut, Delaware, Florida, and Virginia, welfare applicants and recipients were assigned at random to a program group subject to a termination time limit (along with other reforms) or to a control group that was not. The results were fairly consistent: all four programs generated employment impacts in the period before program group members began reaching the time limits, but it is impossible to say how much of this impact was attributable to time limits as opposed to other program features. More to the point, however, in almost all study sites, program group members were no more likely than control group members to leave welfare before people actually began reaching the time limits (Fein and Karweit, 1997; Gordon and Agodini, 1999; Bloom, Kemple, and others, 2000; Bloom, Melton, and others, 2000).

At first glance, this pattern suggests that clients were not "banking" their months for future emergencies. In fact, all four of the programs combined time limits with expanded earned income disregards, and it is possible that two program components worked in opposite directions: the expanded disregards held some people on welfare longer, while other program features (including, perhaps, the time limits) caused other people to leave welfare faster. Indeed, further analysis of data from the Florida study suggests this may have occurred (Grogger and Michalopoulos, 1999). Moreover, the Vermont study, which was designed to isolate the impact of a "work trigger" time limit, found that the limit generated small but statistically significant employment gains and reductions in welfare receipt even before anyone reached it.

In any case, the random assignment studies suggest that the anticipatory impacts of time limits are modest, and if impacts are modest for those most directly affected, it seems likely that impacts on welfare applications would be even smaller. Implementation studies suggest several explanations. First, in many programs, staff did not consistently encourage recipients to bank their months. This is, in part, a symptom of the conflict between disregards and time limits: staff are expected to simultaneously encourage recipients to find jobs and stay on welfare (to benefit from the disregards) and to find jobs and leave welfare (to stop their clock). Interestingly, the one Virginia county where staff encouraged clients to bank months was the only site to generate reductions in welfare receipt in the period before families began reaching the limit.

Second, all of the studies examined early time-limit programs, focusing on some of the first recipients to hear a time-limit message. Many recipients, staff said, did not believe that time limits would be implemented. Conversely, the time-limit message affected some control group members in each study, which reduced the chances that impacts could be measured.

Third, focus groups have found that many recipients are aware of time limits—and believe they will be imposed—but have difficulty translating this awareness into concrete short-term steps; many are understandably focused on day-to-day concerns (paying bills, keeping teenage children out of trouble). To the extent that they discussed welfare reform, recipients focused on policies such as work requirements that affected them more immediately. Ironically, there is even some evidence that time limits can prolong welfare stays: recipients may adopt the time limit as their own schedule for leaving welfare, rather than try to leave sooner.

Finally, although it is the least rigorous way to examine the question, time limits are clearly not necessary to achieve welfare caseload reductions. For example, in Michigan (with no time limit), Oregon (with a time limit that is not emphasized), and Maryland (with a benefit reduction time limit), caseloads have fallen by more than 60 percent since 1994.

Even less evidence is available to test the hypothesis that parents respond to time limits after they reach them, by finding jobs to offset the lost income. Follow-up studies have found that some parents begin working or increase their hours after reaching time limits, but it is impossible to say whether this is attributable to the cancellation of their benefits.

Only two of the random assignment studies have followed sample members beyond the point when program group members began reaching termination time limits. The Connecticut program's impact on employment did not change when people began reaching the limit, although most of the people who were cut off were already working while on welfare. In Florida's pilot FTP, employment impacts grew about the time people began reaching the time limit, but then declined. As in Connecticut, many of those terminated at the time limit were already working. In addition, as shown by an ethnographic study, a number of those who did not work were being supported by family—both before and after leaving welfare—and may not have needed to work.

While the evidence on how time limits affect recipients' behavior is mixed, implementation studies have found that the presence of a time limit can create a sense of urgency for staff and managers, push programs to work harder to identify long-hidden barriers facing their clients, and stimulate creative strategies for helping recipients address such issues.

Circumstances of Families That Have Been Sanctioned or Reached Time Limits

Before examining the results of post-welfare surveys, we briefly discuss how many and what kinds of families have been directly affected by sanctions or time limits.

NUMBER OF FAMILIES AFFECTED. Although precise figures are not available, the number of families nationwide that have been sanctioned is clearly much larger than the number terminated from welfare because of time limits.

A recent study by the U.S. General Accounting Office (GAO, 2000) found that in 1998 an average of 112,700 families a month (4.5 percent of the national TANF caseload) received reduced benefits owing to a sanction. Furthermore, about 16,000 families a month lost benefits owing to full family sanctions. In any given month, however, many families remain off welfare because of full family sanctions imposed in earlier months. One study estimated that 540,000 families lost benefits owing to full family sanctions from 1997 to 1999, and that 370,000 remained off assistance at the end of 1999; in addition, seven states reported that sanctions accounted for one-fifth or more of 1999 case closures (Goldberg and Schott, 2000). Studies that examine a cohort of recipients over time also find high sanction rates: one-quarter to one-half of families subject to work requirements are sanctioned over a twelve- to twenty-four-month period (Fein and Lee, 1999; Hamilton and Scrivener, 1999; Pavetti, Wemmerus, and Johnson, 1999).

In contrast, the number of families whose benefits have been canceled owing to a time limit is still fairly small: perhaps 60,000 nationwide as of mid-2000 (unpublished data from the Center on Budget and Policy Priorities in Washington, D.C.). The figure is low for several reasons. First, as noted earlier, twenty-six states have a sixty-month time limit, and no families will reach those limits until late 2001; another eight states do not have termination time limits. Second, in the states with shorter time limits, relatively few recipients are quickly using up their months of eligibility. For example, in Virginia, of 3,051 cases that were subject to the twenty-four-month time limit by June 1996, only 454 (15 percent) had reached the limit by June 1998. (The speed with which recipients use up their months of eligibility in a particular state is affected by welfare grant levels and earnings disregards, time-limit exemption rules, the nature of work requirements, and the prevalence of full family sanctions, among other factors.) Third, a number of states have granted extensions to a substantial fraction of the recipients who have reached time limits.

CHARACTERISTICS OF RECIPIENTS AFFECTED. Sanctioned families are heterogeneous, but the hard-to-employ appear to be overrepresented. In Tennessee, 60 percent of sanctioned families did not have a general equivalency diploma or a high school diploma compared with 40 percent of families that left TANF for work. In South Carolina, 36 percent of high school dropouts were sanctioned compared with 22 percent of high school graduates. As several studies also indicate, many sanctioned families experience personal and family challenges that may make it difficult for them to comply with program requirements, including chemical dependency, physical and mental health problems, and domestic violence (GAO, 2000; Goldberg and Schott, 2000). Many families also experience logistical barriers such as not being able to find child care or not having access to transportation.

The characteristics of families leaving welfare because of time limits vary from state to state, for reasons mentioned earlier. Four studies have compared the characteristics of families that were cut off at time limits with those of families that left welfare before reaching limits. Not surprisingly, individuals who reached time limits were more likely to have been long-term recipients before becoming subject to the limits. Three studies found that families reaching time limits were larger (recipients with more children need to earn more in order to lose eligibility for welfare). In the three studies with housing status data, those who reached time limits were more likely to live in public or subsidized housing.

At the same time, families that are cut off at time limits are not necessarily the most disadvantaged. In Connecticut, where many extensions were granted, those who were cut off were less disadvantaged, on average, than those who reached the limit but received extensions. Similarly, in Florida's pilot FTP, some of the participants who faced the most serious barriers to employment received medical exemptions and did not reach the limit.

In-depth interviews with people terminated at FTP's time limit reveal some diversity that is masked by aggregate data. Though many of the interviewees had tried without success to find jobs while on welfare, others had been attending college (sometimes without the program's knowledge) or were supported by a parent or partner and did not see an urgent need to work (FTP did not use full family sanctions during most of the study period). Also, administrative data showed that nearly 30 percent of those who reached the time limit had worked in all four quarters of their last year on welfare; many of these individuals would have become ineligible for welfare earlier had it not been for an expanded earned-income disregard.

POST-WELFARE CIRCUMSTANCES. Two sets of data are available to assess the circumstances of families that left welfare because of sanctions or time limits. One set comes from the two random assignment studies that followed their samples past termination time limits. They found that both programs increased average income before program group members began reaching the time limits (owing to expanded disregards), but the income gains disappeared after the limits were reached. In fact, both programs started to reduce income for small groups of families. However, the Florida study, now complete, found no evidence of increased material hardship.

The other source of data is a set of studies of "leavers," that is, families that left welfare owing to sanctions or time limits (see Blank and Schmidt, this volume). Most of these studies compared either the respondents' circumstances before and after leaving welfare (by asking respondents to recall their lives while on welfare) or the post-welfare circumstances of sanction or time-limit families against those of other leavers. Although better than no comparison, neither of these approaches reliably assesses the impact of being cut off welfare (Gordon and others, 1999; Hunter-Manns and Bloom, 1999; Nixon, Kauff, and Losby, 1999; Bloom, Kemple, and others, 2000; GAO, 2000; MDTA, 2000; Richardson and others, 2000). The survey findings are mixed, but several patterns emerge. First, a substantial proportion of the families that left welfare because of sanctions or time limits are struggling. Although each survey measured hardship differently, anywhere from one-third to one-half of the respondents reported that they were having trouble making ends meet. Between 15 percent and 25 percent reported that they sometimes or often did not have enough to eat. On the other hand, it is not clear that the sanction and time-limit families are experiencing much greater levels of hardship than other, broader groups of welfare leavers; the difference, of course, is that time-limit and sanctioned leavers may not be eligible for further assistance. Finally, it is reassuring that extreme housing-related hardship has been rare: no study that examined the post-welfare circumstances of families affected by sanctions or time limits found rates of homelessness above 3 percent.

Second, while employment rates are relatively high among most categories of leavers, sanctioned leavers are less likely to work than individuals who left welfare for other reasons. This finding is consistent with the fact that hard-to-employ families appear to be overrepresented. Summarizing data from nine studies of sanctioned families, the U.S. General Accounting Office (GAO, 2000) estimates that an average of 41 percent of sanctioned families were working after they left TANF. Studies that compare employment rates for sanctioned families and other welfare leavers find a difference of as much as twenty-seven percentage points in the rate of employment for these two groups.

The time-limit story is more complicated and depends on the design and implementation of each state's limit. For example, in Connecticut, where most people who reached the time limit without jobs were granted extensions, the 80 percent employment rate among time-limit leavers is much higher than among other leavers. A similar result was found in Virginia, where recipients were required to work long before reaching the time limit and were subject to full family sanctions if they failed to cooperate; thus those who reached the twenty-four-month time limit were quite likely to be working. Some of the studies found that the employment rate among time-limit leavers increased somewhat after the time limit was reached, although, once again, it is hard to know whether this is related to the termination of welfare benefits.

Third, despite the focus on employment as the key indicator of post-welfare well-being, the studies provide mixed evidence about whether former recipients who are now employed are in fact better off. Employed families typically report higher income, but not necessarily less hardship. In North Carolina and Virginia, employed time-limit leavers were more likely to report that they were having trouble paying for food. In Florida, employed respondents were less likely to have health coverage and more likely to report food insecurity. As noted earlier, many of the parents who were not employed received substantial assistance from their families. It is not clear whether they got help because they were unable to work, or whether the help made it possible for them not to work. There is also no way to know how long the assistance will be available. Finally, some of the studies that tracked individuals after the time limit was reached suggest that those who were not employed may have been more likely to get help from food pantries, soup kitchens, and other community supports.

Fourth, it is clear that, in addition to family and community supports, public assistance programs—notably the Food Stamp program, housing assistance, and Medicaid—are playing a key role in supporting many families that were sanctioned or reached time limits. Without these supports, levels of serious hardship might be higher. In Connecticut, Florida, and Massachusetts, time-limit leavers were more likely than other leavers to continue receiving food stamps after exit.

The situation for sanctioned families is more complicated. States have the option to reduce a noncompliant family's Food Stamp benefit and eliminate Medicaid for the noncompliant adult; however, it is unclear how often these benefits are affected. Seven studies that examined continued participation in the Food Stamp program and Medicaid found relatively high rates of participation in both: 57 to 71 percent of sanctioned recipients received food stamps and 59 to 88 percent received Medicaid benefits (GAO, 2000). However, there is speculation that welfare reform in general, and sanction policies in particular, may be contributing to steep declines in participation in the Food Stamp and Medicaid programs (Dion and Pavetti, 2000).

In short, the rather limited data available to date suggest that most families that have left welfare owing to full family sanctions and time limits are struggling and are far from self-sufficient, but that the policies do not appear to have caused widespread, severe hardship. The critical question is whether families will be able to continue to make ends meet without cash assistance over the long term, particularly if economic conditions worsen.

Shaping a Post-TANF Agenda for Sanction and Time-Limit Policies

Because so little is known about sanctions and time limits, it is difficult to identify specific changes that should be made in reauthorizing TANF, particularly because the current structure already provides so much flexibility. For instance, the data do not support firm conclusions about the adequacy of the 20 percent exemption from the federal time limit. Given the high degree of uncertainty—and the considerable risks involved—if Congress opts to retain this rule, it should create an intensive review process so that midstream changes can be considered quickly if problems emerge. Several broader issues need to be examined before any such changes are proposed.

First, although sanctions received much less attention than time limits in the debate over PRWORA, now that both policies have been implemented, many more families have lost benefits because of sanctions than because of time limits. This may change as time limits draw near in more states, but some families that many feared would reach time limits appear to have already been sanctioned off welfare. More research needs to focus on the implementation of sanctions, their effects on recipients' behavior, and the circumstances of sanctioned families.

Second, whatever occurs at the federal level, the reality of sanctions and time limits will be shaped by the implementation decisions made by states and localities. The early experience suggests a need to focus on fairness and equity, which means avoiding erroneous sanctions, reaching out to sanctioned families to identify and assist those that are unable to comply, ensuring that families reaching time limits receive consistent treatment when extensions are considered, and so forth.

Third, the experiences to date with sanctions and time limits raise two broader issues: how to address the needs of hard-to-employ families and how to support working families in a time-limited environment. The hard-to-employ are overrepresented among sanctioned families, while many of those that reach time limits are employed but earning very low wages.

Over the past decade, most states have implemented work first programs that require able-bodied welfare recipients to find work quickly, but most states are just beginning to explore alternative employment strategies for families that need more assistance. Although states are free to implement such strategies under current law, expanding the range of activities that count toward a state's work participation rate might facilitate these efforts. Also, because such services are often costly, maintaining the level of federal and state TANF funding seems vital.

With appropriate services in place and with intensive efforts to identify recipients facing special challenges, nearly all recipients could be expected to take steps toward self-sufficiency. The risks inherent in full family sanctions would be reduced and time limits could be deemphasized. In a system in which recipients are seriously required to work or engage in productive activities, limits are most likely to affect those least capable of achieving self-sufficiency, namely, recipients with serious problems and those who are working but earning too little to leave welfare.

The latter group is most directly affected by the conflict between disregards and time limits. A few states stop the time-limit clock for working families, but most will simply stop providing aid when the time limit is reached, undercutting the income-enhancing effects of the disregards and leaving families vulnerable if they lose jobs. Although the stop-the-clock strategy is already allowable, Congress could send a strong message by incorporating this option into law. At the same time, as discussed elsewhere in this volume (see Michalopoulos and Berlin), it is still an open question whether the welfare system—still heavily focused on meeting the immediate needs of nonworking families—is the best vehicle for aiding the working poor.

COMMENT BY
Robert Rector

The Personal Responsibility and Work Opportunity Reconciliation Act (PRWORA) of 1996 constitutes the first substantial change in the direction of American welfare policy since the beginning of the War on Poverty in the mid-1960s. To understand this change, it is important to grasp the underlying shift in the philosophy of welfare that accompanied reform.

Welfare policy must inevitably deal with the interrelated issues of material and behavioral poverty. Material poverty involves deprivations in housing, food, or other material living conditions. Having a family income below the official poverty income thresholds is generally treated as synonymous with material poverty. Behavioral poverty is more complex, covering an intertwined cluster of problem behaviors: dependence, illegitimacy, eroded work ethic, crime, and drug abuse.

The traditional welfare system focused mainly on alleviating material poverty. Economic resources were transferred to the poor in an effort to raise incomes. A key assumption was that material poverty harmed the development of children and that raising family income through welfare could significantly improve children's life prospects. Behavioral poverty was treated as a secondary concern or, in the case of illegitimacy, ignored entirely.

Welfare reform shifted the focus from material to behavioral poverty. Dependency and single parenthood per se were seen as harmful to the well-being of children, and the ethos within a family came to be regarded as more critical than its material living conditions in determining personal and social outcomes. To the extent that material poverty remained a concern, reformers felt it could be best addressed by dealing with the underlying behavioral problems that were its root cause. Thus while the old welfare system sought to prop up material living conditions through welfare, the 1996 reforms sought to disrupt the long-term cultures of dependence and the underclass.

It is essential to understand this shift in the conceptual foundations of welfare because most current evaluations, including the bulk of those cited by LaDonna Pavetti and Dan Bloom, continue to assess reform primarily in terms of the goals of the pre-reform system: they emphasize material poverty, particularly short-term changes in family income. Methods for assessing the real goal of reform—the long-term transformation of the debilitating culture of dependence—still need to be developed.

The 1996 reform marked a fundamental shift from a system of unconditional to conditional aid. Under the old system individuals deemed needy were given aid largely without behavioral conditions. Reformers felt this system rewarded idleness and dependence; they sought to create a new system in which aid would be given only if recipients engaged in constructive behaviors to improve their own lives.

As Pavetti and Bloom point out, sanctions and, to a lesser degree, time limits play a pivotal role in the shift from unconditional to conditional welfare. It is now widely accepted that sanctions are necessary to promote responsible behavior. Some debate remains, however, over the appropriate severity of sanctions. At present sanctions may be either full-check (affecting both the adult and child portions of the TANF check) or lenient (affecting only the relatively small adult portion).

Pavetti and Bloom cite research by Lawrence Mead (2000b) and Sarah Youssef and myself (Rector and Youssef, 1999) on the importance of sanctions in disrupting the culture of dependence. In our research, Youssef and I found a positive correlation of 0.496 between prompt full-check sanctions and the rate of caseload decline in a state. Among the ten states with the most rapid caseload reduction, nine employed full-check sanctions. By contrast, among the ten states with the least caseload decline, seven had lenient sanctions. During the eighteen-month period studied, states with a prompt full-check sanction on noncompliant behavior experienced an average drop in caseload of 41.8 percent, while states with lenient sanctions for noncompliance had an average drop of 17.3 percent.

Importantly, states with more rapid drops in caseload did not experience increases in child poverty in comparison with other states. Indeed, Wisconsin, which currently has the most encompassing and strict workfare system in the country, has experienced one of the largest drops in child poverty in the nation since the beginning of its reforms. Specifically, child poverty in Wisconsin—using a Census Bureau measure that takes into account the Earned Income Tax Credit, food stamps, and similar benefits—has been cut roughly in half, falling from about 13.5 percent in the early 1990s to about 6.5 percent in 1997–98.

Evidence suggests that full-check sanctions send an important message that the state is serious about changing behavior. The impact of this message can be wide-ranging. Thus when full-check sanctions were established in Wisconsin, the state saw not only a rapid rise in exits from the welfare rolls but also a dramatic drop in new entrants.

Although Pavetti and Bloom cite the single state of Indiana as counterevidence that full-check sanctions may not be necessary to significantly alter dependent behavior, the fact remains that in the period since PRWORA, Indiana has consistently ranked among the lower states in caseload reduction. The importance of full-check sanctions is emphasized by welfare administrators. Jason Turner designed Wisconsin's highly successful workfare system and is currently commissioner of human resources of the city of New York. He has considerable practical experience with both lenient and strict sanctions in Wisconsin and with lenient sanctions in New York. Turner states:

> Full check sanctions are absolutely essential to a substantial reduction in long-term dependence. Without full check sanctions, it is difficult to get more than half the recipients to even come into the office for an interview let alone to engage full-time in constructive activities leading toward self-sufficiency. Large numbers of recipients simply accept the lenient or partial sanction and remain as part of the idle long-term population on the rolls. (Interview with Jason Turner, January 2001)

Finally, there has been much discussion of the fate of families that have been sanctioned off TANF. Pavetti and Bloom note that these families tend to be less employable and to have multiple dysfunctions. However, a return to permissive and unconditional aid would do little to deal with the underlying problems these families face and is likely to make those problems worse. Instead, what is needed is a work-based system that is

—comprehensive in requiring community service or other constructive job-related behavior immediately upon the recipients' enrollment;

—strict in promptly applying a full-check sanction for noncompliant behavior;

—communicative in seeking to remain in touch with families after they have been sanctioned; and

—forgiving in allowing the family to quickly reenter the rolls once responsible behavior has been resumed.

At the time of passage of PRWORA, time limits received considerable attention and work requirements and sanctions received relatively little. Since then, however, behavioral requirements (including mandatory job search, training, and community service), coupled with meaningful sanctions for noncompliant behavior, are what have led to record declines in dependence. It would be fair to say that work and behavior requirements have already accomplished much of what was expected from time limits and at a far earlier date.

Moreover, as Pavetti and Bloom point out, time limits are likely to have a far smaller impact in the future than was initially anticipated. For one thing, work and behavior requirements have already greatly reduced the number of recipients who will collide with future time limits. For another, exemptions and loopholes make the federal time limits somewhat porous.

It has always been my opinion that serious work requirements would be more effective than time limits in combating dependence. Moreover, work requirements lack the drawbacks of time limits. Despite rhetoric to the contrary, few politicians are eager to cut off aid to a parent who truthfully cannot find private sector employment, no matter how long that parent has been on the rolls. In such circumstances a reasonable alternative is to require the parent to perform community service work in exchange for continuing benefits.

Still, time limits have played an enormous symbolic role in welfare reform. For that reason it is very unlikely that Congress will rescind or weaken them. Nonetheless, it seems that the heyday for time limits as a major mechanism of reform has passed. In the future, attention will shift to other issues such as strengthening work requirements, encouraging marriage, and reducing illegitimacy.

References

Bloom, Dan, James Kemple, Pamela Morris, Susan Scrivener, Nandita Verma, and Richard Hendra. 2000. *FTP: Final Report on Florida's Initial Time-Limited Welfare Program.* New York: Manpower Demonstration Research Corporation.

Bloom, Dan, Laura Melton, Charles Michalopoulos, Susan Scrivener, and Johanna Walter. 2000. *Implementation and Early Impacts of Connecticut's Welfare Reform Initiative.* New York: Manpower Demonstration Research Corporation.

Bloom, Dan, Charles Michalopoulos, Johanna Walter, and Patricia Auspos. 1998. *WRP: Implementation and Early Impacts of Vermont's Welfare Restructuring Project.* New York: Manpower Demonstration Research Corporation.

Brown, Amy, Dan Bloom, and David Butler. 1997. *The View from the Field: As Time Limits Approach, Welfare Recipients and Staff Talk about Their Attitudes and Expectations.* New York: Manpower Demonstration Research Corporation.

Dion, Robin, and LaDonna Pavetti. 2000. *Access to and Participation in the Food Stamp Program.* Washington: Mathematica.

Fein, David, and Jennifer Karweit. 1997. *The ABC Evaluation: The Early Economic Impacts of Delaware's A Better Chance Welfare Reform Program.* Cambridge, Mass.: Abt.

Fein, David, and Wang Lee. 1999. *The ABC Evaluation: Carrying and Using the Stick: Financial Sanctions in Delaware's A Better Chance Program.* Cambridge, Mass.: Abt.

Goldberg, Heidi, and Liz Schott. 2000. *A Compliance-Oriented Approach to Sanctions in State and County TANF Programs.* Washington: Center on Budget and Policy Priorities.

Gordon, Anne, and Roberto Agodini. 1999. *Early Impacts of the Virginia Independence Program: Final Report.* Princeton, N.J.: Mathematica.

Gordon, Anne, Carole Kuhns, Renee Loeffler, and Roberto Agodini. 1999. *Experiences of Virginia Time Limit Families in the 6 Months after Case Closure.* Princeton, N.J.: Mathematica.

Grogger, Jeffrey. 2000. "Time Limits and Welfare Use." Working Paper 7709. Cambridge, Mass.: National Bureau of Economic Research.

Grogger, Jeffrey, and Charles Michalopoulos. 1999. "Welfare Dynamics under Time Limits." Working Paper W7353. Cambridge, Mass.: National Bureau of Economic Research.

Hamilton, Gayle, and Susan Scrivener. 1999. *Promoting Participation: How to Increase Involvement in Welfare-to-Work Activities.* New York: Manpower Demonstration Research Corporation.

Hofferth, Sandra L., Stephen Stanhope, and Kathleen Mullan Harris. 2000. "Exiting Welfare in the 1990s: Did Public Policy Influence Recipients' Behavior?" Population Studies Center Research Report 01-469. University of Michigan.

Hunter-Manns, JoAnna, and Dan Bloom. 1999. *Connecticut Post-Time Limit Tracking Study: Six-Month Survey Results.* New York: Manpower Demonstration Research Corporation.

Massachusetts Department of Transitional Assistance (MDTA). 2000. *After Time Limits: A Study of Households Leaving Welfare between December 1998 and April 1999.* Boston.

Mead, Lawrence M. 1997. "Optimizing JOBS: Evaluation versus Administration." *Public Administration Review* 57 (2): 113–23.

———. 2000a. "Governmental Quality and Welfare Reform." Paper presented at the 2000 Annual Meeting of the American Political Science Association, Washington, D.C., September 1.

———. 2000b. "The Politics of Welfare Reform in Wisconsin." *Polity* 32 (Summer): 533–59.

Nixon, Lucia A., Jacqueline F. Kauff, and Jan L. Losby. 1999. *Second Assignments to Iowa's Limited Benefit Plan.* Washington: Mathematica.

Olson, Krista, and LaDonna Pavetti. 1996. *Personal and Family Challenges to the Successful Transition from Work.* Washington: Urban Institute.

Overby, Russell. 1998. *Summary of Surveys of Welfare Recipients Employed or Sanctioned for Noncompliance.* University of Memphis.

Pavetti, LaDonna, Nancy Wemmerus, and Amy Johnson. 1999. *Implementation of Welfare Reform in Virginia: A Work in Progress.* Washington: Mathematica.

Rector, Robert E., and Sarah E. Youssef. 1999. *The Determinants of Welfare Caseload Decline.* Washington: Heritage Foundation.

Richardson, Philip, Kim Reniero, Mark Tecco, Susan LaFever, and Greg Schoenfeld. 2000. *Study of Families Leaving Work First Due to Time Limits.* Rockville, Md.: Maximus.

State Policy Documentation Project. 2000. www.spdp.org. (Website administered by the Center on Budget and Policy Priorities and the Center on Law and Social Policy.)

Thompson, Terri S., Pamela A. Holcomb, Pamela Loprest, and Kathleen Brennan. 1998. *State Welfare-to-Work Policies for People with Disabilities.* Washington: Urban Institute.

U.S. General Accounting Office (GAO). 2000. *State Sanction Policies and Number of Families Affected.* HEHS-00-44. Government Printing Office.

U.S. Department of Health and Human Services, Office of Inspector General (HHS). 1999. *Temporary Assistance for Needy Families: Educating Clients about Sanctions.* Government Printing Office.

10

CHARLES MICHALOPOULOS
GORDON BERLIN

Financial Work Incentives for Low-Wage Workers

One of the main objectives of the 1996 federal welfare reform law was to move people away from the welfare system and into work. There is substantial evidence, however, that welfare-to-work policies of the last two decades have encouraged work but left parents no better off financially (Gueron and Pauly, 1991; Bloom and Michalopoulos, 2001). Two decades of stagnating wages have made it difficult for many parents, even those working full-time, to lift their families out of poverty through earnings alone. Many low-wage workers are also in part-time or temporary jobs that pay little and provide few opportunities to gain skills or develop careers.

In response to this concern, state governments in the early 1990s began testing a number of new policies that supplemented earnings to provide financial work incentives and to "make work pay," and most states have implemented such policies as part of their welfare reforms. Through expansions of the federal Earned Income Tax Credit (EITC), the federal government has also helped ensure that people who work full-time will not be poor. This chapter reviews these recent policies and what is known about their results, which have been impressive: they have encouraged work, increased income, reduced poverty, and made children better off. Because the state policies that were tested provided financial work incentives on top of the EITC, these results suggest that additional financial work incentives are important to consider in the current policy environment.

At the same time, these programs cost more than previous efforts to encourage work among welfare recipients. In addition, their largest effects on work and poverty are for those who are least likely to work, such as long-term welfare recipients. And they may unintentionally encourage more employable parents—such as those in two-parent welfare families and working poor families not on welfare—to curtail their work effort.

A trade-off appears to exist between increased efficiency for narrowly targeted programs (for example, those aimed at welfare recipients) and increased equity for broadly targeted programs (for example, those aimed at all of the working poor). The challenge for policymakers who want to make work pay is to design policies that further encourage work and reduce poverty among those who would not have worked otherwise without incurring unintended consequences of reduced work effort among the working poor higher up the income stream.

How can policymakers best meet this challenge? The answer depends on their goals. Those who want primarily to reduce poverty while promoting equity could expand the federal or state EITC. Costs would likely be high because eligibility would be spread across the working poor, but they would be equitable and have wide effects. Those who want to increase both employment and income while containing costs could choose a more narrowly focused approach, either by offering earnings supplements to groups such as long-term welfare recipients who are unlikely to work otherwise or by rewarding only full-time work.

A Short History of Financial Work Incentives

An early idea for encouraging work and reducing poverty was the negative income tax (NIT), tested in the United States and Canada in the 1970s. Under the NIT, the government guaranteed families a relatively high level of income, often more than enough to take them out of poverty. The amount received by the families was reduced as their earnings rose, but by less than under the welfare system at the time. It was hoped that this difference would encourage work. It did, but the high guaranteed benefit (the amount of money recipients received when they did not work) overwhelmed the program's modest work incentives, discouraging work overall (SRI International, 1983). In short, the NIT resembled a traditional welfare program: it paid people the highest benefit amounts when they did not work.

Federal policymakers learned a great deal from the NIT tests when they instituted the EITC in 1975. Introduced in part to offset payroll taxes, the

EITC provided a refundable tax credit that was available only to working parents and that increased with earnings up to a maximum credit.

To further reward work and reduce poverty, the federal government significantly expanded the generosity of the EITC in 1990 and 1993. By 1999, taxpayers with two or more children could claim a credit equal to 40 percent of their earnings up to a maximum credit of $3,816—nearly three times the credit available in 1990. The credit was reduced with additional earnings, but some amount was available to families earning as much as $30,000 per year. Fifteen states now also offer EITCs based on the federal credit, with twelve states having expanded their credits since 1997 (Johnson, 2000).

Parallel efforts to reform welfare also focused on work. In 1968, 1971, 1979, and 1988, federal laws toughened work-related requirements for welfare recipients. States experimented with additional requirements during the 1980s and 1990s. These work-focused programs were triple winners, increasing earnings, reducing welfare payments, and saving government funds. But they seldom affected income or poverty because many welfare recipients went to work part-time, most found low-wage work, and the welfare system did not reward work financially. After four months of work, welfare benefits were reduced one dollar for every dollar of earnings.

The 1996 federal welfare reforms went further, tightening work requirements and limiting the number of months federal funds could be used to pay a family's welfare benefits. Virtually unnoticed in the angst surrounding the passage of time-limited welfare, nearly every state also altered the amount of welfare that a working recipient could keep (the welfare earnings disregard; Gallagher and others, 1998). By making their earnings disregards more generous, while requiring welfare recipients to work or prepare for work, officials hoped that more recipients would be encouraged to work and, through work, begin to earn enough to leave welfare entirely.

Work Incentives under Different Policies

A great deal is now known about the effects of policies with financial work incentives because a number of them have been tested using random assignment, which many consider the most credible means of determining the effects of a policy. Each study used a lottery-like process to assign people to one of two groups: one was offered a program that included earnings supplements or enhanced welfare earnings disregards; the other, a control group, was not. Because individuals were assigned at random, any differences that emerged in the average outcomes of the two groups could reliably be attrib-

Figure 10-1. *Income under Various Financial Incentives for Single Parents with Two Children, Earning $6 per Hour*

Monthly income (dollars)

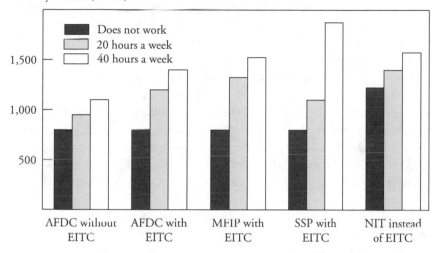

uted to the policy being tested. This section describes these programs, with an emphasis on their work incentives.

Figure 10-1 compares work incentives under Aid to Families with Dependent Children (AFDC), the EITC, and three of the incentive schemes that were tested using random assignment: the NIT, a generous enhanced earnings disregard (the Minnesota Family Investment Program, MFIP; see Miller and others, 2000), and an earnings supplement tied to full-time work (Canada's Self-Sufficiency Project, SSP; see Michalopoulos and others, 2000). Figure 10-1 shows monthly after-tax income from earnings, welfare, and the Food Stamp program (calculated using Minnesota welfare and tax rules for 1996, including the Minnesota EITC) for a single parent with two children who does not work, for a single parent who works twenty hours a week, and for a single parent who works forty hours a week, all at $6.00 an hour.

Under AFDC without the EITC, there was little incentive to work. If the parent represented in Figure 10-1 were to work part-time, her income would have increased by about $170 a month, or about $2 for every hour of work, during the first four months she combined work and welfare (and even less after four months). If she worked full-time, she would lose her eligibility for cash assistance but remain eligible for food stamps, and her income would increase by only about $140 a month.

The expanded EITC provides greater work incentives than AFDC. The low-wage parent would gain nearly $300 a month by working part-time, and another $300 a month by moving from part-time to full-time work.

The pilot MFIP program's enhanced earnings disregard alone provided the strongest financial incentives to work part-time but provided little incentive to work full-time. Under MFIP a parent could earn about 32 percent of her welfare plus Food Stamp guarantee without reducing her benefits. Benefits were reduced 62 cents with each dollar of earnings beyond this point. As a result, families could receive welfare until their earnings were 140 percent of the poverty level. Figure 10-1 shows that working full-time, the parent would receive about $1,400 a month from earnings and the EITC. Working part-time, she would receive more than $1,300 a month. The reduction in income of $100 in moving from full-time to part-time work might be a reasonable price to pay to spend more time with one's children, especially if it also means reduced child care, transportation, and other work-related expenses. In other words, MFIP's part-time incentives might have provided a motive for some people to cut back from full-time to part-time work. About twenty states have instituted earnings disregards that are similar to MFIP's in that they immediately reward work by allowing welfare recipients to keep more of their earnings before benefits are reduced and by lowering the rate at which benefits are reduced when earnings increase. (More than twenty other states have also altered their earnings disregards, but in a way that is much less generous than the MFIP pilot program.)

The pilot MFIP program actually included two separate programs. The MFIP Incentives Only program differed from AFDC only by its enhanced earnings disregard. To further encourage work—especially full-time work—a second version of MFIP, called Full MFIP, required people who had been on welfare for two years in a three-year period to look for work or enroll in education or vocational training in preparation for work. People could avoid these activities if they were already working thirty or more hours a week. (Minnesota's statewide Temporary Assistance for Needy Families, TANF, program is also called MFIP, but it differs from the Full MFIP program by having a less generous earnings disregard, more stringent service requirements that are more focused on job search, and a time limit on welfare receipt.)

SSP provides the strongest incentives to work full-time. The demonstration project offered a three-year earnings supplement to single-parent, long-term welfare recipients who left welfare for full-time work (thirty hours or more a week) within a year of entering the program. Because the program required full-time work, it could be quite generous: for most low-wage job takers, SSP effectively doubled their earnings. Figure 10-1 shows this generosity. The hypothetical SSP scheme shown would provide an earnings supplement of half of the difference between monthly earnings and $2,250 (making it roughly comparable to a version of the program tested in British Columbia). If the parent were to make the jump from part-time to full-time work, her income would increase by about $800 a month, or nearly $10 for every additional hour of work (assuming she uses welfare and the EITC if she works part-time).

The hypothetical NIT shown in Figure 10-1 would lift all families out of poverty by providing a guarantee of $1,200 a month that is reduced 50 cents with each dollar of earnings (the guarantee amounts to about $350 in 1971 dollars, which is roughly equal to the poverty line and similar to the least generous plans tested). As Figure 10-1 shows, however, such an NIT would provide little incentive to work, and its guarantee of income above the poverty level would likely discourage many parents from working at all.

For a higher wage earner (say, someone earning $12.00 rather than $6.00 an hour), the implications of Figure 10-1 generally hold, but there is an important difference: neither the EITC nor MFIP provides much incentive to work full-time. In either program, the parent could cut back her work effort with only a modest loss in income. Thus these policies might encourage high-wage parents to cut back their work effort.

Effects of Policies Tested Using Random Assignment

This section briefly describes program effects on the employment, earnings, and income of single-parent families, as revealed by the random assignment studies (see also Moffitt, 1992; Meyer and Rosenbaum, forthcoming). For single-parent recipients, policies with financial work incentives have increased employment, earnings, and income and have encouraged steady employment. For the children in these families, they have improved school performance, health, and behavior (Duncan and Chase-Lansdale, this volume; Morris and others, 2001). The programs cost more, but their costs have been contained in some cases by tying incentives to full-time work or by targeting the incentives at people who are least likely to work otherwise.

Effects on Employment, Earnings, and Income

Several important findings emerge from these studies.

Financial work incentives can encourage work, and more generous incentives encourage more work. Virtually all of the financial work incentives studied encouraged work to some degree (table 10-1). The effect was largest in SSP

Table 10-1. *Changes in Employment Outcomes for Single-Parent Welfare Recipients Due to Financial Incentive Schemes Tested Using Random Assignment*[a]

Dollars unless otherwise indicated

Programs	Employment (percent)	Monthly earnings	Monthly cash transfers	Monthly income
Financial incentives alone				
Canada SSP	7.1	61	47	107
Minnesota MFIP incentives only	2.2	–22	89	67
New York CAP	3.3	44	–15	17
Vermont WRP incentives only	0.4	–4	3	2
Financial incentives and other policies				
Connecticut Jobs First	7.8	35	46	95
Minnesota full MFIP	6.1	13	61	74
Florida FTP	5.1	50	–12	25
Iowa FIP	3.0	34	–2	32

Sources: For SSP, Michalopoulos and others (1999, 2000); for MFIP, Miller and others (2000); for CAP, Hamilton and others (1996); for WRP, Hendra and Michalopoulos (1999); for Jobs First, Bloom and others (2000a); for FTP, Bloom and others (2000b); for Iowa FIP, Fraker and Jacobson (2000).

a. Averages are for three years of follow-up for SSP long-term recipients, MFIP, WRP, FTP, and Iowa FIP ongoing recipients; two and a half years for SSP applicants; two years for Iowa FIP applicants and Jobs First; and five years for CAP. Indicators of statistical significance are not provided because they were not available for all results. Cash transfers include AFDC/TANF in all studies except SSP. In SSP, cash transfers include Income Assistance and SSP supplement payments. Income is the sum of earnings, AFDC/TANF, and the cash value of food stamps in all studies except SSP. In SSP, income is the sum of cash transfers and earnings.

(an increase in employment of about seven percentage points), which provided the most generous incentive. A relatively less generous earnings disregard in the MFIP Incentives Only program increased employment by only about two percentage points, while Vermont's Welfare Restructuring Project (WRP) Incentives Only (Hendra and Michalopoulos, 1999), which provided little financial work incentive compared with AFDC until after four months of work, had virtually no effect on employment. Results from the Vermont study are especially important because a number of states have taken a similar approach, and they may suggest that people respond more to an immediate offer of an earnings supplement than to the promise of a future supplement.

Results were intriguing for a New York State program called Child Assistance Program (CAP) (Hamilton and others, 1996). The CAP program offered single-parent welfare recipients with a court order for child support a voluntary alternative to welfare that had two features: it provided a basic benefit about one-third lower than regular welfare, and it reduced benefits by only 10 cents for each dollar of earnings up to the poverty line, and 67 cents thereafter. A parent with two children had more income under CAP than AFDC if she earned at least $350 a month (and less income under CAP if she earned less than that). Over a five-year period, the program increased earnings by $44 a month and increased income slightly. Unlike other programs that relied solely on financial incentives, however, CAP reduced benefits from welfare and the Food Stamp program slightly. In other words, it offered a financial incentive that saved the government money while providing a small financial benefit to families. The reduction in public assistance implies that some parents switched to CAP when they earned enough to make the move beneficial but did not reapply for welfare when they lost their jobs. Still other families might have taken jobs because of the program but did not switch to CAP because their earnings were too low or too unstable to make the move worthwhile.

Combining financial work incentives with other policies can increase their effectiveness. Minnesota's Full MFIP and Iowa's FIP (Fraker and Jacobson, 2000) combined earnings supplements with work-related requirements. Connecticut's Jobs First (Bloom and others, 2000a) and Florida's FTP (Bloom and others, 2000b) combined earnings supplements, work-related requirements, and time limits with receipt of welfare. Each of the programs increased employment, and their effect was generally larger than that of programs using earnings supplements alone. The effect on employment ranged from about three percentage points in Iowa's FIP to nearly eight percentage points in Connecticut's Jobs First. Because Jobs First and Full MFIP allowed people to combine work and welfare until their income was well beyond the poverty level, these programs had the greatest effects on income but also increased welfare use and welfare benefits. In contrast, Florida's FTP and Iowa's FIP had virtually no effect on welfare use, perhaps because the less generous welfare benefits in these states meant that many people who went to work quickly lost their eligibility for welfare, or because other elements of the reforms pushed people off welfare.

When the Full MFIP and MFIP Incentives Only programs were compared, the results indicated that adding work-related requirements to an enhanced earnings disregard more than doubled the effects on employment and increased its effects on earnings. The program was nevertheless quite inefficient: most of the effect on income stemmed from increased welfare benefits, not increased earnings.

Financial work incentives may be necessary to increase income. The primary difference between these programs and earlier mandatory welfare-to-work programs that required participation in work-directed services was their effect on income. Two of the most successful welfare-to-work programs studied were in Riverside, California, and Portland, Oregon. Both achieved large employment and earnings gains. In the second year after random assignment, they had increased parents' total earnings by about $100 a month. These results were similar to those in SSP and greater than gains in any of the other programs studied using random assignment. Despite their large effects on earnings, neither program had much effect on income (Bloom and Michalopoulos, 2001). The primary explanation is simple: Riverside and Portland reduced welfare benefits by $1 for every $1 increase in earnings, while the programs with earnings supplements allowed job takers to continue receiving some benefits.

Financial work incentives promote stable employment. Although a number of policies have succeeded in encouraging work, many low-wage workers have trouble retaining jobs (Strawn and Martinson, 2000). Evidence from SSP and MFIP, however, indicates that programs that use financial incentives encourage steady work. In particular, the number of people encouraged by SSP and both MFIP programs to work steadily for a year was almost as large as the number encouraged to work at all. This makes sense. Incentives in MFIP and SSP were available every month, giving people a reason to keep their jobs or find new jobs, and giving them financial resources to weather crises such as problems with child care or transportation.

Reducing Unintended Effects and Containing Costs

As already mentioned, programs with financial work incentives tend to cost more than programs without these incentives. One way to contain costs is to reward only full-time work. Another is to target incentives at less employable groups, such as welfare recipients.

Requiring full-time work can contain costs and reduce unintended effects. Because it rewarded only full-time work, SSP increased income from earnings and cash transfers by the largest amount ($107 a month) but was also fairly efficient, costing only $47 in extra cash transfers (welfare plus the SSP earnings supplements) each month. In other words, each extra dollar of spending on welfare and earnings supplements increased families' income by more than $2. In contrast, the MFIP Incentives Only program increased income significantly but was quite inefficient: an extra $89 dollars in welfare and Food Stamp benefits increased income by only $67 a month because the program reduced earnings slightly. This is a common problem with enhanced earnings disregards: they encourage some parents to work but allow others to cut back their work effort and still enjoy the financial benefits of the earnings supplement.

With the exception of SSP, individuals participating in these experiments were also eligible for the federal EITC, but the EITC was not included in any of the income calculations discussed here. Our analyses indicate that accounting for the EITC would change the impacts on income only slightly and would not change any of our conclusions.

Targeting financial work incentives at welfare recipients may increase their efficiency. By and large, program effects on employment and earnings are concentrated among people most likely to be long-term welfare recipients and are quite small for welfare applicants (table 10-2). Programs that combined incentives and other policies show the most striking results. The Full MFIP program increased employment among long-term welfare recipients by more than twelve percentage points, but only three percentage points for recent welfare applicants. Moreover, the program's mandatory services encouraged long-term recipients to work full-time, but its incentives encouraged recent applicants to work part-time. As a result, the program increased earnings for long-term recipients by $54 a month but left earnings for recent applicants unchanged. In addition, the program for long-term recipients was much more efficient: each dollar of extra cash transfers generated about $2 of increased income for long-term recipients but only $1 of increased income for recent applicants. Results from the Florida FTP and Connecticut Jobs First programs were quite similar. In contrast to these three programs, the Iowa program had somewhat larger effects for welfare applicants than for ongoing recipients, although neither effect was particularly large. It is not clear why the pattern of effects in Iowa differed from those of the other three programs.

Targeting financial work incentives at single-parent families rather than two-parent families may increase their efficiency. Where results for single-parent families can be compared with those for two-parent families—Vermont's WRP and Minnesota's Full MFIP—they again indicate that more narrowly targeted programs may be more efficient. Because two-parent families are likely to have more income than single-parent families, enhanced earnings disregards might actually discourage the secondary worker in two-parent families from working and encourage both parents to cut back their work effort.

MFIP did not increase the income of two-parent families—even though it increased cash transfers by nearly $200 a month—because some parents stopped working. WRP was also less efficient for two-parent families: it increased cash transfers by more than $100 for each two-parent family by making it easier for them to receive welfare but had no effect on cash transfers for single parents.

Table 10-2. *Changes in Employment Outcomes Due to Financial Incentive Schemes Tested Using Random Assignment of Welfare Recipients and Welfare Applicants*[a]

Dollars unless otherwise indicated

Employment outcome	Programs with incentives only			Programs with incentives and services			
	Canada SSP	Minnesota MFIP incentives only	Vermont WRP incentives only	Minnesota full MFIP	Florida FTP	Connecticut Jobs First	Iowa FIP
Welfare recipients							
Employment (percent)	7.1	4.8	1.0	12.2	6.1	10.9	1.7
Monthly earnings	58	–3	9	54	53	63	23
Monthly cash transfers	59	84	–25	49	–12	41	–4
Monthly income	116	81	–16	104	27	116	19
Welfare applicants							
Employment (percent)	7.2	0.9	–0.8	3.0	–3.5	2.8	4.6
Monthly earnings	65	–31	–50	–8	–5	–4	46
Monthly cash transfers	25	91	50	67	–10	58	1
Monthly income	91	59	20	59	–20	72	47

Source: See table 10-1.

a. See table 10-1 for follow-up periods and definitions of cash transfers and income. Recipients in SSP had been on welfare for twelve of the prior thirteen months; in MFIP they had been on welfare for twenty-four of the thirty-six months before random assignment; in Jobs First, WRP, and Iowa FIP, they were on welfare at the time of random assignment; and in FTP they were never on welfare before random assignment. Applicants in SSP had been approved to receive welfare shortly before random assignment after having been off welfare for at least six months; in MFIP applicants had been on welfare for fewer than twenty-four of the thirty-six months before random assignment; in Jobs First, WRP, and Iowa FIP, they were applying for benefits at the time of random assignment; and in FTP they had never been on welfare before random assignment. Results are not presented for CAP because Hamilton and others (1996) did not separately report results for applicants and recipients. Indicators of statistical significance are not provided because they were not available for all results.

Milwaukee's New Hope program (Bos and others, 1999) provides more evidence that targeting single-parent families may increase the efficiency of financial work incentives. New Hope provided a monthly earnings supplement and health and child care subsidies to low-income families in two neighborhoods if one parent worked at least thirty hours a week. In addition, adults who wanted to work full-time could be placed into six-month community service jobs. Because New Hope's incentives were conditioned on full-time work, they motivated people to work and provided no incentive to stop working. The ability to get the earnings supplement encouraged married parents who would have worked anyway to cut back their work effort, however. While the program increased earnings for single-parent families by $22 a month, it reduced earnings for two-parent families by $117 a month. This is not necessarily a bad thing. Many of the parents who cut back their work effort would have been working overtime without the program, and their reduced work effort may have contributed to reduced stress and improved outcomes for their children.

A waiting period may discourage people from applying for welfare to qualify for incentives that are available only to welfare recipients. With financial work incentives targeted at welfare recipients, there is a greater risk that working-poor people will quit their jobs and apply for welfare to qualify for the extra income provided by the incentive. Although entry effects are assumed to be widespread (see, for example, Moffitt, 1996), there is little evidence they actually occur. To measure this effect, welfare applicants assigned to SSP's program group were told that they would be eligible for the program's earnings supplement if they stayed on welfare an entire year. The resulting delayed exit effect was small: the proportion of applicants who received welfare benefits for an entire year increased by a marginally significant 3.1 percentage points (Berlin and others, 1998). Because welfare-based earnings disregards in the United States typically do not have such a waiting period, the entry effect may still be a serious problem. Nevertheless, financial work incentives can be structured to make such effects fairly small.

Evidence on the EITC

Although the EITC has never been studied using random assignment, a number of analyses have produced convincing evidence regarding its effects. This section briefly describes these results (for more details, see Hotz and Scholz, 2001).

Studies of the EITC generally corroborate the findings from the random assignment studies. First, the EITC appears to have encouraged many single mothers to work. According to Meyer and Rosenbaum (2000), for example, EITC expansions caused about 60 percent of the employment increase by single mothers between 1984 and 1996. Since employment by single mothers increased by eleven percentage points between 1984 and 1996, this suggests that expansions of the EITC encouraged about 800,000 single mothers to go to work. Meyer and Rosenbaum also point out that the drop in welfare use by single mothers mirrored their increase in employment.

Like the random assignment evaluations, studies of the EITC suggest that it is a poor means of encouraging work among two-parent families. In comparing couples with children (who might benefit from the expanded EITC) with couples without children (who are unlikely to benefit from the expanded EITC), Eissa and Hoynes (1998) found that the expanded EITC resulted in virtually no change in the employment of married men but caused slight (and statistically insignificant) declines in employment and hours of work for married women. According to their simulation results, the expanded EITC increased family income by $492 a year on average, but it reduced earnings by $40 a year.

These EITC-induced declines in work effort are much smaller than found for more employable participants in programs such as MFIP and New Hope. Differences between the random assignment studies and studies of the EITC might reflect a greater understanding of work incentives among participants in the random assignment studies. Incentives were well explained in those studies, while the link between earnings and the EITC is probably poorly understood by many families. The experimental programs also bolstered families' understanding of the work incentives by supplementing their earnings each month they worked (and stopping those supplements when they stopped working). By contrast, the EITC is paid to most recipients with their annual tax refund. Perhaps the EITC will cause larger reductions in work effort in the long run, as workers become more familiar with its rules.

Of course, a decrease in work effort may be beneficial, particularly if it is accompanied by an increase in income. Parents who reduce their hours of work have more time to spend with their children. By encouraging parents to stop working overtime, for example, New Hope reduced their stress levels and had other beneficial effects. In addition, providing a work incentive is only one of the two main goals of the EITC; reducing poverty is the other. The $30 billion spent on the program in 1999 went to millions of families, making it the largest federal antipoverty program in the United States (Haskins, chapter 4).

If policymakers want to encourage work, however, the EITC may be a somewhat less efficient method. Even the most optimistic estimates imply that the number of people who have gone to work because of expansions of the EITC since 1984 is dwarfed by the number of families receiving the EITC (Meyer and Rosenbaum, 2000; Hotz and Scholz, 2001). In addition, the evidence from MFIP implies that some people will cut back their work effort if they are allowed to receive an earnings supplement for part-time work. In view of the number of families that receive the EITC at its upper end, this may imply that the EITC is providing a considerable incentive for some parents to cut back their work effort.

Policy Recommendations

Given the existence of the EITC and expanded use of earned income disregards by most states, is there any justification for additional work incentives for low-income families? The random assignment evaluations provide two reasons for doing so. First, with the exception of SSP, both program and control group members were eligible for the EITC. The benefits of these programs were therefore in addition to any positive effect that the EITC may have had alone. Second, the disregards now in effect in most states differ from those used in the most effective programs reviewed here: they are not as generous, they are not as well marketed or explained, and they are being implemented along with time-limited welfare.

If officials wanted to increase resources to meet the needs of the working poor, what policy would maximize employment, income, and child well-being while minimizing unintended reductions in work effort among those who would have worked anyway? One strategy would be to increase the generosity of existing incentives programs, for example, by increasing the maximum amount that families can receive from the federal EITC or other federal credits, or by phasing out the EITC at a slower rate (Center on Budget and Policy Priorities, 2000; Cherry and Sawicky, 2000; Ellwood and Liebman, 2000; Sawhill and Thomas, 2001). This might increase the incentives to work full-time and reduce the incentives of some to cut back their work effort. But such a policy would be very expensive and would extend the work disincentives to families not currently eligible for the EITC.

Note, too, that full-time work is more likely than part-time work to provide fringe benefits such as health insurance and to produce skills that would increase a person's chances of becoming self-sufficient. New financial work incentives should therefore be tied to full-time work. This strategy would also limit the work-hour reductions among full-time workers evident in programs such as MFIP and New Hope and would contain the costs of additional incentives. We do not suggest that existing policies such as the EITC or

enhanced earnings disregards should be eliminated, since they provide valuable income to many families. Rather, we recommend that any new expenditures explicitly encourage full-time work. Here are two possibilities.

States could implement new programs like SSP or New Hope that supplement the earnings of those who work full-time. Results from SSP indicate
that the supplement could be quite generous but reasonably inexpensive if
targeted to a subset of the working poor, such as long-term welfare recipients
or the long-term unemployed. Results from New Hope indicate that offering
such a program to a broader group of the working poor would be more
expensive and less cost-effective but would have positive effects for families
even if it encourages some parents who work excessive hours to work less.

Alternatively, Congress could expand the EITC only for people who work
at least thirty hours a week. This strategy would encourage full-time work
while retaining the current program's benefits for parents who work part-
time. Since the federal tax system currently has no means of verifying how
much individuals work, however, the way the EITC is administered would
have to change dramatically. For example, employers might be required to
report information on hours worked to the agency administering the credit.
Although the administrative changes would not be simple, the implementation of full-time work requirements in SSP and New Hope may provide
some useful lessons for implementing such a policy through the EITC.

Another reform Congress should consider is stopping the five-year time
clock for working welfare recipients. Under current law, states can use federal
funds to provide welfare to an individual for only sixty months (states can
exempt 20 percent of the caseload from this limit). In response to this feature
of the law, most states limit welfare receipt to no more than sixty months.
However, policies that combine time limits and enhanced earnings disregards
send mixed messages: time limits encourage recipients to leave the rolls and
thus limit their ability to benefit from enhanced earnings disregards;
enhanced disregards increase income, but families that use them also use up
time-limited benefits. Implementing the two policies together virtually guarantees that a substantial number of people who take jobs while on welfare
will unwittingly exhaust their months of welfare eligibility (Pavetti and
Bloom, this volume). States may then find themselves in the awkward position of having to refuse reentry to welfare to large numbers of people whose
welfare eligibility expired as a result of the incentive. There are at least four
ways to avoid this dilemma.

First, at the federal level, Congress can amend TANF to allow states to
stop the federal time-limit clock but continue to use federal funds to provide
welfare when someone works thirty hours or more a week. This policy would

effectively stop the federal time-limit clock for people who work full-time. Although states can currently stop the federal clock by using state funds, amending the federal law would reduce the need to keep separate track of state and federal funds, help poorer states pay for the policy, and send a powerful signal that the federal government does not want working families to run up against time limits.

Second, states can create a separate or segregated state program for the working poor using maintenance of effort (MOE) payments that states must spend in order to draw down federal TANF funds. In a segregated program, a state can pay earnings supplements within the TANF program, allowing families to remain part of the state's TANF caseload without counting those months of assistance against the federal time limit (an approach currently used in Illinois). Alternatively, the state can provide benefits through a separate state program, so that the affected families do not receive any TANF assistance and are not subject to TANF time limits.

Third, states can structure benefits for working families so that they are not considered "TANF assistance" and therefore do not use up federal time-limited benefits. If properly structured, refundable tax credits, employer subsidies, child care subsidies, periodic bonus payments to reward job retention or to meet work expenses, and individual development accounts to promote savings would not be considered "assistance" under TANF and would not count against the time limit.

Finally, states can use federal TANF and state MOE funds to initiate or expand state EITCs. As mentioned earlier, fifteen states now offer an EITC. TANF and MOE funds can be used, however, only to subsidize that portion of a "refundable" credit that exceeds the amount of taxes owed (Johnson, 2000).

In conclusion, financial incentive policies can encourage work and parental self-sufficiency, reduce poverty, and improve children's outcomes. In designing new financial incentive policies, however, policymakers should remember there are trade-offs. Broadly based programs like the EITC may have an effect on the greatest number of families but would require funds far beyond those available in most TANF programs. For less money, more narrowly targeted programs can be more generous and have greater effects for a smaller number of people. Likewise, supplementing the earnings of people who work part-time will ensure that they are received by a great many people but will also have greater unintended consequences, in that they will encourage those who would have worked a lot to curtail their work effort. Tying new financial work incentives to full-time work will mean that fewer families will receive them, but may make the programs more efficient by reducing their unintended consequences and by increasing the self-sufficiency of those families that increase their work effort to receive the new supplements. With these trade-offs in mind, policymakers merely have to determine their goal and design a program with financial work incentives accordingly.

COMMENT BY

Glenn C. Loury

Charles Michalopoulos and Gordon Berlin present a useful review of recent policy research on efforts to encourage labor market participation among low-skilled workers. Their underlying objective is to identify the fundamental trade-offs faced by public decisionmakers in this area of tax and transfer policy. This is well-trod ground to anyone familiar with the voluminous literature in public finance on the negative income tax. The issues are (a) target efficiency and (b) disincentives to effort.

To encourage work among former or current welfare recipients, a program may narrowly target people now on or only recently off the rolls or may assign its benefits more broadly to all low-wage workers. Programs of the former kind will have lower costs but will raise issues of horizontal equity (because they will treat persons in like circumstances unequally). The latter kind will not leave low-wage nonrecipients out, but costs will skyrocket. In addition, eligibility for any means-tested subsidy can be phased out quickly as beneficiaries' earnings rise, or it can be phased out more slowly and thus make the program more nearly universal. A quick phase-out creates disincentives for program participants to generate relatively higher earnings, but a slow phase-out means substantially greater costs. Michalopoulos and Berlin do a fine job of examining how these conventional trade-offs play out in the context of current and prospective earnings-enhancement policies.

Looking beyond the trade-offs they discuss, I consider some other conflicts among desirable but mutually incompatible objectives created by the commitment articulated in the Temporary Assistance for Needy Families program (TANF) to replace welfare with work. I agree with Michalopoulos and Berlin that the job of policy analysts is to identify and quantify the trade-offs, whereas the job of policymakers is to choose among the competing alternatives while remaining mindful of the opportunity costs thereby entailed. I hope to enrich the discussion of this policy choice problem by bringing attention to some less conventional trade-offs not treated in detail by the authors.

Since raising the remuneration from work also raises the opportunity cost of time spent with one's children at home, it follows that any subsidy to work is necessarily a tax on "home production." This point has not escaped the author's attention, of course. It is worth pointing out, however, that the benefits from greater work effort—in terms of higher family incomes and reduced public transfers—are rather easy to observe and measure. On the other hand, the costs of reduced time at home—in terms of adverse effects on children or diminished well-being for parents—are more difficult to assess. Hence unless policymakers bear this fact in mind, this particular trade-off may get short shrift. This danger is most acute if, as is the case in some quarters, I suspect, there is a tendency to undervalue the contribution to family welfare arising from time spent at home with children by a relatively uneducated, low-wage, single parent. So far as I know, there is no empirical warrant for such undervaluation, particularly in view of the rather poor quality of child care that is within the means of these parents.

A second unconventional trade-off arises from the general equilibrium effects of subsidizing labor market participation among the less skilled. Increasing the supply of low-wage workers (as a policy subsidizing their earnings must do if it is to be effective) necessarily puts downward pressure on the wages of any workers making more than the statutory minimum. This point is nicely illustrated by the senior vice president of the National Alliance of Business who in 1998 said: "Welfare Reform has been a boon for business. . . . It provides a positive way for employers to expand their labor force in a tight labor market" (Miller, 1998, p. 28). Of course, what is a "positive" development for business in this context need not be an unalloyed, positive development for the employees of business, nor need this be seen as "positive" by a policymaker whose objective is to raise the living standards of working poor families.

Yet another unconventional trade-off is that reliance on (subsidized) earnings from work to increase the resources of poor families (in preference to transfers) means exposing these families to the risk of unemployment due to the normal operations of the business cycle. If it is true that a "rising tide lifts all boats," then it is also true that the inevitable arrival of an ebb tide will cause some of those boats to sink again. For instance, Richard Freeman (2000, p. 31) observes:

The experience of the 1990s cautions us that unemployment rates of 4–5 percent may be required to overpower the forces of inequality and improve the condition of low-wage workers. Anything short of those rates, which were once viewed as unsustainable risks returning the

United States to the condition of the 1980s—economic growth without reductions in poverty.

The apparent success of welfare-to-work policy in the 1990s rests to some not inconsiderable degree on the fortuitous circumstance of a recession-free economy. Again, this point has been made often, and the authors are surely not unaware of it. But it is worth pointing out in this context that under current law a worker's Unemployment Insurance (UI) benefits do not count when calculating "earned income" for determining the Earned Income Tax Credit (EITC). Hence, since the EITC has become so central to the strategy of "making work pay," low-wage workers now bear much greater business cycle risks than necessary. It is both feasible and desirable to shift some of this risk onto the public sector by allowing UI benefits to count for the purposes of determining EITC payments. However, even this would not be a perfect solution to the problem since a large fraction of low-wage workers experiencing employment separations are not eligible for UI. Indeed, it has been estimated that more than one-third of low-skilled workers' employment separations are not UI-eligible (Gustafson and Levine, 1998).

In summary, while the conventional trade-offs identified by Michalopolous and Berlin should be kept in view by policymakers, there are some unconventional trade-offs that are also of great importance. Encouraging work discourages time at home with children, for example. Pushing low-skilled workers into the labor market also pushes down their wages. And relying on a strategy of "making work pay" implies that low-wage workers are at greater risks of hardship in times of recession. I maintain that it is crucial to the formulation of good policy for public decisionmakers to remain aware of these latter trade-offs, too.

References

Berlin, Gordon, and others. 1998. *Do Work Incentives Have Unintended Consequences? Measuring "Entry Effects" in the Self-Sufficiency Project.* Ottawa: Social Research and Demonstration Corporation.

Bloom, Dan, and Charles Michalopoulos. 2001. *How Welfare and Work Policies Affect Employment and Income: A Synthesis of Research.* New York: Manpower Demonstration Research Corporation.

Bloom, Dan, and others. 2000a. *Jobs First: Implementation and Early Impacts of Connecticut's Welfare Reform Initiative.* New York: Manpower Demonstration Research Corporation.

———. 2000b. *The Family Transition Program: Final Report on Florida's Initial Time-Limited Welfare Program.* New York: Manpower Demonstration Research Corporation.

Bos, Johannes M., and others. 1999. *New Hope for People with Low Incomes: Two-Year Results of a Program to Reduce Poverty and Reform Welfare.* New York: Manpower Demonstration Research Corporation.

Center on Budget and Policy Priorities. 2000. *Should EITC Benefits Be Enlarged for Families with Three or More Children?* Washington.

Cherry, Robert, and Max Sawicky. 2000. *Giving Tax Credit Where It's Due: A "Universal Unified Child Credit" That Expands the EITC and Cuts Taxes for Working Families.* Washington: Economic Policy Institute.

Eissa, Nada, and Hilary Williamson Hoynes. 1998. "The Earned Income Tax Credit and the Labor Supply of Married Couples." Working Paper W6856. Cambridge, Mass.: National Bureau of Economic Research.

Ellwood, David T., and Jeffrey B. Liebman. 2000. "The Middle-Class Parent Penalty: Child Benefits in the U.S. Tax Code." Working Paper W8031. Cambridge, Mass.: National Bureau of Economic Research.

Fraker, Thomas M., and Jonathan E. Jacobson. 2000. *Iowa's Family Investment Program: Impacts during the First 3-1/2 Years of Welfare Reform.* Washington: Mathematica.

Freeman, Richard. 2000. "The Rising Tide Lifts. . . ?" *Focus* 21 (2): 27–31.

Gallagher, L. Jerome, and others. 1998. "One Year after Federal Welfare Reform: A Description of State Temporary Assistance for Needy Families (TANF) Decisions as of October 1997." Occasional Paper 6. Washington: Urban Institute.

Gueron, Judith M., and Edward Pauly. 1991. *From Welfare to Work.* Russell Sage.

Gustafson, C. K., and P. B. Levine. 1998. "Less-Skilled Workers, Welfare Reform, and the Unemployment Insurance System." Working Paper 6489. Cambridge, Mass.: National Bureau for Economic Research.

Hamilton, William L., and others. 1996. *The New York State Child Assistance Program: Five-Year Impacts, Costs, and Benefits.* Cambridge, Mass.: Abt.

Hendra, Richard, and Charles Michalopoulos. 1999. *Forty Two Month Impacts of Vermont's Welfare Restructuring Project.* New York: Manpower Demonstration Research Corporation.

Hotz, V. Joseph, and J. Karl Scholz. 2001. "The Earned Income Tax Credit." Working Paper W8078. Cambridge, Mass.: National Bureau of Economic Research.

Johnson, Nicholas. 2000. *A Hand Up: How State Earned Income Tax Credits Help Working Families Escape Poverty in 2000.* Washington: Center on Budget and Policy Priorities.

Meyer, Bruce D., and Dan T. Rosenbaum. 2000. "Making Single Mothers Work: Recent Tax and Welfare Policy and Its Effects." *National Tax Journal* 53 (4): 1027–62.

————. Forthcoming. "Welfare, the Earned Income Tax Credit, and the Labor Supply of Single Mothers." *Quarterly Journal of Economics.*

Michalopoulos, Charles, and others. 1999. *When Financial Incentives Pay for Themselves: Early Findings from the Self-Sufficiency Project's Applicant Study.* Ottawa: Social Research and Demonstration Corporation.

————. 2000. *The Self-Sufficiency Project at 36 Months: Effects of a Financial Work Incentive on Employment and Income.* Ottawa: Social Research and Demonstration Corporation.

Miller, Cynthia, and others. 2000. *Reforming Welfare and Rewarding Work: Final Report on the Minnesota Family Investment Program.* Vol. 1: Effects on Adults. New York: Manpower Demonstration Research Corporation.

Miller, William. 1998. "Surprise! Welfare Reform Is Working." *Industry Week* 16: 24–30.

Moffitt, Robert. 1992. "Incentive Effects of the U.S. Welfare System: A Review." *Journal of Economic Literature* 30 (March): 1–61.

————. 1996. "The Effect of Employment and Training Programs on Entry and Exit from the Welfare Caseload." *Journal of Policy Analysis and Management* 15 (1): 32–50.

Morris, Pamela, and others. 2001. *How Welfare and Work Policies Affect Children: A Synthesis of Research.* New York: Manpower Demonstration Research Corporation.

Sawhill, Isabel, and Adam Thomas. 2001. *A Tax Proposal for Working Families with Children. Welfare Reform and Beyond Brief 3.* Brookings.

SRI International. 1983. *Final Report of the Seattle/Denver Income Maintenance Experiment. Vol. 1: Design and Results.* Menlo Park, Calif.

Strawn, Julie, and Karin Martinson. 2000. *Steady Work and Better Jobs: How to Help Low-Income Parents Sustain Employment and Advance in the Workforce.* New York: Manpower Demonstration Research Corporation.

11

JASON A. TURNER
THOMAS MAIN

Work Experience under Welfare Reform

THE SUBJECT OF THIS CHAPTER is work experience programs. These are state or local programs that enroll adult welfare recipients in work activity, usually in government agencies or nonprofit entities, as a condition of receiving cash benefits. Work experience is distinct from public service employment for wages, and from work-promoting activities such as job search or skills training (which may involve some work activity). However, work experience can be and often is combined with other employment readiness activities such as job search, job training, or substance abuse treatment.

The purpose and function of work experience as a welfare-to-work component are somewhat more varied than those of other more narrowly conceived service components such as job search and skills training. It can be said to incorporate four underlying objectives:

1. To increase the employability of participants by offering opportunities to practice work and to learn the habits and social skills necessary to succeed in entry-level employment.

2. To reduce welfare dependency by improving employment prospects and by altering the work/leisure trade-off.

3. To fulfill a social and moral obligation of recipients to contribute to society in exchange for benefits.

4. To attack the culture of poverty, which is related to the notion of social obligation just mentioned, but is not the same. To the extent that the culture

of poverty represents a way of life in which many negative influences become self-reinforcing, the act of working itself may create deep indirect positive personal and social effects (for example, a greater future orientation) that benefit communities and society in general.

Although work while on welfare for those not privately employed was one of the central goals of the Personal Responsibility and Work Opportunity Reconciliation Act (PRWORA) of 1996, and more specifically of the Temporary Assistance for Needy Families (TANF) program created by Title I of PRWORA, it is not now a significant component of the welfare reform programs that most states offer. Given the goals of TANF, this is a surprising and important fact that is not widely recognized and to which we will return.

Work Experience Requirements under TANF

TANF, which replaced the Aid to Families with Dependent Children (AFDC) program, requires adult recipients to engage in work once a state determines the recipient is ready to work, or after twenty-four months of receiving assistance, whichever is earlier (to date, the large majority of TANF recipients who meet this work requirement do so through unsubsidized employment, that is, by working at a regular job while receiving benefits). The authors of TANF clearly intended that work, even while still receiving benefits, should transform the meaning of temporary assistance, and they signaled this intent by setting high levels of weekly work levels and participation rates. In addition, the TANF authors took special care to observe the lessons from past failed attempts to legislate work requirements, for instance, that unless clearly defined, states would not actually require work. Notwithstanding the flexibility otherwise inherent in the TANF block grant, the work requirements and measurements are specifically spelled out. In contrast to earlier federal legislation, especially in light of the disappointing Job Opportunities and Basic Skills Training (JOBS) program created by the Family Support Act in 1988, TANF drafters attempted to lock in higher work levels. They did so in four ways.

First, they insisted on honest counting. The participation standards written into the earlier JOBS program had been beset by the phenomenon of the "shrinking denominator," or the ability of states to exclude large numbers of individuals from being counted as available for work-related activities. Thus states were allowed to announce work participation rates that were misleadingly high. TANF helped resolve this problem by keeping a broad definition of who is available for work, including nearly all adults minus only those with a child under the age of one (a state option for a period of up to twelve months per family) and those cases in sanction status (for no more than three months within the preceding twelve months). Thus few cases can be removed from the denominator of the ratio of those actually working.

Second, the TANF statute defines precisely what counts as work (in the numerator of the calculation), rather than leaving this definition to the states. The definition of work under TANF conforms to the common sense meaning of the word, rather than absorbing into it education, training, and other assorted activities.

Third, the legislation includes substantial required participation rates, beginning with 25 percent of the caseload in 1997, and increasing to 50 percent by 2002 (and higher for two-parent families). Required hours also increase over time, rising from twenty hours per week in 1997 to thirty hours in 2000 and thereafter. Penalties assessed against states for noncompliance with the above standards were set at a realistically low level (5 percent the first year, increasing by two percentage points for each consecutive year of failure). This modest penalty was intended to increase the probability that the penalty would actually be imposed and collected (thereby signaling that program adherence is expected), rather than be blocked in Congress by home state members.

Fourth, TANF requires states to impose serious financial penalties (sanctions) against participants who do not comply with program requirements

A Brief History of Work Experience Programs

The lineage of today's work experience programs might be traced to the Work Progress Administration (WPA) program, which operated between 1935 and 1943 and used federal funds to pay for state and locally managed construction and other projects. Along with its cousin, the Civilian Conservation Corps, the WPA was intended to offer the depression unemployed an alternative to unrestricted government or private charity, bringing into convergence the wishes of both the public and the unemployed themselves. The memory of those honorable 10 million depression laborers who produced shrines to the Roosevelt decade persists in the national consciousness and has played a role in the imagination of welfare reformers ever since.

In the more modern era, work requirements were adopted in 1962 and expanded in 1967 when work or training registration was made mandatory for two-parent households under the Work Incentive Program (WIN). Amendments enacted in 1971 required all able-bodied adults, including women, to register for work or training, but enrollment remained low, and actual participation lower still. When President Ronald Reagan came to office, he enacted legislation as part of the 1981 Omnibus Budget Reconciliation Act that created a variety of work options for states. States were permitted to conduct WIN from welfare agencies (rather than job service agencies), to run work experience programs in government or private nonprofit settings, to mandate job search, and to run on-the-job training programs using welfare grants to subsidize wages. However, with few exceptions states did not exercise these options on a large scale (Brock, Butler, and Long, 1993). Later, the 1988 JOBS program permitted work experience but did not encourage it. JOBS represented the high tide of faith and belief in education as the best long-term strategy for alleviating poverty and dependency. Its most lasting contributions to evolving work programs were that it required and measured participation, did not exempt all mothers with young children, and started to build the state infrastructure for the more ambitious state and federal work-centered reforms to come.

The mandate in TANF for high participation in work experience was not a result of some sudden new impulse in the views of policymakers. Rather, it was an important part of a movement over time among policymakers, primarily conservatives, in favor of work as a reciprocal obligation for people receiving welfare. Although polling figures going back as far as the 1930s showed consistent public support for work obligations among welfare recipients, work as a reciprocal obligation in exchange for benefits was not widely accepted by policymakers until at least the 1980s. By then the problem of long-term dependency was being discussed more openly. Equally important, large and increasing numbers of middle-class women with young children were entering the labor force, greatly weakening the earlier assumptions that mothers should not be expected to work.

Charles Murray's *Losing Ground,* published in 1984, ignited a lively public discussion of the culture of dependency. Two years later in 1986, President Reagan announced in his state of the union address the formation of a task force to study the nation's welfare programs and to propose reforms that would address welfare dependency and associated issues. The task force eventually published a multivolume report entitled *Up from Dependency* (Domestic Policy Council, 1986), which emphasized the importance of work programs in reforming welfare. Also in 1986, Lawrence Mead of New York University published *Beyond Entitlement,* in which he argued that the main problem with the welfare state was not its size but its permissiveness. For Mead, the challenge of welfare reform was to couple benefits with serious work and other obligations that would in turn encourage better functioning of adults dependent on welfare and thus promote their integration into society (Mead, 1986).

The calls for ending dependency were not exclusively made from the right. Around the same time a diverse group of important thinkers and activists convened by the American Enterprise Institute published *The New Consensus on Family and Welfare.* The bipartisan group agreed that able adults should not be allowed to take from the common good without also contributing to it (Novak, 1987). Similarly, a task force on poverty and welfare convened by Governor Mario Cuomo of New York, which included five future members of the Clinton administration (Mary Jo Bane, Peter Edelman, David Ellwood, Robert Reich, and Donna Shalala), concluded in 1986 that society should require work in exchange for public support but guarantee that support will be available by providing jobs if necessary (Task Force, 1986).

Finally, again in 1986, a long and influential article (which became a book in 1992) by Mickey Kaus appeared in the *New Republic,* a standard-bearer of American liberalism. After analyzing and rejecting every alternative welfare reform idea then current, Kaus recommended completely replacing welfare with a single, simple offer of employment in a useful public job at a wage slightly below minimum for those who need assistance. Kaus argued that this approach would undermine the culture of dependency that had been built up over generations of unrestricted cash assistance. Like Mead, he also believed that mandatory work would help the poor by reintegrating them into mainstream society. This culture argument for work experience holds that work programs represent considerably more than merely improving individual employment prospects. Rather, these programs are an agent of the social transformation of the underclass. In discussing the shared experience of work as integral to citizenship, Mead observed:

> The great merit of equal citizenship as a social goal is that it is much more widely achievable than status. It is not competitive. It does not require that the disadvantaged "succeed," something not everyone can do. It requires only that everyone discharge the common obligations, including social ones like work. (Mead, 1986; p. 12)

Two years after he participated in the Cuomo task force, David Ellwood released *Poor Support* (1988), his analysis of the causes of welfare dependency and the need to help adults on welfare work. He endorsed the major tenet of the Cuomo task force, that those who remained on welfare should be required to work, if necessary in a public job. This theme, along with the theme of time limits, was picked up by presidential candidate Bill Clinton. Once in office, the Clinton administration and the Department of Health and Human Services labored over several iterations of reform legislation, all of which featured required work after a period of assistance.

After the 1994 elections, the initiative shifted to congressional Republicans. The Contract with America, which included ten reforms Republicans promised to attempt to enact into law if they were granted control of Congress, contained an ambitious welfare reform proposal that, in a somewhat modified version, Republicans did enact and send to President Clinton in the fall of 1995. During discussions among Republicans around the subject of work requirements, Ways and Means committee staff director Ron Haskins recalls that Republican members generally believed that recipients should work while receiving assistance, were skeptical of the usefulness of nonwork interventions, and believed that if required to actually work in exchange for benefits, many applicants for and recipients of welfare would find private employment on their own. For their part, many Democrats who had opposed work requirements in the past had by this time been influenced by research showing that programs oriented toward job search and immediate employment, as opposed to programs emphasizing education and training, could significantly increase the number of people working and at the same time reduce welfare expenditures. Thus Republicans and many Democrats could come together to support a work-first welfare reform bill, even if they differed over the specific work provisions and other provisions of the legislation.

Low Rate of Usage of Work Experience by States

Interestingly, with all the attention paid to work participation standards by the drafters of TANF, a provision was included in the bill that made achieving high work rates less imperative than it seemed at the time the legislation was enacted. This provision is the caseload reduction credit, which reduces the participation rate requirement by one percentage point for each percentage point a state's welfare caseload falls below 1995 levels. Thus, if a given state's caseload were to fall by 25 percent between 1995 and 1999, the TANF work requirement would fall from the required 1999 level of 35 percent to 10 percent (35 percent − 25 percent = 10 percent). Since well over 10 percent of the caseload in many states already combines private employment with welfare, states such as the one in this example would not need to have any welfare recipient in a work program to meet the 35 percent work standard.

Not surprisingly, given the caseload reduction credit, national data for 1999 show that the typical state had very few welfare recipients in a work experience program at that time. Although over 40 percent of the adult caseload in the average state is involved in some required activity, nearly 70 percent of these are in unsubsidized employment; that is, they are collecting welfare while working at a regular job. By contrast, fewer than 10 percent of all adults who are participating in any activity while receiving welfare benefits are in work experience of any kind. This figure translates to just 4 percent of the entire caseload of 2.1 million adults. Thus the number of adults on TANF who participate in work experience is exceedingly low by any standard. Even the Family Support Act enrolled an estimated 20,000 to 35,000 in work experience on an average monthly basis in 1994, as compared with 78,000 now (U.S. House of Representatives, 1996a, p. 421).

Clearly, states as a group have exercised their option under the TANF caseload reduction credit to focus management attention on other parts of the program. To better understand state intentions relating to work experience, we interviewed responsible state officials from New Jersey, Ohio, and Illinois. New Jersey and Ohio have large work experience programs by state standards, Illinois a small one. The officials from these states each expressed satisfaction with the operations of their work experience programs, although they each acknowledged the high level of effort and resources involved in managing and communicating with work sites and monitoring participation. None of the state officials referenced external political opposition per se as a limitation on program size (at least not at the relatively low levels that characterize these state programs), nor have they encountered bureaucratic resistance. But they did say that initially persuading potential sites to participate can present difficulties. New Jersey and Ohio each use work experience as a program option after a period of unsuccessful job search, with the level of use being left to the discretion of county caseworkers. When used, the component is frequently combined with other activities to meet the number of hours required to count toward the participation rate or to fill gaps between other components such as school vacations. The three state officials said their work experience is often targeted to adults with little prior work history, and all discussed high turnover as a usual program feature.

In each of these three states, work experience is used to the general satisfaction of the state officials we interviewed; however, in none of the states does the use of work experience appear to be communicated from the top of state management as a program priority overriding other considerations, even in the relatively high-use states of New Jersey and Ohio. Thus the significant efforts that would be necessary to organize state programs around a substantial commitment to work have evidently not been generated by TANF as it is currently configured. How one views this development depends partly on one's judgment as to the relative value of maximizing state program flexibility as compared with that of requiring full engagement in work activity as a primary goal of welfare reform. A major management commitment is necessary to mount a large and ongoing work experience program for a high proportion of recipients, and although the policymakers who drafted the TANF program may have anticipated that most recipients would be involved in actual work, implementation by states has simply not produced this result.

Running a Work Experience Program: Early Research

Although work experience has been used as a welfare-to-work strategy for many years, large-scale mandatory program implementation has been rare. In the 1980s West Virginia managed a fairly large program, targeting about 25 percent of women and all men (AFDC-Unemployed Parent cases). Individual counties in Ohio and a few other states have in the past run saturation work experience programs. But currently, only New York City and Wisconsin have large-scale programs in which work experience is required of most adults in the welfare caseload.

One of the few empirical studies of work experience programs, conducted by the Manpower Demonstration Research Corporation (MDRC) during the 1980s, provides information on programs of this kind in seven states: California, Illinois, Virginia, Maryland, Maine, Arkansas, and West Virginia (Brock and others, 1993). Most of these states recorded a low use of work experience; only West Virginia required such experience as part of ongoing participation. The others incorporated work experience for a limited period (usually three months) and even then only after completion of a period of job search. Brock and others reported several other notable findings about work experience.

First, as already indicated, the work experience components had limited use owing to administrative difficulties, insufficient resources, staff opposition, and the greater popularity of other program components among staff, especially education. Second, of the three programs in which MDRC researchers could isolate effects on earnings and employment (San Diego, Cook County, and West Virginia), only the San Diego program for single mothers produced significant impacts (these mothers were employed at the eighteenth month at a rate 5 percent higher than the controls who had job-search only, with earnings over a fifteen-month follow-up of $500 higher). There was no evidence that the mostly three-month work experience components had any impacts on welfare receipt or welfare payments. Work experience combined with job search did lead to small overall reductions in welfare payments and caseloads in San Diego and Cook Counties.

The administering agencies spent $700 to $2,100 (in 1993 dollars) to run a three-month assignment per participant (this included costs associated with intake and assignment, work site development, monitoring, and support services of child care and work allowances). The benefits to taxpayers of running a work experience program, expressed as the value of the output by participants minus all program costs, ranged from about $260 to $1,000 per participant, except in Cook County, which experienced a small net loss to taxpayers. By contrast, the net benefit to welfare recipients, expressed as the difference between total income from earnings and fringe benefits minus new taxes and reduced welfare, was inconsistent. Despite the lack of a consistent impact on participant income, both the participants and their supervisors reported that the work was meaningful and not "make-work."

MDRC suggested the following ingredients were essential to run work experience on a large scale, as opposed to the limited programs studied: strong staff commitment to the program, adequate work site capacity, clear procedures for assigning participants to work sites, monitoring of participation, a procedure for exempting recipients who cannot work, sanctioning for those who do not comply with work requirements, and support for the program (or at least lack of opposition) from advocacy groups and labor unions.

Lessons from New York City and Wisconsin

New York City and Wisconsin are both working toward a fully work based welfare system, which means that for those not in private employment work experience makes up the greater part of a full-time simulated workweek, with other activities such as job search and education included as lesser parts. The work obligation applies to all adults with almost no exceptions, and substantial management attention is devoted to attendance, tracking, and monitoring of sites. In order to ensure suitable work assignments for those of all capabilities, specialized work sites incorporate vocational rehabilitation. Taken together, Wisconsin and New York's work experience programs offer guidance as to what might be expected of a more extensive national program, as reflected in the following observations.

Work Experience Should Constitute Genuine Practice for Private Employment

While empirical evidence is lacking, certain steps appear likely to make work experience more effective in preparing people for actual jobs:

—The program should operate on a standard full-time workweek that conforms to the expectations of private employment. This would allow participants to practice organizing their lives around a realistic work schedule of eight-hour workdays and five-day workweeks.

—Real work must be accomplished. Nothing is more dispiriting to those expecting to work than to remain idle, or worse, ignored, on the job. By contrast, the pride and satisfaction of successfully mastering work tasks often result in a big psychological lift and translate into confidence in the search for private employment.

—Third-party medical review must be available to determine work capability. Medical reviews are essential to ensure the health and safety of participants, and to maintain a uniform work standard not subject to "doctor shopping."

—Work assignments must include close supervision and regular feedback. Those who lack work histories tend to be unfamiliar with workplace norms of professionalism and conduct, and frequently find it difficult to submit to supervisory authority or to get along with co-workers. Supervisors who agree to make part of their task the acculturation of participants play a large role in the success of their charges.

—There must be swift consequences for nonattendance without cause. Such consequences may constitute a new experience for those used to a bureaucratic welfare system in which not much changes. Thus the importance of reliability must be taught, and for this to occur benefits must be closely tied to attendance.

Work Experience Is the Best Alternative to Cash Assistance

Work experience can expand or contract like an accordion to accommodate the ebbs and flows of the private economy. Work experience can absorb those outside of the private labor market while keeping work habits and skills in good repair. Compared with other work-related activities such as grant diversion or public service employment, work experience can be operated on a large scale, can make up the major part of a full-time program week (for example, thirty-five hours), can accommodate participants who remain in the component for extended periods, and can provide an immediate and ever-present work option for individuals rotating into and out of assistance.

Work Experience Exerts Its Greatest Impact at the Time of Enrollment

Where work experience has been required, applicants who do not find private employment within a certain period of time tend to participate in such programs at a far lower level than anticipated. Fewer slots are necessary because individuals who know they must work in exchange for benefits frequently elect not to enroll in the program in the first place. Instead, they find immediate employment or increase their hours at part-time jobs. In other instances they rely on alternatives already present, such as combinations of unreported work, doubling-up, help from relatives, and help from friends.

The use of work experience was clearly lower than expected in the transition from the AFDC entitlement program to the completely work-based W-2 program in Wisconsin. Of the 26,000 AFDC families with an adult head who were required to enroll in the new W-2 program calling for full-time work experience, 45 percent elected not to transfer and closed their case. Another 16 percent accepted W-2 case management services but did not wish to engage in work experience in order to receive cash benefits (Wisconsin, 1999).

Universal Work Programs Require Work Slots for Individuals of All Capabilities

In New York, fully 87 percent of the TANF caseload (excluding child-only cases) is deemed "engageable," meaning that one or more adults are ready for some kind of work assignment. Having a nearly universal expectation of work helps change the culture of the system and channels the energy of recipients in a constructive direction away from attempting to qualify for exemptions.

A work experience program that aims for close to universal applicability must also have an inventory of assignments suitable for participants of varying ability levels. Both New York City and Wisconsin favor a "ladder" of work options that provide real work for adults with all levels of experience and job readiness. Standard work assignments range from outdoor physical work to office jobs in government or nonprofit agencies. For adults with mild disabilities, vocational rehabilitation agencies such as Goodwill Industries can provide work in specialized settings. In New York City, roughly one-third of the mildly disabled who enroll in work rehabilitation have orthopedic limitations such as back weaknesses; another third have mental health problems, especially depression; and the balance have mostly asthma or cardiovascular limitations.

The Incremental Costs of Running a Work Experience Program Are Manageable

MDRC found the annual costs per filled slot in work experience programs range from $700 to $8,000. The incremental cost of running New York City's large-scale program is within the lower part of this range. Total 1999 expenditures on work experience were about $43.1 million, or about $1,400 annually per filled slot excluding child care (because each slot turns over multiple times per year, the cost per participant is lower than the annual amount). Of the $1,400, 67 percent goes to payments to other government agencies for direct costs, including timekeepers, coordinators, and field supervisors as well as tools and equipment (nonprofit agencies that host work experience participants often absorb these costs). Another 24 percent goes to third-party medical assessments. The remaining 9 percent is used for welfare agency administrative costs (New York, 2000).

There Are Benefits for Participating Agencies

Most New York City agencies were reluctant to take on the responsibility for managing large numbers of work experience participants until Mayor Rudolph Giuliani himself made it clear that work opportunities for welfare recipients were a city priority. Once set up to accommodate work experience participants, however, these same agencies came to see significant improvements in the level of service they were able to provide the public. To take one example, immediately before the introduction of large numbers of work experience participants, the city's parks had an "acceptable cleanliness" rating of 74 percent. Largely as a result of the additional labor available beginning in 1995, which peaked at more than 3,000 full-time worker equivalents, the acceptable cleanliness rating of the city's parks climbed to 95 percent. More recently, the sharp caseload declines have resulted in fewer work experience participants for the Parks agency, prompting the department to request an increase in referrals from the city welfare agency.

In 1993 MDRC evaluated the productivity of work experience participants as compared with regular employees. According to the supervisors surveyed, work experience participants were as productive, or nearly as productive, as regular employees (Brock, Butler, and Long, 1993). Using this information, Ellwood and Welty (2000) found hourly output values ranging from $6.31 in West Virginia (1996 dollars) to $9.21 for workers from two-parent San Diego families. Experience in New York City indicates that productivity tends to be somewhat lower than that of regular employees because of higher turnover, more frequent absences, and a tendency for welfare recipients to bring at-home problems to the work site.

Sanction Policies Play a Large Role in Achieving High Levels of Participation

High nonparticipation rates are a feature of most mandatory programs. In Wisconsin, where the W-2 program pays cash benefits only to those who first participate in work activities, compliance by definition is high. However, in states that do not use a version of full-check sanction for nonparticipation (such as New York), a large proportion of families may accept a lower TANF payment rather than engage in work. In a high-intensity program, the number of recipients who accept sanctions to avoid work can actually exceed the number of recipients who meet the participation requirement. For instance, New York recently had 17,000 active TANF work experience participants, along with 15,000 engaged in other primary activities, for a total of 32,000. At the same time, there were 17,500 individuals in sanction status for non-participation, with an additional 17,000 in the sanction determination process, for a total of 34,500, which is slightly higher than the number properly engaged in work experience (New York, 2000). According to a cross state comparison of sanction policies under TANF (see Pavetti and Bloom, chapter 9), programs must enforce work-related mandates in order to achieve high rates of participation.

However, even strong sanction policies will not encourage all potential participants to meet their work obligation. In order to reach greater numbers of nonparticipants, New York City contracted with several faith-based organizations to make home visits to counsel and assist families with problems in an atmosphere of greater trust. Church counselors say that they are usually welcomed into these homes and develop positive relationships with recipients. However, a minority of those encountered have remained isolated at home for such long periods that they lack minimal will and confidence to enter the program. Many of these adults believe that even if they did participate in work experience, they would fail. For this subset, a longer period of relationship building combined with special interventions, perhaps with nongovernment counselors, may be beneficial.

High Turnover Rates Present Management Problems but Lower the Number of Required Work Slots

MDRC found not only high initial no-show rates, but also high work experience turnover for those who do enroll. For those who began a scheduled three-month work experience assignment in Cook County, 35 percent worked the equivalent of a month or less, 60 percent worked for two months or less, and most of the balance worked for three months or less (Brock, Butler, and Long, 1993). In New York, for those who begin a work experience assignment, the 1996 TANF dropout rate was 38 percent after one month, 53 percent after two months, and 61 percent after three months. Since 1996 the turnover rate has continued to increase as the system has approached near universal enrollment and the caseload has declined further.

The high turnover rate stems from at least two factors. One is that those who reliably participate in their work assignments, even for short periods, are able to obtain private employment (experience shows that private employers like to receive attendance information and recommendations from work experience supervisors and take them into account). Fully half of all individuals who participated in New York's work experience program for any period during the first quarter of 2000 found employment the same calendar year (New York, 2000). In addition, normal caseload dynamics in which recipients leave the rolls further increases turnover.

The high work experience turnover rate means that far fewer actual slots are needed to run a universal program than would otherwise be required. For its TANF caseload of 161,000, of which 128,000 have an adult in the household, New York City is able to run a mandatory universal work program with only 17,000 slots (with the caveat that many are not participating even though required to do so), with an additional 15,000 slots for other primary activities such as high school, postsecondary education or training, and initial-stage substance abuse treatment. An additional 10,000 work experience slots are sufficient for a general assistance caseload of 75,000 (New York, 2000).

Work Experience Participants Displace Public Employees

According to a comprehensive analysis of whether work experience participants replace regular employees working in public sector jobs (Ellwood and Welty, 2000), there is almost no empirical information from any of the mandatory work experience programs to suggest this is the case. Hence some would reject the validity of inferences drawn from interviewing supervisors of work experience participants.

When Mayor Giuliani decided to make work activity a central part of the New York City welfare system early in his administration, he negotiated with the public employee unions that he believed might object to extensive use of work experience and assured them that no such substitution would be allowed. The mayor and the unions came to an agreement, the substance of which has remained in effect since then. Nevertheless, lawsuits alleging displacement of regular workers have been filed since 1997, with the city vigorously defending its program. Some of these suits are still pending; none have seriously disrupted the program.

Other lawsuits related to work experience have been filed over the past seven years. Some of these suits allege that insufficient equipment jeopardizes the health and safety of outdoor workers, that home work should count as hours of work activity, and that fair hearing decisions rendered against the city are not acted on in a timely manner. In a major lawsuit filed in 1998, legal aid attorneys argued that the city's job center application procedures violated Food Stamp rules. As of early 2001, this suit remains pending in federal court.

Considerations for Reauthorization

The analysis of work experience presented in this chapter, combined with our experience in administering these programs, leads us to make several recommendations to Congress as it pursues welfare reform reauthorization over the next two years.

Increase the Proportion of TANF Recipients Participating in Work Experience

First and foremost, we strongly recommend that Congress take action to increase the proportion of adult welfare recipients who are subject to a work experience requirement. The level of work experience participation should be increased simply by requiring a higher percentage of the caseload to meet the work requirement so that work becomes an expected standard for those receiving benefits. Every state should be required to have a substantial proportion of its caseload, say 35 percent to 45 percent, in a work program.

Enforce the Pro Rata Reduction of Family Benefits Requirement

The statutory text of the TANF program requires that full-check sanctions be applied whenever there is a complete failure to participate without good cause. In the case of partial participation, the legislation requires reductions equal to the portion of hours of activity missed without good cause. This interpretation of the term "pro rata" (see Section 404(e)(1)(A) of the Social Security Act) was made explicit in the conference report for the 1996 welfare reform legislation. However, regulations of the Department of Health and Human Services (HHS) permit states wide latitude in interpreting the provision, even to the extent of ignoring the provision entirely and retaining the sanction provisions of the former AFDC program.

As a result, several states, including large states such as New York and California, do not as a practical matter require participation in work activities for those who elect to opt out and accept slightly lower benefits. For work to become a meaningful and integrated part of receiving welfare, the original intent of the TANF provisions must be restored so that all states will be required to terminate cash benefits for recipients who refuse to participate in work requirements.

States Should Be Able to Merge TANF and Food Stamp Work Obligations

The 1996 welfare reforms made several important changes to Food Stamp law in order to make administration of the two programs more compatible. For instance, the Simplified Food Stamp Program option is intended to give states greater flexibility in determining benefits, and thus to make procedures more compatible with TANF. Other provisions of the new law allow for greater compatibility with TANF's work program (U.S. House of Representatives, 1996b). However, these statutory changes have been interpreted narrowly by the Department of Agriculture, and the statutory changes themselves do not go far enough.

Constraints on Work Experience Programs Lifted through Legislative Clarification

The interpretation of various federal statutes bearing on work experience programs, issued by both the Department of Labor and HHS, interferes unnecessarily with the operation of work experience and should be clarified by legislation (U.S. Department of Labor, 1999). Among the workplace laws that, according to departmental regulations, can have applicability to work experience programs are the Fair Labor Standards Act (especially the minimum wage), Occupational Safety and Health Administration rules, Unemployment Insurance (at certain nongovernment sites), the Americans with Disabilities Act, titles VI and VII of the Civil Rights Act, the Age Discrimination in Employment Act, and the Equal Pay Act. Because the TANF program is still in its infancy and work experience is not heavily used, many of the provisions just mentioned have not yet generated litigation, but experience suggests that litigation can be expected.

The minimum wage provisions of the Fair Labor Standards Act, which constrain the number of hours recipients can be required to participate in work activity, are being circumvented in states that have deemed work experience a training activity. Other states are restricting the scheduled hours of work experience. However, this rule, after a court test, may constrain work experience in every state because the courts may not agree that work experience is training (U.S. Department of Labor, 1999). Because, as we have argued, work experience is most powerful when it parallels a full-time work schedule of thirty-five hours per week, these rules on allowable hours of work directly reduce the program's effectiveness.

The current federal interpretation of the applicability of workplace law is inappropriate to the context of state-run work experience programs under TANF. Participants in work experience are already covered by the same program standards and protections afforded those in side-by-side activities such as job search, training, and education. Applying federal employment laws to these program operations was clearly not intended under the TANF statute and opens up a whole range of new conflict and litigation based on decades of overlapping laws, regulations, and legal precedents that may have nothing to do with welfare-to-work programs (Dietrich, Emsellem, and Paradise,

2000). The Family Support Act, which preceded TANF, had specific exemptions from several requirements of labor law. These exemptions, which were originally included in the Community Work Experience Program, specified that AFDC benefits were not to be construed as compensation for work performed. The logic of this provision was that work experience assignments for those receiving welfare payments are intended to be educational in the sense of preparing adults to take private employment. Congress should revert to its earlier explicit exemption of work experience from employment law.

Conclusion

The promise of the welfare reform law has been achieved to a far greater degree than was anticipated by most of its critics. Its most distinctive achievement, as shown by the contributors to this volume, has been to greatly increase the number of single mothers who are working in the private economy and who have brought their families out of poverty. Ironically, because of the large number of mothers who have left welfare, and the caseload reduction credit, states now have less need to maintain high levels of participation in work experience programs. A point of continuing concern, however, is that states are not developing the work programs and infrastructure necessary to constructively engage those who remain on assistance and those who are sure to return in the next economic downturn.

For those not able to move into the private labor market quite yet, work experience remains the next best alternative. It can transform the meaning of welfare and may even be capable of affecting the larger culture of poverty. Yet the low level of participation in this important activity means that the promise of the welfare reform revolution remains partly unfulfilled.

COMMENT BY
Clifford M. Johnson

Jason Turner and Thomas Main present a decidedly upbeat assessment of work experience and its potential benefits. It is so upbeat, in fact, that one is left to wonder why sustained efforts to implement such programs at scale are so rare. As the authors note, states have long had the option under federal law to require able-bodied welfare recipients to work in exchange for their benefits. Yet the large-scale, mandatory work experience programs in Wisconsin and New York City stand alone, appearing increasingly idiosyncratic and outside the mainstream of Temporary Assistance for Needy Families (TANF) as state and local policymakers focus on other work force development and caseload reduction strategies.

Why have state and local officials so clearly "voted with their feet" and shunned the approach that Turner and Main advocate? The answer lies in a set of difficult and often controversial policy trade-offs embedded in large-scale, mandatory work experience programs. These trade-offs are obscured or simply ignored by the authors. State and local policymakers typically find them much harder to avoid.

Consider, for example, the threshold decision to require the vast majority of welfare recipients to work in exchange for their benefits. The authors contend that such requirements simultaneously advance the goals of increasing employability and reducing welfare dependency. In practice, however, work experience models such as those implemented in Wisconsin and New York City appear far more effective in producing caseload reductions than employability gains:

—The clear message emerging from the research cited so frequently by Turner and Main is that future work experience programs may yield employment gains, but they generally have not done so in the past.

—As the authors themselves concede, work experience is more likely to trigger caseload reductions by discouraging eligible individuals from seeking assistance than by enhancing their employability.

—Large-scale, mandatory work experience also triggers intense opposition in many communities because its "one-size-fits-all" approach forces many recipients to engage in activities that will not bolster their skills and may prevent them from engaging in other activities that would do so.

—Universal work requirements can be so costly and challenging to implement that they leave administrators without the funds or the capacity to mount complementary work force development initiatives that might compensate for these shortcomings.

While state and local policymakers will occasionally embrace the rhetoric of "social and moral obligations" or of "attacking the culture of poverty," they know that the long-term success of welfare reforms under the TANF program hinges on their ability to move parents into the labor market and construct ladders for career advancement that can help them climb out of poverty. Work experience models of the unpaid, work-for-benefits variety simply have not demonstrated success in achieving these goals.

Turner and Main discuss a variety of operational issues related to work experience but have surprisingly little to say about ways in which its employment impacts could be strengthened. Most work force development experts accept the premise that well-designed work experience programs can bolster the employability of individuals with little or no recent connection to the labor market. The problem in achieving this result through large-scale, mandatory work experience is that a nearly universal work obligation is rarely consistent with the creation of high-quality work sites that promote close supervision, skill development, and successful transitions into permanent employment.

A growing number of state and local officials—including those in Washington, Vermont, and at least fourteen cities nationwide—are turning to transitional jobs programs that provide six to twelve months of paid work experience in the hope of finding a more effective formula for employment gains. Usually operating at a modest scale and targeting individuals who have sought but failed to find or retain unsubsidized jobs, these initiatives seek to replicate the expectations and rewards of regular employment by providing work for wages rather than mandating work for benefits. This shift encourages supervisors, participants, and future employers to view placements as "real jobs" and maintain high expectations regarding performance at the workplace. Wage-based models also defuse much of the controversy and opposition surrounding "workfare" because participants are paid for their work and enjoy many of the rights and benefits of regular employees.

It is possible that the latest wave of transitional work programs will yield outcomes no more promising than those generated by the work experience programs of the past two decades. Nonetheless, the absence of any serious discussion of paid work experience in this chapter is puzzling and unfortunate, given that these innovations have the potential to attain each of the underlying objectives set out by the authors.

In their closing recommendations, Turner and Main seek to accomplish through legislative fiat what proponents of work experience have failed to achieve through powers of persuasion or example. There is no indication that the present statute prevents states from adopting the work programs they believe will be most effective. The authors may disapprove of their choices, but that is hardly reason to override their judgments.

References

Brock, Thomas, David Butler, and David Long. 1993. *Unpaid Work Experience for Welfare Recipients: Findings and Lessons from MDRC Research*. New York: Manpower Demonstration Research Corporation.

Dietrich, Sharon, Maurice Emsellem, and Jennifer Paradise. 2000. *Employment Rights of Workfare Participants and Displaced Workers*, 2d ed. New York: National Employment Law Project.

Domestic Policy Council, Office of the President. 1986. *Up from Dependency.* 8 vols. Government Printing Office.

Ellwood, David. 1988. *Poor Support.* Basic Books.

Ellwood, David, and Elizabeth Welty. 2000. "Public Service Employment and Mandatory Work: A Policy Whose Time Has Come and Gone Again?" In *Finding Jobs,* edited by David Card and Rebecca Blank. Russell Sage Foundation.

Kaus, Mickey. 1986. "The Work Ethic State." *New Republic* 195 (1): 22–33.

———. 1992. *The End of Equality.* Basic Books.

Mead, Lawrence M. 1986. *Beyond Entitlement.* Free Press.

Murray, Charles. 1984. *Losing Ground.* Basic Books.

New York City Human Resources Administration. 2000. Weekly Caseload Engagement Status Report, October 8, 2000.

Novak, Michael. 1987. *The New Consensus on Family and Welfare.* Washington: American Enterprise Institute.

Task Force on Poverty and Welfare. 1986. *A New Social Contract.* Report submitted to New York State Governor Mario Cuomo. Albany.

U.S. Department of Labor. 1999. *How Workplace Laws Apply to Welfare Recipients.* Government Printing Office.

U.S. House of Representatives, Committee on Ways and Means. 1996a. *1996 Green Book.* WMCP: 104-14. Government Printing Office.

———. 1996b. *Summary of Welfare Reforms Made by Public Law 104–193, The Personal Responsibility and Work Opportunity Reconciliation Act and Associated Legislation.* WMCP: 104-15. Government Printing Office.

Wisconsin Department of Workforce Development. 1999. *Wisconsin Works Closure.* Madison.

12

SHEILA R. ZEDLEWSKI
PAMELA LOPREST

Will TANF Work for the Most Disadvantaged Families?

D ESPITE THE RECENT SUCCESS of the Temporary Assistance for Needy Families (TANF) program, there are lingering concerns that some families may not achieve independence from cash assistance. Some adults receiving TANF benefits and some who have left TANF face personal and family challenges that limit their ability to work. Does TANF provide states sufficient flexibility and resources to serve the long-term needs of the most disadvantaged families? TANF allows states to exempt 20 percent of their current caseloads from the federal five-year time limit for receiving benefits, and six states intend to use their own funds to provide some assistance indefinitely. Some states have begun to design programs that target the needs of the most disadvantaged, and more are beginning to focus on these populations. It is not clear, however, whether these programs, in combination with the exemptions and spending flexibility allowed under TANF, will be sufficient to protect all of those who are unable to leave welfare successfully.

This chapter examines the extent of hardship among families on TANF and those who have left TANF but are not working. It also examines TANF programs designed to address the problems faced by the most disadvantaged families. We begin by reviewing information about barriers to work among the welfare population leading up to the development of TANF. The next section shows the incidence of barriers to work among TANF recipients and the most at-risk group of TANF leavers—those who are not working and have no apparent means of financial support. Then we summarize some of the ways states are beginning to address the needs of the most disadvantaged TANF recipients. We conclude with TANF policy recommendations that could assist states in addressing the challenges faced by the most disadvantaged TANF families.

How Does TANF Address the Most Disadvantaged?

During the welfare reform debate, there was little consensus about the extent of disabilities and other challenges among welfare recipients and the extent to which mothers faced with significant personal challenges could leave welfare for work. Research confirmed the relatively high incidence of physical and mental health problems among adults on welfare, disabilities among their children, alcohol and drug abuse, domestic violence, low education levels and cognitive abilities, and limited work experience. Though not all of these issues prevent work, most require special supports to help recipients move into and retain employment. The federal Supplemental Security Income (SSI) program provides an alternative source of income support for adults with a disability serious enough to prevent work at any job, and most states have traditionally advocated enrollment in this program for beneficiaries who qualified. SSI benefits are higher than state cash welfare benefits and, like cash welfare, provide Medicaid eligibility. However, SSI provides eligibility only for those unable to perform any substantial work because of a medical condition expected to last at least one year or result in death. A large proportion of those receiving Aid to Families with Dependent Children (AFDC) experienced health and personal difficulties that did not meet SSI's strict disability definition but still made it difficult to hold a job.

Olson and Pavetti (1996) reviewed fifteen major studies to show the wide disparities in estimates of barriers to employment among AFDC families. They concluded that the incidence of barriers to employment was far greater than in the general population, and that about 25 to 50 percent of the families receiving AFDC would need special intervention to help them move to employment. Their own analyses of the 1992 National Longitudinal Survey of Youth (NLSY) showed that three out of ten welfare recipients reported serious health-related conditions, and another one-third reported modest health-related barriers. Many other recipients had very low levels of education or basic skills, adding to the fraction of the caseload with significant employment barriers.

Despite the high incidence of barriers to employment, many on welfare did work, although the incidence and amount of work diminished with increasing numbers of barriers (Olson and Pavetti, 1996). Though more than half of those with a serious employment barrier had worked in the current or previous year, continuous employment was not common. Other studies showed that the presence of a severe disability significantly reduced a person's probability of leaving welfare (Acs and Loprest, 1999). The literature, however, did not provide policymakers with clear guidance as to the proportion of welfare recipients who could work despite their personal and family challenges, especially if given support services.

TANF provides some safeguards for recipients of cash assistance who may not be able to move to self-sufficiency because of personal or family hardships. States can exempt 20 percent of their average monthly caseload from benefit-termination time limits. The final hardship exemption arose out of compromise between various versions of welfare reform passed by the House and Senate over the 1995–96 period (Weaver, 2000). States can also use their maintenance of effort (MOE) funds to provide state benefits to families that need assistance beyond the federal time limit.

Congress passed two pieces of legislation in 1997 that were designed to help states meet the needs of the most disadvantaged families. Congress authorized the U.S. Department of Labor to award $3 billion in Welfare to Work grants to support state and local efforts to help the hardest-to-serve TANF recipients (as well as noncustodial parents) move into the labor market. Grantees were to spend most of their grant funds on long-term TANF recipients with specific problems affecting their employment prospects (see Perez-Johnson, Hershey, and Bellotti, 2000, on the program's progress to date). Congress also passed the Family Violence Amendment, which allows states to identify domestic violence victims among the caseload and exempt those clients from program requirements. Formal state adoption of the Family Violence Option (FVO) may allow a state to carry more than 20 percent of its caseload past the sixty-month federal lifetime limit (Burt, Zweig, and Schlichter, 2000).

Hardship among TANF Recipients and Leavers

We do not know whether the TANF hardship exemption plus the flexibility states have to use their own money to help these families will be sufficient. The issue is drawing increasing attention because time limits will begin to affect aid recipients in most states in 2002 (see Pavetti and Bloom, chapter 9). If only the able recipients leave welfare for work permanently, the most disadvantaged group will represent an increasing share of states' caseloads. In a scenario in which the disadvantaged part of the caseload exceeds the federal limit of 20 percent, states will need to decide whether to use their own money to support those who meet a benefit time limit without gainful employment, allow these families to go without support, or provide intensive services that might enable a large share of the most disadvantaged group to move into gainful employment.

This section draws on data from a nationally representative survey and from state data to describe the extent of employment barriers among those receiving TANF assistance and those who recently left welfare. These data provide some insight into the size of the group that will require either intensive services or continued state support to avoid economic hardship when the time limit is reached. The National Survey of America's Families (NSAF), which interviewed about 44,000 nonelderly families in 1997 and 1999, with a special emphasis on low-income families, allows us to describe a common set of personal and family characteristics of adults who were on TANF when surveyed and those who had recently left. We augment the NSAF with data from state surveys and case record reviews.

Disadvantage among TANF Recipients, 1997–1999

An analysis of the 1997 NSAF data showed that three-quarters of adults on welfare had at least one potential barrier to employment, including very poor mental or physical health, limited education, minimal or no work experience, and family responsibilities that limited their ability to work, such as caring for an infant or a disabled child (Zedlewski, 1999). All of these characteristics were found to significantly depress work activity. Because the 1997 data represented a point early in the process of welfare reform in most states, the 1999 NSAF can be used to show whether the incidence of obstacles to employment among adults on TANF increased. Caseload decline accelerated after the passage of welfare reform, and the rolls declined by 34 percent between January 1997 and January 1999, roughly the time of the two waves of the NSAF.

As shown in table 12-1, contrary to conventional wisdom, adults on TANF in 1999 were not significantly more disadvantaged than in 1997 (Zedlewski and Alderson, 2001). There were some indications of increases in serious health conditions, but the differences were not statistically significant. In 1999, 28 percent of TANF adults reported very poor mental health; in 1997 the figure was 22 percent. The composite measure of very poor health indicating whether adult recipients reported that their health prevented work, that their health was "poor," or that they had a very poor mental health score increased to 36 percent in 1999 from 32 percent in 1997, but again this difference was not statistically significant.

Table 12-1. *Potential Barriers to Work among Adult TANF Recipients in 1997 and 1999*

Percent

Characteristic	1997	1999
Health prevents work or adult reports poor health	17	17
Very poor mental health score	22	28
Composite: poor health, health prevents work, or very poor mental health	32	36
Less than a high school education	39	44
Last worked three or more years ago	42	27**
Child on Supplemental Security Income (SSI)	8	5
Child under age one	16	17
Does not speak English	6	5

Source: National Survey of America's Families conducted by the Urban Institute; results described more fully in Zedlewski and Alderson (2001).

** p < .05, statistically significant difference between 1997 and 1999.

Adults receiving TANF in 1999 also did not report a significantly higher incidence of non-health-related characteristics found to depress work activity than in 1997. For example, about the same percentage of the caseload was caring for an infant or had a language barrier (for these people, the interview was conducted in Spanish). Although the percentage of adult recipients who had not completed high school or received a GED increased from 39 to 44, the percentage caring for a disabled child decreased from 8 to 5. These changes were not statistically significant.

In contrast, the percentage of adults on TANF who had not worked in the previous three years or longer decreased substantially, from 42 percent in 1997 to 27 percent in 1999. Historically, the lack of recent work experience has been a significant deterrent to employment. The increase in work activity among recipients should enhance their ability to leave TANF for employment.

We also did not find that more adults on TANF had multiple barriers to employment in 1999 than in 1997. Previous research has shown that the number of barriers is the strongest predictor of employment difficulties (Danziger and others, 2000; Olson and Pavetti 1996; Zedlewski 1999). Forty percent of TANF recipients had two or more barriers to work in 1999; the figure was 45 percent in 1997, a difference that is not statistically significant (see table 12-2). Table 12-2 also shows that more than half of those with two or more barriers were engaged in some work activity (including paid work, school or training, or job search) in 1999, significantly more than the 40 percent in 1997. In 1999, 20 percent of those with multiple barriers reported

Table 12-2. *Work Activity and Barriers to Work among TANF Recipients,*
1997 and 1999
Percent

Year	Number of barriers	Percent of recipients	Current activity			
			Working	In school	Looking for work	No activity
1997	0	22	53	17	18	12
	1	33	22	9	28	41
	2+	45	5	9	26	60
	All recipients	100	22	11	25	43
1999	0	20	56	8*	26	10
	1	40*	33*	15	20	32
	2+	40	20**	4*	30	46**
	All recipients	100	32**	9	25	33**

Source: Urban Institute's National Survey of America's Families.
* p < .10, statistically significant difference between 1997 and 1999.
** p < .05, statistically significant difference between 1997 and 1999.

working at a paid job; in 1997 only 5 percent did so. The increase in work
activity indicates the strength of the labor market and strong work incentives
in states' TANF programs.

DISADVANTAGE BY LENGTH OF TIME ON TANF. The numbers describing
all recipients on TANF in tables 12-1 and 12-2 may mask significant differences in barriers to employment among those who have been on TANF for
longer periods of time. Using self-reports of time on welfare, we divided
adult recipients into those who reported entering welfare between 1997 and
1999 ("new entrants"), those who first received welfare before 1997 but had
not received it continuously between 1997 and 1999 ("cyclers"), and those
who first received welfare before 1997 and received it continuously between
1997 and 1999 ("stayers"). The distributions of time on welfare were remarkably similar in 1997 and 1999. In both periods, more than one-quarter of
adults on TANF were new entrants, about one in five were cyclers, and about
half were stayers.

With one exception, new entrants generally had better employment
prospects than stayers (see table 12-3). One-third of new entrants, but only 6
percent of stayers, had an infant, confirming other evidence that low-income
women with infants have more difficulty staying off welfare than low-income
women without infants. Pregnancies among lower-paid women often lead to

Table 12-3. *Adult TANF Recipients Subject to Work Requirements:*
Barriers to Work and Self-Reported Time on Welfare, 1999 [a]
Percent

	Time on welfare		
Barriers to employment	New entrants	Cyclers	Stayers
Percent in each group	26	23	4/
Very poor health	28	41	39
High school dropout	35*	41	50
Last worked three or more years ago	17*	24	34
Child on SSI	3	7	6
Infant at home	33**	20**	6
Does not speak English well	3	5	6
Number of barriers			
0	21	21	16
1	48**	36	32
2+	31**	44	52

Source: Urban Institute's National Survey of America's Families.
* p < .10, statistically significant difference as compared with stayers.
** p < .05, statistically significant difference as compared with stayers.
a. See text for definition of time on welfare.

job disruptions and increased reliance on welfare because their jobs infrequently provide paid maternity leave and infant child care is difficult to find and expensive (Commission on Family and Medical Leave, 1996).

Otherwise, new TANF entrants had fewer barriers to employment than stayers. Sixty-five percent of new entrants and only 50 percent of stayers had completed high school. Twenty-eight percent of new entrants and 39 percent of stayers reported very poor health characteristics; significantly more new entrants had recent work experience. Only 17 percent had no work experience over the previous three years or longer; 34 percent of the welfare stayers had not worked in three years or more. Finally, significantly fewer new entrants than stayers had multiple barriers to employment (31 percent and 52 percent).

The single significant difference between cyclers and stayers was that 20 percent of cyclers and only 6 percent of stayers were caring for an infant. Though the statistics presented in table 12-3 suggest somewhat fewer employment barriers for cyclers than for stayers, these differences were not statistically significant. For example, more cyclers had completed high school, more had recent work experience, and fewer had multiple barriers.

On the other hand, the incidence of very poor health was as high among cyclers as among stayers.

EVIDENCE FROM STATE STUDIES. Various state studies confirm the pervasiveness of obstacles to work among TANF recipients. Sweeny (2000) reviewed recent evidence from states that indicated health was a key reason why parents on TANF were not working. Among recipients not working, from about 20 percent (in Florida, Tennessee, and Utah) to over 30 percent (in Idaho, Indiana, Minnesota, New Jersey, Texas, and Washington) reported that poor health limited their ability to work.

Danziger and her colleagues (2000) have reported extensively on the incidence of disability among women in one Michigan county, as well as how barriers constrained these welfare mothers' employability. Using a sample of recipients between ages 18 and 55 who were not deferred from Michigan's work requirements, they found that 85 percent had at least one of the barriers examined (including physical and mental health problems, low education, low job skills, lack of a driver's license or access to a car, domestic violence, discrimination experiences, substance dependence); and two-thirds had two or more barriers. They also showed that the number of barriers was strongly and negatively associated with employment.

Alameda County, California, has also focused on understanding the hardest-to-serve part of its caseload (Speiglman and others, 1999). It concluded that the number of TANF participants with significant limitations on their ability to work may exceed the 20 percent exemption limit, and that many recipients will need intensive or long-term supports to make the transition to work.

Disadvantage among TANF Leavers

Despite the high percentage of TANF recipients with employment barriers, many recipients have left the welfare rolls. However, leaving welfare does not necessarily mean a successful, permanent transition; some leavers have no visible means of financial support. States' TANF programs also need to address disadvantage among low-income families who have left the program.

One way to assess the extent of disadvantage among those who left TANF is to focus on the leavers who do not successfully get off welfare. We look at this issue in three ways. First, we use the 1999 NSAF to examine employment barriers among nonworking former recipients. Second, we use NSAF and states' administrative data to examine the extent to which former recipients return to welfare. Third, we present some evidence of relatively higher barriers among those who left welfare because of sanctions.

NONWORKING LEAVERS. Many studies have shown that a majority of recipients leaving welfare are employed (Acs and Loprest, 2000; Loprest, 1999; GAO, 1999). However, most of these studies found that a subset of former recipients were not working. The NSAF data on the sample of families that left TANF between 1997 and 1999 and were not back on TANF in 1999 showed these same results. A majority of former recipients were working, 58 percent more than twenty hours a week and another 6 percent fewer than twenty hours per week. Another 9 percent had worked in 1999 (the year of the interview), possibly indicating a group between jobs that would begin working again soon.

Some nonworking former recipients relied on a spouse's earnings. Eleven percent of leavers were not themselves working but had a working spouse or partner. A small number receive federal disability assistance through SSI or Social Security's disability insurance. In our sample, about 2 percent received these benefits in the year before their interview. Individuals' transitions from TANF to a federal disability program are usually permanent. The remaining 15 percent of former recipients were not working, had not recently worked, and did not have a working spouse or partner. Clearly, a majority of former recipients were relying on work. At the same time, the remaining 15 percent, while a minority, had no connection to the labor market. How the group with no connection to the labor market gets by is an important question.

Most would agree that the remaining 15 percent of TANF leavers provides a conservative estimate of the size of the leaver group that should be a target for special concern. This group, referred to here as the "at-risk" group of leavers, shows no evidence of a successful move toward self-sufficiency. Some might argue that the at-risk leaver group should also include those who work part-time or full-time at wages too low to support a family. Our narrow definition excluding everyone with some reliance on work or federal disability benefits allows us to focus on the characteristics of the group likely to be at greatest risk.

Table 12-4 shows that the most at-risk leaver group had far higher levels of personal and family challenges than all leavers or employed former recipients. Almost half of the at-risk group had not worked in three or more years before the interview. Significantly more had a child on SSI (19 percent), very poor health (50 percent), or less than a high school education (38 percent). The level of barriers among this group resembled the level among the more continuous TANF recipients. Slightly more than half of the at-risk TANF leavers had multiple barriers to employment, about the same as TANF stayers (see table 12-3). An even higher percentage of the at-risk group reported very poor health status than the continuous TANF group, 50 percent compared to 39 percent.

Table 12-4. *Barriers to Work Among TANF Leavers, 1999* [a]
Percent

| | Leavers | | |
Barrier	All	Employed	At risk
Percent in group	100.0	64.0	15.0
Does not speak English	3.1	3.7	2.6
Child on SSI	7.4	3.8	18.8
Infant at home	10.7	10.9	7.9
Last worked three or more years ago	12.4	0.0	47.0
Very poor health	32.8	23.9	50.0
Less than a high school education	29.2	22.9	38.2
Number of barriers			
0	40.3	53.1	10.6
1	34.0	32.8	37.8
2+	25.8	14.1	51.6**

Source: Urban Institute's National Survey of America's Families.
** p < .05, statistically significant difference between employed and at-risk leavers.
a. See text for definitions of leaver groups.

TANF CYCLERS. Leaving welfare has traditionally been a gradual process for many recipients: many leave the rolls only to return after a setback and eventually leave again. Some or many of the at-risk TANF leavers may cycle back to welfare. As noted earlier, about one-quarter of those currently on TANF had left welfare in the 1997 to 1999 period but were back on TANF by the time of their interview in 1999. These returnees represented 22 percent of the NSAF sample of TANF leavers during the 1997 to 1999 period. Several state and local studies that examined welfare administrative data for the 1996–98 period found that about one-quarter of the leavers returned to TANF sometime in the year after exit; the NSAF results were similar (Acs and Loprest, 2000). In their study of three cities, Moffitt and Roff (2000) identified only half of the leavers as "dependency leavers," that is, recipients who became significantly less dependent on welfare over time.

These results make clear that transitions off welfare are often not permanent. There have always been families that moved on and off TANF. However, TANF's lifetime time limits will eventually make returning impossible for some families and could be particularly difficult for the subset of leavers who are the most disadvantaged.

SANCTIONED LEAVERS. Other evidence that some families that have left TANF have significant levels of disadvantage comes from studies of families that left because of sanctions rather than voluntarily. As discussed by Pavetti and Bloom elsewhere in this volume, most states use tougher sanctions to enforce compliance with program requirements under TANF than under the old AFDC program. Some sanctioned leavers do not meet program requirements because of the personal barriers discussed earlier, including mental health problems, substance abuse, domestic violence, and low education levels. It is possible that some of the most disadvantaged TANF recipients cannot navigate the system and therefore fall through the cracks and off the rolls.

The limited evidence about sanctioned TANF leavers supports this idea. In general, state leaver studies show lower employment rates for sanctioned cases than the national average for all TANF leavers (Brauner and Loprest, 1999). The U.S. General Accounting Office (2000) summarized ten state studies that reported characteristics and outcomes of sanctioned leavers. Sanctioned families generally had less education, more limited work experience, and longer time on welfare than other families on welfare. Some of the studies suggested that barriers among sanctioned families may have made it more difficult for them to understand complex program requirements or the consequences of noncompliance. One state found that sanctioned families with low education levels were less likely to appeal a sanction and, consequently, more likely to be dropped from TANF. In two studies showing both sanctioned and nonsanctioned leavers, employment rates were about 20 percentage points higher for nonsanctioned leavers than for sanctioned leavers.

How Large Is the Most Disadvantaged TANF Group?

In sum, a sizable group of adults on TANF have significant barriers to employment, and some who had recently left TANF have very similar characteristics. Eighty percent of adults on TANF have at least one significant barrier to employment, and four out of ten have multiple barriers. The good news is that recipients have significantly increased their work activity since 1997 despite these barriers. Twenty percent of recipients with multiple barriers worked at a paid job in 1999; only 5 percent did so in 1997. On the other hand, almost half of the 1999 recipients with multiple barriers were not engaged in work activity, not even job search. Many in this group will need significant interventions to leave welfare successfully. We also identified another group at significant risk. About 15 percent of the group that left TANF in the 1997–99 period were not employed and had not been employed recently, received no disability income, and did not have a working spouse or partner. Half of this group had multiple barriers to employment. It is not clear why these families had not returned to welfare.

These statistics suggest a high level of need among a significant share of families either participating in or recently connected to the TANF program. However, they do not tell us how many families could overcome their challenges and move into employment with the right support services. Moreover, we would argue that these are conservative estimates of need among the TANF population. We have singled out the most at-risk group among TANF leavers as a group in need of other government or private supports, and we allowed the presence of any work to serve as an indicator of some ability to move to independence. In addition, surveys such as NSAF do not identify the hidden barriers among TANF families, such as domestic violence and substance abuse. Nevertheless, we have identified a sizable group that will either need intensive services to move into employment or be declared exempt from benefit time limits so that they can avoid substantial economic hardship.

Addressing Special Needs under TANF

TANF forces states and local welfare agencies to make important decisions about how they will serve the most disadvantaged among their caseloads. States must determine whom they will exempt from work requirements and time limits; they must develop and implement methods for identifying those who qualify for exemptions; and they must decide whether to develop and implement specialized services focused on overcoming barriers to employment. Below we review some state approaches to these decisions and summarize programs that seem to have achieved some success. However, our review showed how little we know about what works for families that have multiple barriers to employment and are reaching their time limits.

Exemptions

States can decide to exempt recipients with serious obstacles to work from work requirements and, eventually, benefit time limits. Current federal work participation requirements, time-limit exemption rates, and many states' shift in philosophy toward promoting work for everyone have pushed about half the states to requiring work activities for all recipients (see Pavetti and Bloom, chapter 9). Some states count nonwork activities toward meeting work requirements, including attending substance abuse or mental health counseling. Many states have moved toward temporary exemptions for the disabled to encourage case workers to revisit hard-to-serve cases (Thompson and others, 2000). Others seem to have taken a wait-and-see attitude toward dealing with the most disadvantaged in their caseload. States can use their own MOE dollars to continue benefits for those who reach their benefit time limits. Although this can be less expensive than providing services that focus on preparing the most disadvantaged for paid employment, it could be a short-sighted solution. Without specialized services to address barriers to employment, the number of families needing exemptions (and continued cash assistance) could increase beyond available state resources over time.

Identifying Those with Special Needs

This is a new responsibility for local welfare offices. Many barriers to employment are not easily identified either because recipients refuse to reveal them or because they do not themselves recognize the barriers. Some states try to identify the so-called "hidden disabilities," such as depression, learning disabilities, and domestic violence, through interviews with trained case workers and use of special assessment tools. Despite these strategies, some recipients with multiple barriers may be identified only through their repeated failure to comply with requirements (such as showing up for assignments). Thus follow-up on sanctioned cases can be an important part of identifying those with special service needs.

Service Provision

Service delivery for the disadvantaged may be the states' most difficult challenge. There is a growing literature on programs designed to serve the most disadvantaged welfare recipients, but there is little definitive information about what really works. Some states are attempting to implement an "inverted pyramid" where all recipients move into "work first" services that provide short-term assistance with the job search, and those who do not successfully find jobs move into increasingly intensive and longer-term services focused on barriers to employment. Postemployment services are also often needed to ensure long-term success. These require a very sophisticated service delivery strategy. Thompson and her colleagues (2000) argue that states still face significant challenges in building institutional capacity to address the needs of the disabled and to develop new links with organizations more equipped to address their needs.

Some TANF programs for the hard-to-serve provide specialized services to address the needs of those with particular barriers to employment, while others provide a more generalized approach that serves a range of disadvantaged individuals rather than a specific segment of the disadvantaged population. Table 12-5 lists some examples of both types of programs.

Table 12-5. *Examples of TANF-Related Programs for the Hardest to Serve*

Location	Program	Type of client	Outcomes
Specialized service programs			
Rhode Island	Domestic violence: All TANF offices have access to specialized counselors (also available in some areas in Massachusetts, Nevada, Washington, Maryland, and Pennsylvania).	Victims of domestic violence	n.a.
Illinois	Substance abuse, Project Next Step: All recipients with substance abuse problems must be in treatment to receive benefits. Colocates health provider in welfare offices to identify abuse problems and refer to providers.	Women who are substance abusers or chemically dependent	Improved client functioning
North Carolina	Substance abuse: Initiative to place qualified substance abuse professionals in every county; Department of Social Services to conduct screening, assessment, treatment, and planning and coordinate care.	Work-first participants with substance abuse issues (61 placed by April 1999)	n.a.
Seattle, Washington	Learning Disabilities Project provides screening, case management, and workplace training for clients with learning disabilities.	Serves 130 clients per year, costs $1,700 per client	n.a.
Generalized service programs			
Chicago, Illinois	Project Match: Individual approach to case management; open-ended commitment to participants; job retention services. Pathways system with incremental stepping stones to employment focuses on hardest to employ (also at sites in Maryland, Iowa, Ohio, and Tennessee).	Families with multiple barriers; 900 clients since 1985, most with multiple barriers	Increased employment

Chicago, Illinois	Chicago Commons: Comprehensive services through multiagency collaboration with staff on site.	Families facing multiple barriers; serves 150 clients per year	After 2.5 years (in Jan. 1998), 67 percent working or in school
Los Angeles, California	Beyond Shelter: Provides housing with home-based management, a one-stop comprehensive service center.	Long-term welfare recipients (200 maximum)	72 percent of enrollees employed after 18 months (one-third unsubsidized)
Phoenix, Arizona	TANF–Vocational Rehabilitation (VR) links VR staff to work with TANF recipients deferred from work participation because of a disability. Counselors develop individualized plans to integrate services.	Disabled TANF recipients	n.a.
Portland, Maine	Contract with Maine Medical Center (MMC) to help individuals with physical, learning, or mental disabilities find employment. MMC dedicates clinical social worker and job development specialists to work with clients, comprehensive services.	TANF recipients with multiple barriers	n.a.

Sources: For information about programs in Rhode Island, see Sweeny and others (2000); Illinois, Welfare Information Network (2000) and Herr and Wagner (1998); North Carolina, National Center on Addiction and Substance Abuse (1999); Washington State, Dion and others (1999); California, Beyond Shelter (1998); Arizona, Thompson and others (2000); and Maine, Thompson and others (2000).

n.a. Not available.

Specialized service programs connect clients to specialists. Several areas, such as sites in Rhode Island, provide access to counselors trained in domestic violence issues. Washington State and some other states have specialized programs that screen for learning disabilities and provide follow-up services. Programs in Illinois and North Carolina locate health providers in welfare offices to identify those with substance abuse problems and connect recipients with treatment. In many instances, this single-issue focus helps to connect the recipient to other services that address additional barriers.

Generalized service programs are programs that work intensively with recipients who have multiple barriers to work. Although the models for these programs differ, they typically deliver a package of services that includes preemployment services, job match services, and postemployment services that take into account a range of special needs. Programs can be run by nonprofit organizations that have long served welfare recipients, such as Project Match in Chicago, which has worked on employment and retention issues for the hard-to-serve since 1985 (Herr and Wagner, 1998). Programs can also be housing-based, such as the Chicago Commons and Beyond Shelter programs. Some TANF agencies establish more formal connections with other government agencies experienced in serving certain populations, such as Vocational Rehabilitation in Phoenix, Arizona; and some include at least one contractor that has experience serving individuals with multiple barriers. Local area Goodwill agencies, long experienced in working with persons with disabilities and multiple barriers, serve as employment service contractors to many welfare agencies across the country.

Considerable effort is focused on serving the most disadvantaged TANF recipients, but so far it is limited in scope and coverage. The majority of programs serve only a few hundred disadvantaged recipients at particular sites in the states. And there is not much information available on program outcomes and effectiveness. At this writing, Wisconsin is the only state that has a comprehensive approach to moving all segments of its TANF caseload into meaningful work activities. Wisconsin moves its disabled recipients into the lowest tier of its Wisconsin Works (W-2) program, where many remain until they gain eligibility for federal disability benefits (Kaplan and Rothe, 1999). However, Wisconsin has been engaged in serious welfare reform since the early 1990s, has a relatively small welfare population and a very positive economic environment, and has the highest level of federal and state TANF resources per recipient. It will be difficult for most other states to achieve something like the Wisconsin model, at least in the near term.

Summary and Implications for TANF Reauthorization

A significant number of families who receive TANF benefits and some who leave TANF have multiple barriers to employment. Poor physical and mental health, low levels of education, drug and alcohol abuse, domestic violence, and children with serious disabilities are prevalent among this population and reduce their ability to move into the labor market and leave TANF. About half of long-term TANF recipients and half of those who leave TANF but have no current or recent employment history have two or more significant barriers to employment. Employment and successful exit from TANF may be only a distant possibility for many of these families. About half of those with two or more barriers and only 10 percent of those without employment barriers reported no current work activity.

Families with significant, long-term barriers to employment present the biggest challenge to state policymakers. Many will begin to face benefit time limits in 2002. However, since the passage of TANF in 1996, most states have not yet put programs in place to help families with significant employment barriers achieve independence from cash assistance. Nearly all states have more to do if they hope to move a large share of this group into gainful employment, a strategy consistent with the goals of TANF. The alternatives are to use state money to continue paying cash benefits beyond five years for more families than allowed under the federal 20 percent exemption or to allow some families with barriers and no jobs to fend for themselves outside of TANF.

We cannot overestimate the difficulty of designing programs that reduce or eliminate some of these families' employment barriers. Administrative challenges include developing processes that identify hidden disabilities, tracking families that have difficulty navigating the "work first" TANF environment, and developing processes that link the most disadvantaged families with appropriate expert services. The diversity and pervasiveness of challenges facing these families have been well documented. Although few states have broad-based programs focused on the most disadvantaged part of their caseload, even fewer have created programs to follow up sanctioned families or provide postemployment support services. The enormity of the challenges still facing states' TANF offices is not widely understood.

This unfinished business of welfare reform must be taken into account when Congress considers TANF reauthorization. States will need ample resources to implement statewide comprehensive programs focused on the needs of families with difficult challenges; states will need more time to develop successful strategies than TANF currently allows; and the federal government will need to allow broader exemptions from benefit time limits, at least in the near term and during periods of high unemployment. TANF needs to mature before we know whether it can address the needs of the most disadvantaged families in America. In the meantime, we need safeguards to protect these families from the potential adverse effects of benefit time limits.

COMMENT BY
Sheldon Danziger

I begin by strongly endorsing two major conclusions in the chapter by Sheila Zedlewski and Pamela Loprest. The first is that a significant number of families that receive Temporary Assistance for Needy Families (TANF) and some of those who have recently left TANF have multiple barriers to employment. These barriers include poor physical and mental health, low levels of education, drug and alcohol abuse, domestic violence, and children with serious disabilities. The second is that few states have broad-based programs focused on the most disadvantaged part of their caseload, and even fewer have programs to follow up sanctioned families or provide postemployment support services. Both of these issues should be taken up by Congress during TANF reauthorization.

Having endorsed these conclusions, I use these brief remarks to argue that Zedlewski and Loprest have not measured some important barriers to employment because they, like most welfare and poverty researchers, have neglected the research of psychiatric epidemiologists, social workers, and others who analyze personal problems and have documented that their prevalence is higher among the poor than in the general population. As a result, the chapter underestimates the extent of barriers to employment and the resulting labor market problems of current and former TANF recipients.

Indeed, the authors mention this issue when they report that the National Survey of America's Families (NSAF) does not identify the hidden barriers among TANF families, such as domestic violence or substance abuse, even though a few states try to identify the so-called hidden disabilities, such as depression, learning disabilities, and domestic violence. These barriers are hidden, however, only because they have been neglected or inadequately measured. The NSAF and similar studies simply ignore a range of available, validated measurements that have been gathered in numerous national surveys.

When barriers are measured rather than ignored, their prevalence is high among welfare recipients. For example, Zedlewski and Loprest report in table 12-1 that in 1997, 22 percent of TANF recipients in the NSAF had a "very poor mental health score." But the NSAF underestimates the extent of mental health problems. The 1997 National Household Survey of Drug Abuse (NHSDA) provides information on six psychiatric disorders (major depression, generalized anxiety disorders, agoraphobia, panic attacks, alcohol dependence, and drug dependence) based on the American Psychiatric Association's DSM-III-R diagnostic screening criteria. In the NHSDA, 30.7 percent of single mothers receiving welfare in 1997 met the criteria for one of these disorders (Pollack and others, 2001). The National Comorbidity Survey (NCS), conducted between 1990 and 1992, measured fourteen psychiatric disorders in a large national sample (Kessler and others, 1994). The NCS does not identify welfare recipients, but 44.5 percent of single mothers with personal incomes below $20,000 met the diagnostic criteria for at least one of the disorders in the previous year (Jayakody, Danziger, and Pollack, 2000).

The Women's Employment Study (WES), a panel study of February 1997 TANF recipients in a Michigan county, shows that about one-third of women in each of the first three waves met diagnostic screening criteria for a psychiatric disorder. In the third wave, in fall 1999, 34.4 percent of all respondents (welfare leavers and stayers) and 50.1 percent of nonworking TANF recipients met criteria for one of six disorders—major depression, generalized anxiety disorder, social phobia, posttraumatic stress disorder, alcohol dependence, or drug dependence.

Poverty researchers know relatively little about how the non–labor market skills and abilities of recipients differ from those of other less-skilled workers because we have not considered it necessary to study their personal attributes. From the mid-1960s to the mid-1990s, liberal researchers tended to argue that welfare receipt was due primarily to structural labor market constraints (skills mismatch, spatial mismatch, discrimination) and recipients' need for further education and training; conservatives tended to argue that dependency was due to recipients' unwillingness to take available jobs, not to personal barriers to work or structural constraints.

The Women's Employment Study was designed to remedy this neglect and link poverty research with mental health research by measuring a range of potential barriers to employment (Danziger and others, 2000; Danziger, 2001). Wave 3 data collection includes measures of nineteen potential barriers covering human capital and skills (such as lack of a high school degree, few prior job skills, low work experience, literacy, and criminal convictions),

physical and mental health (such as self-rated health status, learning disabilities, mother's report of child health problems, and the psychiatric disorders
mentioned above), transportation, severe domestic abuse, and child care.

It is not surprising that the extent of barriers increases if a study measures
additional barriers. Zedlewski and Loprest report (table 12-3) that in 1999,
45 percent of welfare stayers had two or more of the six NSAF barriers
listed. In contrast, in fall 1999, 65 percent of the WES sample and 91.2 percent of nonworking welfare stayers had two or more of the nineteen barriers;
31.1 percent of the former and 73.7 percent of the latter had four or more
barriers.

Table 12-6 shows the extent of each barrier for 594 WES respondents and
for respondents in four mutually exclusive categories based on their work and
TANF status in the survey month (excluding twenty-three individuals who
began receiving Supplemental Security Income during the study period).
Work-reliant mothers reported positive earnings but no TANF; combiners
reported both earnings and TANF; welfare-reliant mothers reported TANF
but no earnings; the final group includes those who were neither working
nor receiving TANF. The first five barriers are measured at wave 1 (fall 1997)
because changes in their prevalence tend to be endogenous with respect to
subsequent work effort. For example, if a woman at wave 1 had not performed at least four of the nine work tasks on a previous job, we classified her
as having low skills. The only way for her not to have low skills at wave 3 was
if she acquired those skills on a job between waves. The remaining fourteen
barriers were evaluated in fall 1999. The last row of the table shows the mean
number of barriers.

The results are striking: the women who were work-reliant (column 2)
were less likely to have the most barriers, and the women who were not
working (columns 4 and 5) were much more likely to have them. The differences are present for human capital, mental health, and health barriers. For
example, 14.2 percent of the work-reliant had fewer than four of the nine
labor market skills measured, compared with 36.3 percent of the welfare-
reliant. Whereas 10.3 percent of the work-reliant met diagnostic screening
criteria for post-traumatic stress disorder, 23.1 percent of the welfare-reliant
met the criteria. Those combining work and welfare tended to have prevalence rates between those of the work-reliant and the welfare-reliant.

The welfare-reliant had the highest prevalence on fourteen of nineteen
barriers. The average number of barriers for the work-reliant was 1.9; it was
2.8 for combiners, 4.7 for the welfare-reliant, and 3.1 for those neither working nor receiving welfare. Note the large differences in the extent of barriers
between working stayers (combiners) and nonworking stayers (welfare-

Table 12-6. Incidence of Work Barriers among Four Groups of Respondents with Varying Degrees of Welfare Use, Fall 1999
Percent

Barriers (year measured)	Total sample	Work-reliant	Combiners	Welfare-reliant	No work/no welfare
Less than high school education (1997)	29.8***	20.3	37.6	48.4	35.2
Low work experience (1997)	14.1**	10.0	18.8	25.3	13.0
Fewer than four job skills (1997)	20.4***	14.2	22.4	36.3	23.1
Knows five or fewer work norms (1997)	9.4	7.7	10.6	11.0	12.0
Perceived discrimination (1997)	13.3*	12.9	10.6	22.0	9.3
Transportation problem (1999)	29.8***	19.4	35.3	57.1	32.4
Major depressive disorder (1999)	17.3*	15.5	14.1	27.5	16.7
Posttraumatic stress disorder (1999)	13.8*	10.3	14.1	23.1	15.7
Generalized anxiety disorder (1999)	10.3*	7.1	10.6	14.3	15.7
Alcohol dependence (1999)	2.2**	0.6	1.2	4.4	5.6
Drug dependence (1999)	3.2***	1.0	0.0	7.7	8.3
Mother's health problem (1999)	21.0***	12.6	21.2	44.0	25.9
Child health problem (1999)	14.0***	10.6	15.3	28.6	10.2
Domestic violence (1999)	12.6**	8.4	11.8	23.1	16.7
Social phobia (1999)	7.6***	4.8	4.7	17.6	9.3
Literacy (1999)	18.2	16.1	20.0	24.2	17.6
Learning disability (1999)	14.*	10.3	12.9	22.0	19.4
Ever convicted of a crime (1999)	5.4	4.5	4.7	11.0	3.7
Child care (1999)	12.3**	7.7	14.1	17.6	19.4
Number in sample	594	310	85	91	108
Percent of sample	100	52	14	15	19
Mean number of barriers	2.7	1.9	2.8	4.7	3.1

Source: Computations by author from Women's Employment Survey data.
*p < .05; **p < .01; ***p < .001 denotes significant difference across the four groups.

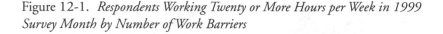

Figure 12-1. *Respondents Working Twenty or More Hours per Week in 1999 Survey Month by Number of Work Barriers*

Percent working

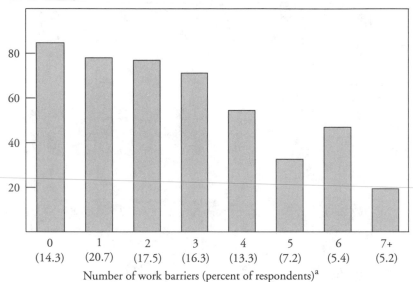

| | 0 | 1 | 2 | 3 | 4 | 5 | 6 | 7+ |
| | (14.3) | (20.7) | (17.5) | (16.3) | (13.3) | (7.2) | (5.4) | (5.2) |

Number of work barriers (percent of respondents)[a]

Source: Computation by author from Women's Employment Survey data, University of Michigan, fall 1999.

a. Numbers in parentheses are percentage of respondents in each barrier category; based on 594 respondents.

reliant). These results suggest that one should use caution in classifying recipients as "stayers" or "leavers" post–welfare reform, and reinforce the distinction Zedlewski and Loprest make between working and nonworking leavers.

Figure 12-1 extends Zedlewski and Loprest's finding that work declines as barriers increase by showing the percentage of all respondents working at least twenty hours, classified by the number of barriers. The number in parentheses below each barrier count is the percentage of respondents with that number of barriers (out of nineteen). The percentage working falls from 84.7 for those with no barriers (14.3 percent of the sample) to only 19.4 for those with seven or more barriers (5.2 percent of the sample). About three-quarters of respondents with the average number of barriers (two to three) were working. This pattern of declining work as the extent of barriers increases is evident at each wave in the WES.

I conclude by emphasizing another conclusion of the authors: namely, that families with significant, long-term barriers to employment present the biggest challenge to policymakers. Despite four years of a booming economy and strong pressures to work from state agencies, many current and former welfare recipients cannot find and keep jobs. Some will be sanctioned or reach their time limit even if they are willing to work, either because employers will not hire them or because personal attributes will prevent them from working steadily. Zedlewski and Loprest are correct that additional resources are needed to identify and provide more and better services to disadvantaged recipients and that many mothers need more time to successfully make the transition from welfare to work. In addition to having their time limits extended, disadvantaged recipients should be offered an opportunity to perform community service in return for continued cash assistance.

References

Acs, Gregory, and Pamela Loprest. 1999. "The Effect of Disabilities on Exits from AFDC." *Journal of Policy Analysis and Management* 18 (1): 28–49.

———. 2000. *Initial Synthesis Report of the Findings from ASPE's Leavers Grants.* Washington: Urban Institute.

Beyond Shelter. 1998. *Service-Enriched Housing: Models and Methodologies.* Los Angeles.

Brauner, Sarah, and Pamela Loprest. 1999. *Where Are They Now? What States' Studies of People Who Left Welfare Tell Us: Assessing the New Federalism.* Policy Brief A-32. Washington: Urban Institute.

Burt, Martha, Janine M. Zweig, and Kathryn Schlichter. 2000. *Strategies for Addressing the Needs of Domestic Violence Victims within the TANF Program: The Experience of Seven Counties.* Washington: Urban Institute.

Commission on Family and Medical Leave. 1996. *A Workable Balance. Report to Congress on Family and Medical Leave Policies.* Washington: Department of Labor.

Danziger, Sandra K., and others. 2000. "Barriers to the Employment of Welfare Recipients." In *Prosperity for All? The Economic Boom and African Americans,* edited by R. Cherry and W. Rodgers. New York: Russell Sage Foundation.

Danziger, Sheldon. 2001. "Approaching the Limit: Early National Lessons from Welfare Reform." In *Welfare Reform, Food Assistance and Rural Poverty,* edited by G. Duncan, B. Weber, and L. Whitener. Kalamazoo, Mich.: Upjohn Institute for Employment Research.

Dion, Robin M., Michelle K. Derr, Jacquelyn Anderson, and LaDonna Pavetti. 1999. *Reaching All Job-Seekers: Employment Programs for Hard-to-Employ Populations.* Washington: Mathematica.

Herr, Toby, and Suzanne L. Wagner. 1998. *Moving from Welfare to Work as Part of a Group: How Pathways Makes Caseload Connections.* Chicago: Erikson Institute.

Jayakody, Rukmalie, Sheldon Danziger, and Harold Pollack. 2000. "Welfare Reform, Substance Use, and Mental Health." *Journal of Health Politics, Policy and Law* 25 (4): 623–51.

Kaplan, Thomas, and Ingrid Rothe. 1999. *New Hope and W-2: Common Challenges, Different Responses.* Madison, Wisc.: Institute for Research on Poverty, University of Wisconsin.

Kessler, Ronald, and others. 1994. "Lifetime and 12 Month Prevalence of DSM-III-R Psychiatric Disorders in the United States: Results from the National Comorbidity Survey." *Archives of General Psychiatry* 51 (1): 8–19.

Loprest, Pamela. 1999. *Families Who Left Welfare: Who Are They and How Are They Doing?* Discussion Paper 99-02. Washington: Urban Institute.

Moffitt, Robert, and Jennifer Roff. 2000. *The Diversity of Welfare Leavers, Welfare, Children and Families, A Three City Study.* Policy Brief 00-02. Baltimore: Johns Hopkins University.

National Center on Addiction and Substance Abuse. 1999. *Building Bridges: States Respond to Substance Abuse and Welfare Reform.* Columbia University.

Olson, Krista, and LaDonna Pavetti. 1996. *Personal and Family Challenges to the Successful Transition from Welfare to Work.* Washington: Urban Institute.

Perez-Johnson, Irma, Alan Hershey, and Jeanne Bellotti. 2000. *Further Progress, Persistent Constraints: Findings from a Second Survey of the Welfare-to-Work Grants Program.* Washington: Mathematica.

Pollack, Harold, and others. 2001. "Drug Testing Welfare Recipients: False Positives, False Negatives, Unanticipated Opportunities." Unpublished paper. Ann Arbor, Mich.: University of Michigan.

Speiglman, Richard, Lynn Fujiwara, Jean Norris, and Rex Green. 1999. *A Look at Potential Health-Related Barriers to Self-Sufficiency.* Berkeley, Calif.: Public Health Institute.

Sweeny, Eileen. 2000. *Recent Studies Indicate that Many Parents Who Are Current or Former Welfare Recipients Have Disabilities or Other Medical Conditions.* Washington: Center on Budget and Policy Priorities.

Sweeny, Eileen, Liz Shultz, Ed Lazere, and others. 2000. *Windows of Opportunity.* Washington: Center on Budget and Policy Priorities.

Thompson, Terri S., Pamela A. Holcomb, Pamela Loprest, and Kathleen Brennan. 2000. *State Welfare-to-Work Policies for People with Disabilities.* U.S. Department of Health and Human Services.

U.S. General Accounting Office. 1999. *Welfare Reform: Information on Former Recipients' Status,* GAO/HEHS-99-48.

———. 2000. *Welfare Reform: State Sanction Policies and Number of Families Affected.* GAO/HEHS-00-44.

Weaver, R. Kent. 2000. *Ending Welfare as We Know It.* Brookings.

Welfare Information Network. 2000. *Promising Practices: Chicago Commons Employment Center.* Washington.

Zedlewski, Sheila. 1999. *Work-Related Activities and Limitations of Current Welfare Recipients.* Discussion Paper 99-01. Washington: Urban Institute.

Zedlewski, Sheila, and Donald Alderson. 2001. *Families on Welfare in the Post-TANF Era: Do They Differ from Their Pre-TANF Counterparts?* Discussion Paper 2001-01. Washington: Urban Institute.

13

ROBERT GREENSTEIN
JOCELYN GUYER

Supporting Work through Medicaid and Food Stamps

THE PRINCIPAL GOAL of the welfare law was to move families from welfare to work and, in so doing, provide them a route out of poverty. Studies of families that have left welfare show, however, that most earn wages that
leave them below the poverty line and that these families usually lack access
to employer-based health insurance. The wages these families earn thus need
to be supplemented with other supports to ease their poverty and ensure that
they are better off working than receiving welfare.

Along with the Earned Income Tax Credit (EITC) and child care, food
stamps and health insurance are the most significant such supports for low-
income working families. A broad bipartisan consensus has developed that
health insurance and food assistance should be available to such families. As
Ron Haskins notes in chapter 4, policymakers broadly concur that families
should not be made worse off by losing health insurance and food assistance
when they leave welfare for work and that families should not have to go on,
or return to, welfare to obtain such assistance. For example, the welfare law
delinked Medicaid eligibility from welfare receipt for families (it had already
been delinked for most children) and accorded states new options to extend
Medicaid broadly to low-income working families not on welfare.

Both programs have had difficulty moving from being adjuncts to welfare
in varying degrees to playing a larger role as work supports. The proportions
of poor families that are served in Medicaid and food stamps have declined

since 1995. Although eligibility for neither program is dependent upon welfare receipt, the dramatic declines in cash assistance rolls appear to have resulted in large numbers of eligible working families failing to receive Medicaid or food stamp assistance for which they qualify, including many families that have moved from welfare to work. Medicaid and food stamps always reached a smaller proportion of eligible working families than of families on welfare. Because of economic growth and welfare reform, this problem has grown in importance. Looking first at Medicaid and then at food stamps, this chapter examines recent developments in these programs and considers policy changes that could enable them to improve service to low-income working families.

The Role of Medicaid

Many families affected by welfare reform have little or no access to affordable employer-based insurance coverage and consequently are at high risk of being uninsured if they do not have Medicaid (Guyer, 2000). Several recent studies indicate that enrollment of low-income parents and children in Medicaid results in greater use of preventive services, reduces the extent to which families do not receive needed health care, and limits their risk for significant out-of-pocket medical expenses (Ku and Broaddus, 2000; Kasper, Giovannini, and Hoffman, 2000).

It is sometimes asserted that many eligible families remain outside Medicaid by choice. Although this may be true for some families, according to a recent study prepared for the Kaiser Commission on the Future of Medicaid (2000), more than nine in ten parents with uninsured children who are eligible for Medicaid would like to enroll their children. and a substantial majority have sought to do so. In surveying parents with uninsured children who are eligible for Medicaid, Kaiser's study found that 67 percent had previously tried to enroll their children. An additional 26 percent of those parents reported they had not tried to enroll their children in the past, often because they did not realize the children were eligible, but would be willing to do so in the future. Among the parents who had previously tried to enroll their children, the majority had been unsuccessful because they had problems completing the application process (which was long and complicated) or because they completed the application process but were denied coverage.

It is also sometimes argued that little harm is done when eligible children and families miss out on Medicaid because they can secure uncompensated care or enroll subsequently if they face a health crisis. Research, however, increasingly suggests otherwise. For example, an Urban Institute analysis found that uninsured children eligible for Medicaid but not enrolled were more likely than their enrolled counterparts to lack a regular source of care, to go without recommended immunizations, and to have unmet medical needs. In addition, their families were more likely to incur out-of-pocket health care costs for children that exceeded $500 a year (Davidoff and others, 2000).

Recent Developments in Medicaid Policy for Families with Children

Before the enactment of the 1996 welfare law, low-income families often had to receive welfare to qualify for Medicaid. Although many of the children in low-income working families not on welfare could qualify for Medicaid because of Medicaid expansions for children instituted since the mid-1980s, parents in low-income working families usually were ineligible. The welfare law made a historic change by delinking Medicaid eligibility for families with children from welfare receipt. Regardless of whether the families receive welfare, states now must make families with children eligible for Medicaid if the families meet the Aid to Families with Dependent Children (AFDC) income, asset, and family composition criteria in effect in their state in July 1996. This is a minimum criterion; the delinking provision accords states broad flexibility to extend coverage to families well beyond these minimum levels. These rules primarily affect eligibility for low-income parents; broader eligibility rules apply to children.

The delinking provision was designed to ensure that changes in welfare policies would not cause low-income families to lose health care coverage. Thus families that reach a time limit in the Temporary Assistance for Needy Families (TANF) program or never apply for welfare remain eligible for Medicaid as long as they continue to meet a state's criteria for family coverage. Delinking also gave states a powerful tool to refashion Medicaid by expanding coverage for low-income working families without simultaneously being required to expand welfare benefits. For example, under delinking, a state can elect to provide Medicaid to all families with children with income up to 200 percent of the poverty level, regardless of their welfare status.

When it delinked welfare and Medicaid eligibility, Congress also modified and continued Transitional Medical Assistance (TMA), a component of Medicaid designed to support welfare reform by preventing families that leave welfare for work from immediately losing their health care coverage. TMA traditionally has provided eligibility for six months of coverage to families leaving welfare for work and an additional six months as long as a family's income, after child care expenses, remains below 185 percent of the poverty line. To qualify for TMA, families had been required to have been on welfare for at least three of the preceding six months. In the welfare law, Congress modified TMA to reflect the fact that Medicaid eligibility is no longer tied to welfare receipt. Families now qualify for up to twelve months of TMA when they lose eligibility for regular Medicaid (rather than when they lose eligibility for welfare), providing they have been enrolled in Medicaid for three of the previous six months.

Delinking and Coverage Expansions

Since 1996, ten states—including several of the largest states—have used the delinking provision to extend coverage to families (that is, to parents along with children) with incomes up to 100 percent of the poverty line and often higher. Wisconsin, for example, extends family coverage to those with incomes up to 185 percent of poverty; once enrolled, families can retain coverage until their incomes reach 200 percent of poverty. These ten states join seven others that previously extended family-based coverage to 100 percent of the poverty line or higher, primarily through use of a Medicaid waiver.

Some other states have used the delinking provision to institute more modest but still significant steps to expand eligibility for working families. Florida, for example, now disregards the first $200 a month in earnings and 50 percent of remaining earnings when evaluating families' eligibility for Medicaid. A mother with two children can earn up to $808 a month (68 percent of poverty) and remain eligible for coverage. Several years ago, such a mother would have become ineligible in Florida when her earnings reached 34 percent of poverty.

Nevertheless, in two-thirds of the states, Medicaid income limits for parents remain at or close to the welfare limits and far below the income limits for health insurance for children. As of July 2001, in the median state, a parent in a family of three loses Medicaid eligibility when her income surpasses 69 percent of poverty. In thirty-seven states a parent working full time for $7 an hour earns too much to qualify for Medicaid (Center on Budget and Policy Priorities, 2001). The states with higher income limits for working parents tend to be more affluent states with greater fiscal capacity.

These gaps in coverage for low-income working families are exacerbated by the fact that many of the working families that are eligible are missing out on coverage. Partly because of administrative problems in breaking the old eligibility link between welfare and Medicaid, some families have not been provided an effective opportunity to apply for Medicaid if they did not apply for welfare or were mistakenly terminated from Medicaid when they left welfare (Schlosberg and Ferber, 1998). In addition, some families do not under-

stand that welfare and Medicaid eligibility rules now differ. A recent study
found that more than seven of ten low-income parents mistakenly believe
welfare time limits apply to Medicaid coverage for children (Kaiser Commission, 2000; see also Quint and Widom, 2001). In response to these problems, several states have instituted aggressive measures to improve the
TANF/Medicaid interface in their programs and are implementing or considering changes to make their Medicaid programs more accessible to working families.

Recent Coverage Expansions for Children in Low-income Working Families

Coverage for children has expanded substantially in recent years, in part as a
result of the creation of the State Children's Health Insurance Program
(SCHIP) in 1997. SCHIP gives states enhanced fiscal incentives (in the form
of a higher federal matching rate than the regular Medicaid program provides) to extend coverage to more children in low-income working families
through Medicaid, through a separate state child health insurance program,
or through a combination of these approaches. All fifty states use SCHIP
funds, and many have adopted major eligibility expansions (Ross and Cox,
2000). As a result, nearly all uninsured children living in families with
incomes up to 200 percent of the poverty level (except certain immigrant
children) now are eligible for Medicaid or a separate SCHIP-funded program
(Broaddus and Ku, 2000).

The establishment of SCHIP also has spurred state campaigns to educate
working families about the availability of health care coverage for their children and to simplify application and re-enrollment procedures. By July 2000
some forty states had eliminated the requirement that families must apply in
person at a welfare or Medicaid office, forty-two states had dropped the asset
test for children in Medicaid and their separate SCHIP programs, and thirty-
nine states were reviewing eligibility at twelve-month intervals so that families do not have to reapply as frequently.

Effects of Welfare Reform on Coverage

But although the eligibility of children for coverage (and, in some states, of
parents as well) has grown, actual enrollment trends have been disappointing,
particularly for parents. An extensive body of research suggests that the sharp
welfare caseload declines of recent years, problems with delinking, and some
confusion among families about Medicaid eligibility rules have had the unintended effect of causing substantial numbers of low-income families to lose
coverage. A reversal of these declines appears to have begun in 1999, particularly among children, who are benefiting from the expansions generated by

SCHIP and state outreach initiatives. In 1999, however, parents in low-income families and many of the poorest children continued to be uninsured at higher rates than they were before the enactment of the welfare law.

The most direct evidence on the connection between welfare reform and health care coverage comes from studies of how families fare after leaving welfare. An Urban Institute study of single-mother families that left welfare between 1997 and 1999 found that close to half of the children in these families—and nearly two-thirds of the parents—lost Medicaid after ceasing to receive welfare (Loprest, 2000). Similarly, a recent review of health insurance data in twenty-five state studies of welfare leavers found that many parents and children lose Medicaid after leaving welfare and are at significant risk of becoming uninsured, even though they often remain eligible (Guyer, 2000). For example, the Colorado leaver study found that 90 percent of children who were uninsured two years after leaving welfare remained eligible for Medicaid or the state's separate SCHIP program. Had these children stayed enrolled, only 3 percent of the children in families that left welfare would have been uninsured. As it was, 31 percent were uninsured. In each of the six state studies that examined this issue, families' unmet medical needs increased after leaving welfare.

Recent census data indicate that some progress was made in 1999, but poor children still were more likely to be uninsured in 1999 than they had been before the enactment of the welfare law (see table 13-1). Between 1995 and 1999 the proportion of children below the poverty line who were enrolled in Medicaid declined from 62.1 percent to 55.6 percent. The proportion without insurance climbed from 22.9 percent to 25.8 percent. By contrast, among children in near-poor families, coverage has improved, partly as a result of expansions in child health programs and outreach initiatives. (States continued to increase enrollment in SCHIP-funded programs in 2000, making it likely that census data for 2000 will show continued improvement in coverage rates for low-income children.)

The insurance situation of low-income parents is of particular concern (see table 13-2). Not only are they less likely to be eligible for coverage than their children, but the proportion of low-income parents enrolled in Medicaid has dropped steadily since 1995 and the proportion of such parents without insurance has increased. The decline in coverage has been sharpest among parents below the poverty line. The share of such parents without insurance rose from 36.5 percent in 1995 to 41.4 percent in 1999, as the proportion with Medicaid plunged from 43.3 percent to 34.2 percent.

Due to the low Medicaid income eligibility limits for parents in many states and the limited availability of employer-based coverage at low-wage

Table 13-1. *Health Insurance Status of Children by Family Income Level, Selected Years*

Percent

Year	Covered by Medicaid	Covered by other insurance	Uninsured
Poor children (0 to 100 percent of poverty)			
1995	62.1	15.0	22.9
1998	54.9	18.1	26.9
1999	55.6	18.6	25.8
Near-poor children (100 to 200 percent of poverty)			
1995	25.5	52.5	22.0
1998	24.6	51.7	23.7
1999	27.4	51.9	20.6
All low-income children (0 to 200 percent of poverty)			
1995	44.1	33.4	22.5
1998	39.8	34.9	25.3
1999	40.7	36.3	23.1

Source. Authors' calculations based on data from the Current Population Survey.

jobs, working-poor parents are at particularly high risk of being uninsured. In 1999 some 46 percent of working parents with incomes below the poverty line were uninsured ("working" is defined here as having annual earnings equal to at least half-time, minimum-wage earnings). This compared to 34 percent of nonworking parents with below-poverty incomes (authors' tabulations of Current Population Survey data).

Erosion in coverage among legal immigrant families also has contributed to the coverage declines. Under the welfare law, most legal immigrants who arrived in the United States on or after August 22, 1996, are ineligible for Medicaid and SCHIP for at least their first five years in the country. Since 1995 (the year preceding enactment of welfare reform) the percentage of low-income immigrant families that have Medicaid coverage has fallen significantly (Ku and Blaney, 2000); the decline has occurred both among immigrants subject to this restriction and among citizen children living in immigrant families, a group that remains eligible for coverage. Several studies indicate that part of the enrollment decline among children and other people in immigrant families who remain eligible is due to confusion among immi-

Table 13-2. *Health Insurance Status of Parents by Income Level, Selected Years*

Year	Covered by Medicaid	Covered by other insurance	Uninsured
Poor parents (0 to 100 percent of poverty)			
1995	43.4	20.2	36.5
1998	35.4	24.9	39.8
1999	34.2	24.7	41.4
Near-poor parents (100 to 200 percent of poverty)			
1995	12.8	59.7	27.5
1998	10.6	60.2	29.2
1999	10.6	60.6	28.8
Low-income parents (0 to 200 percent of poverty)			
1995	25.9	42.8	31.3
1998	21.1	45.2	33.7
1999	20.2	46.0	33.8

Source: Authors' calculations based on data from the Current Population Survey.

grant families about the circumstances under which their children qualify and fears that using means-tested programs could adversely affect family members' immigration status (Zimmermann and Fix, 1998). In addition, a recent Urban Institute study found that children of immigrants were more than two times as likely to be uninsured as children of natives, more than three times as likely to have no usual source of care, and more than twice as likely to be in fair or poor health (Capps, 2001).

Federal Medicaid Reforms

These trends suggest that, either in TANF reauthorization or in separate legislation, it would be advisable for federal policymakers to help states address the significant disparities among states across the country in the eligibility of low-income working parents for coverage, as well as the loss of coverage among many families that move from welfare to work. The positive trends in coverage for children associated with SCHIP-related reforms offer insights into ways to make Medicaid more effective at serving working families. These developments suggest the federal government should consider giving states greater financial incentives to extend eligibility for health insurance to more low-income working parents and increased flexibility to simplify various procedures in order to facilitate the enrollment of more of the eligible families.

Helping States Extend Coverage to Low-Income Working Families

A promising way to enable more low-income working parents to secure coverage would be through a family-based coverage initiative that draws on lessons from SCHIP and recent experiences with child health outreach campaigns. In recent years, some states have extended Medicaid coverage to whole families so that low-income working parents can be covered along with their children. States have instituted such measures to make it easier for families to work without fear of losing health care coverage, to reduce the ranks of the uninsured, and to promote the enrollment of more eligible children (Bartels and Boroniec, 1998). New research finds that family-based Medicaid expansions that cover parents result in a significant increase in Medicaid participation rates among children who already are eligible and may also increase children's use of needed medical services (Ku and Broaddus, 2000; Dubay and Kenney, forthcoming; Lambrew, 2001; and Gifford and Weech-Maldonado, forthcoming).

As noted, however, most states have not yet expanded coverage for parents beyond welfare eligibility levels. A principal barrier appears to be financial. Most of the states that have extended coverage broadly to low-income working parents are in the Northeast or upper Midwest or on the West Coast. These states have greater fiscal capacity, on average, than states in the regions of the country where no state has yet taken such action. One result has been increasing disparities among states in coverage for low-income working families.

The SCHIP experience is instructive here. States were permitted to expand Medicaid eligibility for children beyond the federal minimum eligibility limits long before SCHIP was established, but a number of states did not do so until after SCHIP provided enhanced federal matching rates. Today, with SCHIP in place, all states have expanded coverage for children, most to at least 200 percent of the poverty line.

The most promising recent policy idea in this area for low-income working families is embodied in legislation introduced by a bipartisan group of Senate and House members in July 2000 and expected to be reintroduced on a bipartisan basis in the summer of 2001. This legislation would substantially increase funding for SCHIP and allow states to use these funds, at the enhanced SCHIP matching rate, to cover the parents of children covered under Medicaid and separate SCHIP-funded programs. The parents would be enrolled in the same program as their children. A larger federal matching rate for family coverage would likely lead substantially more states to adopt such coverage. Moreover, a family-based initiative would fill the gaping hole in Medicaid eligibility that has contributed to working-poor parents being uninsured at substantially higher rates than their counterparts who are not working.

Family-based coverage initiatives could be further enhanced if federal law were modified to allow states to apply to family-based coverage the same tools that many of them are using to facilitate children's enrollment, such as the option to guarantee twelve months of continuous coverage and to use health care providers and organizations that work with low-income working families to initiate the enrollment of families in coverage. In addition, Congress could consider giving states the flexibility under a family-based coverage initiative to serve low-income noncustodial parents who meet their child support obligations, as well as custodial parents.

Improving Transitional Medical Assistance (TMA)

TMA needs improvement so that families leaving welfare for work can better maintain health care coverage, particularly if some states elect not to provide broader family coverage. At present, it appears that only a small minority of families working their way off welfare receive the TMA coverage for which they qualify (Kaplan, 1997). Many become uninsured as a consequence. A shortcoming of TMA is that a significant minority of families are not aware of their eligibility for it and do not realize they may need to take steps to secure it when leaving welfare (Guyer, 2000). In addition, families must submit, and states must process, three months of information on earnings and child care costs in the fourth month of TMA coverage, again in the seventh month, and once more in the tenth month to maintain coverage during the second six months of TMA.

TMA and TANF come up for reauthorization at the same time. Congress should strengthen TMA by according several new options to states. As the General Accounting Office has recommended, Congress should give states the option of guaranteeing a full year of TMA to eligible beneficiaries without imposing burdensome reporting requirements and without an income test in the second six months of coverage (GAO, 1999). In addition to simplifying TMA for both families and states, this action would enable states to give TANF families the clear and unambiguous message that they will get at least one year of Medicaid coverage if they work their way off cash assistance.

In addition, policymakers should give states the option of providing TMA to families that find employment quickly. To qualify for TMA, families must have been enrolled in Medicaid for at least three of the preceding six months. This rule is inconsistent with the welfare-reform goal of promoting rapid attachment to the labor force, since it denies TMA to families that move quickly into work. States should be given the option of dropping the three-months-out-of-six rule and providing TMA coverage to any family enrolled in Medicaid when the family's income subsequently rises above the state's regular Medicaid income limit because of increased earnings.

One other TMA-related change also merits consideration. Since TMA's purpose is to provide transitional coverage to families that work their way off welfare but have low or moderate incomes, Congress could give states the option of dropping TMA altogether if the state provides family-based coverage to families with children with incomes up to at least 185 percent of the poverty line. This policy would streamline and simplify Medicaid eligibility and encourage more states to adopt family-based expansions. The House Commerce Committee approved legislation containing such a measure in October 2000.

Coverage for Legal Immigrants

As noted, legal immigrants who arrived in the United States on or after August 22, 1996, are generally ineligible for Medicaid and SCHIP for at least their first five years in the country. Thus legal immigrants with a substantial need for preventive or remedial health care—including pregnant women and children—cannot get Medicaid coverage or SCHIP. If states wish to extend coverage to these individuals, they must pay 100 percent of the cost. Many of these individuals are uninsured and at high risk of going without care or turning to uncompensated care.

Bipartisan legislative proposals have been introduced on Capitol Hill to ease the severity of these coverage restrictions. A strong case can be made that individuals who entered the country legally and otherwise meet all program eligibility criteria should not be denied health insurance solely because they are immigrants. This is particularly strong with regard to children, pregnant women, working parents, and those who have become disabled after arriving in the United States. Granting states more options to cover such individuals merits consideration.

In sum, to help transform Medicaid into a more effective source of health care coverage for low-income working families, Congress should consider giving states new fiscal incentives and options that make it more feasible for them to adopt family-based coverage expansions, make it easier for working families to enroll in TMA and for states to administer this aspect of Medicaid, and enable states to cover more immigrant children, pregnant women, and working parents lawfully residing in the United States. If such changes are enacted, states will have more tools to ensure that welfare reform

improves the health care situation of low-income families rather than intensi-
fying the health insurance problems that such families face.

Food Stamps as a Work Support

Unlike Medicaid, food stamps did not need to be delinked from cash assistance in 1996. Food stamps have long been available to the working and
nonworking poor on essentially the same basis. Working families with gross
incomes up to 130 percent of poverty (almost $18,400 for a family of three
in 2000) generally qualify if they meet the program's asset test. Although parents in a three-person family with full-time minimum-wage earnings are ineligible for Medicaid in the majority of states, such a family qualifies for a substantial food stamp benefit—approximately $175 a month (or $2,100 on an
annualized basis). The food stamp benefits for which such a family qualifies
over the course of a year are nearly equal in size to the maximum EITC payment for a family with one child.

The food stamp program is the only major means-tested benefit program
that covers nearly all types of low-income households. Whether a household
works or receives public assistance, has one or two parents, or is elderly or
disabled does not determine its eligibility. The food stamp program also is
the sole program that places children with their families in the same eligibility-and-benefit structure as the low-income elderly and disabled. This program feature has been particularly beneficial to poor families with children
because they usually are accorded less favorable treatment than the elderly
and disabled poor when separate programs or separate eligibility-and-benefit
rules are established.

Because the benefit level it provides a family depends on the family's disposable income (the poorer the family, the larger its benefit), the food stamp
program narrows the large gaps in income and government assistance
between poor families in more affluent states and families in states where
wages and cash assistance benefit levels are low. The cash assistance for poor
families in the lowest-benefit states is one-fourth that provided in the
highest-payment states. Food stamps cut this gap in half. Thus food stamps
are particularly important in poor states and have been shown to have a
major impact on reducing hunger in very poor areas (Kotz, 1979).

The feature of the program that targets benefits to households with the
lowest incomes after deductions for certain expenses serves other purposes as
well; it reduces inequities between households that secure certain government
subsidies and those that do not. A working-poor family with high child care
or housing costs receives more food stamps than a family that has similar

earnings but does not incur such costs, perhaps because it receives government child care or housing subsidies. In these respects, the program's basic design is sound, and the program helps compensate for gaps and inequities in the structure of other means-tested programs. But the food stamp program also faces a significant problem: eligible working families have historically participated at substantially lower rates than welfare families. As more families have left welfare for low-income work in recent years, the proportion of eligible families not receiving food stamps has increased.

Recent Changes in Food Stamp Participation

Over the decade 1989–99, the percentage of food stamp households receiving welfare fell markedly, and the proportion with earnings climbed. In 1989 some 19.5 percent of food stamp households had earnings, and 42 percent received AFDC (USDA, 1991). By 1999 the percentage with earnings and the percentage receiving TANF benefits were the same: 27 percent (USDA, 2000).

These percentages cover all food stamp households, including the elderly and disabled. Among food stamp households with children, the proportion of households with earnings jumped by more than half between 1989 and 1999, from 26 percent to 42 percent. The proportion receiving AFDC or TANF fell from 67 percent to 48 percent (authors' tabulations of food stamp quality control data).

Even so, the food stamp participation rate—that is, the proportion of eligible households that receives food stamp benefits—remains much lower among working households. The latest data, from September 1998 (Castner, 2000), show that virtually all eligible individuals receiving TANF cash assistance participated in the food stamp program; in contrast, only about half of the eligible individuals in households with children that had earnings but did not receive welfare received food stamps. A portion of this gap can be explained by the fact that eligible working households have higher average incomes and thus qualify for smaller average food stamp benefits than households receiving TANF cash assistance. Studies have long shown that participation rates are higher among those eligible for larger benefits. But after taking this into account, a substantial participation-rate gap remains.

Furthermore, food stamp participation rates have been falling in recent years, in part because of the movement of families from a high participation-rate category (households that receive welfare) to a lower participation-rate category (households with earnings). The Castner (2000) study shows that the percentage of eligible individuals who receive food stamps declined from 71 percent in 1994 to 59 percent in 1998. Among eligible children under 18, the participation rate fell from 86 percent to 69 percent. The decline was particularly large among eligible households with incomes between 50 percent and 100 percent of the poverty level.

These downward participation trends have slowed the reduction of poverty and lessened the effectiveness of efforts to "make work pay." Research indicates that the disposable income of the poorest fifth of single-mother families declined somewhat between 1995 and 1999, despite the booming economy and increased earnings among these families. The decline in food stamp assistance was one of the principal reasons for this decrease. In addition, the "poverty gap" for families with children (the total amount by which the incomes of all poor families with children fall below the poverty line) failed to shrink much between 1995 and 1999 despite economic growth, while the amount by which the average poor child falls below the poverty line was greater in 1999 than in any year since 1979. Here, too, the decline in food stamp receipt played a significant role (Primus, 2000). In a recent study of families that left the food stamp program in Illinois, Mathematica researchers concluded: "Approximately two years after program exit, many food stamp leavers remain poor, experience poor health (without health insurance), have trouble getting enough to eat, and face other hardships. . . . Although food stamp caseloads have declined dramatically in Illinois and nationally in recent years, it is not at all clear that the well-being of those who have left the program has improved" (Rangarajan and Gleason, 2001).

What Is Causing the Decline in Participation Rates?

Given the historic disparities in participation rates between working households and welfare households, one would expect the recent increases in employment and decreases in welfare receipt to result in a drop in food stamp participation rates. An array of studies confirms that many families leaving welfare for work cease receiving food stamps despite remaining eligible for them. Food stamps and Medicaid face parallel problems in this area; in both programs, families that leave welfare and do not return evidently face difficulties in remaining enrolled.

An Urban Institute study found that 66 percent of families with children that were on welfare and food stamps in 1997 but left welfare by 1999 ceased to receive food stamps. Only 43 percent of the welfare-leaver families with incomes below the food stamp eligibility limits were getting stamps in 1999 (Zedlewski, 2001). Indeed, only half of welfare leavers with incomes below *half* of the poverty line were receiving food stamps. Another Urban Institute study found that one-third of the families that left welfare during this period reported that they had cut the size of meals or skipped meals in the past year because they did not have enough food (Loprest, 2000).

Increases in employment, decreases in welfare receipt, and problems in the interaction between food stamps and TANF are not, however, the sole factors responsible for the drop in food stamp participation rates. Other factors also appear to be at play, including an increase in the burdens that working poor households face in seeking to secure or retain food stamps, sharp declines in participation among eligible citizen children in immigrant families, and possibly the reduction in food stamp benefit levels triggered by provisions of the welfare law.

INCREASED BURDENS ON WORKING FAMILIES. Evidence is growing that changes in recent years in how the food stamp program is administered have made it more difficult for eligible households to obtain food stamps and retain benefits after entering the program. This appears particularly true for working families. For example, a substantial number of states have shortened the duration of time for which working families (and in some cases, other families as well) may be certified for food stamps and require them to reapply in person at more frequent intervals. This requirement can cause parents to miss time from work, forgo some wages, and possibly irritate their employers. Between 1994 and 1999, a dozen states increased by 50 percentage points or more the proportion of working households with children assigned food stamp certification periods of three months or less (in other words, the number of households required to reapply every three months to retain their benefits). In these states, the number of working households with children that receive food stamps fell 29 percent over the five-year period. In the remaining states, the number of working households with children receiving food stamps declined less than 1 percent. Similarly, an Urban Institute study found that among families that ceased receiving food stamps after leaving welfare despite continuing to have incomes below the poverty line, the proportion citing administrative problems as the reason for leaving the food stamp program nearly doubled between 1997 and 1999 (Zedlewski, 2001).

The spread of such practices has stemmed not from the welfare law or pursuit of welfare-reform goals but from intensified state efforts to lower food stamp error rates, induced by federal pressures on states to reduce errors. As Gais and his colleagues point out in chapter 2, and as a recent Manpower Demonstration Research Corporation study found, the food stamp quality control system has large effects on state and local administrative behavior (Quint and Widom, 2001). Under that system, any state with an error rate above the national average is potentially subject to fiscal sanctions. Moreover, a state's error rate is the only performance measure the food stamp law sets. States often measure the performance of local food stamp offices, supervisors, and even individual eligibility workers based partly on the error rate of the cases they handle.

The substantial increase in recent years in the proportion of the food stamp caseload that consists of households with earnings has intensified these pressures on states. Because household earnings can fluctuate and food stamp benefits are sensitive to modest changes in monthly income or expenses (each change of $3 in net household income results in a $1 change in benefits), precise benefit accuracy is more difficult to achieve for households with earnings than for other households. Welfare payments usually remain constant from month to month, and if a family's welfare grant level does change, the welfare office—which administers both welfare and food stamps—knows of the change immediately. Among working-poor households, by contrast, hours of work and hence household earnings can fluctuate. It is difficult for food stamp offices (and households) to track these earnings fluctuations from month to month. Until recently, if a working-poor parent worked just one hour more or less per week than the food stamp office had projected, the state was charged with an error. The average error rate in 1998 was nearly twice as high among households with earnings as among those without earnings.

The recent increases in the share of the caseload consisting of working families consequently exert upward pressure on state error rates. Many states have responded by instituting aggressive procedures to reduce the potential for errors among working households, including shorter certification periods and more detailed paperwork and verification requirements. In addition, because of quality control pressures, some states subject categories of households considered to be "error prone" to more exhaustive procedures; in some areas, simply having earnings can place a household in an error-prone category. These practices make it more difficult for families to secure and retain food stamps if they go to work.

CITIZEN CHILDREN OF IMMIGRANT FAMILIES. Another factor that has contributed to decreases in participation rates is the striking decline in food stamp receipt among children who are U.S. citizens but live in a household that contains one or more persons (usually a parent) who is a legal permanent resident. Between 1994 and 1998, the number of such citizen children receiving food stamps fell more than 70 percent despite the fact that children who are citizens did not lose food stamp eligibility. The number of these citizen children who receive food stamps plunged by 1 million, from 1.35 million children in 1994 to 350,000 in 1998 (authors' tabulations of quality control data). This decline accounted for about one-fourth of the national decline in food stamp participation among children between 1994 and 1998. Similarly, the participation rate among citizen children living in a household with one or more noncitizen adults plummeted from 76 percent to 38 percent over this period (Castner, 2000).

This drop appears attributable in part to fears in some immigrant communities that a child's receipt of a means-tested benefit such as food stamps could jeopardize a parent's immigration status. Confusion about the complex food stamp rules that apply to immigrant families also appears to be a factor. Legal immigrant parents are ineligible for food stamps even if they entered the country before the welfare law was signed, but their children are eligible if they are citizens or entered the country before August 22, 1996. Some parents may mistakenly believe that because they are ineligible, their children are too.

REDUCTIONS IN BENEFIT LEVELS. As noted, food stamp participation rates are higher among households eligible for larger benefits than among those eligible for smaller benefits. The welfare law reduced benefits for most households. These reductions may have affected participation rates.

When the welfare law was enacted, the Congressional Budget Office (CBO, 1996) estimated that the law's food stamp provisions would reduce food stamp expenditures by nearly $28 billion over six years, accounting for half of the savings in the welfare legislation, and would eliminate 18 percent of projected food stamp benefit expenditures by 2002. The CBO estimate showed that a substantial majority of these savings did not stem from provisions to restrict eligibility for immigrants or adults without children or from provisions to toughen requirements related to work, payment of child support, or the like. The majority of these savings resulted instead from provisions to reduce benefits, often across the board, for most or all categories of food stamp households, including the working poor and the elderly and disabled. Although a few of these provisions were subsequently scaled back, most remain in effect. A typical family of four with full-time minimum-wage earnings now receives $240 a year less in food stamps as a result. These measures were included in the law primarily to meet austere budget targets the Agriculture Committees were assigned in order to help balance the budget by 2002, rather than for reasons related to welfare-reform goals such as promoting work and marriage. Whatever their justification, these benefit reductions appear to have reduced participation rates modestly.

On at least one front, recent food stamp participation data tell a story that welfare reformers may find reassuring: the data indicate that the food stamp program is not compromising TANF efforts to promote work. A question likely to be examined at reauthorization is whether the presence of the food stamp program is inducing significant numbers of families to escape TANF work requirements by leaving or failing to enroll in TANF and enrolling only in food stamps. Were such an effect present, we would expect to see substantial increases since the enactment of TANF in the numbers of food stamp households with children that receive neither welfare nor earnings. That, however, has not occurred. In 1996 food stamp rules were changed so that benefits no longer increase when welfare benefits are reduced because of a sanction; and the food stamp program's own sanctions for noncompliance with work and other behavioral requirements were toughened. Since then the number of food stamp households with children that have no earnings and do not receive AFDC or TANF has decreased (authors' tabulation of quality control data).

Food Stamp Reforms

Until recently, Medicaid and food stamps have been moving in different directions with respect to serving working families. In Medicaid, many states have eased application-related requirements that burden and impose "transaction costs" on working families and have shortened and simplified Medicaid applications, particularly for children. Federal officials have encouraged such changes.

Until mid-1999, however, the food stamp program was moving in the opposite direction. Federal pressures intensified on states to achieve precise payment accuracy. Along with the increase in the food stamp caseload that consists of working families, this appears to have induced a substantial number of states to institute measures that have the effect of making applying for and remaining enrolled in the food stamp program more burdensome for working families. Rather than requiring fewer visits by working families to welfare offices and adopting less onerous application requirements, these changes in food stamp practices have often required more such visits and more intensive verification.

Since mid-1999, however, federal policymakers have begun to shift course and to grant some new state options and establish other procedures to make food stamps more accessible to working families. For example, recent regulations allow states to fix benefits for working families for six months at a time without having to recalculate benefit levels if family circumstances change during this period (unless the family's income climbs over the program's income limit or the family reports a downward shift in circumstances). These are steps in the right direction. But substantial additional measures are needed.

Improving Participation Rates among Eligible Working Families

Reauthorization offers an opportunity for policymakers to promote welfare reform goals by making food stamps serve working families more effectively. This section explores several proposals. These include reforming the quality control system; simplifying the program; granting states more flexibility over aspects of the delivery of benefits to eligible households; providing funding to states for system improvements in serving working families; and improving the adequacy of food stamp benefits. Some of these changes are connected. Program developments in recent years indicate that when state flexibility is coupled with rigid and unreasonable quality control rules, states can feel compelled to institute measures that have the effect of making food stamps for eligible working families harder to secure. By contrast, if greater state flexibility is coupled with a reformed quality control system, states are more likely to institute measures that improve service to working families, as many states are doing in Medicaid.

REFORMS IN THE QUALITY CONTROL SYSTEM. Because the current quality control (QC) system imposes sanction liabilities on states with error rates above the national average, roughly half the states are subject to sanctions even if states as a group perform well and achieve a low national error rate. In addition, because error rates are higher among working than nonworking families, states that perform better in serving working families increase their risk of exceeding the national average error rate and incurring a sanction, a perverse effect of the QC system. In 1999, USDA announced a long-overdue change under which it adjusts sanctions resulting from error rates downward for states in which the proportion of the caseload consisting of working families exceeds the national average or has risen significantly in recent years. This policy lacks regulatory or statutory status, however, and states are not assured of its continuation.

Cash assistance and Medicaid used to have QC systems similar to that which the food stamp program employs. They no longer do. With 100 percent federal funding of food stamp benefits, some form of food stamp quality control system is necessary, but there is widespread consensus that substantial changes are needed.

In the mid 1980s a blue-ribbon National Academy of Sciences panel studied the food stamp quality control system and called for extensive revision (Affholter and Kramer, 1987). One of the panel's principal recommendations was to cease basing sanctions on measures that subject large numbers of states to sanctions and instead to adopt a standard that focuses sanctions on states whose error rates make them outliers. "When states are operating at attainable levels of performance," the panel stated, "thresholds for sanctions and rewards should be set so that only states at the extremes of good or bad performance are subject to rewards or sanctions." In addition, payment accuracy should not be the sole criterion the federal government uses in measuring state performance. Other measures, including measures related to performance in serving eligible households, and especially working families, should also be used, with possible fiscal incentives attached.

SIMPLIFYING PROGRAM RULES. Various food stamp eligibility and benefit rules are too complex for a program aimed at working families, especially rules related to small amounts of income and unusual forms of nonliquid assets. To ensure that no family gets a dollar more in food stamps than it is considered to need, federal rules address minutia such as when small amounts of money received for giving blood should count as income and when they should be excluded. Such rules should be reviewed with an eye to sharply reducing the number of minor forms of income and assets that must be assessed.

Some simplification of the food stamp program's deductions from gross income, which are used to figure a household's benefit level, also should be considered. Because deductions play an important role in enabling the program to target benefits to need, changes in this area need to be made with some caution. If welfare reauthorization or other legislation includes provisions for greater subsidization of expenses that food stamp deductions recognize—such as child care costs and out-of-pocket medical expenses that elderly individuals incur (such as expenses for prescription drugs)—some of these deductions may no longer be needed.

The most important deduction—the food stamp shelter deduction—should be retained but simplified. This deduction helps narrow the large disparity in assistance between the minority of low-income households (about one-fourth) that receive federal housing assistance and the large majority that do not. This deduction is particularly important for working-poor families that do not receive a housing subsidy. Census data show that in 1999 the number of low-income renter households that had "worst-case housing needs" because they paid more than half of their income in rent stood at 4.6 million households. (An additional 300,000 households had "worst-case needs" because they lived in severely substandard housing.) A substantial majority of these were low-income working households receiving no housing subsidy. Low-income households whose main source of income is earnings constituted 80 percent of the nonelderly, nondisabled households with "worst-case needs" in 1999 (HUD, 2001). The shelter deduction boosts the food stamp benefits of such households by up to $102 a month ($1,224 on an annualized basis). Elimination of this deduction, or changes that would make the deduction much less sensitive to households' housing expenditures, could pose difficulties for working-poor families that pay housing costs that are high in relation to their incomes. Such changes also could drain millions of dollars from states and localities in which housing costs are high.

Accordingly, measures should be explored to simplify this deduction without compromising its role in targeting benefits on households whose high housing costs sharply reduce the income they have available for food and other necessities. Particular attention should be paid to simplifying the program's treatment of utility costs, which add to the deduction's complexity. A household's rent tends to remain constant for months or a year at a time, but its utility costs may fluctuate each month. Simplification of federal rules that limit states' ability to use "standard utility allowances" in lieu of tracking households' monthly utility bills would be helpful.

Also called for are simplification measures that ease the need for working families to provide information, and states to process it, when the earnings of working families fluctuate. In this regard, USDA took two significant steps in November 2000, granting states a new option to freeze benefits for working families for six-month periods (during which time earnings fluctuations do not have to be acted upon and do not cause "errors"), as well as an option to provide a three-month transitional food stamp benefit to families that leave welfare, during which benefits are frozen and states need not fear that changes in a family's circumstances will lead to a food stamp "error."

Simplification efforts also should prove of use in pursuing another objective: the development of simpler joint application forms and procedures through which working families can apply for Medicaid and food stamps together, preferably in settings outside the welfare office. As more states allow working families to apply for Medicaid without going to the welfare office, such joint application procedures will take on added importance.

STATE OPTIONS. If accompanied by enlightened quality control reforms, additional state options regarding procedures under which food stamp benefits are provided should enable states to raise participation among working families. The two new state options just described are examples of such flexibility. So is the option that Congress recently granted states to substitute TANF rules regarding the value of vehicles that households may own for the complicated and restrictive food stamp rules in this area. An examination of food stamp law and regulations should be undertaken to identify further areas where new or expanded state options may make sense, but such flexibility should not undermine the strength of the national benefit structure.

IMPROVING BENEFIT ADEQUACY. As noted, the welfare law included provisions that reduced food stamp benefits for low-income working families and other households. These reductions may have affected participation rates. They certainly have contributed to the income losses that studies have found among the poorest fifth of single-mother families, as well as to the increase in the amount by which the average poor child falls below the poverty line. The adequacy of the food stamp benefit structure warrants reexamination.

FUNDING FOR STATE IMPROVEMENTS. The welfare law established a fund for states to use to address administrative and operational problems in the interaction of Medicaid and TANF after the welfare law's enactment. Such problems have also been significant in the food stamp program, occurring to a much greater degree than was anticipated when the welfare law was passed. Congress may wish to consider establishing a modest fund to help states pay for improvements that can enable their food stamp systems to more effectively serve families moving from welfare to work and other working-poor households. These include computer system changes, staffing improvements, stationing some eligibility workers outside welfare offices, and expanded hours of operation. Such a fund could be modeled on the Medicaid fund; to secure these resources, states would need to provide modest matching funds.

Extending Eligibility to More Low-Income Working Families

In addition to these changes aimed at boosting participation rates among working households, changes also should be considered in at least two aspects of the program's eligibility structure that reduce its effectiveness as a work support: the program's asset rules and its rules governing the eligibility of legal immigrants.

MODERNIZING THE ASSET RULES. Families receiving cash welfare are automatically eligible for food stamps and hence are not subject to the food stamp asset test. Working families, by contrast, are subject to this test, which was designed several decades ago. In states that have modified the asset rules they use in TANF, as many states have done in recent years, working families consequently face more restrictive food stamp asset rules than do families receiving cash assistance. The food stamp asset rules make ineligible for assistance some working-poor families that most policymakers would regard as needy. These rules also are overly complicated.

In short, the food stamp asset rules need modification. Congress took a first step in this direction in October 2000 when it allowed states to substitute their TANF rules regarding the vehicles a family may own for the food stamp program's vehicle rules, as long as the TANF rules are not more restrictive. Other changes in food stamp asset rules Congress should consider include substantially simplifying the rules; excluding all retirement savings from the asset test so that low-income working families are not forced to choose during hard times between depleting modest retirement savings and obtaining food stamps; and raising the $2,000 overall asset limit for nonelderly households (and possibly the $3,000 limit for the elderly). The food stamp asset limits have not been adjusted since 1985, during which time the consumer price index has risen about 60 percent.

Consideration also might be given to allowing states to substitute other aspects of their TANF or Medicaid asset rules for food stamp asset rules, as long as those rules are not more restrictive than the food stamp rules (the Medicaid aspect of this option would apply only in the forty or so states that have Medicaid asset tests for families). At a time when policymakers are encouraging working families to save for retirement, self-employment, college education for a child, or other purposes, the current food stamp asset rules are more restrictive than is desirable.

ELIGIBILITY FOR LEGAL IMMIGRANTS. The food stamp program's restrictions on the eligibility of legal immigrants are more stringent than those that apply in the Supplemental Security Income program, Medicaid, or TANF. Food stamps is the only means-tested program that denies eligibility to large categories of poor legal immigrants who entered the country before August 22, 1996, including most working poor legal immigrants. These restrictions appear to have contributed to the sharp decline in participation by eligible citizen children in immigrant families. And a recent Urban Institute study finds that problems related to affording food were, by 1999, substantially more widespread among immigrant families with children than among their native counterparts (Capps, 2001).

Legal immigrants who entered the United States before August 22, 1996, are ineligible for food stamps unless they are children, were elderly on August 22, 1996, or are disabled. Most individuals who entered the country after August 22, 1996, are also ineligible; unlike in Medicaid or TANF, these individuals cannot become eligible after they have been here five years. These restrictions are too severe and should be changed.

Would Converting Food Stamps to a Block Grant Be a Wise Move?

The final issue we examine is whether the food stamp program should be converted to a block grant. This issue figured prominently in the debate over the 1996 welfare reform law and may reemerge in the reauthorization debate. Such a radical change in the program would be ill-advised for several reasons.

The food stamp program is the most responsive of all means-tested programs to changes in poverty and unemployment. If more households in a state qualify for food stamps because poverty increases, as can occur during a recession or as a result of strong state population growth, the program automatically expands and serves more people. When poverty declines, the program contracts. Under a block grant, the program's ability to respond immediately to fluctuations in the economy and changes in need would be lost. States would receive a fixed amount of funding at the start of the year. If unemployment increased, states would have to choose among bearing 100 percent of added food assistance costs themselves at a time when state revenues were declining, reducing benefits, or placing new applicants on waiting lists in the midst of a downturn when jobs are hard to find.

Some proponents of the block-grant approach argue that because a block grant has not produced problems in the cash assistance area, it would be safe to extend it to food stamps. But the food stamp program is designed to be far more responsive to changes in the economy than AFDC or TANF; food stamp caseloads have risen and fallen much more in response to economic cycles than cash assistance rolls have. Moreover, the TANF block grant had the good fortune to be based on spending in high-expenditure, relatively high unemployment years, providing a cushion for states.

By contrast, food stamp participation is now at its lowest level in twenty-one years, with food stamp costs down substantially as a result. A food stamp block grant tied to current expenditure levels would cause serious hardship when poverty increases.

In addition, the fact that TANF is a block grant, with funding levels that do not respond when need changes, heightens the need for the food stamp program to retain its current responsiveness to changes in the economy. It is doubtful a formula could be designed for a food stamp block grant that would prevent the loss of much of the program's responsiveness to changes in need. Efforts to come up with such a formula when a food stamp block grant was being debated in the mid-1990s were unsuccessful. If one bases state block-grant funding levels on some sort of formula, rather than on expenditures in a base year as TANF does, such a formula would necessarily be based on information that would be outdated when the economy changed. At any point in time, the most recent state-by-state poverty and income data are several years old. State unemployment rate data do not solve this problem either: they do not pick up shifts from full-time to part-time work or erosion in wages that can occur during a downturn; they do not reflect the disproportionate job losses that can occur among the least skilled when the economy sours; and they contain a lag of a number of months, especially since monthly (as distinguished from quarterly) state unemployment rate data are too volatile and imprecise to use.

The conversion of food stamps to a block grant also would represent dubious macroeconomic policy. The food stamp program functions as what economists call an "automatic stabilizer," infusing more purchasing power into the economy when the economy turns down. The late Herbert Stein, chairman of the Council of Economic Advisers under President Nixon, observed several years ago that the increase in means-tested benefits during recessions provides laid-off workers the means to purchase essential goods and services, stimulates demand, and helps stabilize businesses that serve these workers (Haner, 1995).

In addition, conversion to a block grant could render the food stamp program unable to prevent variations among states in the benefit packages that poor children receive from growing larger than they already are. The loss of the national food stamp benefit structure could be injurious to children in another respect as well. The current food stamp benefit structure not only automatically lessens disparities among states in cash benefits for poor children and their families, but it also lessens the wide disparities between cash benefit levels for the elderly poor and for poor families with children. A block grant that did not establish a single benefit structure for all categories of poor households might well result, over time, in changes in benefit structures in some states that favor the low-income elderly (a more politically popular group) at the expense of low-income children and families, even though poor families with children fall farther below the poverty line, on average, than poor elderly households do.

Finally, a food stamp block grant tied to current expenditure levels would provide no room to address the largest problem facing the program: low participation rates among eligible working families. Funds would not be available to improve participation rates among such families unless benefit levels were cut or some categories of households now eligible for assistance were made ineligible.

For these reasons, the block grant course would be unwise to pursue. Nor is a demonstration of the block grant approach recommended; the inherent problems with the approach are too severe. In addition, a demonstration of the block grant approach would not be particularly meaningful unless it covered a recession as well as a recovery period. A demonstration also could create equity problems across states with regard to issues such as food stamp quality control requirements and sanctions. A much sounder approach is to simplify overly detailed and complicated rules, identify areas in which new or expanded state options would be appropriate, strengthen various program features that are particularly important to working families, and reform the part of the program that is the single greatest source of state discord: the quality control system. States can be granted more flexibility in operating the food stamp program without replacing the program with a block grant.

Conclusion

Medicaid and food stamps have important roles to play as work supports that strengthen welfare reform. However, both programs need to become more effective in assisting working families. To this end, states should receive the same type of federal financial support for providing health insurance to low-income working parents that they receive for children. The removal of outdated federal requirements that encumber Transitional Medical Assistance also would be beneficial. The food stamp program's basic design is sound, but the system for delivering benefits to eligible working families needs strengthening. Key aspects of the program should be maintained, such as its entitlement nature, which allows it to respond automatically to changes in need, and its national benefit structure, which allows it to narrow gaps between richer and poorer states. In other areas, reform is needed. Overhauling the quality control system, simplifying federal rules, giving states more options in delivering benefits, modernizing the asset test, and improving benefit adequacy would enable the program to serve working families more effectively and reduce their poverty. Finally, both programs should ease the eligibility restrictions on legal immigrants.

COMMENT BY
Don Winstead

A point made early in the chapter by Robert Greenstein and Jocelyn Guyer is that the declines in cash assistance rolls have resulted in families not receiving Medicaid or food assistance for which they qualify. This statement suggests that the decline in cash assistance caseloads caused a similar result in Medicaid and food stamps as well. In their more detailed discussion of the issues, the authors make a more compelling case that the impact of reductions in cash assistance has had very different results in Medicaid and food stamps due to differences in the programs, differences in the federal regulatory environment, and differences in state operations.

Although Greenstein and Guyer use the latest available data, part of the problem in understanding this issue, particularly in regard to Medicaid, is the delay in the publication of national caseload data.

In my own state of Florida, for example, cash assistance has decreased more than in any other large state. For families containing an adult, the cash assistance caseload declined more than 80 percent from September 1996 (the month before TANF implementation) to December 2000. Even counting "child-only" families, the decline has been 67 percent. If declines in cash assistance have the results described by Greenstein and Guyer, one would expect to see similarly dramatic reductions in Medicaid and food stamps.

In Florida there were about 800,000 children enrolled in Medicaid when welfare reform was implemented in October 1996. By mid-1998 this number had declined to about 700,000. Since then, however, the number has steadily increased, with December 2000 enrollment at 948,000. For adults, even if the data are adjusted to exclude adults enrolled in the Family Planning waiver, the number of nonelderly adults has declined only slightly.

The decline in participation in the food stamp program has not been as dramatic as the decline in cash assistance, but there has been a decline among both children and adults. These trends emphasize that the welfare reform story is different for the two programs, and the needs for further reform of Medicaid and Food Stamps are similarly unique.

Although Florida's experience may not predict the Medicaid caseload trends in every state, reports from other states give me the impression that the declines seen from 1996 to 1998 or 1999 have stopped and that many states are now on an upward trend. As shown in the Greenstein and Guyer analysis of the 1995–2000 Current Population Survey data, although the numbers of poor, near-poor, and low-income children on Medicaid in 1999 are below 1995 levels, the number of children covered is higher in 1999 than in 1998. I think this gives a further indication that Medicaid caseload reductions, particularly among children, have "bottomed-out" and that we will see further increases when data from 2000 are available.

Leaving aside the question of whether Medicaid enrollment is increasing or decreasing, Greenstein and Guyer offer compelling evidence that the children and adults in many low-income families are not covered by Medicaid, the State Children's Health Insurance Program (SCHIP), or employer-based insurance. Although continued progress in enrollment of children is needed, the observation regarding the insurance coverage of low-income parents underscores an area of particular concern.

Greenstein and Guyer offer a number of recommendations for further reform. Many of their recommendations include providing more options for states, coupled with enhanced federal matching rates, to better enable states to overcome the fiscal difficulties posed by increased enrollment. This is a significant issue for states. In Florida one of the most difficult problems for legislators is continuing to fund increases in Medicaid enrollment. Federal funds will be necessary if states are to have the fiscal capacity to provide Medicaid to more families.

Policy options that align and synthesize the Medicaid and SCHIP programs, provide family-based coverage, and simplify Transitional Medical Assistance all have merit and should be considered. The option of a federal-state partnership is important in expanding coverage to legal immigrants who are not currently covered by Medicaid or SCHIP. Immigrants who reside in this country legally and who otherwise meet all eligibility requirements should be eligible for federal programs. It is not in anyone's interest to have legal residents of the country ineligible for health insurance, and national policy should reflect that fact.

Turning to food stamps, Greenstein and Guyer begin with a brief history of the food stamp program. Given the sensitivity of food stamp allotments to changes in family income, it is not surprising that the best economy in a generation should be accompanied by some decline in participation. However, Greenstein and Guyer point to specific statutes and policies that pose significant barriers to participation in the food stamp program. These include the negative consequence of the food stamp program's obsession with quality control errors as the determinant of federal penalties and the hyper-precision with which food stamp policy tries to reflect monthly changes in family earnings.

Measuring payment accuracy is like net fishing. If you want to catch fish of significant size, use a net with large mesh. If your mesh is too fine, you spend your day straining to haul in tons of minnows. The food stamp program has spent far too much time and effort penalizing states for letting the minnows get away. The recommendation by Greenstein and Guyer for enlightened reform of quality control is right on target.

Greenstein and Guyer also recommend additional state options to increase participation among working families. The 1996 law created a simplified food stamp program to permit more uniformity between cash assistance and food stamps. This component has largely failed because of restrictive interpretations of cost neutrality and a narrow focus on current cash assistance recipients. What is needed is a new focus on helping families that are moving to work gain access to food stamps. New rules on issues like treatment of vehicles are good, but much more needs to be done in this area. Policies and administrative practices should support work requirements and families that are working.

With input from the directors of state food stamp programs, the American Public Human Services Association (APHSA) has developed a series of recommendations that would dramatically simplify the calculation of food stamp benefits. There may be room for discussion of specific elements (such as the shelter deduction), but it is clear that much can be done to reduce administrative barriers to participation and to simplify the eligibility process for low-income individuals and families.

Greenstein and Guyer conclude their chapter with a discussion of whether it would be wise to fund the food stamp program as a block grant. I tend to agree that this would not be a wise course of action. However, allocation of administrative funding for food stamps and Medicaid was changed in 1998 in a manner that had a significant impact in some states. States now integrate many of the functions related to eligibility for cash assistance, food stamps, and Medicaid, and consideration should be given to consolidating the funding for the administrative tasks related to these public assistance programs. A block grant with a contingency provision for unanticipated growth merits consideration. Another area of potential reform is the Food Stamp Employment and Training Program. Funding should be consolidated within the policy framework of other work force programs for low-income individuals and families to better coordinate delivery of these services.

COMMENT BY

Gary Stangler

The rhetoric of welfare reform has always stressed the importance and value of work, but welfare programs in the United States have often discouraged work. As soon as welfare recipients got jobs, these programs began to unravel any support to sustain employment. The success since 1996, and the key to sustaining that success, is the support system for working families.

Chief among those supports are health insurance and food assistance. There is abundant evidence that health insurance translates to better health outcomes for children and adults, and that the Food Stamp program is the link to making work pay—along with the Earned Income Tax Credit (EITC) —and reducing the "poverty gap."

The well-documented declines in Medicaid and Food Stamp caseloads that accompanied the decline in enrollment in the Temporary Assistance for Needy Families program (TANF) are complex mixtures of barriers to access, eligibility restrictions, and program designs. Further complicating the use of these work supports is the psychology of welfare reform. Many individuals who go to work are not aware of available supports or are confused by the plethora of eligibility thresholds attending Medicaid, the State Child Health Insurance (SCHIP) program, child care, and food stamps. And the specter of time limits permeates participant perspectives.

Robert Greenstein and Jocelyn Guyer expertly unravel these complexities and set forth proposals for changes that range from broadly conceptual to intricately detailed. My comments are based on my perspective as a former state welfare director and my commitment to a strong system of supports for working families.

First, we need to focus on reforms of the SCHIP program. States have had difficulty enrolling children in SCHIP even when making extensive efforts to do so. In Missouri, we expanded health insurance for children to 300 percent of the poverty level and undertook a massive enrollment initiative with hospitals, schools, social service agencies, and churches. While very successful by many measures, it has been a tough go. Support for the program, as shown by our polling with the hospital association, was very strong, with large majorities supporting the expansion at all age and income levels (up to the top categories in each, where support fell below 50 percent). We found no Medicaid stigma. In fact, Medicaid was more popular than insurance agencies and health maintenance organizations. We reduced the application to two pages front and back and enrolled by phone and mail.

So what is the problem? Why is it still a struggle? In addition to the above-mentioned difficulties associated with TANF caseload declines, there is an issue of incentive, especially for those required to pay monthly premiums or copayments. Because children are generally healthy, parents have less incentive to ensure that they are enrolled in Medicaid. And for those families struggling to make it, health insurance is something you can put off or is just not a top priority until there is an illness or injury. While parental peace of mind is sufficient incentive for some, or access to preventive care for a few, there is usually no urgency.

Contrast this situation with our health insurance expansion for adults. Missouri was the first state to have a waiver to meld Medicaid and SCHIP, and to make it work with our Medicaid waiver. We expanded adult access to health insurance to 100 percent of poverty for adults with children, and to 125 percent for noncustodial fathers current on their child support payments. With no outreach, no advertising, no partnerships to spread the word, enrollment soared. Consistent with the finding of Greenstein and Guyer, helping adults enroll greatly contributed to the enrollment of children. The adults actually need the services, and the provider system abets that enrollment when the adults seek care.

Thus in order to enroll children and to support adults in the labor force, states need federal help on two fronts: additional flexibility to create a seamless—at least to the participant—system of health insurance and strong incentives for states to use Medicaid. Missouri used an approach that merged SCHIP and Medicaid. This approach has alleviated many of the problems attendant to multiplying programs and was easier for the provider system to adjust to.

Our polling showed that it is much easier politically to expand health insurance for children than adults. Adding to the difficulty of expanding coverage for adults is the exploding cost of pharmaceuticals that is draining state budgets and resurrecting the tensions of rising health care costs. Even though the increased costs bear little relationship to the expansion for children, children often take the hit. In Missouri, 90 percent of the increased costs are attributable to the elderly and disabled, which makes intuitive sense when one thinks of who uses pharmaceuticals and remembers that children are inexpensive because they are generally healthy and low health care users.

To increase the use of buy-in with premiums and copays that rise with income and to minimize the burden on the provider system, the financial incentives to the states must be tied to adult eligibility expansions and come with increased flexibility to merge Medicaid and SCHIP. The latter is important because it is politically difficult enough to increase coverage for the poor without raising resistance from the provider system. In addition, as we have discovered in Missouri, it is necessary to work with employers to persuade them to withhold the premiums.

The difficulties in ensuring food assistance are different. Unlike Medicaid, the Food Stamp program has seen its "transaction costs" maintained or increased. For states and participants, this is colloquially known as the "hassle factor" and is the chief culprit in the decline of this needed support. For states, the "best" food stamp case is one in which there are no earnings. Yet in most other programs, states are making great efforts to promote employment and earnings. The federal Food Stamp Quality Control system (QC) retains its exclusive focus on the error rate and uses QC penalties as a club to bludgeon state bureaucrats. Yet virtually no one, with the exception of Greenstein, can explain QC with any degree of competence.

So the public is led to hold onto its interpretation of errors as fraud, and each new round of sanctions leads to a new round of proposals by state legislatures to tighten restrictions and erect more barriers. The hassle factor on states directly translates into hassle factors on participants such as frequent recertifications and face-to-face applications. That means we are hassling the very people who are doing what our rhetoric calls for, namely, those who are working harder, including mothers leaving welfare.

Greenstein and Guyer advance many technical changes that would improve access to food assistance, but I will mention only two: cars and electronic benefits transfer (EBT). First, the asset limit on automobiles has been a bone of contention for years, even decades, becoming a "third rail" politically when President Ronald Reagan deluded the public into the myth of widespread use of Cadillacs by welfare mothers. The food stamp version of the Cadillac myth is recipients using food stamps to buy steaks. Yet, when one talks to employers about what they want in an employee, first and foremost is dependability, showing up at work on time and every day. The most frequent barrier to dependability is transportation, and the most common form of transportation in the United States is the car. But the asset limit for a car virtually ensures that food stamp recipients can only own an undependable car.

Second, the use of EBT has generally not moved beyond fraud reduction or reduced costs. In Missouri, with the leadership of Bob Holden, then treasurer and now governor, free and low-cost bank accounts were provided statewide. Bank accounts have provided a way to bring food stamps from the Neolithic to the modern age.

Finally, Greenstein and Guyer give compelling arguments against a block grant. Any advocate of block granting food stamps must be chilled by the history of attempted raids on TANF and other federal block grants. Barely months had passed on the six-year TANF deal before Congress made attempts to reduce TANF funding levels. Now the states mount an annual battle to fight off the raids, which will become a more difficult chore with TANF reauthorization. Imagine fighting also to maintain food assistance funding levels with the decline in caseloads, especially in a weakening economy. Moreover, the improvements made with Medicaid flexibility demonstrate that the entitlement can be retained while making programs more responsive at the state level.

References

Affholter, Dennis P., and Frederica D. Kramer. 1987. *Rethinking Quality Control: A New System for the Food Stamp Program.* Washington: National Academy Press.

Bartels, Peggy, and Pris Boroniec. 1998. "BadgerCare: A Case Study of the Elusive New Federalism." *Health Affairs* 17 (6): 165–69.

Broaddus, Matthew, and Leighton Ku. 2000. *Nearly 95 Percent of Low-Income Children Now Are Eligible for Medicaid or SCHIP.* Washington: Center on Budget and Policy Priorities.

Capps, Randy. 2001. *Hardship among Children of Immigrants: Findings from the 1999 National Survey of America's Families.* Washington: Urban Institute.

Castner, Laura. 2000. *Trends in Food Stamp Program Participation Rates: Focus on 1994 to 1998.* Washington: Mathematica.

Center on Budget and Policy Priorities. 2001. *Survey of State Officials on Section 1931 Eligibility Rules.* Washington.

Congressional Budget Office (CBO). 1996. *Federal Budgetary Implication of HR 3734, the Personal Responsibility and Work Opportunity Reconciliation Act of 1996.* Washington.

Davidoff, Amy, Bowen Garrett, Diane Makuc, and Matthew Schirmer. 2000. *Children Eligible for Medicaid but Not Enrolled: How Great a Policy Concern?* Washington: Urban Institute.

Dion, Roberta M., and LaDonna Pavetti. 2000. *Access to and Participation in Medicaid and the Food Stamp Program: A Review of the Recent Literature.* Washington: Mathematica.

Dubay, Lisa, and Genevieve Kenney. Forthcoming. *The Effects of Family Coverage on Children's Health Insurance Status.* Washington: Urban Institute.

Gifford, Elizabeth, and Robert Weech-Maldonado. Forthcoming. *Encouraging Preventive Health Services for Young Children: The Effect of Expanding Coverage to Parents.* Pennsylvania State University.

Guyer, Jocelyn. 2000. *Health Care after Welfare: An Update of Findings from State-Level Leaver Studies.* Washington: Center on Budget and Policy Priorities.

Haner, Jim. 1995 "Counting the Cost of Saving Money on Welfare." *Baltimore Sun,* May 31, p. 2.

Kaiser Commission on the Future of Medicaid and the Uninsured. 2000. *Medicaid and Children: Overcoming Barriers to Enrollment.* Washington.

Kaplan, April. 1997. *Transitional Medicaid Assistance.* Washington: Welfare Information Network.

Kasper, Judith, Terence Giovannini, and Catherine Hoffman. 2000. "Gaining and Losing Health Insurance: Strengthening the Evidence for Effects on Access to Care and Health Outcomes." *Medical Care Research and Review* 57 (3): 298 318.

Kotz, Nick. 1979. *Hunger in America: The Federal Response.* New York: Field Foundation.

Ku, Leighton, and Shannon Blaney. 2000. *Health Coverage for Legal Immigrant Children: New Census Data Highlight Importance of Restoring Medicaid and SCHIP Coverage.* Washington: Center on Budget and Policy Priorities.

Ku, Leighton, and Matthew Broaddus. 2000. *The Importance of Family-Based Insurance Expansions: New Research Findings about State Health Reforms.* Washington: Center on Budget and Policy Priorities.

Lambrew, Jeanne M. 2001. *Health Insurance: A Family Affair.* New York: The Commonwealth Fund.

Loprest, Pamela. 2000. *How Are Families Who Left Welfare Doing over Time? A Comparison of Two Cohorts of Welfare Leavers.* Washington: Urban Institute.

Primus, Wendell. 2000. Unpublished tables.

Quint, Janet, and Rebecca Widom. 2001. *Post-TANF and Food Stamp and Medicaid Benefits: Factors That Aid or Impede Their Receipt.* New York: Manpower Demonstration Research Corporation.

Rangarajan, Anu, and Philip M. Gleason. 2001. *Food Stamp Leavers in Illinois: How Are They Doing Two Years Later?* Princeton, N.J.: Mathematica Policy Research.

Ross, Donna Cohen, and Laura Cox. 2000. *Making It Simple: Medicaid for Children and CHIP Income Eligibility Guidelines and Enrollment Procedures, Findings from a 50-State Survey.* Washington: Kaiser Commission on Medicaid and the Uninsured.

Schlosberg, Claudia, and Joel Ferber. 1998. "Access to Medicaid since the Personal Responsibility and Work Opportunity Reconciliation Act." *Clearinghouse Review* 31: 528–47.

U.S. Department of Housing and Urban Development (HUD). 2001. *A Report on Worst Case Housing Needs in 1999: New Opportunity and Continuing Challenges.*

U.S. Department of Agriculture (USDA), Food and Nutrition Service. 1991. *Characteristics of Food Stamp Households: Summer 1989.*

———. 2000. *Characteristics of Food Stamp Households: Fiscal Year 1999* (Advance Report).

U.S. General Accounting Office (GAO). 1999. *Amid Declines, State Efforts to Ensure Coverage after Welfare Reform Vary.* GAO/HEHS-99-163.

Zedlewski, Sheila Rafferty, with Amelia Gruber. 2001. *Former Welfare Families Continue to Leave the Food Stamp Program.* Washington: Urban Institute.

Zimmermann, W., and Michael Fix. 1998. *Declining Immigrant Applications for Medi-Cal and Welfare Benefits in Los Angeles County.* Washington: Urban Institute.

14

GEORGE J. BORJAS

Welfare Reform
and Immigration

It's just obvious that you can't have free immigration and a welfare state.

—Milton Friedman

THE DEBATE OVER IMMIGRATION POLICY has always been concerned with the possibility that immigrants might become "public charges." The expansion of the welfare state in recent decades only increased the intensity with which this question is examined and appraised (Borjas and Trejo, 1991; Smith and Edmonston, 1998). Three related issues dominate the recent discussion. The first is the anxiety over the rapid rise in the number of immigrants who receive public assistance. The second is the worry that the relatively generous welfare programs offered by the United States are a magnet for migrants. Finally, there is a contentious debate over whether immigrants "pay their way" in the welfare state.

Congress responded to these concerns by including a number of immigrant-related provisions in the Personal Responsibility and Work Opportunity Reconciliation Act (PRWORA). This legislation specified a new set of rules for determining the eligibility of foreign-born persons to receive practically all types of public assistance. In rough terms, PRWORA denies

I am grateful to Rebecca Blank, Ron Haskins, and Lawrence Mead for providing many useful comments and suggestions.

most types of means-tested assistance to noncitizens who arrived after the legislation was signed in 1996 and limits the eligibility of many noncitizens already living in the United States.

The available evidence suggests that the rate of welfare participation in immigrant households declined sharply—relative to the decline in native households—after the enactment of PRWORA. This decline is particularly remarkable since most of the provisions for removing immigrants already living in the United States from the welfare rolls were never enforced. Moreover, only a small part of the immigrant population present in the United States in the late 1990s arrived after 1996, making it unlikely that these ineligible new arrivals could have such a dramatic impact on the national trend. The steep decline in immigrant participation rates led an influential study to conclude that "because comparatively few legal immigrants were ineligible for public benefits as of December 1997, it appears that the steeper declines in noncitizens' than citizens' use of welfare . . . owe more to the 'chilling effect' of welfare reform and other policy changes than they do to actual eligibility changes" (Fix and Passel, 1999, p. 8).

This chapter examines the impact of PRWORA on welfare participation in immigrant households. The data reveal that the welfare participation rate of immigrants declined relative to that of natives at the national level. But this national trend is mostly attributable to the trends in California. The decline in welfare use among immigrants living outside California was roughly the same as the decline among natives living in those states. Much of the potential chilling effect of welfare reform on these immigrants was neutralized because both state governments and the immigrants themselves altered their behavior. Some states offered state-funded benefits to their immigrant populations, and immigrants learned they could bypass the new restrictions by becoming naturalized citizens.

Historical Perspective

The limitations on immigrant welfare use included in PRWORA are the latest in a long line of restrictions, dating back to colonial days, designed to reduce the cost that immigration imposes on resident taxpayers. As early as 1645 and 1655, the Massachusetts colony enacted legislation that prohibited the entry of poor and indigent persons (Albright, 1928). In 1691, New York introduced a bonding system to discourage the entry of potential public charges: "All persons that shall come to Inhabit within this Province . . . and hath not a visible Estate, or hath not a manual occupation shall before he be admitted an Inhabitant give sufficient surety, that he shall not be a burden or charge to the respective places, he shall come to Inhabit" (Hutchinson, 1981, p. 391).

The U.S. Congress first considered the problems arising from the immigration of public charges in 1836 and reconsidered the issue several times between 1840 and 1880 without taking any action. In 1876, however, the Supreme Court unambiguously granted the federal government the sole authority to control immigration, invalidating all the state laws that restricted the entry of poor immigrants. The states most affected by immigration lobbied Congress to grant them relief from the costs imposed by (a nonexistent) federal immigration policy, and Congress responded in 1882 by banning the entry of "any persons unable to take care of himself or herself without becoming a public charge." The wording of this exclusion was changed in 1891 to ban the entry of "persons *likely* to become a public charge" (emphasis added). In 1903, Congress went further and approved the deportation of immigrants who became public charges within two years after arrival in the United States "for causes existing prior to their landing."

The current restrictions on public charges have changed little since the beginning of the twentieth century. Section 212(a)(4) of the Immigration and Nationality Act states that "Any alien who, in the opinion of the consular officer at the time of application for a visa, or in the opinion of the Attorney General at the time of application for admission or adjustment of status, is likely at any time to become a public charge is inadmissible." The legislation specifies that the factors to be taken into account in determining whether an alien is excludable include age, health, family status, assets, and education and skills. In addition, Section 237(5) states that "Any alien who, within five years after the date of entry, has become a public charge from causes not affirmatively shown to have arisen since entry is deportable."

Despite the presence of the public charge provisions in immigration law throughout the twentieth century, the Immigration and Naturalization Service (INS) did not interpret the receipt of public assistance by foreign-born persons as a ground for deportation. In fact, only fifty-eight immigrants were deported for being public charges between 1961 and 1980 (U.S. Immigration and Naturalization Service, 1998, p. 226). In 1999 the INS published a regulation that for the first time outlined the link between the receipt of public assistance and the definition of a public charge (U.S. Office of the Federal Register, 1999, pp. 28,676–28,688). In particular, it says, a public charge is an alien who has become "primarily dependent on the government for subsistence, as demonstrated by either the receipt of public cash assistance for income maintenance, or institutionalization for long-term care at government expense." By definition, the receipt of such noncash benefits as Medicaid and food stamps do not enter the determination of whether an immigrant is a public charge. Moreover, even if the immigrant receives cash benefits, the INS must consider other factors—such as age, assets, and skills—in making the public charge determination. Finally, the regulation states that an alien can be deported on public charge grounds only if the alien has failed to comply "with a legally enforceable duty to reimburse the assistance agency for the costs of care."

Perhaps in part because the INS did not link the receipt of public assistance and the public charge provision of immigration law between the 1960s and 1990s, the number of immigrants receiving public assistance rose rapidly. In 1970 immigrants were less likely to receive public assistance than natives. By 1998, however, 20 percent of immigrant households received some type of assistance; in comparison, only 13 percent of native households received assistance.

Congress reacted to this trend by making it increasingly difficult for immigrants to receive public benefits. Beginning in 1980 immigrants began to be subject to "deeming requirements," in which the sponsors' income is deemed to be part of the immigrant's application for particular types of aid. The deeming procedure obviously reduces the chances that new immigrants can qualify for welfare. Initially, deeming rules applied only to Supplemental Security Income (SSI) and lasted only three years, but they were later expanded to Aid to Families with Dependent Children (AFDC) and other programs. These statutes, however, did not halt the increase in immigrant welfare use, mainly because the skill composition of the immigrant population was changing dramatically during that period. Over time, immigrants became relatively less skilled and hence more likely to participate in public assistance programs.

In 1996, Congress tightened the eligibility requirements substantially by including a number of immigrant-related provisions in PRWORA. As signed by President Clinton, the legislation contained two key provisions:

—Immigrants who entered the United States after August 22, 1996, the "postenactment" immigrants, are prohibited from receiving most types of public assistance. The ban is lifted when the immigrant becomes an American citizen. Most noncitizens who arrived in the country before August 22, 1996, the "pre-enactment" immigrants, were to be kicked off the SSI and food stamp rolls within a year.

—Postenactment immigrants are subject to stricter deeming regulations. The eligible income and assets of an immigrant's sponsor are deemed to be part of the immigrant's application for most types of public assistance, and the deeming period may last for up to ten years.

One can loosely interpret the first of these provisions as setting up a five-year "waiting period" before postenactment immigrants can qualify for some types of assistance. After five years in the United States, the immigrant can become a U.S. citizen and the ban on welfare use is lifted. Partly because one must be a citizen in order to receive welfare, the number of immigrants who wished to become naturalized rose rapidly in the mid-1990s. From 1992 to 1994 the INS received only 469,000 petitions for naturalization annually; from 1996 to 1998 the INS received 1.2 million such petitions annually (U.S. Immigration and Naturalization Service, 1998, p. 172). It is doubtful, however, that this increase was induced solely by PRWORA. After all, the number of naturalization applications was already rising before 1996. Moreover, the INS, through the Citizenship USA initiative, took steps to speed up the naturalization process before the 1996 presidential election. Politics and fraud motivated and marred many of the activities in this program (Schippers, 2000).

The restrictions on immigrants' use of welfare brought together a number of powerful interest groups after the 1996 presidential election, all of which lobbied hard for their repeal. And, in fact, many of the immigrant-related provisions of the legislation were never enforced. The balanced-budget agreement reached in 1997 between President Clinton and the Republican-controlled Congress repealed the most draconian aspects of the legislation, such as kicking out the pre-enactment immigrants from the SSI and Food Stamp programs. The five-year waiting period for postenactment immigrants, however, remained on the books. Table 14-1 presents a more detailed summary of the existing restrictions on immigrant welfare use.

Trends in Welfare Recipiency: 1994–98

The Annual Demographic Files of the Current Population Surveys (CPS) provide information on participation in various types of social assistance programs during the calendar year before the survey was conducted. I used data drawn from the 1995–99 files to conduct the empirical analysis reported below. The household is the unit of analysis. A household is classified as an immigrant household if the household head was born outside the United States and is either an alien or a naturalized citizen. All other households are classified as native households.

Table 14-2 reports the percentage of immigrant and native households that received particular types of assistance in each year between 1994 and 1998. The probability that either immigrant or native households received some type of assistance was roughly constant before 1996. About 24 percent

Table 14-1. *Alien Eligibility for Means-Tested Federal Programs*[a]

Category of alien	Program			
	SSI	Food stamps	Medicaid	TANF[b]
Immigrant arrived before August 22, 1996	Eligible, if receiving SSI on August 22, 1996, or subsequently disabled	Eligible, if age 65 or over on August 22, 1996, or under age 18, or subsequently disabled	Eligible, for SSI-derivative benefits; otherwise, eligibility is a state option	Eligibility is a state option
Immigrant arrived after August 22, 1996	Not eligible	Not eligible	Eligible for emergency services only	Not eligible
Refugees and those granted asylum	Eligible	Eligible	Eligible	Eligible
Nonimmigrants and illegal aliens	Not eligible	Not eligible	Eligible for emergency services only	Not eligible

Source: Vialet and Eig (1998, table 1).

a. In this table, "immigrant" refers to a foreign-born person who has a permanent residence visa ("green card"). Nonimmigrants include foreign-born persons who are in the United States temporarily, such as foreign students and tourists. The information provided for immigrants who arrived after August 22, 1996, and for refugees and asylees refers to their eligibility status during the first five years after arrival.

b. TANF = Temporary Assistance for Needy Families.

Table 14-2. *National Trends in Welfare Participation Rates, 1994 to 1998*
Percent of households receiving assistance[a]

Year and group	Any	AFDC or general assistance	SSI	Medicaid	Food stamps
Entire country					
Natives					
1994	15.6	4.6	4.0	13.5	8.7
1995	15.0	4.2	4.0	13.2	8.1
1996	15.3	3.9	4.3	13.5	8.0
1997	14.0	3.1	4.1	12.5	6.8
1998	13.4	2.5	3.9	12.1	6.0
Immigrants					
1994	23.4	7.1	5.7	21.3	12.5
1995	23.8	6.8	5.8	21.9	11.7
1996	21.9	5.7	5.6	20.5	10.1
1997	20.2	4.6	5.3	18.7	9.3
1998	20.0	3.9	5.4	18.8	7.5
Households in California					
Natives					
1994	15.2	5.5	4.2	14.2	5.9
1995	14.5	5.1	4.4	13.6	5.9
1996	13.6	4.9	4.5	13.2	6.1
1997	13.5	4.2	4.0	12.9	5.3
1998	13.6	3.6	3.8	12.7	4.8
Immigrants					
1994	31.2	11.3	7.5	30.3	13.6
1995	31.1	10.6	7.2	29.4	12.4
1996	26.3	7.8	6.2	25.5	8.6
1997	23.7	6.9	5.1	23.0	9.3
1998	23.2	5.1	5.8	22.2	8.3
Households outside California					
Natives					
1994	15.6	4.5	4.0	13.5	8.9
1995	15.1	4.2	3.9	13.2	8.3
1996	15.5	3.8	4.2	13.6	8.1
1997	14.1	3.0	4.1	12.5	7.0
1998	13.4	2.4	3.9	12.0	6.1
Immigrants					
1994	20.0	5.2	5.0	17.4	11.9
1995	20.6	5.1	5.2	18.6	11.3
1996	20.1	4.8	5.3	18.4	10.7
1997	18.8	3.7	5.4	17.0	9.2
1998	18.7	3.5	5.2	17.4	7.2

Source: Current Population Survey.

a. A household is considered to receive "any assistance" if any household member receives cash benefits, Medicaid, or food stamps.

of immigrant households and about 16 percent of native households received some type of assistance in both 1994 and 1995. The participation rate of both groups fell immediately after the enactment of PRWORA, but the post-1996 decline was much steeper in the immigrant population. In particular, the recipiency rate dropped by about 2 percentage points among native households, but by 4 percentage points among immigrant households. In addition, immigrant households experienced a steeper decline in the receipt of specific assistance, including AFDC, SSI, Medicaid, and food stamps.

These national trends seem to suggest that the welfare reform legislation strongly influenced whether immigrant households receive assistance, helping to create the perception that PRWORA had a "chilling effect" on immigrant participation in welfare programs. However, the national trends over the 1994–98 period are misleading, for they do not reflect what went on in much of the country during that period.

The demographic importance of California, a state that is home to almost 30 percent of the nation's immigrants, suggests that it might be of interest to examine the trends separately for California and for other states. As table 14-2 shows, almost all of the relative decline in immigrant welfare participation at the national level can be attributed to what happened to immigrant welfare use in California. The fraction of native households in California that received some type of assistance dropped slightly, by 1.6 percentage points, from 15.2 percent before PRWORA to 13.6 percent afterward. In contrast, the fraction of immigrant households in California that received some type of assistance fell precipitously, from 31.2 to 23.2 percent. Outside California, the welfare participation rate of native-born households declined by about 2.2 percentage points, while the participation rate of immigrant households declined by less than 2 percentage points, from about 20 percent before PRWORA to 18.7 percent in 1998. It is also interesting to note that the timing of the decline in immigrant welfare is different in California than in the rest of the country. The decline began before PRWORA in California but occurred after PRWORA in the rest of the country.

To better assess the role played by PRWORA, I take into account two additional facts that influence how welfare reform affected immigrants. First, not all immigrants were equally targeted. The restrictions in PRWORA mainly affect immigrants who are not naturalized and who did not enter the country as refugees. Second, some states offered their own safety nets to immigrants adversely affected by PRWORA. For instance, the welfare reform legislation makes most immigrants who entered the United States before August 22, 1996, ineligible for many types of assistance, such as food stamps and Medicaid. The legislation, however, also grants states the option to offer these programs to some immigrants, and some states chose to do so (even before any federal restoration took place). In addition, some states also offered state-funded assistance to noncitizens who arrived after August 22, 1996. As noted, these immigrants are ineligible for most types of federal aid.

Zimmerman and Tumlin (1999, table 18) grouped states into four categories according to the generosity of the state safety net. The states where such aid was "most available" to immigrants included California and Illinois; the states where the aid was "somewhat available" included New York and Florida; the states where the aid was "less available" included Arizona and Michigan; and the states where the aid was "least available" included Ohio and Texas. It is worth noting that five of the six states with the largest immigrant populations—the exception being Texas—provided above-average levels of state-funded assistance to immigrants (that is, aid in those states was "most available" or "somewhat available").

I classify the foreign-born households into citizen and noncitizen status based on the naturalization status of the household head. (The results are unchanged if a noncitizen household is defined as one where all persons are noncitizens.) I pool the 1994–95 data to estimate the extent of welfare receipt before welfare reform, and the 1997–98 data to estimate receipt after welfare reform. I also group states into two types: more generous states (states where aid was most available or somewhat available) and less generous states (states where aid was less available and least available).

Table 14-3 shows how the "chilling effect" of welfare reform depends on the actions taken by individual states. The welfare participation rate of noncitizens living in the less generous states dropped by 10 percentage points (from 29.4 to 19.4 percent) during the period. In contrast, the participation rate of noncitizens living in the more generous states dropped by only about 5 percentage points (from 29.7 to 24.4 percent). It is worth noting that the participation rates of native and citizen households do not reveal any such sensitivity to the availability of state-funded assistance.

The effect of the state-funded programs is even stronger when the sample is restricted to the nonrefugee households that live outside California. Although the CPS data do not report the type of visa used by a particular immigrant to enter the country, one can approximate the refugee population by using information on the national origin of the foreign-born households. I classified all households where the household head did not originate in the main refugee-sending countries as nonrefugee households. (The main refugee-sending countries over the 1970–90 period were Afghanistan, Bulgaria, Cambodia, Cuba, Czechoslovakia, Ethiopia, Laos, Poland, Romania, Thailand, the former Soviet Union, and Vietnam.) In the sample of nonrefugee households liv-

Table 14-3. *State-Funded Assistance and Program Participation, pre- and post-1996*

Percent of households receiving assistance[a]

| | Households in: | | | | | |
| | Less generous states | | | More generous states | | |
Households and year	Native	Citizen	Noncitizen	Native	Citizen	Noncitizen
Entire sample						
Pre-1996	16.3	15.5	29.4	14.3	14.9	29.7
Post-1996	14.3	14.4	19.4	13.1	17.0	24.4
Non-California households						
Pre-1996	16.3	15.5	28.4	14.2	13.1	23.9
Post-1996	14.3	14.4	19.4	13.0	16.4	22.6
Nonrefugee households						
Pre-1996	16.3	16.0	28.8	14.3	14.6	27.0
Post-1996	14.3	14.6	19.1	13.1	15.8	22.8
Non-California and nonrefugee households						
Pre-1996	16.3	16.0	28.8	14.2	12.8	21.0
Post-1996	14.3	14.6	19.1	13.1	15.1	20.3

Source: Current Population Survey.

a. A household is considered to receive assistance if any household member receives cash benefits, Medicaid, or food stamps.

ing outside California, the participation rate dropped by almost 10 percentage points for households in the less generous states, and by less than 1 percent for households in the more generous states. The programs offered by the more generous states, therefore, seem to have prevented the chilling effect of federal welfare reform on immigrant welfare participation.

It is tempting to argue that the full impact of PRWORA has yet to manifest itself, because the legislation directly affected relatively few immigrants between 1996 and 1998. But it is far from clear that PRWORA will lower welfare participation rates much more in the long run. After all, "new" immigrants—those in the country for fewer than five years—make up a relatively small fraction of the immigrant population (13 percent in 1999). Moreover, most of the restrictions on immigrant participation in welfare programs vanish once the immigrant becomes a naturalized citizen. The welfare reform legislation may have had a substantial impact on the naturalization incentives of foreign-born persons, with those immigrant groups most likely to be affected by welfare reform being the groups with the highest observed increases in naturalization rates. Finally, the available evidence suggests that welfare participation rates among immigrant households are lowest in the initial years after entry (Borjas and Trejo, 1991). In other words, the historical pattern has been one in which immigrants assimilate into welfare programs. In short, it seems that PRWORA's "waiting period" was designed to reduce immigrant welfare use only in those years when immigrants least use welfare.

Finally, why are the trends in California so distinctive? One possibility is that there were specific items in the PRWORA legislation, or in the waivers granted to individual states before 1996, that had a particularly adverse effect on the eligibility of immigrant households living in California. No such provisions, however, exist either in the welfare reform legislation or in the state-specific waivers. Moreover, California was one of the most generous states in offering state-funded assistance to immigrants after 1996. In short, there is no statutory justification that could explain the sizable difference in the trends between California and the rest of the country.

Nevertheless, any explanation of the "California effect" will have to rely on a hypothesis that there were things going on in California that did not occur in the rest of the country. One obvious candidate is the enactment of Proposition 187 in November 1994. This proposition, supported by 59 percent of California's voters, denied almost all types of assistance (including schooling) to illegal aliens. Although most of the provisions in the proposition were never enforced, its impact on the political and social climate in California is undeniable. Soon after the enactment of Proposition 187, there were numerous newspaper accounts of the chilling effect that the proposition had on aliens applying for particular types of publicly provided benefits.

Welfare Reform and Naturalization

The potential impact of PRWORA on immigrant participation in welfare programs was attenuated by the responses of individual states to the legislation. One additional behavioral response could further attenuate the impact—the actions of the immigrants themselves. The welfare reform legislation drew an important distinction between citizen and noncitizen status. Naturalized citizens are eligible for all programs, but noncitizens are not. This fact obviously raises the incentives for the most affected immigrants to become naturalized.

There was a dramatic increase in naturalization applications in the 1990s. Table 14-4 illustrates this trend. The naturalization rate rose from 42.2 before to 52.6 after welfare reform. But this aggregate statistic masks a great deal of

Table 14-4. *Naturalization Rate, by National Origin*[a]
Percent of immigrants who are naturalized

Country of origin	Year	
	1994–95	*1997–98*
Cambodia	29.1	57.8
Canada	54.1	54.3
China	47.6	69.1
Cuba	52.5	72.7
Dominican Republic	28.8	44.5
El Salvador	18.4	25.4
Germany	78.9	75.7
Greece	75.2	72.5
Haiti	35.8	43.7
India	53.4	59.7
Iran	48.9	66.6
Ireland	68.2	69.6
Italy	72.5	77.5
Jamaica	41.5	60.1
Korea	39.4	55.2
Laos	33.2	40.4
Mexico	16.5	28.2
Nicaragua	16.5	36.2
Philippines	65.4	75.9
Poland	65.5	69.7
Former Soviet Union	65.7	81.2
Taiwan	71.8	73.9
Thailand	37.5	65.5
United Kingdom	54.7	46.3
Vietnam	64.0	73.1
All countries	42.2	52.6

Sources: Current Population Surveys.

a. The calculations use the pooled samples of the 1995–96 and 1998–99 surveys and are restricted to foreign-born persons who are at least 18 years old and who migrated to the United States before 1990.

diversity in naturalization rates across national origin groups. For instance, the naturalization rate increased from 54.1 to only 54.3 percent for Canadian immigrants, but from 16.5 to 28.2 percent for Mexican immigrants and from 65.7 to 81.2 percent for immigrants from the former Soviet Union.

It turns out that there is a strong and positive correlation between the increase in the naturalization rate experienced by an immigrant cohort and the fraction of the immigrant group that received welfare before 1996. A detailed statistical analysis suggests that a 20 percentage point increase in the group's pre-1996 welfare participation rates is associated with a 4 percentage point rise in the group's naturalization rate during the 1994–98 period.[1]

This positive correlation between the immigrant group's pre-PRWORA welfare use and post-PRWORA naturalization rates can be interpreted in two different ways. First, the correlation could be measuring an individual behavioral response. Those immigrants who were most likely to be adversely affected by the welfare reform legislation took a simple action that would neutralize the impact of PRWORA: they became naturalized citizens. It is also possible, however, that the political activists who ran the Citizenship USA initiative, with its goal of naturalizing 1 million foreign-born persons in 1996, targeted particular groups of immigrants, groups that would likely support the incumbent Democratic administration in the 1996 elections. It would be of great interest to determine which of these two hypotheses best fits the data.

Policy Implications

From a historical perspective, the 1996 welfare reform legislation is only the latest attempt to minimize the costs imposed on American taxpayers by the immigration of public charges. Congress could have chosen to achieve many of the same objectives by simply enforcing the public charge provisions of current immigration law—both by denying entry to potential welfare recipients and by deporting immigrants who make extensive use of welfare programs. Instead, the welfare reform legislation aimed to reduce welfare use by immigrants in a more circuitous way. By setting up a five-year waiting period before newly arrived immigrants qualify for many types of assistance, the legislation presumably discourages the immigration of potential public charges. By tightening the eligibility requirements for immigrants already in the

---

1. The regression relates the change in an immigrant cohort's naturalization rate (with the cohort being defined in terms of both country of origin and year of arrival) to the cohort's pre-1996 welfare participation rate. The analysis adjusts for differences in socioeconomic characteristics (such as education and age) across cohorts.

country, the legislation presumably increases the incentives for some immigrants to return to their home countries.

The data summarized in this paper indicate that much of the impact of PRWORA on welfare use by immigrants residing outside California was undone by the actions of state governments. Some states—particularly those where immigrants reside—chose to offer state-funded benefits to the immigrants most affected by welfare reform. In addition, immigrants quickly learned that naturalization allowed them to qualify for many types of public assistance denied to noncitizens. As a result, the national origin groups most likely to receive public assistance in the pre-PRWORA period experienced the largest increases in naturalization rates after 1996. This endogenous response by immigrants further served to neutralize the potential impact of PRWORA on immigrant welfare use.

What should be the next step as Congress considers reauthorization of the welfare reform legislation? What can we infer from the trends in immigrant welfare participation in the post-PRWORA period? Should Congress amend the legislation so as to get more noncitizens on the federal rolls and remove the burden from the generous states? Or should the restrictions on immigrant welfare use be tightened even further?

The answer to all of these questions depends on the objectives of immigration policy. Since colonial days, immigration policy has been partly motivated by a desire to protect native taxpayers. This policy objective obviously conflicts with a humanitarian desire that would open up economic and social opportunities in the United States—including the opportunities provided by the welfare state—to poor persons from around the world.

Welfare programs in the United States, though not generous by Western European standards, stack up pretty well when compared to the standard of living in most of the world's less-developed countries. In 1997 a typical California household with two children receiving Temporary Assistance for Needy Families (TANF) got around $12,600 worth of assistance, including cash assistance, food stamps, Medicaid, and other benefits (Committee on Ways and Means, 1998, pp. 416 and 985). At the same time, per capita income was $3,600 in China, $6,600 in Colombia, and $3,500 in the Philippines (U.S. Central Intelligence Agency, 1999).

Income differences across countries influence a person's decision about moving to the United States, regardless of whether these differences arise in the labor market or in the safety net provided by the welfare state. Thus there are valid reasons to be concerned with the possibility that generous welfare programs might attract a particular type of immigrant. A strong magnetic effect, combined with an ineffective border control policy, can literally break the bank. As a result, the immigration of potential public charges can easily fracture the political legitimacy of the social contract that created and sustains the welfare state. No group of native citizens can be reasonably expected to pick up the tab for subsidizing tens of millions of "the huddled masses." Immigration policy, therefore, will inevitably impose some restriction on the entry of potential public charges. But how should the restrictions work?

One major problem with PRWORA is its explicit link between the receipt of welfare benefits and an immigrant's naturalization status. Before 1996 many immigrants did not bother to become naturalized citizens—only 52.8 percent of those who arrived in 1977 had done so by 1997 (U.S. Immigration and Naturalization Service, 1997, p. 140). The welfare reform legislation changed the incentives for different types of immigrants to become U.S. citizens: those with the largest propensity for receiving public assistance have the most incentive to become naturalized.

This link between citizenship and welfare is problematic. Many immigrants will become citizens not because they want to fully participate in the U.S. political and social systems, but because naturalization is required to receive welfare benefits. It obviously does not constitute good social policy to equate a naturalization certificate with a welfare check. And those immigrants who can make claims on the welfare state will be overrepresented in the sample of those who choose to become citizens. A large number of naturalized citizens combined with the very large size of the current immigrant flow create a real possibility that the link between naturalization and welfare receipt can significantly alter the nature of the political equilibrium in many localities and states.

In 1996 Congress granted individual states the option to supplement the federal benefits available to immigrants. Most of the states with large immigrant populations chose to extend the state-funded safety nets to immigrant households. The political choices made by these states prevented many immigrant households from being removed from the welfare rolls and helped attenuate the impact of welfare reform on immigrant welfare use.

From an economic perspective, the responses of the states with large immigrant populations seem puzzling. One could have easily argued that once states could pursue state-specific policies, many of the states most affected by immigration would have chosen to discourage welfare use by immigrants residing within their borders rather than adopt policies that further encouraged welfare use. Why did the race to the bottom not occur? Was it perhaps because the immigrant population in these states is now sufficiently large that elected officials found it essential—from a political perspective—to cater to the needs of this large minority?

The possibility that the immigrants themselves altered the political decisions in these states is worrisome and raises serious doubts about the wisdom of granting states the right to enhance the benefits that are available to immigrants. A federal policy of allowing states to offer more generous safety nets to the immigrants than the one provided by the federal government could lead to some states' becoming a magnet for immigration from other countries. The states' actions, though sensible from the narrow perspective of local politicians running for elected office, may not be sensible from a national perspective. After all, the state is responsible for the cost of admitting immigrants only in the very short run. As soon as the immigrants become naturalized citizens, much of the burden shifts to the federal government. One state's generosity, therefore, could potentially impose a negative externality on the rest of the country.

It is also interesting to note that the political debate over immigrant welfare use often revolves around the question of whether immigrants use welfare more often or less often than natives. This comparison implicitly adopts a particular "yardstick" for measuring the success or failure of immigration policy and welfare reform.

In an important sense, however, this comparison misses the point. Suppose that immigration policy succeeded in replicating the distribution of skills and income opportunities already present in the native population, so that immigrants used welfare just as often as natives. Would this policy be considered successful from the perspective of the debate over immigration and welfare? I doubt it. After all, this policy would have increased the size of the welfare population considerably, adding to the difficult social and economic problems faced by disadvantaged persons in the United States. One could just as easily argue that the debate should use a very different yardstick, the yardstick that has motivated the public charge restrictions for more than three centuries of U.S. history: Should immigrants be on welfare at all? Put differently, why not take the century-old statutes on the entry and deportation of public charges more seriously?

Finally, it is worth noting that some of the key immigrant-related provisions in PRWORA—removing noncitizens who already live in the United States from some programs, particularly SSI—were revoked soon after they were signed into law. The partial unraveling of the legislation provides an important lesson. Immigrant welfare use did rise rapidly in the last three decades of the twentieth century. So it is hard to argue that the immigrant provisions were based on faulty data or analysis. Congress saw a problem and actually tried to do something about it.

It seems, however, that the American people do not wish to bear the political, social, and economic costs of removing immigrants already in the United States from the welfare rolls. It is naïve, after all, to assume that there are no long-run consequences from denying needy immigrants access to food stamps or medical services. In the end, it is probably easier and cheaper to address the problem raised by the immigration of public charges not by "ending welfare as we know it," but by reforming immigration policy instead.

COMMENT BY
Michael Fix

George Borjas argues that the impacts of the 1996 welfare reforms on immigrants have been dramatically reduced by congressional restorations and state-financed public benefits. The law's effects, he claims, were further attenuated by immigrants' naturalization, which reestablished their eligibility for and use of benefits. He concludes that rationing benefits on the basis of citizenship provides a perverse incentive for naturalization, that permitting states to use their own funds to grant immigrants benefits runs the risk of creating welfare magnets that are not in the nation's larger interest, and that states should be denied the power to extend benefits that exceed federally designated levels. Finally, he concludes that, when all is said and done, perhaps the best way to deal with the immigration of public charges is through the reform of immigration policy and not through the reform of the social welfare system.

I do not view the 1996 reforms as just one in a long line of incremental steps taken by policymakers to limit legal immigrants' access to public benefits. Welfare reform represented a watershed in the nation's immigrant integration policies, for the first time barring legal immigrants from federal means-tested public benefits, and effectively conditioning those benefits on citizenship. Before welfare reform, legal immigrants and citizens were treated on more or less the same terms when it came to public benefits. The law also reversed settled legal policy that barred states from discriminating against legal noncitizens in distributing federal and state benefits. The 1996 reforms, then, represent a fundamental change in policy, not an incremental one.

Despite the chapter's suggestion that the law has been watered down by federal restorations and benefit extensions in states that receive a large number of immigrants, many of the law's most far-reaching exclusions remain in effect. Working-age immigrants who entered the country before 1996 remain ineligible for food stamps. Most postenactment immigrants (those who entered the United States after August 1996) remain ineligible until citizenship for the major federal aid programs: Supplemental Security Income (SSI), food stamps, Temporary Assistance for Needy Families (TANF), Medicaid, and the State Child Health Initiative Program (SCHIP).

Although Borjas claims that all the major immigrant-receiving states except Texas can be viewed as being comparatively generous (a finding based on an Urban Institute report, Zimmermann and Tumlin, 1999), states' generosity varies considerably, particularly toward postenactment immigrants. In fact, postenactment immigrants remain barred from state-funded TANF, SSI, Medicaid, and food stamp replacement programs in all of the major immigrant-receiving states, with the exception of California (Zimmermann and Tumlin, 1999).

Although Borjas dismisses the significance of the law's impact on the postenactment population, the demographic importance of the law should not be underestimated. Indeed, immigrants admitted after August 1996 will make up roughly one-third of the legal permanent resident population in 2002, the year the 1996 reforms must be reauthorized.

Borjas argues that noncitizens have taken advantage of the availability of naturalization in ways that attenuate welfare reform's impacts. It is true that naturalizations rose rapidly beginning in the mid-1990s, and naturalized citizens now represent roughly twice the share of all foreign-born benefit users than they did in 1994. However, rising naturalization rates fall well short of either explaining or offsetting the disproportionately steep drops observed in noncitizens' use of benefits—declines that represent one of welfare reform's most striking legacies.

Food stamp quality control data indicate that legal immigrants' use of food stamps fell by 72 percent between 1994 and 1998; over the same period, use of food stamps by citizen children in families headed by a noncitizen adult fell by 53 percent (Center on Budget and Policy Priorities, 2001). These results make clear one unintended outcome of welfare reform: the substantial loss of public benefits felt by citizen children who live in households headed by noncitizen adults. There is, of course, a strong demographic logic to this outcome: 75 percent of all children in immigrant households are U.S. citizens.

Recent Urban Institute analyses of the 1995–2000 Current Population Surveys reveal that noncitizens' use of food stamps, Medicaid, SSI, and TANF declined faster than use by citizens between 1994 and 1999 (see figure 14-1). Borjas claims that national declines among noncitizens can be attrib-

Figure 14-1. *Change in Use of Four Welfare Programs by Citizens and Noncitizens from 1994 to 1999*

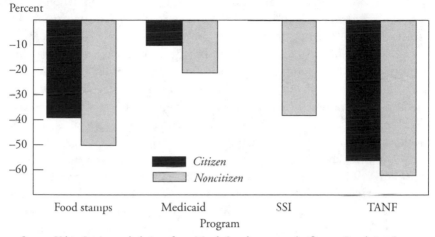

Percent

Program

Source: Urban Institute tabulations from March Supplements to the Current Population Surveys, 1995–2000.

uted to trends in California; in fact, the declines were steeper for noncitizens than for citizens in California, for the nation as a whole, and for states outside California as well. Our differing conclusions are the result of at least two methodological differences. My focus is on nuclear families, which best approximate benefit eligibility units; Borjas uses households as his unit of analysis. Second, Borjas's results are based in part on a composite measure that combines cash welfare, Medicaid, and food stamp use. Because there are so many more recipients of Medicaid than of food stamps or cash welfare, this composite measure is driven by trends in Medicaid use, masking varying use trends in welfare and food stamps.

Here I would highlight Borjas's interesting finding that states with less generous benefit policies have steeper declines than those with more generous policies, a finding that reinforces the fact that welfare reform's effects are being felt beyond California's borders. These disproportionate noncitizen declines are not caused exclusively by changes in eligibility but also by nonparticipation among eligible immigrants, who do not participate out of confusion and fear, or what we have referred to as "chilling effects" (Fix and Passel, 1999).

Another change that reveals the law's broad chilling effects is the extraordinarily steep decline in refugees' use of benefits—use that falls even more sharply than that of other noncitizens. For example, whereas food stamp use by noncitizen families fell 40 percent between 1994 and 1998, it fell 60 percent for refugees. The comparable figures for Medicaid were 17 percent and 39 percent; for TANF, 44 percent and 78 percent. These figures are especially surprising because refugees are a comparatively protected population under the law: they remain eligible for federal means-tested public benefits for five to seven years after entry, depending on the program.

In sum, the effects of the 1996 reforms on immigrants' use of benefits continue to be felt nationally, not just in California. Further, they affect not just noncitizen adults but also citizen children and refugees. And they go beyond cash transfer programs to chill noncitizen use of Medicaid and SCHIP, potentially conflicting with competing national goals of expanding health insurance coverage among the nation's children.

What, then, are some of the implications of these facts for welfare reform's reauthorization? Borjas raises some of the core questions that policymakers might consider. First, he pointedly raises the issue of citizenship policy. Borjas argues—and I agree—that making safety net and work support services contingent on naturalization creates incentives to naturalize that depart from loyalty and other nation-building goals. A recent study of eight industrialized countries showed that only Austria and the United States conditioned benefits on citizenship (Fix and Laglagaron, 2001).

Second, Borjas calls attention to the federalism issues raised by welfare reform's restrictions on immigrants. Here Borjas asks a novel question: should states be denied the authority to extend benefits to immigrants beyond certain minimal, federally designated levels? Should one state be free to extend generous benefits to immigrants, thereby serving as a magnet for migrants who might not otherwise come to or stay in the United States? Borjas seems to think that the federal government should be able to preempt state welfare laws that offer more generous benefits to immigrants than the federal government. However such a proposal appears to me to overreach because it violates the states' right to determine what investments they will make in their own residents.

Moreover, I think that the threat of creating welfare magnets might be overdrawn. A recent study of immigrant settlement patterns in the last half of the 1990s following welfare reform reveals that newly arriving immigrants and longer-term residents are moving disproportionately to the states with the least generous public benefit laws for noncitizens (Passel and Zimmermann, 2001). This analysis sees no overlap between welfare generosity and settlement patterns, raising doubts about the power of the welfare magnet, at least at this time.

To my mind, the most pressing federalism issue is whether Congress should seek to limit the cost shift that restrictions on federal benefits effectively impose on states that are forced to use their own funds to provide benefits to immigrants. This issue of intergovernmental fiscal equity is aggravated by the still rather extreme concentration of immigrants in six major receiving states (California, Florida, Illinois, New Jersey, New York, and Texas).

A third policy domain, one that Borjas does not address, is immigrant integration. Let me make the hoary but necessary points that legal immigrants are mostly here to stay; most of their children are citizens; and noncitizens assume most of the society's heaviest civic obligations—paying taxes and serving in the military. All of these points underline the distributional equity and efficiency questions about their exclusion from benefits.

Further, as this volume attests, the social welfare state is no longer what it used to be. If we accept claims that the welfare system has become an engine of mobility rather than an agent of dependence, the logic of excluding low-income noncitizens not just from the safety net but also from work supports such as health insurance, job training, and transportation subsidies, seems questionable to me.

In short, I would argue that there are citizenship, antidiscrimination, federalism, and integration rationales for revisiting the 1996 law's immigrant restrictions. Specifically, reauthorization might revisit the important issue of how immigrant support obligations should be shared between sponsors and the government. As we have seen, the current system shifts the full burden onto sponsors, begging the question of whether it goes too far. That is, should the sponsor's support obligation and sponsor "deeming" extend to citizenship as it does under the 1996 law, creating in effect an open-ended liability? Or should it be limited to a specific number of years? Should sponsor deeming be extended beyond cash transfer to health insurance programs? I would note that Australia and Britain introduced new sponsor deeming requirements at the same time the United States did, but they excluded health insurance from sponsor obligations (Fix and Laglagaron, 2001).

There are other policy issues that should be revisited during reauthorization:

—Should refugees' eligibility for SSI and Medicaid be limited to their first years after settlement, given the physical and mental health problems they may have suffered? After all, citizens who use these benefits face no comparable time limits. And unlike legal immigrants, refugees do not have sponsors.

—Should other particularly vulnerable postenactment populations (such as pregnant women and children) be made eligible for Medicaid and SCHIP?

—Should states be given the same authority to extend jointly funded federal means-tested programs (Medicaid, SCHIP, and TANF) to postenactment immigrants as to pre-enactment immigrants?

Let me conclude on a somewhat broader note, one that is in the spirit of Borjas's chapter. For citizenship, federalism, and antidiscrimination purposes, I would argue that withholding benefits from legal immigrants is a problematic strategy for reforming immigration policy.

References

Albright, R. E. 1928. "Colonial Immigration Legislation." *Sociology and Social Research* 12 (May): 443–48.

Borjas, George J., and Stephen J. Trejo. 1991. "Immigrant Participation in the Welfare System." *Industrial and Labor Relations Review* 44 (January): 195–211.

Center on Budget and Policy Priorities. 2001. "Tabulations Based on Food Stamp Quality Control Data, 1994–1998." Washington.

Fix, Michael, and Laureen Laglagaron. 2001. "Citizenship and Social Rights," Working Paper. Washington: Urban Institute.

Fix, Michael, and Jeffrey S. Passel. 1999. *Trends in Noncitizens' and Citizens' Use of Public Benefits following Welfare Reform: 1994–97*. Washington: Urban Institute.

Hutchinson, Edward P. 1981. *Legislative History of American Immigration Policy, 1798-1965*. University of Pennsylvania Press.

Passel, Jeffrey, and Wendy Zimmermann. 2001. *Are Immigrants Leaving California? Settlement Patterns of Immigrants in the Late 1990s*. Washington: Urban Institute.

Schippers, David P. 2000. "Abusing the INS," *Wall Street Journal*, August 23, p. A22.

Smith, James P., and Barry Edmonston, eds. 1998. *The New Americans: Economic, Demographic, and Fiscal Effects of Immigration*. Washington: National Research Council.

U.S. Central Intelligence Agency. 1999. *Handbook of International Economic Statistics*. Government Printing Office.

U.S. House of Representatives, Committee on Ways and Means. *1998 Green Book: Background Material and Data on Programs within the Jurisdiction of the Committee on Ways and Means*. Government Printing Office.

U.S. Immigration and Naturalization Service. Various years. *Statistical Yearbook of the Immigration and Naturalization Service*. Government Printing Office.

U.S. Office of the Federal Register. 1999. *Federal Register 64*, no. 101 (May 26). Government Printing Office.

Vialet, Joyce C., and Larry M. Eig. 1998. *Alien Eligibility for Public Assistance*. Washington: Congressional Research Service.

Zimmermann, Wendy, and Karen C. Tumlin. 1999. *Patchwork Policies: State Assistance for Immigrants under Welfare Reform*. Washington: Urban Institute.

15

GREG J. DUNCAN
P. LINDSAY CHASE-LANSDALE

Welfare Reform and Children's Well-Being

ARLY RETURNS ON WELFARE REFORM appear to be stunningly positive. Caseloads fell by half between 1993 and 2000, and many of those who left the welfare rolls joined the work force. But lost in the caseload counts and political rhetoric is the subject of this chapter: the impact of welfare reforms on children's well-being and development. Despite the professed child-based goals of the reform legislation, remarkably little attention has been paid to tracking and understanding its impacts on family functioning and children's well-being.

To be sure, the debate surrounding welfare reform was filled with assumptions and predictions about the proposed reforms and children. Conservative advocates argued that reform-induced transitions from welfare to work benefit children by making positive role models of their working mothers, promoting self-esteem and a sense of control among mothers, introducing productive daily routines into family life, and eventually fostering career advancement and higher earnings on the part of both parents and children. Most prominently, conservatives argued that the reforms would eliminate our welfare "culture" by sending a powerful message to teens that it is in their interest to postpone childbearing until they can support their children within the context of marriage.

On the more liberal side of the aisle, opponents argued that the reforms would overwhelm severely stressed parents, deepen the poverty of many families, force young children into unsafe and unstimulating child care, and reduce parents' abilities to monitor the behavior of their adolescents, leading to deleterious child and adolescent functioning. The direst rhetoric spoke of children "sleeping on the grates."

This chapter sorts through the conflicting theory and evidence regarding the impacts of welfare reform on children by addressing five questions:

—How might reforms affect family functioning and children's well-being?

—Is children's development affected by welfare reforms?

—How do the effects on children vary with the structure of reforms?

—What changes in family functioning account for the effects on children?

—What additional policy changes will enhance children's well-being?

We find strong evidence that welfare reform can be a potent force for enhancing the achievement and positive behavior of children in preschool and elementary school. Even when a welfare reform package does not help children, there is little evidence of harm. On the other hand, reform-induced reductions in maternal supervision may well increase problem behavior among adolescents.

Distinguishing among programs, we find that reforms with work mandates but few supports for working mothers (such as wage and child care subsidies) appear significantly less beneficial for children than programs that provide such supports for full-time workers. Furthermore, and here the evidence is less definitive, changes outside the family—such as use of child care and after-school programs—appear to have more positive impacts on children than changes in parental mental health, family routines, or other aspects of the home environment.

Finally, even though reforms may help reduce problems of poverty, mental health, domestic violence, and children's health and development, those problems remain alarmingly common even among families offered a generous package of work supports.

Our list of policy recommendations includes ways of better supporting work and of addressing safety-net issues for families with barriers to stable, full-time employment.

How Might Reforms Affect Families and Children?

When pushed to discuss how children may be helped or hurt by welfare reforms, federal policymakers, state administrators, state legislators, and advocates identify three key pathways—maternal employment, family structure, and family income (Duncan and Chase-Lansdale, 2001; Moore, 2001). Above all, children are seen to benefit from maternal employment, which is presumed to enhance mothers' self-esteem, as well as from the discipline and structure that work routines, in contrast to welfare dependence, impose on family life. In this view, children's developmental needs are addressed indirectly, but effectively, by policies that promote mothers' transition from welfare to work.

A different, family-structure-based view of how welfare reform might promote children's well-being is featured in the preamble to the 1996 Personal Responsibility and Work Opportunity Reconciliation Act (PRWORA). It identifies marriage as "an essential institution of a successful society which promotes the interests of children," posits that "responsible fatherhood and motherhood [are] integral to successful child rearing and the well-being of children," and declares that the "prevention of out-of-wedlock pregnancy and reduction in out-of-wedlock birth are very important Government interests."

A third, resource-based, view of links between reforms and children's well-being stresses the role of family income. Armed with forecasts of dramatic increases in child poverty, critics of welfare reform focused on the likely detrimental effects on children's well-being stemming from reduced family income. Proponents were more optimistic that earnings growth and marriage would elevate family income above the level provided by welfare benefits.

A more comprehensive framework for assessing how welfare reforms might change children's well-being for better or for worse, presented in figure 15-1, has been formulated by developmental and policy researchers (see, for example, Huston, forthcoming; Chase-Lansdale and Pittman, forthcoming; Moore, 2001). Listed at the far right are outcomes that might be affected by welfare reforms: cognitive development and school achievement, prosocial and problem behavior, mental and physical health, and positive expectations about and aspirations for future achievement.

Welfare Reform Provisions

At the far left of figure 15-1 are key welfare reform provisions: work mandates and incentives, sanctions, time limits, child care policy, and health insurance. Work requirements and time limits on total receipt of assistance are the most widely noted provisions of the 1996 legislation. But the legislation also allowed states to develop sanction policies for noncompliance as well as financial incentives, child care, and health insurance programs to help support welfare-to-work transitions. Other important policy changes, in particular the mid-1990s expansion of the Earned Income Tax Credit and increases in the minimum wage, have also had a bearing on the relative attractiveness of work and welfare. How might these provisions have affected family functioning and children's well-being?

Figure 15-1. *Welfare Reform and Children's Well-Being*

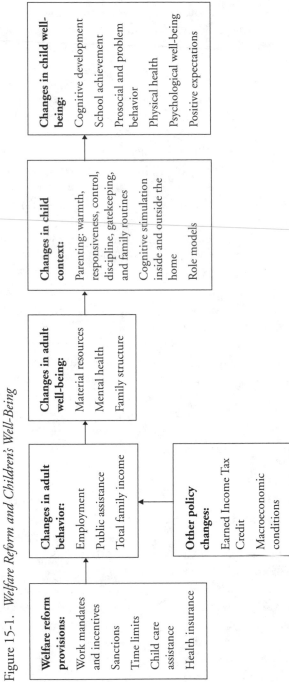

Changes in Adult Behavior and Well-Being

Changes in adult work, welfare receipt, and family income are the primary targets of welfare reform and constitute the first link between reforms and children's well-being shown in figure 15-1. Welfare reform's mandates, sanctions, and incentives, combined with a booming economy and a generous Earned Income Tax Credit, have produced both an extraordinary increase in the fraction of single parents in the labor market (see Blank and Schmidt, chapter 3) and an unprecedented drop in caseloads. The net impact of these changes in work and welfare on total family income and poverty (see Haskins, chapter 4) is important given the evidence that economic deprivation during childhood (and especially early childhood) hinders eventual achievement (Duncan and others, 1998).

Changes in paid work, welfare receipt, and total family income may in turn influence how parents allocate their time; the material resources provided by the cash and in-kind income from their jobs and other sources of public and private support; parental mental health; and even the structure of the family itself.

The net impact of welfare reform–induced changes in work and welfare on families' material resources is likely to vary considerably from one family to the next. Work-related expenses such as child care, transportation, and clothing reduce disposable income by an average of $300 per month (Edin and Lein, 1997). On the plus side, even though the initial jobs taken by former recipients may not pay very much, reformers hope that that earnings growth will eventually boost disposable income far above the level of welfare cash grants.

As for impacts on parents' mental health, many studies have documented extraordinarily high levels of depressive symptoms among welfare-reliant single parents (Bos and others, 1999; Zedlewski and Loprest, chapter 12). McLoyd and her colleagues (1994) found considerably greater stress among unemployed than employed single mothers, a finding that suggested employment may improve mothers' mental health. But a comparison of the mental health of low-skilled, welfare-reliant, and working single mothers found no differences in depression, stress, or sense of control, a finding that suggests that merely exchanging welfare for work may do little to improve maternal mental health (Chase-Lansdale and Pittman, forthcoming).

The collective impact of the labor market and welfare system on family structure—marriage, cohabitation, three-generation living arrangements, and fertility—and of family structure on children's well-being are vital issues for children. Recent trends in those areas are reviewed in the chapters by Murray and by Horn and Sawhill in this volume; the links between family structure and children's well-being are reviewed in McLanahan and Sandefur (1994) and Chase-Lansdale and others (1999).

Changes in Child Context

Parenting and the role models parents provide to their children determine the context within which a child develops. Most of these elements of family functioning could be affected by the work and income changes wrought by welfare reform. Key dimensions of parenting include warmth, responsiveness, and involvement with the child; cognitive stimulation at home; limit-setting and supervision; parents' gatekeeping of the outside world of peers, kin, child care programs, schools, and other neighborhood resources; and the creation of structure and meaning within the home environment (Chase-Lansdale and Pittman, forthcoming).

Infants and toddlers rely on parents or "attachment figures" to provide a secure base from which they actively explore the environment and an important emotional foundation for later development (Cassidy and Shaver, 1999). Although it might be feared that mothers' entry into the labor force could compromise children's attachment, research tends to show that this does not happen (Hoffman and Youngblade, 1999).

The stimulation provided in home environments (see Bradley, 1995), by child care providers, and through community resources such as parks and museums, appears important for the cognitive development of infants, toddlers, and young children. Family income has been shown to be a strong predictor of the quality of these environments, leading both to hopes that reform-induced increases in income will improve children's environments and to fears that income losses will compromise them (Garrett, Ng'andu, and Ferron, 1994). As for child care outside the home, intensive, education-based preschool programs have been shown to provide long-lasting beneficial impacts on the achievement and behavior of low-income children, while more modest differences in child care quality have uncertain impacts on developmental outcomes (NICHD, 1998).

Parents' discipline style and level of supervision are key ingredients in children's healthy development (Bornstein, 1995). Parents who know where their teenagers are and set limits (such as curfews and rules of conduct), but also grant some autonomy, have children with fewer behavior problems, including lower levels of drug and alcohol use, school suspensions and expulsions, and police involvement. Parents who serve effectively as gatekeepers to the world can foster their children's participation in activities and programs outside the home and promote more positive peer interactions, greater feelings of self-worth, and advances in learning (Furstenberg and others, 1999).

Figure 15-2. *Trends in Child Problem Indicators, 1988–99*

Level relative to 1996

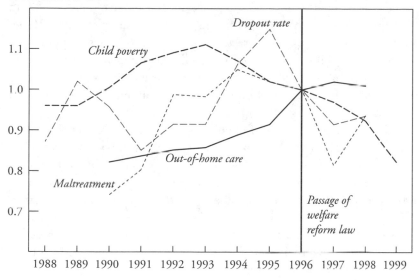

Source: Authors' compilations of data presented in table 15-1.

To the extent that welfare reform provides parents with more economic resources, after-school programs and other community resources become more affordable, as does the possibility of moving to neighborhoods with fewer deviant peers and more community resources. "Social capital" connections secured from co-workers may further link families with community resources. On the negative side, welfare-induced transitions to work may reduce parents' ability to perform their gatekeeping role, particularly during the key period between the end of school and dinnertime, when much delinquent behavior takes place.

Welfare Reform's Impacts on Children's Development

Caseload and employment statistics are compiled and released much more frequently than are indicators of children's well-being. Although we would like to show and account for trends in the cognitive development, school achievement, problem behavior, health, and other domains of children's well-being depicted in figure 15-1, there are few studies that provide pre- and postwelfare reform measures of these outcomes. In figure 15-2 we have compiled time-series data on several relevant indicators, paying particular attention to indicators of problems that might develop if families are harmed by reforms. More complete information on these and several other indicators is presented in table 15-1.

The indicators in figure 15-2 are scaled so that all have values of 100 in 1996, the year before the 1996 welfare reform law was implemented. Values for other years are expressed in relation to their 1996 values. For example, 19.8 percent of children were poor in 1996, and 16.3 percent were poor in 1999. Expressing the 1999 value as a fraction of its 1996 value gives .823 (16.3/19.8) and shows that child poverty fell by about one-sixth between those years.

Had the direst predictions of opponents of the reforms come to pass, we would observe problem indicators in the late 1990s to be well above their 1996 levels. This is the case for none of the indicators, although the rate of children's placements in foster and other out-of-home care and the rate of 6- to 8-year-old children behind in grade for their age was slightly higher than in 1996. In sharp contrast to the predictions of increasing children's poverty during the PRWORA debate, the 1999 poverty rates, regardless of measurement, are well below their 1996 levels (see Haskins, chapter 4). Teen birth and crime rates have fallen as well.

Apart from showing that the sky has not fallen, it is all but impossible to draw firm conclusions from these simplistic comparisons of welfare reform's impacts on children. Waivers granted to most states before the 1996 legislation led to an earlier implementation of many elements of the reforms. More important, the problem-solving impacts of the booming economy of the mid-to-late-1990s may be concealing adverse impacts of reforms that would have appeared under more normal economic conditions and may yet appear as the economy loses some of its luster.

Inferring causal connections between elements of welfare reform and child outcomes from these kinds of data requires consistent state-by-state measurements of the indicator spanning at least the decade of the 1990s (National Research Council, 2001). Furthermore, the data need to be compiled separately for demographic groups (such as single-parent and married-couple families; low- and highly educated women) at differential risk of being affected by the reforms. Among national surveys, only the Current Population Survey is large and frequent enough to provide the needed data on its topics—welfare receipt, work, family poverty, family structure, and education. Vital statistics on fertility and mortality and other administrative data on the details of welfare recipients, child protective services, and juvenile crime have the potential to be used in these ways, although the task of assembling the needed data is formidable (National Research Council, 2001). Sorely lacking as well are data on positive indicators of children's well-being (Moore, 1997).

Table 15-1. *Trends in Negative Indicators of Children's Well-Being, 1988–99*
Percent

Indicator	1988	1989	1990	1991	1992	1993	1994	1995	1996	1997	1998	1999
Poverty rate												
Official												
Children under 18	19.5	19.6	20.6	21.8	22.3	22.7	21.8	20.8	20.5	19.9	18.9	16.9
Related children under 6	21.8	21.9	23.0	24.0	25.7	25.6	24.5	23.7	22.7	21.6	20.6	18.0
After-tax, including additional benefits												
Children under 18	n.a.	n.a.	n.a.	n.a.	n.a.	16.9	15.0	13.8	13.4	13.2	12.5	10.9
Related children under 6	n.a.	n.a.	n.a.	n.a.	n.a.	19.0	17.6	16.3	15.5	14.7	14.0	11.6
Deep poverty rates (income < .50 of poverty threshold)												
Children under 18	9.0	8.2	8.8	9.8	10.2	10.1	9.8	8.5	9.0	9.0	8.1	6.9
Related children under 6	10.2	9.4	10.3	11.2	11.9	11.8	11.5	10.4	10.5	10.1	9.4	7.6
Child maltreatment												
Substantiated reports of child maltreatment (per 1,000)	n.a.	n.a.	11.9	12.9	15.8	15.7	16.7	16.3	16.0	13.1	15.0	n.a.
Children in out-of-home care (per 1,000)	n.a.	n.a.	6.3	6.4	6.6	6.6	6.8	7.0	7.7	7.8	7.8	n.a.
Academic performance												
Children below modal grade, 6–8-year-olds[a]	20.4	21.4	21.5	21.2	19.4	18.7	18.9	17.5	17.9	18.6	19.0	n.a.
Dropout rate, grades 10–12	4.8	4.5	4.0	4.0	4.3	4.3	5.0	5.4	4.7	4.3	4.4	n.a.
Adolescent problem behavior												
Teenage birth rate, 15–17-year-olds (per 1,000 females)	26.4	28.7	29.6	30.9	30.4	30.6	32.0	30.5	29.0	28.2	27.0	n.a.
Juvenile arrests, 10–17-year-olds (per 1,000)	76.0	77.3	80.3	33.8	82.3	84.4	92.8	91.6	95.2	92.2	85.7	n.a.

Sources: U.S. Bureau of the Census, Current Population Survey (poverty rate, children below modal grade, and dropout rate); Paxson and Waldfogel (1999) and Voluntary Cooperative Information System of the American Public Human Services Association (child maltreatment); National Center for Health Statistics (2000) (teenage birth rate); Office of Juvenile Justice and Delinquency Prevention (2000) (juvenile arrests).
n.a. Not available.
a. Modal grade is the year of school in which the largest number of students of a given age are enrolled.

A handful of careful studies have attempted a more complete accounting of the impacts of reforms and the economy on some of these indicators. As reviewed in the Haskins chapter in this volume, some have dispelled fears that reforms have produced a wholesale increase in economic deprivation among children. In analyzing child maltreatment data, Paxson and Waldfogel (1999) found that rates of substantiated maltreatment and out-of-home placements increase systematically with higher rates of family poverty and lower welfare benefit levels. Higher rates of out-of-home placement appear linked to several elements of welfare reform, although the authors hasten to qualify this result with the observation that these placements may be with relatives and represent a way of bringing more resources to the extended family.

The dearth of systematic evidence of national and especially state trends in child outcomes leads us to focus on results from experiments begun in the early-to-mid-1990s that implemented different welfare reform packages and tracked family process and children's well-being (Morris and others, 2001). A great virtue of these experiments is that participants were randomly assigned to a "program group" that received the welfare reform package or to a "control group" that continued to live under the old rules of the Aid to Families with Dependent Children (AFDC) program. Random assignment provides a very strong basis for comparing the causal impacts of the reform packages with those of the old AFDC system.

Relying on evidence from experiments has its limitations, however. Because the states' responses to the 1996 legislation and all of the experimental treatments involve packages of changes, it is difficult to identify which components were the primary influences on children's well-being or family process. The treatments in these experiments represent neither the full range of Temporary Assistance for Needy Families (TANF) programs implemented by states nor the macroeconomic conditions—both good and bad—that states currently face or are likely to face in the next decade. Furthermore, because the experiments were implemented on a small scale, they probably generated few of the larger-scale changes in norms and expectations regarding work and childbearing that might accompany the full-scale implementation of the programs they tested.

The evidence compiled by Morris and her colleagues (2001) comes from five experiments:

—The National Evaluation of Welfare-to-Work Strategies (NEWWS) included two kinds of programs—labor force attachment (LFA) and human capital development (HCD)—offered to welfare recipients in Atlanta; Grand Rapids, Michigan; and Riverside, California (Hamilton, 2000; McGroder and others, 2000). LFA programs required most participants to look immediately for work; HCD programs placed participants in adult basic education and vocational training courses. None of the NEWWS treatments provided wage supplements or other work-related financial incentives.

—The Minnesota Family Investment Program (MFIP) combined participation mandates, "make-work-pay" incentives, and services in a way that constitutes a somewhat more generous version of Minnesota's current TANF program (Gennetian and Miller, 2000). The evaluation focused on two programs: "Mandatory MFIP," which allowed working welfare recipients to keep more of their welfare income when they went to work and included a participation mandate of thirty or more hours per week, and "MFIP Incentives Only," which included all of the features of the Mandatory MFIP program without the participation mandates.

—The Canadian Self-Sufficiency Project (SSP) was a pure "make-work-pay" approach offering a very generous but temporary (three-year) earnings supplement for full-time work (thirty or more hours per week) (Morris and Michalopolous, 2000). The earnings supplement was a monthly cash payment available to single-parent welfare recipients who had been on welfare for at least one year and who left welfare for full-time work within a year of entering the program.

—Milwaukee's New Hope Project combined various "make-work-pay" strategies with employment services (Bos and others, 1999). For parents who worked thirty or more hours per week, New Hope provided an earnings supplement, child care, health insurance subsidies, and if needed, a short-term community service job. Participants in the New Hope experiment volunteered for the program.

—Florida's Family Transition Program (FTP) was the only experiment to include a time limit, in this case twenty-four months of cash assistance in any sixty-month period (Bloom and others, 2000). FTP also had a small earnings supplement, a participation mandate, and fairly intensive case management. Parents with school-age children were required to ensure that their children attended school regularly and to speak with their children's teachers each grading period.

Impacts on Elementary School-Age Children

Figure 15-3, drawn from Morris and others (2001), compares each program's effect on the school achievement of the children in the program with the control groups. Programs are arrayed according to the work supports they provided participants and, for the NEWWS sites (none of which involved

Figure 15-3. *Impacts of Selected Programs on Young Children's Achievement*[a]

Effect size

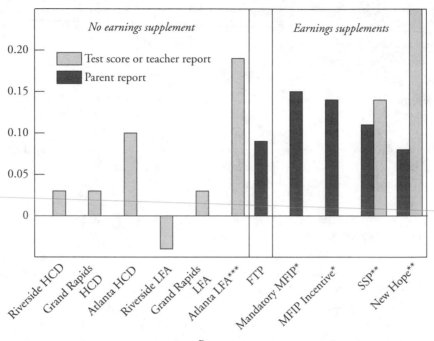

Program

Source: Pamela Morris and others (2001).
*p < .10
**p < .05
***p < .01
a. HCD = human capital development; LFA = labor force attachment; FTP = Family Transition Program (Florida); MFIP = Minnesota Family Investment Program; SSP = Self-Sufficiency Project (Canada).

financial incentives or other work supports), whether the program stressed education or just work. With its modest work supports and time limits, FTP occupies a hard-to-characterize middle category in the figure.

Several important lessons emerge from these experiments:

One lesson is that *welfare reform packages can have positive impacts on children's achievement and behavior.* In the case of New Hope, teachers blind to the experiment reported the academic achievement of program children to be significantly higher than that of control children, with the effect size amounting to one-fourth of a standard deviation. Boys in particular seemed to benefit: for them the program impact was more than one-third of a standard deviation. Smaller, but still significant, achievement impacts were found in the Minnesota MFIP, the Canadian SSP, and the Atlanta LFA site of NEWWS.

Problem behaviors and health were also measured in these studies. Beneficial impacts on children's problem behavior appeared for some but not all of the programs with earnings supplements (data not shown). Among programs with no earnings supplements, only the Atlanta LFA site showed beneficial impacts on behavior. In Florida, there was a significant but negative program impact on children's positive behavior, although no impact—positive or negative—on parents' reports of problem behavior among their young children.

All but one of the studies also asked parents to rate their children's health. There were relatively few program impacts on the health status of these preschool- and early elementary-school-aged children. Small positive health impacts were observed in the SSP and FTP; larger and negative health impacts were observed in the Riverside site of NEWWS. It is hard to know what to make of this latter result. Any harmful child impacts should raise red flags, but in this case there are no other clues in the data that explain the impact.

Morris and her colleagues (2001) investigated differences in program impacts on these elementary-school-aged children across a range of subgroups of interest. Particularly noteworthy was their finding that children in the most disadvantaged long-term recipient families often seemed to benefit the most.

Thus, bearing in mind the exceptional Riverside result, the more general conclusion from the diverse experiments is that *there is little evidence that elementary-school-aged children are harmed by the welfare reform packages built into the experiments.* Critics' fears that preadolescent children's development might be compromised by the stresses and disruptions wrought by welfare-to-work transitions receive virtually no support in these experimental data. We hasten to repeat that the treatments in these experiments do not encompass the full range of reforms implemented by states.

Impacts on Adolescents

For adolescents, the pattern of impacts changes for the worse. Both SSP and FTP evaluated the impacts on various positive and negative indicators of adolescents' well-being (see figure 15-4) (Morris and others, 2001, table A.8). The unfavorable impacts were consistent and striking: positive indicators such as achievement declined, and indicators of negative problem behavior increased. The SSP data showed that teen self-reports of drinking and smoking, as well as parental reports of school achievement and problem behavior, were significantly worse in the program group than in the control group. In the FTP

Figure 15-4. *Effects of Canada's SSP and Florida's FTP Program on Adolescents*[a]

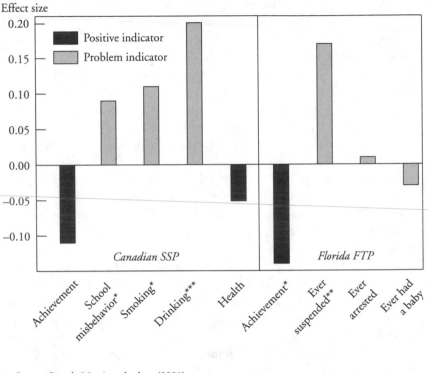

Effect size

Source: Pamela Morris and others (2001).
*p < .10
**p < .05
***p < .01
a. FTP = Family Transition Program (Florida); SSP = Self-Sufficiency Project (Canada).

sample, parents in the experimental group reported lower levels of achievement and more suspensions than did the parents of teenagers in the control group. Thus the experiments showed that *work-focused reforms may put adolescents at greater risk of problem behavior and poor academic achievement.*

Not All Younger Children Are Doing Well

The positive evidence of favorable program impacts on younger children in several studies should not be taken to indicate that all children lucky enough to be randomized into the treatment groups of the most generous program were doing well. The top panel in table 15-2 shows several indicators of problems among children gathered from the reports of the three studies with

Table 15-2. *Negative Indicators of Well-Being among Children, Mothers, and Families in New Hope, MFIP, and SSP*[a]

Indicator	Percent	Study
Child indicator		
Teacher reports child "not making normal progress"	44	New Hope
Child's health "fair" or "poor" as rated by mother	25	MFIP
Child is in special education	18	MFIP
Child has high levels of behavioral or emotional problems	7	MFIP
Child has "long-term problems" (such as asthma, bronchitis, emotional and learning impairments)	26	SSP
Adolescent at risk for depression	46	SSP
Maternal indicator		
Mother at risk of chronic depression	29	MFIP
Mother abused in the past three years	49	MFIP
Mother stressed "much or all of the time"	27	New Hope
Family indicator		
Earned income below the poverty line	65	MFIP
Food insufficiency	6	MFIP
Recent periods without health insurance	44	New Hope

Source: Authors' compilations of data.

a. MFIP = Minnesota Family Investment Program, and data are for long-term AFDC recipients in the program group. SSP = Canadian Self-Sufficiency Project. New Hope data are for long-term AFDC recipients in the program group.

the greatest success in promoting children's well-being: New Hope, MFIP, and SSP. Teachers reported that nearly half the program children were not making "normal progress" in New Hope, and nearly half of the adolescents in SSP reported near-clinical levels of depressive symptoms. Health and developmental problems were also quite widespread, despite the favorable average impacts of the programs that the families of these children had been offered. Thus another lesson of the experiments is that even in families offered generous work supports, there were many children with school or health-related problems.

How Do Child Impacts Vary with the Structure of Reforms?

A crucial message from the experiments is that welfare policies directed largely at adult behavior can have important impacts on children's development. But large positive child impacts were more the exception than the rule. What key features of programs promoted children's development?

To answer this question, Morris and her colleagues (2001) classified experiments by their structure (for example, whether they provided work-conditioned financial and in-kind supports; whether they promoted maternal work or schooling; whether they mandated participation) and then related that structure to the impacts on children. In the following section we look at the experiments that promoted children's well-being to identify the adult behaviors and child contexts that affected children's well-being.

In figure 15-3 the programs are listed from left to right according to the generosity of work supports offered by each one. The pattern of increasingly favorable impacts suggests that *programs with the most generous work supports appear to have more consistently positive impacts on children than programs with no supports.*

This is particularly true for achievement outcomes. All three programs that supported work and required thirty or more hours of work had some positive impacts on achievement outcomes for elementary-school-aged children. Mothers in the program groups of all three demonstrations were more successful in increasing their employment and earnings and in decreasing their reliance on welfare than were mothers in the control groups. Poverty was also significantly reduced in all three demonstrations. Although the Atlanta HCD and LFA sites also produced positive impacts on children's school-readiness test scores, the other HCD and LFA programs in NEWWS did not. Thus the Atlanta result appears to be a site effect rather than a program effect.

Because of its unusual design, MFIP enabled Morris and her colleagues (2001) to disentangle the effects of mandatory and voluntary employment on child outcomes and family functioning (see figure 15-3). The lack of differences suggests that *MFIP's child impacts were about as positive in the mandatory program as in the voluntary program.*

Finally, the FTP evaluation adds important information on the possible impacts of time limits, although in the FTP case the time limit was approached cautiously by welfare officials and bundled together with intensive case management. Subject to these qualifications, the inconsistent and usually insignificant pattern of impacts in Florida suggests that *time limits appear to neither help nor harm children very much.*

What Changes in Family Functioning Account for the Child Impacts?

We turn now to the evidence on which components of family functioning appear to have improved children's well-being. Our summary synthesizes evidence reported in Morris and others (2001) as well as in the detailed project reports.

A first important generalization is that changes in activities outside the family—after-school programs, child care, community programs—appear to be more important than within-family changes in parenting, parental mental health, and family routines in accounting for improved children's well-being. Why is this the case? *Parental gatekeeping was enhanced in most of the studies with positive child impacts.*

In New Hope, SSP, and Mandatory MFIP, mothers in the program groups were more likely to enroll their children in formal child care programs than were mothers in the control group. In New Hope and SSP, program mothers were also more likely to enroll their children (sons more than daughters in New Hope) in after-school programs and extracurricular activities. For MFIP, one of three measures of out-of-school activities found fewer experimental children enrolled in lessons, clubs, and activities, but there were no significant differences in the use of extended-day programs or extracurricular activities. Thus evidence from two of the experiments suggests that parents used their increases in work-related resources to invest in structured programs for their children outside the home.

Dimensions of parenting other than gatekeeping were not much affected by the programs. Evaluations of all five programs showed very few differences in family life and parenting between mothers in the program groups and those in the control groups. The size and nature of the list of "dogs that didn't bark" is impressive and includes parental control, cognitive stimulation in the home, family routines, and harsh parenting. There was a reduction in parental warmth in SSP and NEWWS; however, this was only for the youngest group of children in SSP and for one of the six NEWWS sites. The conclusion can be drawn that *the experiments failed to improve mothers' mental health or parenting.*

Contrary to the hopes of many welfare reformers, work preparation and even employment itself did little to improve mothers' mental health. Only in the MFIP incentives-only group, for whom employment was voluntary, was there a significant reduction in depression. In New Hope, parents in the program group reported less stress and greater hope of achieving life goals, but more time pressures than the control group. These differences were modest, and New Hope program participants did not differ from the control group in depression, self-esteem, mastery, or financial worries. A likely reason for the general lack of improvement in mental health is the continuing difficulty inherent in combining childrearing with employment in the context of economic hardship.

The MFIP study is remarkable in two other ways. First, it produced rather striking impacts on family structure. Single parents in the MFIP program were a little more likely to marry than single parents in the control group (11 percent and 7 percent, respectively), and married parents in the program group were much more likely to stay married than married families in the control group (67 percent and 49 percent). With the exception of the Riverside LFA site, no family-structure impacts were found in NEWWS; nor were they apparent in New Hope or FTP. In SSP, favorable marriage impacts were observed in one of the two Canadian provinces, but only for parents of the older cohort of children. Thus *two-parent family structures were promoted by one of the programs but not by the others.*

Second, MFIP produced a substantial drop in the rates of domestic violence against mothers in the program. The Florida FTP experiment also measured domestic violence but found no program impact. Thus *one of two programs reduced domestic violence.*

Finally, we return to the issue of the distribution of well-being, in this case among families assigned to the program group in the three most generous studies. The middle and bottom panels in table 15-2 show several indicators of negative well-being among program-group mothers and families in the three studies with the greatest success in promoting children's well-being, New Hope, MFIP, and SSP. There were many problems. Despite the reduction in abuse relative to the control group, half of the mothers in the MFIP program group reported having been abused during the three-year course of the experiment, and more than one-fourth of them were at risk of depression. Despite the program-induced increases in income, more than half of MFIP families had incomes from welfare, earnings, and the Earned Income Tax Credit (EITC) that were below the poverty threshold, although few reported episodes of food insufficiency. Nearly half of New Hope program families lacked health insurance for their children. Thus *even among families offered generous work supports, economic problems, domestic violence, and maternal health problems were alarmingly common.*

What Policy Changes Will Enhance Children's Well-Being?

The random-assignment feature of welfare experiments from the 1990s provides unusually strong evidence on which welfare reform provisions, relative to the old AFDC system, appear to enhance children's well-being. Although the evidence does not allow us to judge the likely impacts of the full range of diverse TANF packages implemented by states in the late 1990s, it provides guidance for the implementation of welfare reform and future changes in the federal law. On the basis of this research we recommend that new policies support low-income working families; develop intensive programs to address the needs of problem families unable to secure stable employment; and, more generally, address the developmental needs of low-income children.

Supporting Work

A key finding from the experiments is that child achievement and behavior improved more consistently in programs that provided financial and in-kind supports for work than in those that did not. The packages of work supports were quite diverse. The Canadian SSP offered a powerful but simple financial incentive—a payment of half the difference between a target level of earnings ($30,000 [Canadian] in the New Brunswick site; $37,000 in British Columbia) and an individual's earned income, but no other transfers, conditioned on working at least thirty hours per week. The New Hope program offered a more comprehensive support program that combined a wage supplement, child care assistance, health insurance, a temporary community service job, and supportive caseworkers; again, these supports were available only to families who worked thirty or more hours per week. The Minnesota MFIP program combined higher benefit levels and more generous work disregards, and also required at least thirty hours of work. Thus, *to achieve positive child impacts it appears that states need to go beyond work mandates and provide cash rewards or in-kind supports for the mandated work.*

Although more costly than the "work first" approach taken by NEWWS, both MFIP and New Hope, two of the programs with positive child impacts, had costs within the range of some of the actual welfare reform packages implemented by states in response to the 1996 legislation. The average costs for a participant in the NEWWS labor force attachment and human capital development group were $1,550 and $4,700, respectively. The costs of MFIP ranged from $1,900 to $3,800, depending on the type of recipient family. Owing to intensive case management, Florida's FTP cost totaled nearly $8,000 over a five-year period. New Hope was the most expensive program, at roughly $4,000 annually per program group member over the two-year period.

It would have been extremely useful if the experiments had provided evidence on what particular program components (such as earnings supplements, child care assistance, health insurance) mattered the most. Regrettably, they did not. With positive child impacts found in both the program that only provided a cash earnings supplement (the SSP) and the programs that provided a package of diverse benefits (such as New Hope), it appears that the amount rather than the nature of the increase in family resources matters the most.

Federal policies that support work include funding of the child care block grant, expanding coverage and takeup (actual use) of health insurance for children, and expanding the Earned Income Tax Credit. For states, the challenge is to use TANF and other dollars to fashion support packages that best meet the needs of local populations, labor markets, and politics.

Safety Net Programs

With plunging caseloads capturing most of the publicity about welfare reform, states have only recently begun to pay attention to families facing major barriers to employment (see Zedlewski and Loprest, chapter 12). Maternal depression, physical disabilities, domestic violence, very low levels of skills, and a need to care for other family members who are disabled or ill are common and difficult problems. The magnitude of caseload declines belies fears that large numbers of families are unable to make at least temporary transitions from welfare to work. Yet the experiments reveal that significant numbers of families have problems that are not solved even by generous configurations of work supports. In other words, *for a substantial number of low-income families in our nation, work mandates and supports are not sufficient to foster children's development.*

Since the experimental evidence we review provides little guidance on needed policy responses to these kinds of problems, we note only that possible responses include programs focused on employment (such as supported work arrangements and postplacement trouble-shooting) and safety net programs (Medicaid and food stamps) for families struggling to comply with work-oriented reforms. The former set of programs are described by Zedlewski and Loprest in this volume; strategies for addressing low takeup in the Medicaid and food stamp programs are detailed by Greenstein and Guyer in this volume.

Address Developmental Needs

We are disturbed by the fact that both "children" and "families" are treated as homogeneous entities in the welfare reform rhetoric and by many policies, when in fact families have diverse needs that change as children develop. Research suggests that the development of older children, especially adolescents, is less sensitive to family economic resources and more strongly influenced by the affection, supervision, role modeling, and mentoring from the adults in their lives. There was troubling evidence from two of the experiments that welfare reforms may increase problem behavior among adolescents. After-school and community-based programs would help support working parents' efforts to keep their children focused on school achievement and positive behavior. *Maternal employment creates a need for after-school and community programs that provide supervision and mentoring for preadolescent and adolescent children.*

Indeed, a striking result from the New Hope experiment was that program parents used the extra New Hope resources to secure after-school care and community-based activities for their school-aged boys (Bos and others, 1999). In ethnographic interviews, mothers worried about the temptations of gangs and the drug trade for their boys and appeared to use these programs to counter them.

Only one of the experiments, the Canadian Self-Sufficiency project, assessed impacts on very young children, those aged 0–2 years at the time of program enrollment. In contrast to the favorable picture for somewhat older children, no impacts were found on achievement and behavior thirty-six months after enrollment (Morris and Michalopolous, 2000). It is unwise to generalize from a single source of data, although other studies have shown that very young children may be more vulnerable than older children to the ill effects of an employment-induced separation from their mothers. The economic changes wrought by reforms are probably also more important for very young children than for older children given their apparent greater sensitivity to spells of economic deprivation (Duncan and others, 1998) and the significance of the early years for healthy development later on (National Research Council, 2000).

An implication for policy is that states should be aware of the differential consequences of their policies on children of different ages. Time limits, sanctions, and categorical restrictions may be more detrimental to families with very young children, as may work requirements for mothers in the first months of their children's lives.

Intriguing evidence from at least one of the experiments suggests that welfare reform packages can encourage the formation and continuation of two-parent families. Many existing policies discourage fathers from residing with or providing financial support for their children (see Horn and Sawhill, chapter 16). Financial and time inputs from both parents are crucial to the healthy development of children. In their zeal to ensure that fathers meet their obligations to provide financial support for children, *policies should not discourage fathers from residing with or in other ways spending time with and providing financial support to their children.*

It is also important to emphasize the benefits of delaying the onset of parenthood itself. An ardent hope of welfare reform proponents was to "send a message" to teens at risk of early parenthood. As teen births fall, which they have done over the past decade, more children will be born to more mature and economically self-sufficient parents (see Murray, chapter 5).

We close with two calls to policymakers, advocates, and policy analysts. First, do not assume that meeting children's developmental needs depends only on whether their mothers make successful transitions from welfare to paid employment. The public discourse needs to be broadened beyond caseloads and maternal employment to address the larger issues of children's poverty and the very different developmental needs of children of different ages.

Second, abandon the search for a single answer to how welfare reforms are affecting children's well-being. Reforms will simultaneously help some children and hurt others. It is the distribution of impacts—both good and bad—that will tell the complete story of welfare reform's impacts on children. We need to know which families and children will profit from which components of welfare reform and why; which parents will adapt only if additional work supports are provided; and which children will be at high risk. It is the collection of diverse programs to address the equally diverse needs of children of different ages and in different family circumstances that will determine whether welfare reform accomplishes its lofty goals.

COMMENT BY
Eugene Steuerle

Although welfare is commonly associated with Temporary Assistance for Needy Families (TANF) or its predecessor, Aid to Families with Dependent Children (AFDC), that program makes up only a tiny portion of the federal income assistance budget. What made welfare reform possible in the mid-1990s was in no small part the shrinking importance of AFDC since the mid-1970s (relative to national income) and the rising importance of other income support programs—especially the Earned Income Tax Credit (EITC).

One difficulty with assessing the impact of any single welfare initiative is that it interacts with so much else, not just other public programs but the economy itself. But just as the income assistance budget is a constantly moving target, so also are the many programmatic and societal changes affecting children. Nonetheless, Greg Duncan and Lindsay Chase-Lansdale have addressed as best they can the central question: what is happening to children's well-being as a result of welfare reform?

Duncan and Chase-Lansdale take what are perhaps the only feasible approaches to evaluating the impact of one policy change that has not even experienced one full economic cycle. First, they appeal to rough national measures of the well-being of children in recent years, regardless of cause. These data allow them to conclude that children do not seem to be significantly worse off in a post–welfare reform world. Some even seem to be better off. Second, they try to draw inferences from other more controlled experiments. These experiments are among the few that were designed to track changes in children's behavior and educational success.

Many years ago the economist Robert Lampman tried with limited success to get policymakers and researchers to extend the focus on poverty beyond income poverty and toward its many other dimensions. The analysis by Duncan and Chase-Lansdale is in this tradition. Sometimes its most relevant findings are simply reminders of the difficulties involved. For example, they remind us that half of the mothers in one experiment reported having been abused during the three-year course of the experiment.

Duncan and Chase-Lansdale conclude that resources matter. Again on the basis of the experiments, they find that programs with the most generous work supports appear to have more consistently positive impacts on children than programs with no support. Although I have no quarrel with that conclusion, the data leave one begging for more. In particular, there is not enough information to trace the marginal impact of marginal changes in program design. This issue rises extraordinarily in importance when one is thinking about national changes based on experimental designs.

I return to the debate over whether the mid-1990s welfare reform or the expanding economy caused greater work effort. Either way, one conclusion that is hard to avoid from the late 1990s is that people do seem to respond significantly to incentives. That is, both changes—welfare reform and an expanding economy—increased the differential between the rewards for working and those for not working. In some combination, welfare reform and the growing economy seem to provide the most likely explanation for the remarkable rise in work among low-income women with children (see Blank and Schmidt, chapter 3).

Just as we ideally want to know the income and incentive effects of different program designs on work behavior, so also do we want to understand their effects on other behaviors in the family. Welfare reform and many experiments, for instance, generally do not remove the powerful disincentive for marriage among low-income individuals. Nor do they always, as Duncan and Chase-Lansdale remind us, give children more time in nurturing environments. Thus we want to know what types of incentives and resources respond to these family needs—in particular, time spent by children in a nurturing environment or at least in adult-supervised activities.

A final difficulty with assessing welfare reform is figuring out what happens to the population as a whole. We cannot find that answer simply by looking at a fixed population of beneficiaries. The success of welfare reform is going to be largely determined by two items not yet measured: what is happening among those who are not currently welfare recipients, and what the long-term impact on recipients themselves is, especially once they leave the rolls. This is all the more true if there is only a modest change in well-being among children of welfare recipients in the short run, which seems to be what Duncan and Chase-Lansdale conclude.

For those who are not current recipients, we want to understand the trends in a wide range of behaviors: frequency of out-of-wedlock birth, educational attainment, marriage and commitment rates, job attachment, and much else. This is the fundamental question of whether certain types of welfare breed dependency among those not yet in the system, not just nurture dependency for those already in it.

As for those already in the system, we are especially concerned with long-term impacts over years and decades, not just a year or two of experiments. Pessimists should be reminded of the power of compounding. If increases in work effort simultaneously produce an additional social return of 1 percent, that additional social gain may at first be virtually unmeasurable but could be quite dramatic after many years of compounding.

Unfortunately, the data and the studies now available do not make policy conclusions easy. Not much is known about the marginal effects of particular alternative types of spending: health insurance, travel assistance, or assistance in finding jobs. Much less do we get some indication of whether marginal dollars might be spent even better on community programs that provide supervision and mentoring for children. For their own policy conclusions, Duncan and Chase-Lansdale draw on evidence of some improved social welfare in experiments that provided substantial work supports and on the potential decline in productive behavior by adolescents for whom the mother's work may decrease adult involvement or supervision.

Dodged, however, in the welfare approach is the more fundamental issue of how far one can go toward providing higher and higher levels of support only to welfare recipients—or even of providing some benefits, such as child care or job assistance, to a limited number of others. Policymakers must be concerned about how much a particular benefit package that is available only to a small subset of the population affects the behavior of others. Moreover, there is also a standard of equal justice under the law, or horizontal equity. This standard calls into question programs in which workers with equal pay and equal needs get different treatment from the government. Thus the larger the additional support built into a welfare system or into block grants that provide assistance to a select few, the more the question of how to construct a more universal program applies.

These considerations lead me to suggest one policy that I believe would be effective. It is also expensive and requires thinking outside the "welfare box." It is one that builds off the notion that society now expects work and productive contributions from all families, but it also coincides with one of Duncan and Chase-Lansdale's observations: that positive gains derive from activities in which adults are present with children as mentors, supervisors, or parents.

The policy I envision for children is one that starts with the child rather than the adult. The policy would call for a personal plan to be put in place and updated continually for every child in a community. This plan would attempt at a minimum to ensure that each child is engaged in adult-supervised activities throughout the day—not just in school, but also after school and throughout the summer. That supervision could be in the home, where possible, but it would also be formally available through enhanced educational opportunities, jobs, and extracurricular activities. Rather than trying to develop a one-size-fits-all package, communities and parents should together develop a variety of productive activities. Given what we know about development and about when bad things happen to children and adolescents, such a plan would considerably improve children's well-being and educational attainment while reducing crime rates and out-of-wedlock births. As a by-product it would address most child care needs. Adult programs, in turn, could focus on what they do best, providing job support through such items as the EITC and assistance in finding jobs. Both together would reduce even further the need for welfare supports, however structured.

In sum, the incentives of various welfare reforms—both those that decrease support for adults who do not work and those that increase support for adults who do work—have a significant effect on work behavior. But these reforms are aimed only indirectly at the family or the child via the work incentive door. They often impose large marriage penalties, and they often ignore what children are doing with their time. My opinion, based partly on the issue of equal justice and universality and partly on research findings on changes in children's behavior and well-being, is that children's issues are not likely to be solved within the welfare box. Eventually our society is going to have to ask itself just how our children are spending their time, and it will have to move beyond a model of engaging them only at times when they are not needed to do chores on the farm.

References

Bloom, Dan, and others. 2000. *The Family Transition Program: Final Report on Florida's Initial Time-Limited Welfare Program*. New York: Manpower Demonstration Research Corporation.

Bornstein, Marc H., ed. 1995. *Handbook of Parenting*. Mahwah, N.J.: Lawrence Erlbaum.

Bos, J., and others. 1999. *New Hope for People with Low Incomes: Two-Year Results of a Program to Reduce Poverty and Reform Welfare*. New York: Manpower Demonstration Research Corporation.

Bradley, Robert H. 1995. "Environment and Parenting." In *Handbook of Parenting*, edited by M. H. Bornstein. Mahwah, N.J.: Lawrence Erlbaum.

Cassidy, Jude, and Philip R. Shaver, eds. 1999. *Handbook of Attachment: Theory, Research, and Clinical Applications*. New York: Guilford Press.

Chase-Lansdale, P. Lindsay, and Laura Pittman. Forthcoming. "Parenting and the Home Environment." In *The Future of Children: Impact of Welfare Reform on Children*, vol. 2, no. 2, edited by Margie K. Shields. Los Altos, Calif.: Packard Foundation.

Chase-Lansdale, P. Lindsay, and others. 1999. "Young African American Multigenerational Families in Poverty: The Contexts, Exchanges, and Processes of Their Lives." In *Coping with Divorce, Single Parenting, and Remarriage*, edited by E. M. Hetherington. Mahwah, N.J.: Lawrence Erlbaum.

Duncan, Greg J., and others. 1998. "How Much Does Childhood Poverty Affect the Life Chances of Children?" *American Sociological Review* 63 (3): 406–23.

Duncan, Greg J., and P. Lindsay Chase-Lansdale, eds. 2001. *For Better and for Worse: Welfare Reform and the Well-Being of Children and Families*. Russell Sage.

Edin, Kathryn, and Laura Lein. 1997. *Making Ends Meet*. Russell Sage.

Furstenberg, Frank, and others. 1999. *Managing to Make It: Urban Families and Adolescent Success*. University of Chicago Press.

Garrett, P., N. Ng'andu, and J. Ferron. 1994. "Poverty Experiences of Young Children and the Quality of Their Home Environments." *Child Development* 65 (2): 331–45.

Gennetian, Lisa, and C. Miller. 2000. *Reforming Welfare and Rewarding Work: Final Report of the Minnesota Family Investment Program*. Vol. 2: *Effects on Children*. New York: Manpower Demonstration Research Corporation.

Hamilton, G., with S. Freedman and Sharon McGroder. 2000. *Do Mandatory Welfare-to-Work Programs Affect the Well-Being of Children? A Synthesis of Child Research Conducted as Part of the National Evaluation of Welfare-to-Work Strategies*. U.S. Department of Health and Human Services.

Hoffman, Lois W., and Lisa M. Youngblade. 1999. *Mothers at Work: Effects on Children's Well-Being*. Cambridge University Press.

Huston, Aletha. Forthcoming. "Reforms and Child Development." In *The Future of Children: Impact of Welfare Reform on Children*, vol. 2, no. 2, edited by Margie K. Shields. Los Altos, Calif.: Packard Foundation.

McGroder, Sharon, and others. 2000. *National Evaluation of Welfare-to-Work Strategies: Impacts on Young Children and Their Families Two Years after Enrollment: Findings from the Child Outcomes Study*. U.S. Department of Health and Human Services.

McLanahan, Sara, and Gary Sandefur. 1994. *Growing Up with a Single Parent.* Harvard University Press.

McLoyd, Vonnie, and others. 1994. "Unemployment and Work Interruption among African American Single Mothers: Effects on Parenting and Adolescent Socioemotional Functioning." *Child Development* 65 (2): 562–89.

Moore, Kristin. 1997. "Criteria for Indicators of Child Well-Being." In *Indicators of Children's Well-Being*, edited by R. Hauser, B. Brown, and William Prosser. Russell Sage.

———. 2001. "How Do State Policy Makers Think about Family Process and Child Development in Low-Income Families?" In *For Better and for Worse: Welfare Reform and the Well-Being of Children and Families*, edited by Greg Duncan and Lindsay Chase-Lansdale. Russell Sage.

Morris, Pamela, and Charles Michalopolous. 2000. *The Self-Sufficiency Project at 36 Months: Effects on Children of a Program That Increased Parental Employment and Income.* New York: Manpower Demonstration Research Corporation.

Morris, Pamela, and others. 2001. *How Welfare and Work Policies Affect Children: A Synthesis of Research.* New York: Manpower Demonstration Research Corporation.

National Research Council. 2001. *Evaluating Welfare Reform in an Era of Transition,* edited by Robert Moffitt and Michele Ver Ploeg. Washington: National Academy Press.

National Research Council and Institute of Medicine. 2000. *From Neurons to Neighborhoods: The Science of Early Child Development,* edited by Jack P. Skonkoff and Deborah A. Phillips. Washington: National Academy Press.

NICHD Early Child Care Research Network. 1998. "Early Child Care and Self-Control, Compliance, and Problem Behavior at Twenty-Four and Thirty-Six Months." *Child Development* 68 (4): 1145–70.

Paxson, Christina, and Jane Waldfogel. 1999. "Work, Welfare, and Child Maltreatment." Working Paper 7343. Cambridge, Mass.: National Bureau of Economic Research.

PART IV

*Associated
Program Reforms*

16

WADE F. HORN
ISABEL V. SAWHILL

Fathers, Marriage, and Welfare Reform

IN 1960 THE NUMBER OF CHILDREN in the United States living without their father was less than 10 million. Today that number stands at over 24 million, nearly four out of every ten children. And things are getting worse, not better. By some estimates, 60 percent of children born in the 1990s will spend a significant portion of their childhood in a home without their father (Furstenberg and Cherlin, 1991).

For over 1 million children each year, the pathway to a fatherless family is divorce. The divorce rate doubled from 1960 to 1980 before leveling off and declining slightly in the 1980s and 1990s. Today, forty out of every 100 first marriages end in divorce; in 1960 the figure was sixteen out of every 100. No other industrialized nation has a higher divorce rate than the United States.

The second pathway to a fatherless home is out-of-wedlock childbearing. In 1960 about 5 percent of all children were born to unmarried parents. That number increased to 11 percent in 1970, 18 percent in 1980, 28 percent in 1990, and 33 percent today. The number of children born out of wedlock each year, 1.3 million, is greater than the number whose parents divorce each year: 1 million.

Teenagers who give birth are especially likely to be unmarried. Although teen pregnancy rates declined in the 1990s, the percentage of births to teens that are out of wedlock continued to increase. Today nearly eight of ten teenagers who give birth are unmarried. And although it is true that most out-of-wedlock childbearing occurs among women in their twenties, about half of unmarried mothers begin childbearing in their teens (U.S. House of Representatives, 1998, p. 539). Children born to an unwed teen mother are especially likely to grow up without a consistent relationship with their father, to be poor, and to end up on welfare. A conservative estimate is that births to teens cost taxpayers $8 billion annually (Maynard, 1997).

The absence of fathers in the home has profound consequences for children. Almost 75 percent of American children living in single-parent families will experience poverty before they turn 11 years old, but only 20 percent of children in two-parent families (National Commission on Children, 1993). Indeed, virtually all of the increase in child poverty between 1970 and 1996 was due to growth in the number of single-parent families (Sawhill, 1999). Children who grow up absent their fathers are also more likely to fail at school or drop out, experience behavioral or emotional problems requiring psychiatric treatment, engage in early sexual activity, and develop drug and alcohol problems (McLanahan and Sandefur, 1994).

Despite the emphasis of the 1996 welfare reform legislation on supporting marriage and two-parent families, most state efforts to date have focused on moving previously dependent mothers into the paid labor force. However, simply moving millions of previously welfare-dependent single mothers into low-wage jobs is unlikely to significantly reduce child poverty, especially after they pay reasonable child care expenses. In contrast, two minimum-wage jobs provide an after-tax income of $21,000 a year, enough to lift a family of two adults and three or fewer children out of poverty. Hence, if we wish to decrease the number of children growing up in poverty, public policy must focus not only on helping single mothers get jobs but also on bringing fathers back into the family picture.

Encouraging Male Responsibility and Preventing Premature Fatherhood

Half of first out-of-wedlock births are to women under the age of 20. The fathers of these children are sometimes teenage boys, but often they are older males who, given the age of the young women involved, bear a greater responsibility for the pregnancy (Darroch, Landry, and Oslak, 1999). One solution to the problem of unwed teen pregnancy is to encourage such couples to marry. However, research suggests that when they do their marriages are particularly unstable (National Center for Health Statistics, 1995). This has prompted efforts to prevent teen pregnancies from occurring in the first place, and increasingly such efforts focus on men and boys, not just young women. Strategies have included abstinence education, more comprehensive sex education, family planning services, media campaigns, and state coalitions devoted to preventing teen pregnancy. There has been a substantial increase in such activities, both governmental and private, since the enactment of welfare reform in 1996 (Wertheimer, Jager, and Moore, 2000). For these or other reasons, rates of teen sexual activity (especially among males), teen pregnancy, and births declined during the 1990s.

Some of these efforts have focused on convincing young men that getting a young girl pregnant is a bad idea. The 1996 welfare reform law called for greater use of statutory rape laws, and several states have moved to enforce them more aggressively. However, statutory rape laws are rather blunt instruments that may be ineffective in dealing with deeply ingrained cultural norms.

A better approach may be to provide support to religious and other civic organizations that work with young men and women. Many of these organizations encourage more responsible sexual behavior, including abstinence, but also engage young people in constructive activities such as after-school programs and community service. Some of these efforts have been effective (Kirby, 2001). Sexual attitudes and behaviors, for example, changed quite dramatically in the 1990s. For example, the proportion of college freshmen who believe that it is all right to have sex if two people have known each other for a short time declined from 52 percent in 1987 to 40 percent in 1999. And a careful study by the Urban Institute found that the shift to more conservative attitudes accounted for a majority of the decline in sexual activity among young men between 1988 and 1995 (Ku and others, 1998).

A final way to encourage male responsibility is to strictly enforce child support obligations. Any man who fathers a child ought to be held accountable for helping to support that child financially. Moreover, research generally substantiates that child well-being is improved when nonresident fathers pay child support. And several studies suggest that tougher application of these laws has reduced out-of-wedlock childbearing (see Garfinkel, chapter 17).

Most programmatic efforts to date have focused on reconnecting fathers with their children. But it is worth emphasizing that preventing premature fatherhood is at least as important as trying to reconnect men with children they never planned to have in the first place. Recent efforts to accomplish this objective appear to have had some success.

Helping Fathers Meet Their Responsibilities

The historic policy answer to the problem of absent fathers has been child support enforcement. However, many fathers of children residing in low-income households are undereducated and underemployed themselves and may therefore lack the resources to provide meaningful economic support for their children. Too strong a focus on child support enforcement may lead these already marginally employed men to drop out of the paid labor force in favor of participation in the underground economy and make it even more difficult for them to be involved fathers.

Moreover, an exclusive focus on child support enforcement ignores the many noneconomic contributions that fathers make to the well-being of their children. If we want fathers to be more than cash machines for their children, we need public policies that support their work as nurturers, disciplinarians, mentors, moral instructors, and skill coaches, not just economic providers. Focusing solely on paternity establishment and the payment of child support effectively downgrades fathers to, in the words of social historian Barbara Dafoe Whitehead, "paper dads."

For these reasons, some initiatives have attempted to help fathers support their children, both financially and as involved parents. The best-known and most comprehensively studied of these efforts is the Parents' Fair Share program. Parents' Fair Share was designed to help noncustodial fathers of children on welfare who owe child support to (1) find more stable and better-paying jobs, (2) pay child support consistently, and (3) assume a fuller and more responsible fathering role. Key services include peer support, employment and training services, and voluntary mediation between custodial and noncustodial parents.

A recent report, based on two years of follow-up data, found that Parents' Fair Share produced some increases in employment and earnings among the most disadvantaged subset of fathers, but no impact on the sample as a whole (Martinez and Miller, 2000). Regarding child support payments, Parents' Fair Share participants were significantly more likely to pay child support than the control group (50 percent versus 43 percent) and paid significantly higher amounts ($397 per quarter versus $313). The study also found that many fathers provide informal support to their children and that pressuring them to provide more support through the formal child support system reduces the amount of informal support they provide (Knox and Redcross, 2000).

On the noneconomic aspects of fathers' involvement, Parents' Fair Share reported that the noncustodial fathers seemed genuinely to care about and wanted to be involved with their children. Fathers in the program also reported finding the peer support groups, designed to teach effective fathering skills, helpful. The program did not, on average, increase the amount of visitation, although it did produce some increase in father-child contact in families with very low levels of initial visitation.

One reason that Parents' Fair Share may not have been more effective is its close ties to, and emphasis on, increasing child support rather than on simply encouraging the social and emotional involvement of the father in his children's lives. Such an emphasis may have led many participants to view Parents' Fair Share as a kinder and gentler version of child support enforcement rather than a program to help them be more involved fathers. Indeed, an early process evaluation of a fatherhood program operated by the San Mateo, California, attorney general's office (in which the office of child support enforcement is housed) found many of the nonresident fathers recruited for the program believed it was really a "sting" operation for collecting past-due child support (Price, 1999). These findings suggest that, to be successful, fatherhood programs may need to operate independently of the formal child support system.

Fragile Families Initiatives

Another criticism of Parents' Fair Share is that it intervenes too late. To be included in the program, a nonresident father must have already built up substantial child support arrearages. By that time, many unwed fathers have become disconnected from their children or alienated from their children's mothers, or they have moved on to other partners. Indeed, one study found that 57 percent of unwed fathers with children under 2 years of age visited their children more than once a week, but only 22 percent were in such frequent contact with their children at age 7½ or older (Lerman, 1993). Contrast this with the fact that, at the time of their child's birth, 82 percent of unmarried mothers and fathers are romantically involved with each other, 44 percent are cohabiting, and 99.8 percent of the fathers express a desire to be involved in raising their children in the coming years (Bendheim-Thoman Center, 2000).

This "earlier is better" approach is being implemented in a number of cities throughout the United States. Known as Fragile Families programs, they target low-income, unmarried couples shortly after, and sometimes before, their child's birth and provide the same kinds of services provided by Parents' Fair Share. Although no formal evaluations have yet been reported in the peer-reviewed literature on the effectiveness of Fragile Families programs, several such evaluations are under way.

Thus far, Fragile Families initiatives have been reluctant to integrate a clear marriage message in their programs. Instead, most programs concentrate on helping cohabiting couples strengthen their relationships. Supporters of these programs argue that what is important is the involvement of the father, not the marital status of the parents. They also argue that bringing back marriage to many low-income communities is not realistic.

There is, however, little empirical evidence to support the idea that it is possible to keep fragile families together absent marriage. To the contrary, some existing research indicates that as many as three-fourths of children born to cohabiting parents will see their parents split up before they reach age 16; only about one-third of children born to married parents will see their parents separate before they reach the age of 16 (Popenoe and Whitehead, 1999).

Once a father ceases to cohabit with the mother of his children, that father tends over time to become disconnected, both financially and psychologically, from his children. By one estimate, 40 percent of children with nonresident fathers have not seen their father in over a year. Of the remaining 60 percent, only one in five sleeps even one night a month in the father's home. Only one in six sees his or her father an average of once or more per week (Furstenberg and Nord, 1985). Remarriage, or, in cases of an unwed father, marriage to someone other than the child's mother, makes it especially unlikely that a noncustodial father will remain in contact with his children (Stephens, 1996).

Moreover, even when nonresident fathers do stay involved in their children's lives, the constraints inherent in traditional visitation arrangements often preclude the kind of father-child interactions most associated with improvements in child well-being. That is because when time with one's children is limited, many nonresident fathers strive to make sure their children enjoy themselves when they are with them. As a result, nonresident fathers tend to spend less time than in-the-home fathers helping their children with homework, monitoring their activities, and setting appropriate limits, activities known to enhance child well-being. Rather, nonresident fathers spend more time taking their children to restaurants and movies, activities that have not been found to be associated with enhanced child outcomes (Amato and Gilbreth, 1999).

Another problem with promoting cohabitation is that many men in cohabiting relationships are not the biological father of the children in the household, or at least are not the biological father of all the children in the household. By one estimate, 63 percent of children in cohabiting households are born not to the cohabiting couple, but to a previous union of one of the adult partners, most often the mother (Graefe and Lichter, 1999). This is problematic in that cohabitation with a man who is not biologically related to one's children increases the risk of both physical and sexual child abuse (Daly and Wilson, 1996).

Furthermore, cohabitation seems to reduce future marital stability. The experience of cohabitation appears to alter a couple's attitudes toward marriage and divorce in ways that make the couple more prone to divorce should they subsequently marry (Axinn and Thornton, 1992).

This does not mean that fragile families initiatives are unwise. Children do better when their fathers are actively and positively engaged in their lives. This goes for unmarried fathers as well as married fathers, whether cohabiting with the mother or not. It does suggest, however, that if the goal is to produce lifetime fathers for children, and not merely a temporary increase in father involvement, something else needs to be added to the mix. That something else is marriage.

The Marriage Option

The empirical literature clearly demonstrates that children do best when they grow up in a household with two parents who are married to each other. That this result is not simply due to differences in income is attested to by the fact that step-families, which have household incomes nearly equivalent to continuously married households, offer children few of the benefits of an intact, two-parent household (Horn, 1999).

Some argue that the benefits of marriage are largely due to selection effects. In other words, those who marry have unmeasured characteristics, such as strong interpersonal skills or emotional maturity, that simultaneously make them good partners and good parents. Certainly there is something to this argument. Simple comparisons between the married and the unmarried are not reliable, and even relatively sophisticated efforts to tease out the effects of marriage per se have their limitations. Nonetheless, recent research suggests there is something about marriage itself, such as the expectation of permanency and the commitment and security that this engenders, that produces good outcomes beyond what can be explained by selection effects alone (Waite, 1995).

Of course, not all marriages between a child's biological parents are ideal. Domestic violence and other irreconcilable differences will, at times, necessitate single-parent families. But while acknowledging the reality of domestic violence and accepting the inevitability of divorce and even out-of-wedlock childbearing, it should also be acknowledged that marriage is the most reliable pathway to a lifetime father for children. As Hillary Clinton (1996) pointed out in her book *It Takes a Village*, every society, in order to function properly, requires a critical mass of married, two-parent families, both to raise their own children well and to serve as models for those who are being reared in something other than a married, two-parent family. The great tragedy today is that there are communities, especially low-income communities, that have already lost that critical mass.

The Importance of Social Norms

Given that marriage is good for children and adults, why isn't everyone rushing to the altar to get married? In explaining why people do or do not marry, most social scientists and policy analysts have relied heavily on explanations that emphasize economic changes over time. If marriage has declined, many assert, it is because men's earnings or employment opportunities have declined or because women have independent sources of income in the form of welfare or their own earnings.

There is little doubt that these economic factors have played some role in the decline of marriage, although their effect has not been large (Sawhill, 1999). Certainly they cannot fully explain the rather precipitous changes in marriage rates over the past three decades. Something else must have been at work, and that something else is a massive shift in social norms or public attitudes. Charles Murray (chapter 5) refers to this shift as a change in the zeitgeist. He notes that the merits of the two-parent family came under assault in the 1970s and 1980s and that such attitudes may have at least partially reversed during the 1990s.

Survey data on attitudes suggest that Murray is right. Consider, for example, changes in attitudes toward premarital sex. The proportion of the population that believes premarital sex is always or almost always wrong has declined sharply from close to 70 percent for cohorts born in the early part of this century to close to 20 percent for the youngest age groups (Inter-University Consortium, 1998). This shift in attitudes produced, in turn, a major increase in rates of early sexual activity. The proportion of teenaged girls aged 15 to 19 who were sexually experienced increased from 30 percent in 1970 to 55 percent in 1990 (National Center for Health Statistics, 1995). This growing permissiveness regarding premarital sex, combined with increasing rates of sexual activity and later marriage, has in turn been responsible for the increase in out-of-wedlock births, the most important source of the increase in father-absent families in recent decades.

Social norms concerning the importance, or even desirability, of lifelong marriage have also changed. Forty years ago, for example, there was some consensus that couples in troubled marriages should "stay together for the sake of the kids." Now divorce among couples with children is commonplace. Moreover, surveys consistently find that majorities of teens and young adults consider cohabitation a reasonable substitute for marriage. In a recent survey, for example, three-quarters of high school seniors agreed that a man and woman who live together without being married are either "experimenting with a worthwhile alternative lifestyle or doing their own thing and not affecting anyone else" (Survey Research Center, 1995).

Although the longer-term attitudinal trends have been unfavorable to marriage and family life, the 1990s produced at least a partial reversal of some of these trends. As noted earlier, attitudes about premarital and casual sex have shifted in a more conservative direction, and young people are becoming more interested in marriage (Survey Research Center, 1995). In addition, recent ethnographic research suggests that being an involved father is becoming a more highly respected role among lower-income males (Cohen, 1999).

If norms are not stable, and especially if they can be influenced by public policy, this opens up a whole new arena for public action. It also raises difficult and controversial questions about which norms or values society wants to promote. But if individuals are less autonomous than traditional models imply, and instead can be influenced by the behavior and opinions of others, then it is no longer sufficient to argue that decisions about marriage or childbearing are entirely private. Not only do they have social consequences, they have social determinants as well, including messages embedded in public policy and in the popular media. Social psychologists who have studied this phenomenon have found that behavior is conditioned by individuals' perceptions of what others around them are doing, as well as by what others are likely to approve or disapprove. For example, teens are more likely to become sexually active when they believe that "everyone else is doing it" (Cialdini and Trost, 1998).

This is not to say that the trends we have been describing (less marriage, more divorce, more premarital sex, and more cohabitation) are all bad. The kind of conformity to marriage as a norm that prevailed in an earlier era forced some people to marry who might have been better off single and trapped others in abusive relationships. It is only to say that norm regimes matter, that we must come to some judgments about the kind of regime in which we want to live, and that public policy can influence this regime if policymakers are willing to adopt the kind of public marketing strategies that have been used effectively in other areas, such as smoking.

Economic Disincentives for Marriage

While emphasizing the importance of social norms, it is nevertheless also the case that when couples get married, public policy frequently punishes them economically. The marriage penalty in the U.S. tax code for higher-wage earners is well known. Less well known is the financial penalty for marriage found in the Earned Income Tax Credit (EITC), an income supplement that provides up to $4,000 a year to low-income working parents with children.

This tax credit is now the largest antipoverty measure in the federal arsenal. The good news is that the EITC encourages work because only those with earnings are eligible. The bad news is that it can discourage marriage by making the decision to marry very expensive. That's because a low-wage mother who marries another low-wage earner typically moves into an earnings range that reduces eligibility for the EITC. Thus two low-wage earners are better off, at least as far as the EITC is concerned, if they stay single or cohabit than if they marry.

Admittedly, there is little evidence that low-income couples do not marry in order to keep the EITC (Ellwood, 2000). However, anecdotal evidence suggests there is a sense in low-income communities that if you get married you "lose stuff." They may not know exactly how much "stuff" they stand to lose, but they know marriage is a bad deal. And they are right. A mother earning $10,000 stands to lose $1,600 in EITC benefits alone if she marries a man with similar earnings (Ellwood and Sawhill, 2000). And it is not just the EITC that discourages marriage. The entire panoply of means-tested programs is rife with marriage penalties because benefits are often scaled back when a new wage earner is added to the household. In addition, seventeen states have different rules for two-parent than for one-parent families under the Temporary Assistance for Needy Families (TANF) program, even when both have similarly low incomes (Primus and Beeson, 2000).

When one takes into account the full package of income-tested benefits, the marriage penalty for a single mother who chooses to marry an employed man can be very severe (Steuerle, 1997). For example, when a single mother working full time at the minimum wage marries a full-time worker earning $8 an hour, the marriage penalty is a shocking $8,060. Under such circumstances, marriage simply makes no economic sense. Even if one cannot demonstrate that individual couples alter their marital decisions as a result, such policies no doubt have larger "signaling" effects about the desirability, or in this case undesirability, of marriage, further weakening the social norm of marriage, especially in low-income communities.

The Manpower Demonstration Research Corporation recently reported an example of how the removal of financial disincentives for marriage can positively affect marriage rates and stability in an evaluation of the Minnesota Family Investment Program (MFIP) (Knox, Miller, and Gennetian, 2000). Implemented before 1996, MFIP was an experiment designed to help welfare-dependent families achieve self-sufficiency through work. For MFIP participants, separate eligibility requirements for two-parent families were eliminated. In addition, MFIP allowed two-parent families to disregard more of the money they earned than what was allowed in the traditional AFDC program.

After three years, 11 percent of previously single MFIP recipients were married; in contrast, only 7 percent of single mothers randomly assigned to the traditional AFDC program had married. Even more impressively, 60 percent of two-parent families in the MFIP group were still married after three years; only 49 percent of two-parent families assigned to the traditional AFDC program were still married. This is the first clear demonstration of the positive effects removal of financial disincentives for marriage can have on both marriage formation and marital stability.

Recommendations for the Next Phase of Welfare Reform

If welfare reform is to deliver on its promise not just to reduce caseloads but also to improve the well-being of children, the next phase of welfare reform must recognize the importance of reducing nonmarital childbearing and increasing marriage. Unfortunately, there are no proven remedies for achieving these goals. Nonetheless, given their importance, we urge experimentation with a variety of approaches, some of which will be controversial. As such, they should be tried out on an appropriate scale and carefully evaluated.

First, in reauthorizing TANF, Congress should provide resources to nonprofit and faith-based organizations committed to reducing pregnancy among unmarried teens, engaging fathers, and promoting marriage. Most welfare case workers and many political leaders have been reluctant to address such issues as sex and marriage for fear of offending a particular constituency (Ooms, 1998). This reluctance to bring up the topic of marriage, however, sends the not-so-subtle message that marriage is neither expected nor valued. Although one can hope that the president, governors, members of Congress, and others in public life will use the power of the bully pulpit to encourage childbearing within marriage, faith-based and nonprofit organizations are in a better position than government itself to provide leadership on this set of issues. Indeed, unless faith-based organizations and other civic groups become more strongly involved, and are provided with the resources necessary to do so, any changes induced by political rhetoric alone are unlikely to be sustained.

Second, Congress should take steps to reduce the financial disincentives for marriage. As noted, current policies impose significant penalties on couples who get married. At the very least, the EITC needs to be reformed to ensure that it does not punish low-income couples who choose marriage. There are several ways to accomplish this objective (Ellwood and Sawhill, 2000). One proposal would extend the phase-out range for the EITC by $6,000 for married couples at a cost of roughly $5 billion a year (Sawhill and Thomas, 2001).

In addition, TANF reauthorization could encourage states to treat married couples more favorably, allowing them to keep more of their welfare benefits as earnings rise and eliminating rules that discriminate against families with low incomes and two married parents. Murray (chapter 5) goes one step further and proposes that one state experiment with a plan that would deny all welfare benefits to unmarried mothers under the age of 18.

Third, Congress should consider providing incentives for marriage. Removing financial disincentives for marriage, while helpful, is not the same thing as promoting marriage. Congress should consider earmarking funds to provide explicit financial incentives for low-income couples to marry or at least to avoid bearing children out of wedlock. Currently, West Virginia is the only state that provides an explicit financial incentive for marriage, by adding an extra $100 to the monthly welfare check of low-income couples who choose to marry. Robert Rector of the Heritage Foundation has proposed a more dramatic financial incentive for marriage: giving women at high risk for having a child out of wedlock a $5,000 bonus if they have their first child within marriage. The $5,000 payment would be made in $1,000 annual installments over a five-year period as long as the woman remained married. A less dramatic proposal is for states to suspend the collection of child support arrearages in cases where the biological father and mother get married—and stay married—to each other.

Although controversial, such proposals make an important point: marriage is in trouble, especially in low-income communities. If we are serious about encouraging marriage, public policy may have to do more than simply strive toward marriage neutrality by removing existing financial disincentives for marriage. It will also need to provide a clear message that marriage is valued by rewarding those who choose it for themselves.

Fourth, TANF reauthorization should require states to provide the same employment services to low-income men that they currently provide to low-income women. Admittedly, research on the effectiveness of providing employment services to low-income men has been disappointing (LaLonde, 1995). This may be because many employment programs in the past have emphasized classroom training at the expense of job placement or on-the-job training, have not been adequately linked to employers' needs, and have put too little emphasis on the acquisition of "soft skills" such as dress, attendance, and relationships with supervisors and customers. Nevertheless, improving the employment status of low-income men may encourage marriage by improving their marriageability. Existing Welfare to Work grants can be used for this purpose, but more money could be earmarked for services targeted to this group. In so doing, however, care should be taken not to condition receipt of services on being a noncustodial parent because this might serve to introduce perverse incentives for men to father children out of wedlock, in much the same way the old welfare system provided perverse incentives for women to bear children out of wedlock.

Fifth, TANF reauthorization should include money targeted for programs that enhance the marital and parenting skills of high-risk families. Unfortunately, many men and women lack the necessary skills to sustain a marriage and raise children well. Some may have grown up in broken homes and never experienced positive role models. Others may have had inadequate or abusive parents. Too many African American men, in particular, have never experienced what it means to have a committed father (Patterson, 1998). In order to help couples sustain marriage and be good parents, funding should be provided to religious and civic organizations that offer premarital education and training in parenting skills to low-income couples applying for or receiving public assistance.

Finally, TANF reauthorization should be used to rebuild cultural norms surrounding sex, teen pregnancy, and marriage. It is naïve to think that a single program will yield strong effects if that program operates within a broader culture that regularly and consistently suggests that casual sex outside marriage is the norm, that sexual exploits are a test of one's manhood, that teenage pregnancy and out-of-wedlock childbearing are no big deal, and that marriage itself is old-fashioned. These messages suggest that the next phase of welfare reform might also attempt to change the culture by earmarking some TANF funds for broad-based media campaigns designed to publicize the importance of delaying childbearing until marriage and making lifelong commitments to children, even if they are born outside marriage.

There is reason to believe that well-targeted public education campaigns can affect both attitudes and behavior. Take, for example, the change in social norms concerning smoking. Adult smoking rates declined from 42 percent in 1965 to 24 percent in 1998 (Giovino and others, 1994; HHS, 2000). A multitude of factors contributed to this decline, including evidence establishing a link between smoking and health in the 1950s, the dissemination of this information to the public (particularly in the first Surgeon General's report in 1964), the television and radio antismoking campaigns associated with the 1968 Fairness Doctrine, and the ban on broadcast advertising of tobacco products in 1971 (HHS, 2000). The impact of these external factors was greatly magnified by growing social disapproval of smoking. Once considered a normal social behavior, smoking is now done furtively or apologetically, even among adults, and as the number of people who smoke drops, the social acceptability of the activity further erodes.

Independent evaluations of other media campaigns have shown positive results as well. For example, an evaluation of the National Campaign to Prevent Teen Pregnancy's public service ad campaign found that, among teenaged boys and girls exposed to the ads, teens' awareness increased and attitudes changed, and they had more conversations about sex with their parents. Similarly, an independent evaluation of a statewide responsible-fatherhood media campaign in Virginia found that one year after the implementation of the campaign 40,000 fathers reported they were spending more time with their children and 100,000 nonfathers reported they had reached out to offer support or encouragement to a father in their community (Guterbock and others, 1997).

Media campaigns have thus far been underutilized in the public arena. The fact that corporations spend billions of dollars every year in attempts to get consumers to buy their products, and must justify such expenditures economically, suggests that they can be effective. This is an area in which government has a lot to learn from the private sector.

The new consensus is that fathers matter to the well-being of children. The next phase of welfare reform needs to take this new consensus into account by focusing on effective ways to increase male responsibility and the involvement of fathers in the lives of their children. Part of that work must include promoting the ideal of married fatherhood.

Some will argue that promoting marriage in low-income communities is not just a fool's errand, but also an unwanted imposition of the majority culture's values on minority communities. Data from the Fragile Families and Child Well-Being Study, however, suggest otherwise. When asked their chances of marrying the baby's father, 52 percent of these low-income, unwed mothers answered "certain" or "near certain"; and over 70 percent of them thought the chances of marrying the baby's father were at least "50-50" (Bendheim-Thoman Center, 2000). Rather than being a value foreign to minority communities, the ideal, if not the reality, of marriage seems to be something to which many low-income couples do aspire.

Of course, welfare reform cannot, by itself, solve the problems of unwed parenting, fatherlessness, and marriage any more than it alone will ever solve the problem of poverty. So much depends on both individual choices and broad societal and cultural influences. Moreover, effective mechanisms for reducing out-of-wedlock childbearing and encouraging marriage are scarce. Reauthorization of TANF presents a unique opportunity to experiment with and evaluate some new approaches. If the ultimate goal of welfare reform is not simply to move large numbers of previously dependent single parents into the paid labor force, but to ensure that more children grow up with two parents, then the next phase of welfare reform needs to challenge states, communities, and the nonprofit sector to find creative solutions to this problem.

COMMENT BY
Ronald B. Mincy

Before commenting critically on Wade Horn and Isabell Sawhill's prescription for incorporating fathers into welfare reform, we should consider several points on which their analysis is accurate. First, they correctly place a premium on discouraging out-of-wedlock births, especially among teenaged moms, and emphasize that such efforts should also try to prevent premature fatherhood. Second, their general argument that in the past public policy has discouraged marriage is also correct. We should work to change public policies that still include some marriage disincentives. Third, Horn and Sawhill are right in stating that in the long run child poverty would be lower if more children were born into married families. Marriages last longer than cohabiting and nonresidential relationships between unwed parents, and marriages that occur after cohabitation are more likely to end in divorce. So Congress should include some symbolic language in any reauthorization bill to indicate that it wants states to use their Temporary Assistance for Needy Families (TANF) funds to reduce the number of out-of-wedlock births, engage fathers, and promote marriage. This action would encourage some states to do more than they are currently doing in these important areas given the authority and resources they already have.

However, Horn and Sawhill are too broad in asserting that means-tested programs are rife with marriage penalties, and they are too narrow when they suggest that Congress should remove these barriers for married families only. Moreover, their recommendations for promoting marriage do not inspire great confidence. They suggest large cash bonuses for women at risk of an unwed pregnancy and small cash supplements to cash benefits for cohabiting couples who marry. The former could produce marriages in which the only commitment is to the financial incentive, much like what we feared would occur in arranged marriages between immigrants and citizens. The latter would be of little value because when two parents work, even part time, their earnings exceed the means test for cash benefits in most states.

Another of Horn and Sawhill's recommendations for promoting marriage simply flies in the face of the evidence. They recommend that Congress use TANF to pay for public education campaigns to rebuild cultural norms around marriage. However, new survey evidence, which Horn and Sawhill cite, shows that the majority of young, unwed mothers from low-income communities in which marriage is rare believe that marriage would be best for them and for their children, and the majority of these mothers wanted to marry the fathers of their children (Garfinkel, McLanahan, and Harknett, 1999; Mincy and Dupree, forthcoming). Rather than squandering scarce resources on expensive media campaigns to reinforce existing norms that favor marriage, resources are needed to help young people overcome the barriers that thwart their efforts to fulfill those norms. Appropriate policies include those that support work and supplement earnings among low-skilled men, reduce domestic violence, and improve child support enforcement.

Some demographers now believe that cohabitation before marriage has become so widespread that we should probably assume that the majority of young people who eventually marry will live together first (Smock, 2000). Moreover, births to cohabiting couples account for nearly all of the increase in unwed births in the past fifteen years. Young unwed parents also maintain nonresidential relationships in which they try to support their children. This means that more poor children are raised in poor households with the involvement of both of their biological parents than previous research suggested. So, promoting marriage often means encouraging couples who already cohabit to take the next step and marry.

Besides this, the "fragile family" research is exploring how much child poverty can be reduced by strengthening parental and parent-child bonds in families that delay marriage or in families that never marry—or divorce (Garfinkel, McLanahan, and Harknett, 1999). There are explicit legislative recommendations emerging from this research. Horn and Sawhill treat the fragile families efforts in such a cursory way that it is hard to tell whether they endorse them or not.

A recent paper by Beeson and Primus (2000) shows that researchers have generally overstated the marriage penalties in our income security policies because they fail to distinguish between cohabiting partners with children and cohabiting parents with children in common (hereafter, cohabiting parents), and they ignore child support enforcement. Most means-tested programs treat married parents and unwed cohabiting parents alike. Moreover, at the same level of earnings, these programs make married and cohabiting parents better off than separated families (single-parent families and noncustodial parents), especially when noncustodial parents pay their child support in full.

TANF imposes higher work requirements on states for their two-parent caseload than for their single parent caseload, and seventeen states put additional restrictions on the participation of married and cohabiting parents in

TANF and Medicaid. This reduces the number of married and cohabiting parents that benefit from means-tested programs. Moreover, both married and cohabiting parents are much less likely than single-parent families to know about the child care, food stamps, and other benefits for which they are already eligible. Thus TANF reauthorization should focus on removing the barriers that prevent two-parent families from getting all the help they need. Such efforts are especially important for cohabiting parents because their poverty rate (34 percent) is much closer to the poverty rate of single-parent families (48 percent) than to that of married families (9.5 percent).

The next barrier to marriage that Congress should address is the low earnings of low-skilled men. Recent research shows that male earnings have a larger impact than female earnings on the likelihood that unwed parents marry (Mincy and Dupree, forthcoming). The favorable labor market that helped produce such a dramatic reduction in the welfare rolls had more modest effects on the labor market outcomes of low-skilled men. Since TANF reauthorization is likely to be implemented under less favorable labor market conditions, Horn and Sawhill are right to propose that TANF should pay more attention to the work force development needs of low-skilled men. Responsible fatherhood demonstrations, such as Parents' Fair Share, show that job retention, wage growth, and career growth for low-skilled men are needs that must be addressed (Knox and Redcross, 2000).

The Partners for Fragile Families (PFF) demonstration, which is just getting under way at this writing in early 2001, incorporates the best experience available on increasing job retention, wage growth, and career advancement among low-skilled men (Mincy and Pouncy, 1997). This demonstration is also a laboratory to test several new services and public-private partnerships that will be useful to marriage promotion. These include:

—screening low-income couples for risks of domestic violence and referring low-skilled men for battering services;

—working with community and faith-based organizations to build the communications and team parenting skills of fragile families;

—incorporating marriage exploration and values clarification into peer group services for young disadvantaged men; and

—developing legal and child support mediation services for low-skilled men.

Finally, Horn and Sawhill's criticism of child support enforcement as a focal point for fatherhood services is simply naive. The Personal Responsibility and Work Opportunity Reconciliation Act (PRWORA) dramatically increased the costs states would incur if they failed to make consistent progress in increasing paternity establishment rates and improving their collection of child support payments. As a result, states are now establishing paternity for 1.5 million children every year. This means that child support enforcement offices are coming into contact with increasing numbers of low-income parents. The Fragile Families Survey shows that about 60 percent of young mothers and fathers have more than one child. Anecdotal evidence from PFF suggests that 30 percent of the young mothers and fathers have children with different partners. This raises two important questions that marriage promotion efforts will have to face: Who should marry whom? and How will young, disadvantaged, newlyweds handle the child support obligations they bring from previous relationships?

When Congress reauthorizes TANF, it should support efforts like PFF by helping the partners address certain barriers peculiarly affected by federal law. Using the child support paid by low-income fathers to reimburse states for public expenditures is a particularly important one, because neither the custodial nor the noncustodial parent sees the latter's child support payment as benefiting children. Increasing the amount of child support that is passed through to custodial families on TANF would go a long way toward resolving this problem. If states exercise the option to pass through more child support payments, the federal government should share the cost. Another problem is the inclination of Congress to reduce federal funding for child support. Instead, Congress should increase funding for child support enforcement so that states have the resources necessary to deter unwed births through child support enforcement and, when unwed births occur, to require and enable low-income fathers to meet their responsibilities.

Marriage is becoming a wedge issue in the reauthorization debate, but this is unnecessary. Congress should continue to enact policies designed to reduce the number of unwed births, increase the employment and earnings of low-skilled fathers, ensure that the tax code does not favor cohabitation over marriage, and eliminate barriers that, at the same level of earnings, reduce the participation of two-parent families relative to single-parent families in benefit programs. Congress can also provide incentives in these programs so that, at the same level of earnings, parents who choose more stable family forms (marriage over cohabitation, cohabitation over visiting relationships) are better off. Congress might even include specific symbolic language in TANF to indicate to states that reducing unwed births, engaging fathers, and promoting marriage are important national goals. However, there is every reason to suspect that marriage promotion efforts will be subject to the same slow and deliberate process of development that other attempts at social engineering have experienced. Meanwhile, many children will be born and raised by poor parents who can be helped to jointly contribute to their children's well-being, even if they do not marry. Marriage promotion efforts can learn a lot from responsible fatherhood programs that take on the broader task of strengthening fragile families.

References

Amato, Paul R., and Joan G. Gilbreth. 1999. "Non-Resident Fathers and Children's Well-Being: A Meta-Analysis." *Journal of Marriage and the Family* 61 (3): 557–73.

Axinn, W. G., and A. Thornton. 1992. "The Relationship between Cohabitation and Divorce: Selectivity or Causal Influence?" *Demography* 29 (3): 357–74.

Beeson, Jennifer, and Wendell Primus. 2000. "Safety Net Programs, Marriage and Cohabitation." Unpublished paper. Washington: Center on Budget and Policy Priorities.

Bendheim-Thoman Center for Research on Child Wellbeing. 2000. "Dispelling Myths about Unmarried Fathers." Fragile Families Research Brief 1. Princeton University.

Cialdini, R. B., and M. R. Trost. 1998. "Social Influence: Social Norms, Conformity, and Compliance." In *The Handbook of Social Psychology*, vol. 2, edited by D. T. Gilbert, S. T. Fiske, and G. Lindzey. Boston: McGraw-Hill.

Clinton, Hillary Rodham. 1996. *It Takes a Village—and Other Lessons Children Teach Us.* Simon and Schuster.

Cohen, David. 1999. "The State Dads Are In." In *Map and Track: State Initiatives to Encourage Responsible Fatherhood*, 1999 ed., edited by Stanley Bernard and Jane Knitzer. New York: National Center for Children in Poverty.

Daly, Martin, and Margo Wilson. 1996. "Evolutionary Psychology and Marital Conflict: The Relevance of Stepchildren." In *Sex, Power, Conflict: Evolutionary and Feminist Perspectives*, edited by David M. Buss and Neil Malamuth. New York: Oxford University Press.

Darroch, Jacqueline E., David J. Landry, and Selene Oslak. 1999. "Age Differences between Sexual Partners in the United States." *Family Planning Perspectives* 31 (4): 160–67.

Ellwood, David T. 2000. "The Impact of the Earned Income Tax Credit and Social Policy Reforms on Work, Marriage, and Living Arrangements." Unpublished paper. Kennedy School of Government, Harvard University.

Ellwood, David T., and Isabel V. Sawhill. 2000. "Fixing the Marriage Penalty in the EITC." Children's Roundtable Working Paper. Brookings.

Furstenberg, Frank F., and Andrew J. Cherlin. 1991. *Divided Families: What Happens to Children When Parents Part.* Harvard University Press.

Furstenberg, Frank F., and Christine Winquist Nord. 1985. "Parenting Apart: Patterns of Child Rearing after Marital Disruption." *Journal of Marriage and the Family* 47 (4): 893–905.

Garfinkel, Irwin, Sara McLanahan, and Kristen Harknett. 1999. "Fragile Families and Welfare Reform." Working Paper 99-11. Princeton University.

Giovino, Gary A., and others. 1994. "Surveillance for Selected Tobacco-Use Behaviors United States, 1900–1994." CDC Surveillance Summaries, *Morbidity and Mortality Weekly Report* 43 (SS-3).

Graefe, Deborah R., and Daniel T. Lichter. 1999. "Life Course Transitions of American Children: Parental Cohabitation, Marriage, and Single Motherhood." *Demography* 36 (2): 205–17.

Guterbock, Thomas M., Ted Chang, Robert E. Emery, and Brian J. Meekins. 1997. *Evaluation of the Virginia Fatherhood Media Campaign.* Charlottesville, Va.: Center for Survey Research.

Horn, Wade F. 1999. *Father Facts,* 3d ed. Gaithersburg, Md.: National Fatherhood Initiative.

Inter-University Consortium for Political and Social Research. 1998. *General Social Survey.* University of Michigan.

Kirby, Douglas. 2001. *Emerging Answers.* Washington: National Campaign to Prevent Teen Pregnancy.

Knox, Virginia, Cynthia Miller, and Lisa A. Gennetian. 2000. *Reforming Welfare and Rewarding Work: A Summary of the Final Report on the Minnesota Family Investment Program.* New York: Manpower Demonstration Research Corporation.

Knox, Virginia, and Cindy Redcross. 2000. *Parenting and Providing: The Impact of Parents' Fair Share on Paternal Involvement.* New York: Manpower Demonstration Research Corporation.

Ku, Leighton, and others. 1998. "Understanding Changes in Sexual Activity among Young Metropolitan Men: 1979–1995." *Family Planning Perspectives* 30 (6): 256–62.

LaLonde, Robert J. 1995. "The Promise of Public Sector–Sponsored Training Programs." *Journal of Economic Perspectives* 9 (2): 149–68.

Lerman, Robert I. 1993. "A National Profile of Young Unwed Fathers." In *Young Unwed Fathers: Changing Roles and Emerging Policies,* edited by Robert I. Lerman and Theodora J. Ooms. Temple University Press.

Martinez, John M., and Cynthia Miller. 2000. *Working and Earning: The Impact of Parents' Fair Share on Low-Income Fathers' Employment.* New York: Manpower Demonstration Research Corporation.

Maynard, Rebecca A. 1997. "The Costs of Adolescent Childbearing." In *Kids Having Kids: The Economic Costs and Social Consequences of Teen Pregnancy,* edited by Rebecca A. Maynard. Washington: Urban Institute.

McLanahan, Sara, and Gary Sandefur. 1994. *Growing Up with a Single Parent: What Hurts, What Helps.* Harvard University Press.

Mincy, Ronald B., and Alan Dupree. Forthcoming. "Family Formation in Fragile Families: Can the Next Step in Welfare Reform Achieve PRWORA's Fourth Goal?" *Journal of Children's and Youth Services Review.*

Mincy, Ronald B., and Hillard Pouncy. 1997. "Paternalism, Child Support Enforcement, and Families." In *The New Paternalism: Supervisory Approaches to Poverty,* edited by Lawrence M. Mead. Washington: Brookings.

National Center for Health Statistics. 1995. *National Survey of Family Growth.* U.S. Department of Health and Human Services.

National Commission on Children. 1993. *Just the Facts: A Summary of Recent Information on America's Children and Their Families.* Government Printing Office.

Ooms, Theodora. 1998. *Toward More Perfect Unions: Putting Marriage on the Public Agenda.* Washington: Family Impact Seminar.

Patterson, Orlando. 1998. *Rituals of Blood: Consequences of Slavery in Two American Centuries.* New York: Basic Civitas Books.

Popenoe, David, and Barbara Dafoe Whitehead. 1999. *Should We Live Together? What Young Adults Need to Know about Cohabitation before Marriage.* New Brunswick, N.J.: National Marriage Project.

Price, David. 1999. *Multisite Evaluation and Synthesis of Responsible Fatherhood Projects, Quarterly Progress Report.* 4/1/99-6/30/99. Denver: Policy Studies.

Primus, Wendell, and Jennifer Beeson. 2000. "Safety Net Programs, Marriage and Cohabitation." Paper presented at the conference "Just Living Together: Implications for Children, Families, and Social Policy." Population Research Institute, Pennsylvania State University, October 30–31.

Sawhill, Isabel V. 1999. "Families at Risk." In *Setting National Priorities: The 2000 Election and Beyond,* edited by Henry J. Aaron and Robert Reischauer. Brookings.

Sawhill, Isabel V., and Adam Thomas. 2001. *A Hand Up for the Bottom Third: Toward a New Agenda for Low-Income Working Families.* Brookings.

Smock, Pamela J. 2000. "Cohabitation in the United States: An Appraisal of Research Themes, Findings, and Implications." *Annual Review of Sociology* 26: 1–20.

Stephens, Linda S. 1996. "Will Johnny See Daddy This Week?" *Journal of Family Issues* 17 (4): 466–94.

Steuerle, C. Eugene. 1997. "The Effects of Tax and Welfare Policies on Family Formation." Paper presented at the conference "Strategies to Strengthen Marriage." Family Impact Seminar, Washington, June 23–24.

Survey Research Center. 1995. *Monitoring the Future Survey.* University of Michigan.

U.S. Department of Health and Human Services (HHS). 2000. *Reducing Tobacco Use: A Report of the Surgeon General.* Atlanta.

U.S. House of Representatives, Committee on Ways and Means. 1998. *1998 Green Book: Background Materials and Data on Programs within the Jurisdiction of the Committee on Ways and Means.* Government Printing Office.

Waite, Linda J. 1995. "Does Marriage Matter?" *Demography* 32 (November): 483–507.

Wertheimer, Richard, Justin Jager, and Kristin Moore. 2000. *State Policy Initiatives for Reducing Teen and Adult Nonmarital Childbearing: Family Planning to Family Caps.* Policy Brief A-43. Washington: Urban Institute.

17

IRWIN GARFINKEL

Child Support in the New World of Welfare

T HE AMERICAN SYSTEM of assuring child support directly affects most parents and children. More than half of American children now spend part of their childhood living apart from one of their parents. The system indirectly affects us all because of its impact on welfare costs and, far more important, on future generations of children and adults.

For child support, the reforms that were part of the Personal Responsibility and Work Opportunity Reconciliation Act (PRWORA, 1996) represent a major extension of a series of reforms that began in 1974 when Congress added title IVD to the Social Security Act, thereby creating a new federal/state child support enforcement program. During the next quarter-century, a spate of federal and state legislation transformed child support enforcement from a system of local judicial discretion into one of state and federal administrative regularity, characteristic of social insurance programs (Garfinkel, 1992; Legler, 1996). What prompted this vast change is discussed briefly below. The remainder of the chapter reviews what has been wrought.

Child support enforcement policy in the 1970s condoned parental irresponsibility, was rife with inequity, and contributed to the poverty and welfare dependence of single mothers and their children. Only a bit more than one-third of nonresident fathers paid child support. Paternity was established in only about 10 percent of cases. Except in Michigan, Delaware, and a few other local jurisdictions, child support awards were established on an individual and highly variable basis. In 1979, according to current child support guidelines, American nonresident fathers should have paid $24–30 billion. In fact, they owed only $10 billion and paid only $7 billion. Only a small part, $4 billion, of the total payments gap, $17 billion to $23 billion, was attributable to the fathers of children on welfare (Oellerich, Garfinkel, and Robins, 1991). Nevertheless, if child support had been perfectly enforced, both the poverty gap and expenditures on welfare would have been reduced by about one-quarter (Meyer and others, 1994).

Public assistance to families with children in the early 1970s was limited to single parent families with low incomes. The Aid to Families with Dependent Children (AFDC) program did nothing to prevent poverty; provided meager, below-poverty-level benefits; sharply reduced benefits when mothers earned more; and took away medical care coverage when a mother left welfare. Support for working mothers outside welfare was practically nonexistent. There was no Earned Income Tax Credit (EITC) and virtually no child-care subsidies. For unskilled single mothers who could not earn more than welfare or forgo health insurance, the system was akin to a poverty trap.

Dissatisfaction with both public assistance and child support enforcement was fueled by the growth of single-parenthood, the welfare explosion of the decade following the 1964 War on Poverty, and the continuing high rates of poverty of single-mother families. Politicians and academics alike sought new methods for achieving the long-standing policy objectives of preventing both poverty and dependence on welfare. Prevention requires providing help outside welfare. Free public education and social insurance, pioneered respectively in the United States and Germany and since adopted in all Western industrialized nations, are the most important methods (in addition to capitalism itself) of preventing poverty and welfare dependence. In 1974, Congress enacted two programs championed by Senator Russell Long that have played key roles in providing assistance to poor American families outside welfare—the Earned Income Tax Credit and the new federal/state child support enforcement program. In the years since, federal and state legislation have taken long strides on the enforcement side toward a new child support assurance system, which is akin to social insurance. But there has been no progress on the public benefit side.

The Enforcement Revolution and Its Effects

An unlikely alliance of welfare cutters, women's advocates, and antipoverty warriors produced a near unanimous vote in both houses of Congress for the 1984 Child Support Amendments Act, as well as large majorities for numerous reforms that strengthened the child support program between 1981 and 1999 (Lerman and Sorenson, 2000). Unlike most of the cash provisions of PRWORA that give greater autonomy to states, most of the child support provisions of the federal PRWORA continue a quarter-century trend of imposing successful state practices on other states. PRWORA also intensifies the shift from judicial discretion to administrative regularity in all three collection side components of assuring child support: securing the legal obligation to pay child support, making obligations reasonable and adequate, and ensuring that obligors pay what they owe.

Establishing paternity is a prerequisite to securing a child support obligation for an increasing proportion of children who live apart from their fathers. Paternity establishment laws have their origins in the criminal law. Thus, before the 1980s, paternity establishment in most states was a difficult and costly judicial procedure in which the rights of the accused were relatively well protected. Most courts in the 1970s admitted blood tests as evidence in paternity establishment cases only if they excluded the putative father. During the 1980s, states began requiring courts to admit probabilistic evidence of the putative father's paternity from blood and genetic tests. The 1988 Family Support Act (FSA) required all states to use blood and genetic tests in disputed cases. PRWORA goes much further by requiring states to give administrative agencies authority to order blood and genetic tests without the need for a court order. In perhaps the most far-reaching move away from the judicial system to state/federal administrative regularity, the 1996 PRWORA requires states to have available in hospitals and birth record agencies a paternity acknowledgment form; signing it is voluntary, but when signed it becomes a legal finding of paternity after sixty days. In 1980 paternity was established in only 22 percent of nonmarital births. By 1996 the percentage had reached 57 percent (Garfinkel, Heintze, and Huang, 2000). In view of PRWORA, the percentage is almost certainly higher today.

Before the 1980s, state laws listed factors that courts should consider in establishing how much child support should be paid. But because the factors were so general and even contradictory, all real authority was effectively delegated to local courts. The 1984 Child Support Amendments required states to adopt numerical guidelines for determining child support obligations that courts could use. Then the 1988 FSA required states to make these guidelines the presumptive order. Judges who departed from the guidelines were required to provide a written justification. In addition, the 1988 law required states to use the guidelines to review and adjust every child support award administered by the Office of Child Support Enforcement every three years. PRWORA gives the states greater discretion to update awards.

To ensure that obligors pay what they owe, the 1984 amendments required states to enact laws to require employers to withhold child support obligations of delinquent obligors. The 1988 FSA went further by requiring automatic withholding of child support obligations from the outset for all IV-D cases beginning in 1990 and for all child support cases beginning in 1994. Many states, however, failed to implement withholding for non-IVD cases because they neither had nor wanted to develop the bureaucratic capacity to administer universal withholding of payments.

The 1996 PRWORA requires states to develop the bureaucratic capacity to monitor all child support payments. States must establish central state registries of child support orders and centralized collection and disbursement units. The extra cost to administer universal withholding is trivial.

PRWORA also established a national directory of new hires and requires each state to maintain directories of all state child support orders; the two directories are matched to facilitate the collection of orders. This federal/state directory will greatly facilitate interstate enforcement of child support obligations. PRWORA also expands the federal role in child support collection by requiring that states adopt the Uniform Interstate Family Support Act (UIFSA). The UIFSA, among other provisions, requires all states to have long-arm statutes that apply in other states and allows direct withholding of child support obligations from wages between states.

Finally, although PRWORA generally increases the federal role in child support enforcement, there is one other major exception in addition to the updating provision. Since 1984 states had been required to disregard the first fifty dollars of child support payments in determining benefits to mothers receiving AFDC. PRWORA dropped this requirement.

Effects on Child Support Payments

What has this revolution in child support enforcement wrought? Data on child support receipts of single mothers from the March Current Population Survey from 1979 to 1999 indicate virtually no improvement in the receipt rate for all mothers: it rose from 30 percent to 31 percent. On the other hand, the increase in child support payments from the fathers of children receiving welfare is striking: from 8 percent to 16 percent. Similarly, according to data reported by the fifty state offices of child support enforcement and compiled by the federal Office of Child Support Enforcement (OCSE), the proportion of single mothers who were on welfare and had a child support payment nearly doubled between 1978 and 1998, from 13 percent to 25 percent. Though federal and state offices of child support enforcement in principle are supposed to serve welfare and nonwelfare cases, the focus of legislators and bureaucrats has been on welfare cases. Thus a much larger improvement in child support enforcement for welfare cases than for non-welfare cases is to be expected.

More sophisticated analyses of the data strengthen the story. As documented by Hanson and his colleagues (1996), owing to increases in the proportion of single mothers who are unwed and declines in real wages of non-resident fathers, the child support enforcement system has been forced to swim upstream. Unlike in divorce and separation cases, unwed mothers must establish paternity before a child support order can be secured. Declines in real wages reduce nonresident fathers' ability to pay support. Thus the trends described above understate the effectiveness of the child support enforcement system. Although during a prolonged economic boom, such as we had in the second half of the 1990s, fathers likely have a greater ability to pay, our data go only through 1996 and thus do not reflect the largest effects of the extended boom.

Finally, there are a number of academic studies that document a link between specific child support enforcement laws and increases in child support payments or a particular component of payments. These include blood and genetic testing laws that allow paternity to be established up to age 18, publicizing the availability of IV-D, establishing numerical guidelines for child support, requiring income withholding, requiring payments through a third party, and expenditures on child support enforcement (Garfinkel, Heintze, and Huang, 2000).

In short, the nation's efforts to strengthen child support enforcement have not increased payments from all fathers but have dramatically increased both paternity establishment and child support payments from fathers of children on welfare.

Effects on Welfare Caseloads, Divorce, and Nonmarital Births

Child support enforcement can decrease welfare caseloads both by reducing the proportion of single mothers who receive welfare and by reducing the prevalence of single mothers. Strong child support enforcement reduces entrances into and hastens exits from welfare by increasing the economic security of mothers outside welfare, by complementing work, and by increasing the costs of receiving welfare. Increases in child support increase mothers' income and thereby reduce their need and eligibility for welfare. Child support is also more complementary to work because, as mothers' earnings increase, child support payments fall much less rapidly than welfare benefits, and in many states child support does not decline at all. Finally, by requiring mothers to cooperate in identifying and locating the fathers of their children, strong child support enforcement increases the costs of receiving welfare. A number of studies document that child support reduces poverty and welfare caseloads. Though economic theory does not yield general conclusions about the effects of strong child support enforcement on nonmarital births or divorce, theory suggests that, in the presence of a welfare system, deterrence effects are likely. Stronger enforcement increases the income of the custodial or resident parent (mostly mothers) and reduces the income of the nonresi dent parent (mostly fathers). If child support enforcement were tougher, mothers would be more prone to parent a child out-of-wedlock and divorce, and fathers would be less prone to do either. Which effect would dominate cannot be ascertained in general. But a number of studies find that stronger enforcement reduces both marital disruption and out-of-wedlock childbearing (Garfinkel, Heintze, and Huang, 2000).

Because child support can reduce welfare caseloads via multiple routes, estimates of the effects of strong enforcement on any particular route underestimate the total effect. Consequently, such estimates are likely to be misleading. Suppose, for example, that strong enforcement reduced entrances into welfare by 6 percent, increased exits from welfare by 6 percent, reduced divorce by 6 percent, and reduced nonmarital births by 6 percent. Each effect by itself is quite small and therefore difficult to detect at a statistically significant level. But the aggregate effect of all four taken together would be a reduction in caseloads of about one-fourth!

Three recent studies relate the strength of child support enforcement to recent aggregate declines in welfare caseloads. Mead (1999) shows that variations in county caseload declines in Wisconsin between 1986 and 1994 were very strongly related to the county's success in obtaining child support payments. It is worth noting that Wisconsin has had the largest caseload decline and the strongest child support enforcement system in the nation (Garfinkel, Miller, and others, 1998). In another exploratory note, Mead (2000) finds a similar relationship in national data. Finally, Huang, Garfinkel, and Waldfogel (2000) build on the large body of research devoted to the issue of the determinants of welfare caseloads. Their estimates imply that strengthened child support enforcement explains one-quarter of the caseload decline between 1994 and 1996.

Effects on the Well-being of Mothers, Children, and Fathers

Research indicates that the potential and actual effects of stronger child support enforcement on the incomes of single mothers are large. Meyer and his colleagues (1994) estimated that perfect enforcement of child support would reduce the poverty gap among families potentially eligible for child support by 24 percent. Garfinkel, Heintze, and Huang (2000) found that the increases in child support payments between 1978 and 1998 increased the incomes of single mothers by 16 percent and the incomes of single mothers with a high school degree or less by 21 percent.

Though stronger enforcement increases the incomes of single mothers, even perfect enforcement would leave one-third to one-half of single mothers poor and insecure. Thirty percent of nonresident fathers earn less than $14,000 (Garfinkel, McLanahan, and others, 1998). Child support payments from fathers with low and irregular earnings will be low and irregular at best. To expect more is utopian.

A positive effect on the income of single mothers and even greater father involvement is not inconsistent with negative effects on mother-father relations and children's well-being. There is ample evidence that parental conflict is bad for children and some evidence that strong child support enforcement increases parental conflict. There is also some evidence from a few qualitative studies that unreasonably high child support obligations create undue strains on the relationships between mothers and fathers. Research on whether stronger support enforcement provokes or inhibits domestic violence is sadly lacking. But, though stronger enforcement may have negative unintended consequences, empirical research generally finds positive effects of child support enforcement on average child outcomes (Garfinkel and others, 1998). In short, research indicates that stronger enforcement has benefited both mothers and children.

Has stronger enforcement helped or hurt fathers? Clearly, if it has increased the incomes of mothers, it has reduced the incomes of nonresident fathers. So, how might enforcement help fathers? There are two such avenues. First, rights and responsibilities are the flip side of the same coin. By reinforcing responsibility, child support enforcement strengthens a father's right to be involved in his child's life. Second, assuming greater responsibility for their children, even if at first brought about involuntarily, may be of direct benefit to fathers. Waite (2000) presents persuasive evidence that marriage is good for men's health and well-being. Supporting one's child may well lead to some of the same kinds of benefits. Unfortunately, we have no evidence on the potential beneficial effects of enforcement on fathers.

But, there is ample evidence that stronger child support enforcement has done damage to a large number of fathers, especially those who are poor. A serious problem with the public child support system is that, at its inception, the federal Office of Child Support Enforcement viewed itself exclusively as a law enforcement agency. As a result, fathers have been viewed as lawbreakers rather than clients. Federal and state offices of child support enforcement have come a long way since the early 1980s; they have even cosponsored experiments to help fathers meet their child support obligations (Parents' Fair Share) and to help fathers obtain access to their children. But isolated experiments are not the same as institutional change. It is particularly important for unwed and low-income fathers that child support enforcement become a social welfare as well as a law enforcement agency. These fathers need the most help and suffer most from harsh enforcement.

Only a small proportion of divorced fathers need help meeting their child support obligations. In contrast, a substantial proportion of unwed fathers needs help. Whereas middle-class fathers typically establish visitation rights as part of their divorce agreements, low-income fathers rarely do so. This is because child support orders for low-income fathers are initiated by state agencies whose principal objective is to reduce welfare costs.

Offices of child support enforcement routinely impose much stiffer child support obligations (as a percentage of income) on poor fathers. Low-income fathers are more likely to be ordered to pay amounts that exceed state guidelines than middle- and upper-income fathers. Frequently the child support obligations imposed on low-income fathers are unreasonably high because child support agencies or the courts base their orders not on fathers' actual earnings but on presumptive minimum earnings (for example, full-time, full-year work at the minimum wage) or on how much the father earned in the past. Some fathers are required to pay back the mother's welfare or Medicaid costs. Many fathers who become unemployed or incarcerated build up huge arrearages during these periods of unemployment. Such onerous child support obligations are rarely paid in full, but they do prompt fathers to avoid legitimate work where their wages are easily attached, and they breed resentment on the part of fathers and mothers toward the system and perhaps toward each other. Imprisonment for nonpayment of support exacerbates this negative dynamic. Given what we know about the low earnings capacity of most unwed and virtually all poor fathers, these practices are not likely to be effective and are likely to have unintended negative consequences (Garfinkel and others, 1998a).

Current Policy Issues and Recommendations

Ironically, from a narrow accounting point of view, the federal and state child support enforcement system is a victim of its own success. As child support enforcement became increasingly effective, federal and state savings, as measured by the federal government, increased rapidly, then leveled off, and after 1997 began to decline. In 1998 government savings were about $2.5 billion;

expenditures on enforcement were $3.6 billion. These figures are juxtaposed in the 1999 annual report from the Office of Child Support Enforcement (OCSE) to show that child support enforcement results in a net cost to the federal and state governments of over $1 billion a year. This narrow accounting perspective makes enforcement appear to be a bad financial investment.

Financing Child Support Enforcement

OSCE measures government savings by the amounts of child support paid by nonresident parents of children receiving welfare that are used to offset welfare costs. The increasingly large savings that result from reductions in welfare caseloads due to child support are not counted. This is a case of bad government numbers causing mischief. Our estimates suggest that child support enforcement reduced welfare caseloads in 1996 by 12 to 17 percent. of what they would otherwise have been and thus saved $3 billion to $4 billion. Even if the savings were only half that much, they would be greater than the bogus net cost to government figures published by OCSE. Congress should direct OCSE to cease reporting an indefensible estimate of the financial benefits and costs of child support enforcement and to begin reporting a defensible range of estimates of the financial benefits and costs of child support enforcement.

A better understanding of the true benefits of child support enforcement is especially important now. Because states finance their child support enforcement programs in part from welfare savings arising out of child support collections, the decrease in caseloads threatens state funding and a crisis in child support financing looms. Thus Congress should consider alternative financing mechanisms for child support.

Minimizing Damage from Arrearages

Arrearages owed to the state are increasingly recognized as a problem in child support enforcement. Most of the current discussion focuses on whether states should be allowed to keep arrearages collected for children on welfare or whether they should forward the collections to mothers and children. Under TANF, states must forward to the family collections on arrearages accruing before and after the family is on welfare, with two major exceptions. First, support recouped from federal tax refunds—one-half of all back support collected—is kept by the state. Second, arrearages that accrued before the family was on welfare but that are collected while the family is on welfare are kept by the state. These exceptions vitiate the principle that the family has claim to child support arrearages accrued while not on welfare, and Congress should eliminate them.

An even more fundamental reform would prevent the accrual of unreasonable and unjust arrearages. Nothing would do more to protect the legitimate interests of poor and unwed fathers than to require states to establish child support obligations that are expressed as a flat percentage of the obligor's income. Obligations would automatically go down when the father was unemployed or in jail. And though child support enforcement officials continue to fear that expressing child support obligations as a percentage of the father's income will result in lower payments, the only evidence on the matter suggests that the opposite is true. Bartfeld and Garfinkel (1996) found that percentage child support orders lead to substantially higher, not lower payments. States should also be forbidden from adding repayment of Medicaid costs or welfare to child support obligations. Finally, Congress should require states to revise their guidelines so that the child support obligations imposed on poor and near-poor nonresident fathers can be no higher in percentage terms than those imposed on middle-income nonresident fathers. Routinely imposing more onerous burdens on poor and near-poor men is an ugly practice. Abolishing this practice would be a truly compassionate act.

Treating Cohabitation

One of the most dramatic demographic trends of the 1980s and 1990s is the increase in the proportion of unwed parents who are living together when their child is born. Recent findings from the Fragile Families Study suggest that close to half of all nonmarital births in large cities are to cohabiting couples (Garfinkel and others, forthcoming). How should child support and welfare treat these families?

Welfare and child support need to become father-friendly and family-friendly. If the parents reside together, they should be treated as a family by TANF, and services should be provided to fathers as well as mothers. The services for fathers, like those for mothers in TANF, should be geared primarily toward obtaining employment. If either the mother or father demonstrates the potential to benefit from education and training, TANF should support such programs. Services for both mothers and fathers should also be directed toward educating the parents about their mutual rights and responsibilities, including establishing the paternity of the father.

Aside from establishing paternity, fathers who live with the mother and child should not be required to pay child support. In these cases, a portion of the father's income should be counted in determining welfare eligibility and benefits. But the portion should be well under 100 percent in order to encourage cohabitation.

If the parents live apart, fathers should be required to pay child support, but the amount of the obligation should be proportional to fathers' ability to pay. Paternity establishment and child support enforcement should also help fathers establish their rights to visitation. In short, both child support enforcement and welfare need to provide services to low-income fathers to help them either to make the best possible use of or to upgrade their limited human capital and help them fulfill their other responsibilities and exercise their rights as fathers.

The birth of a child is a very special moment for both parents. Thus establishing the paternity of unwed fathers at the hospital gives the child support enforcement system a unique entrée into the lives of unwed mothers and fathers. Targeting services, such as education and job training, conflict resolution, and drug and alcohol treatment, on fathers soon after the birth of their new baby is also likely to have a greater payoff than offering services to fathers years later, after their relationship with the mother has ended.

Strengthening Bonds in Fragile Families

That public policy should strive to reinforce the bonds between unwed fathers and mothers is not obvious. If a large proportion of either the mothers or the fathers had no interest in, or were hostile to, coparenting their child, attempts to strengthen these fragile family ties might be futile at best and harmful at worst. We know that a high level of parental conflict is harmful to children, and encouraging coparenting by parents who are hostile to each other is likely to increase parental conflict. One of the most important findings from the Fragile Families Study is that the vast majority of unwed parents view themselves as families (Garfinkel, McLanahan, and others, forthcoming) At the time of the child's birth, 83 percent of unwed parents are still in a romantic relationship, nearly 80 percent believe their chances of marriage are good, and over 90 percent of the mothers want the father to be involved in raising the child. These findings suggest that, at a minimum, policies designed to strengthen fragile families are consistent with parents' objectives and therefore not foredoomed to failure.

Similarly, if many unwed fathers were violent toward the mothers, or were drug or alcohol abusers, promoting father involvement might not be in the best interest of mothers and children. Many critics of welfare reform and stronger child support enforcement have argued that these policies are likely to increase domestic violence. Again, early results from the Fragile Families Study indicate that only a small fraction of unwed fathers pose such a threat to the mother and child. Only 12 percent of mothers report that the father has a problem with drugs or alcohol, and only 6 percent report that he is physically abusive. Moreover, some mothers who report that the father is abusive or has a problem with drugs or alcohol are currently in a romantic relationship with the father and want him involved in raising the child. Thus, even in problem cases, there are good reasons for treating unwed parents as a family unit and for trying to shape programs, such as conflict resolution and drug and alcohol treatment, that help them deal with their problems.

In many ways, current welfare and child support policies undermine rather than strengthen fragile family ties. To the extent that welfare policies or practices favor one-parent families over two-parent families, they discourage marriage and cohabitation and push fathers out of the picture. Under the old AFDC program, two-parent families in which the father worked more than 100 hours per month were ineligible for assistance. Many states restricted the eligibility of two-parent families in other ways. More recently, state TANF programs appear to have reduced or eliminated most of these restrictions for two-parent families.

The absence of categorical restrictions, however, is not sufficient to make welfare policy neutral with respect to family formation. Because welfare is income tested and tries to capture the economies of scale that come from living together, it creates an incentive for fathers with earnings and mothers without earnings to live apart (or feign living apart) from one another. Because ascertaining whether a couple lives together is costly and because marriage creates the presumption of cohabitation, welfare encourages cohabitation over marriage. It also encourages living separately over cohabitation.

One way to reduce the disincentives to marriage and cohabitation in welfare policy is to ensure that fathers who live apart from their children pay child support. Child support increases the costs of living separately. Over the past twenty years we have made substantial headway in increasing paternity establishment and child support payments among unwed fathers. Further progress along these lines is desirable. But child support enforcement alone will not be sufficient. Further, as discussed above, if child support obligations are grossly inconsistent with fathers' ability to pay, they may drive fathers away and discourage their involvement.

Another way to reduce the disincentives to marriage and cohabitation in welfare policy is to count only a portion of fathers' earnings when determining eligibility and benefits for TANF (see Horn and Sawhill, chapter 16). The problem with this solution is that it increases welfare costs and caseloads. The time limits and work requirements of the new TANF program, however, limit these extra costs. As suggested above, Congress should require or encourage states to ignore a large proportion—say 50 percent—of fathers' income in determining eligibility for and benefits from TANF.

A third way to encourage marriage among fragile families is to expand policies outside welfare. The Earned Income Tax Credit is a good example of such a policy. A father with earnings of $10,000 and a mother with one child and no earnings stand to gain over $3,000 from the EITC if they live together. On the other hand, the EITC, like the income tax of which it is a part, contains not only marriage bonuses but also marriage penalties.

The incentives in the EITC and child support are more recent, and the former is much less well understood than the disincentives in the welfare system. So part of the problem is knowledge. Welfare, paternity establishment and child support, and other programs need to do a better job of informing unwed parents about the relative benefits and costs of living together and getting married. It would also be helpful, though somewhat costly in terms of revenues lost, to eliminate the marriage penalties in the EITC and, more broadly, the federal income tax.

Creating Financial Incentives for Establishing Paternity and Paying Support

Reducing welfare benefits by one dollar for each dollar of child support paid reduces both mothers' incentive to cooperate with the child support program and fathers' incentive to pay child support. Counting only a portion of support in determining eligibility and benefits would increase cooperation and payments. It would also increase costs, at least in the short run. In the long run, however, if the proportion of fathers paying support increases sufficiently, costs might not even increase. Rather than restoring the old AFDC fifty-dollar set-aside for child support payments, Congress should require or encourage states to ignore a substantial portion—say 50 percent—of child support payments in determining TANF eligibility and payments.

Creating a publicly financed minimum child support benefit that is conditional on being legally entitled to receive private child support will also increase a mother's incentive to cooperate in identifying the father of her child, establishing paternity, and securing a child support award (Garfinkel, 1992). At the same time, a public child support benefit will reduce the poverty and insecurity of single mothers and their children. Finally, a child support benefit will further reduce the dependence of single mothers on TANF.

Minimum benefits are common in social insurance programs. The enforcement features of the American system of assuring child support increasingly resemble social insurance. Adding a minimum benefit to the system is consistent with this evolution.

A publicly assured minimum child support benefit has three costs: an increase in government expenditures; a reduction in incentives for fathers to pay support; and an increase in incentives for living apart. As long as the benefit is conditioned upon legal entitlement to support, the cost of even a very generous minimum benefit is modest: under $5 billion in 1985 (Meyer and others, 1994).

Potentially far more serious is the disincentive to pay support that arises from the guarantee of support. If the public benefit were $300 per month and were reduced by one dollar for each dollar of child support paid, mothers who were owed up to $300 per month would have no incentive to help secure payment from the father and fathers would have no incentive to pay. Although there is no research on how this sort of benefit structure would affect payments, experience with AFDC, even with the $50 set-aside, is not encouraging. But it would be easy to alter the benefit structure to reinforce rather than undermine incentives for payments. For example, a child support assurance program could pay $100 per month to mothers legally entitled to receive child support but not receiving it from the obligor. Child support assurance benefits could increase by $1 for each $1 that the nonresident parent paid, up to $50 per month. For each $1 in excess of $50, the public benefit would be reduced by 50 cents. A child support assurance system with a public benefit structure like this would be even cheaper than the plans costed out by Meyer and his colleagues (1994) and would have all the right incentives for paternity establishment and payment of support.

Unfortunately, there is no way to eliminate the incentive for living apart or pretending to do so that a publicly assured minimum benefit would create. Conditioning part of the benefit on payments by the father reduces but does not eliminate the incentive. This disincentive is a reason for not making the public child support benefit too generous, but it is not a reason for having no public benefit. Targeting benefits on the poor or any other group increases the incentives to belong to the "favored" group. The ill effects of the incentive to live apart must be weighed against the beneficial effects of the incentives to establish paternity and pay support and the increases in the economic security of single mothers and their children.

The 1996 reforms strengthen the dramatic transformation of the federal and state system of assuring child support that has been growing since 1974. Advocates of stronger enforcement hoped that child support would reduce both poverty and welfare dependence by providing a source of income to single mothers outside the welfare system. It is no accident that Senator Russell Long and more recently President Clinton championed both the EITC and child support enforcement. Much has been accomplished, but much remains to be done.

The enforcement system has moved away from local judicial discretion toward the type of state and national administrative regularity that is characteristic of social insurance. This transformation has increased payments dramatically among poor and especially unwed families. Stronger child support enforcement is responsible for a large decline in welfare caseloads and costs and a more modest increase in the incomes of single mothers and their children. The effects on the well-being of children appear, on balance, to be positive. But large numbers of single mothers remain poor, and large numbers of poor fathers are affected adversely.

The reauthorization of PRWORA presents Congress with the opportunity to further strengthen the American system of assuring child support. Congress should build on the solid successes achieved to date by ensuring that low-income mothers and fathers are helped rather than hurt by our child support assurance system, by strengthening the bonds of fragile families, and by creating financial incentives for establishing paternity and paying child support.

COMMENT BY
Robert I. Lerman

The dramatic reduction in the welfare rolls since 1994 is moving public policy toward assisting low-income families outside the cash welfare system. As welfare reforms succeed in drawing millions of single parents from welfare into work, policy can focus on helping low-income families by supplementing their earnings. Child support payments can make an important contribution to this strategy because two-thirds of poor families with children are headed by single parents. For a single mother of two children working thirty-five hours per week at the minimum wage, the addition of a child support payment of $45 per week would raise her family income from 13 percent above the poverty line to 26 percent above the poverty line. Like other non-welfare supplements, child support improves the financial incentives of custodial parents to leave welfare for work. Because child support payments largely offset welfare benefits, they are worth little to families on welfare. But once off welfare, single mothers' incomes should go up a dollar for each dollar paid in child support. With millions of mothers leaving welfare for work, child support is becoming increasingly important.

Certainly, as Irwin Garfinkel explains in his chapter, child support plays many roles in addition to supplementing the incomes of low-income parents outside the cash welfare system. The requirement to pay child support increases equity between custodial and noncustodial parents, reduces the father's incentive to divorce or to parent children outside marriage, and limits the shift of childrearing costs from noncustodial parents to taxpayers. Establishing legal paternity gives children certainty about the identity of their biological fathers and imposes responsibilities on and conveys rights to unwed fathers.

Garfinkel argues that the expansion of the child support system contributed to achieving these goals, but with some negative side effects. Costs are inevitable because of competing objectives. First, if custodial parents received every dollar of child support paid by the noncustodial parent, it would generally increase equity between parents but would do nothing to reduce taxpayer burdens. Second, trying to make sure that all noncustodial parents pay their fair share will typically result in imposing unfair burdens on some. Often, it is hard to know what is fair. How do we distinguish between voluntary and involuntary unemployment, between having a decline in earnings capacity and choosing an easier, lower-wage job to escape formal payments? Although to me, requiring unemployed or incarcerated noncustodial parents to make child support payments is clearly unfair, not all judges agree.

A significant cost, one downplayed by Garfinkel, is the amount of resources used up in administering the child support system. Administrative resources include the federal and state child support offices as well as courts, prosecutors, and jails allocated to the child support systems. In 1998 federal and state direct administrative costs (and excluding some indirect costs) reached $3.6 billion, or about 25 percent of total collections going through the system. Since some of the $14.3 billion paid through the Office of Child Support Enforcement would have been paid anyway, the country is in effect using up $1 of real resources in order to transfer less than $4 from noncustodial parents to custodial parents and to taxpayers.

Garfinkel's chapter yields information relevant to judging whether these costs are worthwhile. First, did expanded support enforcement actually lead to higher payments? Census data reveal little progress; between 1981 and 1995 the percent of custodial mothers receiving at least some payment rose only modestly, as did the real value of payments per custodial mother. Although Garfinkel blames the lack of progress on the increasingly difficult mix of cases (more never-married and fewer divorced mothers), I find that even with no change in the marital status distribution, the 1995 share receiving a payment would have increased by less than 2 percentage points, from 37.4 percent to 39 percent. Still, recent advances in paternity establishment and in administrative reports about collections suggest the child support program is making significant progress.

Second, how do support payments affect the living standards of recipients as well as donors? For the low-income population, Garfinkel sees clear gains for recipients but is pessimistic about the effects on many noncustodial fathers. He projects that improved child support enforcement may have accounted for 25 percent of the decline in welfare rolls. On the other hand, he argues that losses imposed on fathers, especially low-income fathers, at least partly offset the benefits for mothers. He also argues that many fathers have found themselves facing unfair and unrealistic obligations, driving some into the underground economy and leaving them deeply resentful of the child support system. Unfortunately, there is little empirical evidence about the size of these effects on fathers.

Although administrative costs are high and transfer effects mixed though broadly positive, the child support system is apparently exerting significant, desirable behavioral effects. Garfinkel cites studies showing that enhanced child support enforcement reduces marital disruption and nonmarital child-bearing. If the impacts on nonmarital births are robust, the recent dramatic increases in paternity establishment may help the country reap the benefits of reduced nonmarital childbearing for several years to come.

Third, a serious and effective child support system sends a strong moral signal that all parents remain financially responsible for their children even if they never or no longer live with them. Garfinkel does not mention these points in this chapter, though he has often made them forcefully in other venues.

What do all these findings imply for policy? Garfinkel's modest proposals include changing government estimates of the net public benefits of the child support system, ensuring that arrearages accrued on behalf of mothers when they are not on welfare go entirely to the mothers and not to government, preventing the accrual of unjust arrearages, and treating all cohabiting parents as a family for purposes of obtaining cash welfare and gaining access to services. More controversial are recommendations to allow custodial parents on welfare to keep more child support and to assure a minimum child support benefit to all single parents legally due a private support payment.

Although changes in accounting rules make sense, the appropriate questions are not whether the country needs a child support enforcement system but at what level and how to make the system more efficient. What are the benefits of spending an additional $200 million or the costs of reducing spending by $200 million? How best can we use administrative incentives to achieve paternity and collection goals at reasonable costs? Regarding arrearages, Garfinkel is right that states should not claim any payments accrued when the custodial parent was not on welfare. However, what Garfinkel defines as an unjust arrearage is open to question. His argument for limiting obligations to a fixed percentage of actual income has merit, but so does the concern about fathers abusing the system by working in the underground economy or by choosing not to work. One policy not mentioned by Garfinkel would make the system fairer by offering counseling and legal assistance to expand the access of noncustodial parents to visits with their children. Currently, custodial parents receive considerable legal assistance in obtaining support payments, but noncustodial parents have to finance the full legal costs of ensuring their access and visitation rights.

Including cohabiting fathers in the Temporary Assistance for Needy Families (TANF) family unit, another Garfinkel recommendation, was already the legal definition for families receiving Aid to Families with Dependent Children–Unemployed Parent and is still the approach used in the TANF. The real problems are, first, determining when the father is actually in the household (especially when counting his income is likely to cost the family more than the family gains from having an extra person in the unit); and, second, adopting procedures to count the income of cohabiting fathers but not the income of other cohabiting men (which creates perverse incentives). Garfinkel is certainly correct that fathers living with their children should not be required to pay child support, but the fluid living arrangements in many low-income households make benefit calculations difficult. To me, the key to improving incentives for parents to marry and live together is changing benefit structures outside welfare, including the EITC.

Garfinkel's proposal to provide fathers with training, counseling, and drug or alcohol treatment services soon after a nonmarital birth is an excellent idea. At this point, when most unwed parents are still in a romantic relationship and half of fathers are living with their children, fathers are likely to have the highest motivation and the fewest disincentives to succeed. Disappointments about past efforts to raise the earnings of unwed fathers should not discourage us from trying again at this more propitious moment.

Finally, the minimum assured benefit—especially the one sensibly tweaked by Garfinkel to minimize the disincentives of fathers to pay support—deserves another look. We should link the benefit's financing to the state's inability to collect support. States that are more efficient at collecting benefits will pay lower assured benefits. Moreover, paying assured benefits when they fail to collect even a modest amount would encourage states to continue vigorous enforcement policies even after mothers leave welfare. Overall, Garfinkel presents a good case for continuing the federal and state role in enforcing parental financial obligations while doing more to incorporate the needs of noncustodial parents.

References

Bartfeld, Judi, and Irwin Garfinkel. 1996. "The Impact of Percentage-Expressed Child Support Orders on Payments." *Journal of Human Resources* 31 (4): 794–815.

Garfinkel, Irwin. 1992. *Assuring Child Support: An Extension of the Social Security System.* Russell Sage.

Garfinkel, Irwin, Theresa Heintze, and Chien-Chung Huang. 2000. "Child Support Enforcement: Incentives and Well-Being." Paper presented at the Conference on Incentive Effects of Tax and Transfer Policies, Washington, December 8.

Garfinkel, Irwin, Sara McLanahan, Jeanne Brooks-Gunn, and Marta Tienda, eds. Forthcoming. "Fragile Families and Welfare Reform." *Children and Youth Services Review.*

Garfinkel, Irwin, Sara McLanahan, Daniel Meyer, and Judith A. Seltzer, eds. 1998. *Fathers under Fire: The Revolution in Child Support Enforcement.* Russell Sage.

Garfinkel, Irwin, Cynthia Miller, Sara McLanahan, and Thomas Hanson. 1998. "Deadbeat Dads or Inept States?" *Evaluation Review* 22 (6): 717–50.

Hanson, Thomas, Irwin Garfinkel, Sara McLanahan, and Cynthia Miller. 1996. "Trends in Child Support Outcomes." *Demography* 33 (4): 483–96.

Huang, Chien-Chung, Irwin Garfinkel, and Jane Waldfogel. 2000. "Child Support and Welfare Caseloads." Unpublished paper. Columbia University.

Legler, Paul. 1996. "The Coming Revolution in Child Support Policy: Implications of the 1996 Welfare Act." *Family Law Quarterly* 30 (3): 519–63.

Lerman, Robert, and Elaine Sorensen. 2000. *Child Support: Interactions Between Private and Public Transfers.* Paper presented at the Conference on Means-Tested Transfer Programs in the United States, National Bureau of Economic Research, Boston, Mass., May 11.

Mead, Lawrence M. 1999. "The Decline of Welfare in Wisconsin." *Journal of Public Administration Research and Theory* 9 (4): 597–622.

———. 2000. "Caseload Change: An Exploratory Study." *Journal of Policy Analysis and Management* 19 (3): 465–72.

Meyer, Daniel, Irwin Garfinkel, Donald Oellerich, and Philip Robins. 1994. "Who Should Be Eligible for an Assured Child Support Benefit?" In *Child Support and Child Well-Being*, edited by Irwin Garfinkel, Sara S. McLanahan, and Philip K. Robins. Washington: Urban Institute.

Oellerich, Donald T., Irwin Garfinkel, and Philip K. Robins. 1991. "Private Child Support: Current and Potential Impacts." *Journal of Sociology and Social Welfare* 18 (1): 3–23.

U.S. Department of Health and Human Services (HHS), Office of Child Support Enforcement. 1999. *Child Support Enforcement: Twenty-third Annual Report to Congress.*

Waite, Linda J. 2000. "The Family as a Social Organization: Key Ideas for the 21st Century." *Contemporary Sociology* 29 (3): 463–69.

18

DOUGLAS J. BESHAROV
WITH NAZANIN SAMARI

Child Care after Welfare Reform

A KEY OBJECTIVE OF WELFARE REFORM is to move recipients, usually single mothers, into paid employment. For these mothers to go to work, someone must care for their children when the children are too young for school or when school is not in session. Hence providing (or subsidizing) child care has been integral to welfare reform at least since the Kennedy administration. It was certainly a major part of the debate leading up to the passage of welfare reform in 1996.

In this paper we were asked to address three questions: Is child care funding sufficient for the demands of welfare reform? Have states successfully expanded child care programs under welfare reform? What changes, if any, should be made to the child care provisions of federal law when the welfare law is reauthorized in 2002?

Funding

Is child care funding sufficient for the demands of welfare reform? Even though the 1996 welfare reform law considerably consolidated child care funding streams (Besharov, 1996), they are still numerous and complicated. Thus to develop a reasonably accurate estimate of how much money is available (and spent) for child care, one must combine often ambiguous information from many different programs. Even then it is still difficult to determine

461

the sufficiency of child care funding because there is no objective measure of "need."

Spending Increased about 60 Percent

The 1996 welfare law created the Child Care and Development Fund (CCDF), by repealing the legislative authority for three child care programs with differing program rules and combining their funds with additional funds to create the new CCDF block grant.

FEDERAL FUNDING STREAMS. States may use CCDF funds to aid families with incomes up to 85 percent of the state median income for families of the same size as the applicant family. The mother (the father, too, if it is a two-parent family) must be either working or in an employment and training activity, and the child must generally be under age 13. CCDF funds may also be used to subsidize care for children at risk of abuse or neglect or who need child care as a protective service.

The CCDF contains three separate federal funding streams, which, in 1999, were a base allocation of $1.2 billion in entitlement funds for which no state matching is required; an additional $1 billion in entitlement matching funds, available to states that meet a maintenance of effort (MOE) requirement, which is based on their 1994 or 1995 spending level (whichever is higher); and a discretionary fund of about $1 billion (U.S. House, 2000). In 1999, CCDF federal and state spending, not counting transfers from the Temporary Assistance for Needy Families (TANF) program, was $4.6 billion. States must spend at least 4 percent of their CCDF funds to improve the quality and availability of child care, but no more than 5 percent for administrative activities.

States can also use unspent welfare funds for child care. Recognizing that as welfare caseloads fell the need for child care would grow, the welfare law gives states two ways of using unspent TANF funds to pay for child care. They can either transfer up to 30 percent of their TANF block grant to the CCDF or use TANF funds directly to pay for child care. Most states do the former; many do both. In 1999 states transferred $2.4 billion in federal funds from TANF to the CCDF, with $1.7 billion actually spent that year. Direct state spending through TANF totaled an additional $1.1 billion. Thus total TANF spending on child care (through transfers and directly) amounted to about $2.8 billion in 1999 (HHS, 2000; Falk, 2001; and GAO, 2001).

The Social Services Block Grant (SSBG) provides funding to states for a variety of social services, including child care. In 1997 the Children's Defense

Fund estimated that states spent 20 percent of the SSBG on child care (Children's Defense Fund, 1997). If states had continued to spend this portion of their grant on child care, 1999 spending would have been $380 million.

Often overlooked in discussions of child care funding is the Child and Adult Care Food Program (CACFP), which provides meals and snacks to children in child care. The CACFP is an entitlement that goes to licensed child care centers and family or group day care homes serving both low- and middle-income children. In 1999, CACFP subsidized meals for 2.6 million children at a cost of $1.6 billion.

Head Start should also be included in this list because it provides the equivalent of child care services as well as educational and social services for children in families below the poverty line. In 1994, Head Start served about 740,000 children (mostly 3- and 4-year-olds) at a total cost of $3.7 billion, which was almost 43 percent of total federal expenditures on child care. In 1999, Head Start served 831,000 children at a total cost of $4.7 billion, almost one-third of federal child care expenditures (Head Start Bureau, 2000). Most Head Start programs, however, are only part day and part year, so they need to be supplemented if they are used to care for children whose mothers work full time (GAO, 1999a).

FUNDING AMOUNTS. Piecing together an unduplicated total of child care spending is no simple task. Because the welfare caseload began to decline in 1994, it seems appropriate to focus on the increase in spending between 1994 and 1999. During that period, combined federal and related state funding rose by 60 percent, from $8.9 billion to $14.1 billion (both in 1999 dollars) (see table 18-1). But not all of this money was for expanded services; some was designated for "quality" improvements. In 1999, $323 million in CCDF funds and $148 million in Head Start funds were used for quality improvements. These amounts are excluded from the following analysis, leaving $13.6 billion, or an increase of $4.7 billion from 1994, available for direct child care services.

Ample Funding for "Current" Patterns

Was this additional $4.7 billion sufficient to meet the demands of welfare reform? Yes, and more so—but only if the measure is whether funding was sufficient to reflect long-standing patterns of paid and unpaid care within those increases in the labor force participation of low-income mothers. In fact, according to that measurement, most states seem to be providing child care to all CCDF-eligible families with incomes below the poverty line who seek aid.

Table 18-1. *Federal and Related State Child Care Spending in 1994 and 1999*
Millions of 1999 dollars

Program	1994	1999
Head Start	3,738	4,660
Child Care and Development Fund	3,021	4,600
Child and Adult Care Food Program	1,517	1,625
Social Services Block Grant	627	380
TANF transfers[a]	. . .	1,700
TANF spending[a]	. . .	1,139
Total	8,903	14,104

Source: Authors' calculations based on Head Start Bureau (2000); U.S. Department of HHS (2000); Falk (2001); U.S. GAO (2001); U.S. Department of Agriculture, fax received from the Food and Nutrition Service, April 18, 2001; U.S. Office of Management and Budget, *Budget of the United States, Fiscal Year 2000*, Historical Tables (GPO); and Children's Defense Fund (1997).
a. TANF = Temporary Assistance for Needy Families.

Between 1994 and 1999 the national welfare rolls declined by 54 percent. At first glance, this sharp drop in welfare recipiency, involving about 2.7 million families and 4.4 million children, suggests that there must have been a big increase in the need for child care.

LOW TAKE-UP RATES? Surveys of the families that have left welfare, called "leaver studies," indicate that as many as 80 percent do not receive child care subsidies when they leave welfare (Schumacher and Greenberg, 1999). For example, in a review of four leaver studies with representative samples of leavers and sufficient information about child care use, the U.S. General Accounting Office (GAO, 1999b) reported that 17 to 27 percent of all leavers received a child care subsidy at the time of the survey. (Although the caseload may have declined in part because there were fewer entrants, the data to assess these numbers and the reasons for nonentry are not available. Thus we rely on the leaver studies as a proxy for assessing what is happening as a result of the broader caseload decline.)

And yet most observers, including the GAO and even the Children's Defense Fund, have concluded that the child care needs of welfare reform have been accommodated. For example, a 1999 GAO (1999a) report concludes that, in the post-welfare reform period, although low-income parents still face difficulties finding care for infants, for children with special needs, and during nonstandard work hours, "care for preschool children generally was not difficult to find" (p. 11). Thus in testifying before the House Committee on Ways and Means Subcommittee on Human Resources in 1999,

Helen Blank of the Children's Defense Fund said: "New federal child care funds have enabled most states, at least temporarily, to meet the increased child care needs of families on welfare generated by the initial stages of the implementation of the new welfare law. They have also allowed a number of states to help more nonwelfare, low-income working parents with their child care expenses" (p. 2).

EXPLANATIONS. How is it possible for only 20 percent of former welfare mothers to be receiving child care benefits (GAO, 1999b) and yet, in Blank's words, for the states also to be meeting "the increased child care needs of families on welfare"? It turns out that many women who left welfare did not actually "need" child care assistance in order to leave the rolls. We rush to emphasize that this does not mean that child care assistance would not have been financially beneficial to many welfare leavers, just that many did without it. There are several reasons why so many families that left welfare were able to go without child care.

First, many of the mothers who have left welfare are not working. These mothers seem to be relying on other family or household members or other sources of government support such as disability payments (Besharov and Germanis, 2000). The leaver studies and other research suggest that only about 60 percent of welfare leavers are working, and that only 75 percent of them (45 percent of all leavers) are working full time (Isaacs and Lyon, 2000; Schumacher and Greenberg, 1999). In light of these work rates, real world take up rates are substantially higher, as much as two-thirds higher. For example, in its review of leaver studies the GAO found that the take-up rate for employed mothers who left welfare ranged from 27 percent to 38 percent (GAO, 1999b).

Second, many of the children whose mothers had left welfare were already in care. For example, in 1994, even before recent declines in welfare caseloads, about 45 percent of poor 4-year-olds (and 21 percent of poor 3-year-olds) were already in Head Start. Over half of these children were on welfare (in 1999 the figure was about 30 percent).

Third, some of the leaver mothers who work have incomes above the eligibility limits or that require co-payments large enough to make it seem not worthwhile to seek child care assistance. According to the leaver studies, we estimate that about 30 percent of leavers have family incomes above the poverty line, where co-payments begin in earnest, and about 10 percent of leavers have family incomes that make them ineligible for aid.

Fourth, of the leaver mothers who work, many have school-age children who do not need care, or at least not enough hours of care for them to go to the trouble of seeking a government subsidy. Using administrative data from the U.S. Department of Health and Human Services, we estimate that 45 percent of the children who left welfare were between the ages of 6 and 18. Although the regular school day may not permit a parent to work full time without having a child care arrangement as well, many children are involved in after-school activities, such as sports or clubs, reducing the need for such supplemental arrangements.

Summing up, we can perform the following rough calculation: Starting with the children of all leavers, subtract those with mothers apparently not working (40 percent, leaving 60 percent of the total); then subtract those whose family incomes make them ineligible (10 percent, leaving 54 percent of the total); and then subtract those age 13 and older, who are not age-eligible (8 percent, leaving 50 percent of the total). Of the remainder who are theoretically eligible for aid, 32 percent (16 percent of all leavers) are pre-school children with full-time working mothers who, presumably, need full-time child care; 42 percent (21 percent of all leavers) are children in Head Start or school with full-time working mothers and thus do not need full-time child care; 12 percent (6 percent of all leavers) are preschool children with part-time working mothers who, presumably, need only part-time child care; and 14 percent (7 percent of all leavers) are children in Head Start, kindergarten, or school with part-time working mothers and thus probably do not need child care. By our calculation, then, the percentage of all children of leavers who need full-time care is roughly 16 percent, which is less than the percentage of families reported in leaver studies to be receiving child care subsidies (between 17 and 28 percent, according to the GAO, 1999b).

However, if one adds to that figure the children who need part-time care, a somewhat different story emerges. By our calculation, 27 percent would require part-time care. That would mean that 43 percent of all leaver children are theoretically eligible for full- or part-time child care assistance (16 percent plus 27 percent). If we assume that the leaver figures are accurate, then not all leaver children eligible for aid receive it (28 percent as the upward bound in the studies who receive subsidies vs. 43 percent by our calculation of those who are eligible and need care).

Moreover, we hypothesize that the difference between take-up rates and estimated need is caused by the fact that, although most leaver children requiring full-time care receive it, many (if not most) leaver children needing part-time care do not. Instead, we further hypothesize that somewhat higher-income families needing full-time care are being given priority over leaver families needing only part-time child care. A number of state policies formalize this priority, and at least one multistate survey found informal policies to the same effect. (Rules limiting assistance for "in-home" care are another barrier to child care assistance, again one that falls most heavily on families that need only part-time child care.)

Implementation

Have states successfully expanded child care programs under welfare reform? Again, the answer is yes, largely because of the widespread use of child care vouchers. Vouchers have made it easier for low-income parents to use the excess capacity of providers while lowering the barriers of entry into the market for subsidized care for the full range of formal and informal providers. However, state and federal polices place substantial barriers in the way of receiving assistance for part-time care and for care in the family home.

Expansion of Supply

Between 1994 and 1999, about 1.2 million children were added to child care subsidy programs. This expansion, most observers agree, was accomplished with relative smoothness. The major credit seems to go to the widespread use of child care "certificates," which are the equivalent of vouchers (Besharov and Samari, 2000).

TAPPING EXCESS CAPACITY. At least until recent expansions, the child care market had a high level of excess supply, especially for home-based providers (Kisker and others, 1991). Vouchers allowed parents to go directly to providers that had vacancies or that could expand to meet the increased demand, thus avoiding a cumbersome, slow-moving contract and grant-making process. Vouchers also opened the doors to an array of licensed centers and family day care homes by reducing the paperwork and other administrative tasks related to serving subsidized clients. The director of a center in Boston noted that contracts with the state (to purchase slots) required the completion of more than fifty pages of forms each year. Establishing eligibility to serve clients with vouchers, on the other hand, required only the completion of a five-page form.

NEW PROVIDERS. Vouchers also lowered the already low barriers to entry into the child care market. They permitted government funds to flow to unlicensed providers, for whom entry into the child care market requires little more than finding customers. Most states do not require these providers to complete training or make many adjustments to their homes. Even health and safety requirements seem relaxed in operation, if not as a matter of policy.

Vouchers have also made it easier for new center-based providers to enter the market—by giving them the opportunity to attract customers without having to get a large government grant or contract. Providers can start small, with minimal start-up costs, and grow as their business expands. One provider in Milwaukee, who now owns three child care centers, opened her first day care home with a $4,000 personal investment (Besharov and Samari, 1999).

ACCESS TO MORE PROVIDERS. Voucher systems have increased parental choice by allowing government funds to go to all types of providers. First, as mentioned above, vouchers allow parents to use relatives and other unlicensed providers, who can be much more flexible in the hours and form of care they provide. Second, they allow parents to use centers and other providers that previously had served only the more affluent.

Incentives for Low-Quality Care?

The choice that vouchers give parents is constrained by reimbursement and co-payment rules. A major question is whether these rules distort parental decisionmaking by creating incentives for them to use low-quality care or by discouraging them from claiming a subsidy altogether.

REIMBURSEMENT SCHEDULES. Before the 1996 reforms, federal law required states to offer reimbursement rates based on the 75th percentile of local market rates. But because of varying local conditions, this national standard was too high in some communities, and, perhaps, too low in others. In 1996, the Personal Responsibility and Work Opportunity Reconciliation Act (PRWORA) dropped this requirement for the CCDF; it now requires that "payment rates for which assistance is provided must be . . . sufficient to ensure equal access for eligible children to comparable child care services in the State or substate area that are provided to children whose parents are not eligible to receive assistance." (HHS regulations now call the 75th percentile a "benchmark.")

Although about thirty states still base their rates on the 75th percentile (see Gabe, Lyke, and Spar, 1999), many used their new freedom to set lower (or higher) rates. For example, Massachusetts sets reimbursement rates based on the 55th percentile of local market rates, and California reimburses up to the 93d percentile. Some child care experts argue that even the 75th percentile is too low, that it drives many parents to use lower-cost and, hence, lower-quality care. There appears to be a fallacy in such reasoning: Why should government subsidies equal the most expensive care in the community, when most members of the middle class do not use such care because of its cost? The better measure is whether reimbursement rates are set at a reasonably high percentage of what middle-class or more financially comfortable families pay.

But some states do set reimbursement rates lower, sometimes, as with Massachusetts, at least as low as the 55th percentile of local market rates. Depending on the distribution of cost and quality among providers in the same category of care, a very low reimbursement rate could lead some parents to choose inadequate care, but there is no systematic evidence that this is happening.

CO-PAYMENTS AND SLIDING SCALES. A major purpose of co-payments is fairness: Families that can afford to pay for a larger share of child care costs should do so. Thus, and in keeping with the CCDF requirement, most if not all states take family income into account in setting co-payments. Co-payments are generally not required from families below the poverty line, and often quite modest ones are required for families immediately above the line.

As with reimbursement schedules, states must be careful not to set co-payment rates too high, lest they discourage the use of the child care subsidy or encourage the use of inadequate child care; they also must not set it too low, lest they fail to reflect the ability to pay or have no effect on parental decisionmaking. Careful research in other fields establishes that co-payments can do both.

NO APPARENT IMPACT ON USAGE PATTERNS. In theory, therefore, low reimbursement rates and high co-payments might lead low-income parents to use low-cost providers, that is, to use home-based, often unlicensed care instead of center care. The available evidence, however, does not support these fears. Long-standing patterns of child care use have apparently not changed under vouchers and welfare reform.

For example, in 1998 and 1999, Bruce Fuller and Sharon Lynn Kagan (2000) examined the child care experiences of 948 randomly selected single mothers and their children who had recently entered welfare reform programs in California, Connecticut, and Florida. The researchers interviewed the mothers, observed their children's child care environments, and evaluated their children's cognitive and social development.

Fuller and Kagan concluded that "the welfare-to-work push on single mothers is placing a growing number of children in mediocre and disorganized child care settings" (p. 4). But, in fact, according to Fuller and Kagan's own data, the children of "welfare reform" were placed in center-based, family day care, and relative-provided care at about the same rate as all other American children, regardless of income. Moreover, they were more likely than other low-income children to be in licensed centers. Specifically, 34 percent of the children were in center-based care, a figure significantly higher than the national figure for low-income families. The Census Bureau estimates that nationally, 22 percent of preschoolers in care with family incomes below the federal poverty line are in center-based care, and 30 percent of preschoolers in care with family incomes above the federal poverty line are in center-based care (U.S. Census Bureau, 1997, table 6). Figures for family day care and relative-provided care were about the same regardless of income.

These findings are echoed by research conducted by Stefanie Schmidt, Freya Sonenstein, and Jeffrey Capizzano (1999). Using data from the Urban Institute's National Survey of America's Families (NSAF), they showed that in 1997 "the child care arrangements of current welfare recipients, former welfare recipients, and high-income children [did] not differ significantly" (p. 10). The researchers further noted that the proportion of children in each type of care had not changed significantly over time. A comparison of Census Bureau data from 1994 and the 1997 NSAF data reveals similar patterns of use for working mothers with children under 6 years of age. The Urban Institute researchers also noted that "the use of family day care homes or relative/babysitter care does not differ significantly by welfare status and income. While there has been much discussion in the child care policy arena about welfare recipients depending heavily on relatives to care for their children, our results indicate that this group [is] no more likely to use this form of care than other groups" (p. 10).

These studies have some weaknesses, but they suggest strongly that most parents have not turned to informal care in the wake of welfare reform. How should one interpret this lack of change in child care patterns? We believe that it suggests that current child care subsidies are not large enough to shift underlying parental preferences. Parents prefer center-based care for old preschoolers because of its presumed cognitive and social advantages. They prefer family-based care for younger children because they value the warmth of individual care for infants and toddlers. And they rely on family-based or in-home care for part-time care because of its flexibility and convenience. In this context, and in light of the next section, we conclude that child care subsidies are, in essence, a form of financial support for low-income families.

Barriers to Assistance for Part-time and In-home Care

In general, most eligible leaver families seem to have access to the process of obtaining child care aid. There are some reports that mothers do not know that they are eligible for benefits (Schumacher and Greenberg, 1999), or that some caseworkers discourage them from seeking benefits, but these seem to be fairly limited—unless the issue is part-time care or in-home care. To be blunt, it appears that many of the families leaving welfare that use part-time or informal/in-home care are not receiving assistance, while families with somewhat higher incomes are receiving assistance for full-time care.

PART-TIME CARE. Many mothers who have left welfare only need assistance for part-time care. As described above, many of their children are already in school, Head Start, or some other similar program that provides the equivalent of child care. Moreover, using data in the leaver studies, we estimated that 25 percent of employed leavers work part-time (about 15 percent of all leavers) and thus need only part-time care. However, current federal and state child care policies make it difficult—and often not worthwhile—for low-income parents to obtain assistance for part-time care.

An indeterminate number of states have formal or informal policies against providing aid to mothers working part-time. In Pennsylvania, for example, published rules require that parents work at least twenty-five hours a week in order to receive a child care subsidy. This means that families with a full-time earner receive preferential treatment. A Pennsylvania mother with two children, ages 4 and 5, working full time at $10 an hour ($20,000 per year) would be eligible for a child care subsidy. By contrast, a mother with two younger children, a newborn and a child age 1, who prefers working only twenty hours a week so she can spend time with her very young children and who earns only $8 an hour ($8,000 per year), would be ineligible for child care assistance. This bias exists, even though her actual child care expenses might be the same as those of the mother working full time, because child care costs are higher for infants and the discount for part-time care may be limited.

The assumption behind these state policies seems to be that mothers can make informal and less expensive arrangements for part-time care. From the political right, one also sees a tendency to believe that poor mothers should work full time; and from child care advocates, one senses a desire to encourage licensed care. But whatever the intention, the result is the same: Financial need is not the sole basis for deciding who gets assistance, and some families with higher income get benefits while families with lower incomes do not.

In addition, many states have imposed co-payment requirements that do not distinguish between full- and part-time care (and do not even consider the number of children in care), so that the co-payment can be prohibitively high for the amount of care needed. For example, in many states the co-payment for a family with an annual income of $20,000 is about 10 percent, or $2,000 per year. The average cost of full-time family day care for a 4-year-old in full-time care is about $4,000, but only about $2,400 if the care is part-time. In the case of a two-parent family in which the mother works part-time, the amount of the co-payment approaches the cost of family day care and probably exceeds what a relative would be paid. John Pawasarat and Lois M. Quinn (1998) of the University of Wisconsin–Milwaukee Employment and Training Institute, noted this effect in Wisconsin: "Child care payment schedules are tied to family income rather than cost of care. These schedules tend to subsidize high cost, high volume child care use where the co-payment can be ignored and penalize low-cost use for parents employed part-time or with school-age children" (p. 3). In addition, the requirement that eligibility be regularly redetermined, although reasonable, may discourage parents from seeking assistance, especially for small amounts of aid.

IN-HOME CARE. Many of the mothers who have left welfare, like American mothers in general, tend to prefer informal or home-based care, especially for very young children and part-time care. In 1994 about 56 percent of poor preschoolers with employed mothers were in care in their own home (36 percent) or in family day care (20 percent), which is about the same as the 62 percent of preschoolers with employed mothers with annualized incomes above $36,000 (32 percent and 30 percent, respectively), and even about the same as the 58 percent of preschoolers with employed mothers with annualized income above $54,000 (31 percent and 27 percent, respectively).

However, current federal and state child care policies make it difficult, and often not worthwhile, for low-income parents to obtain financial assistance for informal or home-based care, especially if it is part-time. The barriers to obtaining aid for part-time care were described earlier. In addition, many states have imposed prohibitions or limitations on paying family or household members, including subjecting them to the minimum wage and other requirements of the Fair Labor Standards Act; and background check requirements, even for close family members, discourage informal providers from agreeing to accept vouchers. Some informal providers simply do not want any involvement with the government, especially if it means that they have to pay income taxes.

This issue of in-home care is particularly significant. The U.S. Department of Labor has classified in-home child care providers as domestic service workers subject to the Fair Labor Standards Act. Consequently, the U.S. Department of Health and Human Services has advised state child care agencies that in-home providers are covered by the minimum-wage and tax laws.

However, HHS has not provided much guidance on how these rules affect subsidized in-home care and instead says that states have "considerable latitude" in implementing this type of care. But that does not settle the legal issue. As a result, some states appear to ignore the issue, and others require parents who use in-home care to pay the difference between the subsidy rate and the minimum wage (an effective increase in the parental co-payment).

FORMAL AND INFORMAL RATIONING. In many states, the income limits for child care benefits were established far above the incomes of most welfare leavers and without regard to the funds available; that is, more families are eligible than there are funds for them. At the extreme, four states set their income limits at the maximum allowed under CCDF (85 percent of state median income), but they actually provide aid to no more than 9 to 15 percent of eligible children. Most states have set their income limits below the maximum allowed under federal law, as low as 43 percent of state median income, but even under these lower income limits no state serves more than about 30 percent of eligible children, with most serving far less. Rationing, either formal or informal, is the inevitable result.

One way of rationing is to support full-time care rather than part-time care. Another important form of rationing is the widespread use of waiting lists. When income-eligibility levels are higher than the available funding, agencies create waiting lists with internal priorities in an attempt to ensure that they serve the most needy. A common approach is to guarantee benefits to welfare leavers (as long as they are not earning above income limits) and to put other families on a waiting list until it is clear there is enough money to cover them. Apparently, the waiting lists are worked through on a first-come, first-served basis regardless of income, as long as income does not exceed the state eligibility limit. As a result, many families with higher incomes are served before those with lower incomes.

Last, agencies ration child care benefits by not telling eligible families about them. Researchers at the National Center for Children in Poverty and Abt Associates have found that some agencies minimize their outreach efforts "because state and local staff feared that it would create a demand they could not meet" (see Collins and others, 2000, p. 47).

States have apparently not felt the need to address these inequities, probably because the organized community of child care advocates has been eager to create conditions favoring the continued expansion of coverage and use of licensed care. The states have also been discouraged from doing so by uncertainty about current policies and funding levels. As we saw, unspent TANF funds, either transferred to the CCDF or spent directly, account for about 38 percent of what would have otherwise been CCDF expenditures. Because TANF funds are viewed as likely to be only a temporary source of support for child care, states have been reluctant to start the arduous and politically controversial process of developing more elaborate priority systems.

Resolving questions about the future shape and funding levels of both the CCDF and TANF would encourage states and localities to engage in the kind of long-term planning that is needed. Helpful would be a small change that lengthens the accounting period for spending child care funds. One reason that states are so careful about child care spending is that dealing with surpluses and shortfalls at the end of the year can be administratively cumbersome and politically embarrassing. If states had greater flexibility to "bank" funds from one year to the next because they underspent—or to borrow from the next year because they overspent—they might be more willing to give lower-income families the kind of priority now accorded to welfare leavers.

In addition, there appear to be real barriers to some families eligible for subsidies, especially for part-time and in-home care that are caused by restrictive reimbursement and co-payment rules (especially regarding care by other family members), the way waiting lists are administered, the apparent unwillingness of some providers and parents to subject themselves to government scrutiny such as background checks and tax audits, and caseworker and client confusion generally. At the same time, it appears that there has been a partial monetization (providing payments for care that was previously free) of family-provided child care—with some evidence of informal "rebates" to parents. Most states have not addressed these issues with sufficient intensity, largely because of uncertainty about the amount and nature of future federal funding for child care. Depending on how these issues are resolved, they could greatly increase child care expenditures without a corresponding increase in child care slots.

Recommendations

What changes, if any, should be made to the child care provisions of federal law when the welfare law is reauthorized? The following recommendations are made within the context of child care being a predominantly state program, for which there should be a minimum of federal micro management.

Data

Data about child care patterns and spending should be more comprehensive, more reliable, and more timely. The data currently available are not sufficient to understand patterns of child care usage and to identify gaps in coverage. Better data are needed, for example, on the income and demographics of recipients, the nature and hours of care, the hours of work, and parental co-payments.

Funding Streams

Funding streams should be less categorical and less rigid, and there should be a more stable source of key child care funding than unspent welfare funds. To facilitate longer-term policy planning (and budgeting), statutory provisions should be updated to reflect the sharp decline in welfare caseloads and the correspondingly large increases in child care spending. Greater efforts are also needed to coordinate Head Start with the broader world of child care so that it is relevant to working mothers—and to welfare reform.

Barriers to Usage

State and federal policies should not create unnecessary barriers to the use of child care subsidies for part-time care and for care by home-based providers, especially family and household members. Current policies concerning eligible providers, minimum-wage payments for care in the family home, and co-payment requirements serve as barriers to subsidies for part-time care and care by home-based providers, especially family and household members. A good place to start would be to make sure that the Fair Labor Standards Act is not applied to close relatives who provide child care

Income Eligibility

The current federal income limit for receiving child care benefits (85 percent of state median family income) should be replaced by a generalized requirement that states give priority to serving children according to financial need. The current eligibility limit is misleadingly high and causes policy and administrative confusion; in many states, waiting lists rather than financial need are used to ration subsidies.

Vertical and Horizontal Equity

Eligibility and subsidy rules should be better tied to financial need and should reflect differences in family and household composition. Consideration should be given to cashing out child care benefits (or at least making vouchers partially refundable). The current system discriminates against mothers who receive child care help from other family members or who need only part-time care, while giving an unfair bonus to mothers who have other sources of household assistance.

Quality Earmarks

In the year 2000, money devoted to quality improvement amounted to about $750 million. From 1997 through 2000, about $2 billion was spent on various quality initiatives with little discernible result. Despite the rhetoric, knowledge about the characteristics of child care that make the most difference for children is quite rudimentary (Besharov, 2000; Haskins, 1992). Parental judgment, informed by substantially better research, should be harnessed to improve the quality of child care. Efforts to improve the quality of child care (in 1999 about $323 million or 6 percent of CCDF expenditures, and $148 million or 3.2 percent of Head Start expenditures) should focus on a national research agenda of randomized studies of best practices in child care and funding that allows subsidized parents to spend more of their own money on child care and, in return, to have the provider receive a higher payment from the government.

Increased Funding?

This chapter does not suggest what additional funding, if any, should be provided because the answer depends on the resolution of various policy issues, some of which are outlined here. However, it may be helpful to enumerate the most important policy issues that could affect costs: fuller participation of income-eligible families (even if it means the monetization of services already being provided); greater use of licensed and center-based facilities (which are more expensive than informal care); an increase in mandatory activities for welfare recipients (such as work experience and job training) so that more mothers will need care for their children; and a reduction in the amount of unspent welfare funds available for child care (either because caseloads rise or because the welfare block grant is reduced).

COMMENT BY

Kristin Anderson Moore, Martha Zaslow, Sharon McGroder, and Kathryn Tout

Child care is a "twofer." It is one of the components of welfare reform that addresses the needs of both mothers and children. It addresses both the goals of welfare reform and concerns about child well-being and development. It addresses the taxpayer's goal of moving parents from welfare to work, and it has at least the potential to address children's prospects for becoming self-sufficient citizens.

The chapter by Douglas Besharov and Nazanin Samari provides a helpful overview of the first component: the parental perspective. Our first suggestion is to change the title to reflect the content more precisely. The chapter focuses almost entirely on issues of child care funding and supply. Ideally, these issues could be expanded to address what we think is an equally critical issue: the implications of child care for children. Specifically, we think we need to know whether child care quality and stability are sufficient to support the development of children.

Child care as a critical context for young children should not be ignored by society. It is important to all children, but may be especially important as an opportunity for the development of children in poverty. Indeed, it is a source of concern that children are relegated to the "special issue" category in this volume. AFDC was Aid to Families with Dependent *Children*, and the implications of welfare reform for children should continue to be a central concern.

A second set of issues involves the adequacy of child care funding and supply. As noted by Besharov and Samari, government has implemented a series of large increases in funding for child care. The federal and state response has been more supportive than many expected. Nevertheless, we are not convinced that the case is made (or can be made) that the quantity, quality, or stability of available child care is adequate from the perspective of the child.

Even from the perspective of the mother, it is not clear that supply is adequate. On the one hand, there has been a multi-billion-dollar increase in funding. On the other hand, in many places there are long waiting lists. Also, there seems to be a lack of care for parents who work part-time, work non-standard hours, have infants, or have children with special needs. In addition, several studies have found that parents who are given adequate subsidies or vouchers tend to switch to formal care, suggesting the possibility that parental preferences are not actually being realized.

We are uncomfortable arguing that, because broad patterns of care did not change between 1994 and 1997, there are no apparent impacts on usage patterns. Without more recent data, and relying on nonexperimental evidence, we do not know what the child care arrangements would have been. Also, we do not know whether there have been substitutions within a particular category. For example, within a type of care such as family day care, the ratio of children to adults may have risen, but available data do not capture such a change. It may be that even more parents would have gone to work if child care were more available or were more satisfactory to parents. There is some evidence linking duration of participation in welfare-to-work employment activities with parents' perceptions of quality of care. In addition, parents working part-time might work full-time if care were more available. Thus, despite important funding increases, it is not definitively clear that the supply of child care or the funding for child care is adequate even for the needs of welfare reform. This leads to a third point.

There are critical data needs. Besharov and Samari have spliced together what they describe as "ambiguous" numbers from varied sources. It is surprising to us that one might use the level of funding to assess whether supply meets demand. Besharov and Samari are direct about their discomfort with doing so also, arguing that "data about child care patterns and spending should be more comprehensive, more reliable, and more timely." Timeliness is a critical problem. In several places, the survey data used appear to be from 1997, which makes it hard to draw conclusions about the period after states and families accommodated to the 1996 reforms.

Given available data, it is risky enough to conclude that supply is sufficient to meet the needs of welfare reform. It would be unwise to assert that available care meets the needs of children, and the authors have stopped short of drawing this conclusion. Instead, they call for better data. This is the right call.

Not only do we need more comprehensive and timely data; we also need more differentiated measures. At present it is not clear to what extent different aspects of child care quality affect children's development. The chapter is quite critical of available measures to assess quality, and we agree that available measures are merely steps in the right direction. What aspects of care matter for which outcomes for which children? If we measured child care quality in a more differentiated way, would we find that particular child outcomes increase as particular aspects of quality improve? Are there thresholds, such that low-quality care undermines development? Is there improvement after that threshold is crossed? Or does it help a lot to improve quality at the low end, and only help a little to bring care from adequate to good, or from good to excellent? What constitutes quality for children of different ages?

In testimony before the Senate Committee on Health, Education, Labor and Pensions (2000), Besharov argued that there is no strong evidence that child care quality matters. There is considerable disagreement on that point, and as yet, there is no strong evidence that quality has large effects on child development. Moreover, we agree with Besharov and Samari that better measures and better data are needed to better address this billion-dollar question.

It is also time to address the issue of supply more directly. This could be done by conducting a national child care supply study. In addition, we need to have better information about a range of policies, as well as about vouchers. For example, how do the Earned Income Tax Credit and the child care credit fit into the supply and demand picture? The availability of vouchers has probably facilitated welfare reform, but as parents become the working poor and move into the middle class, the tax system plays an increasingly important role. Also, policies vary across states and communities, and information on the implications of these differences has been hard to come by.

Fourth, Besharov and Samari call for a major increase in research on child care. Again, we agree. Child care is not only a multi-billion-dollar issue; it is an issue with possible implications for children's development and school readiness, for subsequent school success among low-income and minority children, and for parental mental health as well as employment. We hope a new series of studies can move on to examine the real question, which is, in our opinion, "What factors enhance or undermine the development of children?" rather than "Does child care inherently benefit or harm children?"

The need for a series of planned variation experimental studies to address this question in the context of welfare reform and the needs of the working poor seems clear. Perhaps, because we as a nation are spending billions of dollars on child care, a research agenda in line with the importance of the issue can now be forthcoming.

There are specific questions about child care quality that should be part of the research agenda. For example: How does training for child care workers affect the quality of care? What are the effects of improving ratios and group sizes? How do wage subsidies for providers affect quality? Do quality improvements affect the hours worked by mothers? What is the role of stability or turbulence in child care?

In sum, our concern about the weakness of the data used by Besharov and Samari to reach the conclusions that the supply of child care is adequate and that states have enough money to meet the child care needs of mothers leaving welfare leads us to strongly endorse their call for better data and more research.

References

Besharov, Douglas J. 2000. Statement before the Senate Committee on Health, Education, Labor and Pensions, Subcommittee on Children and Families, 106 Cong. 2 sess. Government Printing Office.

Besharov, Douglas J., ed. 1996. *Enhancing Early Childhood Programs: Burdens and Opportunities.* Washington: CWLA Press and American Enterprise Institute.

Besharov, Douglas J., and Peter Germanis. 2000. "Welfare Reform—Four Years Later." *Public Interest* (Summer): 17–35.

Besharov, Douglas J., and Nazanin Samari. 1999. "The Other Wisconsin Miracle." *Philanthropy* 13 (3): 30–33.

———. 2000. "Child-Care Vouchers and Cash Payments." In *Vouchers and the Provision of Public Services*, edited by C. Eugene Steuerle, Van Doorn Ooms, George Peterson, and Robert D. Reischauer. Brookings.

Blank, Helen. 1999. Statement of Helen Blank. In "Federal Resources Availability for Child Care." Hearing before the Subcommittee on Human Resources, House Committee on Ways and Means. Serial 106-34, 106 Cong. 2 sess. Government Printing Office.

Children's Defense Fund. 1997. *Federal and State Government: Partners in Child Care.* Washington.

Collins, Ann M., Jean I. Layzer, J. Lee Kreader, Alan Werner, and Fred. B. Glantz. 2000. *National Study of Child Care for Low-Income Families: State and Community Substudy Interim Report.* U.S. Department of Health and Human Services.

Falk, Gene. 2001. *Welfare Reform: Financing and Recent Spending Trends in the TANF Programs.* CRS Report RL30595. Washington: Congressional Research Service.

Fuller, Bruce, and Sharon Lynn Kagan. 2000. *Remember the Children: Mothers Balance Work and Child Care under Welfare Reform.* Berkeley: University of California.

Gabe, Thomas, Bob Lyke, and Karen Spar. 1999. *Child Care Subsidies: Federal Grants and Tax Benefits for Working Families.* Washington: Congressional Research Service.

Haskins, Ron. 1992. "Is Anything More Important Than Day-Care Quality." In *Child Care in the 1990s: Trends and Consequences*, edited by Alan Booth. Hillsdale, N.J.: Lawrence Erlbaum.

Head Start Bureau. 2000. *2000 Head Start Fact Sheet.* Washington.

Isaacs, Julia B., and Matthew R. Lyon. 2000. "A Cross-State Examination of Families Leaving Welfare: Findings from the ASPE-Funded Leavers Studies." Paper presented to the National Association of Welfare Research and Statistics (NAWRS), Phoenix, November 6.

Kisker, Ellen Eliason, Sandra L. Hofferth, Deborah A. Phillips, and Elizabeth Farquhar. 1991. *A Profile of Child Care Settings: Early Education and Care in 1990.* U.S. Department of Education.

NICHD Early Childcare Research Network. 1997. "The Effects of Infant Child Care on the Infant-Mother Attachment Security: Results from the NICHD Study of Early Child Care." *Child Development* 68 (5): 860–79.

———. 2000. "The Relation of Child Care to Cognitive and Language Development." *Child Development* 71 (4): 960–80.

Pawasarat, John, and Lois M. Quin. 1998. *Removing Barriers to Employment: The Child Care-Jobs Equation.* U.S. Department of Education.

Schmidt, Stefanie, Freya Sonenstein, and Jeffrey Capizzano. 1999. *Do the Child Care Arrangements of Current and Former Welfare Recipients Differ from Other Low-Income Families?* Washington: Urban Institute.

Schumacher, Rachel, and Mark Greenberg. 1999. *Child Care after Leaving Welfare: Early Evidence from State Studies.* Washington: Center for Law and Social Policy.

U.S. Census Bureau. 1997. *Who's Minding Our Preschoolers?* Fall 1994 (update). Government Printing Office.

U.S. Department of Health and Human Services (HHS). 2000. *Expenditures in the TANF Program in Fiscal Year 1999.*

U.S. General Accounting Office (GAO). 1999a. *Education and Care: Early Childhood Programs and Services for Low-Income Families.* HEHS-00-11.

————. 1999b. *Welfare Reform: Information on Former Recipients' Status.* HEHS-99-48.

————. 2001. *Child Care: States Increased Spending on Low-Income Families.*

U.S. House of Representatives, Committee on Ways and Means. 2000. *2000 Green Book: Background Material and Data on Programs within the Jurisdiction of the Committee on Ways and Means.* Government Printing Office.

19

LYNN A. KAROLY
JACOB ALEX KLERMAN
JEANNETTE A. ROGOWSKI

Effects of the 1996 Welfare Reform Changes on the SSI Program

THE PERSONAL RESPONSIBILITY AND Work Opportunity Reconciliation Act (PRWORA) of 1996 and the related Contract with America
Advancement Act of 1996 made three major changes to the Supplemental
Security Income (SSI) program administered by the Social Security Administration (SSA). First, it tightened the definition of disability for children. Second, it eliminated the drug addiction and alcoholism (DA&A) diagnosis
from the SSI and Disability Insurance programs. Third, it narrowed the eligibility of legal immigrants for SSI, though this change was partially reversed
by the 1997 Balanced Budget Act.

The changes to each of these segments of the SSI caseload—disabled children, adults with a DA&A diagnosis, and legal immigrants—were motivated
by concerns about the rapid rise in the number of recipients in the years leading up to 1996, as well as by claims that the program was benefiting undeserving populations. For example, the rise in the number of disabled children
occurred primarily among those diagnosed with mental disorders, and there
were media accounts of children being coached to feign such disorders. Similarly, the DA&A caseload had a history of problems with monitoring treatment and successful rehabilitation, leading some to argue that the disability
benefits simply allowed substance abusers to remain drug or alcohol dependent. Finally, legal immigrants, especially elderly immigrants, were perceived
as taking advantage of a generous social safety net, even to the point of

migrating to the United States with the intention of applying for welfare benefits.

Background: PRWORA and SSI Reforms

The SSI program, initiated in 1974 following the 1972 amendments to the Social Security Act, is one of several means-tested programs that form the social safety net for low-income Americans. Specifically, SSI is designed to provide income support to low-income individuals in three categories: those over age 65, disabled adults, and disabled children. Although the federal government establishes uniform national eligibility standards and payment scales, some states supplement the federal benefit levels.

SSI at the Time of the PRWORA Legislation

In December 1995, eight months before PRWORA was signed into law, there were 6.5 million SSI recipients, including 917,000 recipients under age 18 and 2.1 million recipients age 65 and older. As seen in figure 19-1, after remaining relatively stable with about 4 million recipients from 1974 to 1981, the size of the SSI program expanded rapidly through the 1980s and 1990s (SSA, 2000). There was a twofold increase in the number of beneficiaries 18 to 64 years old (from 1.7 million in 1982 to 3.5 million in 1995) and a more than fourfold increase in the number of beneficiaries under age 18 (from 190,000 in 1982 to 917,000 in 1995). In contrast, the number of recipients age 65 and older in 1995 was actually below the level in the 1970s.

Most of the increase in the caseload of children took place in the six years following the 1990 *Sullivan v. Zebley* court ruling, which expanded the eligibility criteria for childhood SSI. As the child caseload rapidly increased, the composition changed dramatically as well. By the time of the passage of PRWORA in 1996, more than two-thirds of the children receiving SSI were eligible because of mental impairment, and about one-quarter were eligible because they had been diagnosed with psychotic or neurotic psychiatric disorders (SSA, 1997a).

The larger number of child SSI recipients has been attributed to several factors, including changes in the program rules in 1984, the expanded eligibility resulting from *Sullivan v. Zebley*, increasing childhood poverty rates, and more SSI outreach activities (Rupp and Stapleton, 1995). There were also concerns, including reports in the media, about families coaching their children to act up in school to cause a behavior problem diagnosis (such as attention deficit disorder), although evidence of this phenomenon was difficult to obtain (U.S. General Accounting Office, 1995a). This concern—

Figure 19-1. *Trends in SSI Caseload, 1974–99*[a]

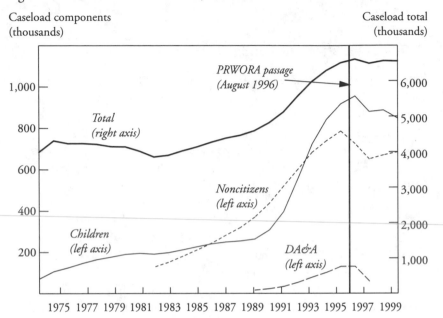

Caseload components
(thousands)

Caseload total
(thousands)

Source: DA&A caseload: Barber (1996) for 1989–95; Stapleton and others (1998) for 1996–97;
all other figures from Social Security Administration (2000).
a. All figures are as of December of the given year. Caseload components excluded from the figure
are adults who qualify on the basis of criteria other than DA&A and citizens aged 65 and over.

combined with the run-up in the caseload, especially for mental disorders—
made this aspect of the SSI program a target for reform during the welfare
reform debates.

Two other segments of the SSI caseload were also targeted as part of welfare reform and related legislation in 1996. As seen in figure 19-1, the number of SSI recipients for whom DA&A was material to their finding of disability increased from approximately 16,000 in 1989 (0.6 percent of the
disabled SSI caseload) to over 130,000 by 1995 (2.8 percent of the caseload),
an increase of over 700 percent in six years. This dramatic rise was unprecedented and unexpected, because the DA&A caseload had actually declined
during the 1970s and into the early 1980s, with only about 3,000 addicts on
the rolls by the end of 1983 (Stapleton and others, 1998).

Providing monthly income and access to medical care and substance abuse
treatment to drug addicts and alcoholics was initially conceived as a way to
move substance abusers toward rehabilitation. The impetus for the elimination of the DA&A disability category, however, was a history of problems

meeting that goal. For example, a study by the inspector general of the U.S. Department of Health and Human Services (HHS) found that among a cohort of approximately 20,000 DA&A individuals enrolled in SSI in 1990, less than 1 percent had resumed work or were rehabilitated by 1994 (U.S. Department of HHS, 1994). There were also problems ensuring that recipients were in treatment and concerns about the effectiveness of representative payees who were supposed to oversee the recipients' use of SSI cash (U.S. General Accounting Office, 1994).

Figure 19-1 also shows the trend in the number of legal immigrants on SSI. Between 1982 and 1995, this segment of the caseload had increased more than sixfold, from 128,000 to 785,000 recipients, representing 12 percent of the SSI caseload in 1995. Analyses document that legal immigrants have somewhat higher rates of welfare use than the native population, although this effect is concentrated among refugees and the elderly, especially for SSI. The high rates of SSI use by elderly immigrants have been attributed to their shorter earnings histories and employment in the uncovered sector that make them less likely to qualify for Social Security benefits; to the more rapid influx of legal immigrants during the 1980s and 1990s; and to the higher program participation rates among more recent cohorts of older immigrants (Hu, 1998).

The inclusion of benefits for legal immigrants had been an issue for the SSI program since its inception (Parrott, Kennedy, and Scott, 1998). In 1980, in response to concerns about SSI use by new immigrants, the income of an immigrant's sponsor was deemed to be available to the noncitizen for purposes of determining SSI eligibility within the first three years (later extended to five years) after their arrival. While this "deeming" was intended to keep newly arrived immigrants from gaining immediate access to the SSI program, the courts determined that sponsors could not be held legally accountable. Claims that recent immigrants were bringing their parents to the United States so that they could receive SSI surfaced during the welfare reform debates and provided part of the impetus for curtailing access to SSI benefits for noncitizens.

The 1996 SSI Reforms

Given the broad-based reforms to means-tested programs, it was not surprising that PRWORA modified the SSI program. The changes appear to have been motivated by two considerations. The first motivation was cost savings: program enrollment and cost had grown rapidly in the 1990s. The second motivation was concern about the unintended consequences of program generosity. Did the definition of a child with a disability include children who were only marginally disabled? Did the DA&A program encourage or support substance abuse? Did the SSI program encourage immigrants to bring disabled or elderly family members to the United States in order to qualify for benefits? Responding to these dual motivations, the 1996 welfare reform legislation restricted SSI eligibility for three groups—children, substance abusers, and immigrants.

CHILDHOOD DISABILITY REFORMS. The PRWORA legislation contained three key components that affected the SSI child caseload (Davies, Iams, and Rupp, 2000). First, the comparable severity criteria for childhood disability were replaced with a more restrictive definition unique to children: "a medically determinable physical or mental impairment, which results in marked and severe functional limitations" (SSA, 1997a). Approximately 264,000 childhood cases that were potentially affected by the new definition were required to be reevaluated to establish whether they met the more restrictive new criteria. Cessation of benefits for those who did not qualify (subject to appeal) was to begin as early as July 1997. The new eligibility rules were also applied to all applications under consideration or appeal and all new applications since August 1996.

Second, PRWORA required that the eligibility of a child on SSI be redetermined at age 18 under the adult disability criteria (SSA, 1997a). Approximately 60,000 children receiving disability benefits would reach age 18 within a year after PRWORA became effective. Third, the legislation required continuing disability reviews not less than once every three years for children under age 18 with impairments considered likely to improve and within the first twelve months of life for infants whose low birth weight contributes to eligibility.

For many disabled children on SSI, Medicaid eligibility may have been based solely on receipt of SSI. At the time of PRWORA's passage, approximately 50,000 children qualified for Medicaid on the basis of receiving SSI. The size of this population and concern over the loss of health insurance led to a provision in the 1997 Balanced Budget Act providing continued categorical eligibility for Medicaid for children who had received SSI and lost eligibility because of the PRWORA provisions, provided they continued to meet the SSI test for low income and resources.

Concern over the implementation of the redetermination process led to a comprehensive review and report by the SSA commissioner, Kenneth Apfel, in December 1997 (SSA, 1997b). The report highlighted the treatment of cases involving a diagnosis of mental retardation (MR), the accuracy of case processing by state and impairment, and the exercising of appeal rights when children were denied continued benefits. Consequently, the commissioner announced that approximately 45,000 cases that had been denied benefits would be rereviewed (primarily MR cases) and a subset reopened. In addition, families of children who had not appealed a cessation would be given another sixty days to do so (and another ten days to request benefit continuation while under appeal). The commissioner's review led to a downward revision in the number of cases expected to be closed as a result of the PRWORA changes, from 135,000 cases to 100,000 cases.

DA&A REFORMS. The Social Security Independence and Program Improvements Act of 1994 and the Contract with America Advancement Act of 1996 dramatically affected the disability benefits available to substance abusers. The 1994 legislation established "referral and monitoring agencies" in each state to ensure that DA&A SSI and Disability Insurance recipients were getting and maintaining substance abuse treatment. Noncompliance with treatment could lead to the suspension and termination of program benefits. The 1994 legislation also limited benefits to thirty-six months and required that a representative payee manage money distributed to DA&A recipients to prevent benefits from being used on drugs and alcohol.

The March 1996 legislation, which superseded the 1994 law, immediately eliminated new DA&A allowances and ended SSI and Disability Insurance benefits for disabled substance abusers beginning on January 1, 1997, where the DA&A diagnosis was material to the finding of disability. Those affected by the terminations were allowed to appeal and could request a new medical determination based on other disabling conditions. Approximately 167,000 SSI and 43,000 Disability Insurance beneficiaries on the rolls in March 1996 received notices in June or July 1996 that their benefits would be terminated. Not all of those beneficiaries were expected to lose benefits: some had other disabling conditions and some who appealed the termination of benefits would be reinstated. SSA's Office of the Actuary estimated that 70 percent of those receiving termination notices would remain on the rolls following the appeals process (Stapleton and others, 1998).

IMMIGRANT REFORMS. The 1996 PRWORA legislation also contained provisions that affected legal immigrants receiving SSI (Parrott, Kennedy, and Scott, 1998; Borjas, chapter 14). The law generally made noncitizens ineligible for SSI, although there were exceptions for specific classes of immigrants, including refugees and asylees (subject to time limits) and those who have contributed to the country through military service or extended periods of work. Noncitizens who did not meet one of the specified exceptions would cease to receive benefits in August 1997. In addition, the deeming provisions were strengthened to be legally binding and to cover immigrants until they were naturalized or had forty quarters of qualifying coverage. These provisions, estimated by the Congressional Budget Office to make nearly 500,000 of the approximately 750,000 noncitizens on the SSI rolls ineligible for benefits after August 1997, represented a large share of the PRWORA's budgetary savings (Primus, 1996–97).

The 1997 Balanced Budget Act (and related legislation passed in 1998) restored or grandfathered SSI benefit eligibility for all legal immigrants who entered the United States before August 1996 and who were or became disabled. However, all new immigrants after August 1996 are ineligible for SSI benefits unless they fall into one of the excepted categories, become citizens, or meet the work requirement.

Effects of PRWORA on SSI Childhood and Age-18 Recipients

With the grandfathering of SSI benefits for current immigrants, disabled children constitute the largest segment of the caseload to be potentially affected by the SSI reforms. In this section, we highlight what is known about the impact of the tightened eligibility standards on disabled children by examining aggregate caseload changes, the net effect on caseloads and costs, and the effects on affected children and families.

Caseload Trends

The 1996 PRWORA legislation required SSA to redetermine the eligibility of the child caseload potentially affected by the new, stricter eligibility standards. In addition, the law required that the eligibility of all children be redetermined using adult criteria after they turn 18. Our analysis of SSA administrative data tracks the outcome of the redetermination process for the 288,000 childhood cases potentially affected by the law, as well as the nearly 69,000 children on the SSI roles in August 1996 who turned 18 between August 22, 1996, and September 30, 1997 (the first cohort affected by the new age-18 rules) (Karoly, Hirscher, and Rogowski, 2000). Table 19-1 summarizes the outcome of the redetermination process as of August 28, 1999, three years after the passage of PRWORA.

Of the 288,000 cases potentially affected by the legislation, nearly 172,000 child cases (62 percent) continued on the SSI rolls, and just over 103,000 (38 percent) had their benefits terminated. Thirteen thousand other cases, not included in the percentage distribution, were terminated for

Table 19-1. *Outcome of SSI Eligibility Redetermination as of August 28, 1999*

	Child caseload		Age-18 caseload	
Total caseload and disposition	Number	Percent	Number	Percent
Total caseload potentially affected by PRWORA	288,000	...	68,854	...
Benefits continued for:				
Cases screened out before redetermination	28,324	...	0	...
Those determined to still be eligible	143,224	...	34,464	...
Total	171,548	62.4	34,464	54.9
Benefits ceased after redetermination of eligibility	103,437	37.6	28,296	45.1
Cessations pending appeal	9,416	9.1	2,219	7.8
Cessation for nondisability reason	9,606	...	3,750	...
Status unknown	3,409	...	2,344	...

Source: Karoly, Hirscher, and Rogowski (2000).

other reasons or their status was unknown. The number of cessations nearly matches the decline in the childhood SSI caseload between 1996 and 1999 (108,000 cases) shown in figure 19-1. For the first cohort subject to the age-18 redetermination process, 55 percent (approximately 34,500 cases) continued to receive benefits based on the adult disability criteria and 45 percent (more than 28,000 cases) were dropped from the rolls, though some of those cases remain on the rolls pending the outcome of the appeals process.

Between 8 and 9 percent of the child and age-18 cases that received a cessation decision were still under appeal in August 1999; so the number of cases that eventually continue on the rolls is likely to increase somewhat when some earlier cessation decisions are overturned on appeal. At the same time, the number of reapplications by those whose benefits were terminated has been quite small (from 2 to 8 percent depending on the length of time considered after the cessation decision), and fewer than one in four cases received a new award. This finding suggests that the extent of return to the SSI rolls is likely to be modest.

SSA data also show that new childhood disability applications have declined about 100,000 each year since 1996 (from about 450,000 in 1996 to about 340,000 each year from 1997 to 1999), although the rate of new allowances (that is, the fraction of applications approved for benefits) has remained about the same as in the pre-PRWORA era (Nibali, 2000). This suggests that the new legislation may be discouraging new applications, especially for children, who are less likely to qualify under the new tighter disability standards.

These are short-run gross impact estimates. Some children would have left SSI anyway because of improvement in their medical condition or increased earnings by their parents (given the robust economic expansion of the late 1990s). And the narrowed eligibility requirements would be expected to reduce the number of new cases. Klerman (2001) builds and simulates a dynamic model to estimate net effects. That model estimates that by 2005, the reforms will cut the size of the childhood SSI caseload relative to what it would have been without reform by about a quarter and the size of the young adult caseload by about a third.

Effects on Children and Families

The intent of the 1996 SSI childhood disability changes was to remove children with less severe disabilities from the program. At the same time, there was concern over the impact of the loss of SSI benefits on children and their families. Limited field interviews suggest that most families are coping with the loss of SSI benefit income, at least in the short term (Inkelas and others, 2000). Even for those with less severe disabilities, retaining Medicaid coverage and transitioning to other sources of health insurance are concerns. Whether the loss of SSI income, along with any changes in access to health care, ultimately affects children's health is an area for future analysis. To make up for the lost income, families have turned to other sources of support, including public and private transfers and work. Whether these sources can be sustained, especially in a less robust economy, remains to be seen. Finally, it appears that there are vulnerable subgroups in the population of terminated children, including those in foster care as well as those who lose SSI benefits upon reaching age 18.

Effects of Other Welfare Reform Changes on the SSI Program

The welfare reform legislation also affected two other segments of the SSI caseload: those with a DA&A diagnosis and legal immigrants. In this section, we review what is know about the impact of the reforms on these populations, as well as evidence of the interactions between the changes to the old Aid to Families with Dependent Children (AFDC) program (which was replaced by the Temporary Assistance for Needy Families [TANF] program) and the changes to SSI.

DA&A Caseload

In June and July 1996, SSA sent termination notices to more than 209,000 SSI and Disability Insurance recipients that their benefits would be terminated under the new provisions. The affected individuals were given the right to appeal the termination or to reapply for benefits on the basis of another disability condition. According to a study by the Lewin Group for SSA based on an analysis of agency administrative data, benefits had been terminated for approximately 108,000 SSI recipients and 31,000 Disability Insurance recipients by December 1997 (Stapleton and others, 1998). However, the Lewin study concluded that 20 to 30 percent of these beneficiaries would have left the rolls during this period for other reasons.

Benefits were retained for about 71,000 recipients, or 34 percent of the target SSI and Disability Insurance caseload. The number who continued to receive benefits fell short of the SSA estimate of 70 percent because fewer recipients than expected (about 60 percent) appealed the termination decision. Nearly 60 percent of those who continued to receive benefits qualified on the basis of a psychiatric disorder and another 10 percent with a diagnosis of mental retardation (Stapleton and others, 1998).

Evidence of the effects of the SSI/Disability Insurance benefit termination on the lives of DA&A beneficiaries is very limited. The authors of the Lewin study visited sites in four states but did not attempt to talk to the beneficiaries themselves. The field interviews with staff at SSA offices and other agencies resulted in "widespread observations" that terminated beneficiaries had experienced sharp income drops and substantial declines in treatment. There were reports that former beneficiaries turned to general assistance (GA) programs for replacement income but little evidence that they returned to work (Stapleton and others, 1998). The study did not comment on the beneficiaries' loss of Medicare or Medicaid and the impact of the changes in health insurance coverage on access to substance abuse treatment or other health care services.

Immigrant Caseload

With the 1997 grandfathering of SSI benefits for legal immigrants in the United States as of August 1996, the changes in the SSI immigrant caseload have not been as dramatic as they would have been under the terms of the 1996 PRWORA legislation. However, figure 19-1 shows that by 1997 the number of legal immigrants receiving SSI had fallen 17 percent from the peak in 1995 (though since that one-time decline the caseload has resumed a slight upward trend). The general downward trend has been attributed to several factors, including a decrease in the number of immigrant applicants to the program following the welfare reform legislation, and a reclassification of SSI recipients from aliens into the citizens category based on updated information on citizenship status (Parrott and others, 1998). Other analysts suggest that evidence of a relative decline in welfare program use by legal immigrants compared with citizens reflects a "chilling effect" of welfare reform rather than actual loss of program eligibility (Fix and Passel, 1999), although Borjas argues (in this volume) that much of this effect is concentrated in California. In the future, it is expected that the SSI immigrant caseload will continue to decline or not grow as rapidly as in the past (see Borjas, this volume).

Interactions between TANF and SSI Reforms

There are reasons to expect the broader TANF changes to potentially affect the SSI caseload and vice versa. As noted above, those who lose SSI benefits may seek income support from TANF or other safety net programs (such as general relief or general assistance). To date, evidence of these program transitions is rather limited, although some of the case study evidence suggests that families of disabled children who lose benefits may turn to TANF for income support, while adult former SSI recipients may apply for GA.

Program shifting in the other direction—from TANF to SSI—is likely to be even more significant. Although we are unaware of any studies exploring this effect, earlier studies of welfare-SSI interactions imply a strong presumption that replacing AFDC with TANF induced some AFDC/TANF recipients to switch to SSI. Garrett and Glied (2000), Kubik (1998), and Brady, Seto, and Meyers (1998) find strong in-flows from AFDC to SSI following the ruling in *Sullivan v. Zebley*. Rupp and Stapleton (1995) find similar evidence with the shrinkage of state general assistance programs. Schmidt and Sevak (2000) document a large movement from AFDC to SSI as a result of the state waivers that preceded the PRWORA legislation. Finally, post-PRWORA leaver studies consistently find that a significant fraction of TANF leavers are collecting SSI.

The plausibility of such interprogram substitution is increased by three complementary considerations. First, surveys of the welfare population consistently find that a sizable minority have low cognitive functioning and that some have severe mental and physical disabilities that limit their ability to work. Thus it seems likely that at least some current welfare recipients are eligible for SSI. Second, recipients often find SSI more attractive than welfare: SSI payments are often higher, a family can collect both SSI and welfare (for different family members), and SSI has no time limits and weaker work requirements.

Third, the difference in the states' cost-sharing between SSI (a federal program) and AFDC (which required state matching funds) and now TANF (a block grant with fixed funding) gives states an incentive to move welfare recipients to SSI, and that incentive grew with the 1996 reforms. Indeed some states are reported to have set up programs to encourage and help potentially qualifying welfare recipients to apply for SSI (Lewin-VHI, 1995; Davies, Iams, and Rupp, 2000). Given the currently robust economy and the states' relative fiscal largesse, the motivation for cross-program shifting since PRWORA has been diminished. However, if the economy worsens or the size of the TANF block grants is reduced, states may face greater fiscal pressure to move as many recipients as possible from TANF to SSI (Kubik, 1998).

Conclusions and Implications for Reauthorization

The 1996 welfare reform provisions that affected the SSI program were motivated in part by rising caseloads and costs for three groups of recipients—disabled children, adults with DA&A diagnoses, and legal immigrants—which together constituted about 28 percent of the SSI caseload in 1995. After the 1997 legislation that reversed the termination of benefits for certain immigrants already in the country by August 1996, an even smaller fraction (16 percent) of the caseload—made up largely of disabled children—was potentially affected. Information available through 1999 indicates that the reforms did result in caseload reductions: about 100,000 adult substance abusers and about 100,000 disabled children were cut from the SSI rolls (although some of them would have left the program in the absence of welfare reform). Since 1996 the total SSI caseload has stabilized at about 6.5 million recipients, and there have been absolute declines in the size of the disabled children and DA&A caseloads, as well as in the number of immigrants on SSI.

Another motivation for the reforms was the perception that many in the targeted groups were not as needy as other recipients, or that the program incentives led to unintended negative consequences. But did the reforms succeed in removing the less deserving recipients from the rolls, and in removing the incentives that could lead to unintended consequences? Presumably some of the potential disincentives of the SSI program have been removed, at least for future immigrant cohorts and adult substance abusers with no other qualifying disability. However, there is only limited evidence to date to suggest how former SSI beneficiaries are faring since the loss of benefits. Some of the case study evidence, especially for disabled children, suggests that there are areas for concern. The concerns include whether children have access to health insurance coverage and appropriate care, and whether the loss of SSI income will make families of disabled children more vulnerable to economic shocks or other crises.

The PRWORA reauthorization debates are likely to focus primarily on the TANF program where the most visible changes to the social safety net were concentrated. Nevertheless, there are issues related to the SSI reforms that merit attention. For disabled children, legislators should consider enhancing transition support (such as health insurance, education, and employment) for SSI recipients who reach age 18 and do not qualify for aid as adults. Likewise, the need for continued health insurance coverage among children with lesser disabilities who no longer qualify for SSI should to be examined, along with the ability of other health insurance programs like SCHIP (State Children's Health Insurance Program) to cover these children. For adult substance abusers who are now ineligible for SSI or Disability Insurance benefits, there is a need to determine whether there are sufficient incentives for addicts to seek the treatment they need and to ensure adequate access to treatment for those who want it. There may be misperceptions in the immigrant community about who remains eligible for SSI and about how eligibility for benefits can be established by future immigrants. Aggressive education and outreach may be required to explain eligibility and application procedures to potential recipients.

Additional information about the effects of the 1996 SSI reforms will be critical for evaluating potential future modifications to the SSI program. Our knowledge base could be improved through additional follow-up studies to measure the longer-term impact of the SSI changes on disabled children, substance abusers, and new immigrants. Options for further SSI changes will also be informed by continued monitoring of the implementation of the 1996 reforms, including the continuing disability reviews for child SSI recipients and the age-18 redeterminations for SSI recipients, as well as the provisions affecting eligibility for future immigrants.

Finally, given the potential for program shifting from TANF to SSI and vice versa, policymakers need to clarify the goals of these two programs and how they are expected to interact, especially for nonelderly adults. The lifetime limits on receipt of TANF assistance assumes that those on welfare are able to work and become self-sufficient. In contrast, SSI benefits are not limited in duration and are available for low-income nonelderly adults who are disabled and for disabled children (where the income support may allow the primary caretaker to remain out of the work force). This suggests a division of responsibility between the two programs: TANF as a time-limited program for those who can reasonably be expected to work, and SSI as a non-time-limited program for those who cannot reasonably be expected to work. For these distinct program roles to be viable, it must be possible to accurately identify adults who are not able to work and to diagnose children with disabling conditions sufficiently severe to limit a parent's work. Evidence to date suggests that the medical determination process is far from perfect and that program incentives may induce unwanted behavior among potential recipients that would make them eligible for benefits.

COMMENT BY
Matt Weidinger

What is most noteworthy about this chapter by Lynn Karoly, Jacob Klerman, and Jeannette Rogowski is what the authors do not say. They do not cite any data confirming the worst fears of "experts" and advocates when reforms were debated and passed. Critics employed a special flair in describing the welfare reforms, and especially the changes in Supplemental Security Income (SSI): "I rise in strong opposition to this deadly and Draconian piece of garbage which will do nothing to reform the conditions of poverty and unemployment suffered by our Nation's most vulnerable. . . . I will not join demopublicans and republicrats in this mean-spirited attack. You can rest assured that I will work to continue to provide equal protection under the law for our Nation's poor, our disabled, our immigrants and our children."[1]

Yet more than four years after welfare reform, as Karoly and her colleagues make clear, there are no data justifying such attacks. In fact, the "limited" data (a phrase the authors repeat several times) "suggest that most families are coping with," for example, the SSI children's reforms. Evidence of outcomes among drug addicts and alcoholics and noncitizens is even more sparse but similarly fails to confirm the fears of critics.

In general, this chapter shows that the reforms are working as intended. Unfortunately, however, the authors have the priorities of reformers backwards. They claim that "the first motivation" for the reforms "was cost savings." Although the reforms have achieved significant savings, those savings were more a by-product of the reformers' primary intent of changing the culture of welfare and its influence on American families and society. This focus on overhauling the values welfare encourages among American families, and especially poor families struggling to get by, shows how far the reform debate

---

1. Rep. Jesse Jackson Jr., *Congressional Record*, daily ed. July 30, 1996, p. H9407.

progressed in the years leading up to 1996. As recently as the debate on the 1988 Family Support Act, those who expected families receiving public benefits to work (a markedly less dramatic change than ending SSI eligibility for certain children) were derided for expecting the poor to "sing for their supper." Not surprisingly and despite much rhetoric to the contrary, the 1988 changes had little to do with boosting personal responsibility or any other fundamental values.

By 1995–96 much had changed. Cash welfare caseloads had exploded to historic highs through both hot and cool economies. As the authors explain, SSI rolls grew even faster. At the same time, increasing concerns were voiced about whether SSI benefits were properly targeted.

The authors highlight some of the concerns expressed about whether certain children should qualify for SSI. The case is equally strong that SSI programs for drug addicts and alcoholics and noncitizens were out of control. Caseloads were exploding, and there were serious questions about whether the ready availability of benefits was encouraging self-destructive behavior and entry into the United States of thousands of noncitizens incapable of supporting themselves, despite our nation's long history of requiring prospective immigrants to prove that they can support themselves. In short, the design of the SSI program was undermining long held values of work and responsibility and was in serious need of reform.

To understand the motives behind the changes affecting drug addicts, alcoholics, and noncitizens, one should consider two simple facts often cited by reformers. First, before reform the primary reason SSI benefits for drug addicts and alcoholics ended was not recovery or work, but death. Second, before reform noncitizens actually received larger average SSI benefits than citizens. Ironically, the relative size of noncitizens' SSI benefits was often due to their relatively shorter work experience in the United States, which made them less likely to qualify for offsetting Social Security benefits. Taxpaying citizens correctly saw as fundamentally unfair the provision of cash benefits to those who had not worked and not paid taxes to earn them. Perhaps the authors should have added the following to their list of questions about the outcomes of the SSI reforms: How could programs that produced such results before reform avoid change for so long? and Is the prereform or the postreform SSI program more likely to earn the support of deserving beneficiaries and taxpayers—including the vast majority of noncitizens who work and avoid welfare?

From the standpoint of reinforcing public support for the SSI program and its benefits, it is hard to argue with the results. Today one finds almost no public concern that SSI benefits are poorly targeted or in need of significant change. Indeed, recent reports have focused more on concerns that some changes were not implemented as intended, resulting in some drug addicts and alcoholics remaining on the rolls (U.S. Social Security Administration, 2000). Before reform the availability of benefits for drug addicts, alcoholics, and noncitizens came to be viewed as an example of how SSI in particular and the nation's welfare system in general were undermining core American values of work and personal responsibility. In retrospect this mistargeting of benefits and the doubts it raised posed a greater threat to SSI and deserving beneficiaries than the 1996 reforms that enjoy widespread support. The authors, in failing to present suggestions for fundamental changes to the 1996 reforms, confirm this basic point: The 1996 reforms were needed and are here to stay.

The authors leave out another important point: the true magnitude of caseload declines resulting from the 1996 reforms. According to the authors, the SSI reforms have succeeded in cutting the caseloads in all three programs significantly, although not as much as was originally expected. But this conclusion is misleading. The authors compare the current caseload only with the 1996 caseload to gauge the decline. The problem with this approach is that to gain a full understanding of the magnitude of caseload reduction, it is necessary to compare the current caseload with the projected caseload as well as the 1996 caseload. Consider recent caseload data alongside projections made by the General Accounting Office as SSI program changes were being debated in early 1995:

SSI beneficiary group	2000 projection	2000 actual	Difference
Children	1,860,000	856,000	−1,004,000
Noncitizens	2,000,000	685,000	−1,315,000
Drug addicts and alcoholics	200,000	0	−200,000

The authors' observation that caseloads have declined only modestly since 1995 tells only half the story, and the less interesting half at that. The reforms have reduced the caseloads dramatically in comparison with projections made before 1996. These figures show that the 1996 reforms prevented some 2.5 million beneficiaries from going on the SSI rolls.

The authors largely ignore this fact, focusing more on current caseload dynamics. This focus on effects on the current caseload rather than on the bigger picture of preventing dramatic future increases is particularly curious in light of the authors' argument that reformers' "first motivation was cost savings." The Congressional Budget Office scores costs and savings by comparing prereform caseload projections with caseloads expected to result after changes. One would expect a discussion of caseload change from the same perspective, which would support my claim that the caseload effects of the SSI reforms were far more significant than the authors suggest.

Assessing the impact of the complex 1996 SSI changes is a difficult task. Passions about SSI and especially its beneficiaries run high, and available outcome data are less than complete, as the authors point out. But it is worth noting that the absence of data can sometimes be telling. Especially considering the doom predicted by opponents of reform, the lack of data and relative silence today among critics of the SSI changes are deafening. Karoly, Klerman, and Rogowski, by making only several rather minor suggestions for revision, implicitly support the basic course charted by the 1996 SSI changes. Representative Clay Shaw, chairman of the House Ways and Means Committee's Subcommittee on Human Resources, said of welfare reform legislation in 1996: "This is not an exercise in politics. This is a rescue mission."[2] That missionary zeal inspired the SSI changes as well. Judging from the results and the converts they have won, the 1996 reforms should continue to strengthen the SSI program for years to come.

References

Barber, Sherry L. 1996. *Supplemental Security Income Recipients for Whom the Alcoholism and Drug Addiction Provisions Apply (DA&A Recipients): December 1995.* Washington: Social Security Administration.

Brady, Henry E., Eva Seto, and Marcia Meyers. 1998. "Tracking the Impact of SSI Program Changes: The Impact of the Zebley Decision on Transition into SSI in California." UC Data Working Paper 13. University of California, Berkeley.

Davies, Paul, Howard Iams, and Kalman Rupp. 2000. "The Effect of Welfare Reform on SSA's Disability Programs: Design of Policy Evaluation and Early Evidence." *Social Security Bulletin* 63 (1): 3–11.

Fix, Michael, and Jeffrey S. Passel. 1999. *Trends in Noncitizens' and Citizens' Use of Public Benefits Following Welfare Reform: 1994–97.* Washington: Urban Institute.

Garrett, Bowen, and Sherry Glied. 2000. "Does State AFDC Generosity Affect Child SSI Participation?" *Journal of Policy Analysis and Management* 19 (2): 275–95.

Hu, Wei-Yin. 1998. "Elderly Immigrants on Welfare." *Journal of Human Resources* 22 (3): 711–41.

Inkelas, Moira, Melissa Rowe, Lynn A. Karoly, and Jeannette A. Rogowski. 2000. *Policy Evaluation of the Effects of the 1996 Welfare Reform Legislation on SSI Benefits for Disabled Children: Second Round Case Study Findings.* DRU-2224-SSA. Santa Monica, Calif.: Rand.

Karoly, Lynn A., Randall A. Hirscher, and Jeannette A. Rogowski. 2000. *A Descriptive Analysis of the SSI Childhood and Age-18 Disability Redetermination Process: Results through August 28, 1999.* DRU-2328-SSA. Santa Monica, Calif.: Rand.

2. *Congressional Record,* daily ed., July 18, 1996, p. H7807.

Klerman, Jacob A. 2001. "The Effects of PRWORA's Childhood SSI Reforms: A Dynamic Model." Mimeo. Santa Monica, Calif.: Rand.

Kubik, Jeffrey D. 1998. "Fiscal Federalism and Welfare Policy: The Role of States in the Growth of Child SSI." Unpublished paper. Syracuse University.

Lewin-VHI. 1995. *Case Studies of State-Level Factors Contributing to DI and SSI Disability Application and Award Growth.* U.S. Department of Health and Human Services and the Social Security Administration.

Nibali, Ken. 2000. "Overview of SSI." Presented at the National Academy of Social Insurance conference "National Dialogue on SSI Childhood Disability."Washington: Social Security Administration.

Parrott, Thomas M., Lena D. Kennedy, and Charles G. Scott. 1998 "Noncitizens and the Supplemental Security Income Program." *Social Security Bulletin* 61 (4): 3–31.

Primus, Wendell. 1996–97. "Immigration Provisions of the New Welfare Law." *Focus* 18 (2): 14–18.

Rupp, Kalman, and David Stapleton. 1995. "Determinants of the Growth in the Social Security Administration's Disability Programs—An Overview." *Social Security Bulletin* 58 (4): 43–70.

Schmidt, Lucie, and Purvi Sevak. 2000. *AFDC, SSI and Welfare Reform Aggressiveness: Caseload Reductions vs. Caseload Shifting.* Working Paper. Department of Economics, University of Michigan.

Social Security Administration. 1997a. *Review of SSA's Implementation of New SSI Childhood Disability Legislation.* Washington.

———. 1997b. *Commissioner's Report.* Washington.

———. 2000. *Annual Statistical Supplement to the Social Security Bulletin.* Government Printing Office.

Stapleton, David, David Wittenburg, Adam Tucker, Garrett E. Moran, Robert Ficke, and Michelle Harmon. 1998. "Policy Evaluation of the Effect of Legislation Prohibiting the Payment of Disability Benefits to Individuals Whose Disability Is Based on Drug Addiction and Alcoholism." Interim Report. Washington: Lewin Group and Westat.

U.S. Department of Health and Human Services (HHS), Office of the Inspector General. 1994. *SSI Payments to Drug Addicts and Alcoholics: Continued Dependence.* OEI-09-94-0071.

U.S. General Accounting Office. 1994. *Social Security: Major Changes Needed for Disability Benefits for Addicts.* GAO/HEHS-94-128. Government Printing Office.

———. 1995a. *Social Security: New Functional Assessments for Children Raise Eligibility Questions.* GAO/HEHS-95-66. Government Printing Office.

———. 1995b. Testimony of Jane L. Ross, Hearings before the Subcommittee on Human Resources, Committee on Ways and Means, 104 Cong. 1 sess. Government Printing Office, January 27.

U.S. Social Security Administration, Office of the Inspector General. 2000 *Audit Report,* A-01-98-61014.

Contributors

Eloise Anderson
Claremont Institute

Gordon Berlin
*Manpower Demonstration Research
    Corporation*

Douglas J. Besharov
American Enterprise Institute

Rebecca M. Blank
*Gerald R. Ford School of Public Policy
University of Michigan*

Dan Bloom
*Manpower Demonstration Research
    Corporation*

George J. Borjas
*John F. Kennedy School of
    Government
Harvard University*

P. Lindsay Chase-Lansdale
*Institute for Policy Research
Northwestern University*

Sheldon Danziger
*School of Social Work
University of Michigan*

Greg J. Duncan
*Center for Urban Affairs
Northwestern University*

Michael Fix
Urban Institute

Thomas L. Gais
*Nelson A. Rockefeller Institute of
    Government
State University of New York–Albany*

Irwin Garfinkel
*School of Social Work
Columbia University*

Susan Golonka
National Governors' Association

Mark Greenberg
Center for Law and Social Policy

Robert Greenstein
Center on Budget and Policy Priorities

Jocelyn Guyer
Center on Budget and Policy Priorities

Ron Haskins
*Brookings Institution and
    Annie E. Casey Foundation*

Hugh Heclo
*Department of Public and
    International Affairs
George Mason University*

Wade F. Horn
*U.S. Department of Health and
    Human Services*

Clifford M. Johnson
National League of Cities

Thomas Kaplan
*Institute for Research on Poverty
University of Wisconsin–Madison*

Lynn A. Karoly
RAND Corporation

Jacob Alex Klerman
RAND Corporation

Robert I. Lerman
*American University and
    Urban Institute*

Pamela Loprest
Urban Institute

Glenn C. Loury
*Department of Economics
Boston University*

Irene Lurie
*Department of Public Administration
    and Policy
State University of New York–Albany*

Sharon McGroder
Child Trends

Thomas Main
*Baruch College
City University of New York*

Rebecca A. Maynard
Mathematica Policy Research

Lawrence M. Mead
*Department of Politics
New York University*

Charles Michalopoulos
*Manpower Demonstration Research
    Corporation*

Ronald B. Mincy
*School of Social Work
Columbia University*

Kristin Anderson Moore
Child Trends

Charles Murray
American Enterprise Institute

Richard P. Nathan
*Nelson A. Rockefeller Institute of
    Government
State University of New York–Albany*

LaDonna Pavetti
Mathematica Policy Research

Wendell Primus
Center on Budget and Policy Priorities

Robert Rector
Heritage Foundation

Jeannette A. Rogowski
RAND Corporation

Nazanin Samari
American Enterprise Institute

Steve Savner
Center for Law and Social Policy

Isabelle V. Sawhill
Brookings Institution

Lucie Schmidt
*Department of Economics
University of Michigan*

Gary Stangler
*Jim Casey Youth Opportunities
    Initiative*

C. Eugene Steuerle
Urban Institute

Julie Strawn
Center for Law and Social Policy

Robert Topel
*Graduate School of Business
University of Chicago*

Kathryn Tout
Child Trends

Jason A. Turner
*Human Resources Administration
New York City*

Matt Weidinger
*Committee on Ways and Means
U.S. House of Representatives*

Don Winstead
*Department of Children and Families
Tallahassee, Florida*

Martha Zaslow
Child Trends

Sheila R. Zedlewski
Urban Institute

Index